D0786840

Aleksander Wat

Aleksander

WAT

Life and Art of an Iconoclast

TOMAS VENCLOVA

Yale University Press   New Haven and London

To my mother,
to my wife, Tanya,
and to my daughter, Maria

Designed by James J. Johnson and
set in Ehrhardt Roman by The Composing
Room of Michigan, Inc., Grand Rapids,
Michigan.
Printed in the United States of America by
Vail-Ballou Press, Binghamton, New York.

*Library of Congress Cataloging-in-Publication
Data*

Venclova, Tomas, 1937–
    Aleksander Wat : life and art of an
iconoclast / Tomas Venclova.
        p.   cm.
    Includes bibliographical references and
index.
    ISBN 0-300-06406-3 (c : alk. paper)

    1. Wat, Aleksander.   2. Authors, Polish—
20th century—Biography.
I. Title.
PG7158.W282V46   1996
891.8′517—dc20
[B]   95-41197
                                              CIP

A catalogue record for this book is available from
the British Library

The paper in this book meets the guidelines for
permanence and durability of the Committee on
Production Guidelines for Book Longevity of
the Council on Library Resources.

10   9   8   7   6   5   4   3   2   1

Contents

Preface

I was introduced to the work of Aleksander Wat more than once. The first time was during my student years in my native Lithuania. It was the curious period of the post-Stalinist "thaw" in Eastern Europe, when my generation was first becoming acquainted with hundreds of previously banned or unavailable texts, including almost all the twentieth-century classics. The experience was happy and demanding. Like archaeologists who come upon an unknown civilization, we communicated the intoxicating news to each other for days and months on end. We discovered, in random order and rapid succession, Hemingway, Proust, Eliot, Wittgenstein, Freud, Pasternak, Tsvetaeva, Russian formalists, and many more. Lithuania, then occupied by the Soviets, was underprivileged by comparison with Poland, where most of these writers were known and widely discussed. We had no access to Western books and newspapers, yet we could subscribe to Polish newspapers and magazines, which from 1956 on became appreciably more informative than Soviet publications. In the Lithuanian capital, Vilnius, there was also a modest Polish bookshop. And so many of us learned Polish, initially with the express goal of cutting open a window to that unknown world. Soon, however, we noticed that Polish literature was interesting in its own right. In some respects, it was more fascinating than the world classics, because it dealt with the experience we all shared. We read Zbigniew Herbert and Wisława Szymborska, poets who reacted to the brutality of totalitarianism by affirming human dignity in their art; we read Stanisław Lem and Sławomir Mrożek, fiction writers of magnificent imagination, who submitted the Communist system to a veiled and incredibly caustic criticism; we even read Witold Gombrowicz and Czesław Miłosz, émigré authors who, though of course unavailable in the bookshop, reached us in roundabout, often curious ways.

One day, while reading a Polish literary magazine, I found a long poem entitled "Evening—Night—Morning" that immediately struck me. It was on a par with poems I had read before, including works by Pasternak and Eliot; classical in design and imagery, it had a dark, disturbing pathos that haunted me for days. The name of the author, Aleksander Wat, meant almost nothing to me. I did not know his life story, though I suspected it was complicated and turbulent. I knew nothing of his literary background, though I knew enough about surrealism to discern it in the work. What I did know was that his work was of an exceptional quality.

Gradually I learned more about Wat. He had belonged to a group of radical futurists that included Bruno Jasieński, a writer who perished during Stalin's purges and whose books I had read. Like Jasieński, Wat apparently became a Communist. (Or was he just a fellow-traveler? The matter was far from clear.) What happened to Wat after that was never discussed in the press, but I knew enough about the fate of old East European Communists to reconstruct much if not all of it. When I first happened upon his work, Wat was living in Poland but spending much of his time in France and Italy. This seemed strange by comparison with Soviet habits, but I knew that Polish habits were a bit different. Several years after reading "Evening—Night—Morning" (I managed to become better acquainted with Wat's work in the meantime), I heard the news: Wat refused to return to Poland. Under the circumstances, his decision was understandable. Friends with whom I shared Polish books and periodicals and I empathized. We even invented a code verb, *to wat*, meaning to emigrate. It was a move some of us considered (despite the impossibility of implementing it). But after that we lost track of Wat: the Iron Curtain was still anything but transparent.

I rediscovered Wat's work unexpectedly in 1977 as my own experience began to parallel aspects of his. As a dissident stripped of my Soviet citizenship (which, to be honest, I never valued very much), I arrived at the University of California, Berkeley, where Wat had lectured and spoken twelve years earlier. He was dead by then, but I was surrounded by people who knew and remembered him well. One of these was Czesław Miłosz, who introduced me to Wat's poetry in its entirety: idiosyncratic and sometimes shocking, it fascinated me anew. I also read *My Century*, Wat's memoirs, the outcome of his tape-recording sessions with Miłosz. It is as significant as any book about communism ever written, on a par with the works of Aleksandr Solzhenitsyn and Nadezhda Mandelstam. Its particular value derives from the fact that Wat spoke about Soviet Russia as an outsider—a Westerner—yet with an intimate knowledge and understanding of the country that rivaled any Russian's, and about communism as an insider, but one who rarely forfeited his ability to evaluate the movement and its ideology from the outside. *My Century* struck a personal note—I knew many people whose lives had to a certain extent paralleled Wat's: young writers of radical and nihilist bent, who became fellow-travelers, then Communists, but never managed to free themselves from that trap. One such man was my father.

Soon I became aware that Wat was a major twentieth-century writer as yet undiscovered by the West. After Wat's death, from the late 1960s to the 1980s, his work was printed only by émigré publishing houses in small editions. A volume of his collected poems appeared in Paris in 1968, his memoirs were first published in London in 1977, and a three-volume set of his fiction and essays, edited by Krzysztof Rutkowski, followed in 1985–88. These generated immense interest in those who were fortunate enough to get hold of them. And in due course they trickled back to Poland, where the young dissidents of the eighties, participants in the Solidarity movement, embraced Wat as their man. The memoirs of Wat's widow, Paulina (Ola) Wat, tape-recorded by Jacek Trznadel and first published in London in 1984, were especially significant, in that they shed light not only on lesser-known aspects of Wat's life but also on the tribulations of Poles in Soviet exile during World War II—a topic on which few testimonies survived, because it was subjected to the strictest taboo in Communist Poland. Aleksander and Ola Wat's writings were reprinted by the Polish underground press, and after the crash of Polish communism they at last reached a general audience, becoming immediate best-sellers. A successful film was made on the life of the Wat family. In addition, a generation of Polish Watologists arose. A full-length study of his poetry by Małgorzata Łukaszuk and a book of studies edited by Wojciech Ligęza appeared, as did numerous scholarly articles. Moreover, Wat's poems continue to have an impact on Polish literature, and in 1992 a definitive edition was published in Kraków by Anna Micińska and Jan Zieliński.

Several of Wat's works have appeared in English translation: two volumes of poems were printed in 1977 and 1989, *My Century* appeared in 1988, and a collection of prewar short stories, *Lucifer Unemployed*, was published in 1990. In 1988 the Beinecke Rare Book and Manuscript Library at Yale University acquired Wat's papers, including his manuscripts, among which was a hitherto unknown, but significant, unfinished novel, "Loth's Flight" (it was published in Polish in 1995). As a result, Wat has now secured a well-deserved reputation as one of the outstanding cultural figures of the twentieth century. Yet he remains only slightly known to Western readers, including most Slavists. This book is an attempt to remedy that situation.

In its essential features, Wat's life is paradigmatic of the lives of the East European men and women of letters of this century. But few authors have identified so closely with the expectations, blunders, and disillusionments of modern times. Wat took part in many intellectual ventures, becoming active in various modernist movements, and for a time was a Marxist journalist and critic of strictly Communist persuasion. By contrast with other writers of similar experience, from Vladimir Mayakovsky and Bertolt Brecht to Paul Eluard and Jean-Paul Sartre, Wat had the good—or bad—fortune to experience the consequences of his literary and political ideas in his life. Through many ordeals, he developed a unique philosophical outlook that led him to reject totalitarian ideology in both its leftist and rightist variants and to subject modernism to a fundamental critique. Wat's works stand out for their consistently high artistic quality, as well as their audacious undermining of traditional notions of literature, history, and life itself. At the same time, the boldness and profundity of his critical approach make him one of the most convincing (and readable) analysts of twentieth-century ideological and cultural trends. His judgments are particularly relevant to the present, postmodern era. Finally, the tragic lyric of Wat's mature period counts among the highest achievements of postwar Polish and East European poetry.

I take an integrated approach to Wat's life and work, analyzing both in chronological order and interrelating them. Wat was an author who transfigured his life and death into art, and vice versa. Of the thirteen chapters of this book, only the first, on Wat's childhood and early youth, is strictly biographical. The rest either combine in varying proportions biography with analysis of poetry, fiction, and essays or are completely devoted to Wat's art and thought.

In Wat's early experiences are found the roots of his lifelong spiritual quest, his attitudes toward cultural traditions, his religious and metaphysical concerns, and the unique amalgam of Polishness and Jewishness that marked both his life and his literary career. His futurist, dadaist, and surrealist poems parallel Western European and Russian trends, breaking literary norms and showing a proclivity for apocalyptic visions. Here Wat distinguishes himself primarily by his parodic undermining of the literary tradition. The landmark work of his early period, *ME from One Side and ME from the Other Side of My Pug Iron Stove*, is an example of *écriture automatique* that predates the experiments of the French surrealists. Comparable in style and quality to Arthur Rimbaud's *Une Saison en enfer* and the Circe episode in James Joyce's *Ulysses*, it merges myths of various origin and subverts not only conformist discourse but the very notion of text and subtext. Wat's prewar short stories (written largely in a satirical vein) examine contemporary social and cultural issues, submitting the key ideas of the twentieth century to crushing criticism. These pieces are successful composites of genres ranging from parables to science fiction and futurological treatises.

Wat found a questionable remedy for his nihilism in Communist ideology, which he espoused with great zeal in the early 1930s and which appeared in his contributions to Polish Marxist criticism. Soon, however, he began to recognize the severely limiting character of Communist dogma. But the final shock—which led to his absolute rejection of totalitarianism—came from his experiences in the 1940s when he was arrested by the Soviet secret police, imprisoned, and exiled in Kazakhstan. The years of imprisonment brought Wat back to poetry, and several lyrical pieces encapsulating his spiritual experiences of that period have become classics.

In postwar years, first in Poland, then in the West, Wat devoted his creative powers mainly, if not exclusively, to deconstructing the totalitarian discourse. He attacked Stalinism primarily as both a manipulation and a perversion of language. He also exposed its historical antecedents, which, in his view, included certain avant-garde trends. This critique found expression first in manuscript notes and later in a series of thought-provoking philosophical and sociological pieces. Wat's unfinished yet revealing memoirs, in which he continued to address totalitarianism and modernism, grew into a monumental attempt at self-analysis. His late poems were, in effect, existential and metaphysical meditations that had much in common with seventeenth-century baroque writing.

Any attempt to write a critical biography of Wat is complicated by his own detailed accounts of his life. *My Century* covers only part of Wat's life, concentrating mainly on his Communist adventure and his incarceration in Stalinist prisons. But it is complemented by other autobiographical texts and by his widow's memoirs. However, other sources that might shed more light on significant periods of Wat's life, especially the 1930s and 1940s are unavailable: there are few documented traces of Wat's Communist activities, and the full story of his imprisonment and exile could be reconstructed, if at all, only after prolonged study of KGB archives (which proved impossible for me). I have therefore frequently had to limit myself to placing Wat's and his widow's testimonies in context, augmenting them whenever possible and correcting obvious lapses of memory contained therein. Both Aleksander and Ola Wat were unique witnesses of their times; but they were also creators of their own myths. Conscious, semiconscious, or unconscious transformation, masking, overstatement, understatement, and sometimes invention of facts to comply with the demands of the authorial myth are the usual stuff of memoirs, even the most truthful. I have tried to avoid or correct any distortions of perspective that may have arisen, though I have hardly been successful in every instance. By contrast, for the postwar period of Wat's life, which remained outside the scope of *My Century* and was treated only summarily in Ola Wat's memoirs, many more sources, archival and otherwise, were available; so the biographical information for these years is more accurate and more detailed.

In discussing Wat's art, the main challenge has been to delimit his focus. Wat wrote in many genres, and I have attempted to present a multifaceted view of his work, including fiction, essays, criticism, and documentary prose. He switched back and forth from poetry to prose and wrote in paroxysms of creativity separated by long periods of sterility. Moreover, because of his difficult circumstances—a succession of prisons and exiles, a debilitating disease, and recurrent spiritual crises—much of his output is in a chaotic and fragmentary state. Part has been compiled from disjointed pieces by his editors and published, but much remains unpublished. Throughout his life Wat aspired to write, but never produced, a major, all-encompassing work. His failure to do so has led some critics to underestimate Wat's writing. "Wat: ruins, where blocks of noble metal lie scattered about," writes Janusz Sławiński. "Perhaps there is nothing in his work except un-accomplishments."[1] Sławiński's evaluation is neither indisputable nor commonly accepted, however. In my view, the fragmentary nature of Wat's output, which reflects the cataclysmic nature of his disas-

trous times, contributes to his fascination. Among these "ruins" are not only
pieces of absolute poetic validity but texts that are intellectually and artistically
far ahead of their time. And they remain powerful more than a quarter of a
century after Wat's death. Incomplete and open-ended, Wat's oeuvre is more
provocative than many of his contemporaries' well-rounded works, which appear dated to the discerning modern reader and are doomed to oblivion.

Although this book presents an overview of Wat's creative legacy in its
entirety, covering all of his published and some of his unpublished writings, I am
interested primarily in Wat's poetry, which I see as the mainstay of his work. Wat
was a poet of the first rank during both his futurist *Lehrjahre* and his mature
Wanderjahre—periods separated by more than three decades of silence and
ordeal. His later poetry may at first appear fundamentally different from his
earlier iconoclastic verse, but he himself saw, not without cause, no major break
between the two, in that they represent two stages of consistent, if critical,
development. I have tried to uncover the unifying qualities of Wat's poetry
despite the seeming divergence between his futurist and metaphysical periods.
At each stage, Wat practiced *poesis docta,* addressing cultural memory (even if his
attitude to it changed considerably) and requiring extensive commentary. A
palpable thread of Gnostic and Kabbalistic thought runs through his work. In
both his early and his later poems, Wat was preoccupied with the corporeal body
and its mysticism. The problems of suffering, revolt, and moral transgression
(accompanied by and embodied in the perversion of language) remained central
in his work: the young Wat was strictly iconoclastic whereas the mature Wat was
an iconoclast of iconoclasm, rejecting nihilism though never relinquishing poignant metaphysical doubts. Wat's late poetry can be defined as the pinnacle of his
lifelong journey toward Self.

My work on Wat, like any such work, has not been a solo enterprise. I am
particularly indebted to the late Ola Wat: our meeting in 1990 was unforgettable,
and it gave me the strength and sense of purpose I needed for my research.
Aleksander and Ola's son, Andrzej, encouraged me along the way, generously
sharing information that would otherwise have been unavailable. Nor would the
book have been written without the assistance of Czesław Miłosz, who first
acquainted me with Wat's memoirs and his entire poetic output and then provided guidance and criticism of my attempts to deal with them.

My warmest appreciation goes to Stanisław Barańczak, friend and tutor,
who proposed the topic to me, read my manuscript chapter by chapter, offered
valuable suggestions and corrections, and helped me in myriad other ways. Alina
Kowalczykowa, a great authority on Wat's published and unpublished work,
provided much information and advice and, with rare generosity, allowed me to
use her extensive personal archive on Wat. (I benefitted greatly from her de-
cipherment of Wat's virtually illegible texts.) I should also like to acknowledge

Vincent Giroud, who facilitated and encouraged my work in the Wat archive of the Beinecke Rare Book and Manuscript Library at Yale University.

I owe a great deal to Polish specialists on Wat's work, whose research and insights precede my own: in many respects, the present work is only a modest complement to the pioneer studies of Włodzimierz Bolecki, Tomasz Burek, Aleksander Fiut, Anna Micińska, Jan Zieliński, and others, correspondence and meetings with whom were enormously valuable. I also thank the colleagues and friends who helped and directed me during my trips to Poland, sharing with me their knowledge of the country, its history and literature, and Wat's creative output: Stanisław Balbus, Jan Błoński, Andrzej Drawicz, Jerzy Jarzębski, Magda Lubelska, Ryszard Nycz, Tadeusz Nyczek, Barbara Toruńczyk, Teresa Walas, and Wiktor Woroszylski.

Joseph Brodsky, Iza and Victor Erlich, Jerzy Giedroyc, Robert Louis Jackson, Vasily Rudich, Alexander Schenker, and Piotr Wandycz offered significant suggestions. Ekaterina Kotreleva and Aleksandr Zhovtis aided my search for materials in Russia and Kazakhstan, and in my discussion of Wat's prison writings, I benefitted much from the insights of Elizabeth Anne Cole.

I owe an inestimable debt to Robert Bird, who struggled with the preliminary editing of the manuscript, teaching me a lot about English (and my idiosyncratic usage of it) and offering additional advice. I am also very appreciative of the editorial work of Nike Agman, Laura Dooley, Tim Sergay, Florence Stankiewicz, Andrei Ukhov, and Jean van Altena.

The writing of this book would not have been possible without a Morse Fellowship awarded to me by Yale College in 1990–91. My numerous trips to Poland were facilitated by generous grants obtained through the Yale Center for International and Area Studies.

Parts of Chapters 2, 3, and 4 have appeared, respectively, in *Literary Tradition and Practice in Russian Culture,* edited by Valentina Polukhina, Joe Andrew, and Robert Reid (Amsterdam: Rodopi, 1993); in *Teksty Drugie* 2 (1994), translated into Polish by Joanna Zach-Błońska; and in *The Mayakovsky Centennial: 1893–1993,* edited by Anne D. Perryman and Patricia J. Thompson (New York: Lehman College, 1993).

The translations throughout are my own unless otherwise indicated. *My Century* is quoted, wherever possible, from the published English translation. But because the English version of Wat's memoirs is significantly abridged, I have complemented the brilliant work of Richard Lourie by much inferior translations of missing paragraphs where these were necessary for my discussion; all such cases are noted. Poems analyzed in detail are quoted both in the Polish original and in English translation; otherwise, only the translation is given.

1

Prehistory, 1900–1918

Aleksander Wat was born in Warsaw on 1 May 1900. The day of his birth, May Day, was symbolic. Radical socialist thought and politics figured strongly in Wat's life. Poland, partitioned by Russia, Prussia, and Austria in 1772–95, never reconciled itself to this division. The struggle for the nation's resurrection shaped nineteenth-century Polish culture and literature and later became amalgamated, to a significant degree, with the workers' movement. In 1892, the Polish Socialist Party (PPS) was formed in Paris. Józef Piłsudski, the most energetic and adventurous of its leaders, became a legendary figure: sword in hand, he won independence for Poland in 1918. Another Polish socialist, Feliks Dzierżyński, chose a different way, repudiating all sentimental ties with Poland and becoming a Russian Communist of strict Leninist persuasion. After the October Revolution, he founded the infamous Cheka, forerunner of the KGB. Dzierżyński's headquarters in Lubyanka Square in Moscow acquired a notoriety that lingers to this day.

Though Wat saw Piłsudski only once[1] and never met Dzierżyński, one may see them as providing a framework for his mature experience and writing. Wat's stint in Lubyanka during World War II was crucial for his subsequent political and creative biography. He therefore listed his birthday, 1 May, as the first in a series of symbolic facts that prefigured his fate. In his words, such facts "occur at the intersection of two perspectives—one real, historical, concrete, the other metahistorical, transcendental."[2]

During Wat's childhood, 1 May seems simply to have been a holiday, a sort of secular Easter: "On the vulgar level of that feeling, I jokingly considered the crowded First of May manifestations as something being done in my honor, and since the day itself has up to our time always been serene, inundated by sun, really the very first day of spring, it was for me, notwithstanding my permanent depressive inclinations, a prognosis of a happy future."[3]

One of his first intuitions, then, was of sunny, tranquil rebirth and plenitude of life. Jokingly—perhaps only half-jokingly—he perceived himself amid that plenitude in an elevated role, worshiped by throngs—a sage, a king, or

1

rather the son of a king. On 26 December 1963 he noted in his diary (which he kept in his native Polish, but omitting the vowels, as in Hebrew): "To be capable of writing, I must feel myself son of a king, at the very least. Just that, not a great writer, not a genius. Fortunately, since such a sentiment is alien to me."[4]

The experience of participating in carnivalistic revelry, of being the first among many, the chosen one, was inseparably entwined with experiences of a more agonizing kind in Wat's earliest childhood. And his later writings contain many reflections on death, including the following, recorded in a notebook dating from his last years: "The fact that I was never afraid of dying was not even a matter of courage. Always, from the very start of my conscious life, or rather from the moment when my consciousness was assailed by the fact of death—the corpse of a hunchbacked neighbor who died of cholera— . . . I had the feeling that Providence, or God, enters human life only at two points: the time of birth and the time of death. . . . In my case, that feeling, at first intuitive, later conscious, was even more inevitable, because I came into the world dead. For the aforesaid discovery, I am indebted to that fact [of being born dead] and to its early assimilation (perhaps at the age of three), as well as to the circumstance that I have experienced countless agonizing states from the year 1941 up to this day."[5]

The son of a king of Wat's early birthday fantasy became a poet who lapsed into silence early in his life. Agony for him took the form of prisons and hospital beds, which crushed him but at the same time contributed miraculously to a creative rebirth. An archetype for Wat's life comes to mind, one that Wat was perfectly well aware of: Calvary.

Wat's family was Jewish, cultured, and proud of its traditions. His father, Mendel Michał Chwat, graduated from Hebrew school at age sixteen. Through-out his life, Mendel Michał continued to study Scripture, winning renown as an expert on the Kabbalah. The grandfather (whose name we do not know) had an estate and owned a smithy, in which he manufactured weapons for the Polish insurrection of 1863; his daughters aided insurgents forced into hiding. (This was nothing exceptional: Jews in Poland were as a rule sympathetic to the uprising, and many took an active part in it.)

It is said that all male members of the family were notable for their Her-culean build, and indeed, that this accounted for their last name. When one of Mendel Michał's ancestors appeared before the Russian committee charged with providing family names for local Jews (at the end of the eighteenth cen-tury), the head of the board is said to have exclaimed: "Vot khvat!" (Now, here is a dashing fellow!). The Russian word—in its Polish form, *Chwat* or *Chwatt*—stuck. Several generations later, Aleksander, who was never distinguished by a strong constitution, dropped the first two letters (which still did not spare him none-too-refined puns on his semi-pseudonym).

At the end of his life, Wat noted with amusement that he was not the only

Chwat interested in his involved lineage. His older brother brought him a bizarre circular letter mailed in New York. The opening of the letter is conscientiously quoted in Wat's notebook published under the title *Kartki na wietrze* (Scraps of Paper in the Wind): "My name is Samuel Chwat and I am 13 years old. For about a year now, I have been working on a family tree, or genealogy that now has over 10,000 people in it, including such famous people as Red Buttons, Eugene and Willie Howard, Sammy Fain, Mitchell Parrich, Jay & the Americans, the Cohns of Columbia Pictures, the Bayliks of Phillias Cigars, Helena Rubinstein, the owners of Golden Farms, Bernard Baruch, Neiman-Marcus, the European nobility, Elia Kazan, Elijah (1720-97), Wilna Gaon, King David and many others."[6] The unintended humor of the list did not escape Wat. That he was a descendant of King David he knew for certain. He was related to one of the most famous commentators on the Bible and the Talmud, Solomon ben Isaac Rashi of Troyes, who came from David's line. Legends are told about Rashi, who attended the Academies of Mainz and Worms, founded an important school himself, and reportedly died while writing the word *pure* in one of his commentaries (which are still considered authoritative). Another ancestor of Wat, on his grandmother's side, was Isaac ben Solomon Luria, known as *ha-Ari* (the Lion), mystic and Kabbalist of Safed, the original proponent of the so-called Lurianic Kabbalah, who also won fame as a liturgical poet.[7]

Coming closer to our times and to Poland, we find in this long line of ancestors one Israel ben Shabbatai Hapstein of Kozienice (Kosnitz), a Hasidic wonder-worker and preacher whose esoteric knowledge gained him friends and followers even among Polish aristocrats.[8] Finally, Wat's mother's great-grandfather was usually referred to as the Gaon of Kutno. Wat says in his memoirs: "I once visited his grave. He had a splendid tomb covered with many little slips of paper. Not ex-votos, just supplications for him to intercede in an illness."[9]

This heritage of sages and saints, of *hasidim* and *geonim*, was passed on to Wat in early childhood. It must have infiltrated his unconscious through hearing his father's prayers, through family celebrations of the Jewish Holy Days, and through his dreams.[10] Yet he felt the full force of his Jewish background only during his long months of imprisonment in Lubyanka and even later, when, confronted by death, he identified with his ancestors and took their side in an unfinished poem, "Próba genealogii" (An Attempt at Genealogy):

> My ancestor Rashi danced during Simhat Torah.
> He taught in the city of Troyes in the times of Philip the First.
> When Godfrey of Bouillon set out for the Holy Land,
> both locked themselves up in his astronomer's tower
> and deliberated, on what? until the late dawn,
> till the disciples came running: "Rabbi, it is already time for the morning
>   prayer."

The coming day was a day of alarm, when the paupers flocked after
    Godfrey,
but Rashi the philosopher danced because it was Simhat Torah.
You know, glosses of my ancestor to the books of the Old Testament
are still preserved, in Aramaic, in every edition.
My grandsons will be subjects of the count of Paris. Thus, the circle will
    close,
including the episode of three-hundred-odd years in my homeland
on the cold Vistula River.

My great-great-grandfather Israel, maggid of Kozienice, danced during
    Simhat Torah,
a wonder-worker and clairvoyant. Prince Adam asked his advice, on what?
It was a stout kin, and a Muscovite styled them Chwatt, the peasants.
In my grandfather's smithy, in the Truskolasy area, they manufactured arms
    for the insurgents,
his brave brother Berek perished in their ranks (as Korzon notes).
My grandfather lived till eighty-seven years. On Simhat Torah, he ate a
    goose,
drank a flask of Rhine wine, said a prayer, turned to the wall, breathed his
    last. That was in 1870.

Much of Wat's life seems encoded in these semiprosaic, matter-of-fact, yet
enigmatic lines. There is learning and magic, stoicism and vigor, epicureanism
and persistent religious anxiety; secret, perplexing dealings with the powerful of
the earth, participation in politics and in battle, judicious advice—and total
disregard of historical disasters in the name of spiritual duty; intertwined images
of warrior, sage, God's fool; and, first and foremost, the pattern of prayer, of holy
dance before the Lord, of the Word recurring throughout the ages.

Wat's grandfather started out as a fairly rich man, but Russian authorities
confiscated part of his estate, presumably as punishment for his ties to the
insurrection. He had a host of children (perhaps twenty-four—nobody knew
the exact number). The sons received a religious education. One of them,
considered a saint, went to Palestine before World War II and died there. Mendel
Michał Chwat was devoted to religion, perhaps no less than his saintly brother.
He was also well read in the Gentile writers, including Plotinus, Nietzsche,
Kierkegaard, and Tolstoy, as well as in Polish classical literature; he had an
especially high regard for Eliza Orzeszkowa, a popular novelist whose *Meir
Ezofowicz* (1878) was an old-fashioned tale about a just Jew impervious to the
intolerance of his provincial milieu.

Perhaps Mendel Michał felt a bit of Meir Ezofowicz in himself. In any case,
the European and ancient philosophical notions probably combined bizarrely in
his mind with the mystical visions of a Kabbalist. He aspired to a pious life,

seeking fulfillment in the purely spiritual and intellectual sphere, but was forced to conform to the practical demands of his situation as youngest scion of a very large, struggling family. "[They] decided to marry him off. . . . [My father and my mother] had never met before their ritual betrothal; they fell in love, mother not immediately, she cried for many months, but father loved her at first sight. Neither my mother nor the father-in-law would hear anything about a rabbinical vocation. . . . Thus they bought for my father a wholesale store of toys, and since he had no idea of trade, a specialist was employed."[11] The specialist promptly got rid of Mendel Michał. New and not always successful business undertakings followed. First there was a small textile factory in Łódź, an industrial city west of Warsaw, the main center of budding Polish capitalism at the end of the nineteenth century. "Łódź was a wild city. My father was inventive, and mother was immensely laborious and energetic, therefore the competitors hired some part-bandits, part-proletarians to scare him away: there was shooting under the windows, masked faces, one had to close the shutters in the evening, threatening letters were mailed, etc."[12]

Better times came when the family moved to Warsaw, but the welfare of Mendel Michał and his wife, Rozalia, had its ups and downs to the end. Mystical and philosophical concerns, as well as a large private library with texts in many languages, mattered much more to Aleksander's father than his erratic enterprises in the none-too-secure realm of trade. "My father never was a gentleman, he was much nobler than that," Wat noted on 7 December 1963.[13] Between the wars, after suffering a heart attack, Mendel Michał lived with Rozalia mainly in a boardinghouse in Otwock, an outer suburb of Warsaw, paid for by their children. "We visited him from time to time, and I still see him sitting in an armchair in the garden, surrounded by old bearded Jews. Staring at him, they listened attentively to his commentaries to the Scripture," Ola Wat recalled in her memoirs.[14] In his old age he thus followed in the footsteps of Solomon ben Isaac Rashi, his more famous forebear.

Mendel Michał suffered from angina pectoris and died in Otwock at the beginning of the Nazi occupation, in January 1940. He was thus spared the fate of most of his kin, who perished in the concentration camps. Still, his death was painful. In the first days of the war, Aleksander fled to Lwów, soon to be occupied by the Soviets, and in January 1940 was imprisoned by them. "[Father's] larynx was half-paralyzed, he just managed to stammer his last words: Aleksander . . . where is Aleksander? . . . And before my flight from Poland I did not bid farewell to him, because of my egoism, though I could have. And that was a great burden, for a long time, till now."[15]

Wat's mother, Rozalia Kronsilber Chwat, was quite unlike her husband—a fact that struck everyone who knew the family. Her father was a wealthy grain dealer. An extremely proud man, strictly Orthodox, he hated Hasidim, members of the mystical sect to which Israel of Kozienice belonged. Their joyful worship of God offended his sense of propriety and decorum. "I remember how he led me through a crowded commercial street, my little fist trembling in his hand," Wat wrote. "With a stick he pushed away Jews in their long black gowns and shouted: 'Let them burn, all the Hasidim!' . . . And that was a bad omen."[16]

But Rozalia was indifferent to religious and scholarly matters. Cheerful and vigorous, she provided much needed assistance to her husband in his commercial undertakings. She was also devoted to worldly pleasures. "My mother was an avid theatergoer, a born actress. She loved dancing to the point of frenzy, she danced, full of joy, even after she grew lame. On any occasion, even in the last year of her life, 1939. That irritated me greatly."[17]

Almost all Wat's relatives on his mother's side perished during the Holocaust, but Rozalia died of cancer in Otwock in July 1939. Aleksander was at her bedside to the end, while Mendel Michał cried silently in the next room. All his life Wat experienced sharp pangs of conscience remembering his mother. "I really wasn't a good son, and very often I treated her with utter indifference. And my mother was the perfection of what is called the Jewish mother. . . . My mother was dying in full consciousness; she had terrible swellings, she couldn't move at all. She was dying in circumstances that might even be called good: her windows were always open and looked out on a forest of fir trees; it was summer, right before the war—six or seven weeks before. The only thing was that her eyes seemed covered by a film—bulging eyes, eyes that were already dead."[18]

Mendel Michał and Rozalia had eight children. One died early, but the other seven were gifted and naturally inclined to learning. The eldest brother, Aron (Arnold), became a Social Democrat, while the next eldest, Moryc (Maurycy), joined the PPS.[19] Aron, a lover of literature and music, was engaged in trade. He died with his wife, son, and daughter, probably at Treblinka. Moryc, a dilettante violinist, emigrated to Belgium before the war and survived. In the 1950s and 1960s, he and his family helped Aleksander and Ola through their émigré misadventures. The third brother, Dadek (Dawid), youngest boy in the family, was a talented painter. Early in the war he managed, like Aleksander, to force his way to Lwów. But the Soviet occupation frightened him so much that he returned to Warsaw, only to be shot, along with his wife, by the Nazis in a nearby forest.

The eldest sister, Seda (Seweryna), became a famous actress. The family did not approve of her theatrical career, at least at the beginning. "When she started to perform," wrote Wat, "my father told her nothing, he still greeted her—she was his darling—but did not speak to her for two years. The blow was too strong."[20] As Seweryna Broniszówna, Wat's sister made her mark on the Polish stage. Ola described her as "full of fantasy, a brilliant actress who really loved her job. And a splendid, honest, obliging human being. She never made compromises. Although her world had little in common with the world of her parents, she was the best of daughters, always, to the very end, caring about their health, their welfare, and peace of mind in their late years."[21]

Seweryna Broniszówna was no stranger to the colorful political life of interwar Poland. She maintained close ties with people in Józef Piłsudski's intimate circle. Some of the preparatory work for the coup d'état of May 1926 (in which Piłsudski and his group gained dictatorial powers) reportedly took place in her Warsaw apartment. For a time in the early 1920s she was engaged to Władysław Anders, a World War II general who fought gallantly at Monte Cassino and died as an émigré. But they never married, and they met for the last time after the war, in London, where she had come on tour with the Polish Theater. Broniszówna continued to appear on stage until she was ninety. "To the very end she possessed a splendid, metallic, vehement voice, and perfect diction as good as any contemporary actor could be proud of. To the end of her life she read and remained interested in everything: art, theater, politics."[22] Positively anti-Communist, she nonetheless never thought about following her brother's example and leaving her native country. She died at ninety-five.

Little is known about the second sister, Czesia (Czesława), to whom Wat dedicated one of his poems.[23] She married Jerzy Gilewicz, an engineer from an aristocratic family. ("[My father], an enlightened though truly pious Orthodox Jew . . . good-naturedly accepted the fact that my sisters married Catholics," Wat observed in the Polish text of his memoirs.).[24] It was Czesława and her husband who took Aleksander and Ola to Lwów at the outbreak of World War II: they had a car, a rarity in Poland at the time.[25] In November 1939, fed up with the Soviet regime, the Gilewiczes returned to Warsaw illegally. They were luckier than Dadek. Both survived: not only Jerzy the Aryan, but his Jewish wife, too.

The youngest sister, Ewa, six years older than Aleksander, became his closest friend in the family. "She was a person of really extravagant fantasy, of great temperament; although she had not the slightest idea about tailoring, she founded a workshop and dressed all the Polish Theater, such actresses as Przybylko-Potocka, Kamińska, Broniszówna (of course), and many others. She created all the designs, splendid indeed. In Paris, she would have made a great career."[26] As a woman of independent means, she was able to help Wat materially during his impecunious futurist years, as well as later, after his marriage. In 1931, when Wat was imprisoned because of his Communist connections, Ewa was instrumental in securing his release. She did not live to see him set free, however. On the day of his release, 4 December 1931, she was hospitalized with typhus and died that night.

This account of Wat's family would be incomplete without mention of one more person who, though not a family member, was nevertheless an important influence on him. This was the Polish maid Anna (Anusia) Mikulak, who raised all the Chwat children. Wat spoke of her with great warmth. Seduced at age sixteen, Anusia had had to leave her native village. She did penance for this for the rest of her life, making pilgrimages to the holy city of Częstochowa, and the Chwats promised her a Catholic funeral with six priests around her coffin. But this last wish proved impossible to fulfill. During the war, Mikulak was arrested by the Nazis, and it is not known what became of her.

Anna Mikulak taught Aleksander Polish, which was not his parents' first language, and she may well have played a part in Wat's emergence as a Polish poet. "A little bit of my dadaism was influenced by some of her nonsense rhymes," Wat said.[27] (Traditional Polish tales influenced Polish poetry of the 1920s and early 1930s, which gravitated toward expressionism and surrealism, usually with a satiric or humorous tinge. In Wat's case, this influence may have been modified by the example of incomprehensible Kabbalistic texts.)

Aleksander's nanny introduced him to the customs and taboos of the Polish peasantry. "Everyone had a sense of the holiness of bread. Bread is holy. . . . I never forgot how she [Anusia] yelled at me; she probably never had yelled at me like that before. She had given me a roll with something on it; I'd had enough and I threw it away. That was something you didn't do."[28] That simple lesson, taught to Polish peasants by ages of deprivation, Wat later had occasion to put into practice in a Soviet prison cell in Saratov. Finally, there was the imprint of Catholicism. Anusia Mikulak was an ardent churchgoer and took her small ward Aleksander to Mass on the sly. The liturgy made a lasting impression on him and was one of the principal sources of the distinctive amalgam of Judaism and Christianity that characterized his mature work. In his last decades Wat professed loyalty to both faiths, unreconciled but similarly endangered by the evil forces of history:

> Our nanny, Anusia Mikulak,
> a peasant from Przasnysz, taught me songs,
> words, and sayings of her wheaten land.
> She was put to death by the Germans, perhaps in a shelter,
> somewhere in Skierniewice. Twenty years after that
> I found her face, a peasant saint,
> turned to stone, on a capital
> in Avignon.
>
> In the summer evenings she took me on the sly
> as far as Bonifratrian Church to the murky vespers.
> There somebody lifted up his eyes to me from the crucifix.
> Oh, how badly I wanted then to become a ministrant in a small white
>   surplice . . .
> And I could become only a minister in Bierut's Warsaw.
> With a hook of bone collectors I raked the rubble
> of a former Jewish quarter, looking for the family menorah,
> as well as for the Bonifratrian cross. It seemed

I heard the treble of a supplicant under the rubble of a former Jewish
  quarter:
Jerusalem, Jerusalem! Delusion. Silence.
When one is all ears: rustle of bugs of a former Jewish quarter.
I ran away. I still run away. And in my ears, the lament:
Jerusalem, Jerusalem.

Here, in a landscape of destruction and death, at the Wailing Wall of the ruthless
century, a perfect blending was achieved: the melted menorah fused with the
broken cross, war-ravaged Warsaw at one with unattainable Jerusalem.

In the year of Aleksander's birth, 1900, the situation of the family seemed
much improved: "A year or a couple of years of abundance, twenty persons at the
table. . . . But good years were invariably followed by bad ones. Glaring poverty,
though dinners with young people still took place, as if by a miracle."[29] The
Chwats had to move from apartment to apartment repeatedly, so providing their
son with a foretaste of his future nomadic life.

Wat's early memories were traumatic, though rooted in what for others
might have seemed ordinary circumstances. One of the first was of a large clock
that stood in a corner facing his cradle. The enigmatic signs on its dial, the
movement of its hands, the monotonous rhythm of seconds, and the uneven
rhythm of striking hours, Wat confessed, gave him an early sense of immobility
versus motion, continuity versus discontinuity, of two time orders—one deterministic, one random but miraculous. But the sharp pendulum frightened him,
and he would wait anxiously for the moment when it would reach him and cut
his throat. "I am not totally sure now, in the sixty-seventh year of my life," wrote
Wat, "if I did not acquire at that time an ability for meditation that was soon lost
during the years of oblivion, censorship, and quarantine described by Freud."[30]
Another early memory that gave him ample material for meditation was
perhaps even more penetrating. Wat wrote about it in the summer of 1964 in a
five-page essay entitled "Dlaczego piszę wiersze?" (Why Do I Write Poetry?). It
is a brilliant piece of psychological insight and self-analysis, naming and describing the most vaguely perceived states between consciousness and unconsciousness, between life, prelife, and nonlife. A gift of colored pencils at age two gave
Aleksander his first experience of creativity. "The *astonishment* that two things
gave birth to a third new and different one; and immediately afterward: that I
made it and can make it at will, whenever I want; this was such an intense and
specific astonishment that I feel it to be the first astonishment of my life, as well
as one of the most powerful emotions."[31] The best approximation to that staggering impression that he was able to find in his adult life was a near-death
experience in May 1944, during his Soviet exile. Exhausted by hunger and
disease and surrounded by a crowd of Asian beggars, Wat passed out on a large,
sunny square in Alma-Ata, capital of Soviet Kazakhstan, with its view of the

Tien Shan Mountains. The borderline experiences of birth, first creative attempt, and near-death seemed to him closely related, if not by their precise physical qualities, then at least in their intensity.

Characteristically, Aleksander's first successful drawing, made before he was three, was a face—something he then deeply feared, as he confessed:

> I was scared by the human face, by its orifices—they made me sick: the merciless teeth, the fleshy tongues. Still, I used to look at them for a long time, I could not, despite my fear and loathing, divert my eyes from repulsive moving lips, from openings and closings bringing out the words which I tried to imitate in vain, with much torment. . . . But eyes frightened me much more than lips. They differed from everything I was used to already. They equaled themselves and were always something more than themselves; that was their challenge. . . . I was scared by every human face, without exception, also by my mother's face, particularly by my mother's face.[32]

In this extraordinary outpouring an orthodox Freudian might easily read signs of castration anxiety. (Wat, an earnest student of psychoanalysis in his youth, as well as later, was aware of that symbolism.) But that would be an oversimplification. What is striking is Wat's attitude to the body, as source of pain and danger, and the ambivalence of his feelings toward it; his characteristic fusing of bodily and linguistic activities; his perception of the eyes as "something more than themselves," something challenging, the locus of the radically other and the site of transcendence; and finally, the cathartic experience of creation— since, when he succeeded in executing his first awkward drawing of a human face, he suddenly felt relieved of his childish fear.

Next Aleksander discovered the similarity between a face and a house. Drawing houses, he invented his first metaphor and simultaneously experienced for the first time an acute sense of his artistic limitations (the shape of a roof eluded him). Still, the houses on paper looked warm and cozy and gave him a sense of security, symbolizing cover, shelter, perhaps a womb ("Their relation to the multistory buildings where I lived was identical to the relation of small children like myself to adults, and I did not want to grow up at all").[33] Two or three years later, during the Revolution of 1905, an older brother showed him a building in Warsaw with barred windows—a Russian prison, as Aleksander already knew. At home he started drawing human faces with thin bars on their wide-open eyes and mouths. Although this phase soon passed, it seemed to be an intimation of his artistic identity. He early perceived the world as a place of social control and coercion, in which human beings were hapless, unwilling participants. Open eyes and mouths were the only, not necessarily adequate, means of coping with this fact—of witnessing and giving testimony. And the body itself was a prison of the soul—or vice versa.

The Revolution of 1905 altered Polish history as a whole and left traces in the life of the Chwat family. Two of Aleksander's older brothers belonged to the socialist movement. His sisters were no less involved in events. "In 1905, when I was five years old," wrote Wat, "my father and sister returned home bloody from the massacre on Theater Square, and I used to sing and lead my playmates around the courtyard with a little red flag. So, you see, that flag 'will flutter above thrones; it bears the thunder of vengeance, for the blood of the workers is on it'—those are things that truly lodge in your heart. Those little demons or angels that enter you along with a song."[34] Elsewhere, he gave more details.[35] Aleksander had seen his brother wounded by cossack swords (his first witnessing of bloodshed), and the revolutionary songs he became fond of during that time included the "Marseillaise," the "Internationale," and a piece written by Maxim Gorky, "The Sun Rises and Sets"—a prisoner's lament that is unexpectedly echoed in Wat's poem of 1956, "W czterech ścianach mego bólu" (In the Four Walls of My Pain).

After 1905–6, a measure of democracy was introduced in Poland and throughout the Russian Empire. Private (though not public) schools were permitted to teach in Polish. The situation of the Jews also improved. A strong, innovative artistic movement, Młoda Polska (Young Poland), born at the end of the nineteenth century, now reached its acme. Young Poland transformed the tradition of Polish romanticism almost beyond recognition, introducing into it all the problematic values of European literary modernism. Innovation and reconsideration of the literary heritage became the order of the day throughout Central and Eastern Europe.

Aleksander attended a Russian school in Warsaw until 1915, when he switched to the Roch Kowalski Polish classical gymnasium there.[36] Russian became virtually a native language for him (one can easily detect Russian borrowings and calques in his writing, particularly in his early poetry). Signs of an ambivalent attitude to Russia (Czarist as well as Communist) are evident in most of Wat's works—an attitude not characteristic of Poles. "Although in our house the family constantly cursed the Muscovites, I did not feel any aversion to them. . . . Things went worse after 1905, and even worse later, when my brother showed me a cossack on horseback, with a sword and a whistle, before the Bristol [hotel]—then I understood: these were wild invaders. . . . [Still] I was sincerely grateful to the Romanov dynasty, especially after the illumination on Theater Square during their 250th anniversary; [I liked] their portraits so much that even now I read with annoyance about their stupidity and degeneration."[37]

Neither his early, childish political sympathies and antipathies nor the school itself were as important for Aleksander's inner development as the activity he preferred above almost any other throughout his life: reading. He was an extremely precocious, avid reader, so much so that Polish critics have compared him in this respect to Jean-Paul Sartre and Jorge Luis Borges. The third name that comes to mind is Osip Mandelstam, the Russian whose life parallels Wat's in more than one respect (he too was born into a Jewish family, albeit nine years before Wat, also in Warsaw, though he soon left it, later becoming a great poet and victim of Stalin's purges). In his autobiographical essay *The Noise of Time* (1925), Mandelstam made an oft-quoted remark to the effect that the biography of a *raznochinets* (an intellectual in the Czarist empire who did not belong to the gentry) consisted exclusively of the books he or she had read.[38] That statement fits Wat better than anyone.

Wat mastered the art of reading at age three by deciphering the title of a newspaper to which his father subscribed. His first two books belonged to the usual repertory of Polish children's reading of the period: the patriotic *24 obrazki z dziejów Polski* (Twenty-four pictures of Poland's history), by Władysław Ludwik Anczyc, whose kitschy illustrations, Wat conceded, might have spoiled his artistic taste somewhat; and *Gucio zaczarowany* (Bobo's Metamorphosis), a popular tale by an obscure female writer.[39] But Aleksander immediately leapt from these artless compositions to the Polish folio edition of Shakespeare. "During my first fourteen years of readership I read perhaps more books than in the following five decades. . . . I read authors nobody had been interested in for a hundred years. . . . Several years ago I talked to Sir Isaiah Berlin, and both of us competed in listing titles and writers for a long time known to nobody except the authors of rather unreadable dissertations."[40]

Of Shakespeare, Wat liked best the chronicles (especially the Falstaff scenes), *The Tempest,* and *A Midsummer Night's Dream,* the last two of which were for him the zenith of poetry, definitely preferable to lyric poetry.[41] Then he discovered Tolstoy, much loved by his father, and was particularly captivated by his diatribes on the harmfulness and immorality of art as such. Hundreds of authors and works followed, among them Cervantes, Pascal, Kant, Novalis, Hoffmann, Kierkegaard, Schopenhauer, Poe, Meredith, Weininger, *The Monk* by Matthew Gregory Lewis, *The Torture Garden* by Octave Mirbeau, "galloping philosophical rhapsodies" by Johann Georg Hamann, and the apotheosis of married love by Coventry Patmore.[42] From early in his life Wat was fluent in German, and he soon mastered French. His Russian, as noted, approached that of a native speaker, but English authors reached him mainly in translation.

When asked by Ola Wat for reminiscences of Aleksander, his older sister Seweryna answered: "I see him sitting on an open drawer of a large glass bookcase. There were many leatherbound books in it with titles in gold on their spines. He used to sit there from early morning to dusk, immersed in reading. Nothing, just nothing could divert him from his occupation. He saw nothing, he heard nothing, he had no idea of what was going on in the house."[43] Wat himself remembered another hide-out where he could indulge his passion at will: he would lie, book in hand, on his stomach under a large table and observe the world of adults. Under this table he once attempted to strangle himself with a towel when his mother punished him for his extreme love of reading. And under this table his favorite activity was once rudely interrupted when his cousin fell on the floor near him in a severe epileptic fit. This was, for Aleksander, a proof that no shelter is safe, that anyone can be threatened in any place at any time.[44]

Certain tendencies in Wat's reading are striking. On the one hand, his interests took him in the direction of metaphysics, epistemology, and ethics; on the other, he developed a taste for grim romantic tales and grotesquerie, tragic stories with mystical overtones, and violence and horror. From childhood he searched passionately for an all-embracing, all-subsuming Weltanschauung, such as his distant ancestors had found in Scripture and the teachings of the Kabbalah. Aiding his search was a fascination with the sensual qualities of life, in particular the sensuous nature of language. "I am easily impressed by words," Wat wrote in *Scraps of Paper in the Wind*, "by their sound, color, and network of meanings and by the possibilities of syntax hidden in that network, syntax which even in my early childhood I considered the mainstay of speech, since it was, so to speak, at the very center of the mysterious, perhaps sacred, marriage of the universe of language and the universe of events."[45]

Polish writing did not play a conspicuous part in Aleksander's self-education. Naturally, he knew nineteenth-century Polish classics, which were so incessantly recited and quoted by his sisters that many lines entered the family discourse as all-purpose proverbs. But his opinions of such universally esteemed authors as Adam Mickiewicz and Henryk Sienkiewicz fall just short of blasphemy: "I barely managed to look through *The Trilogy* [by Sienkiewicz], it was boring and irritating"; "I came to hate . . . *Forefathers' Eve* [by Mickiewicz] for life, except its third part, but "The Great Improvisation" remained in my eyes a nightmare of poetical stupidity and pseudo-philosophical arrogance. Even now, when I take *Forefathers' Eve* into my hands, I always skip that segment."[46] Wat's words, written shortly before his death, are particularly shocking because *Forefathers' Eve*, including the famous monologue of its protagonist, Konrad—usually referred to as "The Great Improvisation"—appears to have influenced Wat's own writing. If in his early texts this influence was disguised through parody, one may yet argue, as Polish critic Jacek Trznadel has done in an unpublished essay, that *My Century* faithfully follows the compositional pattern of Mickiewicz's dramatic poem and develops its philosophical insights.

Virtually the only Polish writers deemed relevant by Aleksander in these years were the modernists of Young Poland, among them Stefan Żeromski, a naturalist of strong neoromantic leanings, and, first and foremost, Stanisław Przybyszewski, a paradigmatic decadent and bohemian whose fascination with demonology and praise of uninhibited libido rendered him influential far beyond Poland.[47]

Religion played a far smaller role in Wat's childhood than might be supposed in view of both the mystical concerns of his father and Wat's profound interest in metaphysical questions in later years. Aleksander came under the spell of the irreverence that coursed through Europe during that era of fading positivism and ascending modernism. His mother, though a believer, was not too overly observant. "During my very early years, as far as I remember," noted Wat, "she used to bless silver candlesticks on Friday evenings, then she put her beautiful noble hands over her eyes. I liked that ritual immensely. Later, only the High Holy Days were observed: Yom Kippur, Rosh Hashana, Passover. . . . But even on the last, Anusia, on the orders of my mother, kept in her chest a hidden piece of black bread for me, which I loved. At that time, I hated matzo."[48] The younger Chwats, influenced by socialist thought, were virtual atheists. At one period in his childhood, Wat studied popular Darwinian pamphlets and liked to tease Anusia and his father that humans were descended from the apes.

Encouraged by Anusia and their furtive visits to the Bonifratrians, young Aleksander had some interest in Catholicism. Later Wat remembered a unrealized project to have him baptized secretly.[49] But his interest in Catholicism went no further than a childish fascination with the external aspects of the liturgy. Only later, in his unending quest for a mathesis universalis, a Weltanschauung that explains everything in a logical, mathematically consistent way, did Wat wrestle seriously with Catholic theology. But this did not mean any cataclysmic change in his world outlook: Aquinas was for him just one more philosopher to be reckoned with.

Growing up without any real grounding in Judaism, among brothers and sisters who chose assimilation, had a predictable effect: an increasing sense of alienation from the Jewish community, which in Poland adhered rigidly to its essentially medieval habits. There were two exceptions, both connected with the image of a stag, a biblical animal that Aleksander once saw painted inside a little wooden Succoth house and came to identify with himself. Pretending one day to be a stag, he met and lightheartedly mocked a young Talmud student whose mother was dying: many years later, he felt compelled to express his shame and repentance in an enigmatic poem.[50] Another day he happened to be running joyfully on a Warsaw street, in harmony with his mythological incarnation, when he dashed against an old Catholic priest who caught him by the hair and hissed angrily, "Oh, you Beilis!"[51] This was in 1913, the time of the notorious Beilis trial.[52] The happy stag was thus cut short: first by the sight of human distress and death, then by a hunter—and thereby given a foretaste of things to come.

Wat's Jewish identity was probably never in conflict with his Polish identity. As both Jew and Pole, he experienced himself as belonging to a humiliated, persecuted people whose opportunities for dignity and independence had been denied over and over again. He felt solidarity with both groups, and they blended in his consciousness, even at times when the tension between them was overweening. The best reflection of that complex attitude may be found in *Moralia*, the notebook he kept probably during 1953–7: "I never felt myself either a Polish Jew or a Jewish Pole. . . . I always felt myself a Jew-Jew and a Pole-Pole (as they would say in French). It is difficult to explain, yet it is true. I have always been proud (if one is permitted at all to be proud of belonging to this or that group) that I am a Pole, that I am a Jew. And simultaneously driven to despair that I am a Pole, that I am a Jew. What a lot of bad luck!"[53]

Immersed in the books of past centuries, young Aleksander paid little attention to his own time. But the century caught up with him in 1914. On 5 August 1915 the Russians left Warsaw, and the German army moved in.

The situation of the family was bleak. Just before the war, Mendel Michał Chwat had been on the way to becoming a well-to-do man. But the German occupation of Warsaw deprived him of a Russian market and left him with huge debts. Wat remembered these years as a period of "ecstasies of famine" and maintained that they molded his personality no less than did the Soviet prisons.[54] If anything, he read more than before. He even wrote, in German, an extensive summary of Kant's *Critique of Pure Reason,* which later so impressed the well-known philosopher Tadeusz Kotarbiński that he accepted Aleksander, a freshman, in a graduate seminar.[55]

Wat's school years "went in a zigzag course, by knight's moves."[56] He attempted to overcome his financial woes by giving private instruction but rarely succeeded because of his overqualification and whimsical nature. Once, for example, invited to help a boy who badly needed a tutor in physics, Wat instead offered him a series of talks on the Italian Renaissance and was immediately sacked.[57] Still, he was fortunate in striking up a number of friendships that proved important in later life. One was his schoolmate Anatol Stern, son of a Jewish Warsaw journalist, a year older than Aleksander and also surviving him by one year. At school Stern was known mainly for his inability to learn mathematics. Later he became one of the most audacious spokesmen of Polish futurism, noted for his distinctive black humor and love of practical jokes. During their futurist phase Wat and Stern were generally perceived as literary twins (an impression they themselves countenanced). Another friend who later played a role in the Polish futurist movement, Stefan Kordian Gacki, was like Wat in his precocious philosophical aspirations. Gacki's role in the futurist enterprise was less than outstanding, but he was a loyal friend in times of adversity.[58]

In his eighteenth year, Aleksander Chwat seems to have been a sensitive, vulnerable youth—a typical neurasthenic. He became afflicted with severe illness only after many ordeals in prison and exile, but at least some of its roots are to be found in Wat's early psychological conflicts. His reading and daydreaming testify to an amazingly rich inner life, accompanied by what one of his sisters later described as a "total absence from the world."[59] What encounters he had with the external world tended to be traumatic. Although beautiful as a small child, he suffered greatly throughout his school years because of his appearance (he had the misfortune to break his nose in an accident at age three). "I convinced myself," he writes in *Scraps of Paper in the Wind*, "that I was hideous, and since I never liked ugly faces, I developed an antipathy, then a disgust, for my own person: thus probably *le moi haïssable* appeared early in my life. My morbid shyness endured perhaps until the Soviet *tiurmy* [prisons]. . . . I learned fast to see myself from the outside in the least advantageous shape: ugly, unpolished, awkward, poor, clumsy, filthy in my dreams and daydreams."[60]

Playmates more often than not rejected him, in part because he was Jewish. Further, his early erotic experiences were frustrating. He was equally inclined to wild games of imagination and unusual exercises in self-imposed discipline. In the summer of 1917 he fasted for three days without drinking a drop of water.[61] "I had been highly excitable all through my youth," Wat confessed. "For quite a long time, in any case for a few years, I imposed certain ideals of castration on myself. I thought that Origen had done exactly the right thing."[62] It is tempting to regard him as a paradigmatic Dostoevskian hero—a man from the underground, a young Raskolnikov or Ivan Karamazov.

He also became oversaturated with books, with philosophy and literature. Wat was intellectually independent, disdaining established artistic conventions, including the conventions of modernism, whose innovative character was fading rapidly anyway. Yet he felt incapable of originality and hence deprived of any means of self-affirmation. As he stated in his memoirs, there was a tinge of Buddhism in his denial of further possibilities for development. Anatol Stern nicknamed him Buddha-Zarathustra, and that oxymoronic definition stuck in his final years at school.[63]

The political situation was conducive to extremist leanings. The February Revolution in Russia gave way to the October Revolution. At that time, and particularly from the vantage point of a Poland still occupied by the Germans, revolution in Russia seemed—if not for everybody, then for many, including young Aleksander Chwat—an event fraught with unknown but perhaps liberating consequences. The German empire fell. In November 1918 an independent Poland reappeared on the map.

A childish fascination with the Russian Revolution resulted in a singular episode in Aleksander's life. By his own account, he planned to flee Warsaw and his family in the spring of 1918, immediately before his final exams at the gymnasium. He persuaded two schoolmates to go with him. Their destination appeared to be Russia. One of Aleksander's sisters reportedly managed to put an end to his adventure at the last moment (which, considering the situation in Russia, was definitely a happy ending).[64]

Aleksander had to pass the exams he was trying to avoid. In the fall of 1918, with that ordeal behind him, he became a university student—and a budding artist. "At the age of eighteen," he wrote, "I revolted—a funny, unsightly, wretched Faust, a little Faust of Warsaw: I wanted to live. Hence, my futurism."[65]

Futurism, 1919–1924

"Boredom and disgust . . . were the midwives of Polish futurist poetry," Wat wrote in 1930, reviewing the crucial literary experience of his youth.[1] A rebellious—even nihilistic—attitude to social and ideological order, to traditional morals and manners, a perennial oedipal gesture repeated by virtually every new generation, undoubtedly contributed to the birth of the futurist movement. World War I left in its wake a poignant feeling of failure. In Poland the years of war resulted not just in torment and death, although the country had its fair share of these—but also, quite miraculously, in the rebirth of the nation. For the first time in more than a century, Polish culture and literature were freed of their obligatory patriotic commitment. It became obvious that habitual patterns of writing were severely limited. Repudiation of previous modes and devices characterized every artistic movement in postwar independent Poland. The futurists simply took the most radical stand.

Poland was now widely receptive to new currents both Eastern and Western. The first futurist manifesto, written by Filippo Tommaso Marinetti, had appeared in Paris in February 1909. Around 1913, Guillaume Apollinaire (a writer of Polish extraction) embraced the new movement, continuing a long, distinguished line of French *poètes maudits*. In 1915 Tristan Tzara and his friends started their iconoclastic performances at Zurich's Café Voltaire, which became a breeding ground for dadaism, related to futurism but even more provocative in its total negation of order and decorum.[2] An even more immediate influence on Poland issued from Russia, where at the beginning of World War I, futurism was already in its prime, led by such men as Vladimir Mayakovsky, a powerful poet who sided with the Communist revolution and was promptly destroyed by it, first as a writer, then as a human being; Velimir Khlebnikov, who created poems in which all the mythologies of humankind converged and verbal experiments abounded; and Aleksei Kruchenykh, who indulged liberally in "transrational language" that excluded all denotative sense.

The qualities that distinguished futurists were above all an inclination to break all taboos, violate all imaginable rules of language and "good taste," and

shock and scandalize. Futurism was also characterized by messianic and eschatological expectations, albeit interwoven with a cult of modern technology,
and a profoundly ambivalent attitude to the city, perceived as at once a source of
fascination and the locus of pathology.

The futurist movement reached Poland only belatedly. In 1919, the great
futurist battles were already a thing of the past in Paris and Moscow. Further,
Poland's native literary tradition, in particular the romantic tradition, was so
powerful and pervasive that to dismantle it required more than sheer boldness
and insolence—the only qualities possessed in abundance by most Polish
acolytes of the futurist faith.

For Wat, futurism was his great adolescent adventure. One of the most
shrewd, perceptive chroniclers of the movement, he also became one of its most
uncompromising critics. For him, futurism was a warning and a foreboding.
Retrospectively, he saw in his futurist poems a rough draft of his mature writing,
a first, if erroneous, approach to his later spiritual concerns. "Wat wrote just a
little," said Adam Ważyk, discussing this particular period, "but each of his
productions was symptomatic, indicating some seminal, as yet undeveloped,
possibilities."[3]

Wat's studies at the University of Warsaw were erratic, to say the least. His
early interest in Kant and Schopenhauer led him to apply to the Department of
Philosophy. He attended lectures and seminars conducted by several professors
of international reputation, more often than not stunning them with his precocious erudition and controversial opinions; but he never took his university
assignments too seriously. He led a bohemian life replete with drinking bouts
and erotic escapades alternating with attempts to write poetry.

Young Aleksander's daredevil flights of fantasy made an impression on
many. In fall 1963, in Paris, he caught up with an old acquaintance who well
remembered it all, as Wat recorded:

> [After World War I] he had just come from Russia, and both of us, Stern
> and myself, questioned him avidly about everything, about Mayakovsky, etc.
> And I immediately, straightaway impressed him as a poet, first and foremost (in
> contrast to Stern, who seemed to him an impostor). I talked for a long time,
> provocatively, with panache, about my decision to become pope. I developed a
> plan: to attain the rank of cardinal very rapidly, and to be elected to the papal
> throne before my thirty-fifth birthday. I spoke so oddly and so vigorously that
> he was totally at a loss: was he dealing with a madman, with a scoffer, or with a
> maniacal visionary? In any case, he was dealing with a poet.[4]

In his university years, Wat cut a striking figure—an elegant eccentric with
an unmistakeable and extraordinary, if not fully developed, talent. He attempted
to overcome the inhibitions of his youth with arrogance and often with alcohol.
The models were at hand: the poètes maudits, Baudelaire, and Rimbaud.

During the years 1919–24, no fewer than a dozen different literary groups appeared in Poland, including expressionists, formists, the Kraków Vanguard, and others. They denounced one another with remarkable zeal. Most of Young Poland's leaders were still active; indeed, some reached their acme only much later. But the avant-garde character of Young Poland had faded. Its vocabulary, syntax, and style smacked of exaggeration and pretention. According to Wat, "the old means of expression, universally imitated, all of a sudden became too facile and lost their impact on perception and imagination. . . . Therefore, the catchy thing was impressiveness, emphasis, grandiloquence, enigmas and gratuitous insinuations, exclamation marks and suspension points, rare and disfigured words and phrases, demonic abstraction, unusual details, ornament and 'grandeur,' overstatement—the whole arsenal of means for 'making strange.' One should not be surprised by Przybyszewski, since even Nietzsche, a writer of genius, did not avoid such things."[5]

The most visible of the new schools called itself Skamander (which was also the name of its literary review). The Scamander (now the Menderes) flowed through the plain of Troy, as sung by Homer—and by Stanisław Wyspiański, the most talented and idiosyncratic of the Young Poland writers. In his dreamlike mythological play *Acropolis,* Wyspiański depicted the Scamander merging with the Vistula, on the banks of which the city of Kraków (and Warsaw) stands. That merging of rivers symbolized an encounter between traditions and myths, the grafting of eternal values onto Polish art. Even if they mistrusted Wyspiański's grandiloquence, the poets of Skamander adhered to that program. They created mainly joyful and lighthearted poetry, classical and cosmopolitan in spirit, employing traditional patterns of metrics and rhyme. Rejecting the extremes of Polish decadence, poking fun at literary clichés, and evincing a mildly disrespectful attitude toward things commonly held sacred, they practiced an art of happy compromise that immediately won the public's heart.

Before they established the review, the Skamandrites used to read their poetry in a Warsaw literary café named Under the Picador, where Aleksander chanced to see them in early 1919. He subsequently became acquainted with eminent members of the group—Antoni Słonimski, Julian Tuwim, Jarosław Iwaszkiewicz, and Jan Lechoń. The performances of the Picadorians were provocative, following, if cautiously, patterns already elaborated by Western and Russian prophets of the new art. In his book *Czyhanie na Boga* (Ambushing God, 1918), Tuwim described himself as "the first Polish futurist," though that was an overstatement.

Wat valued highly the "fantastic formal skill" of the Skamandrites and their exuberant gifts.[6] "A galaxy of talents that occurs once in a hundred years," he wrote in *Scraps of Paper in the Wind.* "[But Poland] was already long ago excluded from conscious circulation of ideas and poetic devices. And the revolution of the Skamandrites was pre-Rimbaldian, naive; it never questioned itself.

They were naive, just naive, completely unaware that the ancient universe had collapsed irreversibly—and what is poetry if not the most intimate signal from the 'universe'?"[7]

Tuwim especially attracted Wat's attention, and the two poets—Wat, always an outcast, and Tuwim, early proclaimed a living classic—became friends.[8] An unfinished article on Tuwim displays a measure of the fascination that this unusual man stirred in Wat. Wat praised the great Skamandrite's campaign that led to the renewal of Polish poetic diction: Tuwim was *the* writer who disclaimed poetry's rhetorical habits and permeated it with voices of the street. Yet Wat mercilessly picked on Tuwim's timidity and lack of determination, the conformism that resulted in his cowardly behavior during the Stalinist years. "If I were an ornithologist, I would form Tuwim's portrait from birds' fragments. A collage of peacock, hummingbird, lark, and vulture. . . . His *daimonion* was birdlike. It was noncarnivorous, it pecked grubs."[9]

Another man of more carnivorous disposition became a father figure of sorts to Wat during his futurist period: Stanisław Ignacy Witkiewicz, the most original Polish writer of the 1920s and 1930s. In Poland between the wars, Witkiewicz—or Witkacy, his common pseudonym—was regarded primarily as an eccentric and was rarely taken seriously as an artist. His bizarre absurdist plays and novels enjoyed little success during his lifetime, and his paintings, though somewhat in vogue, were generally considered the products of a sick imagination. His central, deliberately tedious philosophical treatise *Pojęcia i twierdzenia implikowane przez pojęcie istnienia* (Notions and Assertions Implied by the Notion of Being, 1935) was appreciated by the proverbial happy few. Witkacy committed suicide by a massive drug overdose at the onset of World War II. Only after the war was he recognized as a key figure in the development of the modern mentality and an unusually consistent theoretician of art.[10]

Witkacy praised art as the best manifestation—and root—of metaphysical awareness, but he also maintained that modern mass culture, which he tended to identify with totalitarianism, inevitably led to the extermination of both art and human values. His own creative work was to become a last stand in this hopeless struggle, the acrid fruit of art's agony. It rejected verisimilar logic and conventional psychology and introduced arbitrary actions, incongruous philosophical discussions, and black humor; yet Witkacy's work never became anarchic, because it possessed an almost mathematical precision.

In 1918–22 Witkacy lived primarily in the mountain health resort of Zakopane. His literary activity consisted mainly in penning polemical articles on painting and theater in a highly personal, idiosyncratic style. He had an amazing capacity for work. "His friends maintain," wrote Wat in 1926, "that he executes a painting, writes a play, an answer to criticism, a chapter on aesthetics, and a chapter on philosophy every day."[11] But his towering presence in Polish culture was due less to his creative output than to his unusual, defiant way of life. A bohemian, at once clownish, nonchalant, and deadly serious, he extended his taste for artistic and philosophical experiments to the realm of everyday actions and attitudes. His orgiastic adventures and intermittent drug addictions, publicized widely, made of him a larger-than-life, almost mythical hero. In a constantly stirred, excited atmosphere, he experimented not only on himself but on others, too.

In 1919, an exhibition of Witkacy's paintings at the Polish Artistic Club inspired several of Wat's poems in prose.[12] In turn, Witkacy was quite taken with his younger colleague's work, in which he saw a kindred taste for borderline or extreme experiences. Nevertheless the two did not become acquaintances until 1921, because the trip from Warsaw to Zakopane plus a prolonged stay in that capital of Polish eccentrics and bohemians was expensive. In his memoirs Wat presented the atmosphere of Witkacy's house and circle in picturesque terms: "Straight from the train, I ran to the boardinghouse kept by his mother. . . . He welcomed me stark naked, and while talking and looking at me he immediately urinated into a chamber pot: that was perhaps a test for pederasty—he was not a homosexual himself, but he used to submit his friends, any person at all, to various tests, creating the most extravagant situations for them. I always had a reflexive aversion to pederasty; the mere thought of it made me sick."[13] A prolonged drinking bout followed. Witkacy introduced Wat to his small group of young aristocrats, artists, and liberated ladies as an eccentric count from Romania. (Słonimski, who was present and knew Wat very well, did not betray the secret.) Wat discoursed with relish in dadaist babble, then proclaimed himself an ostrich, took off his clothes, and sat on a hollowed stone with the apparent intent of laying ostrich eggs. Such happenings were repeated more than once, and under Witkacy's influence Wat "accepted death in a gutter as his life's goal."[14]

Their friendship did not last long. Traces persisted during the late 1920s and 1930s.[15] But they parted after Wat joined the Communist movement: Witkacy understood totalitarianism far too well to support Wat's new credo. "Then my attachment to Witkacy turned almost into hate, we virtually scratched each other's eyes out. I, the Communist agitator."[16] Even much later, Wat's attitude to his mentor remained ambivalent.

Of course, Witkacy's and Wat's joint efforts was never confined to drunken escapades and practical jokes. Their artistic paths were almost parallel. Both writers rebelled against conformism, tepid banality, and the submission to common taste characteristic of the Skamandrites. For a considerable period, Witkacy provided young Wat with a model of courage and consistency in challenging Victorian habits. That same relentless consistency, inspired at least in part by Witkacy, is evident in Wat's attitudes even during his Communist phase. Wat was already blessed with a rich, free imagination, but it was Witkacy who taught

him how to subject it to an unbending intellect. The acute sense of crisis so
characteristic of the young Aleksander became, if anything, even more intense
and refined under his older friend's tutelage.

If Wat was less than satisfied with the "pre-Rimbaldian revolution" of the
Skamandrites, in Witkacy he encountered an attitude that was definitely post-
Rimbaldian: "Just imagine Gogol after Rimbaud, moreover, after Marinetti,
after futurism, after Mayakovsky," he said about Witkacy in his memoirs.[17] The
influence was nevertheless mutual. However much he was interested in Witkacy's notion of "pure form" and in his antiutopianism, Wat often surpassed
Witkacy in the mocking refutation of all clichés, as well as in the power of his
tragic imagination.

The seeds of their discord—politics aside—were multiple. Wat never
concealed his doubts about the vestiges of a decadent (and romantic) mentality
in Witkacy's writing. He mocked the all-embracing categories Witkacy used to
interpret his program. Such bombastic terms as "unsatisfied need," "ecstasy,"
"inspiration," and "eternity," strewn profusely in Witkacy's theoretical writings
and artistic pieces, certainly approached clichés.[18] But Wat's ultimate rejection
of Witkacy's platform derived from another source. Attracted by the power of
Witkacy's reasoning and by his intellectual honesty, Wat nevertheless rejected
his dandyish nihilism and extreme individualism, which left no place for human
comfort or transcendental hope. Throughout his career, Witkacy attempted to
erase the dividing line between vital phenomena and artistic phenomena—a line
that Wat felt should not be crossed. In Wat's view, life was too profound and
meaningful to be manipulated solely in pursuit of one's own peculiar creative or
exploratory ends, as raw material for risky experiments on oneself and others.
Here he saw an uncanny kinship between the decadent artist and the totalitarian
dictator. Both considered life to lie lawfully within the sphere of an absolute
subjectivity. For Wat, after his experience of prison and exile, such an attitude
was morally unacceptable—and a sign of weakness.[19]

Friend, mentor, rejected authority, Witkacy fascinated Wat to the end of his
days. One of Wat's last poems, written in March 1967 and not included in his
posthumous book, was conceived as a fragment of a letter to Witkacy. The
poignancy of that apostrophe to a long-departed addressee is striking:

> For very long, now, Ignacy,
> we do not raise our eyelids here: for eyes, here it is forbidden
> to take a simple shape. . . .
> Of course, I choke on those vapors that tumult
> and roar. And it blinds the eyes,
> everything waves. A wave
> adores wave, a wave devours wave,
> a wave renders unto a wave
> its virginity.

Wat and Stern launched their futurist campaign as early as the end of 1918. They published a small leaflet on blue paper with the unequivocal title *Tak* (Yes) that "proclaimed an absolute approval of modernity."[20] The leaflet was presumably written in shocking language, but it is difficult to say anything more about it because not a single copy has survived. On 8 February 1919, Stern and Wat arranged their first poetry reading, which is usually taken as marking the authentic birth of Polish futurism. The reading took place in a concert hall on Mazowiecka Street and was called "Wieczur podtropikalny użądzony przez białych murzynów" (A Subtropical Evening Organized by White Negroes).[21] A large primitivist poster by Henryk Berlewi portended the evening's supposedly exotic and threatening nature.

"That was probably the most grotesque poetry reading in Poland," Wat wrote in 1930.

> Its program consisted of a poem assembled by us from various excerpts of Poe, Verhaeren, Longfellow, et al., translated by Lange [Antoni Lange, a Young Poland poet], and of a poem by Banville. That was the passéist part. The futurist part: a performance by an African, the authentic Yusuf ben Mchim, who danced half-naked, trembling with cold, and sang African songs; a poem by a Picadorian T. Kruk, a musical opus by M. Centnerszwer entitled "Andromeda in a Bathroom" or something of the kind, and poems by myself and Stern marked by outrageous syntax and pornographic Rabelaisian content. There was much about sperm and the passing of intestinal winds, "by which I will disperse you." But the climax of the program was a man in the nude, with a light gauze band on his hips. At the very last moment he got cold feet; we had to push him on stage by force. He read Stern's poem entitled "The Burning of the Fig Leaf." He was expected to burn the fig leaf but did not do it. . . . Afterward, there was much talk and many reviews, none too complimentary.[22]

Seweryna Broniszówna, hardly a futurist sympathizer, was invited by her brother to recite some of his poems. She protested, saying she did not understand a word of them. "That does not matter. It's enough if you read them well," answered Aleksander, unperturbed. Seda yielded to pressure but never reached the end of her reading, because the ill-fated man with the fig leaf took the platform too early. A commotion ensued, and Seda joined Warsaw's stately ladies and young daughters in fleeing the concert hall.[23]

Similar happenings followed. Several took place in the café Under the Picador, where Wat and Stern were assisted by the less provocative Tuwim and others. Most of the pieces presented at these evenings were ephemeral. Created and read impromptu, their sole purpose to stir public resentment, they never made it into print.

"It was hard to single out any stable moments at that period: every month brought a certain fluctuation."[24] One of the fixed points was the closing of Under the Picador at the end of March, following a police search in late February. Futuristic performances, however guileless, gave ample fuel for political suspicions, especially since Warsaw was under martial law. The police had received an anonymous letter suggesting that Under the Picador was a site for bolshevik meetings and a weapons depot. The thorough search that ensued produced nothing, but this did not keep the café from closing. Friendly relations between the futurists and the Skamandrites, cemented by this incident, persisted, however, even after their common breeding ground had disappeared.[25]

The first futurist books began to be printed, including Wat's *JA z jednej strony i JA z drugiej strony mego mopsożelaznego piecyka* (ME from One Side and ME from the Other Side of My Pug Iron Stove). Editorial activity alternated with impish pranks. One fair Sunday in Warsaw Stern pushed Wat on a wheelbarrow along the main avenue from the Belweder Palace to the castle.[26] Another practical joke was less innocent: Wat and Stern (both Jews) presented parodic anti-Semitic lectures to a group of young Zionists, provoking a brawl.[27] (The borderline between such undertakings and futurist poetry readings was rather blurred.)

During 1919, Wat, Stern, and their fellow-traveler Jerzy Jankowski were the only major actors on the Polish futurist scene. But in 1920, their monopoly ended. A new group appeared in Kraków and started performances that, if anything, surpassed the Warsaw happenings in impertinence. The group's leading figure was Bruno Jasieński, a man with a bizarre and tragic fate.[28] He spent his high school years in Moscow, where he absorbed the artistic novelties of the Russian avant-garde. In Poland, he readily took on the role of futurist judge of taste. The member of the Kraków group who made a more serious impression on Wat was Tytus Czyżewski, a poet and painter. Jasieński's work struck Wat as secondary and imitative ("Jasieński had absolute memory for poems, he read a poem and immediately recited it by heart. And that was, for him, a tremendous creative handicap")[29]; by contrast, Czyżewski was more authentic: his futurism came from the depths of his naive personality, which was reminiscent of Henri Rousseau.[30]

The development of Polish futurism was suspended by the Polish-Soviet war, which began in April 1920. Red cossacks approached Warsaw in August but were crushed by Piłsudski's troops on 16–18 August (their defeat immediately became known as "the miracle on the Vistula"). Although most Polish Jews supported Piłsudski and his state, some were preemptively arrested or interned by the authorities as suspected Communist sympathizers. Wat escaped that misfortune: during summer and early fall, he served in a machine gun company in the township of Ostrów Wielkopolski, west of Warsaw.

From the beginning, futurism in Poland was a paradoxical movement. In Wat's words, Polish futurist poets praised modernity and posed as prophets of new times but remained singularly ignorant of the realities of their own country.[31] Their concepts were mainly imported. Neither Italian futurism, with its aggressive imperialist strivings, nor Russian futurism, with its utopian bent, could take root in Poland. In a land with less-than-modern cities and an extremely conservative countryside, with a still powerful feudal ethos and only middling standards of bourgeois life, any attempt at a cult of dynamism, any glorification of the machine, any Russian-style revolutionary slogans, were curiously out of place.[32]

Wat and Stern, moreover, were far from well versed in futurism when they launched their risky enterprise. Wat's assertion that they were unaware of a single futurist work may well be an exaggeration, but rumors about the new movement probably counted more than any direct knowledge.[33] The extratextual aura that surrounded European and Russian futurism had a stronger influence than the texts themselves—all the more so because adepts of that literary movement deliberately erased the boundary between text and nontext, writing and happening.

One might apply to the Polish futurists a famous formula of Osip Mandelstam: they "longed for world culture."[34] They refused to give in to Polish particularism and provincialism. But here yet another paradox became obvious: world culture, for them, was primarily a revelation of crisis. The futurists, especially Wat, the best educated among them, sensed acutely that culture, at least for the time being, had exhausted its resources. Existential anguish, catastrophic premonitions, revolt, and malaise were the order of the day. The slogan of "liberated words," promoted by Marinetti and his followers, fitted that context well. The longing for world culture therefore had to be translated into a triumphant countercultural gesture.

Here, feelings of despair turned almost miraculously into those of joy. The extremist hilarity of the futurists was quite different from the tame, cheery optimism of the Skamandrites, which had been precipitated mainly by the happy change in Poland's political status. The futurists boldly and wittily punctured received myths and stereotypes—especially native ones. Western Europe was considered the heartland of clownery, and Russia enjoyed an ambivalent, vaguely dangerous reputation as the land of creative anarchy.[35]

Futurism in Italy, and even more so in Russia, became a profound revision of all the technical means of art. The futurists emphasized the strictly poetic function of language—even denying its referential function. Interrelations among words were considered far more important than their denotational relations to any phenomena. Yet poetry had no privileged status as compared to other means of communication. Poetry was to be perceived in the same conceptual framework as everyday talk, news accounts, nursery rhymes, electoral slogans, and so on.

That innovative view, which was particularly fruitful in the realm of literary theory, gave rise to far-reaching experiments. The futurists created ephemeral, disposable "languages." Phenomena never before accorded the status of signs were now drawn into the sphere of signification. Free association was proposed as a means of inquiry into the dynamics of modern consciousness; later, under the influence of Freud, it became a tool for the study of the unconscious. The technique of simultaneity led to a nonlinear language. The principle of juxtaposition reigned supreme: futurists advocated that any words, no matter how different their meaning, provenance, and stylistic value, could and should confront one another on the page, marveling at each other and astonishing the reader with their unexpected but unquestionable kinship.

Polish avant-garde poets did their best to learn these techniques of phantasmagorical deformation. There were amusing wordplays, harsh neologisms, fusing of roots, interchanging of affixes, and experiments in typography and punctuation. A cosmic and anthropomorphic metaphor characteristic of Mayakovsky came into vogue, in part because it helped to insinuate into a poem some of the Young Poland patterns that persisted in the young futurists' imaginations.[36] Everyone took it as a point of honor to out-Herod Herod. In an article of 1980, Wat (then an orthodox Marxist) characteristically related this inflation of novelties to postwar economic inflation. It would be farfetched to see in economics the only, or the main, cause of the futurist contest for new devices, but the parallel is instructive. "The law of identity was no longer valid. An object lost its self-consistency. In the morning, it differed substantially from what it had been in the previous evening."[37]

Still, the total reevaluation of the very concept of poetic language, undertaken by such different personalities as Marinetti and Khlebnikov, was alien to Stern and Jasieński, whose task was primarily destructive. The ultimate goal of world futurism was the creation of a coherent if unusual language that would widen the range of human perception and expression. By contrast, the Polish futurists preferred the more modest goal of subverting traditional languages.

One of the first victims was the artificiality of art. Polish futurists made fun of the notion of the artist as a superior being, haughtily apart from the crowd but also leading, educating, and transforming the people—a myth promoted by such Polish classical writers as Mickiewicz and retained, to a degree, by Mayakovsky and Witkacy. The best way to relate to the crowd was to taunt and provoke it.

Decades of humiliation had made Poland into a land of idolatry: petrified, though presumably sacred, values of Polish history and literature constrained the national mind. The futurists boldly assaulted the idols of this self-pitying society. The narrow-minded philistine mentality, mocked already by the Skamandrites, was victim of their scorn. "Polish futurism . . . [became] a crooked mirror in which Caliban scrutinized himself and gave a grimace of disgust."[38]

The entire universe of culture, moreover, was perceived as a repository of signs, codes, and texts that had lost their value and prestige. The rejection and refutation of culture masqueraded as a trivial schoolboyish joke. Polish futurists' standard technique was to employ perfectly correct sentences and traditional forms of metrical verse or unpretentious ditty but charge them with extravagant and disgusting concepts. An extreme example was Jasieński's poem "Mięso kobiet" (Meat of Women), in which he declared that the best way to express one's love of a woman was to devour her raw or, better yet, cooked.

There is a temptation to interpret the Polish futurist enterprise as a variant of carnival, the vagabond merrymaking that occurs during periods of social change and provides an indispensable counterweight to rigid, official culture.[39] That idea draws weight from the futurists' preaching of radical optimism, hedonism, and fervent affirmation of life and its pleasures to the point of inanity. A more immediate predecessor was Alfred Jarry, nineteenth-century French practitioner of black humor and author of the grotesque comedy *Ubu Roi*. Fittingly, the action of that savage, funny play took place in "Poland, that is, nowhere."

In the fall of 1920, as the Polish–Soviet war was nearing an end, Wat and Stern resumed their artistic and para-artistic activities. Their next exercise in "antiliterature" was a twelve-page booklet, *To są niebieskie pięty które trzeba pomalować* (These are the Blue Bare Heels that should be Painted), with two bare feet outlined on the cover. A similar publication was *Nieśmiertelny tom futuryz* (An Immortal Volume of Futurisias). This so-called volume consisted of two pages (one of which was the cover) and four ephemeral, if shocking, poems by Stern and Wat. The largest and most famous of these offensive publications, *gga*, appeared in December 1920, with a print run of five hundred copies.[40] Part manifesto, *gga* also included two cycles of frivolous poems: Stern's part was entitled *muza na czworakach* (Muse on all Fours), and Wat's part presented itself as *fruwające kiecki* (Flying Petticoats).

The manifesto might be described as the first extensive presentation of the Polish futurist credo in print:

the great iridescent monkey known as dionysus has long since bit the dust. we are throwing his rotten legacy out
we proclaim:
I. CIVILIZATION AND CULTURE WITH ITS JUSTICE—TO THE TRASH HEAP.
we choose simplicity vulgarity, gaiety health, triviality, laughter.
laughter fattens the soul and gives it strong sturdy legs.
we renounce voluntarily dignity, seriousness, pietism, we will use laurels by which you crown us for seasoning of our meals.

II. WE ABOLISH HISTORY AND POSTERITY. also rome tolstoy, criticism hats india bavaria and krakow. . . . We *will destroy the city*. all those mechanisms—airplanes, tram cars, inventions the telephone. instead of them the primordial means of communication. the apotheosis of the horse. only homes that are collapsible and mobile. a language of shouts and rhymes.

III. We see the social system as domination by genuine idiots and capitalists. that is the most fertile ground for laughter and for revolution.

IV. **wars should be fought with fists. murder is unhygienic. women should be changed often. . . .**
V. **PRIMITIVE.**
VI. art is only that which produces health and laughter. . . .
from the smoky pub of the infinite we throw out the wretched hysterical creatures known as poets. . . . **instead of aesthetics antigrace. instead of ecstasy—intellect.** conscious and deliberate creation. . . .

. . . .

VIII. poetry. we allow rhyme and rhythm to remain since they are prime and fertile. **destruction of constrictive creative regulations clumsiness is a virtue.** freedom of grammatical forms, spelling and punctuation, depending on the creator. mickiewicz is pedestrian. **slowacki is incomprehensible mumbling.**

WORDS have their weight, sound, color, their contour, THEY OCCUPY SPACE. . . . meaning of a word is subordinate and does not depend on concept attributed to it. . . .

. . . .

X. We glorify reason and therefore reject logic as a limitation, the cowardice of the mind. nonsense is magnificent. . . .

let us open our eyes. then a pig will seem even more enchanting than a nightingale, and a gga of a gander will dazzle us more than a swan's song.[41]

The eclecticism of the Polish futurists' impertinent proclamation is striking. In their repudiation of literary traditions, the authors of *gga* strictly follow their Russian colleagues, who proposed to throw Pushkin, Dostoevsky, and Tolstoy "from the ship of contemporaneity" in a much earlier pamphlet, *A Slap in the Face of Public Taste* (1912).[42] The concept of the autonomous word reiterates the Russian futurist notion of *slovo kak takovoe* (the word as such), developed by Kruchenych and Khlebnikov in 1913.[43] And there is an unmistakeable echo of Marinetti's "words at liberty."[44] Even the "gga of a gander," more bewitching than the decadent swan's song, is a travesty of Mayakovsky's formula *prostoe kak mychanie* (simple as cow's bellowing). To all that, Wat and Stern add a sprinkling of pacifist and anticapitalist catchwords. A magnanimous promise to destroy the cities and the mechanisms supported by "the apotheosis of the horse" forms one of the more original points of the manifesto (a typical futurist would rather affirm the aesthetic validity of modern city life).[45]

The key word is *primitive*—not without reason capitalized and emphasized in the text. This retrogressive utopianism is a recurrent motif in the history of ideas: in the postwar and postrevolutionary years of the early twentieth century it was promulgated by many writers, not all of them futurists. The Russian philosopher Mikhail Gershenzon spoke for many when he wrote in 1920:

> These other-worldly speculations which inevitably fall into systems obeying the laws of logic, this celestial architecture in which so many among us so assiduously engage—I confess that they seem to me idle and hopeless pursuits. Moreover, all these abstractions depress me, and not only they—the whole intellectual heritage of man, all the discoveries, knowledge, values amassed and established through the centuries, have begun to oppress me of late, like an annoying load or too heavy, too stifling clothes. . . . I am thinking what bliss it would be to plunge into Lethe, wash off without trace the mind's memory of all religious and philosophical systems, of all science, art, poetry, and come out naked like the first man, naked, joyous, and light, and freely stretch out to the sky my bare arms, remembering nothing of the past except how heavy and stifling those clothes were, and how easy it is without them.[46]

Adamite and pre-Adamite yearnings, in the case of Wat and Stern, found expression in a taste for the exotic. The metaphor of throwing off "too heavy, too stifling clothes" they took literally, becoming happy exhibitionists.[47] Here the grand gesture of liberation took a specifically defiant and jocular form. Reason, paradoxically and derisively praised as something that transcended its own rules, abolished itself. Alogism and desemanticization were taken to the ultimate—and inexorably comical—limit, in which "gga" and "bellowing" were interpreted literally: "I want to leap as donkeys / I want to moo as cows," proclaimed Stern solemnly in one of his better-known poems.

The insouciant abolition of old values was presented as the victory of laughter over grimness. Entirely in keeping with the carnivalistic tradition, the grotesque body prevailed over soul and spirit ("laughter fattens the soul and gives it strong sturdy legs"). Language was treated as something material, as *bodily:* it, too, was grotesque and unrestrained, self-mocking, and constantly self-regenerating.[48]

However attractive, this cult of immaturity and freedom had its disadvantages. To the extent that words reaffirmed "their weight, sound, color, their contour," so language and art were bound to lose their problematic nature, their cognitive potentialities, their link to truth. Cultural memory, along with the serious and tragic dimension of life, was proclaimed nonexistent—a severe limitation for art. Wat was not totally unaware of that dilemma from the very start of his futurist period.

On 10 February 1921, *gga* was confiscated by government censor on grounds of immorality. The same fate befell *An Immortal Volume of Futurisias*, which only contributed to the literary notoriety of Stern and Wat. On 7 February, three days before the confiscation, they arranged a "Great Recital of World Futurist Poetry" in one of Warsaw's concert halls. At the end of 1920, Jasieński arrived in Warsaw "accompanied by his whole court"—Czyżewski and several budding poets.[49] Determined to conquer the capital, they arranged a poetry reading at the hall of the Philharmonic Society on 9 February. Undaunted by negative reviews, Jasieński and his comrades-in-arms continued their readings throughout February and early March.

A peculiar anecdote conveys the atmosphere of the period. A young provincial who insisted that his name was Aleksander Wat joined Jasieński's retinue. The impostor was exposed in a local café when the leader of the Warsaw futurists and the chief of the Kraków group made their long overdue acquaintance. "Jasieński reddened and blushed: 'How do you dare call yourself Aleksander Wat, when Aleksander Wat came here with us?' And he showed me a very young, extremely likable, and shy man who blushed in turn and began to mumble something—to the effect that, in a sense, so to speak, he feels now and then as if he were someone else, that he just wanted to perform under another man's name for some reason. Of course, Jasieński sacked him at once."[50]

From March 1921, both groups appeared on stage together in various Polish cities. Their poetry reading in Zakopane on 10 August 1921 made history. The evening's program called for "a knife fight" between Stern and Witkacy. That chilling phrase indicated nothing more than a harsh discussion; nevertheless, a real fight broke out. According to Wat's memoirs, one of the Skamandrites, Jan Lechoń, who was on his way to becoming an official state poet and did not shrink from anti-Semitism, had gone the round of the butchers in Zakopane, to alert them that a band of Jews was coming to town intent on insulting the Virgin. During the reading, Lechoń got up on the stage and expressed his disdain for the futurists by slapping Stern in the face. "In the hall, a scuffle broke out indeed. We had to roar the poems at the top of our voices. As a result, I was drubbed," Wat wrote.[51]

Nuż w bżuhu (Knife in the Stomach, or, in futurist phonetic spelling, Nife in the Stomak), a pamphlet that followed in November 1921, marked the peak of the futurists' provocative activities. Its general tenor was signaled by the slogan printed in bold letters below the title: "Hcemy szczać we wszystkih kolorah!" (We want to piss in all colors!). The published poems included the cannibalistic piece by Jasieński discussed above and Wat's "Plodzeńe" (Breeding), which depicted a male giving birth, and "Namopanik barwistanu," a graceful exercise in pure nonsense.

Almost simultaneously, a less shocking publication came out: the first issue of the Warsaw periodical *Nowa Sztuka* (New Art). It was edited by Stern, who as usual initiated the enterprise; the co-editor was Jarosław Iwaszkiewicz, a leading Skamandrite. The first issue, in November 1921, was furnished with theoretical statements that emphasized the synthetic character of the movement and hinted at a change in direction—from purely negative to more constructive and formal.

New Art affiliated itself more with Apollinairian than with dadaist tendencies. This was due in part to the influence of Iwaszkiewicz, whose name served as a guarantee of sustained literary quality and an absence of overly deviant notions. But two men representing the editorial board in Kraków played a particularly important role: Leon Chwistek, an eccentric mathematician and philosopher, and Tadeusz Peiper.

Peiper's artistic output was sparse, but his booklet *Nowe usta* (New Lips, 1925) and a number of essays, later reprinted in book form under the title *Tędy* (The Right Way, 1930), secured him a place among Polish avant-garde thinkers second only to Witkacy. He escaped the commotion and chaos of World War I by moving to neutral Spain, returning to Poland only in 1921. Wat remembered him with humor and sympathy as an unfailingly provincial yet dominant figure: "He was much older than ourselves, a gentleman with a beard, with a wide-brimmed decadent hat. People at that time would swear by Peiper's beard. He smoked cigars. He presided at the café and cultivated a school, very consciously, on the model of Madrid artists, poets, and theoreticians. He prevailed over all of us because of his maturity of thought. His thought was very self-consistent and systematic."[52]

Peiper's school formed around 1925 and entered the history of Polish literature as the Kraków Vanguard. In addition to Peiper, it consisted of the young poets Julian Przyboś, Jan Brzękowski, and several lesser or transitory figures. Members of the Kraków Vanguard opposed the Skamandrites and the futurists. Peiper took a singular stance in his articles. On the one hand, Peiper wrote, the poet had to express his times, to stay abreast of technical and social progress, even venturing a few steps ahead, thereby molding a new consciousness for humanity and teaching it to cope with the modern era. On the other hand, he must remain an aloof master, a hermit whose achievements in word polishing might be appreciated by perhaps a dozen people.

Peiper's intellectual leanings led him into a logical contradiction. He was a man of socialist convictions who adamantly believed in what he called the "three Ms": *miasto, masa, maszyna,* the metropolis, the masses, the machine. In this, he contrasted with Witkacy, for whom progress was fraught with the dangers of totalitarianism and soulless mass culture. At the same time, Peiper, like Witkacy, recognized the autonomous, autotelic character of art. The contradiction proved fruitful. In practice, Peiper's teaching amounted to the promotion of a dense, elliptical line, multilevel metaphor, and rhyme spaced at long intervals; to the rejection of primitive syllabotonic and syllabic verse; and, above all, to an emphasis on technical craftsmanship in contrast to "inspiration."[53]

New Art never became the sustained periodical it set out to be. Its second issue, in February 1922, was its last. Almost immediately, Peiper started a new magazine, *Zwrotnica* (The Switch), which was more successful. The futurists, for a time, remained Peiper's allies, albeit wavering ones. Wat contributed to both *New Art* and *The Switch*, though he recognized that his concept of art and his poetic practice diverged widely from Peiper's postulates. It is tempting to ascribe the discord between the futurists and the Kraków Vanguard primarily to a difference in character: the ludic outlook of Wat and Stern did not sit easily with Peiper's unflinching seriousness. But the disagreement in fact went much deeper. The futurists were reluctant to embrace both Peiper's aestheticism and the Kraków Vanguard's civilizing ambitions, dismissed by Wat (during his Communist period) as "upper-crust capitalist tendencies."[54] As a contemporary Polish critic notes, "Peiper had many positivist traits (incidentally, he appealed to positivism more than once): he believed in progress, in organic work, he was a rationalist. His passion was building, but for the futurists it was destruction."[55] Whereas Peiper's dense, elliptical writing strove toward a condensation of sense, futurist works made ample use of humor and pure nonsense; whereas the Kraków Vanguard stressed technique, Wat and his friends opted for nature, spontaneity, and the unconscious; whereas Peiper in his theoretical articles expressed a serene belief in the forward march of humanity and culture, the futurists, Wat in particular, retained profound (and justified) suspicions concerning progress, language, and art.

An important motif in Wat's critique of the Kraków Vanguard's theory and practice appears in his mature writings. Wat considered metonymic poetics superior to metaphoric poetics. "Metaphoric poetry has reached a dead end," he said in *Dziennik bez samogłosek* (Diary Without Vowels). "Having loosened criteria of similarity to the extreme, it led to a situation where anything could be equated with anything, and, precisely at this point, the very act of equation lost its value. You see, in poetry, as in any art, the proper thing is only what is finally indispensable. Naturally, a poet even there may bundle together and set in a row everything that comes to his mind, but then he will betray himself immediately, because his objects (images, words, concepts) standing next to one another will form a set without his *demarche;* they will lose direction."[56]

That stance (very distinctive in Wat's late poetry) undoubtedly developed in opposition to Peiper, for whom metaphor was the essence of poetic craft. Moreover, it was pointedly aimed at Julian Przyboś, Peiper's most influential disciple. For many years, Wat and Przyboś stood at opposite literary poles. Their conflict was marked, and complicated, by an intense personal animosity. Przyboś never concealed his contempt for the futurists; in turn, Wat did not spare him from ruthless criticism. In 1958, he attacked Przyboś in the press as "a poet with an empty imagination which he industriously and systematically fills up with verbal tricks."[57]

The destinies of Peiper, Przyboś, and Wat intersected more than once. In fall 1939, all three fled the approaching German army and ended up in Soviet-occupied Lwów. Peiper was by then beginning to show symptoms of insanity.[58] He and Wat were both arrested, and the two spent many months in Stalinist prisons, albeit unaware of each other's whereabouts. After the war, Peiper returned to Poland. Although he continued to write and was adored by many young poets, he never showed his new work to anyone; his paranoia was under control, but he suffered from it for the rest of his life.[59] Przyboś, by contrast, established a rather unexpected literary career both in Lwów and in postwar Poland, where by the end of his life, he was considered an official classic. He joined the chorus of indignant loyalists when Wat defected to the West.

The short-lived alliance between the futurists and Peiper and his associates which blossomed in *New Art* and *The Switch* marked the culmination of their attempt to carve out a niche for themselves in literary life. It was an endeavor born of despair. In 1921–23, the young iconoclasts felt more lonely and more troubled than ever before. Their love of scandals and of the fine art of *épater le bourgeois* brought predictable results: both the Polish press and the public took up arms against them. "To be stoned to death . . . was by no means among my ambitions," Jasieński wrote in 1923.[60]

In 1922, the futurists were attacked by several established critics. Most painful was an assault by Stefan Żeromski in his book *Snobizm i postęp* (Snobbery and Progress). Żeromski, an indisputable authority of the Young Poland generation, a man of integrity and broad views, went so far as to accept Apollinaire—and even Mayakovsky—but dismissed their Polish followers as pitiable snobs or pernicious encomiasts of crime or both.

Minor critics of reactionary bent exercised even less restraint. Their charges usually amounted to political denunciation sprinkled liberally with anti-Semitism. Here *Rzeczpospolita* (Res publica), a periodical of the extreme Right, made its mark. In its pages one Jan Żyżnowski characterized Polish futurism as an imitation of deranged Russian and Jewish trends, "a stillborn embryo, with cretin's head and brains afflicted by dropsy."[61] Maciej Wierzbiński, an author of semigraphomaniacal novels, went even further:

> These are not just disengaged and innocent jokes, not just phenomena of sui generis literary trade for the sake of money—but a purposeful, planned, and clever subversive activity. . . . They have instilled [in the reader] a germ of contempt, first for Polish orthography and language, then for Polish art, thus summoning him to launch a hostile action against everything held holy in the nation's collective psyche. . . . And, as somebody assures me, they present the most repugnant images of Our Lady in their "Immortal Volumes of Futurisias." . . . Isn't all of that calculated to prepare the ground for bolshevist seed? Aren't these "poets" the apostles appointed by Trotsky's emissaries?[62]

One result of this campaign was an interpellation in Parliament initiated by Tadeusz Dymowski, a noted anti-Semite. On 28 July 1922 he invoked a government regulation banning posters written in languages other than Polish and lacking a corresponding Polish text. Because the horrible language of futurist posters, Dymowski reasoned, had nothing in common with Polish, and because these monstrosities were never furnished with a standard Polish translation (which would hardly have been possible in any case), displaying them violated the law. The interpellation was ignored, and the Skamandrites added insult to injury by directing public attention to linguistic inaccuracies in Dymowski's own text. At that point, Dymowski took to tearing down the posters with his bare hands.[63]

Such incidents might be anecdotal, but their frequency and increasing intensity made them more than a minor irritant. "The 'Futurization of Polish life' ended in a complete failure," wrote Wat.[64]

Some futurists sought a way out by embracing radical leftist ideology, electing to do precisely what they were accused of.[65] Jasieński's evolution to the left was already apparent in his *Pieśń o głodzie* (Song about Hunger). Later, Stern supported Jasieński's radical leanings. Their development was probably influenced by the evolution of their Russian mentors—Mayakovsky and others—who at that time formed a group called LEF (Levyj Front Iskusstva, Left Front of Art), which was committed to employing futurist tools in social service. That, for all practical purposes, meant service to the Soviet state.

For Stern, the poetry of social engagement was ephemeral; but for Jasieński, it became deadly serious. He preached revolutionary action and praised the salutary values of terror: already in "Śpiew Maszynistów" (The Engine Drivers' Chant), which formed part of the *Song about Hunger*, his voice had acquired a tonality virtually indistinguishable from Fascist rhetoric: "We will crush everything under our boots [since we are] beautiful, huge, and human . . . the world with its back against the wall blinked helplessly like a small, pale manikin, when we raised our butts . . . sorrowful christ bemoaned the souls of his flock while barrels burst in a volley and blood stained the snow."[66] In 1924, Jasieński moved to Lwów, where he became one of the editors of a communist newspaper and a translator of Lenin. In Wat's words, "Not very much remained of the arch-snob with the monocle and the curl on his forehead, always on the prowl and surrounded by young women as he had been in Warsaw and Kraków."[67] Now Jasieński referred to himself as "a former futurist."

The last venture of the futurist movement was initiated by Gacki. In early 1924, he founded *Almanach Nowej Sztuki* (The Almanac of New Art), which brought under one umbrella the writers of the avant-garde, including Peiper and Witkacy. *Almanac* also bore the parallel title *F 24*, easily decoded as "futurism of the year 1924," but it hardly continued the futurist practice of the preceding years. "If one can mark the terminal point of Futurism," Ważyk noted in his book on the Polish avant-garde, "it was just *Almanac:* end of the great hyperbole, of the grotesque, of absurd exhortations and dreams, transition to poetry that is a representation of the world—external as well as internal—a vision, a new lyric."[68] Writers who contributed to *Almanac* displayed an interest in Apollinaire and Picasso, Walt Whitman and G. K. Chesterton, African sculpture and Russian formalist theory. Wat was one of *Almanac*'s leaders. In sum, *Almanac* was a civilized and civilizing enterprise that inclined toward what Gacki and Stern defined somewhat vaguely as the "new classicism."

Almanac ended after its fourth issue, at the beginning of 1925. "Futurism ceased its existence as an independent movement, but it sank into the whole of Polish culture, giving it a distinct coloring."[69]

Wat continued to move back and forth between his irregular studies, bohemian pranks, and literary enterprises. Between 1919 and 1921, he appears to have supported himself by writing anonymous stories, which were sold at newsstands for twenty *groszes* (Polish pennies) each. In his later years, Wat remembered, of these, only a cycle of booklets on Charlie Chaplin. With Stern, he also appears to have concocted a parodic booklet abusing their mutual friend Tuwim. This mimicked the worst traditions of the Polish yellow press and had the appropriate title *Żydek-Literat* (A Kike Posing as a Man of Letters). It is said that much later a certain scholar misunderstood its satirical intent and quoted it in all seriousness as proof of the harassment experienced by Tuwim in the interwar years.[70]

Wat also tried his hand at advertising. In 1924, backed by the painter Henryk Berlewi and a poet of the *New Art* group Stanisław Brucz, he started a short-lived advertising agency, Reklama-Mechano. According to the agency's brochure,[71] it set out to edit texts of advertisements "in the direction of ellipsis, acuity and impetus, employing the latest achievements of modern literature."[72]

A parodic intent is probably in evidence even here. When, many years later, Berlewi referred to him publicly as the author of some promotional texts, Wat, in a letter to him (December 1966), expressed his profound displeasure: "I wrote them 40 years ago for the money, anonymously, and also *for malicious fun*—I went out of my way to make them *maximally banal* and vulgar. Without these explanations, the texts by themselves discredit me."[73]

Wat took some pains to enter the literary establishment. In 1922 he became a member of the Union of Polish Writers. Later, in 1926, he enlisted in the Polish chapter of PEN (a circumstance that was to play a role in Wat's life after World War II).

"In the year 1924, I decided to stop writing poetry," Wat noted in *Scraps of Paper in the Wind*.[74] At this time, several of his friends, including Gacki and Ważyk, abandoned poetry either temporarily or for ever. In fact, even in his futurist years, Wat was far from a prolific poet. His reputation—limited to a narrow milieu—was largely made by his very first poetic text, *Pug Iron Stove*.

The rest of Wat's creative output as a futurist was too meager to comprise a book, consisting merely of a dozen-odd poems scattered among various periodicals. In later years, Wat ventured to reprint fewer than half his short futurist texts.[75]

The poems of *gga* are the least significant. Light and frivolous, they lack direction and betray no trace of assiduous work. Their obvious aim was to provide a jocular complement to Stern's poems, which formed the first half of the collection. Taken together, Stern's and Wat's contributions give a good idea of early, still immature Polish futurist writing. In his "Muse on All Fours," Stern did his best to *épater le bourgeois*, presenting his muse as a drunken prostitute, employing outrageous orthography, and describing vividly, if long-windedly, a gentleman masturbating in a pissoir. In "Flying Petticoats," Wat responded in kind. Thus, the very first poem of his cycle, "Ranek" (The Morning), is a classical sonnet in French style—perhaps influenced by such *poètes maudits* as Tristan Corbière, Jules Laforgue, and Laurent Tailhade—overflowing with exotic words, highlighting risqué images, and introducing unusual punctuation. It ends on a pedophiliac, blasphemous note, the narrator's occupation consisting in the procurement of little girls for Roman Catholic cardinals.

For the most part, the poems that make up "Flying Petticoats" can hardly be called futurist. They employ themes (and borrow masks) common to symbolist and post-symbolist poetry: ennui and the senselessness of being, horror and pity in the face of an absurd world and a powerless God, the poet as gloomy dandy universally adored by women, and finally a fantastic soul-liberating journey to unknown lands. The imagery is still ornamental to a large degree, the verse still within the confines of tradition. Wat is nevertheless an innovator: he weakens the logic of the narration and the composition, bringing it to the verge of nonsense; shows an uncommon skill in balancing hyperbolic or contradictory ideas; reaches the outer regions of style; and, while still infatuated with romantic and symbolic *écriture*, mocks its affectation and explodes it from within.

A short poem that Wat deemed worthy to reprint in the 1960s was the most popular among the *gga* texts, one frequently recited by Wat during futurist happenings ("Wat, with his flattened nose and olive complexion, often delivered . . . a dadaist verse which I memorized in full," Ważyk wrote in 1966[76]):

JA MAM NIEBIESKI KROK.	I HAVE BLUE STRIDE.
ON ROK WYPUSZCZA Z RĄK.	HE LETS THE YEAR SLIP THROUGH HIS
i mówi: "Tak	FINGERS.
Jam jest ptak	and says: "Yes
Któremu niebios brak"	I'm a bird
A ja skanduję: tyk, tyk, tak	who lacks sky"
i myślę sobie skrycie:	And I scan: tick, tick, tack
Tyś jest niebieski kulawy ptak	and think secretly to myself:
wiszący na suficie.[77]	You are a blue lame bird
	hanging from the ceiling.

The most striking trait of the poem is its sprightly, dancelike rhythm, which corresponds to the image of "stride." The prevalent pattern is a regular iambic trimeter, and the poem has an energetic, measured movement. This may be considered a distinctly futurist feature—the more so if one retains a "background" memory, as Wat undoubtedly did, of Mayakovsky's verses, which reproduced the dance rhythms or march of presumably victorious proletarian legions.

The insistent beat is intensified by the prevalence of short, stressed words. The poem consists of thirty-one words (not counting prepositions and conjunctions). Among these, one-syllable nouns, pronouns, verbs, adverbs, and interjections make up more than half, most of them strongly linked phonetically: for example, the sequence KROK–ROK–RONK in the first two lines (onomatopoetically reinforcing the aural impression of the clear-cut *krok*, "stride") and the group of interjections *tyk, tyk, tak* (contrasted and intensified by *tyś*), which imitates the acoustic movement of verse-scanning and, at the same time, the ticking of a clock.

Thus, primarily by means of rhythm and sound-patterning, Wat introduces a complex semantic theme. A lively dance with *accelerando* and *ritardando* passages combines with the monotonous, regular ticking that marks the passage of time, and also with scansion—that is, with a metapoetic reference to the process of creating verse. As we know, Wat counted the awareness of two distinct time orders, a deterministic one and a miraculous one, among his earliest and most important recollections.

Still, the subject of the text is far from clear. The poem has all the makings of playful, provocative absurdity. But a close reading reveals something more. The opening serves as both its title and its summary. In it, two characters are introduced: JA (I) and ON (HE), as first words of the first and second lines.

"I" and "he" are opposed both grammatically and semantically. Moreover, their fates, equally strange, are different. "I" has "blue stride." A semantic discrepancy between a modified noun and a modifying adjective is a typical futurist device, and *niebieski* (blue), a frequent word in Polish futurist poetry, could be applied to almost anything. But the etymological connection between *niebieski* and *niebo, niebiosa* (sky, heaven) should also be noted: for the adjective may also mean "heavenly" or "celestial." "Blue stride" may thus be read as "heavenly stride," thereby connoting in characteristic futurist style a victorious poet conquering space and time in a Mayakovskian "assault on Heaven." By contrast, "he" is weak and passive, unable to control time—"lets the year slip through his fingers"—and space—"lacks sky." In this way, "I" represents the futurist, "he" the passéist.

Predictably, "he" poses as a romantic hero—"a bird," a winged creature subject to earthly bondage, striving for the unattainable. His condition is completely demythologized. "I" describes him as a "blue lame bird / hanging from the ceiling." Here, a specific meaning of "blue bird" is employed" *niebieski ptak* in Polish urban slang denotes "swindler," "impostor." The lachrymose antagonist of the poet is a disgusting wretch—a stuffed bird? a rogue punished by hanging? a suicide?)[78] The adjective *kulawy* (lame) with all its devilish, chthonic connotations, contrasts with the triumphant, heavenly "stride" of "I."[79]

Glorification of futurist youthfulness and boldness, denunciation of passéist values, and joyful celebration of an art that vanquishes time—all these goals are attained here, in the tight space of nine lines, by means of sound and graphic patterning, changes of tempo, parallelism, and wordplay.

Wat took up a different artistic task in the poems identified with the strange generic term *namopaniki*. These were the outcome of pure linguistic experimentation, in Khlebnikov vein, rarities in the corpus of Polish futurist poetry. "Namopanik charuna," included in *An Immortal Volume of Futurisias*, marks the high point of this experimentation. Totally untranslatable, it may still impress the reader in its original quasi-Polish, its linguistic density rivaling certain passages of Joyce's *Finnegans Wake:*

1. Ptachorenki rozchorongwił roz i grajoncy na pstrych charmonikach w pachnurach chromawy charun chrapał w chmurach i wbarwistach. A chmurawie munrawy ogroi i grujce rozgrai na grajkatych guranach. W ranach gorun garbi ogury gromach i gromadach pagur. Na pagurach chrabonszczy lew o chrabonczyna o chrabonczyki rozchrabonczyn i lew chrabonszczony onże chrabonszcz.

A charmoniki—w poronionych charmonjach sfer—chdyiście jach ja chruwały garbus w fturach ochrągłych i pszystych! chdyiście jach ja po-Drzewiach chroplistych postali! o! charmoniki charmonki rozchramonki charmoniuny charmoniętr o pocharmonik charmoniacze! . . .

2. O chdyiścia chrufały, o chruwajonce archamiołły chorongwiazy! Gwiazy jamiołłów goronce granaty źrą i wiagzdy w chabrach stronch skrzydałrenki dromader skradocha garbani srebroje—on że kokodryl w złotawach, i chorongwicze i chorongwioncze pochorongw o chorongi rozchorongwy chorongewie choronginy chorongawy chorongwii chorongwiecze rozchonwigcze rozchongwicze chorongwiuny o rozchonrogw chorongwij i pochorongw horongwiassy![80]

Most of the words here are either phonetically spelled—*grajoncy* for *grający* (playing), for example—or slightly distorted. Thus, an initial letter *h* is changed to *ch*, and *harmoniki* (harmonicas, accordions) become *charmoniki*, for example. The same misfortune regularly befalls initial *f, k,* and *g*. The text, in effect, wheezes. It comes to be oversaturated with *ch*, the first sound of the mysterious titular word *charun*.

In addition to these "orderly," "regular" distortions are many unpredictable, unsystematic ones. Thus, *gwiazdy* (stars) may turn into *gwiazy* and *wiagzdy; archanioły* (archangels) into disturbing *archamiołły*, a mixture of *archanioł* and *cham* (boor, cad); or a capital letter may appear unexpectedly in the middle of a word.

The poem appears to consist in an idiosyncratic narrative of the exploits and adventures of a certain Charun. It is tempting to read the name as Harun, referring to Harun ar-Rashid, the main hero of *The Arabian Nights*. But Charun might be also Charon (the ferryman of Hades), or indeed anybody.

It would be an exercise in futility to seek the poem's precise meaning. Its only logic may be defined as the logic of sound- and morphological patterns. Starting with a seemingly fortuitous word, quasi-sentences swell and stretch like the bellows of an accordion until they have exhausted, for all practical purposes, the harmonious possibilities latent within the originating word. Wat generates neologisms and runs the entire gamut of derivatives, his aim primarily a musical modulation and transformation of some fundamental themes.[81] This is especially obvious in the second part of the poem, which consists mainly of transmogrifications of the word *chorągiew* (banner). "The linguistic sign becomes palpable, since attention is wholly turned upon it as carrying the magic function."[82]

But there is something perverse in that incantation. The magic harmony achieved by the poet is constantly undermined by funny and absurd distortions, as well as by tongue-in-cheek changes of mood. Saturation of the text with *ch* gives it the semblance of an effusion discharged by a less-than-cultivated person, since *ch* in Polish has obscene connotations as the first sound of the word *chuj* (penis).

Most of the words of the poem fall into three classes: they belong to the semantic field of either sound or religion or both—witness *gromach* (loc. pl. of "thunder"), *chury* (a distortion of *chóry* [choirs]), *ranach* (loc. pl. of "wound," probably referring to the wounds of Christ), *cheruBy* (slightly distorted "cherubs"), and *duchże* (distortion of *duże* [big], which can also be read as *duch że* [and spirit]). An interesting amalgam is *cHramy*, which may be read as *chramy* (temples, fanes) or *gramy* (we play). The sound semantics is supported by the very structure of the poem, with its unending echoes and modulations reminiscent of peals of thunder and Gregorian chant; the religious semantics, in turn, is corroborated by words denoting height (hills, mountains), celestial phenomena (stars, clouds), and a paradisiacal nature (soft grass, birds).

A fourth class of words subverts that imagery of a divine, perfected realm, however. These are words pertaining to physical handicap, illness, and old age, such as *garbus* (hunchback), *jedookchi* (distortion of *jednooki* [one-eyed]), *staruch* (old man). Likewise, music is intruded upon by such verbs as *chrapał* (snored), and the paradise is populated by dromedaries that happen to be identical with crocodiles.

Thus the vocabulary of the poem, together with its phonetic and syntactic devices, evokes disharmony. "Namopanik charuna" is not only a celebration of the magic qualities inherent in language, but also an avowal of its inferiority, its defectiveness. The words "w poronionych charmonjach sfer" (in the aborted music of the spheres) reveal the poem's message in maximally condensed form.

Far from an imitation of Khlebnikov's triumphant "Incantation by Laughter," Wat's "Namopanik charuna" is its annulment, its bitter parody.

A further complex and interesting example of Wat's art is a rather extensive poem entitled "Wieś" (The Countryside), printed in *The Switch* in 1922:

I

Biskup stojący nad rzeką
błogoslawił poród ryb;
wieloryb przed nim uciekał
pod grzędy pachnące lip.

Wiatraki rwały chmury
i chaty unosiły w krąg.
Wyciągał mnie ktoś z góry
za włosy z grzywy łąk.

W chałupach skulonych w skrzypce
mchem porosły wdowy.
Czerwone parne jak lipiec
modliły się w chmurach krowy.

Chciałbym płaski jak ryba
rozpruwać chmurę wód
chciałbym Lewiatan niby
uciec pod ziemi spód.

Z krzykiem mkną stodoły
z sioła w pustelnię pól.
Gwiazd morderczy ołów
oblepi ziemi puls.

Dziobami nas zadziobią
miedziane hufce kur.
Złe ptaki nas wytropią
strzałami zatrutych piór.

A w czerwonym kurniku nieba
kogut żelazny zemstą piał;
padały podziobane
stosy anielskich ciał.

I

The bishop who stood at the river
blessed the spawning of fish;
a whale was escaping him
under the fragrant beds of lindens.

The windmills tore the clouds   5
and carried away the huts in a circle.
Somebody from above pulled me
by the hair from the mane of
    meadows.

In the cabins cuddled up into violins
the widows were overgrown by moss.   10
Red and sultry as July,
the cows prayed in the clouds.

Flat as a fish I would like
to rip open the watery cloud
I would like to turn Leviathan   15
and escape under the earth.

The barns run screaming
from the village to the hermitage of
    the fields.
Murderous lead of the stars   20
will stick over the pulse of the earth.

Copper legions of hens
will pick us to death with their beaks.
Evil birds will track us down
with the arrows of their poisoned
    feathers.

And in the red coop of heaven   25
an iron rooster crowed vengeance;
heaps of angels' bodies
fell, pecked.

Krzycząc potrząsam zły bałagan:
"Przyjdź królestwo miast i maszyn!"
Lecz krzyk mój zatrzymał szłaban,
jak ratujących się wstrzymuje
lokomotywy żelaznym śledziem.

I shake the evil mess screaming:
"Come the kingdom of cities and   30
   machines!"
But the barrier halted my scream,
as rescuers are halted
by the locomotive's herringbone
   grate.

II

Zwierząt królestwo boże
roztacza pęki barw.
Księżyc jak brzytwa gorze:
zgolić wiejski parch!

II

God's animal kingdom
displays the buds of colors.   35
The moon shines like a razor:
to shave the scab of the village!

Kury zakwitły w koniczynie
konie wyrosły w gołębniku
po niebie mkną obłoki-świnie
liczę lica: lic bez liku.

Hens blossomed among the clovers,
horses grew up in the dovecote
swine-clouds fly in the sky   40
I count the faces: the faces are
   countless.

Wozy na oślep łamane bykami
pędzącymi wszerz i wzdłuż.
Niebiosa ryczą nad nami
łykając męczacy kurz.

The wagons are blindly crushed by
   the bulls
who race lengthwise and crosswise.
The skies roar above us   45
swallowing the tiresome dust.

Obory dymią jak moloch
rojem gnijących iskr.
Na dachach gromów golem,
od deszczów spuchł mu pysk.

The cow barns fume like molech
with a swarm of rotting sparks.
On the roofs sits the golem of
   thunders,
his mug is swollen from rains.

Z flaszek domów wysysa
dymów porwany kłak,
wieś rozłożoną jak misa
toczy niebiosów rak.

From the flasks of the houses he   50
   sucks
the drifting shred of smoke,
the village, spread open like a bowl,
is devoured by a cancer of heavens.

Między sprzychami biednych wozów
siedzą staruszkowie z przytułków
chciwie wdychają zapach nawozu
który skacze na kółku.

Among the spokes of the poor
   wagons   55
sit little old men from a hospice
they inhale greedily the smell of
   manure,
that jumps on the wheel.

Odbija pacierz kocioł kościoła
na wzgórzu stercząc jak gruby kloc.
Okryła pola niebo i sioła
wymalowana w figurę mą noc.

The cauldron of the church echoes
   the prayer
and protrudes on the hill like a thick   60
   log.
The night painted into my figure has
   covered
the sky and the villages with its lap.

Bocian jak igła, okiem i bokiem
i głową kiwa, chudy jak francuz,
dziobem ostrym wykluwa oko
na mojej twarzy złotym bizancjum.

The stork, like a needle, nods his eye
   and
side and head, he is lean as a
   Frenchman,   65
with a sharp beak he picks out an eye
from the golden byzantium of my
   face.

I czyjaś ręka, zda się niczyja
wbiła w łeb mój na niebie ćwiek.
I pękając buchnęła ma gruba szyja
i pożarem zalała wiek.

And somebody's hand, seemingly
   nobody's,
drove a nail into my forehead on the
   sky.
And my thick neck gushed bursting
and engulfed the century with fire.

In its innovative spirit, "The Countryside" is typical of Polish modernist writing of the 1920s. It rejects the normative poetics of Peiper and the Kraków Vanguard based on a rigorous practice of free verse, elliptical line, and refined, multi-tiered metaphor. Even if the lyrical persona of the poem summons "the kingdom of cities and machines," thus echoing Peiper's famous formula "the metropolis, the masses, the machine," the appeal is in vain. The poet evidently prefers "God's animal kingdom" and the nonurban landscape; presented as site of a murderous clash of elemental forces, it is nevertheless a source of fascination and awe. That the poem should have appeared in Peiper's periodical seems paradoxical, for one would expect to find its counterparts among the likes of Czyżewski's pastoral poems.

The pattern of bold, flexible accentual verse, far removed from traditional Polish syllabic and syllabotonic versification, has itself the value of a sign, denoting the poem's modern, nonpasséist character. The same can be said of its rhyme pattern. The rhymes are rich and expressive but usually only approximate, entailing the repetition of a vowel and several consonants, the order of which may vary. A rhyme is often elongated, embracing the preceding word or words and blending with sound patterning —"*stodoły—gwiazd morderczy ołów*," for example.

The poem may be described as a sequence of striking, condensed, rural scenes. Far from being a pastoral *locus amoenus*, the countryside is full of dynamic transformations. Everything is caught in a circular, upward movement, as if in the vortex of a tornado. Here Wat employs images that smack of naive folk art ("Hens blossomed among the clovers, / horses grew up in the dovecote, / swine-clouds fly in the sky"), sometimes Chagallesque in their boldness ("Red and sultry as July, / the cows prayed in the clouds"). Yet the narrator remains a denizen of the city who observes the rustic landscape and its stunning changes from without. This is signaled to the reader by vocabulary drawing on ancient cultural and mythological—sometimes Jewish—tradition (molech, golem, byzantium, and so on).

The countryside is not only the locus of elemental collisions; it is also the sacral space of fertility. Mighty nature constantly overflows all boundaries and limits, giving birth to legions of creatures, actual, fictitious, and mythological. Thus the poem abounds in wildly metaphorical and prosopopoeic images that celebrate triumphant biology, the tremendous uproar of nature and its furious dynamism. Here, Wat's fresh, unbridled imagination, as well as his mastery of phonetics, are at their best. Take, for instance, lines 48–49, where thunder becomes a personified, palpably biological yet at the same time godlike being. The dense sound patterning of these lines has an obvious onomatopoetic quality: "Na *da*chach *gro*mów *go*lem, / od *deszcz*ów *spu*chł mu *py*sk."

Nevertheless, the poet's attitude to nature is far from being one of pure enthusiasm. In this respect, lines 3–4 and 13–16 are particularly indicative: a whale and Leviathan belong to the core of Wat's imagery.[83] In the first part of "The Countryside," the poet identifies himself with these creatures that *escape* the blessing and refuse to take part in nature's feast. The Old Testament and Talmudic symbolism of Leviathan is complicated. Food of the righteous when the Messiah comes, Leviathan is a sea monster, a chthonic creature inimical to God. Moreover, as well as having strong satanic connotations, it constitutes a variant of an archetypal symbol encountered in Indo-European (and Slavic) mythology—a dragon slain by the god of thunder.[84] In the Book of Job, however, Leviathan effectively loses its evil character, serving instead as testimony to God's omnipotence and the inscrutability of his designs.

Characteristically, Wat reconstructs the scene of the cosmic struggle between the god of thunder and the primordial dragon who represents chaos. He also re-creates the ancient mythological opposition between fish and birds. "We," the denizens of the lower world, are killed by "them," the inhabitants of the upper world—"copper legions of hens" and mythic Stymphalides who destroy with the arrows of their feathers.[85] The sixth stanza, which describes that fight to the death, is key to the poem. Not without reason is it emphasized graphically and given an exceptionally tight sound pattern.

The image of the poet-Leviathan should not necessarily be interpreted as demonic, or the birds as heavenly forces (for in their rage they murder even the angels). The poem may be read in a different way, one that brings us closer to the semantic nucleus of Wat's mature poetry. A human being represents a rupture, a hiatus in the order of nature. For humankind, the fertile chaos and eternal regeneration of nature signify the inevitability of death, and the human body, which belongs to the nature's realm, by the same token becomes a source of pain and decay. Humans are pecked to death by birds—that is, by the forces of nature. They are the ones who are sacrificed.

In the final stanzas, the poet is presented as both a Christlike figure[86] and Prometheus preyed upon by an eagle. His face becomes a golden Byzantine icon. He is tortured, blinded, and crucified, and the blood that gushes from his bursting neck ignites the universal conflagration.[87] Thus, a noncommittal futurist verse comes to be a prophecy of Wat's personal fate in a century of fire and ruin.

3

Pug Iron Stove

The main piece from Wat's futurist period (and virtually the only extensive text of Polish futurism of appreciable value), *ME from One Side and ME from the Other Side of My Pug Iron Stove,* hardly fits the framework devised in *gga* and *Knife in the Stomach.* It consists to a large degree of parodic mockery, but it is more than that and, like many important works of art, resists any one-sided interpretation. It oscillates between parody and nonparody, between tragedy and Rabelaisian grotesque, between hallucinatory confession and clownish grimace. If Polish futurism saw as its goal a happy return to a pre-Adamite paradise, *Pug Iron Stove* might be described as a journey through a Dantesque or Brueghelian hell with no paradise in sight.

Pug Iron Stove predates most futurist works. Written during the period of the early futurist performances on Mazowiecka Street and in the Picador café, in January–March 1919,[1] it was published in the fall of the same year (though dated 1920). A long prose poem, *Pug Iron Stove* was an experiment in *écriture automatique* conducted independently of French surrealists, several years before André Breton introduced the term. Wat wrote it in a state of high fever, seated beside a small stove in his Warsaw apartment at which he tried in vain to warm himself after his nocturnal adventures. Four or five onsets of a trancelike condition resulted in several dozen (all but unreadable) pages, which the young author took straight to the printing-house. The printer, a friendly alcoholic with a taste for futurism, deciphered Wat's scrawl with limited success, adding his own errors to Wat's numerous slips of the pen. Wat neither read the proofs nor revised a single letter. Having composed the work in a borderline state, rejected any control by reason, and given free rein to his unconscious, he thus allowed a comparable element of chance to enter the text at the next stage of production.[2]

Thus, the poem was to be read as a mediumistic, Sibylline work, dictated by a *daimon* and possessing prophetic qualities. "There are words given to us prematurely, and perhaps they later determine the poet's vocation. Knowledge of words, a premature knowledge is given to some young people. . . . That is magic. Magic and poetry that possesses an immense charge of consolation."[3]

In later years, Wat was to insist that the entire pattern of his life was revealed in *Pug Iron Stove*.[4] Even the geographical names might be seen as prophetic. Wat mentions dens of San Francisco (*Sanct* Francisco, thanks to the printer, who seems to have confused the Californian city with St. [Sankt] Petersburg), dens that were to become his favorite haunts in the 1960s. Another toponym of the poem was Mount Gargan, which Wat was to observe with an intensely nostalgic feeling in 1957.[5] Such echoes could of course be dismissed as purely coincidental. But what was far from fortuitous was the obsession with torment, disease, demoniac temptations, and suicide that found ample expression in his poem—and later became embodied in real-life events.

When it was first published, the poem attracted little critical attention. There was probably only one genuine enthusiast, but he was a significant one— Witkacy.[6] Supposedly, he embarrassed Wat by asserting publicly that *Pug Iron Stove* was a work of genius. Moreover, he bought twelve copies, distributing them among friends (whom he loved to tease by reading aloud its more shocking passages).[7] Witkacy also wrote, in May 1921, the sole extensive review of *Pug Iron Stove*.[8]

Departing from the usual futurist stance, *Pug Iron Stove* was a work of high epistemological ambition. It was concerned with cognition, which supposedly could be obtained only at the price of total self-denial, even self-sacrifice. The knowledge in question was, first and foremost, self-knowledge.

As befits an esoteric text, Wat's poem shocks the reader by its apparent incoherence. Formally, it is divided into three parts, which in turn consist of short sections with titles such as "Choroba" (Disease), "Bunt" (Rebellion), "Szaleństwo" (Madness), and quite unexpectedly, "Rozporekmędrca" (Wizard's Slit). Long series of dizzying metaphors are from time to time interrupted by a blasphemous prayer, an obscure imperative, a catechism-like set of questions and answers, an exclamation, or a mocking apostrophe to fellow writers. But the bulk of the poem consists of only marginally intelligible narrative sentences, which freely mix biblical, classical, medieval, exotic, and modern imagery. Thus:

> Girls die on the white sow thistle of the horizons. (226)[9]

> Flat disheveled witches weep, roll, crawl in a church porch, on the earthen floor, from the archbishop's seat to the walled up niche of sad widowed Dione. (227)

> While jackals wander and howl between gray beards that grow during every somnambulic full moon. (229)

> Centauresses defending the throne soared to the highest summits of cinnabar mornings, slowly and harmoniously fluttering their wings. (230)

Dead God Panurge in his Chalcedon sarcophagus of onyx and selenite still directs the army of Silenuses, maenads and archangels whose leader is Michael. (254–55)

My birth and growth are fed by electrons speeding from an immense brass Roentgen's vial of trembling space. (270)

Self-knowledge is revealed primarily as knowledge of the text. Wat's attitude toward inherited cultural codes can be characterized only as deeply ambivalent. Human personality, to all intents and purposes, consists solely of words, of cultural symbols, of language that bewitches and promises but also limits and enslaves. People live in cages of language—or, to be precise, of overlapping sign systems. But in the final analysis, all codes and texts prove valueless and comical. Here, Wat occupies a middle ground between the romantic tradition, for which all codes were inhibiting, and the postmodern concept of pantextuality, of "people being thought by language."

We have already seen how prodigious a reader Wat was in his early years. He observed in his diary in 1964: "Writers, at least the modern ones, are recruited among young and frantic readers; memory at that age is sticky, and the impression left on a young mind by a book is sometimes more powerful, profound and lasting than personal impressions. Originality is very often, perhaps most often, the *contre façons* of the model, its negation, its counterpoise."[10] *Pug Iron Stove* is a corroboration of that maxim. In it, dozens of writers and literary works are alluded to—either directly or, more often, through thinly veiled quotation, the name of a character, or a hint. Among them one finds European medieval romance, Jacobus de Voragine, Raymond Lully, Dante, Rabelais, Shakespeare, Cervantes, Benvenuto Cellini, Abbé Prévost, Edgar Allan Poe, Charles Baudelaire, Gustave Flaubert, and many many others. One may confidently point to an allusion to François Villon in the melancholic sigh "What has become of pagodas and of dull heaving of Deities' Sunday? What has become of them?" (269), a misquotation of Dostoevsky in the sentence "The tear of a common man tipped the scale" (268), and a hint of Mayakovsky in the mention of the "yellow jacket" (229).[11] It would be hard, however, to recognize in the bizarre Greek word *symparanekromenoi* (the fellowship of buried lives) a reference to Kierkegaard, had not Wat revealed it himself, at least twice, in later writings.[12] References to native Polish writers are also frequent, albeit, if anything, even more concealed than references to world literature.

The first and most essential textual source for Wat's poem is undoubtedly the Bible. The Kabbalah, diligently studied by Wat's father and mentioned in the poem, also figures as a paradigm, the most obscure segments of *Pug Iron Stove* resembling some enigmatic parts of the *Zohar*. The reader is further struck by Wat's obvious interest in alchemy, and indeed in all sorts of occult science and demonology—witness, "One is attracted and tickled by a retort swollen with red smoke, in which a dwarf-incubus hisses with twisted limbs, legs spread wide as a cupola" (240). The quasi-Jungian apparatus of heretical and para-heretical mysticism is intimately interwoven with the more official codes of established religions: "Through the disagreeable alchemies of the forests, seven candlesticks of Solomon, through the seven pilgrimages of Jesus—the stone-block answer: Amen venerabilis Domine" (233). There is at least one common denominator, however, in that set of references: Wat's fascination with the enigma of being, his predilection for the unconscious, for magic formulae and apocalyptic visions.

To a considerable extent, *Pug Iron Stove* parallels such monuments of world literature as Flaubert's *The Temptation of Saint Anthony* (with which Wat was certainly acquainted in 1919) and, even more so, the Circe episode of Joyce's *Ulysses* (published only in 1922). All three make use of endless quotations; in all three, heterogeneous myths and traditions merge into a vague, syncretic whole. (Another example of this kind of practice is Khlebnikov's poetry.) What confronts the reader is tantamount to an immense library gone mad. Symbols belonging to different spheres do not merely intersect; often as not, they are conflated. Thus, Don Juan and Don Quixote commingle in "Don Juan from La Mancha" (259–60). Monna Vanna, heroine of a popular play by Maeterlinck, and Da Vinci's Mona Lisa become "Monna Vanna Gioconda" (249). One cannot fail to recognize the mythical motif of Pan's death in "dead God Panurge" (254); yet Pan (blended with "demiurge") becomes one with Rabelais's likable rogue.

Wat's poem is as much an exercise in mysticism[13] as a denial of the validity of mystical cognition. If, as the Gnostics and Kabbalists (as well as the romantics and symbolists) maintained, the universe *is* the Book, then the Book cannot be decoded. The unknown author—if there is one—sends random signals, and it may well be Satan himself who tempts and mocks us with senseless splinters off the Tree of Knowledge.

A source that is noted by virtually all the critics is Arthur Rimbaud's poetry in prose, his *Une saison en enfer* and *Les Illuminations*.[14] This is supported by Wat's own admission and by his estimation of Rimbaud as constituting a turning point in the history of literature. In fact, at the very time that Wat was writing *Pug Iron Stove*, the Skamandrites Iwaszkiewicz and Tuwim were preparing a volume of Rimbaud in translation, which was published in 1921.

Many biographical parallels can be detected between Rimbaud and Wat: indeed, to some extent, Wat deliberately patterned his life on that of Rimbaud. Both poets lapsed into silence after a precocious, promising start, although with Rimbaud, the silence was final, whereas with Wat, it subsequently gave way to new periods of fertility. Both were addicted to reading and took an interest in mystical philosophy. Both were representative of the type of the young nihilist who rejects traditional moral values and shows total contempt for literary rules. Both strove for the status of seer and prophet. In his famous letter to Paul

Demeny of 15 May 1871, Rimbaud stated: "The Poet makes himself a *seer* by a long, gigantic and rational *derangement* of *all the senses*. All forms of love, suffering and madness."[15] Wat was unaware of that letter while working on *Pug Iron Stove*, but his attitudes and internal needs, as reflected in the poem, were clearly in accord with Rimbaud's program.[16]

Shades of Rimbaud are abundant in *Pug Iron Stove*. He is directly, if patronizingly, mentioned in the second part, in a section entitled "The end of Aleksander Wat." Rimbaud here blends with the hero of Flaubert's well-known novel: "Here loiters the 'sentimentally educated' youngster and nincompoop Rimbaud" (254).[17] Earlier, there is the following indirect, but immediately recognizable reference: "Seventeen years; Africa! the awakening fang. Down with consciousness. I go 'To liberate my witches.' An unsuccessful escape! Dislocation, disgust, hunger for life and lack of appetite. Sloth. 'I am a walking cloaca.' After two years of suppurating drowsiness and shrinking, of loitering among the people—consciousness—the withering of the hands—now I take up theology and go to Paris then to Tibet to the monasteries of the gray ones or to Sanct Francisco" (232). This is a good example of Wat's mastery in manipulating sources. "Seventeen years" refers equally to the popular image of youthful Rimbaud and to the first line of his poem "Roman." "Hunger for life," a seemingly abstract notion, in fact, relates to the famous "Fêtes de la faim." The motifs of escape and particularly of Africa are inseparable from the Rimbaldian myth.[18] In this context, two quotes set off graphically—"To liberate my witches" and "I am a walking cloaca"—have the appearance of direct quotations from Rimbaud, though they are not found in his corpus; instead, they represent a brilliant pastiche, brief summaries of his favorite topics.[19]

Another pastiche that picks up—and characteristically perverts—Rimbaldian motifs and intonation is as follows: "For the sake of returning to the primeval state of the ruler, I have stretched myself into a magnificent arch on the firmament and am playing with your heads, o stupid people!" (238). In this arrogant apostrophe, it is easy to detect an echo of the most popular of Rimbaud's "Phrases": "J'ai tendu des cordes de clocher à clocher; des guirlandes de fenêtre à fenêtre; des chaines d'or d'étoile à étoile, et je danse."

Wat develops the persistent Rimbaldian theme of the curious, wandering youth who experiences all the pain of adolescence and commits himself wholly to a dramatic spiritual adventure.[20] The youth represents "the poet opposing his civilization, his historical moment, and yet at the same time revealing its very instability, its quaking torment."[21] One of the few integrating motifs of *Pug Iron Stove*, reiterated throughout, is precisely the figure of the poet, referred to alternately in the first and third person, in the present and in the past:

> I extract the sky-blue color from the essence of gray hours between midnight and midday. (230)

Endowed with the art of actually feeling every possibility, I rejoiced exceedingly. For insofar as the ballet of potentialities is infinite in its splendor, I believed that my life will be colorful and free of boredom. (231)

By day, I sleep. By night, I sneak into sickly back streets [I am] very radiant very radiating. When it is already late I fall on my back in gutters and hide my rumpled and blind face in the dazed humps of lanterns. (235)

And serpents whispered to him of the greatness of civilized cities, electric lampions, God, and of the beastly speed of funny cars. Trams uncovered their bald heads before him and lisped: "How prodigious and unfathomable is the motto of unlocked doors." (249)

That self-image may look like the stereotyped mask of a poète maudit; but behind the generalized picture is the particular persona of Rimbaud. Alchemist of intellect and imagination, the poet is not just a victim of the city; he is also a visionary who broadens the scope of human perception and directs the splendid "ballet of potentialities." He is the savior—even if he fails.

The intoxicated, hallucinatory moods, the spirit of despair and disgust, of aggression and anguish, and the taste for extraordinary metamorphoses are all Rimbaldian traits. Like Rimbaud too, Wat attempts to overcome art by going beyond it, into the realm of pure *nihil*. But there is an important difference between the two: Wat is not just a visionary, he is also boldly parodic and auto-parodic. Rimbaud did not avoid humor, mockery, or self-mockery; but he strictly maintained a distance between the serious and the nonserious in his work.[22] There are no comic passages in either *Les Illuminations* or *Une saison en enfer;* however unconventional, these poems preserve a tonal unity, remaining ecstatic and exalted throughout. In *Pug Iron Stove,* by contrast, one cannot draw a dividing line between grim nihilism and grotesque merrymaking. Elevated hallucinatory images are constantly undermined by a powerful admixture of "transcendental buffoonery"[23]—and vice versa. Esoteric signs that defy decoding yet demand it are mixed with absurdities that neither demand nor defy. It is precisely this tension between opposed registers, between desperate and "amused" kinds of iconoclasm, that determines the originality and vividness of *Pug Iron Stove.*[24]

To a large extent, the nonsensical in Wat's poem harks back to folkloric sources, often resembling typical Slavic children's ditties, enumerations, and tongue-twisters. The overall effect of such passages can be described only as a reckless, if amusing dance of phonemes, morphemes, and semes with no overall semantic input whatsoever.

Another kind of playful absurdity in *Pug Iron Stove* harks back to the theme of carnival, mentioned in connection with futurist iconoclasm. As Mikhail

Bakhtin has amply demonstrated, carnivalistic ritual, associated with Dionysian mythology, utilizes a specific body language. It emphasizes nature's—hence humankind's—potential for consumption and fertility, assigning special prominence to *bottom* as opposed to *top*, overturning the official system of values, and freely employing scatological (as well as unabashedly sexual) vocabulary and imagery.[25] One cannot fail to recognize such carnivalesque gestures in many passages of Wat's poem:

> On that night small luminous chamber-pots were marvelously hung in the sky. Pretty coopers' wives surrendered perversely to adolescent knights and portly monks. (235)

> Calm incidentally poured down on a friend of Benvenuto Cellini, when he shat from horror in bushes of ripe golden berries. (235)[26]

> Beata Beatrix will recite the last *Requiem* at the pedestal and will withdraw into the current of blessed shadows. Into blissful moments of lassitude and misty days which nevertheless have displayed before you their delightful hind hemispheres? (237–38)

> And in the blue distance (illusory as you know) throngs of singing bards, shepherds and Lancelots entertain sorrowful visionary virgins with the jingling of phalli. (250–51)

> Thus it is for me as if slender fakirs lightly, slowly and solemnly rose from their knees around a high pile of shit and turning away proclaimed to all the generations of the regions my *apotheosis*. (264)

The semantic mechanism in all these passages is identical: conventional discourse marked by a biblical and traditionally poetic idiom is unexpectedly compromised by an inadmissible image, exhibitionism, or a scoffing grimace. In Bakhtinian terms, this might be seen as a relic of ancient folk practices (ambivalent praise and abuse, mock crowning and decrowning, upended apotheosis). An echo of such practices permeates numerous texts well known to Wat, including Greek comedy and the four Gospels. One of the most conspicuous traits of his poem is an obsession with filth, impurity, the "unnameable," an ongoing violation of conformist discourse underwritten by the violation of even the rules of language.

Significantly, allusions to carnivalistic processions, masks, and monsters, as well as to the ancient phallic and Dionysian cults that were the immediate predecessors of the medieval and Renaissance practice of carnival, are scattered throughout *Pug Iron Stove*. Yet even here, Wat is ambiguous. Carnival and Dionysian imagery is not for him the profuse, uproarious disorder that leads to Paradise regained; often, it is grim, unnatural, morbid, marked by irremediable degeneration and rot:

My being moans in an orgy at turbid white walls. And on the highest
tower my peeling skull watches for the approaching carnival. (240–41)

The gaslight scatters small yellow jewels on my paper. They grow to
blossom and adorn vast meadows on which exhausted Narcissus and moribund
Dionysus traverse. (251)

Two years later, in the opening statement of the *gga* manifesto, this motif of
a "moribund Dionysus" reached its logical conclusion: "the great iridescent
monkey known as dionysus has long since bit the dust."

Pug Iron Stove may be described as parody made total. Its quasi-structure
challenges the very notion of structure. Wat manipulates and conflates his
quotations and pseudo-quotations as if striving to sabotage the very mechanism
of intertextuality and design of palimpsest. A *Pug Iron Stove* sentence mocks, as
it were, that poststructuralist term *avant la lettre*: "From the pages of a palimpsest gray kerchiefs of lice sneak out" (241). Not for nothing does Wat invoke
Cain: ("Traditions have surrounded me and ask: Where is thy brother?" (247).
For Wat *is* the murderer of tradition, code, even writing itself.

Wat's principal target is easily recognizable: the literary modernism of
Young Poland bent.[27] *Pug Iron Stove* debunks its unfounded pretensions, artificial concepts, and counterfeit presentations of art and self, all the while reveling
in Young Poland's convoluted, highly ornamental, hypnotizing style:[28] "when
out of the amethyst distance thou wilt weave the baldaquin of thy hands, when
trifoliate roses will wither and I shall see on my palm the sparkling cicatrice of
thy forehead—I will come to the meeting where, trembling in tears and be-
numbed, thou wilt surrender, you will surrender, he (she) will surrender, we will
surrender, you will surrender, they will surrender" (242).

This passage, in which a ceremonial meeting between two celestial lovers in
a Pre-Raphaelite landscape unexpectedly slips into a grammatical spree, is probably the best specimen of Wat's parodistic skills. But many other instances can be
found in *Pug Iron Stove*. Thus, the Faustian narrator invokes "the spirit of
decay" in the fitting environment of "deep damp dungeons" and then un-
ceremoniously hangs that spirit up on hooks (230); angels meditate on the
paradisiacal radiance of colored bulbs "in the buzzing crucible of a cabaret"
(256–57); the heavens give off a fragrance "of sweetness and of flies" (259)—
and so on. Yet it is not only the modernist style (or any artistic style) that is
challenged in *Pug Iron Stove*. Wat questions language as such and creates a
parody of communication that subverts the habits and violates the expectations
of the reader. The ability of language to convey sense is itself disputed.

Mistrust of language, exacerbated by the experience of Stalinist "semantic
experimentation," constituted one of the pivotal motifs of Wat's thought in later
years.[29] At that time, he did his best to stay on the invisible borderline where

mistrust could be counterbalanced by trust and love. In his youth, however, hatred for the word predominated, which was in perfect keeping with the general futurist program.

Wat achieved his goal of compromising language by employing numerous devices, not all of which could be described as parodic. One such device was the juxtaposition of two stereotypes. An even more common device (not always easily distinguishable from the first) was defined by Wat as "an attempt at creating an image—by analogy with modern physics—that would be alien to our intuition (*Anschauung*), unimaginable":[30] namely, the generation of purely verbal objects without any plausible denotation, the description of actions and situations bearing no reference to any conceivable reality, or, at the very least, the use of adjectives ill-suited to the nouns they modify. Thus:

> Stony spherical sanctuaries of consciousness applied to the baton of a little long-nosed bandmaster pull out trunks of metropolitan elephants and tusks of hippopotamuses. (239)

> Green thresholds. Rosy and succulent hiccup. Translucent downpour of hairs. Rabid funnel of striped ethers. Unity-snare. (242)

> Queen Mab entertains herself by fairy-play of a rocket on a white tram made of peacocks' heads and golden-blind simooms. (247)

> Dogs bark at the boreal moon, whose parchment taste rustles in a coffee-colored hirsute paw of the Demiurge. (253)

> I will send far away my ears—powerful reservoirs for storms of four sides of night. (260)

In these examples, both devices are at work. Virtually all the sentences consist of "regular," if insufferably bombastic, images in the decadent style, which nevertheless explode by reason of their juxtaposition. Wat pretends to establish a referent and negates it, betraying any kind of *mimesis* for the sake of pure *semiosis*.[31] Logically uncoordinated semantic features clash and cancel one another out. Thus, a grim image of dogs barking "at the boreal moon" possesses mythological overtones consistent with the Gnostic concept of an ape-like "Demiurge," the presumed creator of all evil. "The parchment taste" of the moon may seem a bit strained but is nevertheless a rather impressive metaphor. It is only when Wat places the taste in a paw and, to top it off, makes it rustle that the synesthetic discourse is derailed.

Wat usually opposed such triumphant refutation of logic to correct, logical grammar, which could not fail to reinforce the general feeling of absurdity.[32] As a rule, he preserved the rigid structure of the sentence—the skeleton of thought—while inverting the rules of thinking, the relation of cause and effect, and so on. The resulting conflict between grammatical form and "agrammatical" content provided one more tension in a text constructed of multiple tensions and contradictions. But now and then Wat indulged in strictly linguistic experimentation.

Among the mild syntactical licenses in *Pug Iron Stove* are a large proportion of nominal and infinitival phrases, some of which remain within the limits of Young Poland stylistics, even if their shocking imagery more often than not transcends it. Perhaps more unusual are Wat's ellipses and aborted sentences. The punctuation generally is loose, and here and there a sentence stutters as if on a broken record, reminding one of Gertrude Stein's experimental writing:

> Thresholds green, green thresholds, green. (242)

> I watchful will be awakened by rattles, as if by seagulls thrown overboard. I watchful will be awakened by rattles, as if by seagulls thrown overboard. I watchful will be awakened. (256).

A special kind of gibberish is created by employing series of unrelated verbs connected only by their rhythm and sometimes also by rhyme: "The dreams scorched, chewed, danced, crowed" (232); "They revolved wept hugged whine whine whine. They repent, chatter, invite" (233). The last sentence, translated here literally, definitely makes more "sense" in the free translation provided by Bogdana Carpenter: "They tattle babble gabble." Here again we encounter the pure nonsense of Anusia's folk ditties and of nursery rhymes.[33] Rhyming, alliteration, and sound repetition appear in many phrases of *Pug Iron Stove*.

It is well known that futurists, especially in Russia, extended their renovation of poetic speech to the point of "transrational language" consisting of neologisms and specific "sound-images"—that is, clusters of sounds without obvious denotations.[34] Such notions were far from unknown to Polish futurists. But in *Pug Iron Stove* Wat takes a different approach, one that is closer to the Western poetry of his time: his war against sense is waged on the level not of the individual word but of the sentence. Nevertheless, he comes close to the transrational language of Khlebnikov and Kruchenykh in certain respects, by employing words that are so uncommon that virtually no reader would recall their definition. Such is the word *elektuarze*, which means, if anything, "a medicine made by mixing drugs with honey or syrup to form a paste"; but it is unlikely that anyone would understand it, all the more so because Wat gives it in maimed form (something between Latin *electuarium* and Old Polish *elektwarz*) and in an absurd context ("Embroidered Rivieras of the electuaries," 248–49; "The electuaries are abortive," 251). Another word used by Wat, *sembtajon*, is not found in any dictionary and remains unexplained by Wat's commentators, although it too is probably not pure invention. Such words could be classified as "functional transrational language," by contrast with the "pure transrational language" of Kruchenykh's bent.

Wat indulges this tendency through several more devices. He is fond of archaisms, dialecticisms, and rare variants of common Polish words. His stint in a Russian high school resulted in a large number of Russian loanwords, which contribute to the displacement of meaning. In his afterword to *Pug Iron Stove*, Wat confesses, for example, that he introduced the Russian noun *konura* (kennel, 226) in place of the Polish word *buda* because it seemed to be in tune with the Polish (and Russian) adjective *ponury* (gloomy).[35] Nor can one complain of a lack of Greek, Latin, English, German, French, Italian, Hebrew, and Japanese vocabulary.

This bending and torturing of language is sometimes taken to its logical limit, with the word breaking apart, as if it were a body torn asunder in some Dionysian ecstasy ("To re-mem-ber," 246; "Tomorrow, To morrow w?" 254; "Fingers, ers fiifi f fi-fi," 258). Finally, language dissolves into purely phonic sequences, onomatopoeias, and grimaces. The following scene, furnished with stage directions as well as with an onomatopoetic sequence reminiscent of Aristophanes' comedies, sums up the process in a picturesque way: "Only the phantasmagorias of moons would awaken me from my torpor: wrinkling and contracting incredibly my face in an ashen glow, bent on the left side and lifting the right arm and the right little finger; this way, and the left little finger a bit lower and bending the right knee: that way! I trot and squeak: **tim tiu tju tua tm tru tia tiam tiamtiom tium tiu tium tium**" (229–30).

Is this sheer clownery? Or is it authentic madness? Isolated, tormented, destroyed, the word in *Pug Iron Stove* loses its symbolism. Only its metalinguistic quality remains: a word is a word, and nothing else. Any word may be juxtaposed and interrelated with any other, together with any images that may result; pure stochastics reigns in the poem, leading ultimately to void and silence. The authority *of* sign and language is revealed to be an empty one, even if authority *over* sign and language proves to be just as empty in the final accounting.

At the same time, it is clear that the victimizer is profoundly fascinated by his victim. Phonic qualities of the language, the infinite richness of its vocabulary, the intricate patterns of grammar and syntax, and subtle constellations of semantic units all attract Wat, even while he relishes subverting them. Wat described this love-hate complex splendidly in *Scraps of Paper on the Wind*:

> *Trust:* language (logos) is the only social (I + you) vehicle of truth.

> *Distrust:* words pervert the thought, the thought perverts the Being.

> *Love:* joy granted first to the senses, then to the intellect by the very stuff of language. It is analogous to the joy granted to painters of the Quattrocento (and to modern painters) by color.

Hate: the resistance of verbal material, the incommensurability of words with their ideal prototype that resides in the brain of the poet.

Adoration: initiation into the transcendent which is revealed to the poet (to the initiate) by every word, even by punctuation marks.

Aversion: the weakness of any language in the face of the transcendent.

Love-Hate: the poet is an offspring of language and the transcendent, he wishes to possess the language and to murder the transcendent—sometimes, vice versa.[36]

At first glance, the text appears to be confined to the endless, wanton game of construction and destruction; there would appear to be no guiding principle that could help render it comprehensible outside the notion of contradiction. Wat himself provided his future critics with a warning: "Those who see there a puzzle and arrange significant ensembles from shreds are crazy."[37] Nevertheless, *Pug Iron Stove* comes across as a sort of narrative not devoid of development. It may be classified as a modern, tortuous, convoluted transformation of a folk legend or, better still, of a medieval romance. Viewed in this way, several motifs that run through the text, integrating it, stand out. They relate mainly, if not exclusively, to religious archetypes or to the Gnostic mythology of the Self.[38]

Transmitted through various channels, reflected and distorted by a multiplicity of ideological mirrors, the Gnostic spirit was never far from the center of European culture. Its teachings impregnate European philosophy and art, particularly the work of Jakob Boehme, William Blake, and Friedrich Schelling, German and French romanticism, the symbolist and surrealist movements, and Jungian analysis.[39] To that impressive list one should add the work of Polish romantics and Messianists of the nineteenth century—first and foremost, Adam Mickiewicz and Juliusz Słowacki, both of whom were influenced by Andrzej Towiański, a mystic of dubious reputation, in whose doctrine Gnostic ideas are fairly obvious.[40] The Messianist message, even when contested, contradicted, or mocked, never failed to inspire the writers of Young Poland and their successors. Wat's poem thus constitutes a late, idiosyncratic link in that esteemed tradition.

The religious dimension of *Pug Iron Stove* is obvious. The whole poem might be described as an exercise in blasphemy. In subverting all languages, Wat does not spare the language of religious experience and mysticism. His sacrilegious passages appear even more extreme and shocking than those of Nietzsche and Rimbaud, especially when viewed within the context of the provincial Polish Catholicism (or, for that matter, Orthodox Judaism) of his time. Wat's debasement of God borders on nihilism, even if one cannot fail to discern a despairing personal note in his imprecations. In any case, his stance has nothing in common with the complacent, indifferent atheism of the late nineteenth

century: it reminds one rather of Gnostic and romantic theomachy,[41] as expressed in Mickiewicz's *Forefathers' Eve*, the protagonist of which challenged
the Creator in a Czarist prison, asserting his own moral superiority over a God
who serenely tolerates human suffering. But in *Pug Iron Stove*, Wat goes far
beyond Mickiewicz or Young Poland writers such as Tadeusz Miciński and
Przybyszewski, mocking and compromising all the fundamental symbols of
Catholicism and of any faith:

> Saints ran away in horrible fear grabbing all the property they came
> across. Young elegant Andalusian witches averted their eyes from the fleeing
> Bashkir god: that old stinking limper hardly slipped down from his throne and
> skipping dragged himself along a desolate road; and still for a long time turned
> his face to us slavering suppurating curses madly threatening us with his
> crutch and exhaling an unbearable stench. (230–31)

> Strings never shattered by despair, on which only God with swelled
> watery body shivers from cold and loneliness. A monotonous procession de-
> scends from snowy mountains, like a throng of hooded pilgrims. A feast of
> mountain spring overwhelms baby roes who suck their mother's breast and a
> lonely Onanist who jerks the sky. (246)

> From the unlit windows the Angel will descend with a lily of
> Annunciation.—Will it be artificial? (253)

> And from the darkness of the third corner Jesus Christ will come out, and
> will cover the company of drunks with the smoke of a cigarette. (258)

> King Cophetua stands at the house and invites guests to the wedding.

> An idiot! he does not know that the actor given the role of God the Father
> in a mystery play went insane, the actor playing God the Son got drunk, and
> the actress, the only real one among them, indulges in lewdness with the
> menials in the corners. (262–63)

These grotesque and comic images, predictably, did not escape the censor:
"Jesus Christ" in the pub scene was blackened out, although one can still
decipher it under the thin layer of paint in the few surviving copies of the 1919
edition. All religion—or, to be precise, all established religious symbolism—is
presented as a total fraud. Yet the very bitterness of Wat's scoffing and the
delirious quality of his invectives testify to a profound involvement with metaphysics and to the despair of a poet in a world from which God is absent.

Wat's blasphemies can easily be linked to the psychological trials of his
youth: after several traumatic experiences, he lost his virginity in his eighteenth
year, shortly before writing *Pug Iron Stove*.[42] In his memoirs, he confessed that

"between my fourteenth and sixteenth year I went through hell, but at that time I had an ideal of purity, 'the ideal of Madonna' of Dmitri Karamazov."[43] The repressed libido took its toll. Characteristically, "the ideal of Madonna" was the ideal most fundamentally discredited in the poem; and no less typically, it was presented as "the only real one" among moral and religious ideals.

The Madonna appears in the poem in several guises. Wat alludes to many versions of the cult of the Eternal Feminine, so entangling himself in a virtually endless intertextual game. Thus, at the beginning of *Pug Iron Stove* the reader encounters an image that refers to a number of major writers: "A wandering knight tears out his own heart with his spear and *dedicates it to the Madonna* red, alive, sloshing" (227). The motif of the wandering knight derives from *Don Quixote* and the whole tradition of medieval romance developed in half-parodic manner by Cervantes. But it also refers more specifically to Pushkin's poem "Once upon a Time There Was a Poor Knight," the hero of which, having fallen in love with the Virgin Mary, dedicates to her all his exploits and his very life. The poem (not part of the corpus of Pushkin's work studied in Russian high schools) might have been known to Wat in a roundabout way, since it is quoted by Dostoevsky in *The Idiot,* where it explains the character of the titular hero. The motif of the courageous man who tears out his own heart for a noble reason is absent in all three of the above-mentioned texts. Most likely it harks back to Maxim Gorky's heavily stylized tale *Old Woman Izergil,* which was very popular before World War I. Thus the image is multilayered. Moreover, it is placed within a context of similar images all suggesting medieval symbolism, in a section entitled "The Heavenly Legend"[44] where they form an ensemble of Romantic and Pre-Raphaelite bent. But the moving, if unlikely, tableau is undermined by the vulgar word *człopiące* (sloshing)—characteristically, Wat uses a substandard form in place of the correct *człapiące.*

The next scene of "the heavenly legend" impairs the idealistic message of chastity and self-denial: "a flogged slave, a servant of Onania, met thirteen-year-old Beatrice on his path, on the third step of Krzywe Koło. And since there was twilight which drove off all the inclement weather and inopportune maledictions by its long velvet eyelash—thus, he took her by her little fingers and led her to his scarlet lonely bed. But exhausted (weakness rolled up his spine and his withered hands) he turned his back on her. And after being pushed, he slid down soundlessly through the square aperture in the treasury of the thirteen heavenly thieves" (227–28).

Dante's beloved appears here as a child prostitute, and Dante himself (clearly identified with the author) as both lecherous and impotent. The third rung of the heavenly ladder in the third part of the *Divine Comedy* is replaced by "the third step of Krzywe Koło" (Crooked Circle, a lane with steps in the old part of Warsaw, which enjoyed a dubious reputation at the time and was allegedly frequented by young Wat).[45] The thirteen thieves in whose treasury the unlucky hero finds himself are an allusion to *Ali Baba and the Forty Thieves* (a well-known tale in the *Arabian Nights*). But their number is also that of the participants at the Last Supper, as well as the age of the Lolita-like Beatrice.

It would be pointless to enumerate all the feminine myths that Wat demystifies and destroys in *Pug Iron Stove*. Among the characters who either take part in the "action" of the poem or are merely mentioned in passing (usually in a shocking context) are not only symbols of purity and love (Iseult,[46] Rachel, Solveig) but also symbols of debauchery and dissoluteness (Messalina, Manon Lescaut). Thus two complementary aspects of the Eternal Feminine are attacked. An important role is assigned to Lilith, a character taken from the Talmudic and Kabbalistic tradition,[47] who accompanies the narrator in his melancholy wanderings. In accordance with her magical habit of changing form, as well as her traditional representation in decadent art, she appears as a *demimondaine* from the paintings of Henri de Toulouse-Lautrec.

Another esoteric symbol that appears at strategic points in the poem is "Ulalume on a Pink Pig" (235). Here is yet another typical amalgam: of the chaste heroine of Edgar Allan Poe's poem with no less than the Whore of Babylon (see Rev. 17:3 and 17:6: "So he carried me away in the spirit into the wilderness: and I saw a woman sit upon a scarlet coloured beast, full of names of blasphemy, having seven heads and ten horns"). As usual, Wat engages in multilevel parody. The two texts clash and negate each other; moreover, the apocalyptic "scarlet coloured beast" becomes a commonplace pink pig that is unimaginable in either the Revelation of St. John the Divine or Poe's poetry.

Thus the image of the Madonna is multiplied and reflected in dozens of (mostly crooked) mirrors. The undisguised Virgin appears only once, in a sadomasochistic scene decidedly offensive to conventional morality. At the same time, Wat makes here a metaliterary statement that could serve as a motto to the poem as a whole: "The Byzantine Mother of God and resurrecting Lazarus flagellate themselves accompanied by orgiastic organs. In a tiny cell, I illuminate the Life of the Most Holy Virgin. Thus, I while away my hours" (253).

The meaning and function of Wat's blasphemies are manifold. While they undoubtedly reflect a primitive wish to shock the reader by any means, as well as a rather commonplace history of deliverance from pubescent trauma, on another level, one may see a typical case of de-automatization. Wat assaults traditional religious symbolism and the symbolism of the Eternal Feminine in the same way that he attacks language, thereby forcing the reader to reconsider the sign system rather than mindlessly recognize (and reproduce) it. The defilement, pollution, and corruption of mythology and imagery respected from time immemorial may provoke disgust. But destruction and desecration, paradoxically, are close to— even become—reconstruction and consecration, just as the torturing of language proves to be inseparable from a fascination with its potentialities.

It should also be noted that Wat, while appearing to discredit all myths of

Godhead and Femininity, remains well within the limits of the Gnostic myth concerning Sophia (Achamoth). In that myth (espoused in the twentieth century by Russian symbolists whose work was familiar to Wat), Sophia, or Divine Wisdom, the feminine principle underlying the universe, falls from primordial unity in the pleroma and becomes imprisoned in the world of matter, disharmony, and sin. She passes from one female body to another, anxiously awaiting the savior who is to redeem her. In the semi-apocryphal story of Simon Magus, she is incarnated as a whore of the lowest imaginable rank.[48] Wat's debased Beatrices, Iseults, and Madonnas fit perfectly with that image of captive though divine femininity. The Kabbalistic tradition does not recognize Achamoth but has a similar notion of "sparks of divinity" imprisoned in the world of evil and inextricably mixed up with it. The demonic and the heavenly touch each other closely and even, in a sense, coincide. This, in turn, seems consonant with many of Wat's visions of corrupt and abused Godhead.

The violation of the rules of language and the violence perpetrated on traditional (for example, artistic and religious) sign systems that are so characteristic of *Pug Iron Stove* have their logical extension in the bodily sphere. In the poem the human body is tormented and destroyed as mercilessly and thoroughly as language itself. Language and body form perfect counterparts.[49] Infringement of logic and grammar is accompanied by abundant imagery of bodily transgression.

For Wat, as for the mystical systems of antiquity and the Middle Ages, the body constitutes a microcosm corresponding to the physical, as well as the cultural, macrocosm. At the same time, the body is open and grotesque in the Bakhtinian sense: it interacts with its environment, its borders are continually breached. Wat is obsessed with filth and pollution, with bodily excretions (saliva, blood, sperm, pus, excrement) and parasites: this impurity of the body is underscored by his "pollution" and "impurity" of style. Typically, writing is identified with bodily activity. Wat speaks of writing in blood, and the poem ends with a shocking scene in which the climax of the metaphysical and poetic pursuit is virtually inseparable from (rather particular) ejaculation:[50]

> Amen. In thy hands is the might so that heavens may rejoice immeasurably. . . . The eye swells and bursts oozing sperm and beautiful blue posters. . . . The sharp point is the twisting the summons into the Immeasurability. Thus the member gets sharp before the discharge. (269–70)

Also, characteristically, Wat emphasizes the diachronic extremities of the human body—its initial and final stages. The body is presented either as an embryo, not yet fully formed, not yet independent, or as old, exhausted, and withered, on the verge of death, decomposition, and blending back into its environment. A fully formed, not disfigured body is a rarity in *Pug Iron Stove*.

And when it occurs, Wat compromises its wholeness, showing it in some extreme state (drunkenness, madness, pain, despair) that obliterates its borders, as it were. Or, more usually, it is represented metonymically, through its parts.[51] Nor is this metonymic "cutting up" of the body in *Pug Iron Stove* ever far from "realistic" dismemberment.

Predictably, the code of human sexuality is subverted in Wat's poem no less than all the other linguistic and bodily codes. In inventing a "counter-language," Wat at the same time celebrates all that is "contra-natural."[52] *Pug Iron Stove* more often than not resembles a study of so-called deviant practices such as Richard Krafft-Ebing's *Psychopathia Sexualis* (1886), a book popular during Wat's youth. Wat highlights incest, pedophilia, cunnilingus, sadomasochism, homosexuality (male as well as female) and relishes scenes of masturbation. All this, like Wat's blasphemies, can be explained, up to a point, by the typical futurist urge to *épater les bourgeois*. The impression made on the reader of this seemingly endless catalogue of unconventional sexual behavior borders on the comical. At the same time, it fits into the general semantic pattern of the poem. The violation of all codes and the transgression of all boundaries are, for Wat, a necessary stage in the search for selfhood.[53]

The next, no less visible layer of bodily motifs in *Pug Iron Stove* consists of images of disease and physical degeneration. They can be classified as yet another type of transgression. Here we are dealing with the overturning of the code of health:[54]

> Sick early youth, yellow sides of the head, Maria's fingers bless a hollow chest. Harmony, fantastic navigations of the studies, when red roses horribly swayed on the small altar of a sick heart. (231)

> DISEASE. Disease upon arrival first of all strained facings of the eyelids. The eyeballs vibrated in shallow very mesmeric convulsions. . . . And that was already the second day of the bloody diarrhea. (234)

> Dance of the sex on small misshapen rachitic legs. Balançons. (242)

> Tuberculosis reads from very long books. (258)

> Brother Disease and a blessed leprous jester. And the exhaustion will come true. (259)

> Brown death and black typhoid fever embrace each other, withdraw and again, once more again. (267)

Dozens of other illnesses, including scrofula, dropsy, and blindness, could be added to this list. Wat seems to have been positively fascinated by all imaginable symptoms of bodily deterioration: rot, jaundice, hollowness, grayness, impotence, and so on.[55] Naturally, there is no lack of alcoholism, drug addiction, or that paradigmatic disease of the fin de siècle, syphilis, and tabes dorsalis. Cultural references, which abound here, include "Brother Disease," which brings to mind—and parodies—the *Canticle of the Sun* by St. Francis, in which Brother Sun, Sister Moon, Brother Wind, Sister Water, Brother Fire—and, significantly, Sister Bodily Death—are praised. Saint Francis, who cared for lepers but was never himself infected, is juxtaposed with "a blessed leprous jester."[56] Here, the reader is again faced with a set of Gnostic concepts, introduced this time in Manichean guise: nature as *the* polluted sphere is virtually identical with malady.

The ultimate metaphor for the alienation, sterility, and unnaturalness of the God-forsaken world is castration, which figures prominently in *Pug Iron Stove:* "And in the corners of the grotesque arcade sleepy castrates moan" (246); "A withered swarm of the castrates admires the smoke of the cigarettes" (256). But the final form of transgression in the poem is death, which usually equals suicide.

The density of imagery involving (usually voluntary) physical suffering, dismemberment, execution, and self-destruction is striking.[57] Among the trials presented in terms of Romantic or modern imagination are encountered, usually in travestied and/or ironic form, the ancient agonies of the decapitated St. John the Baptist, the crucified Christ, and the torn Dionysus:

> At midnight one should always lay down one's head under the dazzling, yes! dazzling blade of a guillotine. And the tribades will dance far and away with a bloody torso. (245)

> The knife and the poison have equal gastronomic value. The knife and the poison, the lamp, the mask. (247)

> A viperine flash of Her breast in a mocking descent from the cross. (250)

> The sun torn by the maenads melancholic "bluestockings." (252)

> Torrents of severed heads, and the bell in the shape of Priapus destroy all memory. (255)

> When I came out from the green inn it was already very late. Laundresses who danced in a ring in the suburb caught me: Having raped me, they hung [parts of] my body, like linen, on the thick ropes of a cemetery. Some salamanders wetted with saliva my feet, lips, and eyelids. (262)

> I like [the moment] when an executioner saws seams of my skull obliquely, when I lay down pink ends of my nerves under the falling guillotine of hours.

I like so much [the moment] when the one-eyed lame dunce, the auto-
mobile, spits out the pulp of my intestines and marrow. (263)

Here, Wat characteristically mocks the symbolism of martyrology as well as
the very figure of the martyr: in this filthy universe, there can be only false
prophets and fake martyrs. Likewise, destruction takes the most horrible forms
(highlighted by the palpability of the images) but remains farcical. The hero
enjoys the "gastronomic value" of his own mutilation and death.

The motif of multiplication may be noted here. The head of the victim
turns into "torrents of severed heads," and the body is hung on ropes like so
many pieces of washing. Moreover, death itself is repeated endlessly: one should
lay one's head under the blade of a guillotine and present one's bleeding torso to
Dionysian dancers every midnight. Here, Wat's strategy is double-edged. On
one hand, he faithfully re-creates the ancient archetype of the dismembered
deity (which in Gnostic and other Hermetic teachings symbolized the destruction of the primordial unity, the pleroma, *'en-sof*). Death and dismemberment,
in this tradition, anticipate reconstruction and rebirth and are an indispensable
aspect of the metaphysical drama.[58] Significantly, some sections of *Pug Iron
Stove* carry titles which refer to that myth: "Death," "Disintegration," "Regeneration," "Resurrection." The titles do not altogether correspond to the content
of the sections, but at least they appear "in the right order," even if their
progression is interrupted by titles of a different kind. On the other hand, in
Wat's poem death and dismemberment lack any transcendental aspect. They are
easily reversible and eternally repeatable. It is as if the hero cannot escape from
an immense hall of mirrors in which his earthly predicament is reiterated endlessly.

In his afterword to *Pug Iron Stove*, Wat says that the poem was, for him, like
a psychoanalytic session. "For a long time, I intended to commit suicide as a
poète maudit, at the latest before the age of 25, which seemed to me the last
barrier before debasement."[59] In the poem itself, he indulges in a ceaseless
ironical game with the idea of suicide. The final annihilation is longed for yet left
in doubt. It escapes the poet, giving birth to characteristically Romantic lines
that, in contrast to the majority of his statements, are virtually deprived of irony:

The nightingales sing for my death. Blind Solveig and also the peacocks. And
the golden dreams, shaking their spear.[60] Should I go to the ponds. Or perhaps
I should wind, around the soft neck, a warm shawl of tears? Or an intoxicating
bell of hair? The nightingales sing already for death. (244)

Here, the ravings of a nineteen-year-old futurist attain the status of grim
prophecy. For in 1956, during a bout of his incurable disease, Wat found himself
in the French hospital of Saint-Mandé, which stood in a garden (bringing to
mind, unerringly, the garden of Gethsemane) where nightingales sang in old
acacia trees. There he wrote a poem entitled "Noc w szpitalu" (A Night in a

Hospital), which ended with the following self-quotation: "and the night filters pain, its black essences, / and the nightingales, the nightingales sing for my death." Suicide, postponed for many years, was now in sight.

The Gnostic tradition also provides a hermeneutic framework for the unusual metamorphoses of the "I" in Wat's poem. Insofar as an overall narrative pattern can be discerned in *Pug Iron Stove*, it is the story of a quest, a journey, a *rite de passage*. Presented mockingly and parodically, the story nevertheless retains obvious Hermetic overtones.

The "I" of the poem is multifaceted. On one level, what the reader encounters is a young Warsaw poet with a name and a distinctive appearance, who is not without social status and who sports the loud futurist garment made fashionable by Mayakovsky.[61] The reader is given his address, even his phone number: "ME Aleksander Wat a youth with a flat broken nose in a gaudy yellow waistcoat, with protruding ears and weak-sighted eyes. Studiosus philosophiae Niecała str. 8 apt. 31 tel. 282-42" (260). Characteristically, this empirical "I" appears only near the end of *Pug Iron Stove*. Prior to that, it changes masks and undergoes a myriad transformations: into Cro-Magnon man, a medieval alchemist and magician, a tramp, an emperor of the globe,[62] a (pre-Ionesco) rhinoceros, and so on. The narrator also assumes numerous literary personae, including Hamlet, Faust, and Don Juan. In these, a touch of narcissism is usually present.

It is possible to describe roughly the "course of events" in the poem. A young man experiences all the temptations and ordeals of the earthly world. He immerses himself in the realm of legends and myths. He is tested by love, power, and wisdom. He is afflicted by fear, physical calamity, and revolts. He takes an enchanted sea-journey (reminiscent of Homer's *Odyssey* and Rimbaud's "Le Bateau ivre"). He "speaks in tongues," like the Apostles at Pentecost, and undergoes passion, resurrection, apotheosis, albeit of a mock variety. At the end of the poem, we find him in a feverish, ecstatic state, facing his double. He has lived his human adventure to the full.

This is the story of a search for identity. The empirical identity of a "studiosus philosophiae" who lives on Niecała Street belongs to the world of disintegration and meaningless diversity: even the name of the street carries this connotation, *niecała* meaning "incomplete," "imperfect." In an uncanny passage from the first part of *Pug Iron Stove*, which is echoed at the end of its second part, we read: "Having possessed the joyous science[63] of the mask, I burned with a marvelous desire: to spatialize![64] But I was once frightened by a bottomless gap, which I discovered immediately *behind* the surface of [my] nose, while looking at it by the right eye. A damned gap, a damned principium individuationis, it frightens, harasses, lashes, twists, paralyzes me like a yellow jacket.[65] Where could one find the might to step over it! Where!" (229).

This laughable "gap" connotes the world out of joint. *Principium individua-*

tionis, a technical term in metaphysics, means "basic distinguishing trait." All things marked by it—that is, separated from the pleroma—are considered imperfect, hence nonexistent.[66] The hero of the poem meditates on this fallen state of the world in the posture characteristic of Job: "And once more an emaciated Jew sits on a dunghill holding on to it convulsively by sharp hooks of fingers of both hands and once more smashes his brains on the principium individuationis, on the stiff cold canopy of heaven" (263).

According to Gnostic doctrine, the empirical "I," the subject immersed in the world of "earthly sleep," can return to his true home, "step over" the *principium individuationis*, only by finding his real self—which is to say, only by meeting his celestial counterpart.[67] Gnosis—"the purification of the spiritual being and at the same time knowledge of the Whole"[68]—is obtained on the path of mystical quest and ecstasy precisely at the point where descent of the soul to the lowest depths gives way to ascent, and destruction changes places with creation. In that search for meaning, in which the satanic pole has to be reached before one can return to heaven, spiritual creativity is virtually indistinguishable from the poetic imagination. The essence of self, attained by gnosis, is at one with the essence of essences, God (or Being).[69] Gnosis also has an eschatological aspect, since it leads back to the pleroma. "The end will coincide, thus, with the *restitutio*, or restoration, of the original spiritual body, whose members are dispersed in the darkness."[70]

Here, the motif of androgyny needs investigating.[71] The blending of male and female occurs in *Pug Iron Stove* in various contexts. Sometimes it is mentioned only in passing; at other times it is developed in refined, erotically charged, mysterious scenes. "In the silence, pain and tension of every moment that burns without a rustle on the black candelabrum of the night—I feel how it stirred inside me—and with a golden and spotted head of an embryo or a serpent[72] flashed and spirally filled the church of my soul: the Female. And my vigorous and round legs in dumb hunger for pleasure rub under the shiver, under the lisping shiver of bisexuality" (238).

Androgyny is one of the most fundamental concepts of Gnostic thought, according to which God is unity, without beginning or end, who therefore makes no distinction between male and female. "The symbolism of the androgyne, so widespread in the history of religions and found alive in ancient mythological thought also by virtue of the particular good fortune enjoyed by the Platonic androgyne, tends to express as its most general content the concept of *coniunctio oppositorum*, or joining of opposites, to embody the conquest of all duality in an image that for the most part is constructed on a sexual paradox."[73]

This symbolism repeats itself on the lower rungs of the Gnostic universe. The Protennoia (First Thought of God) in the treatise of the same name is presented as androgynous, simultaneously performing the roles of mother and father and copulating with itself.[74] (Parenthetically, Wat's scenes of self-abuse and his image of Godhead as "a lonely Onanist who jerks the sky" may be interpreted as parodic representations of that notion.) The first man, Adam, is also androgynous.[75]

A pivotal section of *Pug Iron Stove* entitled "Gindry" alludes to these Gnostic concepts. It is a sort of love poem (patterned, in part, on The Song of Solomon), the addressee of which possesses somewhat baffling traits:

> Hark, Gindry, hark! when the surf of strings dreams—I go to greet the backbone of my Gindry. (241)

> About Gindry they dreamed, light rosy palaces filled with heavy cruses of pearls, pale withered hands of the prince of Siberian tundras and a sad harlequin from the shop window on Traugutt street. . . . Gindry has blind fingers and Gindry does not know where, in what country and in which regions are the stalls where a sanguine huckstress sells cinnabar and golden springs. (242)

> Who is the lonely one pacing through night and mist? Who is he, a late guest entering an alien house amidst night and mist?

> It is Gindry, it is Gindry who knocks at my door, at the door abounding in Sesame of mahogany. In a minor key. I have anathematized every alien power in the area of the great magic circle. For Gindry, there is nothing to fear, for Gindry, there is nothing to cry about. The unhealthy pulse of the driven away dawn will not disturb the tranquility of our first night. (243)

The mysterious creature Gindry, depicted in a fin de siècle manner, has all the characteristics of a heavenly being, like one more incarnation of the *ewig Weibliche*. At the same time, he is a dark male spirit whom the hero, a latter-day Doctor Faustus, summons to the magic circle: "Already the tenth night I summon thee in vain, o Doctor of darkness" (243; see also 244). The name Gindry, presented in the original Polish text in various syntactic positions requiring different cases, remains undeclined so could refer to a person of either gender. It is sometimes modified by a feminine possessive pronoun—"mojej Gindry"— but is always replaced by masculine adjectives and nouns. The all-inclusive explanation for this is that Gindry is simultaneously male and female. Gindry is an embodiment of the Absolute, which is defined in another part of the poem in quite explicit terms: "THE ABSOLUTE. A sexless whore with a bronze forehead, motionless throughout the vibrations of years and universes" (266). Nor can one fail to notice that the word *Gindry* is an anagram of the word *androgyne*.[76]

A complementary interpretation of the androgynous figure of Gindry, who is so anxiously awaited by the "I," reveals its role as divine messenger, Savior— and, at the same time, the real Self of the hero. In Gnostic thought, joining with the Savior (often presented in terms of a marital union) means salvation, "the definitive return to the divine world, one's real homeland."[77] The messenger communicates the only knowledge that counts, knowledge of one's own *archē* (beginning) and *telos* (end.).[78] "Thus the Gnostic reaches the end of his long, perilous journey. What awaits him is the last repose, the final conquest of struggles, dissensions and lacerations. . . . The individuals, reconstructed in androgynous unity, can now rest in themselves."[79]

Rebirth to the true life, the end of the Gnostic journey, equals reunion with one's celestial counterpart—the real "I," as opposed to the empirical "I." This may be described as an encounter with one's double. The motif of the double remains ambiguous in Wat's poem. It usually signifies, not the true Self, but the nightmarish dissolution of identity.[80] The double is presented as a hallucinatory delusion, which does not bring exoneration but instead fills a person with horror: *"Behind a counter, you will see your own pale image. How terrible it is to meet one's own pale image at midnight. What?"* (238).

The final identification of the Self with God does not in fact take place. One of the most memorable parts of *Pug Iron Stove* presents the predicament through the symbolism of Jacob's ladder (Gen. 28:10–17) and Jacob wrestling with the angel (Gen. 32:24–29): "A ladder to heaven, on which I climb arduously with eternal desire: enough. And then comes my own angel and hurls me down; I rise slowly with broken limbs. I am blind, flies hatch instead of eyes in their burned out orbits. Stars stick over me and torment me, [they are] sticky like brown tiny baby apes" (268).

The epilogue sums up the hero's failure. He undergoes the experience of mystical burning (inseparable, in Gnosticism as well as in the Kabbalah, from ecstasy and ascent of the soul).[81] But the inner burning of the ascetic saint is presented in very earthly terms: as a trivial fever caught on a Warsaw street and aggravated by the smothering warmth of an iron stove. Once more, the hero encounters the menacing gap of *principium individuationis*: "But I see only one thing: that, that: a (black) empty fissure between the palms" (270). This parodic scene (and the whole poem) concludes on a desperate note:

> This is ME who burns in the inquisitorial bowels of my pug iron stove, this is ME who burns in the middle between myself lying together on one side and myself as well on the other side of the stove.[82] Hurr! I behold the ominous palms of this one from one side and that one from the other side.

> On one and on the other side sits ME.

> This is ME from one side and ME from the other side. (271)

The closing lines recall the baffling title of the poem and explain it, if only partially.[83] In the statement about "the Other" observed by the hero, one may easily discern a counterpart to the declaration in Rimbaud's letter to Paul Demeny (15 May 1871): "Car *Je* est un autre" (For *I* is someone else). The manifold interpretations that are accorded these words by Rimbaldian scholars usually converge on the view that the empirical "I" is created by an inner power, the unconscious, or whatever, and that a human being is thus capable of transcending his or her limits.[84] This is what makes the poet's passage from subjectivity to objective, dehumanized writing possible.[85] Here, one is dealing with "the impersonal, original, objective, cosmically-rooted self, the 'other' behind the social 'I.'"[86] The Gnostic root of this idea is obvious.

In the most feasible reading of the final scene, the double turns out to be the same "ME," observed from a different perspective. The true Self comes near to the hero but escapes him. All the spiritual power of the hero having been exhausted, the end result is a split personality. Thus the concluding passage of *Pug Iron Stove* restates the motif of dismemberment and disintegration that pervades the entire work. The split of the "I" indicates "both his being at odds with society, his uniqueness, and, in another direction, his being at odds with himself, constituting what would be, if pathological, schizophrenia."[87]

The possibility of another reading is not annulled, however. The real Self temptingly shimmers through the veil of the schizophrenic self. In Wat's universe, the serious is always undermined by the parodic, but the parodic is just as likely to turn out to be serious. There are no uncontested solutions, positive or negative; there are no definitive, closed readings, comforting or disquieting. There is only pure speech. This is the only form of mysticism available to the reader of *Pug Iron Stove:* Wat's poem is an immense chord left unresolved.

4

Radical Left, 1924–1928

In the early 1960s, Wat wrote an imaginative essay entitled "The Death of an Old Bolshevik."[1] The titular hero was Yury Steklov-Nakhamkes, an associate of Lenin and a victim of Stalin's purges, whom Wat met in Saratov prison hospital shortly before his demise. Faced with death, Steklov attempted to come to terms with the dismal history of the movement in which both he and Wat had previously participated. Wat listened to the half-mad ranting attentively, in his mind comparing Steklov and his generation to faithful Catholics who had lost all hope of salvation. Repeatedly, the moribund man entreated: "When you return to Poland, tell people how old Nakhamkes Steklov died." Wat complied with Steklov's request, spreading the story first by word of mouth, then in writing. "The Death of an Old Bolshevik" is full of understanding, compassion, and, to a considerable degree, identification with the hero. For many years, Wat continued to perform the task bequeathed to him by Steklov: to comprehend and explain the system that had deformed both their lives, as well as those of innumerable other men and women.

Wat treated communism in theological and psychological, rather than sociological, terms. He saw his own involvement in the Communist movement as a sin he could never expiate, a disease from which he could never fully recover. It would be easy to dismiss Wat's interpretation of communism as a product of mythologizing (and in Wat's lifetime it was repeatedly rejected as the ravings of a defeated émigré). But Wat's interpretation may also be understood as a great metaphor comparable to the metaphors employed by Dostoevsky in *The Possessed* or by Thomas Mann in *Doctor Faustus*.

In Soviet prisons Wat learned the powerful lesson that there may never have been a movement so fraught with cruel paradoxes as communism. Insisting on rationalism, it created the most far-fetched myths. Assuring happiness, it caused untold sufferings, for its adherents as well as others. Allegedly possessing the key to all economic problems, it failed miserably in the very field it had staked out for itself. Instead of abolishing inequality, homelessness, and hunger once and for all, it exacerbated these conditions longer than did its historical enemy, capitalism. Rather than promoting international cooperation for the common good, it gave rise to chauvinistic and militaristic states, the manipulation and perversion of language, and an incredible waste of human potential. In short, it translated into reality the chilling words of Dostoevsky's character Shigalyov: "Starting from unlimited freedom, I arrived at unlimited despotism."[2] Parenthetically, the next sentence by Shigalyov, quoted less often, is much more frightening: "I will add, however, that there can be no other solution of the social formula than mine."[3]

But is this true? Wat was probably tormented by this question to the very end. He did not live to see the collapse of communism and may have assumed its invincibility. Yet he felt it his moral duty to become a witness and give a philosophical interpretation of the phenomenon that determined the course of his disgraced century.

While in power after World War II, Polish Communists attempted to appropriate all the traditions of the Polish workers' movement—and, moreover, all the Polish traditions they deemed "progressive," including the heritage of the Enlightenment and of Romantic poetry. In reality, their patrimony was modest. They were the direct successors of the SDKPiL (1900–1918), a Social Democratic party that took the Leninist path, disregarding Polish aspirations to independence. The party did not lack outstanding leaders (not only Dzierżyński, but Rosa Luxemburg were participants), but it remained a distant second to Piłsudski's PPS in influence. After the October Revolution SDKPiL merged with the so-called PPS Left (a wing of the PPS in opposition to Piłsudski) and changed its name to the Polish Communist Party (KPRP; from 1925, KPP). It now lent its unconditional, unswerving support to the first Communist state, Soviet Russia, which it aided by any and all means possible. This led to a decline in the KPP's political significance. Considered, not without reason, an instrument of a foreign power, it was relegated to the political margin.

In 1929 the party could claim, at best, twelve thousand members; workers made up only 10 percent, whereas intellectuals constituted no less than 59 percent.[4] Moreover, the party remained uncommonly narrow-minded and sectarian. If at times it enjoyed a modicum of popular support, it was primarily among Poland's ethnic minorities. A small, but visible, group of Communists came from a Jewish background. Although most Jews in Poland were either Orthodox or Zionist, some were attracted to the party for various reasons, not least the fact that in Russia state anti-Semitism was at that time virtually nonexistent, so offering a ray of hope to many young, naive people. That, in turn, furnished rich soil for the hatemongers of the Polish Right, who promoted the derisory expression *żydokomuna* (the Jewish Commune).[5]

In May 1923, a rightist government took power. After three years, on 12–14

May 1926, Piłsudski carried out a coup d'état and established an authoritarian regime (the so-called *sanacja*) that lasted even beyond his death in 1935, up to World War II. Although the KPP openly supported Piłsudski's coup, he did not acknowledge a debt to the Communists and gave orders for their demonstrations in his favor to be dispersed immediately. What was worse, Moscow declared Piłsudski a Fascist (which was far from true) and denounced the KPP's support of the coup as scandalously erroneous. The attempt to form a broadly leftist Popular Front in the 1930s largely failed, not least because the KPP leadership promoted it with ill-concealed mental reservations.

Finally, in 1937-38, the party was disbanded and decimated by Stalin, an exceptional fate even in a period that did not lack unbelievable and terrifying developments. Accused of being infiltrated by *sanacja* provocateurs and Trotskyites, the KPP faced the liquidation of virtually all its leaders, as well as quite a few rank-and-file members who happened to be in the USSR. The outbreak of World War II found the handful of Communist survivors in Poland in a state of shock and total disarray.

Wat repeatedly said that he never joined the party, although he is listed as a member in some sources.[6] Bearing in mind that the party records were in a state of permanent disarray and that members and sympathizers were not always distinguished between either by the party itself or by the police,[7] that may not mean anything, however. What is *not* disputed is that Wat's involvement in Communist activities was of long duration and significant, if tortuous.

In September 1920, when Wat and Stern were planning their *gga* manifesto, the KPRP saw fit to establish a cultural and educational association, Kultura Robotnicza (Worker's Culture), which, in February 1922, started a periodical of the same name. To all intents and purposes, it was an offshoot of the Russian Proletkult, an organization that came into being at the time of the October Revolution.[8] The underlying concept was disarmingly simple. Since bourgeois culture was in a state of decay and disintegration, as its own brightest spokesmen acknowledged, new, distinctly proletarian art and literature were in order. This was to be created mainly, though perhaps not exclusively, by the proletarians themselves.

The task of creating proletarian culture in Poland was undertaken by two people, both of them remarkable, if deluded. Antonina Sokolicz had started as a member of the PPS and then of the PPS Left. She had some personal ties to Piłsudski, and represented, in the not-too-conducive environment of the KPP, the old Polish positivist and socialist traditions. During World War II, she joined the anti-Nazi resistance and perished at Auschwitz. A friend and collaborator of Sokolicz, Jan Hempel, played an even more significant role. An eccentric who had spent his youth traveling to the Far East and Brazil, he toyed with theosophy and was for a time intellectually close to Witkacy.[9] But after joining the KPRP in 1921, he became a loyal party ideologue. In 1932, he emigrated to the USSR, only to share there the lot of other Polish Communist leaders.

Sokolicz and Hempel represented a communist cultural elite. For them, the alliance of avant-garde literature and the party seemed natural enough. Moreover, they knew of such an alliance in Russia, where Mayakovsky and his friends had dedicated their talents to the revolutionary cause. They actively sought contacts with young futurists.

It would be an error to suggest that the theoretical postulates of Lenin (or of any of his collaborators) could have made a strong impression on Wat, the budding intellectual, or on his friends.[10] The "workers' poetry" promoted by Polish adherents of the Proletkult was an even sorrier spectacle. Rhetorical and stereotyped, it endlessly repeated the motifs of chains, dawn, storm, Prometheus, and similar clichés long outworn by Romanticism.[11] "The principal poet was Słowik [Nightingale]. That was his family name. A sworn poet, a sort of Konopnicka full of a nightingale's fervor. Besides this, total graphomany."[12]

All the same, the pitiable efforts of Słowiks might be considered an aberration. Lenin may have been an amateurish philosopher, but his revolutionary endeavor was far from unimpressive. Wat and his friends experienced a sort of Nietzschean fascination with the primeval forces of revolt, with the dark, cruel, yet purifying, Dionysian explosion occurring in semi-mythological Eastern lands. This attitude was shared, if only for a time, by the Russian symbolists Aleksandr Blok and Andrei Bely, as well as by countless European intellectuals. If futurists advocated discarding old books and destroying museums, Russian Communists practiced such iconoclasm on a scale hitherto unknown. Revolution seemed a *Pug Iron Stove* translated into reality, a great negating, mocking gesture that might clear the field for one's true Self.

While demystifying old values, revolution at the same time contained a strong utopian, eschatological element. Revolutionary activity could be interpreted as a spontaneous realization of ideals as old as mankind itself: brotherhood, freedom, creativity, and participation in life to the full. The blood of oneself and others, spilled together in the name of the future, was a kind of communion. That was the attitude of Mayakovsky and Khlebnikov: on Polish ground, it was expressed primarily by Jasieński.

Nor should other factors be underestimated. In the Polish milieu, communism could easily be taken as an antidote to provincialism and stagnation. It emphasized activism, promising everyone a chance to influence history. The Communist world view might look tough, but it was consistent and seemingly devoid of illusions. The declared goal of the Communists, fighting social injustice, was attractive in a poor country. Finally, although one might question the artistic taste of the Communist leaders, they at least assigned art an important place in the life of the society, giving it an almost sacred function. It is hardly surprising, then, that the leading futurists gradually moved towards the party. They had nothing to lose, since they were poignantly aware of their literary and social isolation and, in any case, had already been accused of bolshevism.

The periodical *Workers' Culture* did not last long. It ceased publication in May 1923. Already on 1 July its direct successor, *Nowa Kultura* (*New Culture*) appeared, continuing the same program under the same guidance. An organ of the banned KPRP, it was run by Hempel, although for conspiratorial reasons he was never announced as its official editor. In January 1924, Jasieński, Stern, and Wat came into the periodical's orbit, contributing to it several of their poems, as well as translations from Mayakovsky and Apollinaire. In the first issue of 1924 Wat published a short story, "Prowokator" (An Agent Provocateur) and in the third a poem, "Policjant" (The Cop).

These writings were typical of Wat, in both their paradoxical wit and their theomachic fervor. The poem described God as "a cop with a bulldog's eyes," as merciless as simple-minded:

> he divided the light from the darkness
> to see clearly and at once
> whom to punish by darkness
> whom to punish by light
>
> he tethered to the belt of zodiac
> the might of leo the love of virgo and the libra
>
> and he crucified his own son
> for a violation of the law.

The cosmic imagery and sharp rhythm of the poem recall to mind early Mayakovsky. The opposition of Christ as victim to Jehovah as evil despot has Gnostic overtones that remind one of *Pug Iron Stove*. This set the poem apart from the dull, anti-religious material produced en masse by so-called proletarian authors.[13] Hempel, an ardent propagandist for atheism, could accept the poem for its subject matter (even if it was more blasphemous than atheist) and also took note of its technical deftness. But, as a party ideologue, he was probably unhappy with its too obvious ties to "anarchist and petty bourgeois art."

The story looked even more suspicious. Nor did Wat value "An Agent Provocateur" in later life.[14] It was not reprinted until 1988, more than twenty years after his death. Nevertheless, it is not without interest. Even the topic was sensitive—and ominous. Double agents bedeviled conspiratorial parties throughout Russia, Poland, and virtually every country for many years. The hero of the story, Grzegorz, a party functionary and police informer, is a classical case of split personality, here described in terms of "class consciousness" that are exaggerated to the point of parody, perhaps not entirely an undesired effect. The

contrast between the tough proletarian (who is also a hard-boiled agent provocateur) and the "tearful intellectual" springs from experiences of Grzegorz's
childhood and youth: he was brought up by a devout mother and studied at the
university before joining the party ranks. At the beginning of the story, he
observes a religious procession, the sight of which leads to a revelation whereby
his double life acquires its metaphysical sanction.

> Thereby Grzegorz, the police informer No. 37, suddenly felt himself a
> prophet, the likeness and imitator of God; discovered a new religion, the
> religion of the provocation; recognized a religious mission in his calling, saw
> the plan and the goal before his eyes: precipitating the last day, advancement
> of the Heavenly Kingdom. The sooner the measure of evil overflows, the
> sooner the Heavenly Kingdom will come.
>
> Grzegorz understood the Day of Judgment thus: an untold number of
> electric chairs, a revolutionary in every one of them, a policeman before every
> one of them, and somewhere high up, on the highest podium he, the agent
> provocateur, presents a speech: then he rings the bell, each policeman presses
> the button, a revolutionary is electrocuted in each chair.
>
> That vision split into two now and then. Everything as it was, but now the
> policemen in the chairs and the revolutionaries before them.

Overpowered by his newly found religious mission, Grzegorz becomes
fanatical: he attempts to inveigle all the proletariat into terrorist actions and then
plans to denounce everybody. The police finally detect the instigator and set him
before a firing squad (not on an electric chair, as Grzegorz remarks regretfully).
"And Grzegorz imagined that the glittering barrels of the guns were directed not
at him, not at the miserable agent No. 37, not at him the clumsy imitator, but
higher, higher, at the highest agent provocateur whose name must not be taken in
vain."

Here, once more, we find Wat's typical motifs. God, in full accordance with
Catholic belief, appears as a coniunctio oppositorum, reconciling order and
mutiny. This leads to the realm of theological disputes and heresies. Evil may be
interpreted as a shortcut to good, and theomachy and blasphemy may bring one
nearer to the Lord. But there is more to it: Wat, like Dostoevsky before him,
perceives acutely the moral and religious dimension of the revolutionary
struggle and realizes that its logic may lead to absurd antinomies. In this sense,
his "crazy short story" prefigures the writings of his mature years.

Even the form of "An Agent Provocateur" proved significant. Here, for the
first time, Wat attempts a short, ironic, philosophical parable, a genre that
became his trademark as a fiction writer. The best features of the story consist in
apt paradoxical formulas that subvert philosophical clichés by setting them in a
twentieth-century context: witness the Socratic signboard "Know Thyself.
Paint and Mirror Shop"—not by accident did the motif of mirror image determine the structure of the piece.

This technique is reminiscent of G. K. Chesterton, and "An Agent Provocateur" was obviously patterned on *The Man Who Was Thursday* (1908), Chesterton's popular novel on terrorism in which the head of the terrorist squad proved to be the police chief (and, for that matter, most likely the Lord himself). Such a story, which hinted at the perfect interchangeability of revolutionaries and policemen, was hardly calculated to make a positive impression on party ideologues. Nor can one deny its prophetic nature. "The Heavenly Kingdom, as Grzegorz imagined, would come when everyone attained perfection, i.e. when everyone became an agent provocateur. Everyone would be a policeman on the one hand, and a revolutionary on the other." This delirious dream was to be translated into reality. In Stalin's Russia, the entire Polish Communist movement, Wat included, was accused of being in the pay of the Polish intelligence service, an accusation made, ironically, by Stalin, a godlike man who, according to a widespread rumor, had himself been a double agent in his youth.

The involvement of the former futurists with *New Culture* was precarious and, predictably, short-lived. Liberal-minded by comparison with most Communists, Hempel could not afford any hesitation in promoting the party line. "We must," he wrote in one of his editorials, "unmask the so-called non-class or supra-class character of previous culture and reveal, even if quite brutally, the concealed class nature of artistic flight of fancy, the sophisticated philosophical arguments or, finally, the eternal religious legends."[15] If all the futurists were guilty of bourgeois anarchism and muddled beliefs, some of them, including Jasieński, still held out a certain promise. But Wat's addiction to individualistic values appeared to be incurable.[16] As early as March 1924, Hempel printed in his periodical an article that expressed the attitude of the editorial board to the published futurist texts: "Very soon, unfortunately, it became clear that these writings were artistically unintelligible for our readers. And not for the reason of their oversophistication, but simply since they were ideologically alien to the workers' movement."[17]

The rapprochement between *New Culture* and the futurists was declared a "misunderstanding" and an aberration. The "readers" mentioned by Hempel were by no means workers: it was the leader of the KPRP who had declared Wat and his friends "ideologically alien" and had decided to nip Hempel's liberal experiments in the bud. Nevertheless, some contacts and personal friendships between the futurists and the Communists survived. Wat still felt much warmth for Hempel, with whom he was to collaborate again in the near future, and several other acquaintances that he had struck up during this period proved to be even more important.

Among them was Władysław Broniewski, a poet whose colorful personality did not allow him to conform too closely to Communist ideology. His career was paradoxical. At eighteen he enlisted in Piłsudski's legions and in 1920 fought gallantly against the Soviets. Soon afterward, he became a radical revolutionary and secretary of *New Culture*.[18] Poetically, Wat and Broniewski were opposites: Broniewski wrote in the vein of Romanticism and *Skamander* and was praised, among others, by Lechoń, who "took him for an idiot but valued him as a great talent."[19] Still, Broniewski's poems, with their vigor, conciseness, and macho tinge, made a strong impression on Wat (as well as on mass audiences).[20] Later, Wat had a chance to observe Broniewski's honorable behavior in a Soviet prison, as well as his decay during the postwar years, when he concocted the obligatory ode to Stalin, was proclaimed national poet of Communist Poland, and consoled himself with alcoholic orgies, cursing everybody and everything in a language that was the last and only reminder of his soldierly past.[21]

In circles close to *New Culture*, Wat also met Andrzej Stawar (Edward Janus), a critic who became both friend and mentor (although, by a strange coincidence, they were born on exactly the same date). "It is hard to characterize [Stawar] by any other word than sectarian. This critic's dispassionate, terse, and stylistically wooden articles, imperturbably confident of his judgment, strongly suggest such a classification,"[22] noted a historian of Polish literature, who nevertheless admitted Stawar's perspicacity and acumen. In 1927 Stawar, together with a constructivist artist Mieczysław Szczuka, became the moving spirit of *Dźwignia* (*Lever*), the monthly of the leftist artistic avant-garde to which Broniewski, Hempel, and many others contributed.[23]

During the postwar years, Stawar (who became an anti-Stalinist of semi-Trotskyite bent in the 1930s) managed to escape direct repression while still stubbornly defending his intellectual independence. "Stawar's name could not appear in the press. He was requested to carry out self-criticism but he refused. He kept his eyes open for the truth of life, and was a profoundly honest human being,"[24] Ola Wat wrote. In 1961, while visiting Paris, Stawar approached the émigré publishing house "Literary Institute," offering it his prewar anti-Stalinist essays with extensive commentary. At the time he realized that he was dying, and shortly thereafter he passed away in a French hospital. His remains were taken to Warsaw for a state funeral—a fate he had hoped to evade by publishing a scandalous book, but the book did not appear until several months later.

Wat's involvement with *New Culture* coincided with a momentous event in his private life. In spring 1923, at a party at the Warsaw School of Drama, he met a young drama student, Paulina Lew, called "Ola" by her friends. They fell in love immediately. A prose poem by Wat, "Moje serce" (My Heart), published in 1924 and dedicated to Ola, leaves no doubt about that:

> I used to address my heart: oh you bomb of my heart, oh you red bomb
> that so long, so long, so long do not want to tear me asunder! . . .
> Then once at midnight I understood its real nature. That was some day

in April 1923 between Żórawia street 26 and Marszałkowska street. Having
looked at my heart through my eye, as if through a keyhole,
        I noticed:
    my heart is the compass which always points to O.

Wat's futurist conceit, reminiscent of typical baroque *concetti*, finds its echo
in Ola's straightforward words: "Even now I get the creeps at the very thought
that I could have skipped the School of Drama and that our paths could never
have crossed. I feel that my life in such a case would have been abortive, invalid,
inessential. And very meager. Although hardly a believer, I have always felt that
we had to meet, since that was a predestined event."[25]

Ola came from a well-to-do Jewish family who lived on Żurawia (Żórawia):
the street figured prominently in "My Heart," as well as in Wat's poem of 1942
"Willows in Alma-Ata,"[26] in which the poet, exiled from Warsaw by imprisonment and war, called the gas lamps of Żuravia Street "the stations of the Calvary
of my love."

The relationship was harmonious, and it cured Wat of his youthful despair,
postponing for many years the suicide he had considered in the period of *Pug
Iron Stove*. The main problem was Ola's father, who did not look kindly on this
penniless futurist, notorious for his crazy poems and his drinking. The family
conflict lasted almost four years. During that period, Wat abandoned his university studies for good and wrote a book of iconoclastic short stories entitled
Lucifer Unemployed, which he subsequently gave to Ola as a wedding gift.

In the middle of his courtship of Ola, Aleksander left Warsaw for Paris. For
the first time, he saw the West and the much-touted world capital of modernists
and bohemians (no wonder Paris became the locus of several of his more idiosyncratic tales). Wat's first, and almost only, contact in the city was Jasieński.
Like many young newcomers to Paris, they both spent a lot of time exploring the
city's seamy side. Because of their penury, aggravated by raging inflation, they
just drank beer and observed the girls.[27] "In sum, it was an abridged view of
society. Not of society, of course, but of its certain reflection. One of the mirrors
standing by the road."[28]

The sojourn in Paris lasted several months (from May to early October
1926), almost all of them marked by extreme poverty. In his memoirs, Wat
vividly describes a time when, awaiting a money order from home, he was forced
to leave his student's room and make do for three long days on morning coffee
and a croissant. After finding a cheap hotel on rue Jacob, overcome by fatigue, he
slept for twenty-four hours.[29]

Three months after his return to Warsaw, he and Ola were married in a
synagogue, on 24 January 1927. In her memoirs, Ola provides some details:
"The family stood around. But Julian Tuwim stood together with our close
relatives as well, since he was very much set on taking part in the ritual. It had a
strong effect on his poetic imagination. He, like us, saw it with Chagall's eyes,

and the rabbi was straight from Rembrandt's paintings."[30] Ola's father took revenge on his wayward daughter and her futurist husband: Ola received no dowry, and the young couple had to start from scratch.

Aleksander was extremely proud of his wife, one of the prettiest, most elegant women in Warsaw. Moreover, she was just what he needed. Later, in *Scraps of Paper in the Wind*, Wat was to write: "Forty years of faithful affection and devotion . . . Whenever prospects of a career, of a comfortable and glittering life opened before me, she was the one to protect me against the temptations of conformism. Whenever I happened to be at the bottom of illness and despair, she was on the relentless alert and supported me every minute. . . . I entreat God—although I do not know, I cannot know if I believe in Him—to give her serene old age without me."[31]

Paulina (Ola) Wat died in Paris on 9 February 1991, having survived her husband by twenty-three years, during which time she became a keeper of his memory, an editor of his works, and a writer in her own right. Born in 1903, she reached the age of eighty-seven.

After the wedding, Aleksander considered it a point of honor to provide Ola with the comfortable way of life to which she was accustomed. Fortunately, *Lucifer Unemployed* was a success. It did not provide enough to live on by way of royalties, but it did put Wat at the center of Warsaw's literary life. Moreover, his knowledge of languages paid off handsomely. In 1927–30, he was able to make a living mainly as a translator from Russian, French, and English. The books he translated into Polish during that relatively short period include major works such as *The Brothers Karamazov* as well as important contemporary books like *The Star of Satan*, a celebrated novel by the French Catholic author Georges Bernanos. Wat's work was highly praised. To quote a typical review of *The Star of Satan:* "Against the background of the present flood of translations, usually poor and hastily done, the translation by Wat looks monumental indeed, due to its precision of thought, richness of language and empathy, not just with the text but with the spiritual world of the author as well. Owing to Wat's work, *The Star of Satan* will remain forever in our literature, and the present translation will be enjoyed not only by our generation, but also by future ones."[32] (The reviewer was right: Wat's translation, which appeared in 1928, was successfully reprinted after World War II.)

Wat tended to translate works consonant with his own literary and philosophical leanings. The motifs and thought patterns of *The Brothers Karamazov* reverberated throughout his later work, and the same could be said of *The Star of Satan*, a novel dealing with asceticism and diabolical temptation. He also translated grotesque stories by Ilya Ehrenburg and tales by O. Henry written in a similar vein to *Lucifer Unemployed*. Parenthetically, during his stays in Soviet prisons, Wat used to retell O. Henry's stories to his cellmates—a salutary practice in that criminal environment.

During this period, Wat was also active as literary critic, polemist, and popularizer. His polemical article concerning plans to establish a Polish academy (analogous to the French and Swedish academies),[33] caused quite a scandal. In the name of the younger generation, Wat rejected the very notion of an academy, seeing such an institution as a haven of "literary statism," "senility, obscurantism, routine, inertia, cowardly and envious ignoring of the most essential problems." Many older writers were never able to forgive Wat this insolence.[34] There was a rumor that Piłsudski was impressed by Wat's essay and that this was why he postponed inauguration of the Academy for two years.[35]

Two other articles by Wat seem particularly important. In an extensive survey entitled "Teatr w dzisiejszej Rosji Sowieckiej" (Theater in the Present Soviet Russia)[36] he analyzed the work of Vsevolod Meyerhold, Sergei Eisenstein, Aleksandr Tairov, and other directors who at that time had transformed Moscow into the world capital of the avant-garde stage (a feat as short-lived as it was spectacular). Wat's enthusiasm for the "powerful, improvisational, propagandistic, collective" art of Meyerhold "directed against the bourgeoisie and religion" presaged his Communist phase. It was nevertheless balanced by equal enthusiasm for Tairov, a proponent of "pure," antinaturalistic theater devoid of propaganda.

The same contradictory pattern of ideological aggressiveness combined with an attempt to separate art from ideology is found in the article "Nieporozumienia krytyki literackiej" (The Misunderstandings in Literary Criticism).[37] Here Wat tried his hand as a theoretician, discussing problems of literary terminology and attempting to reveal semantic fallacies that led to confused statements about modern writing. Wat's theoretical stance once again betrays his fascination with the Russian avant-garde—and particularly with the formalist trend in literary criticism developed at that time by Viktor Shklovsky, Boris Eikhenbaum, and others. The influence of Marxist criticism can also be seen, although Wat was cautious in his attitude to Marxism, denouncing the oversimplification and sectarianism typical of the "proletarian" ideologues who had spurned him and his friends not long ago:

> One may request ideology from a writer as a human being and a working person, but in any case one may not *request* it immediately from a literary work. The whole point is that ideology in literature, in the main, does not manifest immediately; it usually plays . . . the role of a *catalyst*. Nevertheless in our country, in accordance with the apostolic tradition of our literature and under the influence of certain Russian critics, literature is expected to dispel all doubts, to solve the problems that can be solved, at the very best, by a sociologist or an economist, to organize life (!), etc. What nonsense!

His harangue, however clumsy and naive, was nevertheless a defense—if only a limited one—of literary freedom. Wat succeeded in giving an appropriate answer to Hempel and his superiors: as a matter of fact, he accused them of being more Catholic than the Pope.

Wat's attraction to the literature, art, and criticism of Soviet Russia never blunted his interest in nonproletarian cultural developments elsewhere, however. He became a reader for the Warsaw publishing house "Rój" (The Swarm), a job that expanded his literary horizons. One of the writers who attracted Wat's attention was Franz Kafka, who had died several years before and was still relatively unknown. Reading *The Castle,* Wat was dazzled by Kafka's prose— "perhaps not so much by his vision yet, but by his German, his crystal-clear German."[38] He was only too eager to translate Kafka's novel; but unfortunately some of the reviews convinced the publisher that *The Castle* was an exercise in graphomany, so Wat did not get the go-ahead.[39]

It is difficult to imagine two writers more different than Kafka and Mayakovsky—an introvert creator of phantasmagorias and an energetic agitator for social causes. Yet Wat felt an affinity to both. There was perhaps only one trait common to the Austrian and the Russian, but it was one that weighed heavily on Wat's sensitivity: both expressed, in their work and their lives, the tragic quality of their times.

Wat never met Kafka, but his meeting with Mayakovsky was an important event in his life. Mayakovsky arrived in Poland in 1927, at the height of his career though not of his creative power. His early futurist extravagances and triumphs already belonged to the realm of legend. Much more committed than a fellow-traveler—although this was a label that many party ideologues tried to stick on him—Mayakovsky was virtually the only bard of communism who performed his agitational duties with the flamboyance of a major talent. His career became, for many, proof that Communist dictatorship was not incompatible with authentic avant-garde art. Mayakovsky was eager to support this myth, whose ruin eventually contributed to his suicide.

His sojourn in Warsaw constituted one episode in a longer trip to several European countries. The first Soviet poet to visit Poland, Mayakovsky was aware that he was playing three roles at once: as delegate of the enigmatic and intimidating Communist power, as representative of a country presumed barbarous yet full of vague promise, and as paradigmatic avant-garde artist. All three merged in one persona, which Mayakovsky cultivated successfully. He startled his Polish interlocutors with demonstrations of physical power, as well as with his disrespectful wit. When Broniewski started glorifying Esenin, who wrote his last poem in his own blood, Mayakovsky cut him short by saying that blood was too expensive and that he preferred a fountain pen.[40] Others felt nonplussed by Mayakovsky's statement that a well-designed bath was aesthetically as valuable as the Venus of Milo.[41] Mayakovsky's stay in Warsaw resulted in three essays and two poems describing his experiences in a strictly Soviet, heavily ironical vein. While still in Poland, he wrote an introduction to a Polish book of his poems, the proofs of which were presented to him by Stern.[42]

In his essay "Ezdil ja tak" (How I Traveled) Mayakovsky described Wat as an "author of fiction and translator."[43] A more colorful mention has survived in one of Mayakovsky's notebooks, in which he made short comments on the people he met—for example, "Hempel—an economist, man of letters," "Stawar—a critic," "Broniewski—a poet," "Tuwim—a poet writing for the cabaret." There, Wat is described as "a born futurist"—a phrase marked as much by its aptness as by its sympathetic tonality (the only comment to denote not the occupation but the artistic and behavioral preferences of the writer).[44] Many years later, Wat described Mayakovsky, no less aptly though less flatteringly, as "a very great author of very dubious poetry."[45] Even early on, Mayakovsky fascinated him (in contrast to Jasieński and Stern) not so much for his lyrical voice as for the force of his personality, especially those traits of his public image that made communism and artistry look perfectly compatible. "Mayakovsky's influence was like an inclined plane, a gangplank that conveniently led from the avant-garde position, formal innovation, to communist, revolutionary writing."[46]

Wat met Mayakovsky in Warsaw on further occasions and developed a closer relationship with him than did most of Mayakovsky's Polish hosts, aided by his perfect knowledge of Russian. Both Aleksander and Ola were present at a party in Mayakovsky's honor at the Soviet embassy. In her memoirs, Ola said of it: "I do not know why they seated me next to him [Mayakovsky], but thanks to this I could size him up well and listen to his speech. Aleksander sat opposite us. Of course during the party there was no serious talk. Everybody drank a lot, and food was abundant. For the first time in my life, I became quite tipsy and could not get up from the table. Mayakovsky availed himself of it and lifted me together with my chair."[47] From then on, he had a tender spot for Ola. He would call her endearingly "Vatochka" (a tiny piece of cotton wool).[48]

Both Ola and Aleksander were immensely impressed by Mayakovsky's histrionic gifts. Wat depicted the effects of Mayakovsky's reading thus: "A voice like Chaliapin's, a powerful voice, an imperious voice and words. . . . That wasn't a man, that wasn't a poet; that was an empire, the coming world empire."[49] This opinion was shared by many. Suffice it to quote another witness: "An unusual effect. Pronaszko who sat next to me could not keep his composure: —Well, you know. . . . What a might! Just a cosmic voice! Are they all of such stature over there across the border? Grenadiers! Isn't it a miracle that in the year 1920 . . . He was interrupted by the noisy applause of everybody present."[50]

Mayakovsky's performance hit its target: his image as a consummate revolutionary orator, someone voluntarily and totally identified with the victorious power of the future, was etched into the collective memory of his Polish audience. He did his best to reaffirm this impression in his interviews. Returning to Moscow, Mayakovsky could say that he had carried out his duties in a bourgeois country well. All the same, the reality was more complex than his persona suggested, and Mayakovsky knew it.

The image of a triumphant proletarian bard, a leader and educator of his people, was at odds with the frustration and alienation that Mayakovsky felt increasingly throughout the 1920s.[51] His almost mystical faith in the coming transformation of the universe into a place where poetry would reign supreme seemed natural enough during the immediate postrevolutionary years. By the second half of the decade, however, it already smacked of hypocrisy and conformism. Individual poetic voices were becoming excluded by the all-pervading totalitarian discourse. Mayakovsky, who hated and censured any form of apostasy, was himself gradually forced out of the ranks of the victors into those of the apostates (or time-servers). A love affair, as unsuccessful as any in Mayakovsky's life, finished off the job.

Aleksander and Ola could not fail to notice the cracks developing in Mayakovsky's personality. Both relate them not to his first, but his mysterious second stay in Warsaw. It appears that Mayakovsky visited Warsaw on the way back from Paris to Moscow in 1929.[52] This visit must have been incognito or semi-incognito, since it left no traces in the press. In a letter to Mayakovsky's biographer, Wat stated: "during his [Mayakovsky's] *second* stay in Warsaw, we parted only late at night, and also during the time he spent playing billiards in the polpredstvo [embassy]. That was the period of my blindness, therefore I did not understand, just shamefully did not understand anything of his dejection."[53] According to Wat's memoirs, little of the previous revolutionary tribune remained by the time of Mayakovsky's second visit: Mayakovsky had grown gloomy, drank excessively, and had no desire to talk about politics or Soviet life.

The most interesting of the conversations between Mayakovsky and Wat were about Russian writers ruined by the Communist regime: Aleksandr Blok, who died of hunger and neglect, and Sergei Esenin, whose suicide foreshadowed Mayakovsky's. "I think he said that Blok had been right and he had been wrong—something to that effect. I could not accept that idea because I was a neophyte, full of enthusiasm, but it left some trace."[54] Ola recalled Mayakovsky making a phone call to his beloved Tatyana Yakovleva in Paris: "The conversation took place in the next room [of the embassy]. After it, Mayakovsky came back completely changed. One could sense that he had received a blow, that something irrevocable had happened. He had talked to a woman he loved very much at the time. He had tried to persuade her, he had perhaps implored her, to leave Paris and go with him to Moscow. And just then, in my presence, he was ultimately rejected."[55] Mayakovsky tried to meet Tatyana Yakovleva in Paris one more time, in October 1929, but was supposedly refused a Soviet exit visa.[56] The suspicion that he might defect was not without some ground, it appears. In any case, Ola's story of the telephone conversation is plausible in light of our knowledge of the affair. It may even be that Mayakovsky's behavior during his alleged second visit to Warsaw exacerbated his visa problem that fall.

That visit, which is not recorded in any of the existing biographies of

Mayakovsky, can only have taken place at the end of April 1929, since on 24 April Mayakovsky was still in Paris with Tatyana,[57] and on 2 May, in fulfillment of his promise to his common-law wife Lili Brik, he returned to Moscow.[58] He could have made a stopover in Warsaw between these two dates, although his stay would have had to have been shorter than Wat maintained. As it is, this second visit to Warsaw remains a conjecture, albeit a plausible one, not a fact established beyond doubt. On the whole, Aleksander and Ola can be considered veracious witnesses, yet they were susceptible to changes of accent and emphasis, and their memories sometimes failed them. Thus, both describe Mayakovsky in 1927 successfully reciting his "Stixi o sovetskom pasporte" (My Soviet passport), a poem that expressed, with a skillful mix of didacticism, satire, and high rhetoric, the author's joy at being a Soviet.[59] But this is patently incorrect, since the poem was not written until July 1929. It is not difficult to detect a possible psychological reason for the mistake. During their Kazakhstan exile in 1943, a Soviet passport became, for Wat and his wife, a symbol of oppression. Wat's refusal to become a Soviet citizen was perhaps the most courageous decision he ever made.[60] "My Soviet Passport," a poem that was crammed into students' heads in every Soviet high school, clashed with the Wats' personal myth so sharply that it may have led to an error in perception: in their memoirs, both, stressing the sinister spell of the poem, misplaced it in time.

But whatever the case, Wat's account of his meetings with Mayakovsky forms a focal point of his memoirs. It also fulfills a structural function in *My Century*, furnishing a kind of semantic rhyme to the story of the old Bolshevik Yury Steklov. The ravings of the dying Steklov echo the confessions of Mayakovsky heading for self-inflicted death. Both feel themselves beyond redemption, and Wat identifies with both. Whatever factual inaccuracies there may be, the stories have an artistic integrity that is indisputable.

5

The Early Fiction

In the years 1924–27 Wat mastered a new genre: from a budding controversial poet, he developed into a provocative prose writer. The change took place in a shifting literary context. The era of programs and manifestoes was largely over, and Polish prose had reached a maturity, marked, on the one hand, by rich, complicated realist writing and, on the other, by a refined aestheticism. There was also a generational change of the guard. The grand old men of Young Poland gradually left the literary scene, their place being taken by writers who had started work when the country was independent.

"Proletarian culture," less than successfully promoted by the KPP in the early 1920s, also chalked up some achievements at this time. A major gain for proletarian literature was Jasieński, who embraced collectivist values without equivocation. But he soon turned to an international (rather than a Polish) audience and switched to Russian as his preferred language.

Wat was reluctant to abandon his individualistic, nihilistic stance. Yet he was too ambitious to allow himself to be pushed to the margins. After 1925, he moved to center stage—for the first, though by no means the last, time in his motley literary career. If *Pug Iron Stove* remained an esoteric work enjoyed by few, *Lucifer Unemployed* became a success that transformed Wat into a much-admired, much-talked-about writer.

In February 1922, Wat published in the second issue of *New Art* a prose piece entitled "Powieść" (A Story). It was envisaged as consisting of seven chapters, but only the first and the beginning of the second survive. The opening sentences plunge the reader into the delirious atmosphere of *Pug Iron Stove:* "Six legs of the old lady crawled on the concave walls of my room, fluttered in the air, calling desperately for help. They could not find a footing. Since the equilibrium was still totally absent, and my room was of a spheroid egg shape."

Having started with an image of cosmic chaos, the text subsequently becomes somewhat more coherent, though less than predictable. It is as if a universe of bizarre objects and events hatches from the egg, as in ancient mythologies. The old lady encounters the soul of the narrator, described as a machine-like object with a steel spring inside and a brass larynx. They begin a lengthy philosophical discussion, in which the soul quotes Voltaire in the original French and the old lady answers with a quotation in Old German. All this takes place during and after an abortive revolution against Alfonso XIII, a bizarre king-cum-astronomer.[1] The lady then procures a little girl. While the girl is being sexually abused by the soul, the narrator goes mad and ends up in a psychiatric hospital, where he listens to the monologues of the inmates. After his escape "via Paris," he finds his soul, the lady, and the girl once more, and they all go for dinner to his bachelor's apartment.

It would be futile to try to judge "A Story" from the point of view of common sense. Wat's work is strongly reminiscent of French surrealist texts (including films). The juxtaposition of incongruous ideas, a distinctive trait of *Pug Iron Stove*, is also a pivotal element of the story's poetics. Both works are displays of bizarre erudition. In both, parody and sheer mockery alternate with outpourings of genuine despair. Other features common to both include identical phrases, certain technical devices (such as numbering the paragraphs), and an obsession with motifs such as pedophilia.

On the most general level, the story continues the theme of split personality that was so crucial for the poem. But there is a significant innovation: the double (the soul) is strikingly modern, a kind of robot[2] deprived of any spiritual qualities. Already in *Pug Iron Stove*, Wat had introduced a concept that might be termed *spatialization*. Here, it is taken to its logical limit: since the soul is represented as a mechanical being detached from the person and deprived of any temporal dimension, the very idea of an "inner man" is subverted more fundamentally than in *Pug Iron Stove*.

In his later years, Wat saw the undermining of the "inner man" as a key characteristic of the Communist world view.[3] Rejection of an "interior" to the personality is tantamount to the commonplace idea that a human being is totally determined by—and dependent upon—external (biological, social) factors. Such determinism, by making choice illusory, deprives the person of his or her future; hence, according to Wat, it also amounts to a substitution of space for time: "And to philosophize a little about communism again: in distinction to what we call Western civilization—the name doesn't matter—our civilization (maybe it's not Christian, maybe it's not Western, but it is our civilization), communism is space, spatialization. . . . And that's why numbers matter so much, mathematics, numbers. Spatial relations, not temporal relations."[4]

With characteristic boldness, Wat explored in his story the ultimate consequences of the Weltanschauung that he was to discard. In this regard, one surrealist sequence in his work may be charged with a deeper significance. During the narrator's stint in a psychiatric hospital, his enigmatic room is destroyed, and five hundred half-decomposed cadavers are found bricked up in its walls: this leads to a propagation of vermin and to an epidemic that takes 12,720 victims. One may easily dismiss this part of the text as a disrespectful parody of the horror story à la Edgar Allan Poe. But Adam Ważyk has rightly noted that this kind of black humor would have been unthinkable before World War I.[5] It might also be added that it anticipates the experience of totalitarian dictatorships: "numbers matter so much, mathematics, numbers."

Another early story by Wat, "Sprzedawca snów" (Seller of Dreams) was more traditional and, appropriately enough, was accepted for publication in *Skamander*, in December 1922. As its title suggests, it is a specimen of the so-called oneiric fiction that was much in vogue in Poland during the 1920s;[6] and, like most texts of its kind, it is oversaturated with baroque rhetoric and decorative symbolist imagery. But typical traits of Wat's writing can also be discerned: his interest in metaphysics and Gnosticism, his nihilist leanings, and his incurable bent for parody.[7]

The action of "Seller of Dreams" takes place in the imaginary English town of Whiteflower at some indeterminate time (anywhere from the eighteenth to the twentieth century). Wat arranges the setting conventionally: there is humdrum downtown to the south and medieval, sinister uptown to the north. The two main characters are an antiquary with the telltale name Thomas Traum ("dream") and a budding poet, Gabriel Moor. Thomas Traum, an outsider who disturbs the citizens of Whiteflower by his bizarre habits, has his shop uptown, and the catalogue of his hodgepodge merchandise brings to mind the hallucinatory mixture of mythology and history in *Pug Iron Stove*. He may be a crank or a madman or a charlatan or all of the above, yet his Hofmannesque shop holds the attraction of an enigma. A sign in capital letters at its entrance proclaims: "Here all desires come true," which may be read as a brazen misadvertisement or as a promise of a higher, mystical, or poetic reality.

The interplay of two levels is even more perceptible in the case of Gabriel Moor. After mailing one of his poems to a periodical, Moor has a strange dream. He meets, in the uncannily changed setting of a city, the editor of the periodical, "a Spaniard of strange, ecstatic looks," and a Jew "with the face of an anchorite of Tiberias, in the attire of a ghetto rabbi." They hand him a parchment with the galleys of his work. On the other side of the parchment, Moor finds a heretical poem of ineffable beauty entitled "Jesus." From the moment of awakening, his life becomes a delirious search for that poem. Although he has forgotten its words, he knows for sure that it would bring him immortality.

In the course of Moor's quest, the border between dream and reality becomes more and more blurred. One night, he finds himself in front of Traum's shop, now detached from its quotidian environment. He draws the curtain and enters the forbidden realm, where Traum appears before him in his higher identity of Lord of hosts. Traum's daughter, Leonora (with whom Gabriel Moor is in love), is transformed into the "Mother of Mothers." From then on, the poet spends almost all his time in the dreamlike kingdom. The poem he is looking for is revealed to him. During one of his short and increasingly rare outings into the world of Whiteflower, he meets a madman, who murders Leonora. After her funeral, the whole town follows in Moor's footsteps and immerses itself in the dreamworld: "everybody and everything dreamed. All the workshops, all the stores and offices closed. Craftsmen in their workshops saw themselves in the palaces of gold and nacre. They worked with golden tools set out with jewels. Shopkeepers saw themselves on the Oriental pillows, among carpets and lanterns, surrounded by clouds of incense; they lay smoking narghile and spitting on long rows of backs of naked black slaves."

Whereas Traum, "the seller of dreams," is to be crowned king of the earth, Moor attempts to escape this ambivalent universe which, for him, is becoming increasingly nightmarish. To his horror, he finds that the land surrounding Whiteflower has disappeared, and that the town is now just a small island encircled by primordial waters. Moreover, its inhabitants turn into strange, half-vegetable, half-crystalline forms. After an unsuccessful gesture of rebellion, the poet dissolves into a final dream, which equals nothingness.

The story may appear derivative, and it is easy to perceive in it traces of nineteenth-century Romanticism. More immediate antecedents also suggest themselves: the work of German expressionists such as Gustav Meyrink, whose dreamlike novel *Der Golem* (1915), which made ample use of Kabbalistic mythology, was popular at the time. Yet "Seller of Dreams" has a distinctly autobiographical dimension, in the form of some curious hints of the author's environment. While the Jew in the first dream of Moor, redolent of the Kabbalists who used to visit Wat's father, still smacks of literary cliché, the ecstatic editor of the literary periodical is a friendly, half-mocking version of Peiper.[8] Moreover, Moor's argument regarding the "perfectly constructed" poem employs some of Peiper's terminology.

As usual, Wat plays with commonplace notions and literary *topoi*, subverting and overturning them at every step. The concept of two realms—a lower, dull, prosaic reality and a higher, metaphysical kingdom—is, of course, as old as humankind (or, at least, as old as Plato). Gabriel Moor is presented as a mediator between "high" and "low," between dream and reality; his first name, significantly, is that of a divine messenger. The transcendent universe, concealed behind the curtain of humdrum events, discloses itself to the poet, and in that universe he achieves a state of blissful nirvana.

On another level, "Seller of Dreams" is a story of madness. The quest for the ideal turns out to be mortally dangerous. The identity of Gabriel Moor becomes blurred in more than one sense. Transformed into "the king of poets," he encounters "the king of the mad," who murders his bride Leonora. The murderer may well be his double—parenthetically, it is far from clear who delivers the frenzied monologue that comprises the central portion of the story. Following this line of interpretation, we conclude that the transformation of Whiteflower into the dream kingdom takes place only in Gabriel Moor's sick brain, the ocean encircling the town being merely a projection of his regression. The end of the story thus represents his immersion in the darkness of psychosis.

One more reading, no less consistent than the previous two, is based on another ambiguity, that of Thomas Traum, the titular "seller of dreams." His habit of presenting items of garbage as enigmatic, significant objects fits into the framework of Romantic irony. Half-mad eccentrics who turn out to be supernatural figures are common enough in early nineteenth-century literature. In folkloric texts such behavior often points to the Devil.

After Gabriel Moor violates the taboo and enters the secret room behind the curtain, Traum is revealed to him as the Lord. At the end of the story, Traum's transcendent aspect is again emphasized. On this reading, Leonora, the "Mother of Mothers," is Sophia or Achamoth. Moreover, the whole story can be interpreted as a variation on the ancient topos of the universe as a dream of the divinity. But too many signs point to the deceptive nature of Traum's power. He "obscures the sky"; he is called "king of the earth" (an obvious reference to the Devil); Moor's final confrontation with him is described as the "forty days of Christ's temptation." Traum is most likely the evil demiurge of Gnostic texts, the father of all illusion. (Significantly, Whiteflower, when turned into a dream-world, appears as a fraud. In their comic orgy of dreaming, petty craftsmen and shopkeepers produce only kitschy pseudo-exotic images—or perhaps they are deceived by the Devil who presents trash as gold and jewels). In his rebellion, Moor attempts to escape from the evil labyrinth designed by Traum, but he never succeeds.

These readings are far from being mutually exclusive. Rather, they interact and complement each other. The message generated by their juxtaposition is one of relativism. Two world orders ("higher" and "lower," "divine" and "demon-iac," "objective" and "subjective") continually exchange places. Both are compromised and undermined, and their confusion leads to the annihilation of both.

Ultimately, one may understand the story as self-referential: "selling dreams" is a metaphor for art. Art's power to change reality and create uncanny objects gives it the dual status of prophecy and deadly temptation. The miracle of art continually reveals the falsity and deceptiveness that underlie it. Thomas Traum, a divine yet satanic being who serves as a father figure for Moor, is the archetypal artist. And the story itself, with its giddy interplay of meanings, likewise possesses an archetypal quality. It can be identified with the "perfectly constructed" work of art, combining metaphysical belief with nihilist heresy— like the work of art dreamt by Moor at the outset of his delirious quest.[9]

In "Seller of Dreams," as well as in "A Story," Wat tried his hand at a genre that was subsequently to become his own: the philosophical parable that explores the limits and consequences of a particular doctrine. The crucial devices in both works are parody and *reductio ad absurdum*, and both remained critical in the stories that make up *Lucifer Unemployed*. Like *Pug Iron Stove*, the book was a devastating attack on culture, a playful dismantling of its values, myths, and stereotypes, a mockery stretched to the limit. But this time, the assault also used different means. Instead of a prodigious stream of disjointed surrealistic images, Wat here created perfectly comprehensible, intriguing fiction, almost classical in its clarity and terseness. Rimbaud and Apollinaire have here yielded to Voltaire and Anatole France.

The book was published at the end of 1926, although dated 1927. It consisted of nine short stories: "Bezrobotny Lucyfer" (Lucifer Unemployed), "Żyd Wieczny Tułacz" (The Eternally Wandering Jew), "Królowie na wygnaniu" (Kings in Exile), "Historia ostatniej rewolucji w Anglii" (The History of the Last Revolution in England), "Czyście nie widzieli ulicy Gołębiej?" (Has Anyone Seen Pigeon Street?), "Prima Aprilis" (April Fool), "Hermafrodyta" (Hermaphrodite), "Niech żyje Europa!" (Long Live Europe!), and "Tom Bill, szampion ciężkiej wagi" (Tom Bill: Heavyweight Champion). Not all the fictional works that Wat wrote during this period were included—"just because they would spoil its systematics,"[10] as he put it in 1964. The texts were supposedly chosen to form a logical, functional whole. That logic was violated in the second edition, however. Wat had intended to reprint the book in 1948, but it appeared only in 1960, with a new introduction and truncated. Two stories were missing: "Long Live Europe!" perhaps because it could easily be construed as deliberately insulting Chinese Communists, and "The History of the Last Revolution in England," because it ridiculed English Communists even more mercilessly. A politically suspect paragraph from the titular story and several fragments too frank for Victorian taste from "Hermaphrodite" were excised as well. Wat acknowledged these changes in his introduction, noting with some pride that he "did not add anything and did not alter the content, spirit and style of the original"[11] (which was not always the case in Communist Poland at that time).

The introduction to the proposed edition of 1948 gives what is perhaps the best account of the book in its entirety:

> This collection of short stories presents to its author, and will perhaps present to the reader, a consistent testimony and an exaggerated reflection of a certain state of mind preceding the great disaster of 1939–45. The critics . . . noted the scepticism of the book, its ironic grotesquerie; they even perceived despair at the base of its contradictory paradoxes. Nevertheless they did not perceive the consistency of its comprehensive assault: it demolished, page after page, not only the reality of the times (the titular story), but also the idea of direction and sense inherent in history (*The Eternally Wandering Jew, Kings in Exile*), the sense of collective action (*The History of the Last Revolution in England*), the notion of people and religious faith (*The Eternally Wandering Jew, Long Live Europe*), the notion of personality (*April Fool*), the sense of

moral norms (*Tom Bill*) and creativity (*Has Anyone Seen Pigeon Street?*), even
of biological impulses (*Hermaphrodite*). The book unquestionably lodged a
protest against the inhumanity that was at the time growing progressively
worse, but simultaneously it deprived humanism of its justification. . . . Moreover, by its realistic design of paradoxes, by lending the air of verisimilitude to
anything that could be thought up, it attempted to undermine not just Realism
but the very concept of verisimilitude as well, and herein lies—as I less than
modestly suppose—its relative originality. If anything can become verisimilar,
what is then *veri*similitude and what becomes of verity as such? If anything is
plausible and can be made probable, what becomes of our world?

The answer to the question formulated was soon provided by the world
itself, where everything became plausible![12]

Lucifer Unemployed received almost unanimous acclaim from the critics. A
typical appraisal is that of Leon Pomirowski, a leftist man of letters endowed
with aesthetic sensitivity and taste: "A bold, militant fiction. *Lucifer Unemployed*
is not just the first book of a young author, but, to a degree, a new type of writing.
An ambitious attempt to break out of the prison cell of more or less sentimental
psychologism and to throw one's descriptive net into the wider waters of artistic
dialectic."[13] Nor were the reviews by less well-known critics lacking in rapture
and rhapsodizing: "intellect," "modernity," and "formal perfection" were key
words. Wat was not overstating the case when he noted in his memoirs: "After
Lucifer my literary position was excellent; my stock, so to speak, was high. Three
books received good reviews at the time, and mine may have been the best of
them. That is, besides my book, *People from Over There* by Dąbrowska and
Youth, Love, Adventure by Choynowski. Those were the three books of the
year. . . . In *Literary News*, there was a cartoon by Daszewski: a map of the sky
and myself—a star of first magnitude."[14] Virtually the only negative reactions
were those of the hard-line Marxists Witold Wandurski and Isaac Deutscher,
who, predictably, accused Wat of petty bourgeois nihilism and decadence.[15]

A powerful and original work, *Lucifer Unemployed* stood out against its
literary background. By contrast with the two other "books of the year"—*People
from Over There*, a typical cycle of realist stories, and *Youth, Love, Adventure*,
which depicted Poland's struggle for independence in the same traditional vein
with Romantic overtones—Wat's book, with its crisp, concise, conceptual writing, broke with such practices. It played freely with the notions of space and
time, truth and fiction, logic and paradox. Full of accusatory passion, it extended
its methodological anarchism to itself, making fun of its own catastrophist
forebodings.

Wat was not the only Polish writer to try his hand at grotesque stories
dealing philosophically with history or the future at that time. His friend Antoni
Słonimski was perhaps the first. In his *Torpeda czasu* (*Torpedo of Time*) of 1924,
people of the twenty-second century go back to the eighteenth with the express

goal of annulling the unsavory consequences of the French Revolution (a task that proves to be beyond their abilities). Later, in 1937, Słonimski produced a witty, if ominous, book entitled *Dwa końce świata* (*Two Ends of the World*), which describes the annihilation of Warsaw by a mad dictator named Retlich (a transparent anagram of Hitler) and its subsequent ambivalent liberation by the Lapps, a totalitarian power from the Northeast.

Witkacy's novel *Pożegnanie jesieni* (1927) *Farewell to Autumn* and his *Nienasycenie* (*Insatiability*) of 1930 also belong to this genre. Written in an inimitable style, they also played with futurology. *Insatiability* parodies the stereotyped concept of the "yellow peril," giving a picture of Poland conquered by the Chinese Red Army.[16] (It is quite clear that China, like Lapland in Słonimski's *Two Ends of the World*, serves primarily as a pseudonym for Red Russia.) The famous novel *I Burn Paris* by Jasieński has a similar plot though a contrasting vision of history. In it, the self-satisfied bourgeois "capital of the world" is all but destroyed by an epidemic of plague, caused by a vengeful worker. As a result of the deaths of many millions, Paris is transformed into a proletarian fortress, governed, significantly, by a Communist of Chinese origin.

The large number of such endeavors in futurological and historiosophical fantasy, as well as their relative weight in Polish letters, testifies to the influence of *Lucifer Unemployed*, which preceded all other efforts of this kind except the weaker *Torpedo of Time*. Most of the ideas and devices utilized by other authors of the genre can be traced to Wat's short, irreverent stories, which are distinguished by the perfect equilibrium of tragic and ludic elements, of sensational plot and philosophical intensity, an equilibrium that escaped his rivals.

However innovative and bold in the Polish context, Wat's book followed a characteristic Western European and Russian literary trend, and most critics have pointed to its kinship with Ehrenburg's works. The first, and arguably the best, novel by Ehrenburg, *The Extraordinary Adventures of Julio Jurenito* (1922), a biting, nihilist satire that did not spare any aspect of Western culture or the Russian Revolution, resembles Wat's book in its mockery and fervor. Also relevant here is his *Trust D. E.* (1923), half science fiction, half fantasy, on the destruction of Europe by American capitalists.

Dozens more of Wat's contemporaries might also be mentioned—not least H. G. Wells, patron of the trend, at the end of the preceding century. But Wat's most immediate model was an ardent opponent of Wells, namely G. K. Chesterton.

During the 1920s, Chesterton's popularity in Poland (and elsewhere) was at its peak.[17] "The author of *The Man Who Was Thursday* enjoyed a particular respect in the circle connected with *Almanac of New Art;* he attracted [us] by his paradoxical plots uniting suspense and philosophy, by his slightly adventurous Thomism, by his slogan of seeing everything anew and simultaneous praise of intellect," Adam Ważyk wrote.[18] In 1927, Wat mentioned Chesterton along with Voltaire as among the influences he was striving to overcome.[19]

A fascinating, controversial, many-sided writer, Chesterton used his narrative skill to explode conventional ideologies. In the words of a modern critic, he was "a voice of sanity sadly needed in the battle against the mythopoetic currents of thought of the new twentieth century, evolutionary, racialist, and historicist, which have helped to mould our present life and thought."[20] Such a stance could not but appeal to Wat, who was interested in both the structural characteristics of Chesterton's work (fantasy, grotesque, juxtaposition of the picaresque, and science fiction) and its substance, since most of it addressed the problems of the coexistence and conflict between Christianity and socialism, and thus spoke to Wat, a man of leftist leanings combined with metaphysical anxieties.[21]

Immediately after *Lucifer Unemployed*, Wat published, at short intervals, three essays: "Uwagi o Chestertonie" (Notes on Chesterton), "Czego broni Chesterton" (What Chesterton Defends), and "Chestertonica."[22] The last two took the form of reviews of Polish translations of Chesterton, even if they surpassed the limits of that genre, becoming passionate, extensive treatises on a major writer, probably the best Wat ever wrote. Starting from a position of almost unconditional praise and fascination, Wat gradually became profoundly disillusioned with Chesterton. The last essay, his farewell to Chesterton, was also, to a degree, a farewell to himself. All three essays have an unmistakeable air of self-description and self-interpretation.

Wat sees Chesterton as an essentially Romantic writer who has rejected one of the main tenets of Romanticism: namely, psychologism. As a result, his characters, deprived of "inner life," become no more than vehicles for certain moral and ideological concepts. Flights of imagination, which had provided rebellious Romantic writers with their mythology of the soul, serve, for Chesterton, a different purpose: they illuminate the "incomparable theater of ideas."[23] It is this synthesis of Romantic fancy and Cartesian rationalism that appeals to Wat more than anything else. He calls it the control of the imagination by the "lenses of learning"[24] and sees in it a great opportunity for Polish literature.

This attitude of Chesterton, according to Wat, has consequences that are embedded in the very fabric of his writing. First, the rejection of the psyche results in a visual, spatial imagery. Second, Chesterton disregards history, evolution, and time. For him, ideas are preexistent and substantial, with history merely providing an arena for their manifestation. Thus, Chesterton's stance is Platonic—albeit not without a difference: "While the idealism of Plato allows one to create a lofty, univocal, solemn universe, alien and even inimical to Romantic humor—the universe of Chesterton is a Romantic treasure-house of humorous dissipation. This occurs because Chesterton has managed to recognize the principle of the substantiality of ideas, which do not depend upon time, and to utilize simultaneously the relativity, mutability and ambiguity of their conceptual content. He has succeeded in becoming Socrates and Protagoras at the same time."[25]

This insightful characterization undoubtedly pertains to Wat's own literary concerns. Wat had already developed a strictly spatial, visual technique of literary presentation in "A Story," and all the stories in *Lucifer Unemployed* are exercises in Romantic humor utilizing "eternal ideas" and playing with the plurality of meanings they could assume.

The negative judgments of Chesterton expressed in Wat's essays are no less significant. With characteristic astuteness, Wat noted that Chesterton's paradoxical dialectic could destroy the very values he was fighting for. Moreover, that dialectic had its shortcomings: Chesterton frequently attacked not an ideology in its entirety but only isolated fragments: "After chopping off the hand of his enemy, Chesterton challenges it to a joust."[26] In the course of time, Wat came to see in his mentor a tendency to verbal jugglery and excessive theatricality. Last but not least, Chesterton lacked a penchant for metonymy. "Literature is founded mainly on the rule *pars pro toto.* . . .[In Chesterton's writing] everything is equally (and too strongly) illuminated. But for that reason, Chesterton's reality is perhaps less fictional, fantastic, dreamlike or poetic, than artificial."[27] Most if not all of these criticisms could equally well be leveled at *Lucifer Unemployed*.

"The Eternally Wandering Jew" was probably the first work to provide Wat with a taste of literary success. The story remains of interest today, even if some of its passages sound jarring after the experience of World War II and the Holocaust. It is a satirical parable about anti-Semitism. Wat's subversion of a dangerous myth looks particularly perfidious here, since the depersonalized narrator appears to take the myth at face value.

The Chestertonian approach reigns supreme. The characters, devoid of a traditional psyche, are merely puppets in the "theater of ideas." Time is effectively abolished, and the play of paradoxes and inversions is nothing short of dizzying. The reader is introduced *in medias res* from the very first line, a snatch of a telephone conversation that ends abruptly. The speaker, Baron Gould, is a stereotypical Jewish businessman in New York, "a croupier, raking in gold from the gambling table of Europe."[28] He plans to become a reformer who will change the course of history. In the second chapter, the narrative switches from New York to Zebrzydowo, a murky Polish shtetl and the birthplace of Nathan, who represents the opposite pole of mythologized Jewishness. After losing his parents in a pogrom, Nathan becomes a budding rabbinical scholar. But one evening, something happens that changes all that, when he takes the local Catholic priest for the rabbi. Upon leaving the yeshiva, he decides to go and see Baron Gould (at whose expense he has been studying) for guidance and advice.

Their meeting in New York triggers an avalanche of incredible events.

Nathan, hired by Gould as a secretary, resolves to become the savior of European civilization in its apocalyptic crisis (by now, time has switched to the not-too-distant future, the year 1935). His goal is to unify the two most powerful ideological systems of the age: Catholicism and communism. But the task of establishing the desired Communist theocracy is to be entrusted to Jews, who must, therefore, convert to Catholicism en masse. With Gould's help, Nathan succeeds in this mind-boggling undertaking; in the year 1965, he is elected Pope Urban IX, and in 1985, Baron Gould is canonized. A new and perfect system is established throughout the world, with the Pope as dictator and all ecclesiastical positions being held by people of Jewish origin (the priestly vow of celibacy having been abolished, clerics may marry, but only within their own group).

The sole enemies of the new world order are the anti-Semites who reject Jewish Catholicism and, in time, become segregated from the rest of the society. After many years of discrimination, they find, in Zebrzydowo, the last Jew still practicing the religion of his forefathers. Impressed by his firmness and wisdom, the anti-Semites (whose leader is a certain John Ford, descendant of a family of Jew-haters) begin to study the Talmud and, in the year 2320, convert to Judaism *in toto*. The Church reacts by reviving the office of the Holy Inquisition, with the Pope's confessor as its head. This "monk with the heart of a dove"[29] sends to the stake by the thousands the born-again people of Israel.

In the year 2900, there is a gifted student in the yeshiva at Zebrzydowo once again. His remote ancestors were anti-Semitic, he lost his parents in a pogrom, and his name, predictably, is Nathan. One evening he meets in the street a man whom he takes for a rabbi. "When the so-called rabbi turned around, Nathan was horrified to see his mistake: instead of the anticipated towheaded, blue-eyed face of the rabbi, the jaundiced, freckled face of the parish priest stared back at him with its hook nose and eyes veiled with a cosmic melancholy." The wheel of the history has completed its turn.

From an artistic point of view, the story is perhaps the most successful in the book. Short and crisp, matter-of-fact and discreet, it applies the most eccentric concept imaginable, shocking equally to Jew and to Gentile, to a religious person and a positivist, and develops it with truly Voltairean gusto. Wat explodes two opposing myths simultaneously: the nineteenth-century myth of progress and the twentieth-century myth of the "decline of the West" promoted by Oswald Spengler.

It could be said that time is the main topic of the story, emphasized and exposed from the outset: "Time is the enemy, thought the baron." It is his awareness of his own mortality that causes Gould to launch a crusade against the temporal dimension of the universe. In a sense, he succeeds. Not only is he elevated to the supra-temporal status of a Catholic saint, but history itself is ultimately revealed as static. The world has been literally turned upside down, yet the year 2900 repeats the year 1900 to the letter.

Such a picture of eternal return is what one might expect from an enthusiastic student of Nietzsche, but at the same time, it is profoundly parodic. Characteristically, "cosmic melancholy" can hardly be distinguished from irreverent fun. The sense of repetition and standstill, of history's mills turning in vain, is supported by a simple but powerful device. Wat repeats many fragments of the text almost verbatim, thereby giving it a particular rhythmic quality. Most prominent among the repeated images is that of mud surrounding the yeshiva:

> There is always mud in Zebrzydowo. In the spring it runs in wavy streams; in the summer it is thick, deep and black; in the fall it is sticky and gummy; and in the winter it crunches underfoot. In Zebrzydowo there is an old yeshiva. Marks left by Chmielnicki's bullets are still visible on its pockmarked walls.

> In the year 2900 there was mud in Zebrzydowo, the ancient, immortal mud of Zebrzydowo. In the old yeshiva, still recalling Chmielnicki's bullets, the most capable student was Nathan.

The structurally inverted repetition at the end of the story has a Heinean air in its mocking repudiation of both faiths and both ways of life.

The rhythm of the story is strikingly uneven. The first chapter describes, in detail and with flashbacks, a July evening in Baron Gould's life. The second presents chronologically Nathan's biography, comprising more than twenty years. Then the spark falls on the tinder, and history explodes. We are suddenly hurled into the future, into the apocalypse that makes fun of all Marxist predictions: "The bourgeoisie gathered its forces and defended itself with a heroism never before known in history. Here and there it died Herostrates' death; here and there, it was utterly pauperized; in vain did it sigh after communism. The proletariat was vanishing in the vortex of the general chaos." The last chapters give short summaries of events that took centuries. The spasmodic temporal leaps are counterbalanced by the perverse, yet highly comical, vision of ideal timelessness embodied in the mud at Zebrzydowo.

Throughout, biblical imagery predominates. Both Gould and Nathan perceive modern reality in scriptural terms and Mosaic ritual. Yet, while parts of "The Eternally Wandering Jew" are obviously patterned on the Bible, in their rhythm and their intonation, the element of parody is never lacking. (Suffice it to cite Wat's eschatological prophecies: "There was talk of signs that would precede the final day. In Paris, a fifty-five-year-old newspaper vendor who had never known a man gave birth to a son with radiating skin. In London, bloody swords and riders on red horses were seen in the sky in the evenings. In Berlin, the owner of a fashion house pronounced herself the savior of the world.") The principal biblical source for the story, however, is the Book of Ecclesiastes: "Vanity of vanities, saith the Preacher, vanity of vanities; all is vanity. . . . Is there any thing whereof it may be said, See, this is new? it hath been already of old time, which was before us. . . . Therefore I hated life; because the work that is wrought under the sun is grievous unto me: for all is vanity and vexation of spirit" (Eccles. 1:2, 10, 2:17).

Subverting and ridiculing the notion of historical progress, as well as catastrophist myths, Wat demolishes several more ideological stereotypes. First, he transforms (and parodies) the titular concept of "the eternally wandering Jew," presenting Jewishness not as an innate, racial condition but as a social role that may be taken by any minority. The anti-Semites illustrate this idea in the most provocative manner imaginable. The Jew wanders not only through the centuries but also through "racial slots." Thus, total relativity is affirmed, and, by the same token, any concept of "superior and inferior races" is destroyed. In passing, as Wat noted in 1948, even the notions of a people and a religious faith disintegrate.

One may argue with Wat the relativist, but one cannot deny the inventiveness and boldness of Wat the writer. His story may be compared to an elegantly devised algebraic formula or a problem in chess, the solution of which is thrust upon the reader with intellectual rigor.

Wat's mockery undermined the unsavory myth of the all-pervading power of the Jews and of a "universal Jewish conspiracy"—a myth heartily supported and promoted at the time by a significant portion of Polish public opinion. "The Eternal Wandering Jew" can also be seen as parodying, to a degree, the famous drama *Nie-Boska Komedia* (*The Undivine Comedy*) by the nineteenth-century Romantic bard Zygmunt Krasiński. *The Undivine Comedy*, like Wat's story, portrayed a futurological vision of coming revolution. A powerful—even prophetic—piece, it was nevertheless marred by the roles of villains being assigned to Jewish converts who manipulated the revolution out of hatred for Christians.[30]

Wat as narrator pretends to take the anti-Semitic myth at face value. Yet, in his game of unending mystification and demystification he moves on slippery terrain, and signs of irony and distance are infrequent. "The Eternally Wandering Jew" overflows with situations and sentences that confirm the virulent stereotype. Yet these are mixed with "positive stereotypes" and with statements that probably convey Wat's real view.

Baron Gould, all-powerful convert multimillionaire, is truly eclectic and subsidizes "missions, convents, sects, Tibetan monasteries, Beth Ha-Midrashim." Nor does he flinch at the idea of financing communism. Like Krasiński's revolutionary heroes, he is also endowed with satanic traits. Wat introduces into his story a modicum of ominous number magic:

> "Hello! Hello! This is New York speaking. A pound 3.20. In the morning I leave by dirigible R 5. See you at five in London."

The telephone was disconnected. The hand of Baron Gould rested motionless on the support of the armchair. . . . A hand with swollen veins—a railway junction, obscured by strands of cigarette smoke—with five wide fingers, wide tracks to five capitals, to five parts of the world. . . .

The July evening lay on the terrace of the seventeenth story of the Hotel Livingston. . . . Baron Gould daydreamed. . . . The oval of the murky Galician town, the silver candlesticks spattered with melted wax. Friday evening.

In this opening passage, two numbers are emphasized. One of them is five: 3.20 (3 + 2 = 5), R 5, at five, five fingers, five capitals, five parts of the world, Friday (in Polish, *piątek*, the fifth day). The other, less exposed number is seven: July (the seventh month), the seventeenth story, the candlesticks (with their seven candles). While seven may be defined as "magical number par excellence," providing the text with a certain enigmatic tinge, five is more complex. It is considered *the* diabolical number. Here it qualifies not only the fingers of the powerful (and greedy) Gould and the continents that submit to his will; it also refers to the magical pentagram (as well as to the five points of the Red Star).

Another device employed by Wat pertains to onomastics. Gould's name is, of course, reminiscent of gold (and God), thus making of him a latter-day Mammon. He lives in Hotel Livingston (perhaps a reference less to the explorer of Africa than to Gould's "stony heart"). Nathan—Natan in the original—is provided with a palindromic name that reflects the reversal of time.

In the general economy of the story, these subliminal allusions acquire a parodic value. Rather than an uncanny revelation, "The Eternally Wandering Jew" is no more than a playful testing of stereotypical concepts, a reductio ad absurdum of ideological extremes.

Wat the satirist does not restrict himself to mocking and destroying anti-Semitic ideology. The unbelievable project of Nathan entails an amalgam of concepts that were in wide circulation in the 1920s (and, to some extent, before and after). The notion of a "new Middle Ages" was being promoted at the time by Chesterton and a number of other thinkers, including Jacques Maritain and Nikolai Berdyaev (whose influential book with that title appeared in 1924). A synthesis of Christian and radical leftist values had been preached in Poland by Stanisław Brzozowski and in Western Europe by philosophers too numerous to list. Hence the seemingly perverse idea of a Communist theocracy, referring back to Dostoevsky's *The Legend of the Grand Inquisitor,* was in the air all the time.

A perfectly cerebral literary game, "The Eternally Wandering Jew" does not lack a personal element. It is not hard to recognize the young Wat in Nathan, the self-oblivious reader who goes through contrary stages in his quest for all-embracing Weltanschauung. The story is Wat's first, if less than serious, attempt to come to grips with his Jewishness (and Polishness). We also find here the core of Wat's personal religious experience. Nathan's project and its consequences are purely provocative. But grotesque notions developed by a young atheist became matters of grave concern for a writer facing death. In a letter to Baron Gould, Nathan says: "The Eternally Wandering Jew wants to rest. He will find death under the cross, death, followed by a rebirth." In the context of Wat's life, these words have a prophetic—and deeply poignant ring.

During the 1950s, Wat reflected on the typology of fiction frequently. Two of his notions are particularly relevant:

> The difference between a short story and a novel [is the same] as between a delineated route and a city map.[31]

> The final stage of the development of the novel will consist in a novel-note. . . . One should write a collection of novel-notes like a manual of chess endgames. All the rest—"just literature"—may be skipped or replaced by *stage directions* in the manner of "scene, situation, dialogue."[32]

"The Eternally Wandering Jew" could be called a "note" of this kind: it squeezes the content of a long futurological novel into the space of several pages, omitting all that is not absolutely necessary for the unfolding of the paradoxical conceit. This trait is even more striking in three other futuristic stories dealing with social, political, and cultural issues, even if, overall, they are less successful than "The Eternally Wandering Jew."

"Kings in Exile" consists of twenty-two short chapters, each of which summarizes a protracted series of events. It oscillates between socio-philosophical treatise and disrespectful anecdote. Wat himself defined the story as a "monarchic opera buffa." The plot has Czar Nicholas II and his son Aleksei escaping from the Bolsheviks and reaching England.[33] This provides ample grounds for satire. One of the main targets, of course, was Poland, which took great pride in having thrown off the Czarist yoke: "In Poland the blue generals, landholders, clergy, student fraternities and guild masters dragged out and dusted off lithographic portraits of the Czar's family and felt a rising tide of nostalgia for savings accounts books, gold braid, samovars, the Czarist police and kopecks, the sunshine of bygone days." The miraculous appearance of the dethroned monarch—and subsequent surge of retrogressive dreams—gave rise to a question typical of any postrevolutionary period: can the course of history be reversed, and if so, to what extent? Here, Wat found an ironic, elegant solution: he took the metaphor of "reversed time" literally.

The main devices of the story are borrowed from the cinema. A sequence of shots is developed, which, at a certain moment, starts to run backward. Nicholas II and other kings who have been exiled from their countries decide to exercise their sovereign power on a small island in the Indian Ocean and thereby preserve the purity of the monarchic ideal for a better future. The globe is thus divided into two realms, in which time, literally, runs in opposite directions. At the beginning, the island is a perfect conservative utopia, a paradise regained. But unfortunately for the traditionalists, this happy state of affairs is just an intermediary stage. Once reversed, time does not stop there but flows backward to the bitter end. Isolated from the rest of the world, the island passes unflinchingly through the periods described in history books, albeit in the reverse direction. In the twenty-fifth century, when the so-called Isle of Kings is rediscovered by a team of black scientists, its inhabitants are found to be living in a state of barbarity, and the hairy, half-naked king of the Franks is trying to pierce the hairy, half-naked king of the Germans with a javelin.

The story thus becomes a humorous anti-utopia in the vein of Anatole France,[34] which demolishes the monarchist myth and, in its wake, myths of "primeval Arcadia" and the "noble savage." The beginning and end of the story mirror each other. In the opening chapter, the first mate of the English ship scorns "natives," whereas in the last one, the enlightened but condescending Black professor Anarchasis Hualalai speaks of "a typical scene in the life of barbarians" (who, ironically, are related to the very highest European aristocracy). Notions of civilization and barbarity prove to be interchangeable—like the notions of Jew and Gentile in the preceding story. The hierarchy can be overturned, "central" and "marginal" phenomena can be put in place of one another, but the structure survives. Here, Wat is a faithful student of Witkacy— and, even more, of the famous anthropologist Bronisław Malinowski, who was Witkacy's friend and mentor.

Although it is distinguished by its cinematographic technique, innovative for the 1920s, the story may seem simplistic in its symmetry. Once the reader has become accustomed to Wat's paradoxes, many of the plots appear predictable. Still, Wat's taste for perversity and his truly Chestertonian ability for upside-down vision provide good comic effects. The effect of the central reversal is augmented by marginal reversals, in which Wat turns ideological clichés and conventional slogans inside out—witness the rallying cry for Nicholas II and his comrades, "Monarchs of the World Unite!" Monarchy is praised as "the only just system of distribution of material goods" and as "the sole defender of the proletariat, a representation of the battle and harmony of the classes." Moreover, the Soviet foreign minister, Chicherin, proposes "the formation of a soviet of kings in the Crimea." No matter how strong Wat's Communist sympathies were at the time, communism did not escape the net of his all-pervading derision.

The story "Long Live Europe!" may be seen as a third variation on the theme of interchangeability. It deals with another popular stereotype, the myth of the yellow peril. Arising in Germany at the end of the nineteenth century, it assumed currency in the work of Russian symbolists, particularly Andrei Bely in his influential novel *Petersburg.*[35] The traditional notion of Poland as "the bulwark of Christianity" made Polish culture particularly susceptible to speculation about the forthcoming clash between the "cultivated West" and the "wild East" (the Polish-Soviet war of 1920–21 was considered by many a dire portent).[36]

Wat's story opens with a veritable paean: the narrator speaks at length of his overflowing love for Europe, "that great eternal Europe which, after centuries of toil, was climbing endless rungs of contradictions and antinomies, shooting toward the heavens with the religiosity of its virtue and vice, bursting with the momentum of progress, bonded by dynamism in every one of its atoms, its creative, productive tradition speeding in eternal restlessness from unity to complexity, from multiplicity to simplicity." But one may sense an ambivalence lurking behind the dithyramb. Is the narrator right? Is he being completely sincere? Whatever the answers, he is too rhetorical. He employs clichés and juxtaposes things in a less than meaningful way, all but losing the thread of his argument amidst the hyperboles and redundancies. The author maliciously indicates that the rapturous monologue was spoken on the eve of World War I. But the disaster of the war does not stifle the enthusiasm of the narrator (who, incidentally, loses his right hand in battle). Once again, Wat is in his element: there is an interplay between narrative levels, a juxtaposition of points of view, and a distancing that makes any statement double-faced and relative.

The story is then given a bizarre twist. The narrator imbues with his excessive ecstasy two friends who represent races enslaved by Europeans: an African, Jusuf ben Mchim, and an Asian, Chang Wu Pei.[37] The first perishes in the war as a French soldier; the second becomes a warlord and dictator, "a Peter the Great of China," who, in a sense, takes revenge for the African's death. In the year 193–, his modern, well-organized army overruns Europe. The irony of the situation consists in the fact that Chang Wu Pei acts mainly, if not exclusively, out of adoration for Europe (though for him European civilization is, first and foremost, the source of innovations in military technology).

Together with all the natives of Europe, the narrator is deported to the Eurasian steppe, where Chinese bureaucrats force him to work as a teacher in a benighted village.[38] After twenty years, he is ordered to return to Paris, where, to his utter amazement, he finds defeated Europe once more European, "bursting with creative dynamism," although populated exclusively by Chinese. The turn of the wheel has come full circle.

The message of the story may seem optimistic: Europe proves to be eternal and imperishable indeed. But at a deeper level, the vision of a victorious European culture sits uneasily with an ironic grimace. The very concept of a people—and, consequently, of a distinctive culture—is pronounced illusory. "Europe" becomes an abstract notion. The structure remains intact, but all its elements have been interchanged. All that is left is a "creative dynamism" mischievously embodied in a total absence of movement: the threadbare clichés of the beginning of the story are repeated almost verbatim at the end.

That perverse game of dynamism and stasis, optimism and pessimism, is further complicated by the fact that the author and the narrator are alternately identified with each other and distanced. The story reiterates, to some extent, the structural pattern of "The Eternally Wandering Jew," but it has a tension and an originality of its own, which compensate for its weaker points, such as the simplistic cartoon-like characters and rather primitive "telegraphic style."

"Long Live Europe!" may also be read as a refutation of commonly held opinions about the Communist revolution. In Wat's view, revolution does not bring incurable disaster, but neither does it bring progress or even real change. Such a view would have been equally insulting to right-wingers and Marxists: which may have been precisely Wat's intention.

The fourth sociopolitical tale, "The History of the Last Revolution in England," deserves no more than a passing mention. It is an unassuming, mildly humorous story that plays up stereotypic notions of the English national character. A bloody encounter between proletarians and government forces is imperceptibly transformed into a soccer match, which provides a perfect, agreeably safe way to vent class hatred. Wat achieves a comic effect here mainly by juxtaposing two dialects of journalese (the first pertaining to revolution, the second to sport), that change places and merge as smoothly as the actions themselves.

A counterweight to the sociopolitical stories is furnished by stories that are more abstract, poetic, and philosophical—though no less nihilist. There are also four of them: "Has Anyone Seen Pigeon Street?"; "April Fool"; "Hermaphrodite"; "Tom Bill: Heavyweight Champion." Each attempts to demystify a concept at the core of our habitual world outlook.

"April Fool," which deals with the notion of personality, is one of Wat's weakest tales. Its hero, a librarian named Peter Moreau, leads a responsible, ordered life, "pondering the superiority of order and system over anarchy, humor, and all spirits of revolt." All of a sudden, he becomes derailed: the unconscious overtakes him, forcing him to proclaim himself, first, a serial murderer, then a semibiblical prophet, a latter-day Savonarola. In the same abrupt, unforeseen way, he returns to monotonous, regular existence.

The story mocks the idea of behavioral consistency—one may exchange personalities at whim. It may also be read as a metaliterary essay, which explores—and questions—the borders between reality and art. When, in the middle of a theatrical production, Peter climbs onto the stage and confesses his imaginary crimes, he is acting; but the audience takes what he says for truth (and, in a sense, it becomes the truth). But the story is uneven and convoluted, its comicality too strained, its philosophical message too obtrusive, and its denouement trivial.

"Tom Bill: Heavyweight Champion," another paradoxical story, touches on problems of ethics, juxtaposing the moral codes of Christianity and Nietzsche. Wat characteristically exhibits a subversive attitude to both. He shows no preference and makes the very notion of choice between them whimsical.

From the standpoint of genre, the story is an exception in *Lucifer Unemployed:* rather than a grotesque fantasy, it is like a quasi-psychological novella. Its fascination lies not in its plot (which is simpler than those of the other tales) but in its lengthy descriptions of the melancholic world of the Parisian suburbs in which the titular hero spends his years and in an almost Proustian analysis of his daydreams:

> Lying with a woman, he grew lost not in love's ecstasy but in whispers reaching him from the courtyard, in the shouts and playful hubbub of children's voices, perhaps seeking in this twittering choir his own voice, perhaps hearing this same sweet, tormenting echo of life from thirty years ago listening in a room where he lay sick and lonely, perhaps hunting the feeble shadows of a paradise lost. . . . Under the asphalt of the street his soles felt the rough-hewn stones of the courtyard on which, as a child, his feet were so often bruised. The maps doubled, streets fell away and sometimes he froze, forgetting himself in the misty rising and falling of memories.[39]

By contrast, "Hermaphrodite" is the very essence of grotesque and is reminiscent of certain segments of *Pug Iron Stove*. Like the latter, it is embellished with esoteric mottoes and Latin quotations (one of them, from Juvenal, decidedly un-Victorian) and overflows with shocking portraits of every imaginable sexual deviation, including voyeurism, coprophilia, and necrophilia. The style is a heavy pastiche of typical Young Poland prose. The hero, Peter, awakens indomitable desire in his female companions but is a sexless hermaphrodite; his only carnal experience worthy of note dates from his stint in a lyceum and concerns his pal, "a heavyset Frenchman from Cairo . . . to whom Peter yielded one cruel stormy night." A lady in love with him, Mrs. Cleopatra Van Hymenseel (!), a virgin lesbian, undergoes "a Golgotha of monstrous agony" in her relationship with Peter, but eventually succeeds in arousing in him manly feelings and furnishing him with a functional penis. The consummation comes too late: "Peter did not notice that he had impregnated a dead woman. Her heart had burst." The rest of Peter's story is said to be "a story about a Don Juan," which the author tantalizingly promises to "write some other time."

This summary, faithful to the parodic quality of the story, does not do full justice to its finer nuances. Peter has a friend and double of sorts, Hamilkar Pater, who is his exact opposite: endowed with an aggressive masculine sexuality, he nevertheless repels all women by his unseemly appearance. The story includes two tales narrated by Hamilkar in the manner of Scheherazade, which deal mainly with the psychological torments of sexual frustration. His lust and bizarre exercises in self-discipline are exaggerated versions of young Aleksander's:

> At eighteen, in a metaphysical desire for purity, I mortified my flesh, surrendered to ascetic practices, wore a hair shirt, and struggled with an enemy

of the law of the species which considered itself my more real "self." Lying on the couch for hours I dreamed about the bellies of women, about the damp vegetation of Venus's mound, about breasts swollen with heat; I wallowed in the imaginary debauchery of bodies. Feminine shapes became the archetypes of all shapes. The red of genitals contemplated in paraoptic vision became primal red, the Platonic idea of colors. The body of a woman realized in desire was the abc of all impressions, observations, and their transcendental a priori form—like space and time.

All the labyrinthine tangle of Wat's student years is present in "Hermaphrodite": his philosophical interests, his castration fantasies, his self-love and self-hatred. But the dominant tonality of the story is, as usual, derisive. Wat presents the sexual urge as one more instance of universal illusion and deceit. The most immediate instincts of a human being turn out to be relative and changeable, just like everything else. The mystical concept of the primordial, androgynous figure, so important in *Pug Iron Stove,* degenerates into pure clownery. The story's last sentence deals with "the incredible transformation" of Peter's body now that it has ben endowed with a penis; but that penile display can be interpreted only as the ultimate gesture of contempt, directed at society at large.

"Has Anyone Seen Pigeon Street?" no less shocking in its message, reveals a very different aspect of Wat's writing: its poetic, Romantic side, and more than one critic has judged it the best tale in the collection. The hero, Raphael, is faced with an inexplicable occurrence: Pigeon Street, where he used to live, has disappeared, together with his wife and child. The remainder of the story consists of his abortive attempts to find the street and so restore sense and direction to his life. He becomes a regular at the Café on the Hill, where an odd collection of people meet, chaired by a philosophizing anarchist known as the "professor." As Raphael comes to suspect, he is the man responsible for the disappearance of street, wife, and child. A masterful dose of suspense compels the reader to share this belief, but the denouement violates expectations:

> Raphael did not find Pigeon Street, because it never existed in that town (nor will you ever find the town on any map. Nevertheless, does that make the disappearance of Pigeon Street less of a mysterious riddle?) He did not find his wife or child because they, too, never existed. Raphael was a known bluffer and spinner of tall tales. Now, for example, it is Sunday evening. Raphael is sitting on the veranda of the Rotunda. Through the clouds of smoke rising from his cigarette he imagines dramatized heretical landscapes.

The most striking part of the story concerns the enigmatic professor and his ragtag band, which includes a couple of Wat's stock characters—a less-than-successful poet and a sex maniac. These characters are probably patterned on the group of supposed anarchists in Chesterton's *The Man who was Thursday.* The professor is a new incarnation of the antiquary Thomas Traum, demoniac figure, tempter, and prophet of nihilism. Once again, it is an ironic self-portrait of Wat that we are presented with.

The text is saturated in symbolism, most of which is ambivalent. Thus, Raphael is a paradigmatic name for an artist. Pigeon Street is in the shape of the letter T, the shape of gallows and early versions of the cross, as Raphael notes; it thus stands for law and faith, both of which are denied by its disappearance. The name "Pigeon" (Gołębia, dove in the Polish original) may be construed as a reference to the Holy Spirit. The story is thus a metaphysical allegory of the artist's quest, with strong religious overtones. On the other hand, "pigeon" in Polish connotes "a kind person," and in several other languages, "a person easily deceived or gulled." This last meaning, well known to Wat, adds an element of mockery to the plot.

The story seems to be an exercise in art for art's sake. The border between art and life is erased; or, to be precise, there is nothing except the "dramatized heretical landscapes" of storytelling. But Wat teases the reader with a double perspective. Is the Rotunda real—and is it identical with the famous Café Rotonde in Paris? Is Sunday evening real? Is Raphael real—or did he create himself ex nihilo, just as he created Pigeon Street and the story? This giddy ambiguity—reminiscent of "Seller of Dreams"—forms the main structural principle of the tale.

The titular story is both the most straightforward and one of the finest in the book. A pungent satire worthy of a latter-day Voltaire, it presents an all-encompassing survey, as well as an indictment, of twentieth-century civilization. Its structure is clear and follows the format of the traditional philosophical novella: there are seventeen loosely connected episodes, each demolishing a particular aspect of culture (or a particular social institution) in toto. The language is elegant, lucid, and concise. The story sparkles with witticisms, metaphors, and newly invented proverbs; many of its scenes are genuinely hilarious, even if its message overall is far from amusing.

The hero, the Prince of Darkness himself, visits the earth in search of a job. He fails all his interviews miserably. The modern world, whose ruling principle is the total mechanization of society, has no place for the Devil, representative of a vanquished era in which evil was personal and devoid of banality. His "haphazard" miracles, such as transporting elderly ladies through the air on brooms, are unnecessary and unimpressive in a society in which all miracles are utilitarian. His plots and intrigues pale by comparison with the methods of modern diplomacy, and his crimes look pitiable compared to twentieth-century warfare. His penchant for temptation and perversion falls flat in a universe in which everything is permitted. Having lost all hope of employment, Lucifer chooses a typical way out and tries to commit suicide. His final monologue sums up his desperate search: "The modern world doesn't need me. It is cleansed of all that is demonic. . . . The world is *plus diabolique que le diable même*. No, not even that. It is an infernal cocktail, in which God himself cannot distinguish his ingredients from mine."

On the verge of the self-annihilation, Lucifer nevertheless changes his mind—a decision made inevitable by the fact that he is immortal, after all. Following wise advice, he becomes a film artist, and a well-known one at that: Charlie Chaplin. Artistry turns out to be a last refuge for the spirit of anarchy and tragic despair—in short, for the human soul.

Almost seven decades after it was first published, *Lucifer Unemployed* still seems astonishingly up-to-date. In it, Wat grasped "something of the sinister dynamics peculiar to our own time," as Czesław Miłosz put it.[40] Here is found Hannah Arendt's concept of the "banality of evil," as well as notions developed by Marshall McLuhan and Herbert Marcuse. The permissive society described in the story has developed into a full-blown reality only recently, and one cannot but admire Wat's comprehension of its traits, including its capacity to tame almost any rebel.

Making the Devil the judge of civilization is a literary topos with a distinguished history, stretching back at least as far as Le Sage (*Le Diable boiteux*) and Goethe (*Faust*). In the early twentieth century, it was employed, before Wat, by Ehrenburg.[41] It suited perfectly Wat's frame of mind and his pronounced demonological interests. Wat always tended to identify himself with a fallen angel. Moreover, he gradually came to the conclusion that "for a contemporary person, it is incredibly difficult to believe in God, but terribly difficult, perhaps even more difficult, to disbelieve in the Devil."[42] Nevertheless, in the 1920s, he treated Lucifer more as a literary motif than a metaphysical entity.

Characteristically, Wat inverted the commonplace: in his tale, the tempter is rendered impotent and obsolete by society. Demonism is dissolved in the mechanism of alienation. Rebellious, self-affirming Lucifer is replaced by faceless Ahriman, spirit of pure nonbeing. Paradoxically, the old-fashioned Devil turns out to be the last believer in any norms, hierarchies, and values, and even in the existence of God.

An appeal to Chaplin as ultimate arbiter was typical of Wat's generation of writers and intellectuals, who saw in Chaplin's art a way out of the all-embracing cultural crisis. Adam Ważyk praised his "silent, absurd, philosophical humor"[43] and noted: "I was not alone in ascribing an exceptional artistic value to Chaplin. . . . He seemed more contemporary than any poet, writer or painter. For many, he was the most contemporary artist."[44] Wat himself write booklets about Chaplin and remained under his spell for many years. As late as 1941, exiled in Kazakhstan, he wrote a film script that proved to be an unintentional imitation of *The Great Dictator*.[45]

The fate of art in modern society, one of Wat's chief concerns, is the focus of the story. One episode concerns the author of a poem about the crucified

Antichrist who meditates on the degradation of metaphysics in the modern world and then commits suicide—the exit refused to Lucifer in the denouement of the story. The poem, quoted in full, is among the best of Wat's early works, and the poet is, once again, a self-portrait. Thus, Wat kills his disillusioned hero as a stand-in for himself—and survives as Lucifer-become-Chaplin. All that remains of art is a sarcastic gesture that remonstrates against the era and the universe. "For you are sufficiently wise to understand that humanity demands anarchy to the end."

Wat's iconoclastic tales, full of playful but controlled imagination, provided the impulse for a series of utopian and dystopian fantasies, which were among the most original trends in Polish literature in the interwar period. But their influence extended much further than that. An echo of them may be found in the so-called Polish catastrophism of the 1930s.[46] Even closer links can be established between the author of *Lucifer Unemployed* and Witold Gombrowicz, the great iconoclast who brought the art of parody and irreverent gesture to perfection in his novels and plays. The visionary prose of Bruno Schulz, a Polish counterpart to Franz Kafka, frequently betrays the same quality—in part oneiric, in part ironic—as Wat's tale about the unsuccessful search for Pigeon Street (and, to an even higher degree, his "Seller of Dreams"). In contemporary Polish letters, a relation to Wat is evident in such disparate phenomena as Stanisław Lem's satirical futurology and Sławomir Mrożek's demystifying attacks on totalitarian patterns in human life and thought.

A trait that singles out new Polish writing against the background of world literature has been described as "a tonality of cunning philosophical grotesque and all-embracing mockery."[47] Although it must be conceded that this trend was never limited to Polish letters—in the era of postmodernism it is probably the dominant tendency of art overall—the Polish contribution to this development is significant and beyond dispute, and here Wat is one of the great precursors. His jocular "multivariant history" certainly does not lack predictive value, even if he did not foresee the phenomena that were to define his own life: the Holocaust and Stalinism.

Communism, 1928–1939

By the time of Mayakovsky's visit to Poland in 1927, Wat had become a frequent visitor to the Soviet embassy in Warsaw. In this, he was far from an exception; many Polish writers and cultural figures—and not only professed leftists—were attracted to the mysterious land to the east that boasted of conducting a social experiment on a scale unequaled in the history of humankind. The Soviet embassy in Warsaw was more fascinating than any Soviet diplomatic institution was to become during the mature Stalinist period. True, there was much shady activity, including financial and logistical support for subversive actions within Poland and perhaps direct involvement with terrorism. But there were also some cultured Soviet officials of broader awareness, with views that were more attractive than those of the average Western diplomat of the time, although almost all such people were subsequently wiped out by Stalin.

Social life at the embassy included viewings of new Soviet films[1] and meetings with Russian writers. Besides Mayakovsky, visitors to Poland at the time included Lidia Seifullina (in 1927) and Boris Pilnyak (in 1931). Wat was fascinated by Seifullina's exotic appearance, which reminded him of the archetypal Spirit of Earth—an earth upturned by the revolutionary plow.[2] Pilnyak was a more significant literary figure, almost equal to Mayakovsky in fame, whose ornamental prose dealt with the aspect of communism that interested Wat more than any other—namely, the revolutionary savagery that, by a peculiar mental trick, was perceived by many as a justification for Red October. Pilnyak was also interested in Asia and became enamored of Japan when he visited it in 1926. In his view, Japan combined Eastern tradition with Western elements more successfully than the USSR,[3] a none-too-orthodox stance that he paid for with his life during the purges, when he was accused of being a Japanese spy. While in Warsaw, Pilnyak visited the Wats in their apartment. But even there, "he spoke with set teeth, he was extremely cautious. A man doubtlessly full of falseness. In my opinion, he was an anti-Communist in disguise."[4]

At the very least, Wat's visits to the Soviet embassy provided him with relatively enlightened interlocutors, who represented an antidote to the provincialism of Poland and a much needed alternative to the total nihilism of his younger years. In 1924 or 1925, his attitude to communism was marked by the same profound, biting irony that characterized his views on any social system and ideology: "When Herling-Grudziński [Gustaw Herling-Grudziński, a Polish émigré essayist] received a copy of the second postwar edition of *Lucifer Unemployed* in 1959, he wrote me a letter: 'Aleksander, did you write this after you became disenchanted with communism?' And really I thought it was an entirely logical supposition because that little collection of stories contains some utterly sober judgments about communism—communism that had shattered on the atom of the soul."[5]

This perfect iconoclasm could not hold its own, however. It led to an intense spiritual search and, finally, to an iconolatry more thoroughgoing than the traditional iconolatry that he had rejected in *Pug Iron Stove*. In this, Wat was like many Europeans who embraced communism after emerging from their respective expressionist, dadaist, surrealist, or futurist periods, including Bertolt Brecht, Louis Aragon, Paul Eluard, and, most important, Mayakovsky. Where he differed from them was in not then settling down, in not opting for an exit into death after facing disillusionment. Wat had the will to proceed to the next, more mature iconoclastic period and then, retrospectively, to analyze his conversion to communism in detail and with insight.

Among his reasons for taking the Communist option, the one that Wat highlighted in his memoirs was of a religious nature. An appendix to *My Century* found among Wat's papers after his death and not yet translated into English deals with his religious crisis at length and makes a crucial point: "I was pushed toward communism not by the hunger for faith, but by the inability to endure an absolute, thorough scepticism and, consequently, senselessness of existence. Not without a belated envy, I think at present of those who could endure it with Stoic fortitude, like Camus, and even of these who wallow in the senselessness of existence with early Romantic *delectatio morosa*, like Beckett and his followers."[6]

Paradoxically, the main shortcoming of Communist ideology, its excessively simplistic nature, was viewed as an asset by the oversophisticated intellectual that Wat undoubtedly was. In his memoirs, he confesses that his refined, penetrating mind could not cope with the proliferation of mutually exclusive, self-contradictory philosophical and ideological doctrines of the twentieth century. It is tempting to describe this reasoning as deconstructionist avant la lettre: its very subtleness provides some justification for the Communist simplistic approach. "Today, in order to advance even a *coherent* train of thought, not to mention a system, one has to be dishonest. One has to tacitly reject the counterarguments implicitly offered by one's intelligence, memory and education. One must make a choice based on intellectual dishonesty. Only a simpleton can be intellectually honest in the full sense of the word—or a person with an ability for self-deception."[7]

Communism became, under these circumstances, the kind of universal calculus that Wat had searched for during his school and university years. It also had the advantage that it could be shared with the masses, thereby alleviating his profound sense of alienation. It furnished uncomplicated answers to any question, the counter-arguments being declared either irrelevant, or, much frequently, the result of bad faith. Such thinking led directly to the worst excesses of Stalinism, but there was no denying its coherence.

The quasi-religious catechism of communism advanced an eschatological view of a future in which all contradictions would be resolved forever. Anyone who did not join the victorious march incurred the risk of being excluded from history. Communism also provided a savior, a new Christ leading to the future and expiating his faithful followers in the process. Lenin was an idol to which the free will of a person, ever bound to err, must be surrendered. His heirs constituted a quasi-church that provided not only an ideology but also precise prescriptions for acting. This action would supposedly lead to the salvation of the human species. In light of this comprehensive goal, the destruction of an isolated individual or individuals was of no importance.

Even in his Communist years, Wat was far too astute to embrace such a Weltanschauung without reservation. But the temptation to do so was great. To one threatened by social rejection, as Wat was, communism held out a unique appeal of collective warmth and the promise of universal brotherhood. Further, his long-nurtured scorn for bourgeois mentality was in perfect agreement with Marxist doctrine, so much so that the inevitable doubts and ironies could be dismissed, at least for the time being, as remnants of an individualistic attitude. (Moreover, one might cherish reservations in private: that was the practice of doublethink taught by the likes of Boris Pilnyak.)

In addition, there was the sheer thrill of political (and mental) adventure. Nevertheless, the most important cause of Wat's conversion was that described by Miłosz in *Zniewolony umysł* (The Captive Mind): fear of "the *suction* of the absurd."[8] As Communist fellow-traveler, Wat became the epitome of the captive mind, the heyday of which lay in the future.

The year 1928 was marked by the closing of *Lever,* the leftist monthly that had sponsored Mayakovsky's visit to Warsaw the previous year. The intellectuals who had been connected with *Lever* then formed a Marxist circle with the express goal of maintaining and developing mutual contact. The group included Broniewski, Hempel, Stawar, Stanisław Stande, the avant-garde painter and set-designer Władysław Daszewski, and Leon Schiller, a stage director of international repute. Wat's memoirs are the only significant source of information about the circle's activities: other members seem not to have written about them at length, for various reasons, and there are few traces of the group's existence in the archival documents.

Meetings of the circle took place either in the sumptuous apartment of Schiller or in the Wats' more modest abode in Hoża 13.[9] The format of each meeting was a lecture followed by prolonged discussion. The participants were avid readers of the national and international Communist press, as well as of classical Marxist texts (with the conspicuous exception of *Das Kapital,* considered too boring).[10] "Someone from the party always came, sometimes some anonymous person, probably from the Central Committee, sometimes somebody who was in hiding. . . . Then Schiller would sit at the piano and play. Sometimes he would play 'My girlfriend's so ugly her teeth fall out' or 'The wind is laughing at the window, dammit, life is vile. . . .' A beautifully furnished apartment and so on."[11] Police observers were never far away.

Soon, the idea of founding a legal Communist periodical arose. The planned journal was perceived as a natural successor to *Workers' Culture* and *New Culture,* as well as, to a degree, *Lever.* The project was promoted—perhaps even initiated—by Stawar.[12] Wat was considered by him, as well as by Hempel and others, to be the least proletarian member of the circle. Paradoxically, this worked in Wat's favor: a licit journal required the editorship of someone not necessarily known for an unflinching stance, who could maintain connections among the liberal intelligentsia. Wat consented eagerly.[13]

Before the periodical was founded, however, an important event took place, one that contributed to Wat's reputation as a workers' advocate and at the same time provided him with financial means for his second trip to Western Europe. It throws an interesting light on the tenuous coexistence between the Polish government and those who sought to subvert it. In 1929, an exhibition commemorating the tenth anniversary of Polish independence opened in Poznań. Among its organizers was Alfred Krygier, an influential member of Piłsudski's PPS. He put forward the idea of staging a propaganda play entitled *Social Policy of R.[epublic of] P.[oland]* that would graphically demonstrate the achievements— and shortcomings—of the country's social legislation. To this end, he enlisted the services of several left-wing artists, including Schiller, Wat, and an avant-garde filmmaker, Leon Trystan.[14] The project was consonant with the modernist experiments being conducted at the time by Meyerhold in Russia and Erwin Piscator in Germany. Its genre was defined as "facto-montage," which, according to Schiller, "discards the anecdotal part and the dramatic design and, following the plotless films of Eisenstein, Pudovkin, Turin or Ruttmann, or imitating a cabaret revue, connects individual facts taken from collective life to the ideological links and explains their sense."[15]

Wat was given abundant material about conditions in Polish industry. It revealed the backwardness of the country and the extensiveness of brazen exploitation in its factories. The realistic picture of the proletarians' situation that Wat obtained from the sources made accessible to him could not help but consolidate his pro-Communist stance: "I immersed myself in those materials, but I just did not have the time to recast them, to digest them. It was all raw and superficial, and so the script was abominable. . . . The announcer would read a short paragraph from the labor laws, and then the telephone would ring. He'd answer the phone and receive information from various large factories as to how many violations of the laws had been recorded there in the course of the year. In a word, I showed that all the laws had been broken. And naturally, to top it off, there was a chorus of unemployed workers."[16]

In a letter to Schiller's widow, Wat also mentioned *tableaux vivants*, on-screen statistics, songs, skits, and so on.[17] Part of the "abominable" script has survived, since it was published in the socialist periodical *Pobudka* (Signal). It consists of short factual statements pronounced by workers, accompanied by sound effects. Very straightforward and unassuming, it is not devoid of suggestiveness:

> *A Farm Laborer.* A woman worker covered her head with a kerchief close to a thresher. The drum of the machine caught the ends of the kerchief, pulled her head in and smashed the skull.
> *A Young Worker.* We are killed by the electric current, we perish in furnaces, from the explosions, gases, poisoned exhausts.
> *A Woman Worker.* Lead condenses in our blood. Dust glues up our lungs. Alcohol fumes eat away our eyes. We are poisoned by raw materials, machines, manufactured products.[18]

A small hall was constructed for the performances, which ran twice a day, and any publicity was carefully avoided. Nevertheless—or perhaps for that very reason—Wat's "facto-montage" caused a sensation. In September, Piłsudski's wife, accompanied by Labor Minister Aleksander Prystor, attended a performance, following which the enterprise was shut down immediately.[19] But in spite of the trouble, Wat and his friends were paid handsomely.[20]

Wat's second trip to the West was more significant than his first timid venture in 1926. This time he was accompanied by Ola. No longer a young, naive tourist, but prospective editor of a Communist monthly—hence a Communist functionary *in spe*—he had a specific task: to contact writers and journalists of the same ilk in Germany and France. To be sure, there were contacts of a less literary sort. Józef Kowalski, a correspondent for the Soviet newspaper *Pravda*, had given him the name of Grigory Besedovsky, counselor at the Soviet embassy in Paris and someone involved in intelligence activities and various shady intrigues.[21]

In the first volume of his memoirs, Wat gives the time of his trip as the summer of 1928, and this date has found its way into the literature on Wat. But all circumstances point to the summer of the following year, 1929, and in the second volume, Wat himself gives this date.[22]

Those years saw a crisis in the history of communism—and of Europe. In the USSR, the struggle for Lenin's succession had already been won by Stalin in 1927. In the West, extreme right-wing movements were growing apace. Hitler's *Mein Kampf* had already been published, even if it enjoyed only modest success at the time. More troublesome, perhaps, the middle ground was shrinking. Liberal and democratic ideas were discarded by Communists and Fascists alike, being regarded by a large and growing body of intellectuals as either outdated or mendacious or both.

The year 1929 was climactic: not without reason, was it later glorified by Stalinists as "the year of the great change." In April, Stalin and his supporters succeeded in thrusting on the country their program of breakneck industrialization and total agricultural collectivization. In the same year, the Great Depression in Europe contributed to the growth of mass support for the Nazis.

On his way from Warsaw to France, Wat stopped in Berlin, at that time still buzzing with political activity, avant-garde artistic experimentation, and all kinds of cosmopolitan fads. Berlin was one of the nerve centers of the world Communist movement. The KPP, to a considerable degree, was manipulated from Berlin.[23]

The German Communist party enjoyed a position quite unlike that of the KPP: far from being illegal, it was at the height of its power and influence. Wat made contact with the staff of the pro-Communist *Die Linkskurve*, visiting its office on Alexanderplatz. Of particular importance was his meeting with Friedrich Wolff,[24] whose play *Cyanide* was soon thereafter staged by Schiller in Poland, where it provoked tear-gas attacks by right-wing rowdies.[25]

What struck Wat about Berlin was its contrasts—a city of tumultuous night life, rampant unemployment, and brazen-faced poverty: "Decadence, decadence, a Babylon of debauchery."[26] His experiences of that debauchery were depressing rather than fascinating: a voyeuristic visit to a gay nightclub with a friend, Stefan Napierski, a homosexual writer; an evening or two in a lesbian café, the name of which Wat could not even remember; an encounter with an elderly prostitute who offered Wat the services of her fifteen-year-old daughter; a foray into a neighborhood of bad repute where people were literally dying of hunger.[27] More than Paris, the capital of the Weimar Republic seemed to Wat to be the paradigmatic Rimbaldian city of transgression and alienation that he had imagined in *Pug Iron Stove* and "Hermaphrodite."

Against this background, the Communist movement offered a sense of direction and common sense. The people connected with *Die Linkskurve* represented an upcoming generation that strongly dissociated itself from the hysterical decadents who had supported communism in Germany immediately after the October Revolution. Brecht, with his cult of irony and reason, was the epitome of this new wave.[28] The work of the Comintern, which Wat had an opportunity to observe in Berlin—if only in part and only on the sly—

conformed to his idea of a great revolutionary upheaval in the making. Later, his experience crystallized into the uneasy sense "that there was a certain international community of people, heterogeneously connected, like the neurons of the cortex, and between them ran an alternating current—currents of various tension and strength, of various phases, currents of ideas and money."[29] But in 1929, he felt inspired.

His stay in France was anticlimatic. He arrived in Paris on 14 July, in the middle of the dead season. He was struck mostly by France's adherence to tradition, stability, and provincialism, all of which were repellent to a young revolutionary. The only French author of any stature whom Wat met in Paris was Henri Barbusse, who later put his name to a bizarre eulogy of Stalin (*Stalin*, 1935). In *My Century*, Wat sketched a portrait of Barbusse, the precision of which is exquisite: "Barbusse—an unbelievable courtesy, a beautiful profile, a lean and tall body. Such a thoughtful head that the back had to hunch, a very pretty contour of the profile, and magnificent, refined French. . . . An elderly man—for me, he was then a very old one. An old gentleman, whose concepts of communism looked (to the very naive pro-Communist I was at the time) the apex of the nineteenth century, the apex of nineteenth-century misunderstandings— and here, incidentally, I was right. Well, that was France."[30]

The one incident in Paris potentially fraught with serious consequences was Wat's meeting with Grigory Besedovsky. Dealings with a Soviet agent could have drawn Wat into the underground activities of the Comintern more deeply than anything else—indeed, that may well have been Kowalski's goal. But thanks to the attendant circumstances, the visit to the Soviet embassy on rue Grenelle was a failure. Besedovsky paid almost no attention to his Polish guest, being too concerned with his own predicament. Enmeshed in various initiatives that lacked official approval and, supposedly, having lost all faith in communism, he was under threat of arrest by the Soviet security force and on the verge of defection, which he undertook on 3 October 1929.[31]

On his return from France, Wat continued to attend meetings of his Marxist circle. According to his autobiography, he also took part in the activities of Leon Schiller's theater studio[32] and gave lectures to workers at the People's University—less than successfully, since he felt inhibited before a proletarian audience. Allegedly, he was even considered for a nomination to Parliament (the KPP, though formally banned, still had a faction there) but rejected the offer.[33]

As before, he contributed to the mainstream magazine *Wiadomości Literackie* (Literary News) and in the late summer and early autumn printed two essays: one on the novel *Zavist'* (Envy) by Soviet author Yury Olesha,[34] the other on the "literature of fact" promoted in the USSR by theoreticians of LEF.[35] Both testify eloquently to his Marxist faith. An incident in his memoirs gives a taste of the atmosphere of the era. The editor of *Literary News*, Mieczysław Grydzewski, an enlightened man of leftist bent, was eager to enlist contributors representing all shades of radical opinion. Still, the extreme left was allowed only a low profile. But Broniewski, then secretary of the editorial board, taking advantage of a leave of absence on the part of Grydzewski, published Wat's brazenly pro-Soviet article on the first page, thereby provoking a scandal.[36]

Such tactical moves became unnecessary in December 1929, when a legal Communist periodical entitled *Miesięcznik Literacki* (The Literary Monthly) got under way. As arranged previously, Wat was appointed editor-in-chief.

In a typical socialist realist narrative, such an appointment would be considered an event of mythic magnitude, a rite de passage exposing the hero to all kinds of challenges, through which, after numerous ordeals, he would be transformed from a semi-bourgeois nihilist into a hardened knight of the Great Cause. Wat did in fact assign mythical status to the period of the *Literary Monthly*, creating, however, an iconoclastic anti-myth: for him, it became the nadir of his journey, the zero point from which his tortuous reascent toward Paradise Lost started. On New Year's Eve of 1954, Stawar presented him with a complete set of their old periodical (already a rarity by then) with the inscription: "For Olek. In memory of the shared sins of our youth—Edward." Almost ten years later, as an émigré during a particularly bad night when he thought death was just around the corner, Wat supplemented his friend's inscription with his own: "This is the *corpus delicti* of degradation. The history of my degradation in communism, by communism. It was in a Communist prison that I came fully to my senses, and from that time on, in prison, in exile, and in Communist Poland, I never allowed myself to forget my basic duty: to settle accounts, to pay for those two or three years of moral insanity. And I paid. 23 June 1964. Berkeley."[37]

The editorial board of the *Literary Monthly* (never made entirely public) included Hempel and Broniewski, the latter not formally a member of the party. The liaison with the KPP was originally Hempel, then Mojżesz Nowogródzki, who belonged to the party elite and later fell victim to the Nazis.[38] Ola had the triple role of secretary, typist, and distributor.[39] Aleksander and Ola were paid handsomely enough for Wat to be able to give up his labor as a translator.[40]

The number of subscribers, according to Wat's memoirs, was close to two thousand, and the general circulation about five thousand, quite substantial for Poland at that time, especially when one recalls that each issue (being rather expensive) was read by dozens of people.[41] Many of them belonged to the younger generation of intellectuals who came to the fore after World War II, and the influence of the periodical on their views and tastes—and, consequently, on the entire ideological landscape of postwar Poland—should not be underestimated. During a taping session with Wat in California, Czesław Miłosz confessed to being among the passionate readers of the *Literary Monthly*.[42] On the other hand, no less of a fan, presumably, was Jerzy Putrament, Miłosz's opposite number in Polish culture, a conformist who later became a Communist hard-liner. In his autobiography, he claimed to have dedicated his first poem of political commitment, "Aleksander Chwat," to Wat, unknown to him personally but revered as the persecuted Communist poet and editor.[43] Nonetheless, this dedication did not prevent Putrament from attacking Wat fiercely throughout the Stalinist years.[44]

All Wat's activities in connection with the *Literary Monthly* were marked by zealotry. Later, he analyzed his motives as a yearning for brotherhood and mutual love and the desire to overcome the stigma of a "bourgeois mentality." Wat, the most extreme of the radicals, was considered an "eternal outsider," too unruly to be of real value. As recently as 1982, one of the former leaders of the KPP dismissed Wat in the following words: "You see, Wat wasn't ours! . . . Deuce take it, he was probably nobody's. Just a bourgeois man of letters."[45] That opinion, even if influenced by Wat's subsequent emigration, was already current in the late 1920s; indeed, Wat's postwar behavior only corroborated the party's original judgment.

Wat's predicament was not unlike that of the outsider incisively analyzed in Sander Gilman's recent book *Jewish Self-Hatred*. Attracted to a group by the promise of a share in its power, and thereby obliged to abide by its rules, the outsider is rejected again and again. The more he or she adapts, the more the group's sense of its own value is confirmed, and the more the newcomer is seen as a self-interested cheat. In many Jewish writers this dilemma has generated an all-consuming urge to master the language of the ruling group better than any native speaker.[46] Examples abound, from Franz Kafka to Osip Mandelstam, Julian Tuwim, and Bruno Schulz. Yet, while they surpassed virtually all their non-Jewish counterparts in the precision and fluency of their respective German, Russian, and Polish, they were unable to erase the label "undesirable alien" assigned to them by countless contemporaries. Substituting "decadent heritage" for "Jewish background" and "Communist discourse" for "language of the ruling group," we have a description of Wat's problem. Moreover, he was a Jew, and in the Stalinist years, "bourgeois decadence" and "Jewishness" gradually became synonymous in the eyes of the party.

No wonder that the *Literary Monthly* was, from its beginning, an eminently radical enterprise, much riskier than its initiators and sponsors had envisioned. The KPP would have preferred a periodical of a different kind, one that could have served as a front for covert activities and attracted liberal intellectuals (such periodicals were in fact being published at that time in more than one country).

The mixture of political involvement and literary verve, however fraught with contradictions, provided Wat, at least temporarily, with much emotional satisfaction. "Those few years were very happy ones, perhaps the happiest time of my life," Wat noted later. "Ola and I were very much in love. I had extricated myself from desperation, hopelessness, and the sense of absolute absurdity. . . . I had a cause, I had a goal, and once again I had . . . what intellectuals in our time dream of: a *vita activa*. Not only to interpret, but to change the world with your own hands. . . . And one more thing: the game was fundamentally honest. For after all, there could be no doubt that it would end with prison."[47]

   Yet, the years of desperation had resulted in significant books (as happened yet again in Wat's old age), whereas during the happy, active years, Wat's creative output was almost negligible, consisting of literary polemics and a few articles. To be sure, there was more of it than meets the eye; for, after publishing *Lucifer Unemployed,* Wat apparently wrote some philosophical stories that have not survived. Nor did he abandon poetry altogether. In his memoirs, he mentions several "lyrical cycles" dating from that time.[48] However, the stories, as well as the poetry, fell victim to his increased political involvement, combined with his idea of artistic honesty: "I was then in the course of writing stories, the continuation of *Lucifer Unemployed,* more than ten rather extensive philosophical stories. And that was squaring the circle. To bring myself in line with the Communist worldview meant the destruction of their value, their element of beauty, their literary merit. Just imagine stories in the vein of *Lucifer Unemployed* on the topic of communism, treated dialectically."[49]

   In the first issue of the *Literary Monthly* Wat published an article entitled "Pacifist Literature in Germany," a specimen of crude, dogmatic Marxist criticism. It was a rabid attack on "bourgeois decadent" writing, the more rabid on account of Wat's own inner struggle with bourgeois temptations. The bulk of the article consisted in an analysis of Erich Maria Remarque's novel *All Quiet on the Western Front* (1929), a world best-seller that had just been translated into Polish by Wat's friend Napierski. Wat's criticism was not devoid of perspicaciousness, wit, and almost futurist audacity in exposing the weak points of the celebrated literary figure, particularly Remarque's sentimentality. Nevertheless, in presenting Remarque's novel as a cleverly masked attempt at war propaganda, the article displays a primitive sociological approach and a flagrant disdain of literary factors.

   Many critics of *All Quiet on the Western Front* have noticed its fatalistic concept of war as natural disaster and its somewhat disquieting cult of martial solidarity. But for Wat, these were neither traits of Remarque's world view and style nor characteristics of a literary trend (which could be agreeable or disagreeable, determined in part by historical or sociological circumstances, liable or not to self-interested utilization by certain groups and political movements, and so on). Rather, the whole book was ill-intentioned, an artful trap for the masses driven toward a massacre, and Remarque no more than a skillful counterfeiter, part and parcel of the international conspiracy of profit-seekers.

Wat's fanaticism was ridiculed by his old friend Antoni Słonimski, who published a merciless survey of the magazine's first issue in *Literary News*. The most politically sensitive aspect of Słonimski's article was his lack of respect for the USSR. He pointed out, not without grounds, that "the tyranny of the Medicis was more conducive to art than the Soviet terror," and had the impudence to turn the problem of militarist imperialism on its head: "It is a pity that Mr. Wat did not add where one should look for proletarian 'antimilitarism.' In Russia, scarcely, since the militarist education there is brought to heights of perfection. Soviet antimilitarism at present finds its expression in the powerful Red Army and in a bloody war with China. Please do not try to suggest that Russia is fighting the aggressive imperialism of capitalist China in the name of Communist ideals. It is hard to discover any class-oriented antimilitarism in the struggle for the profits of the Manchurian railway."[50]

The *Literary Monthly* responded in full accord with Stalinist precepts, stooping to a below-the-belt answer that included a hint at Słonimski's Jewishness.[51] The invective went unsigned, almost everyone on the staff of the *Literary Monthly* having contributed a vitriolic remark or two, but the responsibility was Wat's, and his relations with Słonimski were ruined for several years.[52]

The essays that Wat published in the next issues of the *Literary Monthly* conformed just as strictly to the party line as his onslaught on German pacifists. Two semi-memoir articles on the history of Polish futurism exhibit a similar, less-than-sophisticated Marxist analysis. In May 1930, Wat published an extensive obituary of Mayakovsky,[53] interpreting his suicide, in accordance with the opinion hastily manufactured by Soviet critics, as the result of a conflict between Mayakovsky's revolutionary élan and the new tasks of the reconstruction period, a conflict that had been temporary and not particularly significant but had become aggravated by purely personal circumstances.[54]

Like almost every avant-garde author of the 1920s, Wat was struck by the new literary vistas opened up by Proust and Joyce. His immediate reaction to both was unequivocal: "An absolute love, absolute enchantment for one and for the other."[55] In 1931, this enthusiasm was as strong as ever, but the Communist faith required the demolition of old idols, and Wat volunteered for the task. All the same, Wat's subsequent essay on Proust and Joyce,[56] marked by admirable methodological stringency, has some valid points. It does justice to Proust's artistic subtlety, to the innovative psychological theory implicit in his work, and to his extraordinary skill in handling the element of time. In Wat's comments on Joyce, the insight of a critic is sharpened by personal experience, and his evaluation of *Ulysses* may be read as a self-evaluation by the author of *Pug Iron Stove:* "In Joyce's novel, the world is perceived as a hellish bunch of contradictions, a nightmarish chaos galvanized by blind instincts. . . . [Nevertheless] the Kabbalah of the structure is consistent up to the smallest detail. This order, invisible to the naked eye, without an explicit analysis, is transcendent to the object of description (a causeless, chaotic universe)."[57]

Wat stressed the "workshop" quality of the modernists' writing. In his view, they were not concerned with the straightforward ideological message, leaving this to "applied" literature and reserving for themselves the task of testing new methods and styles.[58] This approach could easily lead to a Marxist (or semi-Marxist) justification of the literary experiment, which Wat gave in 1948, in express opposition to the Communist zealots of the postwar period. But in the *Literary Monthly,* Wat's delight in Proust's and Joyce's work and in the boldness of their experiments yielded to simplistic, tiresome analysis in terms of class struggle, with both authors, not unlike Remarque, being transformed into insidious defenders of capitalist power. The treatment of time as subjective and elastic in *The Remembrance of Things Past* and the "dissociation of the ideas" in *Ulysses* were, in Wat's view, invented for the sole purpose of concealing social contradictions and distracting proletarian attention from the real problems of life.

Later, in *My Century,* Wat maintained that his essay on Proust and Joyce was a watershed of sorts: "I started to return to intellectual health, but I could see the catastrophic elements in their work—I mean, the extent of their decadence. As I remember it, my interest was simply in the problem of the human personality, the disintegration of the personality. The ego. The 'I.' So it was rather personalistic criticism."[59] This may be the psychological truth, but the term "personalistic criticism" hardly seems appropriate. The problem of the ego was raised—and, supposedly, solved—in a manner indistinguishable from that of the most grotesque Soviet criticism of the period. Political pragmatism was all that counted. And the rules of conduct were defined—and continuously redefined—by the pronouncements of the collective (or, rather, individual) father.[60]

The only admissible literature was that of socialist realism, and Wat, if only because of his futurist training, perceived its handicaps acutely. One way out of the predicament was proposed by LEF. The Russian ex-futurists and ex-formalists who contributed to it pronounced the death of fiction (allegedly an outdated, nineteenth-century genre). In the new historical and social environment, it was to be replaced by a "literature of the fact"—that is, by reportage, sketches, feature stories, travelogues, memoirs, biographies, and so on. The concept was given a scholarly aura, first and foremost, by Victor Shklovsky. It looked tempting enough, since it encapsulated a growing trend in modern art. Yet it was supposed to minimize the danger of outright falsity and misrepresentation while allowing maintenance of a staunch prorevolutionary stance.

Wat's engagement with literature of the fact preceded his editorial activity, his "facto-montage" staged at the Poznań exhibition being a specimen of the genre. He had also produced, in *Literary News*, a comprehensive review of the Soviet book *The Literature of the Fact*, written by a group of critics that included Shklovsky and Mayakovsky's friend Osip Brik. Wat pointed out that the trend was by no means limited to the USSR, analogies being found in German *Neue Sachlichkeit*, French biographical novels, and even, up to a point, in that odious concoction *All Quiet on the Western Front*. Now, in the *Literary Monthly*, he started a veritable campaign to promote literature of the fact. Background was provided by two of his articles: "Reportage as a Literary Genre"[61] and "More on Reportage."[62]

Following Soviet theoreticians, Wat wrote that the opposition between fiction and fact was strictly historical. In the modern environment, a profound crisis in fiction was taking place, since the device of plot had become petrified, hence, ineffective. Modernists had attempted to resolve the dilemma by creating two kinds of plots: totally unrealistic, improbable plots or plots that imitate the capriciousness and fortuitousness of real-life events. (Here it should be noted that Wat had utilized extremes of both types in *Lucifer Unemployed*.)

Up to that point, Wat's reasoning (and that of his mentors) was sound; but now it took a new, ominous turn, with Wat maintaining that fiction as such was the product of the victorious bourgeoisie—and, consequently, was inherently contaminated by the bourgeois world view. Fiction's multiplicity of meanings and complexity of style provided a covert means for promoting the ideology of the class enemy. The remedy was literature of the fact, the proletarian form of art par excellence.[63] In literature of the fact, ideology supposedly assumed the role of traditional devices and stylistic conventions.[64]

Did this mean that the straightforward, honest description of facts was all that was demanded of the proletarian writer? Yes and no. It was still necessary to choose and juxtapose facts in order to obtain the required effect; but—more important—the choice, juxtaposition, and emphasis were to be determined by the correct ideology. Yet, the concept of fact itself remained somewhat vague: "One has to take into account something very important, namely, that the 'fact' is far from being fixed and simple, that it is a set of varying relations: therefore the writer who describes a certain fact or process, sees and describes a specific set of relations, and no others. A bourgeois writer, for example, would produce a completely different report or novel about a certain phenomenon than a proletarian writer."[65]

The dialectics went even further: "The members of LEF . . . distinguish between the fact as effect and the fact as defect, the friendly fact and the hostile fact. Choice, montage of the facts and their expedient arrangement—those are the fundamental requirements of the literature of the fact. Not every fact is good and suitable: here, the role of the ideology starts."[66]

The distinction between "friendly" and "hostile" facts opened the door to every imaginable distortion and false emphasis, thereby turning literature of the fact (in LEF's sense) into the worst kind of socialist realist fakery. The coup de grace for Soviet literature of the fact was wielded by the notorious *Stalin Canal: History of the Construction,*[67] product of a writers' outing to one of the dictator's favorite projects. The book, in Orwellian fashion, presented slave labor as a glorious exercise in creative work and the executioners as benevolent teachers. Among the authors who contributed to that incredible book were Maxim Gorky, Shklovsky, and Jasieński, the last of whom, with only five years left before his death in a prison camp, wrote part of a section entitled "To Deal the Final Blow to the Class Enemy."

A further paradox is evident here. In what amounted to a powerful display of historical irony, literature of the fact had its grand revival during the post-Stalin years. Gradually freeing itself from Orwellian discourse, it contributed significantly to the fall of the system it was designed to serve. Wat's *My Century,* together with Solzhenitsyn's *The Gulag Archipelago,* are among the most characteristic examples of that literature.

"I have to remind you," Wat once said to Miłosz, "that my enthusiasm for the reportage campaign was supported by a certain illusion: I believed that the working class would bring forth persons of natural gifts who would probably write something worthwhile."[68] In the USSR, there was a centrally promoted and supervised movement of *rabkors* (worker-correspondents), who were to produce a new socialist literature; but before long, it descended to the level of blunt political denunciations (which was probably the purpose for which the authorities called it forth in the first place). In Poland, where violations of workers' rights could be genuinely exposed, an analogous movement seemed to hold more promise.

For the education of prospective correspondents, Wat published in the *Literary Monthly* examples of professional reporting. He maintained contacts with the German journalist Egon Erwin Kisch and with the journal *New Masses* in New York.[69] Among the material that found its way into the *Literary Monthly* should be mentioned sketches by Agnes Smedley and Larisa Reisner, a Soviet writer of some stature. A competition was announced in the seventh issue, as a result of which: "I maintained an immense correspondence. . . . But as far as that new hope was concerned, it fell flat. The authors were teachers, sometimes officials, one starosta [governor], an enthusiast of the *Monthly,* who later came to me and said that as starosta he had had to use a pseudonym."[70]

If the goal of training a cadre of proletarian Polish authors was never achieved, some of the reportage published by Wat was not entirely devoid of value, and the censor (indifferent to furious articles pushing Communist dogma) felt obliged to intervene. The eighth issue was confiscated in its entirety, and subsequent issues, often as not, contained blank spots, where excised material had once been.

To make matters worse, the *Literary Monthly* became increasingly Stalinist. Indicative of this was the case of the Franco-Romanian writer Panait Istrati, one of whose books, *Massacre in the Desert*, Wat had translated. Supported by Barbussc and others, Istrati became an enthusiast of the Communist "transformation of life." But a short visit to the USSR was enough to disillusion him, and he expressed his disillusionment publicly. Soviet writers reacted by branding Istrati an enemy—in Wat's words, "a snake, a scorpion fed by their own breasts, and an agent of Siguranza [the Romanian secret police]."[71] Their attack was published in the *Literary Monthly*, which, in a show of solidarity with the Soviets, continued the defamatory campaign against Istrati in two further issues. By 1931, it was on its way to becoming a vehicle of the Soviet embassy.

The twelfth issue of the *Literary Monthly*, which was to give the results of reportage competition, was also confiscated. Moreover, Wat was advised by the district attorney that this second confiscation was tantamount to a final warning.[72] But curiously enough, Poland's laws provided an escape clause. The regulations of the old partitioning powers were still valid in the regions administered by the respective powers before Polish independence. Hence, an act constituting a misdemeanor in Warsaw (previously governed by Czarist Russia) did not necessarily constitute a misdemeanor in Kraków and Lwów (which were previously part of the Habsburg Empire) or in Poznań (previously part of Germany). Wat started to move the nominal seat of the editorial board between various cities, playing cat-and-mouse with the authorities (while he himself usually stayed in Warsaw). By this means, he was able to extend the life span of the journal to twenty issues.[73]

The temporary transfer of the journal to Lwów resulted in inter-ethnic collaboration. Lwów was an important center of Ukrainian culture. It was also the hub of the autonomous Communist party of western Ukraine. The idea of printing two simultaneous issues (a Ukrainian issue in Polish, a Polish issue in Ukrainian), thereby emphasizing the Communist solidarity of both nationalities, seemed natural enough.[74] Thus, the sixteenth issue of the *Literary Monthly* presented a small anthology of Ukrainian leftist writing. Wat's opinion of these works was far from positive, though the shaky Ukrainian of the Polish contributors to the issue may have been partly to blame. (One translator later confessed that he did not know any Ukrainian at all—though, strangely enough, the first time he read Blok's *The Twelve*, it was in the Ukrainian translation.[75]) This effort is worth mentioning, however, since ties with Ukrainian writers were to play a further role in Wat's life during his stay in Lwów under Soviet occupation in 1939–40.

Editorial activities became increasingly clandestine. Wat advised his collaborators to mail materials for the *Literary Monthly* not to its official address, but to "boxes." "The 'boxes' were far from being permanent; these were the addresses of people involved in party work who were caught red-handed more often than not, hence the necessity of frequent changes."[76] Clues for the rendezvous between correspondents and the editor were inserted inconspicuously into some of the reportages.[77] Such necessities provided a bit of spice, but they went against Wat's nature: he was unfit for conspiracy, and everyone knew it.

The *Literary Monthly* was only the most visible aspect of the Communist literary undertaking. The party had also established a legal publishing house called "Tom" (A Volume), which put out literature of various kinds, ranging from a booklet about contraception (a taboo topic in Catholic Poland) to Marxist classics.[78] Wat was one of the managers of "Tom," bringing his habitual overzealousness to all its activities.[79]

The reportage campaign was only one facet of the periodical's Sovietization. Other traits were reflected in its so-called internationalist stance. Contacts between writers of various countries were the order of the day—all the more so in Poland, whose culture had long suffered from provincialism. But Stalinist internationalism in literature meant simply the establishment of a world canon of "progressive" and "revolutionary" authors who unconditionally supported the meandering political course of the USSR. The activities of such international writers' organizations as the PEN Club were deemed hypocritical and harmful. In 1930, the International PEN Congress took place in Warsaw. In the ninth issue of the *Literary Monthly*, Wat, who never cancelled his membership in PEN, printed a ferocious though not terribly witty feuilleton entitled "Łosoś w majonezie, Liga Narodów i radosny cień króla Stasia" (Salmon in Mayonnaise, League of Nations and the Joyous Shadow of King Staś), in which he attacked the Congress in the typically Soviet style of "unmasking."[80]

A Communist response to the activities of PEN was provided by the International Conference of Revolutionary Writers, which took place in Kharkov (then capital of Soviet Ukraine) in November 1930. The conference attracted authors from twenty-two countries, including such left-wing luminaries as Louis Aragon, Johannes Becher, Michael Gold, and Anna Seghers. Jasieński, who had already emigrated to the USSR, played a leading role. Characteristically, the organizers sent their letter of invitation to the official address of the *Literary Monthly* by regular mail, with the result that even Wat, himself a bungling conspirator, was nonplussed by such blatant disregard for the rules.[81]

Since no one from the "group of Polish proletarian writers" connected with the *Literary Monthly* could go to Kharkov, "subject to circumstances beyond [their] control," this attempt to establish strict organizational ties with the Moscow-directed writers' movement fizzled. Nevertheless, the nineteenth issue of the journal was filled with materials from the conference, which doubtless furnished one more ground for police action.

The activity of the *Literary Monthly* that finally triggered repression was its protest against conditions in Polish jails. In the fifteenth issue, Wat had attempted to publish an open letter about the torture of Ukrainian political prisoners in the city of Łuck. "That was not an invention, there were real tortures, awful tortures. I knew about them firsthand from the sister of a tortured poetess. Nina Matulivna[82] came to Warsaw for that reason and told me the details. Moreover, I had a corroboration of the fact."[83] The censors forbade publication of the letter,[84] but in the twentieth issue, a forthcoming collective protest was announced in response to a circular promulgated by the Polish Minister of Justice, Czesław Michałowski, conferring on political prisoners the status of common criminals. Michałowski took it as a personal insult. To make matters worse, Wat planned to send the protest to foreign correspondents stationed in Poland, which was equivalent to "slandering Poland abroad."[85]

Of all the political activities of the *Literary Monthly,* this looked the most honest. Nevertheless, it was marked by more than a tinge of moral ambiguity. The man who exposed its double standard was, once again, Słonimski. "Słonimski said to me," Wat later wrote, "'Of course, I'd be glad to sign, but on condition that there's some mention of Soviet prisons.' . . . I remember clearly my amazement, my pain, even my contempt for that Słonimski, who would combine such things. Why couldn't he understand that it is one thing to imprison the enemies of freedom and another to put the defenders of freedom in prison? . . . I consider that distinction as one of my intellectual low points."[86]

Wat was to learn the falseness of his logic the hard way when he found himself in a Soviet prison, where the distinction between enemies of freedom and defenders thereof was irrelevant. (The unfortunate minister, Michałowski, was murdered by the Soviet secret police in 1939, without the slightest semblance of due process.) But that lay in the future. For now, Wat was cast into the first of the fourteen prisons in which he was to spend the most significant period of his life.[87]

The timing was unfortunate. On 23 July 1931 Ola gave birth to their only child, a boy named Andrzej. In late August or early September, released from the maternity clinic but still weak, she moved to her parents' five-room apartment on Żurawia Street. Wat went with her and on 10 September called a routine editorial meeting of the *Literary Monthly* there. At midnight, a large group of armed police entered the apartment. Six men were found in the living room: Broniewski, Hempel, Nowogródzki, Stawar, Wat, and Ola's brother, Ignacy Lew, a twenty-year-old medical student who had no connection with the Communist underground. All were arrested on the spot and put into a large cell (no. 13) in the basement of Warsaw Central Prison, together with a group of Jewish bakers, members of a Communist trade union.[88] Lew was released after a few weeks, but his health was affected, and he subsequently died of consumption in 1938, at the age of twenty-seven. Wat anticipated a five-year sentence at worst and worried mainly about Ola, the baby, and the ill-starred Ignacy.[89]

The yellow and right-wing press publicized the event extensively, presenting it as the unveiling of a major Comintern conspiracy and playing up the Jewish background of some of those arrested. The crimes imputed to Wat and his friends were publishing translations from the Soviet and German Communist press and promoting their views through "Tom"—activities that had never been concealed. Many of Wat's colleagues rushed to his defense. Słonimski published an article mocking reports that the editors of the *Literary Monthly* "disposed personally of huge sums of money," adding ironically: "I can tell you in secret, that Broniewski and Stawar bathed in gold. Broniewski recently bought twelve dozen 'Omega' golden watches."[90] Boy-Żeleński, a senior leftist, struck a more earnest note: "They have jailed several writers on charge of publishing—for two years—a Communist periodical (incidentally, very bourgeois in its tediousness) that was public and known to everybody including the censor. The orgy of ravings we read in the press the day after the arrest gives us a sample of the atmosphere in which the 'independent' judges would pass sentence, if the jury trial takes place. In Lwów, these writers would be sentenced to hang at least."[91]

A taste of the experience has been preserved not only in Wat's memoirs but also in Broniewski's poem "Magnitogorsk albo rozmowa z Janem" (Magnitogorsk, or A Talk with Jan), which was widely anthologized in postwar Poland. The narrator of the poem (essentially a short story in verse) describes his circumstances, employing the careless, ironical intonation that was Broniewski's trademark:

> I sit with Jan in the thirteenth cell
> in the Town Hall, downtown.
> They took us both three days ago,
> put into jail, keep there, that'll do.
>
> Sleeping on the floor is less than comfortable,
> they gave us soup, unfit for a dog,
> Jan is protected by a chain-mail of dialectics,
> I—by a light cloud of poetry.
>
> Stench, insects, heavy snoring . . .
> Well, such things happen in life.
> Somebody scrawled on the wall with a piece of coal:
> "Long live the bakers' struggle!"

The titular Jan, a man "with a stomach ulcer, and nearing fifty," was Hempel. In the poem's denouement, Jan effected a catharsis for his companion in distress through his words: "You know, two blast furnaces are being fired today in Magnitogorsk." The words were indeed pronounced by Hempel— Wat, who is never mentioned in the poem, also heard them[92]—and their vivifying effect was far from Broniewski's invention. The USSR was still perceived as the proletarian Promised Land, and its industrialization was supposedly bringing near the golden age of no hunger and no prisons.

Bourgeois Poland, however, ensured some benefits unheard of in the Soviet Union. Wat was allowed to see Ola frequently. He also received packages from her containing herrings, with letters hidden in the fishes' heads.[93] At an arranged hour, Ola would approach the prison wall from the street, and Aleksander would communicate with her in sign language.[94]

For Wat, his imprisonment became the rite de passage he had been longing for. He was fascinated by the valiant behavior of his friends and flattered himself with the thought that he was not necessarily inferior to them. Nor did the prison experience last too long. By the beginning of November, Broniewski was already free.[95] Hempel got out probably in the middle of November. According to Wat, he was released on condition that he go to Russia, and the party agreed to it.[96] In May 1932, Hempel joined his old associates Jasieński and Wandurski, whose unenviable fate he was to share. Stawar, Nowogródzki, and Wat remained in prison a bit longer, but finally a fake medical certificate was arranged for Wat, stating that he needed treatment for a heart problem.[97] He then rejoined Ola in her parents' apartment, having spent approximately three months in the Polish jail.

The years between Wat's first imprisonment and World War II were the least striking—although, in a sense, the most momentous—in his life. After his boisterous futurist youth and awkward apprenticeship in the Communist underground, Wat established himself as a rank-and-file member of the cultural community. He found a job at the publishing house of Gebethner and Wolff, a reputable company founded in 1857, which published mainly post-Romantic Polish writers and for many years enjoyed a virtual monopoly in the field. The head of the company, Jan Stanisław Gebethner, himself a pious Catholic and later, in 1938, a right-wing Member of Parliament,[98] may have had his doubts about Wat but soon recognized his gifts and energy. In 1932, Wat was made editor of the advertising bulletin and in 1933 was promoted to the key post of director of the publishing department.

The dynamic spirit Wat introduced into the work of Gebethner and Wolff helped to revive public interest in some of the Polish classics.[99] Thanks to his literary connections, he also attracted to the house most contemporary authors of any stature. His duties consisted mainly in reading, evaluating, and correcting manuscripts and giving writers advice. Of this work, he wrote: "Incidentally, I liked the work very much—to analyze the manuscript in such a way that, you know, one catches the thread and when one pulls it, all the pieces go apart. That is, one catches the thread and then analyzes. Therefore I did it all the time with all the authors, though I never forced anything on anyone. . . . I argued, I talked and explained a lot and went page by page, sometimes sentence by sentence, but as a matter of principle, if the author jibbed after my argumentation, I supposed that he was probably right, even if he wasn't."[100]

The writers Wat worked with included many of his friends, like Iwaszkiewicz, and a considerable number of new authors, whom Wat managed to furnish with a literary niche. They all frequented Wat's apartment, and most of them struck up friendships with him that lasted many years. One of the new acquaintances was the brilliant and idiosyncratic Bruno Schulz.[101] Another was an avowed Communist named Leon Kruczkowski, for whom Wat secured a contract, enabling him to quit his teacher's job and become a full-time writer.[102] Wat made only one blunder while working for Gebethner and Wolff, it seems; but it concerned a major talent, Witold Gombrowicz. This is strange, given that Gombrowicz followed, to some extent, in Wat's footsteps. His novel, which had the untranslatable title *Ferdydurke* (1938), was a grotesque book that thoroughly demolished the stereotypes of Polish culture. It interested Wat, but he did not like its striking originality and therefore did not fight for it; the novel was eventually published by another company.[103]

During this time, Wat all but stopped writing. Between 1933 and 1939, a few translations were all that appeared under his name: two books by Ehrenburg, the first volume of *Young Henry of Navarre* by Heinrich Mann, and *The False Weight* by Joseph Roth.

For some time after his release, Wat probably remained involved in underground work. A conspiratorial trip to Berlin appears to have been planned, though it was never realized.[104] The party intended to launch a new official periodical, a successor to the *Literary Monthly,* to be directed by Wat and Stawar but edited nominally by people who had not been "burned." But it never got off the ground, although conspiratory contacts, more often than not with the top level of the KPP, continued at least until 1936.[105] Wat also belonged to a Communist front organization, the League of Human and Civil Rights, from 1931 to its disbanding in 1938, though his participation in its activities seems to have been minimal.[106]

Naturally, Wat's name remained in the police files.[107] To make matters worse, Wat displayed his leftist convictions ostentatiously: he was the only person employed by Gebethner and Wolff who took part in the May Day demonstrations (a habit he discarded in Communist Poland).[108] Hence, the label "Communist agitator" stuck to him, resulting in petty—though not necessarily groundless—harassment. In her book, Ola supplies some interesting details:

> From time to time, they came to search us, in particular before the First of May. I remember these searches as not brutal, as they are usually described—

throwing books on the floor, disemboweling drawers, etc. The people who did the search often became engrossed in specific books, displaying a real interest in them, to such a degree that I sometimes forgot what was going on, and proposed to them to sit down, even to have a cup of tea. . . . I remember a search in the presence of Stawar. He stood close to the bookshelves and after a certain moment ceased to move completely. I even got angry at him, since he impeded the work, and told him to sit down somewhere. He just gave me an irritated glance—I did not understand what the matter was. Only when the cops left, did he scold me. It turned out that he had been standing on a certain dangerously illegal document—I do not remember which one—and held tight, pretending to observe the work of the police. We commended him for that very much.[109]

The Seventh Congress of the Comintern in 1935 adopted the program of the so-called Popular Front, which meant a partial revision of the earlier Stalinist doctrine: the enmity toward Social Democrats and other leftist groups was replaced by a tactical alliance. The program was never implemented in Poland, and it proved to be short-lived elsewhere. Yet it left some traces in Polish cultural life and in Wat's political biography. In October 1935, an appeal entitled "Za porozumieniem" (For Concord) was published, calling for an alliance between left-oriented and liberal authors in their struggle "for freedom of speech, for writer's independence" and "in defence of progress, peace and culture."[110] Wat signed the appeal, together with Broniewski, Kruczkowski, Putrament, Ważyk, and others, including a rising star of socialist realist literature, Wanda Wasilewska, who was later to play a role in his life—and in the lives of many others—as a particularly influential member of the Polish and Soviet Communist establishment. Moreover, according to his memoirs, Wat was one of four coauthors of the appeal's text.[111]

"For Concord" followed the precepts of the Congress of Writers in Defence of Culture held in Paris in June–July 1935 and attended by such celebrities as André Gide, André Malraux, and Boris Pasternak. The Congress was, in all probability, the brainchild of the non-Stalinist wing of the Soviet Communist party headed by Bukharin and supported by Gorky. Although Louis Aragon was formally the initiator of the entire enterprise, its moving spirit was Ehrenburg.[112] The avowedly anti-Fascist character of the Congress and the general breadth and vagueness of its program made it acceptable to a multitude of writers of democratic persuasion. Wat felt able to support its line, though by the following year, his doubts were strong enough to keep him from attending the Congress of Cultural Workers in Lwów—a Polish replica of the Paris meeting.[113]

Wat was considered a dangerous Communist, a member of the *żydokomuna,* to the very end of the interwar period. According to extant document listing alleged subversives who must be arrested in the event of war, Wat figured on a par with Broniewski and Wasilewska,[114] even if the confusion generated by the Nazi attack prevented the plan from being implemented.

In fact, Wat's connections with the party loosened every year, for several reasons: the natural cautiousness of a man who had undergone the ordeal of imprisonment and felt responsible not only for himself but for his wife and child as well; the less-than-favorable opinion of party functionaries, who never ceased to regard Wat as no more than a fellow-traveler; and, last but not least, a steadily growing disenchantment with Communist dogma and praxis. Wat's change of heart probably started with the rise of Hitler. He had enough acumen to perceive that Stalinist policy toward Hitler in the early 1930s was not only wrong but insane. In his Popular Front activities, he was driven mainly by anti-Nazi sentiment.[115]

Several of Wat's Marxist friends adopted an anti-Stalinist position, the most influential of whom, Isaac Deutscher, was expelled from the KPP in 1932 as a Trotskyite. Wat fell out with him, since at that time he still considered it unfair to attack Soviet Russia.[116] The story of Stawar was more complex. The demystifying passion so characteristic of Stawar drove him into open conflict with the party—and, since he was also critical of Trotsky (whom he nevertheless preferred to Stalin), into total isolation. In 1934–36, he edited a radically Marxist—and heretical—magazine named *Pod Prąd* (Against the Stream), writing at that time under the pen name Pawel Trestka. Wat confessed that he would probably have contributed to Stawar's periodical had it survived longer.[117] Stawar did his best to remain an orthodox Marxist-Leninist—the *only* orthodox Marxist-Leninist, in his opinion—whereas Wat started to entertain suspicions concerning the whole ideological framework so dear to his friend. In any event, Wat's association with Stawar was fraught with consequences: it may even have contributed to his arrest by the Soviets.[118]

The next stage in Wat's inner development came in 1937–38, the years of the Great Purge. During that period, around five thousand Polish Communists perished in the USSR,[119] in addition to millions of Russians, Ukrainians, and others. Hempel, Jasieński, and many others close to Wat were among Stalin's victims, and Wat knew it. All attempts to discuss the purges with Communist friends and acquaintances led nowhere. There were several standard answers, including the most typical and most frustrating: "People at the top know better." At the same time, the mortal danger represented by Hitler and the weakness of Western democracies in the face of this threat were becoming increasingly obvious. Imperialist and semi-Fascist traits in Polish politics continued to develop, as the ruling circles followed the dubious example of totalitarian powers. This resulted in comically petty, but unsavory, practices: for example, in March 1938, Poland threatened the small neighboring country of Lithuania, demanding political concessions, which were granted. The Jewish community was subjected to discrimination, much milder than in Nazi Germany but humiliating nonetheless.

During the 1920s and early 1930s, Jews (who comprised around 10 percent of Poland's population) felt integrated into society. True, anti-Semitic attitudes remained widespread, but almost half the country's lawyers and doctors were Jewish, and writers of Jewish background such as Tuwim and Słonimski succeeded in building brilliant careers. But now the number of Jewish students in the universities became limited by law, and they were harassed in classes. Jan Gebethner was forced to hire a non-Jewish literary historian as official director of the publishing department, though Wat continued to work under his cover.[120] Even more threatening was public encouragement of anti-Semitism in everyday life. Little Andrzej Wat was infected by the voice of the common people, insisting to Ola that Jews were awful, ugly, and dirty. When Aleksander explained to him that Ola was Jewish, Andrzej answered: "Well, I would love her more if she were not a Jewess."[121]

Such incidents and the growing threat of war led the family to consider emigration. Supposedly, there was a possibility of going to the United States and establishing a small Polish publishing house there. But it came to nought.[122] The mood of impending doom was exacerbated by the deaths of Ignacy Lew and Wat's mother and by the terminal illness of Mendel Michał Chwat. A few lines in *My Century* say it all: "Sadness and the certainty that terrible things were going to happen. In general, and to me. Not death, but horrendous experiences that would make the living envy the dead."[123]

7

Prison and Kazakhstan, 1939–1946

The Wat family spent part of the summer of 1939 at Jastarnia, a Polish spa on the Baltic Sea, not far from Gdańsk, then the German-speaking free city of Danzig, which was to provide Hitler with an excuse for starting World War II. They returned to Warsaw at the end of July. The mood in the capital was tense, although most of its inhabitants did not foresee the scope of forthcoming events. The Molotov-Ribbentrop Pact of 23 August had put the USSR on the side of Nazi Germany, but no one among Wat's immediate acquaintances—nor, it seems, among Polish politicians—was aware of its secret protocols, which outlined a division of Eastern Europe into German and Soviet spheres of influence and a new partitioning of Poland.

When the first bombs of World War II fell, on 1 September, they brought a paradoxical sense of relief: the long wait had ended. But panic spread rapidly. On 6 September, Wat's brother-in-law Jerzy Gilewicz told him that he was fleeing the city and had two extra seats in his car. Aleksander destroyed part of his library, and Ola tore in pieces one of his letters for fear that it might fall into the wrong hands. As they walked to Gilewicz's house, the Nazi bombers struck, and the family sought shelter in a church. They left Warsaw without any belongings except for a fur, which they later exchanged for a modicum of food.[1]

The journey was a nightmare. The car headed southeast, in the general direction of Lwów, which was considered a safer place; but the roads were bad, the heat exhausting, and fuel scarce. They could travel only at night, since German bombers controlled the sky during the day. Many thousands of refugees were fleeing in the same direction, among them Witkacy, who committed suicide in a small Belorussian village on 18 September, after getting word that Soviets had struck from the east, and that there was nowhere else to go.[2]

On the eve of the Soviet invasion, Wat accidentally became separated from his family. He spent the early chaotic days of the Soviet occupation in the Western Ukrainian city of Łuck, where he distributed hundreds of cards with his address along with a desperate plea for information regarding his wife and child. In this way, the new authorities became aware of his identity.[3] He was persona non grata to all the powers around: the Polish government (now in disarray and fleeing to Romania) considered him subversive; the Nazis would have destroyed him and his family without ado, if not as Communists, then as Jews; and the fate of his former friends who had emigrated to the Soviet Union before the war had given him sufficient warning about his own chances in Stalin's empire.

Still, the Wats survived the first days of the new regime virtually unscathed. Ola and Andrzej were first in the small town of Dubno, where Ola experienced more tribulations than Aleksander; but by the end of September she and Andrzej were in the relative safety of Lwów, where Aleksander soon joined them.

Russian troops invaded Poland on the seventeenth day of the war, encountering little resistance. Stalin allowed his Nazi ally to crush the core of the Polish forces—and to take the brunt of the blame for the aggression. The eastern frontier of the country had been left virtually undefended. Soviet propaganda presented the invasion as "the liberation of Western Ukraine and Western Belorussia," which, left to their fate by the defeated Polish government, had welcomed Stalin's troops as rescuing them from a foreign yoke (as well as from the vagaries of a European war).

Nor was this without some basis in fact. There were indeed Ukrainians (and, to a lesser degree, Belorussians) who attacked Polish detachments and welcomed the Soviet tanks. The Jewish population, quite substantial in these regions, preferred Stalin to Hitler—and, often as not, to their former, notoriously anti-Semitic rulers. In the chaos that reigned, even certain Polish officers considered the Soviets the "lesser evil," as fellow Slavs who were perhaps coming as allies in the war against Germany. All these illusions proved to be short-lived, but only after they had had their day.[4]

Most historians agree that the atmosphere in the Soviet-occupied part of Poland was, at first, less stifling than that in the Western part seized by the Nazis. The invaders, far from behaving as *Herrenvolk*, seemed to be confused and intimidated. More threatening was the behavior of some of the local inhabitants, who, after the collapse of state authority, decided to settle accounts with their former superiors, often resorting to violence. The establishment of a Soviet administration on the local level curtailed the most flagrant excesses and brought some seemingly positive developments, such as full employment, free education, promotion of the local language, and removal of restrictions on people of Ukrainian and Jewish stock. But the repressive nature of the regime became increasingly obvious. To begin with, fear was the outcome of a general unrest; now, it became an ever-present element of settled, everyday life. The Stalinist police (known at that period as the NKVD) seemed to be the only efficient organization around. People were arrested either systematically, by social category (landowners, factory owners, members of various prewar parties, and so on), or at random, in order to instill into people a feeling of helplessness in the face of the state machine.[5]

Everyone, from Molotov to the average street agitator, repeated the stock phrase "There will be no Poland." The Polish state was judged to have been illegal from the beginning—the result of an oversight now happily corrected through its obliteration from the map. Polish speakers automatically became second-class citizens. The secret protocol affixed to the German-Soviet Boundary and Friendship Treaty signed in Moscow on 28 September unequivocally stated: "Both parties will tolerate in their territories no Polish agitation which affects the territories of the other party. They will suppress in their territories all beginnings of such agitation and inform each other concerning suitable measures for this purpose."[6]

On 4 October, a Soviet-style election campaign was launched. A rally in Lwów was addressed by, among others, Nikita Khrushchev, at that time First Secretary of the Ukrainian Communist party. The elections took place, on 22 October. The general consensus was that neither voting nor non-voting could influence the results: hence the majority performed the ritual task simply to avoid trouble. The outcome of the elections was the establishment of the People's Assemblies of the Western Ukraine and Western Belorussia, which promptly requested the merger of their lands with the respective Soviet republics. In November, the Polish government-in-exile reestablished itself in France, headed by General Władysław Sikorski. Most Poles in the occupied country pledged their allegiance to this body, which took the position that Poland should be restored within its prewar (if not more favorable) borders.

Occupied Lwów has been described by several writers who were there at the same time as the Wats. Adolf Rudnicki depicted it in a story entitled "Wielki Stefan Koniecki" (The Great Stefan Koniecki). Written and published during the Stalin years and therefore subject to self-censorship, the story nevertheless conveys a sense of extreme confusion and insecurity under Soviet rule:

> The city was reminiscent of an Oriental bazaar; at every turn, one met *bieżency* [refugees] in grotesque clothes, but those weird garments attracted nobody's eye, and similarly the tales of that recent September attracted nobody's ear. . . . No one exhibited any interest in personal biographies: only world history seemed worthy of attention. . . . After nightfall, when the streets emptied, the refugees lay in their rooms—overcrowded like bathhouses and swollen with beds and mattresses—with radio-sets, listening to the voice of history. . . . "Nothing is happening," they said to each other, stricken with horror.[7]

The refugees included a number of artists and public figures: Boy-Żeleński, Broniewski, Chwistek, Daszewski, Peiper, Przyboś, Putrament, Stern, Wasilewska, and Ważyk, as well as Rudnicki. They belonged mainly to the left wing of prewar Polish society, albeit with some exceptions. Thus, the critic Ostap Ortwin, who was definitely anti-Communist, continued his duties as head of the local Union of Polish Writers.[8] But as early as the end of September, a Ukrainian socialist realist, Oleksandr Korneichuk, arrived from Kiev with the express task of organizing a Soviet-style literary life in the city.

Wat chaired the first meeting of Polish leftist writers with Korneichuk,[9] his repute as a pro-Communist playing a role in his being awarded that dubious distinction. On 13 October, a larger gathering took place. Although the fate of Lwów and the surrounding region was technically still in limbo, Korneichuk asserted that it had already been sealed: "After elections to the Ukrainian National Assembly, after the nationalization of land and banks, after the incorporation of the [Western] Ukraine into the USSR, then we can start reorganization of the Writers' Union."[10]

Several Soviet writers and artists visited Lwów with Korneichuk. One of them was Shklovsky, whose work Wat knew well, although he had never seen him before; another was Pavlenko, whose work had featured in the *Literary Monthly* as the epitome of Soviet literature of the fact. (A person of ill fame, Pavlenko was held by many to be responsible for Mandelstam's death.[11]) Wat also met Semen Kirsanov, a minor futurist and a member of LEF. Most if not all of the visiting writers were in uniform, having been assigned military rank as war correspondents.[12] The meetings provided the Poles with countless opportunities for horrifying insights into the Soviet mentality. Thus, Polish writers used to refer matter-of-factly, if naively, to arrested "nonpersons," such as Jasieński or Pilnyak. "At the mention of any of these names the casual Soviet interlocutor would blanch with terror. . . . Therefore we soon ceased to mention any name, just to be on the safe side, at least for the time being."[13]

By 20 October, the organizational committee of the Writers' Union (the so-called *Orgkomitet* or *Komorg*) was already operating. Wat was a member of its board, together with Boy-Żeleński, Broniewski, and Wasilewska.[14] The spacious palace of Count Bielski was given by the Soviet authorities to the *Orgkomitet*. The count continued to live on the second floor of the palace, treating the newcomers as his personal guests. In a conversation with Boy-Żeleński, the count supposedly expressed his joy that the property had been presented to writers, since he had been afraid that the Bolsheviks would transform it into a stable. (Later, Count Bielski was deported to Kazakhstan. He did not survive the war.)[15]

Before the *Orgkomitet* was set up (and perhaps before Korneichuk's arrival), a Soviet newspaper in Polish, *Czerwony Sztandar* (The Red Banner) was founded. Today, it is a bibliographic rarity. It merits attention, however, as the first—and almost the only—Polish newspaper to employ immaculate Stalinist newspeak.[16] The vocabulary and syntax of almost every sentence were formulaic: for example, "The working people of the Western Ukraine, having languished for several decades under the yoke of Polish landowners and capitalists, can take only one decision. With pride and joy, they declare their desire to live under the sun of Stalin's Constitution, in the united family of happy Soviet people!"[17] The Sovietization of style extended to rules for spelling. Thus, the names of Goethe and Dickens were given in Latin letters, but according to Russian transcription, as Gete and Dikens. A prominent place was assigned to Hitler's speeches and to the pacifist musings of an English writer introduced as "Bernard Szou." Gradually, the *Red Banner* enticed into the ranks of its contributors more than one Polish writer living in Lwów.

Wat took an active part in the cultural life of the Sovietized city. On 19 November, he put his signature to the declaration "Polish Writers Hail the Unification of the Ukraine," which unequivocally supported the annexation of Lwów and the surrounding region to the USSR. (Among the signatories were Broniewski, Boy-Żeleński, Ważyk, and several lesser known figures.)[18] To Polish patriots, this amounted to high treason.

Another source concerning the moral climate in Lwów at the time, an autobiographical novel by Julian Stryjkowski published in 1980 also sheds light on Wat. During the first Soviet occupation, Stryjkowski was in Lwów as a budding leftist critic and essayist. His novel—under the appropriate title *Wielki strach* (*The Great Fright*)—was first printed in an underground journal, the express goal of which was to overcome Communist censorship.[19] The principal character, Artur, meets one of the contributors to the *Red Banner* in the newspaper's office: "A head rose. It had large, black, heavy eyes, bushy eyebrows, crooked nose and thick lips. The eyes looked at Artur suspiciously, and as if a shadow of a smile appeared on the downcast, scared face. A dark cloak hung on his shoulders, although it was warm."[20] The man, obviously expecting the worst, is Wat.[21] Later, this same "famous writer with bushy eyebrows and bent head on stiff neck" appears in the proofreaders' room, where his informal talk about literature conforms only too well to the party line:

> —The times of Khlebnikov are over. . . . In twenty years, maybe more, talents greater than Pushkin will explode. A golden age of poetry will come. The new poetry will conquer the whole world and will pave the road for our ideology. In the beginning was the word.
> —And Mayakovsky?
> The famous writer became thoughtful and put his finger to a highly raised eyebrow.
> —Was it an unhappy love?—asked Robert.
> —I don't know.
> —An act of despair?
> —As any suicide. Esenin . . .
> —I have in mind the reality . . . disillusionment . . .
> —There are no proofs.

—Pasternak? Mandelstam?
—The defeated past.[22]

It is clear enough that the writer described by Stryjkowski is wearing a mask, although it does not help him much—ten pages later, he is arrested.

Wat maintained that his behavior was motivated by fear—not so much for himself as for his family. His memoirs testify not only to "the great fright" but to a profound sense of alienation and remorse as well: "I would say that those few weeks in Lwów were the most disgusting period of my life. . . . I knew that they would arrest me, that Ola and Andrzej would go under. I was trembling in my boots. I pretended that, yes, I had regained my faith in communism. I did not harm anyone. On the contrary. And I wrote no poetry about Stalin."[23] This last self-justification may sound pathetic; but for Wat, as for more than one other person under Soviet rule, glorifying Stalin constituted the ultimate in moral degradation.

The line between collaboration and resistance was in fact tenuous and blurred. There were as many variants of behavior as there were people. Thus, Ważyk espoused the Communist cause with a blind faith that made his repudiation of Marxist ideology after 1956 all the more poignant. Broniewski could not cope with the fact that his beloved Red Army, instead of helping Poland, had become an ally of the Wehrmacht: he drank heavily, made ironical remarks, and wrote anti-Nazi poems that could not get past the censor.[24] Boy-Żeleński, by contrast, simply did his best to continue his scholarly work.[25]

A special case was Wanda Wasilewska, whose loyalty did not waver in the slightest after the clash with Soviet reality. She succeeded in establishing personal contacts with Stalin, who liked her literary work, and his henchmen, including Khrushchev, which made her into "the grande dame" of the regime. As such, she sometimes used her influence to help people, although she did much harm as well.[26] She married Korneichuk and remained in the USSR after the war; she was reluctant to return to Poland, since people there, not without justification, considered her a traitor of the first rank.

Wat's memoirs testify to a certain ambivalence toward his new circumstances. True, life was gray, ragged, and shabby: but its very hardness made it preferable, in some way, to the grotesque, theatrical life of the immediate prewar years: "As a matter of fact, one had the impression that it is Asia, it is something horrible, but real indeed. . . . Here, it's terrible, it's dirty, it's lousy, it is tarred, but such is earth, such is actual life, such is actual reality, such is being. *Condition humaine*. One had that feel."[27]

Certain elements of the new life could be construed as positive. Whereas the old Union of Writers in Lwów was strictly Polish, the new one accepted Poles, Ukrainians, and Yiddish writers on an equal basis (while of course requiring absolute loyalty to the regime). The Ukrainian members made a favorable impression overall, and memoirists of the period are unanimous in their praise of Stepan Tudor and Oleksandr Havryliuk, two leftist authors who may have been second-rate talents but struck many as singularly worthy human beings.[28] Tudor went so far as to challenge Khrushchev on behalf of the Poles murdered by self-styled "people's avengers" in the countryside.[29] (Both Tudor and Havryliuk were subsequently killed by a Nazi bomb on the first day of the German-Soviet war.)

The diplomatic stance of Korneichuk, Pavlenko, and others helped, for a while, to maintain the illusion that tolerable conditions for creative work might be guaranteed. In the words of one eyewitness, Pavlenko "assured that it is not only allowed, but even appropriate, and necessarily so, to preserve the organic unity and to continue the development of traditional topics and styles of Polish literature."[30] Like many others, Wat may have taken such assurances at face value. There were hopes that the Soviets might create in Lwów a center of Polish anti-Nazi activities, a "cultural Piedmont" that would serve as a model for a future Poland liberated from Hitler. Wat and Broniewski were naive enough to present the project of a "cultural Piedmont" to Pavlenko, of all people. Naturally, he treated them as madmen.[31] In 1939-40, the Soviets did not have the slightest intention of either condoning anti-fascism or recreating Poland in any shape or form. The project of a "new Socialist Poland" received official support only after the start of the German–Soviet war—and, by then, it had lost all connection with Lwów.

On 25 November the *Red Banner* advised its readers that "Aleksander Wat is preparing a volume of short stories on political prisoners and his recent war experiences."[32] This was undoubtedly pure invention, promulgated for the sake of buying time. Wat joined the staff of the newspaper but, according to *My Century*, worked there for only six or seven weeks (that is, in December 1939 and January 1940). The items in the *Red Banner* signed by Wat were diverse: he commented on the autobiographical manuscript of a female worker in Lwów,[33] and wrote about links between Lwów writers and Soviet literary organizations[34] and about a former political prisoner delegated to a trade union congress in Moscow.[35] One article described a meeting in a factory, which, naturally, sent a congratulatory telegram to Comrade Stalin.[36] An essay on Lwów was also published in *Literaturnaia Gazeta* in Moscow.[37] The editors, without notifying Wat, apparently made certain crucial changes, thus rendering his language perfectly Soviet (a practice typical of the period).[38]

By a certain stretch of the imagination, one might view articles in a Soviet newspaper as a direct continuation of the reportage campaign of the early 1930s. But this would be a delusion. It was impossible to maintain any artistic and moral standards in the Stalinist press. The sin of lying was committed passively, by adopting the prescribed discourse and erasing inconvenient facts. There were also other problems peculiar to the work of a Soviet journalist, some of them quite incredible. The most responsible position held by Wat was that of proof-reader. And a responsible position it was, since an error in one letter was considered a punishable offense. Unfortunately, the name of Stalin could easily be distorted to "Sralin"—that is, "Shitlin." Such a misprint was a *lèse majesté* of the first rank and might lead to the death penalty for the proofreader, as well as for the typesetter.[39] The constant search for that error proved to be too much for Wat's nerves, and he resigned the proofreader's job.[40]

The office of the *Red Banner* was flooded with anonymous letters, in which the authors expressed their opinions of the regime without undue courtesy. Showing a letter to a higher authority meant collaboration with the secret police, whereas throwing it out was fraught with consequences, since it could have been forged by the NKVD in order to test the loyalty of the staff.[41]

Another nerve-racking experience was the mandatory public interrogation by a group of party functionaries, called "self-criticism," of every employee of the editorial office about his or her past. Wat passed the exam with flying colors, but at the expense of a virtually split personality.[42]

Under Soviet occupation, Lwów became a textbook case of the gradual atomization of society, as former voluntary organizations and associations were banned, traditional groups dispersed, and all natural human ties broken. The variegated, multilevel loyalties that constituted the framework of civic society were to be replaced by a single loyalty to the state. The suppression of traditional ideologies, savage censorship, official lies, and, not least, the militant atheism of the authorities contributed to the general feeling of loneliness and alienation. The very concept of law and order collapsed, and in the resulting chaos, hun-dreds, if not thousands, of people pursued private interests and squared personal accounts by denunciations and collaboration with the NKVD.[43]

The first series of searches and arrests took place in the middle of October; the second, a veritable witch hunt, followed in the middle of November. At that time, the following maxim was already making the rounds in Lwów and its vicinity: "In the Soviet Union there are only three categories of people—those who were in prison, those who are in prison, and those who will be in prison."[44] The third wave of repression struck in January 1940. It was followed by four mass deportations, in February, April, and June 1940 and June 1941, the last of which was interrupted, on 22 June, by the Nazi invasion, greeted as liberation by many people.[45]

Wat fell victim to the third wave. From his dealings with the interrogator in Lubyanka, he concluded that there had been a decision to arrest a certain number of Polish leftist writers, but that the composition of the group was "rather a matter of chance."[46] The circumstances of the arrest were nothing short of bizarre. Both Wat and Ola insisted that the agent provocateur who arranged the arrest was Władysław Daszewski. This cannot be proved, however.[47] At that time, Daszewski worked at the central Lwów theater. An eyewitness remembers him as supervisor of a group of painters who produced innumerable portraits of Stalin and his military commissars: "[The portraits were] as big as houses, as mustachioed as scarabs, as smooth as vaseline. Byzantine icons in green, red and gold of the marshals' full-dress coats."[48] Daszewski threw a party at a restaurant, to which some of Wat's former friends were also invited. The ill-fated party took place on 23 January. At a certain moment Daszewski, playing the role of host, introduced a stranger, supposedly a Soviet art historian or theater critic eager for a friendly talk with the Poles. But almost immediately the newcomer started a brawl, whereupon a group of NKVD agents burst into the room. Wat was struck, and he fainted. Daszewski escaped unhindered by the police, but most of the other men were placed in NKVD vans that were waiting outside the restaurant, and driven to the Zamarstynów prison.[49]

Among the writers who were arrested were Broniewski, Peiper, Stern, Wat, and a peasant poet named Wojciech Skuza. On the same night, the NKVD visited the apartments of several more writers, their arrest furnishing further proof that the episode in the restaurant was far from accidental. In sum, approximately twenty Polish men and women of letters were imprisoned.[50] Stern was released within a few months, but Skuza died in a prison camp.

On 26 January, the *Red Banner* published an article under the unambiguous heading "Zgnieść gadzinę nacjonalistyczną" (To Crush the Nationalist Viper), signed by W. Kolski, which portrayed the arrested writers as inveterate enemies of the people. Broniewski was described as a reactionary and a worshiper of Piłsudski, Peiper as an author of degenerate bourgeois poetry, and Wat as a Trotskyite.[51] For the families and friends of those imprisoned, this was authoritative confirmation that their release was out of the question.

Wat spent several months in Zamarstynów prison in appalling conditions. A cautious estimate reveals that during the Soviet occupation of 1939–41, Polish prisons were filled to about five times their original capacity.[52] Thus Wat shared a thirty-eight-square-foot cell with twenty-eight other inmates of various backgrounds.[53] To make matters worse, the winter of 1940 was unusually severe, and the spring turned out to be unbearably hot.[54]

In 1931, when Wat and his friends had landed in a Polish jail, an impressive public action had been undertaken on their behalf. This time, no such action was possible. The only imaginable (and requested) response was immediate condemnation of the imprisoned, in the manner of Kolski. According to Michał Borwicz, two writers, one of whom was Putrament, started collecting signatures to a declaration censuring the victims.[55] Refusal to sign it became the only conceivable manifestation of civic courage.[56]

Fortunately, help from family was not yet forbidden, even if it was far more difficult than in prewar Poland. Ola and Maria Zarębińska, wife of Broniewski, were able to find out their husbands' whereabouts and were allowed to send them food and a change of underwear. On the dirty underwear that was returned, Ola found stains of Aleksander's blood and also lice: "Lice that tormented him and yet cohabited with him, stayed with him so recently, fed on his blood. Well, I was touched."[57]

There was no question of seeing the prosecutor or consulting a lawyer, however. The wives' main concern was their husbands' survival. Nor did the Writers' Union provide any help. Ola witnessed one gesture of solidarity, nevertheless, when she was approached by a man unknown to her, who secretly gave her a thousand rubles, saying that he was confident the money would be returned after Wat's release. He was a cabaret musician who had known Wat in Warsaw.[58]

Wasilewska told Ola and other prisoners' wives that an error had been made which would doubtless be corrected, and that their husbands would return home. She pulled some of the levers accessible to her and even went to Khrushchev, who happened to be in Lwów at the time. But Khrushchev advised her, in his typically rough manner, to mind her own business.[59]

By that time, Ola's own fate had already been decided. On the night of 13–14 April 1940, several armed soldiers entered her apartment, giving her and Andrzej fifteen minutes to pack. This was the second mass deportation of Poles from occupied regions. The freight cars with the deportees stood on a side-track for three days. Those inside included all kinds of people, from a milkmaid to scholars, officers, aristocrats, and the wife of Lwów's mayor. Some of them suspected Ola of being an NKVD spy; others were anti-Semitic. The agonizing journey to an unknown destination lasted three weeks. Finally, they reached a small group of mud huts inhabited by Kazakh herdsmen. This was their assigned place of life and work: the state farm "Red Cattle-Breeder" in Ivanovka, less than two hundred miles from the Chinese border.[60]

If the year 1940 was one of the most sinister in recorded history, it was particularly disastrous for the citizens of prewar Poland. The Wat family shared the fate of innumerable others. In western Ukraine and western Belorussia, there were probably as many as 150,000 people imprisoned at any one time.[61] Mass deportations from the region took a much larger toll, approximately a million and a half people.[62] In May 1940, several thousand Polish prisoners of war, almost all of them officers, were shot by the NKVD in Katyń forest near Smolensk. In the part of the country occupied by the Nazis, much the same pattern prevailed. Between May and August, some ten thousand Polish intellectuals were transported to Dachau, Buchenwald, and Sachsenhausen; in June, the death camp at Auschwitz was established; and in November, the gates of the Warsaw ghetto closed, separating Poles, condemned to oppression, humiliation, and violence, from Jews, doomed to death.

Ola spent the summer, fall, and winter of 1940 and most of 1941 in Ivanovka. The work assigned to her consisted of making bricks and chopping manure for fuel. For that, she was paid seventy kopecks a month (a loaf of bread at the Zharma bazaar cost 180 rubles).[63] The deportees could avoid starvation only by exchanging their clothes for food and stealing grain. At the end of the fall, Ola managed to rent a bed in a hut belonging to a family of Kazakhs. An extreme culture shock contributed to her plight: relations with local people (who were also hungry and struggling for survival) were tense and marked by a mutual lack of understanding. Failure to report for the job or any minor infraction could result in a prison sentence, in which case Andrzej would be put in a children's home, where his chances of survival would have been negligible.

Ola's only link with the outer world was correspondence with Maria Zarębińska. One of Zarębińska's letters, written in Lwów on 5 September 1940, furnished some information about Aleksander: that he was still imprisoned but alive, presumably in adequate health and good spirits but unaware of the whereabouts of his family. Ola then ventured to approach Ehrenburg, to whom she sent a letter via the Writers' Union in Moscow. Ehrenburg mailed her 300 rubles and a telegram: "Have talked to Wanda Wasilewska. We'll do everything necessary and possible for easing your lot."[64] But the promise was empty. Ola's and Aleksander's fates were changed only by a circumstance beyond the control of any well-wisher: the start of the German–Soviet war and consequent shift in the political constellation.

In Zamarstynów, Wat was interrogated for many days and nights in succession: "[In a Soviet prison] there is nothing except interrogation, and the prisoner faces an alternative: either the investigator or he himself has gone crazy," he noted in his memoirs.[65] The range of accusations ran from being a Zionist to being a Polish nationalist to being a Trotskyite. Once, Wat was even accused of being an agent of the Vatican.[66] But his greatest liability was the fact that he had edited a Communist monthly in the early 1930s. Jerzy Borejsza, a journalist who was to become supervisor of essentially all Polish culture in the early postwar period, had apparently testified that Wat founded and directed the *Literary Monthly* in collaboration with Hempel, Stande, and others, alleged agents of Polish intelligence who had already been executed during the Great Purge.[67] This could easily have qualified Wat for the death penalty.

Beatings and torture were not unknown in Zamarstynów, but only the Ukrainians were subject to them; the Poles seem to have been exempt for some reason.[68] Nevertheless, all interrogations were conducted under duress. They took place nonstop, usually at night, and lasted for very long periods: "They'd use the conveyor belt system . . . you stood on your feet for long hours during the interrogations by a very hot stove with your back to the fire all the time, and with a light shining in your eyes."[69] (One cannot help but be struck here by an uncanny echo of Wat's youth, when he wrote his delirious poem by a stove in a state of high fever; and one may presume that some of his confessions were no less surreal than his poetic ravings of 1919.) For an attempt to communicate with Broniewski, Wat was consigned for five days and nights to a punishment cell. A poem by Broniewski, written in Zamarstynów, conveys the mood and feelings of both of them with precision:

Old Mother History, Queen of Them All,
how you enjoy raising a stink!
Orion peeps through the bars in the wall,
and here we sit, you and me, in clink. . . .

Immortal madam, why and whence
the passion for paradox you display?
Do you really think that it makes sense
to poison the world's blood in this way? . . . .

Why should a revolutionary poet
rot to death in this Soviet hole?
Dear History, it strikes a jarring note.
Surely one of us is playing the fool?[70]

Wat maintains in his memoirs that he spent nine or ten months in Zamarstynów,[71] but this is most likely a misperception caused by a disturbance of his sense of time (magnificently described by Wat himself). According to the aforementioned letter of Zarębińska, he was moved on 9 August after six and a half months. His next port of call was Brygidki, another prison in Lwów, where he stayed a week or more.[72] From there, he was taken to Kiev. (He was fortunate to leave Brygidki so early: at the start of the German-Soviet war, in June 1941, some twelve thousand inmates of that prison were shot by the NKVD.)[73]

In early fall of 1940, Wat was moved by train to Moscow. There, he found himself in Lubyanka, the nerve center of the NKVD.

The inner prison of the Cheka-NKVD-KGB offices was reserved for the most important political offenders. Imprisonment in Lubyanka was thus a privilege, if a dubious one. Wat became aware of his privileged status immediately: there was no shouting or humiliation, the cells were kept clean, and the searches, although thorough, were carried out skillfully and in silence. After several days in a solitary cell, he was placed in cell no. 34, where he slept in a bed formerly occupied by General Anders (former fiancé, incidentally, of his sister Seda), who had been removed from the cell not long before and who had yet to play his role in the history of Poland.[74] There were only four inmates to twelve or thirteen square meters, and the prisoners were fed adequately by Soviet standards. But what mattered most of all was that Wat could satisfy his appetite for reading, since prisoners were allowed to take books from Lubyanka library. This was made up of the confiscated private libraries of "state criminals" and was, by many accounts, one of the best in the country. During his long stint in Lubyanka, Wat read an enormous amount, from St. Augustine to Machiavelli to Proust.

Torture was as much a feature of Lubyanka as of Zamarstynów and was perhaps conducted with a more refined cruelty. But some screams that appeared to issue from those being tortured were probably stage-managed for the benefit of other inmates—a detail corroborated by the experience of Mandelstam and other victims of the NKVD.[75] In any case, Wat was lucky enough to escape physical abuse, the main method of coercion applied to him being strictly psychological: "The rule here was strict and permanent closure, a cutting off of ties with the outer world, the world of authentic reality and logic, in order to drive the prisoner, by the devastation of his mind and moral degradation, into a universe which was not an imaginary one, as people usually suppose, but fundamentally different, governed by laws unintelligible to the prisoner."[76]

Still, the interrogators, in pursuit of their own goals, unwittingly helped the prisoner obtain some knowledge of developments outside the prison gates. Thus, Wat was given a copy of *Nowe Widnokręgi* (New Horizons), a Polish monthly that had started to appear in Lwów in January 1941. It was less crude than the *Red Banner* and aspired to certain standards of literary art and political honesty. Edited by Wasilewska, it enlisted the services of such diverse people as Boy-Żeleński, Przyboś, Rudnicki, and Ważyk.

New Horizons, whose proclaimed goal was the preservation and development of Polish culture, reflected a new trend in Soviet policy. As relations between Hitler and Stalin began to sour, an alternative design for Poland's fate arose. This might have explained the behavior of the interrogators, who were polite and seemingly benevolent. It was proposed to Wat that he write a lengthy paper about the state of Polish literature and the attitudes of Polish intellectuals, which he did, albeit attempting to withhold—though perhaps with varying degrees of success—any information liable to harm anyone.[77] The requested analysis was probably intended for use in working out a new line in dealings with the Polish cultural elite.

Wat's time in Lubyanka was cut short by the outbreak of the German-Soviet war on 22 June 1941. The inner prison of Lubyanka was hurriedly evacuated, and Wat and the other inmates were put on a train to Saratov, 450 miles southeast of Moscow. Conditions in Saratov prison were almost as atrocious as they had been in Zamarstynów. That fall, Wat all but died of starvation. Further, he had dysentery and a temperature of 106 degrees. But that was not the only reason for reckoning with the possibility of death: rumor had it that all the prisoners were to be shot before the arrival of the Germans, who were supposedly approaching Saratov. This marked a turning point for Wat: from that time on, he was to embrace a distinctly religious outlook, if a private, idiosyncratic one.[78]

Relief came for Wat, as for many thousands of Poles, with the so-called Sikorski-Maiski pact. At the start of the German-Soviet war, Poland and Russia found themselves faced with a common enemy. As early as 23 June 1941, General Sikorski, head of the Polish government-in-exile (which had, by that time, moved to London), expressed his hopes for Russo-Polish reconciliation. An understanding—which proved to be only temporary, however—was very soon reached, the rapid German advance toward Moscow serving as a potent catalyst for Stalin's softening. On 30 July, an agreement was signed, which, among other things, provided for the release of all Polish prisoners and deportees in Russia. A Polish army was to be organized in the USSR, with General Anders, a recent inmate of Lubyanka, as commander.

Predictably, Stalin developed a two-track policy. On 1 December 1941, a conference of pro-Soviet Polish politicians (including Wasilewska) was convened in Saratov. It established the so-called Union of Polish Patriots, whose main task would be the Sovietization of Poland at the appropriate moment.

The amnesty for Polish detainees who had managed to survive the first two years of Soviet occupation was carried out only gradually, however. At first, Wat did not believe that it would affect him, but on 20 November 1941 he was shaved, given two loaves of bread, and summoned before a senior officer of the NKVD who announced his release. Ola had been released earlier in the summer. She had ended up in the village of Antonovka, where conditions were, if anything, worse than at her place of confinement.

Upon his release, the first thing Wat did was to look for his family. He was told that Ola and Andrzej must be somewhere in the south of Kazakhstan, where most Polish deportees lived at the time. Therefore he made for Alma-Ata, the capital of Kazakhstan. Wat's appearance as he set out has been vividly described by A. Krakowski, a Jewish student from Wilno and a chance companion:

> At Saratov station, where all of us, seated in freight cars, were waiting for departure, the doors were suddenly opened, and with the help of those near them a man was pulled in: he stood out distinctly against the background of all present since he had a fur coat with an otter collar and . . . a bowler hat. How tremendous an impression this made on us might be seen from the fact that after so many years and experiences that image is still incised in our memories. And just as he stood on the car's wooden floor, he collapsed. He was so weak that he could not stand by himself.[79]

Helped and fed by Krakowski and his wife, Wat managed to reach Dzhambul, a town in southern Kazakhstan. His family was staying not too far from there, though he did not know it. In Dzhambul, he was examined by a doctor, who told him that he had at most two weeks to live. Finally, he arrived in the capital of Kazakhstan, where, in the only hotel, the Polish delegation was located (in accordance with the Sikorski-Maiski agreement, it was to care for Polish citizens).[80] The first night, he slept in the hall of the hotel, behind a large statue of Lenin. "At one point I woke up to find that a search was on, documents were being checked. I had no right to be in Alma-Ata. Lenin saved me."[81]

The delegation appears to have treated Wat, still considered a notorious Communist, in a lukewarm way. First, he was sent to a hospital, where he spent approximately a month recovering from exhaustion and scurvy.[82] After that, he could find neither a job nor a place to live. Fortunately, the hotel was also serving as home for several evacuated Soviet writers. There Wat met his old acquaintance Victor Shklovsky, who invited him to stay incognito in his room. Later, Wat moved to a house on the outskirts of the city belonging to a Russian night watchman, where he was given a bed that was so narrow that his hands dangled down on both sides.[83]

Wat's frantic search for Ola and Andrzej lasted two months. After he had finally managed to locate them, Ola and Andrzej left Antonovka, on 1 February 1942, for Alma-Ata.

> Finally, we stopped before a small wooden hut. . . . I entered a room straight away: it was stuffy and filthy. In the middle of it stood a wooden rocking cradle, and in it was a baby, all covered with red spots. On a stool, an old man smoking a pipe, at the stove a woman in a kerchief, girded with an apron.
>
> I asked about Aleksander. The old man, almost without a word, motioned his head to the right, and there in the middle of another room stood Aleksander who was jotting down something on a card. He had grown grey, I saw a large black cross under his unbuttoned shirt. He did not hear me entering since he was absorbed in writing. When I saw him for the last time getting into that black car after the arrest, he was forty. He was young and strong, he had very dark hair and large shining eyes. Now, virtually an aged man stood before me, grizzled, thin, exhausted.[84]

The baby in the cradle was dead from scarlet fever. Andrzej was not much better: he "looked like a child from the Warsaw ghetto."[85] Fortunately, the Soviet writers with whom Wat associated were very helpful: "the Moscow intellectuals provided us with food, they treated us as fellow sufferers. A bit like 'Muscovite friends' in the times of Mickiewicz. I just don't know whether as much courage was demanded in these days as in our era," Ola wrote in her book.[86]

Most of the survivors from that period testify to the fact that circumstances had relaxed moods and created expectations of imminent change. Shklovsky, who had been trim and cautious in his role as war correspondent in 1939, now exuded human warmth. Among those with whom Aleksander and Ola became friends was Mikhail Zoshchenko, the renowned Soviet satirist; Konstantin Paustovsky, a liberal writer; Sergei Eisenstein, the great film director; Mikhail Shneider, a script-writer, "a sterling character and a most precise mind";[87] and Serafima Narbut, widow of the poet Vladimir Narbut (a close friend of Mandelstam and likewise a victim of the Great Purge). Wat also became acquainted with Mukhtar Auezov, a Kazakh scholar and writer apparently as enlightened as the Russians.

Shklovsky, Paustovsky, Shneider, and Serafima Narbut made up a kind of club in which the conversation was amazingly free by Soviet standards. Its members hardly concealed their hatred for the regime and their disdain for its official art. The only thing Soviet that they still supported heartily was the war effort. But there was a general expectation that after the war the Stalinist dictatorship would inevitably be abolished.[88] The only one of Wat's Russian friends who doubted this was Eisenstein, who, unfortunately, proved to be right.

It seemed that the hardest times were past. The Polish embassy, located at that time in Kuibyshev, offered Wat some material support, and the delegation in Alma-Ata eventually allowed the family to visit its privileged shop. "The shop was placed in hidden premises in a courtyard," Ola wrote." "It is difficult to believe what the privileged were entitled to, while lots of people were starving. The choice and the quantities were incredible. One could get absolutely every-thing including caviar, cakes, wine and chocolate."[89] But Aleksander's health had been damaged irreversibly. In March 1943, he was diagnosed as suffering from dystrophy of the heart muscle and atheroma of the aorta.[90]

Shklovsky attempted to find Wat a job in the screen-writing department of Mosfilm, the Russian state film company, which had been evacuated to Alma-Ata. Wat allegedly drafted two scripts, both of which were rejected.[91] He also received a substantial offer to write about Mayakovsky, but he felt uneasy about this topic so intimately connected with his Communist period.[92]

One advantage of being in Alma-Ata was its Pushkin Library, which had an archive containing some unusual Polish materials. Kazakhstan, like Siberia, was a notorious place of exile even in the nineteenth century: many participants in Polish conspiracies and insurrections had been banished there by the Czarist regime. Wat was extremely interested in the fate of these people, so obviously parallel to his own. A two-page proposal pertaining to USSR polonica collec-tions survives among his papers.[93] Certain texts discovered by Wat were of a sensitive nature. He found a toadyish appeal to Nicholas I concocted in exile by Tomasz Zan (1796–1855), who had always been considered an irreproachable revolutionary.[94] Even more controversial was a petition to the Czar written by Mickiewicz while in exile in Russia in 1827, asking for a permit to establish *Irys*, a Polish periodical "which was to promote Russian–Polish friendship, one would like to say Soviet–Polish friendship."[95] (This was already known to Polish scholars, but they preferred to keep silent about it.) Mickiewicz's project excited Wat so much that he proposed to revive the idea in the new circumstances.[96] It would be easy to dismiss that plan as reflecting conformism. But another explanation is conceivable, in that Wat, who had already established ties with semi-dissident Russian writers (like Mickiewicz with his "Muscovite friends"), might have envisaged such a periodical as holding out promise of an authentic cultural exchange.

In any case, the war was a time in which Wat broke his vow of silence. One of the first signs of his creative rebirth, as well as of the inner change that had taken place, was an obituary for Stanisław Rogoż—virtually an essay—written in Alma-Ata in May 1942 and published in the periodical *Polska* (Poland) in Kuibyshev.[97] Stanisław Rogoż, journalist and literary critic, was a longtime friend of Wat, who had shared his experience of Soviet prisons. The Polish delegation cared for him, but he succumbed to typhus after a few weeks. Wat's obituary became a declaration of the world view formed by years of ordeal: "He spoke about all of us, ex-inmates of concentration camps and prisoners, in bitter words that were also filled with profound kindness. We said to each other that we were eyewitnesses to a confounding of the language, an apocalyptic ruin of cultures and civilizations that had craved to rule themselves solely by the laws of human reason."[98]

With a courage nothing short of amazing, Wat revealed his disagreement with communism, an ideology that claimed to be rational and truthful yet resulted in semantic subversion and the outright lie. His obituary for Rogoż contained in a nutshell all the main themes of Wat's mature writing. It also allegedly figured among the charges brought against him when he was next arrested, in 1943.[99]

In a letter to Ola of 19 January 1942, in which Wat stated that he was coming through "the curious stage of a certain second maturing and forming,"[100] he also mentioned a renewed interest in poetry. In Saratov and even earlier in Zamarstynów, he had apparently managed to write down more than a dozen poems.[101] Included in the posthumous volume of 1968 are a poem entitled "Ballada Więzienna" (Prison Ballad), labeled "Zamarstynów, 1940," and another entitled "Jak drzewo wypróchniałe" (Like a Rotten Tree), designated "In Saratov prison, November 1941." Both are short and succinct, as befits texts composed in extremity.

Another poem, "Wierzby w Ałma-Acie" (Willows in Alma-Ata), was written during his search for Ola and Andrzej, and Wat had planned to publish it in the Polish press in the hope that Ola might spot it and get in touch.[102] But it came out, in *Poland,* only in April 1942, after the family had been reunited. Reprinted by the underground press in Poland,[103] it became widely known and was memorized by many as a testimony of fidelity and remembrance, one of the very best in literature of the time.

General Anders's army left Soviet Central Asia for Iran, in two stages, in March and August 1942. There it joined the Western allies in the Middle East. Among Wat's many friends who took the opportunity to enlist and leave

Kazakhstan was Broniewski. From this time on, the Soviets were preparing for their formal break with the Polish government-in-exile. Their relations with the Polish embassy in Kuibyshev (and the delegation in Alma-Ata) started to sour, and the friendly atmosphere of the Alma-Ata intellectual circle gradually dissipated. After the arrest of several functionaries of the delegation, Wat remained one of only two representatives of the Polish government-in-exile for the entire territory of Kazakhstan. Finally, he was told to leave the capital within forty-eight hours. He was allowed to choose any district in Alma-Ata province, and, after some procrastination, he opted for Ili, a town—or rather, a workers' settlement—about fifty miles northeast of Alma-Ata, on both the railway line and a river (also called Ili) that at one time had served the shipping trade with Xinjiang in western China. The departure to Ili took place around February 1943, though both Ola and Wat assign it an earlier date.

> The workers' settlement Ili to which we were deported in 1943 was long, intersected along the middle by a long potholed road covered by dirty sand. At the slightest wind the sand rose as a dark rusty cloud. In the zenith of summer, the heat reached 50 degrees Celsius, and there was no vegetation around, not the slightest oasis for an eye sick for verdure. Just some filthy anemic growth here and there.
>
> At both sides of the road stood rows of Kazakh huts built of mud and cow dung. At the end of the road, a large marketplace. For several hours in early morning, while the sun was still merciful, old Kazakh men and women sat there squatting on the earth, similar to it, just as gray, as if carved out of dust and lumps of dry mud. . . . In the rough wooden stalls nestled around the place, those among them who were richer sold pieces of fat mutton speckled with flies. All that was unavailable for us, worth its weight in gold.[104]

Ola maintained that Ili had been Trotsky's place of exile in 1928–29. Presumably that was a local legend, if an incorrect one, given that Trotsky had stayed in the relative comfort of Alma-Ata and had visited the Ili valley only for hunting parties.[105] For the Wat family, the new location represented a huge change for the worse. It also became, for Wat, a kind of hermitage, where his new Weltanschauung could mature.

Ili was inhabited almost exclusively by observant Jews deported from eastern Poland, many of them Hasidim. Wat wore a cross, which would have been considered a punishable insult in most Jewish neighborhoods in independent Poland, where strict Talmudic rules still prevailed. But, an ecumenical spirit had developed in Ili, which had the flavor of antiquity before the division of faiths. Wat even became a leader of the community, almost a patriarch. With good reason, he later defined the year 1943 as "the most important, heroic year," without equal in his life.[106]

In March 1943, the NKVD started a campaign of so-called passportization, forcing Polish deportees in Kazakhstan to accept Soviet passports. Acceptance, in the opinion of those affected, would cut off all their hopes of ever returning to their fatherland. The campaign was coordinated with other actions implementing Stalin's "alternative plan" for Poland. At about the same time, the Union of Polish Patriots (ZPP) emerged into the open. It had representatives in Alma-Ata and even in Ili.[107] The ZPP took a decision to organize a new pro-Soviet Polish army in the USSR, consisting of people left behind by Anders's army, which had already departed. Stalin broke off diplomatic relations with the Polish government-in-exile on 25 April. Any holder of a "London" passport became, by definition, a hostile foreigner.

At that time, Wat assumed the role of organizer of an anti-Soviet revolt. His experience of the 1930s, as a Communist agitator, now came in handy in diametrically opposed circumstances. "First in private conversation, then at meetings, he presented people with the situation, but chiefly he roused their violated sense of dignity and their awareness of what submission would mean in this case."[108] When the NKVD commission led by Colonel Omarkhadzhev arrived, it was astounded by the people's unanimous refusal to accept Soviet passports. Wat was arrested, along with many other Poles.

Shortly thereafter, Ola was also jailed. Her experiences in jail did not differ too much from those of people in Nazi death camps. On arriving at Alma-Ata station, those arrested were marched to the city. The guards "kept speeding up the pace, beating those who couldn't keep up, especially the old Jews. They beat them on the head, on the back, with whatever was at hand. And that was how we ran the more than eight kilometers to the center of the city."[109] (Half a year before, in September 1942, Ola's parents and sister had perished—perhaps under similar circumstances—in Treblinka, though she did not know it.) After being placed with women criminals, who beat her and other Polish inmates, Ola agreed to accept a Soviet passport.

Aleksander was first in custody in Ili, in less ominous conditions: "After all of my experiences, I was touched by the idyllic character of the jail to which I was brought by two teenagers in shabby students' coats and armed with ancient carbines. It was a sunny morning of March 1943. . . . Therefore, the ward was light, its walls cream-colored, here moderately smeared with excrement, there covered by more or less—yet always—philosophical thoughts, aphorisms and signals of young and old bandits. Sometimes one found both excrement and thoughts together."[110] From there he was transferred to an Alma-Ata prison, the so-called Second Section, and finally to the notorious Third Section, where "I was in a group of thirty thieves, the worst kind of *urks* [bandits], and young prostitutes. . . . I walked stiff as a ramrod. I have never walked with pride like that before, my head held high. Poor Ola ran after us. . . . She followed me all the way to the gate, the large wooden gate of the Third Section, and then for the last time I saw a face without a face. Ola's face."[111]

Aleksander was more fortunate than Ola: his courage and stubbornness impressed the inmates, and the leader of the cell, Valentin, took him under his protection.[112] Moreover, a sort of friendship evolved between him and Omarkhadzhev, who was visibly fascinated by his obstinate ward. The relationship with Omarkhadzhev, which Wat described on several occasions, would provide material for an unusual psychological novella.[113] One cannot fail to notice an almost erotic element in Wat's attitude to that "magnificent Genghis Khan."[114] The NKVD colonel became a metonymy for Asia and its nomadic hordes. This fascination with the mysterious nomads was an important feature of Wat's world view, albeit one not without masochistic overtones.

Be that as it may, Wat finally had his London passport returned to him.[115] He came back to Ili, where his family was waiting for him, probably in June 1943.[116]

He was to remain there three more years. Outwardly, life was monotonous, interrupted only by bouts of illness. The only medicine available was aspirin, which Wat found "no more helpful than toothpaste."[117] The Wats worked as hired laborers and received ration cards entitling them each to 400 grams of rye bread. To supplement these rations, they frequented the second-hand bazaar in Alma-Ata, selling whatever they could.[118]

Later, Wat was employed as a teacher in the settlement's Polish school, where he was required to use a textbook whose opening page was adorned with a photo of Stalin kissing children.[119] Subsequently, he was manager of a dining hall, keeper of a bread store, and, finally, production manager of Ili's *sel'po* (general village stores). A surviving record states: "Citizen Khvat A. is a serious, honest and conscientious worker"[120]—a stock Soviet formula that did not necessarily correspond to reality. (Jobs in dining halls or stores in the USSR were considered lucrative, since they provided opportunities for stealing and thus supporting one's family.)

Among the odd jobs Wat took was, supposedly, that of seizing turtles in the River Ili, described with horrifying verve in a poem of 1962, "Żółw z Oxfordu" (A Turtle from Oxford) in which an English turtle addresses the narrator:

> "You gulped the blood of my cousins, is not that enough? Seizing
> them in whole fistfuls in the bulrushes by the river Ili, crushing and
> smashing them with a rolling pin, on the rough table in the kitchen
> of the Promkombinat where you helped the dirty woman cook to
> steal food. The blood of my brothers splashed into your eyes,
> bespattered your face, your rags, you waded in their blood, still you
> didn't have enough. You have never had enough. Not
> enough. Not enough. Not
> enough . . ."[121]

The poem (which probably exaggerates the author's murderous feats) has an obvious metonymic quality.[122] The literal meaning has to do with ecocide.

But the opposition of predatory and defenseless may also be interpreted on the allegorical level, as in a classical fable, with the animal realm standing for humankind, the tyrant splashed in blood for a totalitarian dictator. Still deeper layers of meaning also appear, one relating to Wat's all-pervading sense of some moral transgression committed in his youth, another to the inscrutable God, Master of the universe, who nevertheless permits evil—a problem that had troubled many, from medieval thinkers to Dostoevsky, and that came glaringly to the fore again after Stalinism and the Holocaust. One cannot fail to detect a desperate note of self-reproach, as well as an echo of the theomachic harangues of Wat in his younger years.

The metaphysical, ethical, historical, and ecological interpretations of the poem form a hierarchy; different but contiguous levels of being—God, man, society, nature—are reflected in each other, while the final interpretation escapes the reader and transcends language. Even the excerpt quoted is complex enough to warrant a fourfold reading (literal, allegorical, moral, and anagogical) of the type postulated by early Christian thinkers, yet rarely applicable to works of the twentieth century.

"A Turtle from Oxford" contains references to the war and to Wat's exile, although it was written much later. This temporal separation between the events narrated and the moment of narration, as well as the psychological distance between the narrator in the kitchen of the Ili Promkombinat and the far more mature narrator on the lawns of Oxford, contributes to its meaning and overall effect.

Such distance is absent in two poems that belong entirely to the period of the Kazakhstan exile, poems that are powerful in their immediacy. The narrator both suffers his ordeal and assigns to it a suprapersonal significance by relating it to ancient texts and archetypal patterns.

"Willows in Alma-Ata," written in January 1942, is a good example of Wat's new, noniconoclastic treatment of the biblical tradition:

> Wierzby są wszędzie wierzbami
>
> Pięknaś w szronie i blasku, wierzbo ałmaatyńska.
> Lecz jeśli cię zapomnę, sucha wierzbo z ulicy Rozbrat,
> niech uschnie moja ręka!
>
> Góry są wszędzie górami   5
>
> Przede mną Tiań Szań żegluje w fioletach,
> pianka światła, głaz barw, blednie i niknie.
> Lecz jeśli cię zapomnę, daleki szczycie tatrzański,
> potoku Białej, gdzie z synem barwne roiłem zeglugi

żegnani cichym uśmiechem naszej dobrej patronki—   10
niech się w kamień tianszański obrócę!

> *Jeśli was zapomnę*
> *Jeśli cię zapomnę miasto rodzinne,*

nocy warszawska, desczczu i bramo, gdzie   15

> *w bramie dziad wyciąga rękę*
> *pies rozerwał mu sukienkę.*
> *Śpij Jędrusiu . . .*

Rozrzucam ręce żałośnie, jak polska płacząca wierzba

Jeśli was zapomnę,
lampy gazowe Żórawiej, stacje mej męki miłosnej—   20
świetliste serca wtulone w ciemną wstydliwość liści
i szept i szmer i deszcz, w Alei turkot dorożki
i złotopióry świt gołębi.

Jeśli cię zapomnę, walcząca Warszawo
w krwi spieniona Warszawo   25

jeśli Cię zapomnę
jeśli Was zapomnę

Willows are willows everywhere

Beautiful in rime and luster art thou, O willow of Alma-Ata.
Yet if I forget thee, O dead willow from the Rozbrat street,
let my hand forget her cunning!

Mountains are mountains everywhere

Before me Tian Shan sails in violet hues,
froth of light, stone of colors, it grows pale and vanishes.
Yet if I forget thee, O distant summit of Tatry,
O stream of Biała where I with my son imagined colorful sailings,
both of us blessed by the silent smile of our good patroness—
let me turn into the Tian Shan stone!

> *If I forget you*
> *If I forget thee O my native city*

O Warsaw night, rain and gateway, where

> *a beggar stretches his hand in the gateway*
> *a dog has torn his coat.*
> *Sleep Jędruś . . .*

I spread my hands sorrowfully, like a Polish weeping willow

If I forget you,
O gas lamps of the Żórawia street, the stations of the Calvary of my love
shining hearts nestled in the dark bashfulness of leaves
and whisper and rustle and rain, rumble of a carriage in the Alley
and golden-feathered dawn of doves.

If I forget thee, O fighting Warsaw
O Warsaw foaming with blood

If I forget Thee
If I forget You

The poem is rooted in the landscape of Kazakhstan. The willows of Alma-Ata and the Asian mountains looming south of the city and closing the perspective of its avenues are often mentioned in Wat's memoirs. The tree and the mountain belong to the repertoire of images mediating between heaven and earth, between the transcendent and the immanent, the atemporal and the temporal. The tree also came to assume special significance for Wat during his imprisonment, as a powerful symbol of freedom and creativity: "There is no greater miracle than a green tree. To be born, in my next incarnation, a hamadryad. To grow with a tree, to live with a tree and to die together with it."[123] And "In the tree, all essential symbols merge. If one must write a great novel, it should be about a tree. About one particular tree."[124]

The exotic land of the East where Wat was to spend his exile could easily be identified with Babylon, land of exile for the ancient Judeans.[125] An obvious source text for the poem is the opening of Psalm 137: "By the rivers of Babylon, there we sat down, yea, we wept, when we remembered Zion. We hanged our harps upon the willows in the midst thereof." Yet, "a Polish weeping willow" (line 18) is also redolent of numerous Polish texts including nonliterary ones, such as the famous statue of Chopin by Wacław Szymanowski in Warsaw's Łazienki Park.

Technically, the poem differs significantly from Wat's early works. It employs neither absurdities nor unusual images designed to shock: on the contrary, it is free of confusion, highly consistent in tone, and almost classical in its lucidity. The only nonstandard word *złotopióry* (golden-feathered, line 23), even if it has its counterparts in Wat's early writing, brings to mind a Romantic and Skamandrite vocabulary rather than futurist "transrational language."[126] The integral stylistic pattern that unites the biblical tenor with the tonality of Skamandrite urban poems is broken only once, in lines 15–17, which quote a typical ditty of Anusia Mikulak[127]—a folklore lullaby she sang for Aleksander, which Aleksander, in turn, sang for Andrzej (Jędruś), his only, lost son.

The poem is written in free verse, but the insistence on feminine endings, as well as the pattern of caesuras in the long lines, brings it close to classical Polish versification à la Mickiewicz. Moreover, the second line, which serves as the true opening of the poem, virtually conforms to the model of Polish thirteen-syllable verse and cannot fail to bring to mind the opening of Mickiewicz's "Pan Tadeusz"—that most famous Polish thirteen-syllable poetic line which presents the experience of exile in the condensed, moving words: "Litwo! Ojczyzno moja! ty jesteś jak zdrowie" (Lithuania, my fatherland, thou art like health), the argument being that health, like one's fatherland, begins to be valued only after it has been lost.

"Willows in Alma-Ata" juxtaposes and mixes a number of different styles. Structurally, it consists of two parts, the middle line (14), in which the name of Warsaw is first introduced, albeit indirectly, constituting the dividing line. It is flanked, on one side by a solemn biblical distich and on the other by a ditty, both given in italics. The first part of the poem, built around images of willows and mountains, might be described as mythological; the second part, focused on the city where Wat consummated his love for Ola—a city now fighting against an enemy and being destroyed thereby—is, by contrast, historical, so opposing culture to nature (and the auditory experience to visual).

The first part could be called "a commonplace disproved." *A* is not *-A:* willows are *not* willows everywhere, and mountains are *not* mountains everywhere. By comparison with the sensual, palpable Polish images, the Kazakhstan images take on an air of artificiality and unreality. Simultaneously, the Polish images obtain a dimension of depth. Certain elements of the poem are inevitably lost in the English translation, unfortunately. Thus, *sucha wierzba* (literally "dry willow") corresponds to the idiom *niech uschnie moja ręka* ("let my hand forget her cunning"—literally "let my hand dry up"). The name of the street, Rozbrat (literally "breach, discord"), albeit real, also reflects the general picture of dislocation and alienation. The image of the narrator, his wife, and son has a manifest mythological connotation, of the Holy Family. Here, the words *żegnani* and *patronka* take on a particular role. *Żegnać* has several meanings—"to bid farewell," "to bless," "to make the sign of the cross"—all of which contribute to the religious connotations of the scene.[128] *Patronka* (patroness) in Polish primarily denotes "patron saint"; thus the wife of the narrator is referred to as the Virgin Mary. Consistently, *fiolety*, translated "violet hues," refers, first and foremost, to "a bishop's attire." Thus, both Tian Shan and Tatry become immersed in the atmosphere of a solemn Catholic Mass.

A captive carried away to a strange land comes back to his own country appropriating the semi-mythological space superimposed on the none-too-real

Asiatic landscape, as in a double-exposed snapshot. The memory of the sacred, embodied in nature and family, gives him a feeling of world order and divine presence on earth. The dreamlike passage about a father and son who imagine "colorful sailings" under the gaze of the mother (or blessing of the heavenly Madonna) has the quality of a Renaissance painting.[129]

Just as the narrator's family substitutes for the Holy Family, so Warsaw substitutes for Jerusalem (never mentioned by name in the poem). The two parts of the poem are connected by the biblical "If I forget thee" (Isa. 49:15), as well as by many subtler echoes. Thus, *świetliste* (shining, line 21) and *świt* (dawn, line 23) connect with *światła* (genitive of "light," line 7). The same play on a common root assumes a tragic tonality in the correspondence of *pianka* (froth, line 7) and *w krwi spieniona* (foaming with blood, line 25).

As noted already, the second part starts with a ditty impressed on Wat in childhood—and, significantly, connected in his memory to an early trauma: "I imagined vividly our long arched gateway under the number 5 on a small residential Kupiecka street, where there were no shops except a grocery, a gateway paved with marble slabs on which I had broken my nose. . . . I imagined a beggar with a long white beard, a black dog tearing his coat, and the wind which is still my enemy."[130] The motifs of alienation, injury, and sorrow recede in the passage that follows (lines 19–23), which is distinguished by its rhythmic and syntactic structure, as well as by its amalgam of sensual and spiritual. The urban landscape surrounding the lovers becomes an incorporeal vision, though lamps and leaves paradoxically acquire the immediate presence of bodies; a fine onomatopoeia *i szept i szmer i deszcz* (and whisper and rustle and rain) is followed by a strong visual image of dawn. Moreover, the entire scene has religious connotations: love is not only a Calvary but also a Pentecost, marked by the appearance of both a dove and the gift of speaking in tongues—that is, poetry.

The imagined encounter of a lonely exile with the nature, city, and love of his youth leads to an affirmation of his identity. He is torn away from his country and family (both emphasized by capital letters, which are habitually reserved for the name of God) but remains inseparable from them. The last lines of the poem (cf. Isa. 49:15) are open. Now, the ellipsis has revealed its meaning: forgetting is inconceivable. The polyphonic structure juxtaposing Old and New Testaments, the voices of a Jew in Babylon, the narrator, and Anusia Mikulak has found its resolution.

A poem dated April 1943, when Wat was in Alma-Ata prison under the supervision of Colonel Omarkhadzhev, is simpler and more straightforward, though paradoxical. With a daring that would befit a seventeenth-century metaphysical poet, it unites the discordant concepts of theomachy and theophany and unites two opposite characters of the Gospel:

Długo broniłem się przed Tobą
długo nie chciałem Ciebie poznać
długo przed Tobą umykałem
w zaułki ślepe
w absynt poezji
i w zapał walki
i w zgiełk jarmarku,
gdzie antreprener z somnambuliczką
wyczarowują
raj utracony.

For so long I protected myself from
    Thee
for so long I did not desire to know
    Thee
for so long I escaped Thee   5
into blind alleys
into the absinthe of poetry
and into the fury of struggle
and into the uproar of a fair
where an entrepreneur and a   10
    somnambulist lady
call forth by their magic
paradise lost.

Gdy mnie dopadłeś i znienacka
na pal mnie wbiłeś!
Między łotrami mnie powiesiłeś!
Potem wbijałeś mi gwoździe w czoło
w ręce i nogi!
Bok mi przebiłeś włócznią
odjętą żołnierzowi!
I napoiłeś mnie piołunem
i octem!
Gdy napisałeś: król żydowski,
to z głowy zdjąłeś
koronę z cierni
i rozkrwawiłeś moje czoło.
Noc wtedy była, trzęsienie ziemi.

Then Thou overtook me and by
    surprise
impaled me!
Thou hung me up between the
    thieves!   15
Then, Thou hammered nails into my
    forehead
my hands and feet!
Thou pierced my side with a spear
taken from the soldier!   20
And Thou gave me to drink
    wormwood
and vinegar!
When Thou wrote: King of the Jews,
Thou took off my head
the crown of thorns
and bloodied my forehead.
There was darkness, and the earth
    did quake.

Wtedy przejrzałem
wtedy poznałem
Eli krzyknąłem
lamma sabahtani.

Then I recovered my sight   25
then I gained my awareness
I cried Eli
lama sabachthani.

Like the previous poem, this one employs free verse with a perceptible tendency to regularity. This regularity reaches a climax in the lines 25–27, which are rhythmically identical, syntactically parallel, and, moreover, closely connected by sound patterning and a rhyme. (The rhyme *przejrzałem–*

poznałem– krzyknąłem, the only one in the entire poem, is of a primitive variety that refers back to Polish medieval and baroque religious poetry.)

It is a poem of confession and prayer that transforms itself into a wail *de profundis.* The text is divided into three parts according to the classical triad of thesis, antithesis, and synthesis. The first part consists of one long sentence without punctuation; it creates an image of the poet as renegade and apostate. The second part, by contrast, breaks down into a series of short energetic sentences, which depict the crucifixion of the poet, with imagery taken from Matthew and John, albeit with significant changes to be discussed later. The third part, the most condensed and, technically, the most refined, speaks of clarity of vision gained in the midst of suffering.

All this is in the great tradition of religious poetry. The additional factor stems from Romanticism—specifically, Polish Romanticism, the central topic of which was a dramatic dialogue with God, leading to spiritual awakening (*The Great Improvisation* by Mickiewicz is undoubtedly the most influential text of this kind, though many examples may be found in the works of Słowacki, Krasiński, and others.[131]) The deepest layer of the poem refers to anthropological motifs that predate Christianity—namely, to the rite de passage of shaman and poet: the inner change and attainment of maturity engendered by physical torture and ritual dismemberment.[132]

It is not hard to detect an autobiographical note superimposed here on the multilayered traditional pattern. "Blind alleys" is, of course, a cliché, but it can also be interpreted literally, as the back streets in Warsaw where the poet experienced his frustrations. "The absinthe of poetry" harks back to *Pug Iron Stove,* in which Lilith drank "pale-turquoise absinthe," the paradigmatic decadent liquor. "The fury of struggle" refers to political fury, "the uproar of a fair" to the frivolous literary scene of futurist and post-futurist Warsaw. "Paradise lost" probably alludes less to Milton (or, for that matter, Proust) than to the Romantic topos of *les paradis artificiels,* traditionally demythologized and rejected by a religious convert.[133] Similarly, the crucifixion in the second part is imbued with Wat's experience of the Kazakhstan prison where he, quite literally, found himself among thieves—and socialized with them, following Christ's example.

God appears here in the guise of merciless executioner. His acts remind one of the tyrant in Wat's blasphemous poem of 1924, "The Cop."[134] In Wat's description of the Passion are a wealth of details with a sadomasochistic tinge, with God himself replacing human torturers. Crucifixion is equated to and, in a sense, complemented by two other forms of execution—impaling and hanging. God hammers nails not only into the sinner's hands and feet but also into his forehead (a detail absent in the Gospels, though symbolically present in the sign of the cross). It is God himself who seizes the spear out of the hands of the Roman soldier in order to pierce the man's side. He gives him wormwood to drink instead of the traditional gall.[135] It is he, not Pilate, who inscribes "King of the Jews" over the renegade poet's head and then removes his crown of thorns, stripping him of even this sign of kingship. All this goes to prove that there is no escape from God—witness Job 10:16: "Thou huntest me as a fierce lion: and again thou shewest thyself marvelous upon me." Consequently, one must acquiesce (Job 13:15: "Though he slay me, yet will I trust in him"). The experience of God's wrath leads to an ultimate darkness, which nevertheless results in the recovery of sight (lines 24–25).

All the "stations" of the crucifixion serve as metaphors for an inner collision and anxiety that find their resolution in a metaphysical awareness gained through Golgotha. An involuntary sacrifice becomes voluntary. This paradox, transcending the bounds of human logic, is revealed in its fullness in the closing lines: the awareness of the highest and loving force finds its expression in the desperate words of Psalm 22: *lama sabachthani* (My God, my God, why hast thou forsaken me), which, on the surface, say the opposite.

In assuming an involved, antithetic, and contradictory way of thought, the poem imitates medieval (or Baroque) meditation closely enough. It was clearly influenced by the fifteenth-century treatise on asceticism *De Imitatione Christi*, usually attributed to the Augustinian monk Thomas à Kempis. This was almost the only book Wat had in Alma-Ata and Ili. Distributed by the London government to Polish exiles, together with old shoes and cans of corned beef,[136] it made an immense impression on Wat. Echoes of the following passage from the *Imitation* are easily discernible in the poem:

> Thou shalt be sometimes as if thou were forsaken by God. Sometimes thou shalt be vexed with thy neighbour; and what is yet more painful, thou shalt be sometimes grievous to thyself. And thou shalt find no means to be delivered, but that it behoveth thee to suffer till it shall please almighty God of his goodness otherwise to dispose with thee; for he desired thou shalt learn to suffer tribulation without consolation, so that thou mayst thereby learn wholly to submit thyself to him, and by tribulation to be made more meek than thou were first. No man feeleth the Passion of Christ so effectuously as he that feeleth like pain as Christ did.[138]

In the 1960s, Wat still had *De Imitatione Christi*—"a small book bound in black cloth with a pale cross, published in 1941 in London by F. Mildner & Sons"[137]—in his possession, and he continued to consult it frequently.

In Postwar Poland, 1946–1957

Life in Ili could justifiably be called an inferno, marked by despair and a monotony that obliterated all sense of time. Wat wrote in his *Diary without Vowels:* "And my only fright and fear was to be buried in that desert earth, in the Ili cemetery where the last dogs, still roaming free and savage, were dragging the bodies out of the graves, in that entirely disgraced earth."[1]

Yet history proceeded inexorably, with grave consequences for the Polish exiles. On 19 July 1944, Soviet troops reached the River Bug, which had been chosen by Stalin as the eastern border of the future Polish state. On 22 July the recently established Polish Committee of National Liberation published its manifesto, whose text had been approved by Stalin himself. It declared that democracy was to be restored in Poland but added, ominously: "Nevertheless, democratic liberties should not be allowed to serve the enemies of democracy." Wasilewska, Borejsza, Putrament, and many other Communist acquaintances of Wat now enjoyed an hour of triumph, exerting their authority—limited, of course, by the Soviet occupiers—over a large (and growing) segment of the Polish population.

Lwów was once again proclaimed part of Soviet Ukraine. In Warsaw, events took a turn for the worse. On 1 August, the Home Army (Polish guerrilla units) rose up against the Nazis, counting on help from Russian troops. But Stalin ordered the Red Army to refrain from action, thereby giving Hitler enough time to crush the "reactionary" uprising. After two months of desperate fighting, Warsaw was forced to capitulate, by which time it had been reduced to a pile of ruins comparable to Hiroshima.

Six million of Poland's citizens perished, either in the war and the uprisings or at the hands of the Nazis. This amounted to a loss of 22 percent of the population, unmatched by any other country involved in the war, the USSR and Germany included. The German withdrawal revealed a network of death camps, which boggled the imagination. Approximately half the victims in Poland were Jews, with the result that the thriving prewar Jewish community was effectively wiped out. Thousands of Polish intellectuals were among the dead.

Power in the country, responsible directly to Stalin, was vested in a group of Communist hard-liners who had spent the war years in the USSR. Headed by Boleslaw Bierut and Jakub Berman, it soon gained the upper hand over Wladyslaw Gomułka, who had remained in Poland under the Nazi occupation and was considered a relative liberal attentive to Polish national interest.

Nevertheless, the early postwar period witnessed an impressive revival of Polish culture. Communist cultural policy between 1944 and 1949 might be described as relatively enlightened.[2] The tight control over culture reintroduced in the USSR after the notorious 1946 speech by party hack Andrei Zhdanov was not automatically extended to Poland. Only after Zhdanov's death, in the fall of 1948, did an article in the Polish press state: "The role of Zhdanov as a theoretician and propagandist of Marxism in the areas of science, philosophy, art, and literature in particular, doubtless far exceeds the bounds of the inner cultural politics of the Soviet Union."[3]

The first literary weekly in the new Polish state, *Odrodzenie* (Rebirth), served the tactical needs of the party by promoting the so-called *rewolucja łagodna* (soft revolution) and embracing a tolerant attitude to tradition. The next, and perhaps more important, periodical was *Kuźnica* (The Forge), which was under the editorship of the Marxist intellectual Stefan Żółkiewski. In Kraków, the Catholic *Tygodnik Powszechny* (The Universal Weekly) was also established, and for a time, its polemic aimed at the Marxist press was tolerated by the censors. Finally, a rather elitist monthly entitled *Twórczość* (The Creative Work) joined the literary scene, under the editorship first of Kruczkowski, then of the brilliant scholar Kazimierz Wyka. Several publishing houses either appeared or reappeared, including private ones such as the old Gebethner and Wolff. Arguably the most visible among them was the publishing cooperative "Czytelnik" (The Reader), which became an undisguised party enterprise only at the end of 1947.

Polish writers and artists, scattered over the entire globe, started returning to Poland. Some of them, including Ważyk, entered the country with the Communist army organized in the USSR. Broniewski, who had joined Anders and fought in his ranks,[4] came back from the West in 1945, the same year as another staunch leftist, Leon Schiller. The more cautious Tuwim returned from emigration only in 1946, and Słonimski as late as 1951. Several writers, including Iwaszkiewicz, Przyboś, and Miłosz, who had spent the years of occupation in their native land, resumed their positions at the core of Polish literary life. Nevertheless, more than one representative of the older generation (for example, Lechoń), as well as of the younger one (for example, Gombrowicz), opted for permanent exile, with the result that a lively émigré literature gradually developed in the West. The prewar *Literary News* reappeared in exile under the shorter title *Wiadomości* (News), but its reputation was soon eclipsed by the monthly *Kultura* (Culture), established in Paris.

The Polish Writers' Union held a meeting in Lublin as early as 1 September 1944. At that meeting Wat, among others, was reinstated as a Union member *in absentia*.[5] A certificate concerning the restoration of his rights was sent to his address at Ili.[6]

The Wats did their best to get in touch with their relatives and friends in Poland. With the help of the well-known actor Stefan Jaracz and Iwaszkiewicz, they managed to contact Seda Broniszówna. She wrote in early June 1945 from Łódź, informing Aleksander of his family's fate—"several words . . . and how horrible they were," Wat answered on 7 July.[7]

A rumor sprang up that Poles exiled to Kazakhstan would be allowed to return to the country of their birth. There was a further rumor that Jews would be ineligible for repatriation (in Soviet passports, such as the one Ola had received, there was a category "nationality," and those listed as Jewish were by that very fact separated from ethnic Poles). The alleged restriction caused an outcry and was seemingly dropped.[8] But the strain on the exiles' nerves continued. When the Wats were called to appear before the authorities, it turned out that Aleksander's victory in obtaining a Polish passport went against him. Ola and Andrzej, together with all the other Polish inhabitants of Ili who had accepted Soviet citizenship, were given permission to leave immediately, while Aleksander was not.[9] He had to turn to several influential acquaintances in Poland for help in speeding up his repatriation.[10]

Finally, Ważyk wrote an appeal entitled "Troska o człowieka" (Care for a Human Being), which was published in the *Forge* on 14 January 1946. There he noted that Wat, "a war émigré" who "is dying of a grave heart condition and pining away with nostalgia several thousand kilometers from his native land," might be useful in the new Poland. After paying less than subtle compliments to the Soviets, Ważyk urged the Polish authorities to display their much-touted tolerance. He also emphasized Wat's Catholic views, probably intending thereby to make an impression on Polish anti-Communists and émigrés. The fact that Ważyk's appeal was widely commented on in émigré circles certainly did no harm.[11] In spring 1946, the Wats were finally allowed to return to Poland, together.

After packing their meager belongings and buying some dried bread crumbs (originally intended for cows), they traveled to Alma-Ata. There they spent many days trying to obtain a train ticket. Ola described the long, exhausting journey through the Asian part of the Soviet Union as if it were an alien planet:

> During our trip from Alma-Ata to Moscow we were astonished by the immeasurable spaces, tracts of empty ashen land. . . . From the car windows one could not see any houses, any plot or tree. We rushed through these desert lands under the vault of the leaden sky. From time to time our train stopped

suddenly. Why here and not there? No station, no trace of huts or any human dwellings. Only some wretched ghostlike bodies loaded with bags appeared at the train. At the car windows some other people ambushed already, also with bags. They exchanged contents with lightning speed. Later, we got an explanation. A sack of salt for a sack of fish. After several dozens of kilometers, a repeat. A sack of tea for a sack of cords, or threads, or something else. Thus, up to Moscow, the Soviet trade went on: it was banned and punished most harshly, but those people waiting outside most likely could not survive without it.[12]

Finally, Aleksander, Ola, and Andrzej reached Poland, arriving on 16 April 1946,[13] during Holy Week.

Like most Polish exiles, Wat returned unaware of the extent of the destruction wrought by the Nazis upon his native city. His prewar house, like almost all houses in Warsaw, stood in ruin. In Ola's words:

Andrzej's room . . . was simply squashed, as a heavy tree bough or an architectural drawing torn asunder. The room of our son was no more; the white wall which joined it with our dining room remained, washed by rain and marked by the stains of time. Then I saw hundreds of thousands of such children's and adults' rooms that did not exist anymore. The people who once upon a time had climbed the stairs hanging over the abyss were dead. Thus I understood that my Warsaw was no more, that something had perished forever, and that the old life and the approaching new life would never be able to grow together, as two halves of a broken nut.[14]

Nevertheless, the atmosphere in Warsaw was unexpectedly fresh and bracing. "I came back to Poland," Wat wrote, "and at the beginning Poland looked to me a paradise of freedom. In particular, Polish literature: it seemed as if censorship was entirely absent. . . . Therefore, once again I succumbed to a tremendous illusion: it seemed to me it would stay that way."[15] And again:

In the ruins, people took their roots, the roots of their freedom: the ruins seemed to be its price. True, there were invaders in the office buildings, and victims of their raids sat behind the small barred windows of the basements. But perhaps they were marauders? The driver of a black limousine, who did not want to wait for his guest, a general, picked us up in a field, several kilometers from Warsaw, where we had been forced to get off from the train with our bags full of tin plates, dried bread crumbs, rags and other goods and chattels belonging to us. He told us on the way, how "our lads" beat lonely Russians, whom they catch on dark streets. "Our lads?" I asked him to repeat. "Yes, I'm a driver at Radkiewicz's office, the Ministry of State Security." Making us disembark one or two hundred meters from the Wilno Station, he refused to take a hundred rouble note: "I do not request payment from martyrs."[16]

The Wat family found Broniszówna's apartment not too far from the station: she lived in the Praga area, a relatively unscathed neighborhood.[17] After a few days, Borejsza contacted Wat, proposing to him various jobs (allegedly, there was even talk about a ministerial position).[18] Reluctant to align himself with the new regime, Wat restricted himself to free-lance activities. But in June 1946, he accepted an offer of the directorship of the newly organized Państwowy Instytut Wydawniczy (State Publishing Institute). An old friend, Alfred Krygier, who was now responsible for the distribution of flats in Warsaw, provided the Wats with a good apartment on Niemcewicz Street, where they lived until their emigration in 1957.[19] In a very short time, Wat joined the management of *Rebirth*, as well as a number of bodies and commissions concerned with Polish culture.[20]

Notwithstanding his ambivalent reputation, Wat was able to maintain contacts with many members of the new Communist elite. For them, he was the semi-legendary editor of the *Literary Monthly,* hence a sort of mentor. The periodical was still ignored officially, and most of its contributors were rehabilitated no earlier than 1955–56. Nevertheless, it enjoyed respect in the "inner party."[21]

A special relationship developed between Wat and the *Forge,* the most sophisticated of the Marxist periodicals, which laid claim to the inheritance of the Polish radical philosophical tradition and had a particularly soft spot for the Enlightenment. It also emphasized its anti-fascism. "The people at the *Forge* essentially followed the myth of Boethius: to civilize the barbarians, to save everything that can be saved among the great values of the doomed culture."[22] Wat liked those young men who, in his opinion, were engaged in the ritual repetition of his old errors.[23]

In 1947–49, Wat's public activities were conducted, to a significant degree, under the auspices of the Polish PEN Club. Wat renewed his membership in the Polish branch as soon as it was reactivated, in 1947, and continued to be a leading figure of its executive board for many years.

In 1963, looking back on this time from the viewpoint of an anti-Communist émigré, Wat wrote that the PEN Club was, "at that time, in the immense empire of Stalin, the only one, let me emphasize, perhaps the only one secular institution not controlled by the authorities. . . . Why did the authorities tolerate the PEN Club? For so many years? Of course . . . the party and the Security mostly ignored those meetings of old and placid intellectuals, 'the has-beens,' as the Russian saying goes . . . [and] reckoned with the international reputation of the Polish PEN Club. The reputation was merited precisely because of its independent stand." Another reason for the toleration of such an independent group was, according to Wat, the presence of "marranos" among the Communist functionaries.[24]

As an active member of the PEN Club, Wat found it easy to travel to the West, which was particularly welcome after his wartime confinement. In early

June 1947, he left Warsaw for the Nineteenth International PEN Congress in Zurich and apparently visited Paris as well.[25] For the Zurich meeting, he prepared an extensive speech,[26] in which he told the writers of the world about the staggering losses suffered by Poland in World War II. The main part of his statement was nevertheless optimistic. He emphasized the variety of trends and styles in postwar Polish literary life, in which Catholics, Marxists, and existentialists, hermetic and avant-garde poets, realists of an American bent, followers of Proust and Joyce, and pupils of Kafka and Alain-Fournier could compete on equal terms. (In 1947, this was not yet an untruth, although it already contained a tinge of wishful thinking.)

It is difficult to determine how far Wat was being sincere. His excessive praise of pluralism in Poland before a forum of world writers could be construed as a defence of the liberal trend in cultural policy against hard-liners (though, at the same time, it helped to camouflage their designs). Wat was far from being alone in this predicament. The same dilemma, writ large, bedeviled Ehrenburg and other liberal Soviets used by Stalin as his spokesmen in the West. In his speech, Wat couched his love-hate attitude to the Western world in typically Ehrenburgian terms:

> Our links with European culture are indissoluble. We love every stone of Europe, we love Gothic cathedrals, we love the antinomies and contradictions that enabled the Europeans to go upward, we love the great libertarian traditions of Western culture and civilization. But don't wonder when we ask: what is the West? Since crime, and murder, and fire, and the supercivilized scientific methods of our destruction, and the ovens of the crematoria where millions of our peace-loving people perished, came to us from the West. . . . For us, who are profoundly attached to the great European traditions, who accept them with confidence and love, the world, just like peace and morality, is one and indivisible, and the partition of the world into West and East is false, worthless and ominous. That partition has always been conducted on our living body. It crushes our bones.[27]

Like Ehrenburg, Wat was so shaken by the magnitude of Nazi crimes— brought to a halt only by the victory of the Allies, including the Soviets—that he seems to have considered it morally defensible to pass over in silence Stalinist crimes, at least for the time being. In his account of the congress, he even went so far as to equate anti-Russian attitudes with anti-Polish ones, so denying the reality of the Soviet occupation.[28] It is also striking that he, a Jew, many of whose near ones had perished in the death camps, never mentioned Jewish suffering in his speech: in perfect conformity with the Stalinist censors, he simply subsumed Jews under the general category of "peace-loving people." Such compromises were all but unavoidable at that time for Eastern European intellectuals—for those who did not intend to defect or remain silent, at least. This does not alter their reprehensibility, however, something that Wat soon came to recognize.

The main controversy at the Zurich Congress flared up around the question of whether to readmit German writers to the PEN Club. After the enthusiastic greeting extended to such guests of the congress as Thomas Mann and Erich Kästner, the matter seemed settled. It was Wat, a leading member of the Polish delegation, who protested the blanket rehabilitation of Germans and advocated scrutiny of each individual case. Once again, a complex motivation was at work: Wat doubtless hated the idea of associating with people who might have supported Hitler, but his stance also coincided with the official policy of Polish Communists. Notwithstanding strong appeals by Thomas Mann and even by the Communist Johannes Becher, Wat's proposal was finally approved by a vote of twenty-six to four.

Following his successful performance in Zurich, Wat was an official Polish delegate at the next two International PEN congresses, in Copenhagen and Venice. The Copenhagen Congress took place in late May to early June 1948. In Wat's words, "it was essentially boring and sterile."[29] "Perhaps this was caused by the very place of our meeting, by the *genius loci*, the phlegmatic, awkward and slightly disobedient spirit of that most beautiful city, which still lives on the memories of an ancient adventurous power and mercantile abundance, while vegetating in postwar poverty," he wrote in his account of the congress.[30] But the underlying cause of the congress's failure was the gap between Western and Eastern Europe that was widening relentlessly. Wat here rendered a service to the Communist cause, perhaps his last. In his speech, he said that a resolution addressing the Communist coup in Czechoslovakia would only increase hatred and harm prospects for world peace. The congress passed over the coup in silence.[31]

From Copenhagen, Wat went to Brussels, where his brother Moryc lived.[32] The meeting was more than just a happy occasion: it led Wat to ponder—for the first time in his life—the possibility of emigrating to the West.

In 1949, Wat was invited to the bicentennial of Goethe's birth in Weimar. At that time, Poland was becoming increasingly Sovietized, and Wat had every reason to believe that his journeys to the West would soon be severely curtailed.[33] From Weimar, he made a side trip to Erfurt.[34] Following his return to Weimar, there was an awkward scene, which, Wat maintained, was a crucial factor in his decision to become an open dissenter. He was to present a speech during a gathering of writers, with the indispensable toast to Stalin at the end. Wat, however numerous his compromises with the authorities may have been, still prided himself on having never mentioned the name of the dictator in a positive context. He arrived late and was scared to death by the unannounced presence of Russian high officials and generals. His delivery was a source of embarrassment, both to himself and to his audience. Allegedly, it ended with an inarticulate mutter that was taken for the required toast—and presented as such in the West German press.

Following the celebrations in Weimar, Wat went to Venice, to the next International PEN Congress. "Venice astonished me, one could not imagine it," he wrote.[35] "This is not even the result of all those charms present here in absolute plenty, but . . . of the ambiance in which I feel myself at home like a fish in water. A completely uncanny upsurge of strength."[36] Significantly, he avoided contributing in any way to the congress and did not publish an account of it.[37] He devoted a considerable part of September to simply enjoying the city and its art, as well as to making private contacts with Western writers and ordinary Italians, with whom he felt more at ease than with many of his Polish colleagues.

After the congress, Wat traveled through Italy, to Florence, then to Rome and on down to Naples and Capri. This first encounter with the Mediterranean environment was to play an important role in his poetry in the 1950s and 1960s. Wat's description of the Neapolitan landscape contains a mixture of mythologization and demythologization, exultant anthropomorphism and pervasive, erudite, postmodern irony, a mixture that was to become a trademark of his mature work:

> The wild beauty—here, one cannot fail to become an animist, one sees in the rocks and the sea the deities, who have for sure grown wild after so many centuries, but have retained ancient good looks even in their wild state—a certain wrinkled Apollo or Dionysus, a certain grizzled hag Venus, the spirits of mountains and rivers—in a word, *Faust II*, the antique Walpurgisnacht. . . . The line between the sky and the sea was as if prismatic, and the sky together with the sea looked like God's face, with the roaming eye of the moon and the pupil of a planet . . . in a word, a face of strange inhuman beauty—Picasso attempts to communicate something of the kind."[38]

In Rome, Wat came face to face with his Jewishness more directly than ever before. Standing in front of the Arch of Titus in the Roman Forum, he went through an extremely powerful, crushing emotional crisis. This experience was so significant for him that he described it three times, in three different genres: first, in a letter to Ola of 29 September 1949;[39] then, in the first poem of the cycle *Na melodie hebrajskie* (Hebrew Melodies), written in 1949 but not published until 1957; and, finally, in a note that forms a section of his notebook *Moralia*. This last is perhaps the most telling:

> When I passed the Arch of Titus, the beauty of which from a distance, against the background of the sky and next to the lonely columns of Castor and Pollux, had shaken my heart—I planted my feet upon the earth as a donkey and: oh, barbarian!—spat, seized by a sudden hatred. Only after a moment did I look attentively at the inner relief, where my ancestors in chains, driven to slavery, carried the Jerusalem menorah, and among them, among the first ones, was my father's face! . . .
>
> And I wanted, I wanted very much to pass under the Arch of Titus. Later I learned that at no time, for two millennia, had a Jew (at least a Roman Jew,

and there were extremely enlightened people among them) passed there—
while at the day of the announcement of the State of Israel Roman Jews passed
under it openly, in a crowd, to the sound of music, joyfully and triumphantly.
Thus atavism explodes in a human being, even in one who is, supposedly, fully
denationalized, deprived of ethnic feelings, the most cosmopolitan.[40]

Seemingly dismissed as "atavism," it was, in fact, a confession of belonging, an assertion of common roots and a shared fate, one that was subsequently to
weigh heavily on Wat.

At approximately that time, Wat conceived the intention of visiting the
United States. Confident that the planned three-month trip would translate into
reality, he made arrangements with the periodical *Nowiny Literackie* (Literary
Tidings) to write a series of essays on American life and culture. But his Communist past and his semi-official standing in Poland resulted in his being refused
a visa by the American consulate. In an ironic essay that Wat composed about his
interrogation by American authorities, he states, in an offhand manner, that it
"had awoken in him some scary memories."[41]

Meanwhile, the scary atmosphere of Lwów and Lubyanka was resurfacing
in Polish public life. The year 1948 was crucial. In Poland, the new political
climate was ushered in by the defeat of Gomułka, who lost his leading position in
September and was reportedly put under house arrest. The PPR (Polish
Workers' Party, successor to the KPP) and the remnants of the PPS formed the
so-called Polish United Workers' Party (PZPR), which dismissed all calls for
political pluralism. Many intellectuals, including Broniewski and Tuwim, glorified the event; Wat added his signature to a joint statement by fifty-five writers
(among whom were Iwaszkiewicz and Stawar) but did not publish any congratulatory text of his own.[42] In the mid-1960s, he noted: "I do not remember the
dates well, it was most likely in December 1948: late in the evening, I was going
home by tram No. 9 from a meeting. . . . Already, one felt everywhere the race to
become like Saratov or Simbirsk—I could smell the dirty breath of that race. I
could not any longer remain lost in a sweet illusion. . . . 'How long will it last,
the *bezobrazie* [outrage]?' a female conductor (perhaps a chief one, neat, good-
looking and well-clad) asked an officer. 'For a long time,' he answered and
emitted a sort of whistle, either of regret or of satisfaction."[43]

The Iron Curtain was descending. In 1949, Wat resigned from the State
Publishing Institute and gave up almost all his other positions. Like many other
Polish intellectuals, he crossed the divide, accepting the status of "internal
émigré."

During the period 1946–49, Wat was a regular contributor to the Polish
press, though he remained a less than prolific author. He did write and publish

some poetry, however. In 1948, he placed in the *Literary Tidings* his cycle *Pięć wierszy z notatnika* (Five Poems from a Notebook).[44] Three of the poems were written much earlier, in Soviet prison and exile. The other two formed a counterpart to the "Gulag poems," since they dealt with another version of the totalitarian experience—Auschwitz and its crematoria.

One more poem published in 1948, "Sąd ostateczny" (The Last Judgment),[45] is a grotesque variation on the medieval theme that is nevertheless impressive for its manifest religious tonality. A long list of nationalities summoned for judgment—"Ainu, Tibetans, Tungus and Koreans . . . / Bashkirs, Chuvash, Mordva and Cheremis, / Dungans, Kurds, Aimaks and Khazars . . ."—while following the paradigm of biblical enumerations, obviously refers to Stalinism as well: they are, almost without exception, ethnic groups enslaved by the Communist dictatorship and observed by Wat during his Asian exile.

The most striking work of this period had to wait until 1957 to be published. It is a short (four-couplet) verse entitled "Imagerie d'Épinal," a Kafkaesque parable about a little girl who joins a joyful parade, carrying on a pole the severed head of her father, who is alleged to be an enemy of the people. In Wat's collection of 1957,[46] the poem was given the subtitle "On the Death of X . . . Y . . . Z. . . ." Editing it while an émigré, Wat spelled out the cryptogram (which was in any case intelligible to many readers of the earlier version): now the poem was subtitled "On the Death of Rajk, Slansky and Thousands of Others." Written probably soon after the execution of the Hungarian Communist leader Laszlo Rajk, but before the trial and execution of his Czech counterpart, Rudolf Slansky, it marked the end of Wat's attempts to work within the system. Its very inclusion in the 1957 book constituted an act of defiance.

Up to 1949, Wat was also active as an essayist and literary critic. None of his essays of this period has lasting significance. But in most of them, Wat manages to promote his own ideas. Thus, in one essay Thomas à Kempis rather unexpectedly appears by way of advice as to how to achieve salvation in the totalitarian world. Some passages of the essay on the reconstruction of Warsaw develop into a fine eulogy of architecture as opposed to literature, which only too easily succumbs to ideological manipulation: "Here, everything is firm, immediately verifiable and usable, one can touch it, concrete is concrete, marble is marble, it does not cheat, in contrast to the writers' material—always ambivalent, always unsteady, too pliable and slippery. . . . I would persuade my son to study architecture."[47]

Perhaps the most unusual piece of this period was "Druga zbrodnia Salome" (The Second Crime of Salome), published in the popular magazine *Przekrój* (Cross-Section), which for many years was an outlet for writers of liberal artistic taste and belief.[48] Outwardly, "The Second Crime of Salome" is an unprepossessing story intended strictly for entertainment, with a strong element of parody. Yet, it would hardly be out of place in *Lucifer Unemployed,* in that it presents some provocative (and definitely un-Marxist) thoughts about the nature of art and its relation to life.

The story revolves around several well-known masterpieces in the Louvre, including *La Gioconda, The Man with the Glove* by Titian, and the titular *Salome* by Bernardino Luini. At first, they are admired by tourists, who, significantly, imitate art in their behavior, repeating gestures of the painted persons and so on. This scene mockingly inverts the Marxist notion of "art as reflection of reality," which Wat frequently assailed in his theoretical statements.[49] The game of subversion continues as the plot develops. A young, "slightly somnambulistic" painter falls in love with *Salome* and Salome answers him with a wink and an ironic smile. A parallel love develops between a famous actress and *The Man with the Glove.* After the museum closes, the paintings come to life and step out of their frames. Salome, the paradigmatic criminal temptress of European decadence, entices the enamored painter to decapitate his girlfriend. The love between the actress and the Man with the Glove results in the lady becoming profoundly fearful and unhappy. Thus, the mingling of life and art proves to be disastrous: human beings, born to earthly existence, cannot tolerate suprapersonal existence embodied in the paintings, which must go back into their frames and be confined again.

The ideological guardsmen hardly noticed the subversive message of this story printed in a frivolous magazine. But in another, more important enterprise of the fateful year 1948, Wat was less fortunate.

From 1947, a new generation of writers started to make its mark in Polish letters. These were the so-called *pryszczaci* (pimple faces), mainly young men who sincerely believed in communism and their own role in preparing the ground for the coming millennium. Their program, formulated in the student periodical *Po prostu* (Point-Blank), left no place for illusions: "We will openly condemn the forces that attempt to set young intellectuals in opposition to the new reality."[50] Characteristically, most of the "pimple faces"—Wiktor Woroszylski, Tadeusz Konwicki, and others—became dissidents around 1956 and contributed to the liberation of Polish culture and society.[51] But in 1947-49, their writing followed the worst traditions of the prewar Communist press, boding ill for the future.

The advent of an active group of young adherents was a mixed blessing as far as the party ideologues were concerned. More than once before, such groups had gone astray; therefore, they must be educated—that is, tamed and disciplined. The educational campaign included a seminar for the young writers in Nieborów (an old princely palace near Warsaw), 11-17 January 1948. Forty-seven literati, including all the leading pimple faces, attended. The most remarkable among them was Tadeusz Borowski, who had been a prisoner at Auschwitz

and wrote highly talented stories about it. In 1948, Borowski was a "true believer" of the narrowest kind. Three years later, he was to commit suicide as a
result of a crisis in his Communist ideology—an act comparable, in the Polish
context, to the suicide of Mayakovsky. Among the lecturers were Żółkiewski,
Iwaszkiewicz, Stawar, and Wyka. (One of the functions of the seminar was
probably to test the orthodoxy not only of the students but also of the teachers.)
Wat was invited as well, and his performance was scandalous.

Wat's paper, "Antyzoil albo rekolekcje na zakończenie roku" (Anti-Zoilus,
or Meditations at the End of the Year),[52] was actually a long, "slightly labyrinthine"[53] essay that wittily disproved the main tenets of socialist realism, its
Zhdanovist version in particular.

The recipe for socialist realism, concocted in the 1930s, was simple.[54] The
traditional, sociologically minded realism of the preceding century (Balzac and
perhaps Tolstoy, but certainly not Dostoevsky) was accepted as the one and only
norm of structure and style. It was to be complemented by "revolutionary
Romanticism." In practice, this meant that literature must affirm the Soviet (or
Soviet-like) way of life rather than criticize it. This led to brazen deformations,
concealed, in part, by a heavily mimetic technique.

Wat made the following patently heretical statement: "I do not assert that
representation of the objective truth is unattainable for a writer, that it isn't, in
fact, his calling! But I assert that realism in our present situation cannot be the
exclusive and supreme means of attaining it."[55] The pet Marxist metaphor of
literature as "mirror of life" was, in Wat's opinion, wrong. A good example was
provided by the German literature of the Weimar Republic, the greatest of which
was pacifist. Taking the mirror metaphor at face value, one would thus perceive
Germany as a country on the eve of profound, positive change. The truth about
the condition of German society, according to Wat, was to be found only in
third-rate nationalist novels or in the disturbing works of expressionism.

"The slogan of Realism propped up by Romanticism sounds even more
pitiful," Wat wrote, attacking another of the holy of holies of socialist realism.[56]
He reminded his listeners of Romanticism's negative potential: that "Hitlerism,
on the plane of culture, is the successor of German Romanticism, albeit a
degenerate one."[57] The eschatological scheme of socialist realism—"the
struggle of good and bad, the chosen and the accursed, the last judgment and
salvatory triumph"—was, in Wat's view, a ludicrous imitation of the great
religious archetype: "I do not deny that one may write *one or ten good novels*
employing the scheme, but *what next?* After all, the entire flourishing of secular
literature came, if not due to, then in the process of the destruction of that
scheme, just as the flowering of modern painting was caused by the surmounting
of the—however magnificent—Byzantine canon. Thus, in a sense, the history
of literature is a process of gradual liberation from canons, rules and conventions. And that process is, in my opinion, historically irreversible."[58]

The explosive potential of that argument cannot be overestimated. Far from casting away the Marxist paradigm, it called into question the very strait-jacket that the party was putting on the arts. If the notion of progress is accepted, then the "canons, rules and conventions" of socialist realism are something to be surmounted: moreover, their destruction is to some extent guaranteed by that Marxist idol, history itself. On the other hand, neither expressionism nor Dostoevsky nor Proust nor Joseph Conrad could be eliminated from literature without irremediable harm.

Here, Wat became a precursor. During the thaw of the 1950s and 1960s, this line of thought was picked up by countless critics and philosophers, in Eastern Europe as well as in the Soviet Union. Furiously denounced, but never convincingly countered by hard-line theoreticians, it contributed to the demise of Stalinist culture and, indirectly, of Stalinism itself.

A further heretical notion of Wat was his distinction between "high" literature (which could and should be completely free in both method and style) and "applied writing" (which could follow the precepts of didacticism). The former answers to the spiritual and epistemological needs of the individual human being, whereas the latter has an educational function (which, however, does not release it from the requirements of good and honest craft).[59]

In sum, Wat's entire paper was a defense of authentic art. It opted for a literature that would serve the cause of the "humanist development" of society, broadly understood; but it was to be a literature "with a wide margin of intellectual and artistic licenses and variations, and, first of all, without catechism or the birch rod."[60]

The participants in the Nieborów seminar were nonplussed, to say the least. In his account of the proceedings, Borowski wrote: "The paper by A. Wat was brilliant but incorrect in its too hasty denial of the value of Realism."[61] The party mentors of the pimple faces reacted even more strongly. A veritable press campaign was launched against Wat. An anonymous teacher assailed him in a popular daily for the alleged obscurity of his text, which was much overloaded, in the teacher's opinion, by foreign borrowings. Wat responded in a disdainful manner, which led to a new round of accusations. But the teacher (perhaps an invention of the party authorities) was far from being the only attacker. More ominous were polemical articles signed by two leading Marxist ideologues, Borejsza and Żółkiewski.

Borejsza, for the most part, limited himself to the kind of arguments set forth by the anonymous teacher: he accused Wat of being elitist and looking down on ordinary people. This populist harangue was fully consonant with the "anti-cosmopolitan" campaign that had broken out in the Soviet Union in 1947–48 and continued until Stalin's death. Żółkiewski was more straightforward. In an outwardly friendly but heavily ironic article, he exposed the essence of Wat's position and made clear its unacceptability to an orthodox Marxist. According to Żółkiewski, Wat's argument could be summarized in two points:

1. "One should not put dolphins in cages." Ideological intervention into literary life is undesirable.

2. The sense of literature does not consist in engagement, in contribution to the creation of certain extraliterary facts and social situations, does not consist in struggle, educational activity, opposing correct politics to wrong politics, but in meditation upon the passing time, in a reflective catching of the images of transient life.[62]

However simplistic, the summary was certainly not devoid of perspicacity. Żółkiewski, who at that time sincerely believed in the salutary qualities of a consistent Marxist approach, may have considered his polemics with Wat part of a purely ideological struggle and may not have intended to cause any personal harm to his opponent. Nonetheless, his article was, in effect, a political denunciation of the worst kind. In the context of Stalinism, honest Marxists might easily present a greater danger to their non-Marxist colleagues than time-servers and demagogues.

To Wat's credit, he did not recant. He repeated calmly his most subversive statements: that good literature should *not* mirror life and should *not* perform didactic tasks.[63] But "Anti-Zoilus" was virtually the last visible manifestation of Wat's presence in Polish literary life during the Stalinist period. He published a few more pieces in 1948 and 1949, but from then on engaged in a "speech campaign," as the only way of registering his dissent:

From 1949, I spoke systematically at all imaginable literary or semi-literary meetings. Of course, I did it in a cautious but unambiguous way and always got a thrashing! . . . Why did I do it? I am not a Don Quixote. There is a moment, when one cannot stand it any longer, when one is choking with anger.[64]

I made speeches in the Writers' Union up to 1952 . . . incidentally also for the young ones, "the pimple faces," to reveal to them the primitivism of their tutors, the caddishness and anachronism of Communist doctrine, and to fascinate them with the richness of Western thought.[65]

He evidently made ten or twelve such speeches,[66] though their texts have not survived. (It seems that the records of the meetings at which Wat spoke were destroyed.[67]) Still, Wat's words are corroborated by numerous witnesses who were influenced by his courageous stance. Interestingly, one of them was Wiktor Woroszylski, perhaps the staunchest of the pimple faces and later a leading Polish dissident:

During the Stalinist period, Aleksander Wat used to climb the podium at the Writers' Union and make speeches that were completely intolerable from the system's point of view. I listened to these speeches and boiled with hatred. I thought it was pretty abominable stuff, the twaddle of a class enemy. Yet it never entered my mind at the time that one should deal with the problem by means of the police or something of the kind. . . . I believed that on the whole it was correct, that he had the right to speak that way. But it seemed horrible to me that there was a guy who said these things. Incidentally, the funny part of the affair was that it had a certain effect upon my life. I felt myself intellectually powerless confronting his speeches, and at the same time I was infuriated, I believed that they surely could be disproved, I just did not know how to do it. Therefore it influenced my decision to go to the Soviet Union for postgraduate studies. I went there since I hoped to learn magnificent arguments for disproving everything that Aleksander Wat had said against us. You know the results. There I found arguments which rather supported Aleksander Wat's stance, and quite soon at that.[68]

The only means of economic survival now available to Wat was translation. Having become accustomed to such work during the 1920s and 1930s, he pursued it now with even greater intensity, often jointly with Ola. But even here, censorship and ideological supervision had to be reckoned with. For the most part, only Soviet literature or, at best, Russian classics could be translated. The author on whom Wat's survival primarily depended was Arkady Gaidar, a tremendously popular Soviet journalist and children's writer who perished in World War II. Gaidar's stories were published and republished in Poland, as well as in the USSR, literally every year. Dealing with Young Pioneers helping old and disabled people and similar topics, they were nevertheless not without some artistic and ethical value. "A talented and very honest man," Wat said of Gaidar in his memoirs. "A pearl, if one considers his honesty against the background of Soviet literature; not a demoralized one, very brave, courageous. . . . I must confess that I translated him with real pleasure, it was very pure atmosphere."[69] But what impressed Wat most was that Gaidar never mentioned Stalin's name in his writings.[70]

"I hardly eked out a living: from time to time they gave me translations, the most difficult ones and on a meagre rate; my sister [Broniszówna] had to support me for many months; sleuths followed me on the street, pestered the concierge; the oldest friends, with the exception of two, did not recognize me; the most decent among them, such as the poet J . . .[71] (like Proust's Monsieur Legrandin) displayed warm sympathy for me in one eye and glassy indifference in the other, which faced bystanders," Wat wrote in the 1960s about his life in Stalinist Poland.[72] Two former friends who kept up relations with the Wat family were Stawar and Broniewski, the first as isolated as Aleksander, the second becoming increasingly ruined by alcoholism.

In the early 1950s, totalitarianism became virtually all-pervading in Poland. Defection or death looked like the only options for an honest writer: in 1951, Miłosz joined the community of exiles, and Borowski committed suicide. Such major authors as Słonimski and Tuwim compromised themselves, albeit to varying degrees. By contrast, Wat made only small concessions to the political establishment (such as attending obligatory May Day demonstrations), of which he was deeply ashamed.[73] Nor did he renounce his "speech campaign," which he continued even in "the blackest year" of 1952.

"I wrote: in the blackest year 1952. One must specify," Wat noted several years later. "It was the blackest one until the XIX Congress,[74] since from the proceedings of the XIX Congress of the CPSU one could easily infer the decline and ruin of the great and immortal Stalinist era. One had to be blind not to see the fiery writing: *Mene Tekel Peres.* I remember how I, unable to conceal my joy, loudly harangued on that topic in the presence of two scared colleagues. . . . They did not write a denunciation."[75]

Wat's words seem like an overstatement. At the time, someone with his political experience and insight might indeed have been able to predict the appearance of the first cracks in the system, but joy was premature. A reflection of this was the brutal attack on Wat in the same year, 1952, probably around the time of the Congress. At the writers' meeting, Putrament cut short Wat's "counter-revolutionary" speech, quoting a Russian proverb: "Kogda medved' vorchit, dash' emu dubinoi po golove, i togda on molchit" (When a bear growls, hit him on the head with a bludgeon to make him silent). An old Communist, Żanna Kormanowa, seconded him by asserting that Wat was the last adversary of the new order among the literati. On reaching home, Aleksander told Ola: "They held a first-class funeral for me."[76]

Wat now had to reckon with the possibility of a new arrest and imprisonment. He noticed signs of his impending doom, reminding him of his Lwów experience. People whom he considered agents of the secret police began to greet him gregariously.[77] The extent to which his anxiety was well-founded versus the extent to which these signs aroused in him a persecution mania is unclear; each feeds on the other. Be that as it may, Wat was twelve years older and far more exhausted by his misfortunes than he had been in Lwów. All that followed was essentially predictable.

On the night of 11 January 1953, Wat fell seriously ill. Three days later, he was taken to a Warsaw hospital (which, strangely enough, still had the prewar name of the Infant Jesus). The exact diagnosis was *thrombosis arteriae cerebelli posterioris inferioris,* otherwise known as Wallenberg's syndrome.

> For a layman, it would be enough to tell, that I felt as if a tank had smashed my skull and all my body. Piercing pain in the left side of the torso and in the right extremities. Contraction of the larynx, nausea, hiccup, aversion to light, dizziness and headache, double vision. I could not stand on my feet and always fell

to the left side (left-wing deviation, in contrast with the suspicions of my colleagues from the Writers' Union). . . . Lying in the most regular manner on a reliable bed, I felt all the time that I was about to fall, that the physician standing close by on his sturdy legs would collapse, that the walls would also collapse.[78]

Like all the other patients, most of whom were in critical condition, Wat was exposed to education by radio: in obedience to an Orwellian decree, the loudspeaker was switched on early in the morning and switched off only at 10 P.M. "Most tolerable were the agricultural talks: one could learn many things, for instance, how to convert refuse into compost. The worst were optimistic songs or choral howlings and recitations, and the very worst—the sports news, which, to make it more intolerable, was broadcast late in the evening."[79] Wat probably missed the most ominous news, which coincided with the onset of his disease. On 14 January, the day he was taken to the hospital, *Pravda* announced the discovery of the so-called doctors' plot: a group of (mainly Jewish) Kremlin physicians was arrested and accused of "terrorist activities"—that is, an attempt to poison Stalin. It was the signal for a new purge, which most likely was to exceed in thoroughness the bloody purges of the prewar years. A mortal fear grasped the Soviet Union and all Eastern Europe. But in early March came a second announcement, that Stalin was "temporarily withdrawing" from the leadership of the party and the state due to grave illness.

On 5 March, Ola arrived at the hospital, only to find a group of silent, brooding doctors and nurses at the entrance to Aleksander's ward. In a trembling voice, she asked about his condition. One of the women whispered: "Do you fancy that we've gathered here because of your husband? Stalin died, and we arranged a mourning chapel in your husband's ward." There were candles, flowers, and a large portrait hung with black crepe. An old nurse lamented: "Our dear little Stalin, such a powerful man, and now he's dead. To say nothing of us, the small people." In the calendar that lay on his desk, Wat wrote in capital letters: "AT LAST." Then he tore out the page, to be on the safe side.[80]

Wat's illness was a decisive factor in his life for the next fourteen years. After Stalin's death, he spent some time in the hospital of the Ministry of Health. By the time he was released, most of the incapacitating symptoms had vanished, but one continued: severe burning and a biting pain, mainly in the left side of his face and in his right leg, radiating to other parts of the body. Almost any attempt to concentrate for even a quarter of an hour resulted in a fit of pain followed by excruciating insomnia.

In 1954, Wat was allowed to visit Stockholm, where he was examined by a world-class neurosurgeon, Professor Olivecrone. After a series of tests, Olivecrone ascertained that Wat's illness was caused by a small blood clot in his thalamus, the part of the forebrain involved in the transmission and integration of sensations of pain. Any discomfort in any part of the body was, as it were, magnified by the condition. Surgery was not recommended, since it could result in paralysis, blindness, deafness, and mental incapacitation. But Olivecrone consoled Wat with the promise that his suffering would subside in seven years— a prognosis that unfortunately proved to be wrong.[81]

Many of Wat's acquaintances dismissed his health problem as hypochondria. When Wat opted for political exile, the Communist authorities hinted that he had exaggerated his physical torment so as to facilitate his defection to the West. Even Wat's friends often accused him of hysteria, self-pity, and "escape into illness" to avoid facing difficult situations.[82] It cannot be doubted that Wat suffered enormously: but there is also no doubt that his condition was, to a large degree, psychosomatic in origin. In his last years, Wat analyzed it with extraordinary incisiveness. His *Diary without Vowels* presents one of the most refined and intriguing examples of self-analysis in world literature.

"For pain thou art, and unto pain thou shalt return. Or: in the beginning was pain. One may continue it endlessly," Wat wrote in the 1950s.[83] He searched desperately for circumstances that might have predisposed him to this suffering. Was it genetics, the result of a hereditary dissonance between a phlegmatic father and a sanguine, hysterical mother? Was it the innate asymmetry of his body noticed by portrait-painters? A disturbance of body thermodynamics? The manic-depressive disposition that was already noticeable in his youth? The traumas of his early years, the ordeals of prison and exile, his near-hopeless resistance to Stalinism in postwar Poland? Perhaps all that, and much more.[84] Before long, Wat was interpreting his illness as the result of demonic possession, a punishment meted out by a transcendental power. He was aware of the metaphorical nature of this interpretation yet insisted on a literal reading of it, on its "realization" (in formalist terms)—its translation into metaphysical reality:

> I cannot mediate upon the topics I want to, upon those I have decided and am obliged to, and that is a far from ordinary occurrence caused by the loosening of control or mental laziness. Quite the opposite, it happens when I concentrate and control myself, when I make an effort of will and industriousness, and it intensifies to the degree the latter intensify. Therefore, this is something more powerful than myself, this is *the Interferer* (the main and most primeval function of the biblical devil). It is he who thinks, by means of my thought, about what he, the capricious one, wants to; he directs my choice, he picks and changes the topic, and when I resist him, he splits into a multitude of demons, he lets in a horde of them, and then I feel giddy, as if the wind has swept up bits of old trash and scattered them, and whirled them into the tortured space of my brain.[85]

Motifs of split personality, disintegration, and dismemberment, already conspicuous in *Pug Iron Stove*, are evident here. But what was a nihilistic literary "play with the devil" in Wat's early years has now become deadly serious: art has been transformed into life.

"If I had lived three or four centuries ago, a good exorcist might have cured me of my disease," Wat asserted.[86] (In fact, in 1957, Wat did seek help from an exorcist, the controversial Italian Padre Pio, an experience that ended in bitter disappointment).[87] He therefore turned to the best that the twentieth century had to offer: drugs. Pills of percodan alleviated the pain by deadening its main— if not only—source, his imagination, sensitivity, and memory—in short, his inner life.[88] Pharmacology, for Wat, was a new embodiment of an old enemy, in that it resulted in exteriorization, in making a person completely determined by material factors.[89] Hence, he considered it to be one more diabolical ruse.[90]

An important element in the fabric of Wat's psyche was his ambivalence toward the body. In line with an age-old religious tradition, Wat perceived the body, first and foremost, as the "seat of sin, of blasphemous transgression."[91] Sensitive to all signals from the perceptible universe, it was also hapless and isolated, subject to decay and death, the prison of the soul—and, simultaneously, a prisoner of it, awaiting a deserved punishment.

This punishment—or, to be precise, self-punishment—had all the relentlessness of Sophocles' *Oedipus* and Kafka's *The Trial*. Wat experienced a profound and multifarious sense of guilt:[92] vis-à-vis his father, whom he had left to die alone under the Nazi occupation; his mother, whom he had treated with indifference for many years; Ignacy Lew, who was arrested when found with Wat and presumably died because of this association; and Ola, who had suffered because of his political stands. Symbolically, all these transgressions amounted to one: the sin of apostasy, of rejecting one's own kin. In his early youth, Wat had repudiated his Jewishness, choosing instead assimilation; then he had repudiated his Polishness (and its Christianity), opting for the pseudo-international Stalinist faith. But it was communism that he perceived as the ultimate apostasy, a disease both of mankind and of history, involvement in which was therefore punishable by a physical disease, according to the rule *similia similiaribus curantur.*

Moreover, playing into this was the Romantic and post-Romantic notion of a link between disease and art.[93] According to this view—which became much more than an abstract idea—art was a destructive force, intimately connected to the Dionysian side of life. With its innate interest in the morbid aspect of being, art both promoted illness and insanity and thrived on them.

Traces of Wat's Communist experience further complicated the picture. Thus, in the period of the *Literary Monthly* he virtually rejected art as a bourgeois trap, corrupted by its links with a degenerate social order. Consistent Marxists—as well as modernists—considered all genuine art to be punishable. This could not fail to have intensified Wat's predicament, however strong his repudiation of Marxism and Stalinism might have been. The experience of a split personality was, to a significant degree, an outcome of Wat's Communist years and, in particular, of his Lwów period. Even his pattern of soul-searching was consistent with the practice of self-criticism that Wat had become acquainted with in Lwów (and probably during his interrogations in Lubyanka). To quote a contemporary critic, "Wat's confession of his Communist heresy seems singular since it is patterned after a method borrowed from the enemy with whom he is wrestling."[94]

To sum up, Wat's suffering was a metaphor that had attained the status of reality—and reality transformed into a metaphor. Wat perceived it as situated on the border between the physical and the metaphysical and as oscillating continuously between the two. It was both penance and martyrdom: moreover, it had a suprapersonal dimension, in that it was also "a figure of the existence of the contemporary world."[95]

One of the principal sources of his illness, art, was also its remedy. Wat complained bitterly that his persistent pain hampered his literary work: nevertheless, most of his oeuvre stems from these years of illness. During the last decade of his life, Wat wrote (or dictated) several volumes of essays and memoirs, as well as a volume of poetry that far surpassed his early lyrics in quantity while never yielding to them in quality. The borderline existence of an incurably sick man was as conducive to writing in Wat's case as in Proust's (a comparison he was aware of). In a poem of 1956, "Przed Breughelem starszym" (Before Breughel the Elder), he described this:

Work is a blessing.
I tell you that, I—a professional loafer!
Who bedded down in so many prisons! Fourteen!
And in so many hospitals! Ten! And innumerable hotels!

Work is a blessing.
How else could we deal with the lava of fratricidal love towards our fellow
        men?
With those storms of extermination of all by all?
With brutality that has no bottom, no measure?[96]

Wat's commitment to writing was, in his last years, a commitment to self-knowledge as well as to his fellow human beings. Finding an authentic Self would for him have been equivalent to finding the solution to the "biggest riddle, our riddle, the riddle of history,"[97] namely, the problem of communism. It was also the key to self-healing. But neither complete self-knowledge and recovery nor the final solution of the historical enigma proved to be attainable. There was to be no last word that would mean the end of writing: writing was all.

The political sea change that followed Stalin's death affected Aleksander and Ola as much as anybody. Outwardly, the dictator's death did not alter anything. There was an outbreak of mass sorrow, for the most part of dubious sincerity, with the best-known Polish intellectuals taking the lead and filling the pages of newspapers with effusions in the vein of the old nurse's lament in the hospital where Wat was convalescing. Some limited themselves to standard statements: "Stalin died, but his great idea, the idea of socialism and peace lives," for example, from Iwaszkiewicz. Others waxed rhapsodic; thus, Przyboś: "The death of Joseph Stalin bereaves us of speech. . . . But Stalin's work is more lasting than his life and is indestructible."[98] The *Universal Weekly* was the only periodical that refused to comply with the express order to print Stalin's photograph in a black border with the caption "the greatest man of our era," justifying its disobedience in terms of the fact that Stalin was not the head of the Polish state. For this infringement, publication was suspended indefinitely.[99] Fortunate in having the excuse of his illness, Wat sat on the sidelines, cautiously but impatiently awaiting better times.

On 6 April 1953, a communiqué appeared in the press, stating that the Kremlin doctors accused of poisoning their patients were innocent and adding the extraordinary admission that their self-incriminating depositions had been obtained by torture. Soon, the Polish office of state security was criticized in a closed meeting of the PZPR leadership, and Gomułka was released from detention. A series of formal rehabilitations followed in 1955–56. Among many others, Jasieński and Hempel were declared innocent victims of the Stalinist secret police.

The Wat family suffered its share of harassment even after Stalin's death. In 1953 Andrzej, then a student of art history, was threatened with expulsion from school, which would have meant assignment to work in the mines or service in a penal unit of the army. But Ola managed to rescue him by using her connections.[100] There was more such petty obstruction, since Wat was still, not without justification, considered "a class enemy." Nor did he do anything to try to change that image. Quite the contrary, he did not conceal his growing attraction to Catholicism, an attraction that culminated in the baptism of both him and Ola, conducted in secret, not so much out of caution perhaps as out of deference to the intimate nature of the ritual.

Wat gives the year of his baptism as 1953, but it probably took place in 1954, when he was considering brain surgery that could have resulted in death or total disability.[101] He and Ola were prepared for baptism by two nuns, Sister Maria and Sister Katarzyna, both of whom were Jews who had converted to Catholicism before the war. Prior to their conversion, they had been active in Communist circles and knew many leading members of the party (their acquaintance with the Wat family also dated from before the war). After living out the war in a convent, they managed to use some of their old contacts to help political prisoners.[102]

Wat's feelings about religion were deeply ambivalent. Two religions, Catholicism and Judaism, opposed to each other both theologically and historically, dwelled in his consciousness, at the same time remaining distinct and unreconciled. Naturally, he felt an aversion to the Church's record of anti-Semitism: "Jews, thanks to their distinctiveness, mysterious fate and loyalty (which withstood the massacres) to the habits and superstitions formed a couple of thousand years ago, evoked anti-Semitic prejudice everywhere in the diaspora . . . but only the Church furnished these antipathies with a philosophy, a system of motivations, crystallized and organized them, just as Hitlerism in our own times organized the xenophobia of the Central European and East European masses."[103] This constituted a weighty argument against conversion, since it would mean being unfaithful to his kin: "My road to Damascus was impeded by an obstacle, certainly not the only, but an imperative one: the voice of my father, *remember, remember.* I say this in a figurative sense, since my father was the most tolerant of all men."[104]

What attracted Wat to Christianity was not the entire corpus of its teachings, never mind its historical record, but a single figure, that of the suffering Christ. He had first identified himself with the crucified Christ in Zamarstynów, where he also saw the Crucifixion as an archetype of the distress of countless peoples under totalitarian rule. This identification was paradoxical, since at the time Wat was not a believer. He perceived himself simultaneously as Christ and doubting Thomas, a contradiction that remained in his thought and writing for many years,[105] although one for which there is a precedent, in such apocryphal texts as the *Acts of Thomas,* where Christ appears as Thomas's twin, virtually indistinguishable from him. Moreover, Christ became, in Wat's imagination, an archetypal image of Jewishness: "Jesus, the Jewish son of Mary, was for me then—and always—a Jew from alpha to omega, the highest incarnation not only of the Jewish psyche but also of the Jewish fate . . . in the image of Christ there was a personified unity of Jewish martyrology. How often I met, precisely among the pious [Jews], *naturaliter* Christian souls!"[106]

This concept provided a bridge between the two faiths and quenched, if only in part, Wat's thirst for metaphysics. Nevertheless, his baptism did not lead to inner harmony: "Even at the moment of that act I felt with despair that it failed, that it was not accepted, 'did not take' on me, that I was called but not chosen, that I was an outcast. I never received the eucharist."[107] Wat's last wish was to be buried in a Christian cemetery in Israel,[108] and nothing could reveal the paradoxical nature of his conversion more clearly. But it was a wish that was not fulfilled.

At the end of 1955, Wat was allowed to go abroad for treatment once more, with Ola accompanying him. Obtaining permission, as well as material support for a stay in the West, was far from easy because of Wat's political reputation. But the legend of the *Literary Monthly* was alive, and former influential acquaintances helped, if only to a degree. In late fall of 1955, Aleksander and Ola left for France, and on 30 November they were already in Paris.[109]

What was originally planned as a winter outing lasted more than a year and a half. The Wats spent most of this time in the French Riviera, where they stayed at Menton-Garavan and later in Vence. In early 1957, they undertook a long trip to Italy, once more visiting Rome, Venice, Florence, Naples, and Capri and spending three months in Sicily, mainly in Taormina. Aleksander also underwent treatment in Paris, in the hospital Saint-Mandé. They returned to Warsaw on 8 July 1957.[110]

Notwithstanding his ongoing physical suffering, this stay in Western Europe was a happy period for Wat. He caught its mood in a short and simple poem entitled "Piosnka dla żony" (A Song for My Wife), written in Menton on his fifty-sixth birthday:

> I have visited more than one hell,
> I have run through more than one country,
> I was never so glad
> as here, in this winter camp of birds,
> under this pink rock,
> over this green wave. . . . Although there is pain *in every breath*,
> don't weep poor girl—
> I was never so glad,
> I was never in such a bliss!

The Wats rented an apartment in a rather exclusive Menton house: "Two terraces smelling of violet wisteria, the rooms full of paintings, antique furniture, carpets and silver. At the kitchen door, immense bushes of camellia in bloom. . . . We were visited by our Paris friends, Aleksander's brother came for a short time from Brussels."[111]

During their stay in Western Europe, Aleksander and Ola met more than one important cultural figure. The Wats were resident in the Pension Chapignac in Vence with Gordon Craig, aged eighty-four at the time. "The old man is charming and young indeed," Wat wrote to Broniszówna.[112] Ola left a concise account of Craig in her memoirs: "He screamed out separate French words in a torrent of English speech and whistled like a bird. . . . In a black cape, with a large black hat and flying gray hair, he was beautiful. . . . He pronounced emphatic monologues. At the day of our departure he played the role of Romeo under my window for a farewell."[113] A meeting in Rome with Italian man of letters Ignazio Silone led to a close friendship. Wat and Silone had traveled similar paths, first embracing communism, then rejecting it and opting for a religious world outlook. They had even been born "together with the century," on the same day, 1 May 1900.

Mixing with old acquaintances of an anti-Communist persuasion and engaging in long discussions became quite natural. In Naples, Aleksander and Ola stayed with Gustaw Herling-Grudziński, alias Gustaw Herling, a former Soviet prisoner who had left the USSR with Anders's army and later became a brilliant writer and one of the founders of *Culture*.[114] At that time, the Wats were considering the possibility of leaving Poland for good. Wat even toyed with the idea of trying for the position of Polish cultural attaché in Athens, which was, of course, wishful thinking.[115] Defection seemed a more realistic option. But there was an obstacle: in accordance with the Communist practice of "hostages," Andrzej (an art historian by this time) would not be able to join his parents, because he had been denied permission to leave Poland while they were abroad. Moreover, Wat was ill-prepared to take on responsibility for a new life. If he defected, he would have to support not only himself but also Ola and perhaps Andrzej, and he was fifty-seven years old and feeling much older than this.

At the same time, he was in the midst of a veritable explosion of creativity. In France and Italy, he wrote more lyric poems than he had in the rest of his life put together, poems that were highly regarded by the discriminating readers to whom he showed them in private.[116] On 15 December 1956, Ola mailed a typescript of Wat's new book of poetry from Paris to the state publishing house "Wydawnictwo Literackie" in Kraków.[117] There was still some hope that Wat might be able to participate actively in the literary life of his homeland.

The year and a half that the Wats spent abroad was fraught with events that proved to be fateful for the history of Eastern Europe. The Twentieth Congress of the Communist Party of the Soviet Union, which took place in February 1956, was marked by Khrushchev's secret speech in which he denounced Stalin and some Stalinist practices. The text leaked abroad, generating a worldwide sensation, and Wat, like all Poles in the West, had ample opportunity to become acquainted with it.

Khrushchev's denunciation of Stalin fell on fertile ground. Gradually, Poland became one of the leaders in the liberalization of the entire Communist world, strongly influencing other countries—including the USSR itself. Most steadfast Marxists of the previous period, among them Żołkiewski (Borejsza had died in 1952), now opted for democratization. They were seconded by virtually all the writers. At a meeting in late March 1956, Przyboś declared: "Socialist realism was nothing but a stick created by Zhdanov for killing art." Słonimski was, if anything, even more direct, ridiculing the official concept of the so-called personality cult: "First of all, not a personality cult, but a person. Not a person, but a system which is conducive to such harmful activity of the person." Infuriated by this attack, a certain General Witaszewski entreated workers in Łódź to "take a gas pipe and drive away that kike Słonimski," but the only effect of his appeal was that he was given the nickname "General Gas Pipe."[118]

An early instance of a disobedient writer was Ważyk. Six months before the Twentieth Congress, he published his "Poemat dla dorosłych" (Poem for Adults) in *New Culture*, generating quite a commotion. The poem, a long, semi-journalistic harangue against Stalinism, was well timed: "Two years earlier such a poem could not have been published without the threat of immediate arrest, and no editor would have risked his neck to publish it."[119] Artistically, "Poem for Adults" was mediocre, and it ended on a note of continuing belief in the party. But its emotional intensity and, most of all, its blunt account of conditions in Stalinist Poland made it a revelation. Wat read the poem of his old friend and adversary before leaving for France, in Nieborów, where he spent part of the summer of 1955: "I remember that . . . somebody brought the poem from Warsaw, fresh off the printing press. We sat on the terrace, it was getting dark. Szyfman[120] was there with us, among others. Everybody wanted to read it first, then Aleksander said he would read it aloud, *a vista*. He did it, and then Szyfman (we were amused by his words) said: 'Aleksander, I give you an engagement at the Polish Theater. None of my actors would be able to read a poem in such a brilliant way.'"[121]

An even more important event was the takeover of the student publication *Point-Blank* by a group of young revisionists, who made it into a platform for the anti-Stalinist camp. Many if not most of its contributors were former pimple faces. Leading roles were played by a dissident philosopher, Leszek Kołakowski, and a young writer of rebellious existentialist bent, Marek Hłasko.

The political crisis in Poland emptied into the open in June 1956, when workers in the city of Poznań went on strike, and seventy-three people were killed.[122] The mood of the country became redolent of the Revolution of 1905. The reformers took the upper hand, attempting to control events through a combination of threats and concessions. Gomułka was rehabilitated and on 21 October 1956 became leader of the party. After several days of extreme tension, the so-called Polish October ended in far-reaching concessions to the people. Bloodshed was avoided, in contrast to Hungary, where a parallel movement for democratization, much influenced by the Polish example, was crushed by the Soviet Army on 4 November.

When Wat returned, in July 1957, it was to a country quite different from the one he had left not long before. Socialist realism was dead and forgotten, and once again, Poland was in touch with modern trends in world literature, art, and philosophy. The old demands of Wat's "Anti-Zoilus" were satisfied. Dissident authors who had been driven into "internal emigration" during the Stalinist period, such as Zbigniew Herbert and Miron Białoszewski, made impressive débuts. Witkacy, Bruno Schulz, and even some émigrés (such as Gombrowicz) were published again; there was also revived interest in the futurist and *New Art* heritage. Most important, the climate of fear and servility had dissipated. Under these circumstances, Wat's writing became emblematic of the new epoch.

"Loth's Flight": An Attempt at Reconstruction

News that Wat was working on a major novel made its way into the press as early as January 1949.[1] In an interview with *Express Wieczorny* (The Evening Express) Wat stated that the controversies about realism seemed futile to him and that he preferred creative work.[2] The novel he was planning was about a small town in Nazi Germany and one of its inhabitants, a Jew saved miraculously from extermination. Its title was to be "Ucieczka Lotha" (Loth's Flight). The name of the protagonist refers to Lot, the righteous man in the Book of Genesis who pitched his tent on the plain close to the city of Sodom and managed to escape when God's punishment befell it: "I said—Sodom, but the whole point is that Sodom consists of decent people. . . . It was an important task to record the martyrology of human beings and nations, to show those who suffered. But a more important task, in my opinion, and a more difficult one, is the description of those who caused the suffering."[3]

Wat's project was prompted in part by his own vulnerability as an avowed dissident and by considerations of survival. Work on an anti-Nazi novel furnished an excuse to withdraw from public life and wait until the worst was over by providing a sort of loyalty certificate. " 'The Reader' paid me a modest advance for a year or even longer, which helped me to survive somehow, without dedicating too much of my time to money-earning. Even after my numerous speeches at the Writers' Union, when blows fell on me thick and fast and my best friends did not visit me anymore, Leon Kruczkowski . . . passed on to me what Berman had said: 'Let him write his novel, and then we'll see.' "[4]

It would be wrong to claim that Wat was motivated only by pragmatic concerns, however. The nature of the Nazi regime and the problem of German guilt were undoubtedly matters of great interest to him. His was a philosophic and artistic task that any serious writer would have found challenging: first, to ferret out the roots of the Nazi crime in the European tradition (which he had already criticized mercilessly in his early iconoclastic works), and second, to ponder the similarities and differences between the Nazi regime and the other version of twentieth-century totalitarianism, the one known to him from personal experience.

In the West, there had already been one work of fiction that had attempted to elucidate the cultural background of the Nazi phenomenon: Thomas Mann's *Doctor Faustus* (1947). Wat had met Mann at the Zurich Congress, where Mann's speech had left him less than happy because, in Wat's opinion, Mann was too ready to absolve his country's sins.[5] "Loth's Flight" seems to have been intended as an Eastern European (and Jewish) answer to the German author's great novel.[6]

It was because he wanted to visit Erfurt, where the novel's action was to take place, that Wat accepted the invitation to the Goethe bicentennial.[7] Wat's account of this trip, considered by him to have been a high point of his life,[8] gives some insight into his creative process:

> The book's point of departure had been a bronze plate I had seen on a crematory oven at Auschwitz. It read, "Topf und Söhne, gegründet in 1886, Erfurt." I imagined the two junior Topfs, one of whom I saw as a classical philologist by education and calling who had ordered reliefs of the Grecian image of the spirit of death to be put on the doors of the luxurious ovens and who would have used quotations from the *Iliad* on his brochures, in particular the passage in which Hector's spirit implores Achilles that his remains be burned. [While in Weimar, I went to] Erfurt and was in the office of Mr. Topf, who had taken refuge in West Germany, and on his book shelf I saw Sophocles, Epictetus, Seneca, and so forth in German and also Kiesewatter's books on Homer. His younger brother had committed suicide as I had planned for him to do in my novel. . . . The chief engineer said to me, "There's nothing to see here. Yes, we exported crematoria during the war, and they were used in Buchenwald too. Buchenwald is a small German town; people die there like they do everywhere else. They used to bring the bodies to the cemetery in Weimar, but transportation is expensive in wartime and so we installed crematoria there." I rebuked the engineer, who was pasty from his fear of me. Then I ran out with a welter of emotions and wandered around the old city.[9]

The complete story of Topf and Söhne was revealed only in 1993, by Gerald Fleming, an English writer who obtained access to Soviet archives containing materials about the firm. According to his account,[10] Ludwig Topf, the managing director, committed suicide in May 1945, and his brother, Ernst-Wolfgang, fled the Soviet zone. One of the firm's senior engineers, Kurt Prüfer, had been interrogated by the Americans but had been released by them after convincing them—as one of his colleagues later attempted to convince Wat— that the crematoria had been used exclusively for health reasons. In 1946, he was arrested by the Soviets, and in 1952 he died in a Soviet prison camp.[11]

"Loth's Flight" was never completed. A long excerpt appeared in issue 8 of *Creative Work* (1949), with a statement by Wat that the entire work would be

published by "The Reader." Eight years later, during the thaw, another considerably shorter fragment was published in issue 45 of *New Culture* (1957). For a
long time, these fragments were the only traces of Wat's projected novel.

Wat was hindered in his work by the need to eke out a living by making
translations. But this was not the only thing that interfered with work on the
novel. In *Scraps of Paper in the Wind,* Wat noted: "I already had heaps of paper,
dozens of scenes and characters, dialogues, hundreds of situational sketches, but
the more I got to know German matters, the more distinctly I came to understand that my genuine intent could not and should not be realized in that
manner. . . . The only thing I needed and wanted to say was my truth about the
Soviets and communism. That was in my heart of hearts, that demanded my
voice, in that I saw my mission. . . . Totalitarian Germany was, for me, only a
coverup."[12] But the anti-Communist message of the novel would be detected
only too easily by the censorship. In addition, Wat's intention to hand down an
indictment of totalitarianism was undermined by the fact that the differences he
discovered between its two versions proved to be more profound than he had
bargained for.

Nevertheless, a large portion of "Loth's Flight" has survived. In 1991, a
typescript of it was discovered in the Wat archive, having eluded the attention of
several scholars who had previously studied the writer's legacy. The text[13]
consists of a short introduction, the six chapters of Part I, and three chapters of
part 2, the last of which is short and probably incomplete. Thus, the episodes of
"Loth's Flight" long known to readers because they were published can now be
seen as part of a significantly larger whole, which is probably a final draft of the
novel's opening. How large a fraction of the novel the extant typescript represents can only be guessed, though it seems safe to surmise that "Loth's Flight"
was conceived as an extensive work on the scale of *Doctor Faustus,* comprising
four or five hundred pages or more. What we have is polished enough to be
perceived as a coherent whole. Moreover, its "open-endedness" contributes to
its overall effect.

The "heaps of paper" and "hundreds of situational sketches" that Wat
mentions in his notes are by no means an exaggeration. In addition to the
typescript, fourteen notebooks containing materials for the novel are preserved in the Wat archive. They include entire scenes of the novel, summaries
thereof, chronological notes, excerpts from newspapers, a draft of a map of
the Brandenburg-Saxony-Thuringia region, notes on German Renaissance
painters, comments on the Severikirche in Erfurt, an extract from the minutes of
a survey of Auschwitz, and a rough sketch of the crematorium design. There is a
list of fifty-four characters, including a narrator (who is also referred to as
Johann Sebastian M***). All this enables one to reconstruct the design of the
novel, if only in a very tentative way.[14]

The action of the novel takes place in the German town of S***, a code

name for Erfurt, starting in the critical year 1931. The town is the epitome of
provincial Germany—a peaceful conurbation in the shadow of a medieval cathe-
dral, with its own intellectual tradition and also some industry, represented by
the factory J. S. Topf & Söhne. The eponymous hero, Jacob Loth, is a successful
surgeon, whose background is summarized in the first chapter. Only son of
Commercial Councillor Samuel Loth, he has a foster brother Klaus, illegitimate
child of his wet nurse. Both are active in World War I. Jacob comes back with an
aversion to all warfare, whereas Klaus goes on to see action in Palestine, where he
develops a predilection for violence, and, after the war, joins the Nazi movement.
By contrast with Klaus, who feels rootless and alienated, Jacob is committed
emotionally to his ancestors and family (which consists, according to the archetypal pattern, of a beloved wife and two daughters). Whereas Klaus is an Aryan
and proletarian, Jacob is a middle-class Jew, equally proud of his German bourgeois tradition and his ties to rabbis of yore. Whereas Klaus is brutal and
uncouth, Jacob is a refined if amateurish intellectual, who spends much of his life
in the local library and writes a paper entitled "Music as the Language of the
Soul." After becoming a *Gauleiter* (a local boss of the Nazi party), Klaus was
presumably to have played a role in Jacob's fate. But the precise nature of the role
remains unclear, since, starting with the second chapter, Klaus is relegated to the
background. After a traditional kind of narrative telescoping the life stories of
several characters, the genre shifts and we find ourselves in the midst of a heated
political and philosophical debate—a transition obviously patterned on *The
Brothers Karamazov.*

The argument develops in the club "Prometheus" attended by Jacob and
several of his intellectual friends. A group of new characters is introduced, the
most significant of whom is Carl Topf, a classical scholar by training, co-owner
and director of J. S. Topf & Söhne by occupation. He embodies, in a sense, the
ancient ideal of a harmoniously developed personality: an erudite thinker enamored of Renaissance Italy, he is also a musician and an athlete. There is
nevertheless a touch of spiritual malaise in Topf: like many of Thomas Mann's
characters, he feels acutely the approach of old age and death, which at the same
time arouses in him a sort of sexual excitement. The next most important
character seems to be Ernst Grolle. A biting critic of German tradition, he plays
the role of a "tabloid Nietzsche"[15] and is reminiscent of the heroes of Wat's early
fiction (or of Ehrenburg's Julio Jurenito). The third discussant is Kurt Glücks,
an architect suspected of homosexuality, though this is probably a false accusation. He stands out among the clubmen by virtue of his rightist views. ("Prometheus" is, in general, left-leaning.) Knowledgeable about biblical texts, Glücks
provides a counterpoint to Topf, quoting Scripture as frequently as Topf quotes
Latin aphorisms.

The long, involved argument, full of brilliant formulas, presents a survey of
the German political situation and a fascinating critique of German culture,

Goethe in particular. Almost all the discussants are anti-Nazi, albeit for varying and even contradictory reasons; but the only one who does not underestimate the danger represented by Hitler and his followers is the shady ironist and hater of Goethe, Ernst Grolle.

After this long detour, the story once more gets moving. The Nazis grow in strength, and a refrain, "It was worse and worse," accompanies the development of the plot. "Almost imperceptibly and without particular surprise,"[16] Jacob finds himself in the new reality of Hitler's Third Reich. Samuel Loth passes away to the accompaniment of one of Hitler's speeches, while the old, previously faithful servant Johann Puffke listens with approval to the rabid voice of the dictator coming from the radio set. One of the Jewish inhabitants of S***, Professor Frankfurter, a historian who has devoted his life to the glorification of authoritarianism, is taken out of the café where he once sat in elegant company and is dragged through the street in a Calvary-like march. One of the many who passively observe his ordeal is Carl Topf; but the most ominous rabble-rouser is Erika Pokorny, daughter of a well-known ethnologist who now indulges in supplying her father's scholarly articles with racist interpolations.[17]

More new characters are introduced at this point, one of whom is Father Johannes Thyl, a Jesuit who bravely opposes the Nazis and defends the Jewish people in his sermons. The topic of Christianity in a totalitarian state was to be developed further, in relation to the fate of Loth's twin daughters, Else and Rose, both of whom are fascinated by Catholicism and dream of baptism (their mother is Aryan and an indifferent Lutheran), but are inhibited by their esteem for their grandfather, a practicing Jew.

Wat's drafts and notes provide clues to the novel's missing parts. More sources for the re-creation of the overall design are provided by its biblical archetype and by various intertextual considerations. Wat undoubtedly intended the most significant theme of the novel to be with the "surrender and destruction of intellectuals in the face of the totalitarian regime," to use the description of a Soviet dissident, Arkadii Belinkov, who applied it to Russian intelligentsia. Almost all the people who expressed their scorn for Hitler in the "Prometheus" scene were eventually to become conformists and seekers of privilege in the world ruled by the Nazis.

Carl Topf was to furnish Auschwitz with crematoria (and then commit suicide). The Mephistopheles-like Ernst Grolle, who gave a provocative though sober analysis of the German internal situation in the second chapter of the novel, was to join the Nazis,[18] which was predictable in light of his earlier confession that he would always opt for the side of the winner.[19] Wat also envisaged Grolle as a participant in a great metaphysical scene à la Dostoevsky. Moreover, he planned a collateral plot line whereby Grolle's son Willy, involved in an anti-Nazi movement, would land in prison and undergo there a profound religious experience, patterned on Wat's spiritual crisis in Saratov.[20] His comrade-in-arms was to be the Communist son of the prosecutor Herbert Wolff. The fate of Kurt Glücks was to be of a different sort. Wat planned to introduce in the text Glücks's inner monologues and hinted at "Glücks's case." Glücks appears to have been conceived by Wat as an ambivalent figure: he is constantly refereed to as someone who "had not yet said his last word"[21] and was "always in the process of spontaneous crystallization, unfortunately without any visible signs of its progress."[22] Depicted in an ironic vein, Glücks is to some extent an autobiographical character.

Numerous notes relate to the titular character, Jacob Loth, and his family. Loth's trial and imprisonment are both mentioned and a short typewritten fragment of one of Loth's monologues survives: " 'Once upon a time there was a man whose name was Loth, there was such and such a personality,' he thought, 'there was the future of such and such a personality and the fate of Loth, and suddenly there was no future, and no man whose name was Loth, and no personality altogether, there were only imaginary numbers in the calculation, the purpose and necessity of which were unintelligible.' "

One of Loth's humiliations was to be particularly bizarre. According to several notes, he was to become a clown—or, rather, a caged exhibit—in a circus. This poignant plot-twist had a precedent in Heinrich Mann's novel *Professor Unrat* and in its popular screen version, *The Blue Angel* (1932), in which a respectable citizen degenerates into a pitiful circus performer.[23] Yet, it is possible that the circus was to have played a role in Loth's eventual escape.

Interestingly, the narrator, who in the extant text takes no part in the action, was to enter the plot and join Loth's supporters. Loth's wife, rarely mentioned in the extant text, was to repeat the biblical pattern and be turned, figuratively, into a pillar of salt. An Aryan, she was probably reluctant to leave S*** and Germany, and the notes refer to her delirium and death.

Wat apparently intended to multiply the references to the Book of Genesis at the end of the novel. His notes include intriguing remarks pertaining to the "bringing of the angels" and "the daughters' conversation with the angels." In the biblical story, the final proof of Lot's righteousness is the hospitality he extends to the heavenly messengers. When the men of Sodom demand that he hand over the angels to them, Lot offers them his daughters instead; the angels then save the entire family and prompt them to leave the condemned city. In the novel, the role of the angels was obviously to be taken by human beings—Willy Grolle and Herbert Wolff's son come to mind, although this is no more than a guess. In any event, a happy ending was planned: Wat's notes point to Loth's ultimate success.[24] The book was to end with an epilogue, perhaps summarizing the subsequent fates of all the characters in the classic tradition of the eighteenth and nineteenth centuries.

The genre of "Loth's Flight" may be roughly defined with reference to two classes of modern novels. First, it is a conscious transformation of a myth, like *Ulysses, Doctor Faustus*, and John Updike's *The Centaur*. This device, which goes back to the roots of the modernist Weltanschauung (the Nietzschean concept of eternal return and so on), presents marvelous possibilities for intertextual games. Second, "Loth's Flight" has aspects of the novel as philosophical discussion, juxtaposing various points of view on metaphysics, morals, politics, and so on. This genre found its early embodiment and acme in Dostoevsky's "dialogical" writing,[25] in particular in *The Brothers Karamazov*. Among its later adherents, one might name Thomas Mann (*The Magic Mountain*) and Albert Camus (*The Plague*). The two types tend to overlap, however, *Doctor Faustus* being a case in point.

The mythical source texts of "Loth's Flight" are manifold. The story of the righteous nephew of Abraham, his unlucky wife, their daughters, and the escape of the family from the wicked city forms the backbone of the plot—the very name of the city, S***, plainly stands for Sodom. But other stories, both biblical and nonbiblical, are superimposed on this, and, to a significant degree, interpret and elucidate each other. Thus, Loth's first name, Jacob, and his relationship to Klaus obviously allude to the story of the twin sons born to Isaac: Jacob, the "smooth man" (Gen. 27:11), and Esau, the red, hirsute man who loses his birthright and his father's blessing. Not without reason is Klaus older than Jacob Loth, if only by three weeks.[26] According to the Talmud,[27] Esau was a hunter of people and a murderer—which fits perfectly with the role of Klaus as Nazi functionary. Esau was traditionally depicted as a nomad and as ancestor of people who live by the sword (as well as of Gentiles in general). Wat continually hints at the archetypal pattern by stressing Klaus's love for horses, his warlike preoccupations, and his wanderings throughout the Middle East, "among red rocks and ruins of the ancient cities, under the scorching sky without clouds and rain."[28] Further, other pairs of contrasting biblical brothers are visible here: Isaac and Ishmael, Abel and Cain. In the last analysis, Wat has employed the archetypal motif of the divine twins (one bright, one dark) known to virtually all mythologies,[29] as well as the time-honored literary device of the double.[30]

Klaus is an Antichrist figure, who, significantly, loses his Christian faith and becomes anti-Semitic in Palestine, where he spends time in the Christian holy places of Bethlehem, Nazareth, and Jerusalem.[31] At the end of the war he finds himself in Damascus (where, unlike St. Paul, he becomes even more hardened in his anti-Christian stance). Loth, by contrast, has some of the qualities of Christ, although these are not his only qualities. At the beginning of the book, he is compared to Job.[32] He is a man of "the Golden Age" who must nevertheless live in the Iron Age, symbolized by the iron cross he receives for his service.[33] Unlike Jacob in the Book of Genesis, he loses his dying father's

blessing by sleeping through his agony—like "the disciples of Gethsemane."[34]
(This may be interpreted only too readily as a symbol of the failure of the entire
Western cultural tradition, even at its best, in the century of totalitarianism.)

Another significant archetypal thread in the novel was to be the medieval
myth of Faust. After Goethe, the Faust motif became virtually unavoidable in
any major work dealing with German culture and Germany's historical predicament. Faust's pact with Mephistopheles, as embodied in the cultural trends that
were paving the way for totalitarianism, could not fail to fascinate Wat.

The symbolic role of Mephistopheles was to be assigned to Ernst Grolle.
The key to his character is offered in Glücks's monologue: "Grolle wants to be
everywhere and in everything, but since one cannot be present everywhere
simultaneously, actually he is nowhere, and he masks the fact of his nonexistence
by pure noise, by the fermentation of intellect, which exhausts itself by itself and
within itself, and is unable to create. . . . Only one thing is relatively stable in
him: hatred! I hate, therefore I am—that is the principle of Grolle's functioning.
Just that hatred gives him a semblance of existence, only a semblance, since
hatred itself is also an illusion."[35] These lines unambiguously point to the
theological concept of Satan. As in many passages of the novel, the tone is
ironic—especially since this is spoken by Glücks and is refracted through his
slightly parodic discourse. Grolle himself is furnished with a telltale name, a trait
he shares with several other characters in the book, since *Ernst* means "serious,
earnest" and *grollen* means "to be angry." His name is highlighted by the
attention paid to it by his fellow members of "Prometheus." "Grolle's debate
with the Creator," envisaged by Wat in his notes, could refer to Satan's wager
with God concerning Job's fate, as well as to the prologue of *Faust*. It is not hard
to imagine the grotesque tinge that Wat the iconoclast would have given to these
textual allusions (as Dostoevsky did so frequently in his most metaphysical
passages).

Wat's plan was for Grolle's son Willy, imprisoned by the Nazis, to face
Satan in person. This was to be one of the high points, if not *the* high point, of
the entire novel. Presumably the meeting was to be patterned not only on Wat's
own experience in Saratov prison, which he saw as a turning point in his life, but
also on Ivan Karamazov's dialogue with the Devil (repeated, in altered form, in
Doctor Faustus).[36]

The religious element in the novel could hardly be limited to demonology,
and Christian themes were to play a crucial role in its general economy. In accord
with his iconoclastic predilections, Wat portrays Christianity in an ambivalent
light, emphasizing its spiritual message as well as its potential for perversion.
Doubtless, he also intended to develop a subject that was of great importance for
his inner life—namely, the relation between Christianity and Judaism, their
conflict and their imaginary amalgam.[37]

Memories of the Holocaust and of Stalinism could not fail to lead to a more profound evaluation of the diabolical element in history than was the case in the halcyon days of *Lucifer Unemployed*. However banal and however ridiculous in its banality, evil was nevertheless deadly. Embedded in politics, in social crisis, and in spiritual degeneration, it led to Auschwitz and also to Lubyanka. Here, Wat's unfinished novel was consonant with the best European and Polish writing of the period—not only that of Thomas Mann but also that of Czesław Miłosz, Wat's younger friend whose life's work was to deal primarily with the Christian-Manichaean debate on the nature, roots, and poisonous fruit of evil.

There is an inner contradiction in "Loth's Flight" that it shares with many novels on Nazism. Like *Doctor Faustus*, it destroys the totalitarian myth by invoking another myth (or myths), of an allegedly opposite nature. This *similia similiaribus curantur* approach might be justified on the grounds of the tremendous sociopsychological power of myth. But Wat was clearsighted enough to see that to deal with the totalitarian threat requires, first and foremost, its *demythologization:* thus, the synthetic approach, utilizing artistic images related to archetypal patterns, must be complemented by an analytic approach that examines the phenomenon with epistemological and scholarly rigor, places it in its social and historical context, and deconstructs it by finding gaps and fractures in its discourse. Irony and parody are always on the side of demythologization.

In a review of Kruczkowski's play *The Germans*, Wat had already attempted to juxtapose mythic thought, characteristic of totalitarian movements, with logical thought, intended to ensure their overcoming. One of the underlying causes of the degeneration of the German psyche was, in his view, the atomization of society. (He was among the first critics of totalitarianism to dwell on this phenomenon.[38]) Wat quoted Friedrich Hölderlin, whom he saw as having coined "a brilliant formula" in his novel *Hyperion:* "I can think of no people more at odds with themselves than the Germans. You see artisans, but no men, thinkers, but no men, priests, but no men, masters and servants, but no men, minors and adults, but no men—is this not like a battlefield on which hacked-off hands and arms and every other member are scattered about, while the lifeblood flows from them to vanish in the sand?"[39] Confined within the limits of his or her social position, lacking intimate ties with neighbor, deprived of a traditional moral framework equally binding for all, the individual becomes merely a cog in the machine of the state, with his or her responsibility devolved and transferred to the anonymous power.

Wat cautiously hinted that such atomization was by no means limited to Germany:

> Doesn't it appear, perhaps less pronouncedly, on a smaller and different scale than in Germany, among other people and in other countries as well—at present, of course, mainly where the imperialist powers prepare once again to commit crimes against mankind? Let us say to ourselves clearly: the problem of evading moral responsibility for everybody and everything—in the epoch of

the unconditional interdependence of everybody and everything—or, to put it differently, the problem of evading political responsibility—does not only belong to Germany or to the past.[40]

This passage is a classic case of double entendre. The censorship could interpret criminal "imperialist powers" as referring solely to the capitalist West (the very suspicion that the expression might be applied to its adversary as well would be construed as testimony to a counterrevolutionary frame of mind). Wat's harangue against "evading political responsibility" was even more ambiguous, since it smacked of Stalinist vocabulary. At the same time, there were plenty of people in Poland who understood Wat's Aesopian message only too well: "other countries" were the USSR and its satellites, and responsibility for crimes belonged to them no less than to the Nazis.

The atomization of society and the transformation of people into "screws" (to use Stalin's boastful idiom) resulted in a rupture between mind and conscience. The story of Topf & Söhne was only one, albeit striking example of that state of affairs. But the roots of the phenomenon preceded the totalitarian movements of the twentieth century: Wat saw them as part and parcel of the general crisis of post-Renaissance culture, a crisis that he had experienced acutely in his youth.

A long divagation on Loth's reading, which parallels, intellectually as well as stylistically, typical passages in such modern classics as the works of Robert Musil and Elias Canetti, picks up a subject broached in both *Pug Iron Stove* and *Lucifer Unemployed:* the cultural oversaturation and utter relativization of values. At first, the library, "the great garden of mankind," has a soothing effect on Loth, but this proves to be short-lived, since the world of culture is as atomized and as antagonistic as everything else: "Now, mankind's paradisiacal garden, where one could taste fruits from every tree without punishment, was out of the question; there was, indeed, selva selvaggia[41] in that spacious comfortable room, into the windows of which lush ivy leaves looked. . . . There was no maxim which could not find here its counter-maxim, one argument opposed another, one truth opposed another, and there was no thought, no event, no crime, which could not affirm here its reason."[42] This predicament is conducive to cultural retrogression: a primitive idea, which simplifies one's view of the moral and social universe and draws a clear division between "one's own kind" and "the enemy" (be it the class enemy or an inferior race), now stands a good chance of winning over the masses, and even some refined minds, to its side.

As befits a major novel in the realist tradition, "Loth's Flight" pays much attention to the German sociopolitical and intellectual context of the 1930s and the preceding era. The great debate in "Prometheus," as we have seen, included an extensive survey of the situation in Germany on the eve of the Nazi takeover. The most straightforward evaluation is given to Grolle, who states that Germany faces a choice between two simple (though not particularly happy) options: Nazism and communism, *tertium non datur.* Grolle's analysis is essentially Marx-ist, which by no means deprives it of acuity. He quotes, with approval, Napoleon's words pronounced during his meeting with Goethe, that "politics is fate."[43] This formula was of central importance to Wat, who repeated it on various occasions as well as in his memoirs.[44] The concept of politics as fate connoted, for Marxists and socialist realists, the inevitability and desirability of conforming to the "laws of history" embodied in the party line. But for Wat, it meant something much closer to the spirit of Greek tragedy: that although fate—that is, politics—may be invincible, it is still to be challenged by the human spirit.

The discussion of "spirit versus politics" culminates in an argument about the arch-German poet Goethe. Wat presents three typical opinions of Goethe: Grolle attacks him as a pitiable Philistine responsible for the rupture of German consciousness;[45] Topf defends him as a "Faustian spirit that never stops but continuously, unrelentingly strives forward from one goal to another";[46] and Loth (as well as Glücks) praises him as one who overcame the opposition "politics–spirit" and so embodies inner harmony, tranquility, and integrity.[47] This entire section of the novel may be described as an exercise in characteristic-ally Dostoevskian technique.[48] The monologues consist mainly of clichés, each of which nevertheless reveals an aspect of the truth; and no definite statement about Goethe—as well as about the fate of Germany—is possible, though it is continuously being attempted in the dialogue and glimmers through the surface of ever-imperfect human speech.

Like Thomas Mann, Wat considered Nazism a characteristically German phenomenon, "an extreme manifestation and incarnation of forces long dor-mant in the nation's soul, or, at least, a syndrome of a specifically German disease."[49] As a result of the vagaries of history, the rupture between free cognitive spirit and mindless conformism became more pronounced in Ger-many than in other modern countries, even if they all experienced it to some degree. Yet the treatment of Nazism as an essentially German phenomenon, intimately bound up with the peculiarities of a particular country's history and inseparable from the dislocations of its cultural framework, contradicted the central thesis of Wat's project, and during the course of his work, he became increasingly aware of the fact that one could not—and should not—identify the two variants of twentieth-century totalitarianism too closely and treat them as interchangeable.

Not that it was not commonplace in Eastern Europe and the USSR during the 1950s and 1960s to use Hitler as a stand-in for Stalin: numerous writers, à la Evgeny Evtushenko and Andrei Voznesensky, denounced the vanquished Nazis with great gusto. Virtually the only claim that Communist governments had to legitimacy was their contribution to the victory over Hitler: consequently, they encouraged the "unmasking" of their former enemy by all means. Yet many readers (though not necessarily the censors) would have understood that Hitlerite atrocities stood for Stalinist ones. Wat was much too serious a writer to indulge himself in such games, however. Unmasking Hitler tongue in cheek was, to him, morally unacceptable. Substitution of one regime for another was also a cheap shot from a strictly artistic standpoint, especially in a major novel subject to the norms of the realist tradition.

In the extant text of "Loth's Flight" there is almost no discussion of Nazism vis-à-vis communism. The only exception is provided by Loth's boss, Dr. Voigt, who entreats Loth to stay on at his job in the hospital, notwithstanding the anti-Semitic campaign going on, and notes in passing: "Do you think it would be better if the Reds took power? You should read the memoirs of the Russian revolution. Our coup, you see, is much more benign, there are far fewer victims, less terror! That probably reveals something—the good-na-tu-red-ness of our people, the German culture, moreover, it shows them up [i.e., the Russians] as well."[50]

This passage is, of course, a bitterly ironic testimony to a myopia common among Voigt's compatriots and also among noncompatriots. Wat may have been aware of the fact that Stalin's victims outnumbered Hitler's, but he would have been the last to define the Nazi coup as "more benign." The Stalinist phenomenon and the Nazi phenomenon had a common denominator; yet there were real and profound differences between the two regimes, which Wat attempted to disclose, if only gropingly. The goal was to avoid any double standard yet expose the contrast.

Wat's thoughts on this topic found their way into some of his later writings. He tended to deny any links between communism and Russia's past while emphasizing the links between Nazism and Germany's past. Thus he assumed a rather isolated stance among anti-totalitarian thinkers, a stance echoed later by Solzhenitsyn. Wat's judgment of Nazism and communism found its final expression in a letter to Józef Czapski, written less than three months before Wat's death, on 6 May 1967. Defying Czapski's assertion that the German people bore no guilt for Hitler's crimes, Wat stated:

> Certainly, the crimes of Bolshevism did not yield to the German crimes quantitatively, in sum, but—and here the fundamental, essential difference lies—they were committed at the expense of the Russian nation itself, they were perpetrated by a handful of usurpers who managed to enslave the entire people, since everything had disintegrated there. While Germans not only voted for Hitler, but supported him en masse and profited from it (elimination of unemployment; national power, conquests and plunder). That crime would have never taken place without the general and organized support of the entire people. . . . The number of 138 fighters against Hitlerism [is] pitiful and

denouncing by its very ridiculousness (just realize how many hundreds of thousands of the Russian peasants fought the Bolsheviks), etc., etc.[51]

Some of Wat's remarks concerning the relation between communism and Nazism are particularly fascinating, in that his strictly aesthetic preoccupations come to the fore. Thus, he employs the Nietzschean opposition of Dionysus versus Apollo, so popular during his youth, in order to draw a further dividing line between the two regimes. The Nazi crimes, in Wat's views, were irrational and orgiastic (Dionysian) by nature, whereas Stalin's crimes were dictated by perverted reason. "Pockmarked, abominable Stalin as an Apollo! There is nothing outrageous in the comparison. One forgets that Apollo skinned Marsyas alive, and the readers of Holy Writ know that it foretold the spirit of darkness in Apollo."[52]

Another comparison refers to the "anxiety of influence"—in an unexpected context and many years before Harold Bloom:

> The borrowings of Hitlerism from bolshevism (e.g., the system of prison camps and *vice versa:* the reform of the Soviet camps after the pattern of Dachau, the purges of 1937–38 patterned on the liquidation of Röhm in Germany in 1934) have their analogy in the influences of one writer of the same age upon another, which oscillate between imitation and controversy. The more influenced is writer Y by writer X and the more he actually imitates him, the more assiduously he attempts to distinguish himself by controversy, and one may estimate the degree of influence by the degree of the controversy on the very ground common to both writers. Here, one should not forget that the promoters of both fascism and communism came from artistic Bohemia, that Marx wrote poetry, that Trotsky, Lunacharsky, Bogdanov, Lenin were men of letters, that Stalin started [his career] by publishing his poems in a Georgian [periodical] *Iveria* (see his biography by Deutscher), that Mao and Ho Chi Minh are poets.[53]

One may take issue with certain statements made by Wat on the two versions of totalitarianism. Nevertheless, they seem refreshing even today, after so many considerations and reconsiderations of the topic. And the main point made by Wat is perfectly valid: Nazism and communism, however interrelated and however equally noxious, are still virtual opposites. The first is nationalism gone mad, whereas the second is internationalism gone mad. The first sacrifices "inferior" races and nations to the *Herrenvolk;* the second sacrifices *all* nations and races to an abstract, perverted set of ideas. This trait of communism becomes even more pronounced when it attempts to invoke national feelings and values for its own ends (as it did during World War II and afterward). The ensuing contradiction is one of the central causes, if not *the* central cause, of its crisis and collapse.

Anyone familiar with Wat's life and work cannot help but be struck by the extent to which "Loth's Flight" is saturated with autobiographical material. As a prospective *magnum opus*, it set out to incorporate all the events and reflections that had had a critical mental or emotional impact on Wat. It seems safe to assume that not only the subplots of "Loth's Flight" but also its overall design were intended to be autobiographical. Thus "Loth's Flight" is "Wat's Flight": his flight from the totalitarian world of Lubyanka and Ili and from the formative background of that world—that is, from the mental framework that generated the totalitarian temptation.

Echoes of situations known from Wat's memoirs and other writings abound from the beginning. One might speak here of auto-intertextuality. The family of Commercial Councillor Samuel Loth is, to a significant degree, patterned on the family of Mendel Michał Chwat. Jacob's wet-nurse, seduced at sixteen and crushed by her predicament, is, of course, Anusia Mikulak. Samuel Loth's death, which occurs at the climactic moment of the Nazi takeover, echoes the death of Mendel Michał Chwat in January 1940, in a Poland recently occupied by Hitler. During his childhood, Jacob Loth, like young Aleksander, despises and teases "eastern" Jews. He cruelly mocks a young Talmudist, not realizing that the boy's mother is dying in the same room. The event becomes deeply ingrained in both his consciousness and his unconscious, perhaps playing a part in his decision to become a physician.[54] All this is clearly autobiographical.[55]

Perhaps the most interesting clue to the actual—if only partial— identification of the author with his character is the defiant motto that Loth chooses in his youth: *ad logicam pergo, quae mortis non timet ergo* (I strive for logic since it does not fear death).[56] This medieval Latin line, which Wat found in *The Golden Legend,* had been employed by him before. It formed part of an epigraph for *Pug Iron Stove,* where it highlighted the unrelenting logic with which Wat had pursued his avant-garde experiment.

In many respects, "Loth's Flight" was to be patterned on such classical models as the works of Balzac and Tolstoy. The narrative develops consistently and slowly. Each character is introduced gradually and with care, the narrator dwelling at length on his or her background, circumstances, and views and usually painting a detailed physical and emotional portrait, as in much nineteenth-century prose. Landscapes, interiors, and spiritual states are described in syntactically rich, involved sentences that rival the best that can be found in Polish and international novels of the past. At first sight, Wat appears to be following the prescriptions of Communist critics: "learn from the classics". There could be no stronger contrast to the immoderate experimentation of Wat's futurist youth or to the concise, paradoxical style of *Lucifer Unemployed.*

Nevertheless, a more careful look at the novel reveals traits that entail a break with the nineteenth-century model. In this respect, Wat was particularly

close to Thomas Mann, also a traditionalist on the surface but a deeply disturbing modernist in essence. One notes, for instance, that the borders between
author, narrator, and characters continuously shift. As we have seen, Wat intended to present the narrator as one of the inhabitants of S***, someone with a
specific background and biography, who was to take an active part in the development of the plot. But at the beginning of "Loth's Flight" the reader is unaware
of this. The author seems to be omniscient, portraying Loth, Topf, and the rest
"from inside." Moreover, he describes the meeting in Zurich in 1947 and the
speech of Thomas Mann as only someone who was part of the audience could.[57]
The author (or narrator?) is very much present in the pages of the novel,
addressing the reader directly with his arguments and comments, which are
often introduced in a heavily stylized, old-fashioned, and semi-parodic manner.
He admits his limitations: his field of vision is restricted to "Prometheus" and is
not necessarily representative of all Germany or even of S***, but he does not
have "enough data and courage to explore other terrain."[58] This admission
serves as an introduction to a long erudite argument about the inevitable one-
sidedness and deformation inherent in any novel.

The reader thus becomes involved in a continual game. We are dealing
simultaneously with Aleksander Wat, a Polish writer who exercises his freedom
in the creation of characters and a plot; with the traditional image of the
omniscient author who observes events and human beings from a neutral position; and with the persona of the narrator (a certain Johann Sebastian M***,
according to Wat's notes), who knows Loth and the other characters well, does
his best to record what happens, and is painfully aware of his limitations. These
three images are constantly confounded and merged.[59] Often as not, the reader
cannot make out which one of the three is speaking. To further complicate
matters, some episodes are narrated from the point of view of some other
characters; thus, the ordeal of Professor Frankfurter is observed by Langleben, a
psychoanalyst who treats Topf.[60] Wat also intended to employ the device of a
"story within a story,"[61] which would further confound things.

Thus, Wat's narrative games supplied "Loth's Flight" with a metaliterary
dimension. Revealing the conventional character of any writing, they allowed
Wat to mediate on the very concept of truth and meaning in a novel. For Wat,
history itself became a partner in the play:

> Oh, we challenge it, History, we provoke it: let it pronounce its confirmations
> and its denials, let it outdistance us continuously, since we love it to the base of
> our essence, we love historical time, the time which is over, just at the moment
> it is over, with everything that belongs to it—and while we say it we reveal,
> immediately and without any cover, our most secret depravity, our immeasura-
> bly profound depravity! Well, let it help us, let it complement and straighten
> out the monologue of the narrator—silently, but knowledgeably and unforget-
> fully, and thus perhaps a dialogue would be generated, consisting of less

weighty words and weighty silence: a natural form, in which the human spirit finds its expression.[62]

In the dialogue with history, everything is in flux. Almost everyone is *nel mezzo del cammin,* facing the most important decision of his or her life.[63] This aspect of "Loth's Flight" once more places it in the category of modern novel that traces its ancestry to Dostoevsky; and "the moral responsibility of everybody for everything" emphasized by Wat is also a strictly Dostoevskian concept.

The involved narrative technique is supplemented by a technique of leitmotifs and refrains, most of which pertain to the realm of culture. Dante and Goethe, Racine and Shakespeare, Homer and Euripides, are quoted and cited on innumerable occasions. These allusions form a dense network that is almost musical in structure.[64] Characteristically, the counterpoint of these other texts is accompanied by the counterpoint of languages. Most of the characters are polyglot, as was Wat himself, and the text is full of Greek, Italian, French, English, and other expressions that Wat makes no attempt to translate into Polish.

Only a fragment of Wat's great design survives. But a part of a ruin may be sufficient for imagining—and even reconstructing—a major building, if the general principle of its architecture is visible enough in the columns, reliefs, and scattered stones that remain. The structure of "Loth's Flight" is so tight and so well thought-out that such a task is not beyond the realm of possibility. Moreover, one thing can be said with certainty: "Loth's Flight" was to be a *polyphonic novel,* a specimen of twentieth-century novel that disdains all authoritative discourse. Countless sign systems were to interact in its text, counterbalanced by the "weighty silence" of history. Wat intended to show the young generation of Polish writers how one could—and should—oppose and surmount the deafening monophony promoted by totalitarian ideologues. He did not succeed; nor, perhaps, could he have done. But the surviving fragments of "Loth's Flight" are more than a testimony to Wat's uncompromising stance: they constitute a monument of art, as fascinating today as in their own time.

10

The New Poetics

The typescript of Wat's new collection of poems reached the Kraków publishing house around New Year 1957, while Wat was still in Paris. He added several new texts in the first half of 1957, which he spent mainly in Sicily, and the last poem in the collection as published was written immediately after his return to Poland. It had the provocative title "Sen (bez żadnego tzw. głębszego znaczenia)," which might be rendered in English as "A Dream (Without Any So-called Deeper Meaning)." This anti-Freudian sally was a subterfuge: the poem did indeed have hidden meanings, and its final lines can be read as referring the ambiguous situation of a poet returning from self-imposed exile:

Perhaps I'll return to the water and sit over it with a fishing rod?
It would be better for me if I had never left it,
never returned after leaving,
so that I could not be convinced that I am and am not,
that I am here and not here, that I was and will not be.

This bitterly ironic rendering of the Odysseus myth refers also to lost identity, life in the shadow of death, and the inescapable force of history:

What could I do? I took refreshment. I fell asleep. And I sleep.
I sleep until history ends. And it has no intention of ending.

Until now, history had been Wat's enemy. Now, its meaning for him was unclear. His return to Poland, was, in a sense, a return to historical time and, as such, fraught with both dangers and unexpected possibilities.

Wat's unprepossessingly titled book *Wiersze* (Poems) appeared in December 1957. It was a slim volume of 180 pages. The edition of 2,500 copies sold out almost immediately.[1] "Such a demand for poetry was never known before in Poland. . . . Once again, one of the few merits of the system: perhaps under the oppression of boorish usurpers one's inner life secretly develops best of all," Wat noted a decade later.[2] Not that he had ever aspired to be a popular poet: "I really don't want you to think that I care about fame," he wrote to an émigré friend; "if I were rich, I would print my poems in 200 copies, believe me. . . . Yet one needs some lively response, a voice of several, of *a dozen,* but real *readers*—you know how, in our nasty craft, doubts lie in wait everywhere."[3]

The success of Wat's poetry was given an immediate stamp of recognition. In January 1958, Wat's *Poems* won *New Culture's* prize for best book of the year. The competition was stiff. Among the unsuccessful bids were several works that proved to be of more than momentary importance: anti-totalitarian novels by Jerzy Andrzejewski and Kazimierz Brandys, the brilliant collection of lyrics by Zbigniew Herbert, a book of fierce satirical stories by Slawomir Mrożek, as well as essays by Stawar and Kolakowski.[4]

News of the prize reached Wat in one of the hospitals that were now his habitual abode. After returning to Poland, he fell ill with typhus:

> I had actually a temperature of 106 . . . when they called Ola at the hospital advising her that I had received the prize. All of it seemed distant to me. It was the decisive night, leading either to recovery or to death. . . . Ola came and told me: there was a call from Słonimski, you got the prize for the best book, the decision of the jury was unanimous. I listened to it and understood it perfectly, I was interested, I asked something, but all of it was reminiscent of the roar of a distant sea, that is, unrelated to me.[5]

Wat's book was exceptional in more than one respect. First of all, it was the work of a writer who was reentering literature at the age of fifty-seven. Throughout the postwar decade, Wat was a famous (if, for some, notorious) literary figure. Yet he was known mainly for his defiant political stance. "Loth's Flight" was never completed. *Pug Iron Stove* (to say nothing of Wat's other futurist poems) belonged to the realm of literary legend, and *Lucifer Unemployed* was considered important only by a few critics knowledgeable in prewar literature. Wyka was justified when he said of Wat's book: "In the artistic sense, this is virtually a début. In the moral and philosophical sense, this is a summation."[6]

Second, Wat remained a daring innovator and avant-garde poet, even if he had virtually cut his ties with the poetics of the 1920s. His old, light-minded iconoclasm was now imbued with the attitude of one who is aware of the fragility of cultural values, as well as of their uncanny ability to survive. The sense of the tragic dimension of being, already present on the pages of *Pug Iron Stove,* was complemented by the meditations of a much older man who had gone through all the trials anticipated, but hardly taken seriously by the young poéte maudit. And the outcry of a rebel who had faced the absurdity of the universe in a half-indignant, half-amused way merged with the thoughts of one who had come to understand the absurdity of history and human suffering, as well as the powerlessness and value of human protest.

As thirty years before, Wat found himself at the center of literary discussion. Many of the critics who reviewed the book were pursuing their own agendas. Thus, Wat's old comrade Stern saw the success of Wat's poetry as a signal for the full rehabilitation and renaissance of Polish futurism, in which he himself had taken a leading part. According to Stern, Wat's new poems were an extension of prewar futurist writing. By contrast, Andrzej Drawicz, a writer of the young generation who was to become a leading figure in the Polish liberation movement in the 1970s, dismissed such attempts to read Wat's poetics as a revival of the old: "Now, a new volume of verses continues the previous develop-ments. It continues and disproves them simultaneously. By the law of creative evolution, it shows us Wat completely opposed to the young and disorderly futurist of the same name. The false conventionality of the elements is sup-planted by their simplicity. The play of unexpected associations yields to a precision of thought. Mature tranquility supersedes youthful effrontery, bold-ness, and provocativeness of tone."[7] Stanisław Grochowiak, a poet who had made his début in 1956 and was soon acclaimed leader of the "Turpists,"[8] a rebellious group of writers who focused on the more unsavory aspects of Polish life, was more outspoken: "Neither Przyboś nor Stern, but precisely Wat should be accepted by young Polish poets with all the respect due not to a new mentor and master, but to a formidable rival and brilliant colleague."[9]

The pro-government press reacted to Wat's success in a guarded manner, to put it mildly. A review by Włodzimierz Maciąg with the malicious title "Poezja rozstrojonego instrumentu" (Poetry of an Out-of Tune Instrument) attempted to demolish Wat by harking back to the old disagreements between the futurists and the Kraków Vanguard. "Reading the uncontrolled chains of sentences which so often appear [in Wat's book], one can understand all the sharpness of the prewar critic's struggles for verbal frugality, for discipline, construction and uniqueness of expression. . . . In Wat's volume, there is simply too much bad metaphysical twaddle which harks back to the beginning of the century, remind-ing one of Przybyszewski's flow of words," Maciąg wrote, with more irritation than justification.[10]

In his article, Maciąg does not once mention Przyboś, who then enjoyed the official status of living classic (however strong his disagreement with Zhdanovist aesthetics might be); yet Maciąg's entire criticism of Wat's work was founded on dogmas developed by Przyboś (and, before him, by Peiper).[11] The pedantic "discipline of the imagination" characteristic of poets of the Kraków Vanguard was as incompatible with Wat's free style as was their elliptical metaphor with his metonymic way of thinking. Moreover, the steadfast belief in the blessings of civilization that led Przyboś to his guarded acceptance of the postwar system in Poland was profoundly discordant with Wat's apocalyptic world view.

Maciąg remained rather isolated in his opinions, however, and most re-viewers took Wat's side in the controversy. A case in point was an essay by Witold Wirpsza, one of the outstanding spokesmen of the young. Wirpsza described Przyboś as "the most outdated" among living Polish poets: "as a matter of fact, the condensed metaphorical chain of his poetry is of a delicate, brittle, fragile nature, not equal to the task of addressing contemporary philosophical and moral problems and prohibiting the rough, dry prose sentence, where metaphor consists not in a shallow amalgam based on sensual impressions but in a broad arc of multi-layered thought. Aleksander Wat copes with this task very well."[12]

Wirpsza praised the natural flow of Wat's verse, deprived of the artificial poetical figures, "strangeness," and coquetry so characteristic of the poets of the Kraków Vanguard who, through the years, tended to become their own epigones. The lack of any unifying formal principle in Wat's poetry—anathema to a disciple of Peiper—was, in Wirpsza's eyes, not a vice but a virtue:

> Aleksander Wat is a thoroughly modern artist. He practices restraint, even a diffident kind of restraint; but at the same time, he does not renounce any of the means of expression available to him: he rhymes when necessary; he employs regular rhythm when necessary; he uses descriptive metaphors and comparisons when necessary; he brings rhythm and syntax close to prose when necessary. Yet he permits none of these "modes" to become prevalent in his poetry, he does not give exclusive rights to any one of them; never a slave, he is always sovereign.[13]

The same reasoning could be extended to Wat's Weltanschauung: far from being the servant of a particular ideology (or of a modernist utopia, as in the cases of Peiper and Przyboś), Wat juxtaposed various ideologies and utopias in his poetry, maintaining a distance between himself and each of them, while revealing the limitations of all. This was a continuation of the road tested many years before in *Lucifer Unemployed*, albeit by different means. The playful jeering of the 1920s had yielded to a better understanding of a world threatened by all-consuming ideologization. Wat's main service to postwar Polish literature was his crucial contribution to its deliverance from ideological chains.

Kazimierz Wyka, who wrote the most extensive and insightful essay on Wat's book, approached the topic from a different point of view, placing Wat's lyrics in a broad perspective of Polish and European thought. The most relevant context here was Polish catastrophism, a current to which early Miłosz (and, to a degree, Witkacy) subscribed. Catastrophism was more than an artistic tendency; it might be described as an original Polish contribution to the intellectual landscape of Europe in the first half of the twentieth century. The principal representative of catastrophist thought was Marian Zdziechowski, an authority on Romanticism and religious philosophy who considered profound pessimism a condition for the renewal of Christianity. Also deserving mention is Czesław Miłosz's older relative Oscar Miłosz, a poet of Polish origin who opted for Lithuanian citizenship, wrote in French, and indulged in apocalyptic prophecies that came true—even if only in part—before, during, and after World War II.

Polish catastrophism, paralleled to some extent in the West by the teachings of Oswald Spengler and José Ortega y Gasset, remained an idiosyncratic philosophical trend. For catastrophists, the economic and political crisis of the twentieth century assumed cosmic, not merely historical, proportions. They attempted to incorporate the tragic dimension of life and the notion of an inevitable decline in morals and culture into a general economy of the universe: at the same time, they proclaimed redemption beyond the human power of understanding and expression. Far from being aloof to the ordeals of ordinary people, they avoided commitments that might undercut their liberty; in particular, the young catastrophists of the 1930s "hesitated between their sympathies for Marxism and their metaphysical frame of reference."[14]

The war and the postwar era translated the dark visions of Polish catastrophism into quotidian reality. In poetry, a trend arose that might be called post-catastrophist, Miłosz's book of 1945, *Ocalenie* (Rescue), being its best-known representative.[15] Wyka, a critic instrumental in defining this new tendency in Polish literature, situated Wat's poems in its perspective thus:

> The work of Aleksander Wat is more than catastrophic . . . It is apocalyptic, undertaken already after the catastrophe, after the apocalypse which has been fulfilled within the framework of this moral universe, and is being fulfilled continuously. Its dimensions are proclaimed by its omnipresent angels of old age, night, anguish and suffering. And, finally, by that very modern angel who was still unknown to the prophet-evangelist from the island of Patmos: the angel of being. The angel of living and existence as such.[16]

Wat's poetry, according to Wyka, was concerned with ontological and epistemological problems that did not necessarily enter the field of vision of other catastrophist writers: "The emptiness of Being around the person. The loneliness of human existence vis-à-vis Being. Escape from existence into nothingness. Modes of existence. Existence and the body. The unity of the personality. Limits of cognition, from the ancient sceptical arguments of Zeno of Elea to modern cognitive problems."[17] This list of philosophical topics pointed to the next, broader context of Wat's thought: the European existentialism of Heidegger and Sartre. Wat's existentialist background was complemented by his continuing attachment to the implicit philosophy of surrealism, which emphasized the lack of coherence in the objective universe and insisted that if it could be considered familiar and manageable, it was only because of our wrong habits and wrong patterns of thinking. The web of interrelated influences determining Wat's thought included, according to Wyka, at least one more thread: the Russian philosophy of history created on the eve of revolution: "In the rhythm of the images and in the historiosophical pulse of these works one distinctly hears the Scythian hoofs originating in Aleksandr Blok. He was similarly fascinated by perishing civilizations and 'the footprint of a Mongol horse on the golden sand that covered the labyrinths of the cities.' The Polish poet, who has come to visit the ruins of ancient civilizations from nowhere else but Warsaw, merely has more arguments and observations than Blok."[18]

Wyka's search for the cultural and ideological framework of Wat's poetry was taken up by several critics of lesser stature. More than one reviewer pointed to Cyprian Kamil Norwid (1821–83), a cryptic, idiosyncratic late Romantic poet of philosophical bent, as one of Wat's most obvious predecessors.[19]

The Polish émigré community was no less fascinated by Wat's work than readers in the old country. Konstanty A. Jeleński, guiding spirit of *Culture* and a renowned member of the international literary community, was the first to discuss Wat's poetry in the world press. In the American journal *Partisan Review,* he stated: "Aleksander Wat, one of the rare intellectual poets of Poland, analyzes himself and the world in terms of a poetic Imaginary Museum. His work has features in common with Eliot and Auden."[20] Later, he examined Wat in a broader perspective:

> He is . . . like T. S. Eliot, Ezra Pound, Valéry Larbaud, W. H. Auden, Pierre-Jean Jouve (who are not necessarily brothers, though Wat is a brother to every one of them), a poet of memory. Mineral memory, biological memory, archetypal and mythological memory, historical memory, psychological memory, which superpose each other. . . . Besides, this poet of erudition, this renewer of the most cultivated Baroque "concetto," has lived passionately through history, as have few of his contemporaries, both as its protagonist and its victim.[21]

Gustaw Herling-Grudziński stressed the religious dimension of Wat's poetry. This approach, indispensable for an understanding of Wat's creative imagination, was still frowned upon—though not entirely banned—in Poland. Herling-Grudziński noted the tension in Wat's world view: a hunger for metaphysics combined with a lack of inner harmony, mysticism combined with doubt. This state of being convinced of the necessity of transcendence while profoundly uncertain as to its accessibility underlay, in the critic's opinion, Wat's kinship with Eliot, as well as with the baroque. A poet of "pure black," Wat was among those who explore the limits of literature and human experience, the regions where our knowledge "does not conform any more to our five senses, where the borders of the visible world become obliterated and firm ground escapes our feet."[22]

Many of these critical judgments are sound. One cannot but agree with Wyka's assertion of Wat's kinship with catastrophism. Wat's poetic imagination was marked from the very beginning by an acute sense of ruin and calamity. His futurist works, notwithstanding their grotesque and parodic character, had strong apocalyptic overtones and to a considerable degree presaged the catastrophism of the 1930s. He was far better acquainted with Russian prerevolutionary thought (which provided an impulse for, and a foretaste of catastrophism) than most Polish writers and was attuned to it more than anyone, with the possible exception of Witkacy. Evil and suffering, cosmic disorder and the metaphysical nonsense of existence, were among Wat's main themes. During the war and the postwar years, his intimation of the impending end of the world gave way to a sense that the final disaster had already occurred: the civilization of yesteryear had been obliterated, and the promise of salvation proffered by Marxist ideology had proved deceptive. Now, the despair was much more profound than it had been in the wake of World War I. Yet, however paradoxical it might appear, this time the despair led to stoicism and an intense metaphysical quest, rather than to nihilism.

The observations regarding the importance of existentialist thought for Wat are no less valid, although specifically *Christian* existentialism can hardly be traced to Heidegger or Sartre. The most obvious philosophical influence here is Søren Kierkegaard, whom Wat had studied and admired from childhood: "I read *Diary of the Seducer* at the age of seven, and at ten, when I already possessed an adequate knowledge of German, I read the large volume *Entweder-Oder* [Either/Or], a favorite book of my father."[23]

A philosopher of metaphysical anguish, Kierkegaard was deeply aware of human limitations and the threat of nothingness. At the same time, he was a philosopher of freedom, who emphasized the uniqueness and openness of human existence more powerfully than perhaps any thinker before or after him. Kierkegaard demanded a metaphysical choice not backed by outside criteria, in the face of uncertainty and doubt. Such a risky "leap of faith" appealed to Wat far more than any submission to traditional religious teachings, be they Catholic or Jewish. A born agnostic and doubter, Wat had made his leap of faith in Ili, when he had opted for resistance against all the odds. It was a choice that he was faced with again and again, and he oscillated to the very end between religion and rebellion, tradition and innovation, Judaism and Christianity.

One of the most prominent traits of Kierkegaard's thought was his critical attitude toward historical Christianity—and indeed toward any historical religion. This provided an antidote to the narrowness of Polish Catholicism, with its anachronistic mind-set, which Wat had already mocked in his futurist years: "Can the Polish mind, brought up on the Polish Catholicism of collators, peasants, and Jesuits, and Piarists, get to the core of Kierkegaard? What a discovery it would be! How negligible in comparison with Kierkegaard (for the Polish way of thinking) are Maritain and Neothomists, who in fact gave the signal for the contemporary revival of Catholicism in Poland! He would cure it immediately of all that sentimentality. . . . He would show that communication with God is the most difficult of all struggles, a never-ending struggle of souls and minds."[24]

Kierkegaard was a precursor of catastrophism in his acceptance of the tragic quality of human existence and his rejection of superficial consolation. Moreover, he introduced a theomachic note into his thinking, a note that was particularly resonant for Wat (and, incidentally, reverberated through the best works of Polish Romanticism). In his imperviousness to doctrines and his insis-

tence on testing everything by personal experience, he surpassed the existentialists of the twentieth century, who, often as not, yielded to abstract schemas. A
modern poet could not but recognize in Kierkegaard a kindred spirit.

But Kierkegaard's impact on Wat extended beyond the realm of poetry. A
critic of Christianity, Kierkegaard was also the most convincing critic of Hegel,
whose concept of the "spirit of history" had contributed so significantly to
Marxist dogma. An ironist and satirist of the first rank, Kierkegaard was very
close to Wat in his attacks on anonymity and the concern with numbers; he was
among those who early on recognized the depersonalization and social atomization that were to become hallmarks of the new era.

Both Wyka and Herling-Grudziński emphasized that Wat's philosophical
predilections were complemented by his surrealist background. This background contributed to the success of his poetry, reducing its dependence on
abstract concepts and creating a dreamlike atmosphere conducive to the free
flow of associations. Nevertheless, the psychoanalytical doctrine underlying
Wat's surrealism was far from orthodox. An assiduous student of Freud
throughout his life, Wat nevertheless tended to deride and parody pansexualism.
He was also suspicious of Freud's attempts to construe dreams as readable
without remainder: "Despite Freud, I maintain that the majority of dreams are
caprices of the imagination, like the caprices of clouds. Sometimes, however, in a
dream you are aware that the dream has meaning. . . . Of course, you don't know
what the meaning is, and here Freud is certainly right in part."[25] In his mature
years, Wat was more interested in Jung, as witnessed by one of his surviving
letters, written in a Paris hospital: "C. G. Jung is the Einstein or Copernicus of
psychology, ethnology, etc., and in order to write, e.g., on art, one decidedly
must know his work."[26]

Jung's mystical, spiritual approach to the world of the imagination strongly
distinguished him from Freud, and in this he was far more in tune with Wat's
metaphysical leanings. It could even be said that Wat elaborated some of the
tenets of Jungian psychology independently of Jung (and earlier than him).
Wat's interest in mythology, Gnosticism, and alchemy, so obvious in *Pug Iron
Stove*, predated Jung's fundamental studies of the same phenomena, and his
quest for the Self was markedly similar to, if not coincident with, the Jungian
path of individuation.[27] In Wat's late poetry, the symbolism of the unconscious
and the mythology of the Self become increasingly evident, and the Jungian
overtones of his work are more often traceable to direct knowledge of Jungian
thought.

In strictly literary terms, the most important forebears of Wat's book of
poems were the metaphysical poets of the Baroque and Counter-Reformation.[28]
The baroque is often considered, not without justification, a recurrent phenomenon in art. It may also be noted that metaphysical poetry tends to appear, in

various guises, during periods of transition. The relationship between meta-physical poetry and the baroque is far from unambiguous. The two overlap but do not coincide, either logically or chronologically: not all baroque poetry is metaphysical, and metaphysical poetry also features during the ascendancy of nonbaroque traits. Nevertheless, both metaphysical poetry and the baroque are associated with periods of turmoil. The religious upheaval, social breakdown, and political chaos of the late sixteenth and seventeenth centuries, together with the scientific revolution that denied humankind its privileged position in the universe, were conducive to the emergence of poetic schools which refined intellectual wit and cultivated a multiplicity of tonalities, dramatic paradox and oxymoron, grotesquerie and free forms, introspection and a capacity for "de-vouring all kinds of experience," to use Eliot's much-quoted phrase. Very simi-lar, albeit exacerbated, conditions in the twentieth century could not help but contribute to the flourishing of similar poetic strains.

The metaphysical poetry of Donne, George Herbert, Jean de Sponde, Luis de Góngora, Angelus Silesius, and, in the Polish context, Mikołaj Sęp Szarzyński thus constituted an important part of the background of Wat's later work. An avid reader, Wat had been fascinated by this poetry for many years. In this, he preceded most, if not all other, Polish writers. The rediscovery and reevaluation of metaphysical poetry that took place in Europe at the turn of the twentieth century did not reach Poland in earnest until 1956—and then, to a significant degree, due to Wat's influence. Wat studied St. John of the Cross and Donne and was particularly fond of Maurice Scève, an early representative of the baroque in France. In 1958, he undertook a translation of Scève's *Délie*, which was published by the émigré press in 1964. "Scève is really a metaphysical French poet, perhaps the only one in France, in each of his poems one finds the *apex animae* of the mystics and metaphysicians: he spent his nights indeed on esoteric and mystical studies and meditation, you can feel it everywhere in *Délie*," Wat told Miłosz in November 1963. "*Délie* is Psyche in the Neoplatonic sense, as well as the corporeal one: spurs, 'lusts,' the philosophical and sensual *appetitus*."[29]

Wat's late poetry resembled baroque poetry in its flexibility of form, ellipti-cal and compact wording, caustic irony, and mixture of abstract notions and sensual images. It was marked by the keen sense of disharmony and disequilib-rium that is usually taken as distinguishing "baroque" trends in art from "classi-cal" ones. It was also typically baroque in being learned, utilizing dialectical argument and bordering at times on pedantry, traits that prompted critics like Maciąg to accuse Wat of artificiality. For Wat, as well as for Donne and Scève, a poem was primarily a means for addressing spiritual issues. Nevertheless, the religious context provided ample scope for the profane: it accommodated realis-tic imagery, as well as sheer mockery. Already perceptible in *Pug Iron Stove*, these traits were now displayed in a more fully developed form, as Wat reestablished his ties with the tradition that he had so joyously disrupted during his early iconoclastic period.

Wat was a first-rate critic himself, but in accordance with his philosophy of criticism, he rarely if ever made his remarks in scholarly language: fragmentary and figurative notes sufficed. This was also consistent with his "passive" attitude to method and style: "I do not choose poetics: they choose me, and I just do not resist," he wrote in 1963.[30] But, from seemingly causal comments scattered throughout his writings, more than one brilliant essay on his own poetry and on poetry in general could be cobbled together. Some of these remarks actually became an unfinished article, "O ciemnych poetach i ciemnych czytelnikach" (On Obscure Poets and Obscurant Readers), included in the *Diary without Vowels*.

Striving to explain his art to himself and his readers, Wat was keenly aware of the elusiveness of the subject and the limits of criticism in general:

> However the relationship between a particular writer and his particular critics (and scholars) may form, the fundamental attitude is one of conflict. A conflict of interest and of disposition. As a matter of fact, the scholar (and the critic) attempts to understand and communicate the underlying principles of the work's or writer's *knowhow*, and to summarize in his own words what the writer wants to say. At the same time, the writer is most profoundly reluctant to obtain any knowledge of these principles and intentions. He is terrified by this self-revelation, as if by the exposure of a magic secret. Since every authentic writer, notwithstanding his idea of himself and the structure of his mind, however rationalist it might be, perceives his work as valuable only when he feels in it the supreme presence of something which was absent in his brain before he started writing, and only this conscious or unconscious feeling of a mysterious gain, of a surplus value presented to him, becomes his anointment. . . . His relationship to his creation is demiurgic: he wants to tell himself: "And saw that it was good," as in *Genesis*, yet more obviously and much more powerfully he does not want to know, why and how it is good. . . . The exposed creation turns immediately into a depersonalized set of mechanical devices and soulless tricks.[31]

The next-to-impossible undertaking entailed positioning oneself on the thin line where poetry turns into meta-poetry without losing its essence and where poetic unconsciousness reaches the threshold of consciousness without actually overstepping it. There, and only there, would the study of the poetic craft not deprive it of the "mysterious gain" born in the course of writing.

The mature Wat took a critical attitude toward the iconoclastic currents of the early twentieth century and was mistrustful of their striving for continuous innovation. Change for its own sake tended to be at the expense of psychological and artistic relevance in Wat's view.

It is known that nothing ages as fast as novelty. . . . Nothing becomes conventional as fast as intentional anti-conventionalism. . . . Anyone who entered that devilish circle would never come out of it. The only salvation: to ignore the existence of conventions, all of them, to be aware and unaware of them simultaneously.[32]

Now I think that a return to the clear, most simple poem in a traditional form, with a theme, is not just desirable but possible. Yet what a difficult path it is, how many superstitions and small vanities have to be repudiated.[33]

In this regard, the poetry of the Skamandrites, with its cult of clarity, seemed to Wat a promising trend in the history of Polish literature, whereas the Kraków Vanguard was, in his opinion, "a disastrous retrogression,"[34] the epitome of innovation for innovation's sake. Yet, Tuwim and other Skamandrites were wrong in emphasizing the musicality of poetic language while dismissing its intellectual content. The nineteenth-century works of Norwid, marked by a roughness of texture and complexity of thought, were a more important model for a true avant-garde.

A new poetry capable of accommodating the experience of the twentieth century could not be other than intellectual. At the same time, the profound difference between poetry and science (including philosophy) must be taken into account: "The power and dignity of poetry consist in its discord with scholarly thought."[35] Poetry is opposed to history and, in particular, to the latter's tendency to depersonalization: it remains on the side of the individual. Moreover, the specificity of poetic thought is inherent not only in its personal character but also in its dialogical nature:

It is known that there are various ways of thinking: there is common sense comprehension and strictly logical comprehension, there is contemplative or mystical, intuitive or eidetic, prophetic or premonitory comprehension, comprehension by heart, body, senses, etc., etc. . . . Modern poetry refers to pure poetic comprehension. Moreover, it merely develops this comprehension as its *organon*. . . . This way, authentic new poetry forms and perfects its readers, it does not come to a prepared soil, and this is perhaps its greatest credit, as well as the principle of its dynamism: the reader is "in the making," exists only and continuously *im Werden*, and develops from poem to poem, together with the poet. In contemporary poetry, in contrast with old poetry, a poem, even the best one, means little or even nothing! You should follow your poet from one poem to another and from one cycle to another. Is it worth such an effort?—a reader would ask. Certainly it is: since independently of the result, if a poet is authentic, the very road, the very effort becomes, for the reader, a way of self-improvement, revealing new horizons and leading to inner transformation in the process of "individuation," found by C. G. Jung in the practice of the alchemists.[36]

It should be added that this model includes feedback: each side can take the role of therapist and patient alternately. The poet achieves inner transformation by taking into account changes in the reader (or readers). It is a dynamic relationship, a molding of interdependent personalities gradually attaining self-knowledge through doubt and pain.

Writing—and, correspondingly, the perception of the poetry—can take place under two opposite conditions: either by the light of full consciousness illuminating inner torment or in a state of "obscured consciousness" that gives way to intuition, recollections of childhood, half-forgotten historical memories, and mythical archetypes.[37] The second of these conditions was described by Wat, characteristically, in an alien language (French):

> One turns into a poet when one ceases to be him: when one comes back to the state of primeval consciousness of a six-month-old infant, just a receptacle for voices which do not come from us, although they are in us. The universe is full of voices. And when you are empty enough to perceive them, a real problem appears: how to discern the propitious voices from those disadvantageous for your work. The representation of these mysteries in *Faust* and in Mickiewicz's work is naive and simplistic, since good and ominous voices are juxtaposed there in a geometric manner. Actually, they mix.[38]

This half-mystical, half-depth-psychological approach to poetry also determined Wat's attitude to time. Wat saw the passage of time as a "chaotic swaying toward and away from death," interrupted by moments of remembrance that allowed him to discern the timeless core of his personality. Here is an echo of Wat's early perception of two temporal orders: a deterministic one and a miraculous one.[39] In fact, the matter was even more complicated. In Wat's words, "the same experience, or, to put it otherwise, the same situation or arrangement of objects repeats itself on various planes of time . . . the planes of time cross according to their geometry, and the points of crossing or interference make up a figure which is . . . the enriched present time. I would perish one hundredfold in my predicaments, if I were not endowed with the gift of enriched present time."[40]

The main formal quality of modern metaphysical poetry, in Wat's view, was its proteanism: "not Apollo, but Proteus is the father of art."[41] All forms were acceptable, traditional as well as nontraditional ones, on the sole condition that the reader be challenged sufficiently: "A continuous play of changing shapes, a continuous equilibrium between the expected and the unexpected."[42] This is a reference to the notion of "defamiliarization" developed by Russian formalists: that the perception of a work of art (and of the reality lurking behind it) never be allowed to settle into a static, automatic pattern. In practice, this meant continuous oscillation—from poem to poem, as well as within the limits of a single poem—between metrical lines and free verse, convoluted and simple syntax,

poesis docta and folk ditty, gnomic precision and surrealist logorrhea. Wat consciously erased even the distinction between poetic and nonpoetic genres. In
1967, he confessed: "The so-called means of technique in my case consist perhaps solely in an attempt to place myself and hold my ground on the narrow
borderline between prose-prose (not poetic prose, God forbid!) and poetry-
poetry (if only that it be nonprosaic). One should define here the meaning of
these two terms, but let us leave to the scholars what is properly theirs."[43]

This liberty with regard to means of expression did not exclude poetic
discipline, but required a discipline of a very specific kind, consisting of an
almost mathematical symmetry and a precise—yet always endangered—
balance of opposing psychological and linguistic forces. "I am satisfied only by
those of my poems," Wat wrote, "the structure of which . . . is somewhat related to mathematical structures; to put it differently, by those that evoke in me
the feelings I experienced long ago, when I indulged in mathematics."[44]

An essential element in this precarious balance was the interdependence of
the phonetic quality of words and lines and their meaning.[45] The disorderly,
grating lines of Norwid (and the futurists) Wat saw as among the best examples
of the harmony treasured by a contemporary poet.[46] When it came to vocabulary, Wat opted for "linguistic simultaneism or syncretism," attempting to make
words "independent of their spatiotemporal grid"—that is, using them indis-
criminately with regard to their provenance and age.[47] Still another problem was
rhyme:

> Rhyming was introduced by medieval poets. *Dies Irae. Stabat Mater.*
> Their rhymes astounded, the accord of sounds at the end of the line evoked
> the different, final accord between earthly destinies and God's judgment. It
> was a misunderstanding to employ rhyming for secular, empiric, rational
> topics! . . . A fault of Petrarch and Dante, and before them of the trouvères
> and Islamic poets.[48]

> The most primitive reader assumes that it is precisely rhyming that makes
> poetry . . . Whereas for common sense rhyming is absurd.[49]

Wat did not eschew rhymes (or classical metric and stanzaic patterns)
altogether, but he used them sparingly. There is the occasional rhymed poem in
his book of 1957 in the midst of free verse and unrhymed traditional verse, where
rhyme is one way of violating the reader's expectations. When Wat did employ
rhyming, it was mainly in contexts in which it had semantic value, either by
linking metaphysical concepts, as in medieval poetry, or by referring ironically to
the outdated poetics of the era of Young Poland. Thus, the "absurd" device
became informative once again.

In his theoretical pronouncements, Wat did not limit himself to the precepts of the Russian formalists; rather, it might be said that he developed
formalist ideas in the direction of structural poetics, especially as represented by

the Tartu-Moscow school, which began to take shape during this same period of post-Stalinist thaw. There is a distinct similarity between Wat's implicit poetic theory and the views of Yury Lotman, the head and most accomplished scholar of the Tartu-Moscow school.[50] Wat's notes cannot stand comparison with Lotman's extensive, systematic treatises, even if some of his insights preceded Lotman's by several years. Still, the general accord of the two thinkers is clear, especially their approach to the structural function of sound patterns and rhyme in poetry. It appears that Lotman and Wat were unaware of each other's existence; thus, one is dealing here with a striking case of parallel development from a common point of departure, rooted in a similar style of thought.

In the 1960s, Wat took a lively interest in the works of Claude Lévi-Strauss and Roman Jakobson, who, together with the Russian formalists, exerted a formative influence on Lotman as well. He mentions both of them in his article "On Obscure Poets and Obscurant Readers," which is an attempt to define modern poetry: "It is, therefore, intellectual or cerebral poetry, which ignores logical discourse and refers to other dispositions (functions) of reason: the imagination—this is metaphoric poetry; and/or to the senses and memory— this is metonymic poetry, to use the excellent terminology of Roman Jakobson. . . . The kinship of metaphoric or metonymic thought and imagery with magic—by similarity, or by contiguity in space or time, respectively—was established by Lévi-Strauss and Jakobson perhaps beyond any doubt."[51]

As we know, Wat was suspicious of metaphoric thought, which, in his view, led to a dead end: "anything could be equated with anything and, precisely at that point, the very act of equation loses its value."[52] For him, as for Pasternak, the preferred figure was metonymy, the substitution of one word or sequence of words for another on the basis of contiguity. According to Jakobson, metonymic thinking results either in the intersection and interpenetration of different objects in the poetic text or in their splitting, analogous to the splitting of objects in Cubist paintings. It leads to a displacement of reality by emotion—that is, to a projection of the poet's being onto reality, which then appears as an endless chain of the lyrical persona's subjective states. Metonymy, in Jakobson's view, is characteristic more of prose than of poetry.[53] This complex of traits is found already in Wat's futurist works, but it becomes, if anything, even more pronounced in his mature poems, which situate themselves on the borderline between "poetry-poetry" and "prose-prose."

One more analogy between Wat's theoretical statements and structural/poststructural poetics concerns his treatment of intertextuality. As early as *Pug Iron Stove*, he implicitly defined human consciousness as totally determined by cultural codes. Whatever else might be said about *Pug Iron Stove*, one characteristic is striking: the text is relative to an almost infinite number of other texts, yet without any ultimate referent that would stabilize its meaning. In his mature years, Wat came close to considering intertextuality the fundamental quality of any literary text, although he (like Lotman) avoided the extreme position typical of some poststructuralist thinkers.

Since the autonomy of a literary work is, in Wat's view, an illusion, since every text is "plagiaristic by its very essence,"[54] the whole concept of authorship and of a work's uniqueness and intrinsic value is called into question. In *Scraps of Paper in the Wind*, Wat tells of a Western poetess he knew, who concocted her poems, not without success, from fortuitous fragments of Pierre-Jean Jouve, Robert Desnos, Jules Laforgue, and others. Under such conditions, how does one distinguish between an authentic poet and the thousands of mediocre compilers and imitators? But, in contrast to many poststructuralist critics, Wat postulates a means of discernment in the extra-literary realm: "I think that today the only verifiable criterion is the face of the poet, that is, the poetic personality and fate, something that—unfortunately—places itself outside poetry as such. The only tangible guarantee is sincerity—that is, a moral quality. And the price which the poet has paid for the poem, paid in his own flesh and blood—a question of biography which, according to the critics, should not be anybody's business."[55]

Thus, the last word of Wat's theory of poetics is an affirmation of the interdependence of the *literary text* and the *text of life*. Biography and creative work encode and pattern each other.[56] Problems of morality, personal sacrifice, and fate, however distant from literature they might appear, cannot be excluded from the critic's field of vision: indeed, they belong at its center, as in ancient times. Suffering, pity, and terror, the formative factors in Aristotelian catharsis, are, for Wat, the very substance of poetry.

Wat's book consisted of two parts of unequal length: *Wiersze nowe* (New Poems) and *Z wierszy dawniej drukowanych* (From the Previously Printed Poems). The first part was divided into four cycles: *W okolicach cierpienia* (In the Environs of Suffering), *Sny* (Dreams), *Inne* (Varia), and *Obce miejsca, obce twarze* (Alien Places, Alien Faces). The book could be described—and was in fact described by some critics—as a singular poetic travelogue. The author travels in space and time simultaneously. Imagery of cities, landscapes, and European monuments is interlaced with memories of childhood and youth, war and prison, the Central Asian desert and innumerable hospitals. Sketches of nature alternate with examinations of moral, psychological, and political attitudes. In the final analysis, travel in physical space and time is seen to have a metaphysical correlate: it is a medieval pilgrimage, a Dantean journey—and the road to Golgotha.

The biblical and mystical connotations are especially evident in the first cycle. It opens with a short poem, "W czterech ścianach mego bólu" (In the Four Walls of My Pain), that serves as an epigraph to the entire book. It describes the poet's incurable illness and his life experience generally in terms of life imprisonment. The cycle includes poems with such telling titles as "W szpitalu"

(In a Hospital), "Noc w szpitalu" (A Night in a Hospital), and "Kołysanka dla konającego" (A Lullaby for a Dying Person) and it is a veritable encyclopedia of pain, both physical and spiritual. There are poems born of Kierkegaardian "fear and trembling"; poems on the hopeless search for a place to hide or escape to; nightmarish visions and hallucinations in which baroque images of corpses and skeletons reign supreme; reminiscences of youthful creativity that become, in retrospect, portents of sufferings to come; meditations on agony and nothingness in a language that is almost technical in its striving for precision yet transcends the bounds of everyday logic:

> Here neither space nor will exists
> here is only non-time, without-will
> non-nothing and without-thing—mirage and stone—
> anti-energy in the void of illusions.
>
> Agony is not death, nor is it life,
> nor Sein zum Tod of Heidegger the Wise,
> it is also neither life in death nor death in life,
> nor is it their struggle, although it does mean struggle in Greek . . .

Some poems allude to Wat's prison experiences[57] and exile in Kazakhstan, but projected onto the background of "the great and terrible wilderness" of Exodus: "There I will be called to the Last Judgment by the bellowing throats of wild donkeys, / who will copulate furiously over me, under Satan's burning sun."[58] Pivotal to the entire cycle is a set of poems entitled "Trzy sonety" (Three Sonnets), incorporating motifs of the garden of Gethsemane and the Crucifixion. In a denouement, the boldness of which had no rivals in Polish literature[59] or even in world literature perhaps, Christ refuses to resurrect until "man is also free of death and pain."

The second, short cycle (entirely in free verse) is limited to poems recording dreams (most of them probably authentic). Their main emotional tenor is one of vulnerability and insecurity. Especially striking is the profusion of water imagery. For the most part, water is presented as dangerous, polluted, and defiled. The resulting fear of water reaches a poignant, grotesque level in the poem "Sen flaminga" (A Flamingo's Dream):

> Water water water. And nothing but water.
> If only one inch of land! An inch of no-matter-what land!
> To set foot on! Just an inch!
>
> We begged the gods for that! All of them!
> Water gods, land gods, southern gods, northern gods.
> For an inch, a strip, a scrap of any kind of land!
> No more than just enough to support the claw of one foot!
> And nothing. Only water. Nothing except water.

Water water water.
If only a speck of land!
There is no salvation.[60]

The cycle *Varia*, in keeping with its name, is the most diversified in content as well as form. It includes short epigrammatic verses and long narrative poems, ironic sketches and intricate philosophical meditations, and ballads, songs, and polemical stylizations of Romantic or Young Poland lyrics. A significant part of the cycle consists of biblical and Oriental parables: "Z perskich przypowieści" (From Persian Parables); "Sługa królowej Kandaki" (The Servant of Queen Candace); "Japońskie łucznictwo" (Japanese Archery). Meditations on slavery and exile, based on Wat's personal experience, are often presented under the guise of a legend or motif from the Old Testament and take on a symbolic quality: thus, Chechen girls deported by Stalin from their homeland in the Caucasus to Ili turn into captives from the land of Ophir[61] on the banks of the alien river Iola in "Panienki cudne" (The Wonderful Maidens).[62] Several poems record impressions of paintings, thereby providing occasion for psychological and metaphysical reflection.

Some of the *Varia* texts reflect the ludicrous, horrifying events of postwar Poland, from the alcoholic escapades of a humiliated Broniewski ("Z notatnika oborskiego" [From Notes Written in Obory]) to the ambiguous experience of the thaw ("I tak się własną krew pompuje" [And Thus One Pumps One's Own Blood]). The theme of Stalinism is closely interwoven with that of Nazism. The race of "magnificent supermen of the future" born from the loins of a grotesque degenerate ("Chyba nie widział" [He Perhaps Could Not See]) could refer to both the Nazi *Übermensch* and the "new Soviet man," and an eight-line aphoristic poem may be read as an epitaph for all the victims of both Stalinism and the Holocaust:

We left the dominion of the old telluric gods long ago,
we have been going deep into the realm of the chthonic gods for a long
    time.
We drag our feet in a disorderly herd, millions of wheezing phantoms
who escaped from the torture-chambers and crematoria, from the graves,
    excavations and charred ruins.
We make nothing of the initiations, assemblies, symbols, marches,
your bestial obsequies, and even of your base repentance.
We have our route—we hasten to the marriage,
where blood will turn into wine in the name of the Holy Spirit.

Generically, the fourth cycle, *Alien Places, Alien Faces,* corresponds most closely to the poetic travelogue idea. It opens with "Dytyramb" (A Dithyramb), a poem written in 1949 on Capri that is striking for its dark tonality, a foretaste of the mood that was to inform Wat's later lyric. More poems dedicated to Italy follow, including a grim sketch of cadaverous Venetian water ("Przypomnienie Wenecji" [A Recollection of Venice]) and a meditation on the ruins of Rome, which merge in Wat's imagination with the ruins of Warsaw ("Do przyjaciela rzymianina" [To a Roman, My Friend]). These are followed by poems on France, mostly about Paris. They are quite different in intonation and style from the Italian poems, being for the most part imbued with a cheerful feeling of newly found life (albeit not without poignant overtones) or, at least, of tranquility and reconciliation. The cycle ends with two long poems, "Odjazd na Sycylię" (Leaving for Sicily) and "Wieczór—noc—ranek" (Evening—Night—Morning), that recapitulate the main themes and moods of the book. The latter is arguably the most complicated and most important of Wat's works of the years 1956–57.[63]

Like the book as a whole, *Alien Places, Alien Faces* contrasts the beauty of earthly things and forms with ugliness, misery, and nothingness. Technically, the cycle (like the first and third cycles) includes a mixture of free verse and metrical lines, and shout alternates with whisper and prayer. The breaking and rupturing of form is justified by—and reflects—the experience of unremitting pain, which becomes, for Wat, a universal principle.

The short poem "Trochę mitologii" (A Bit of Mythology),[64] which posits a link between suffering and creativity and shares the function of epigraph to the book with the aforementioned "In the Four Walls of My Pain," is a good example of Wat's mature art:

Ja nie jestem Heraklesem
ani Ola Dejanirą,
wrogi moje nie centaury.
Lecz koszuli ja Nessosa
już się nie pozbędę nigdy.
Ona wlewa w żyły ołów,
ona trawi w wolnym ogniu
limf rysunek, nerwów deseń.
Ona tkankę miażdży żywą,
kość rozkrusza, mózg zaciska.
Żeby wyżąć z krwawym potem
słowa słowa słowa.

I am not a Hercules,
nor is Ola a Deianeira,
my enemies are not centaurs.
But I'll never get rid
of the shirt of Nessos.   5
It pours lead into my veins,
it etches in its slow fire
the outline of lymphatics, the design
    of nerves.
It grinds the living tissue,   10
crushes the bone, squeezes the brain.
To wring out with a bloody sweat
words words words.[65]

"A Bit of Mythology" belongs to the group of minimalist poems that constitutes one of the poles of Wat's book and indeed of his entire lyric.[66] One might describe it as *centripetal* verse, as opposed to *centrifugal* poetry, which is marked by verbosity, stylistic complexity, and a certain disorder of rhythm, syntax, and imagery.[67] An ascetic text, it is almost classical in its formal elegance.

The poem is written in a trochaic meter, which is striking by dint of its

monotonous, almost doggerel-like quality. It stands out against the free verse
that is so prevalent elsewhere in the book. The lines are tightly knit. The
impression of monotony and symmetry is reinforced by numerous structural
devices. The periods always coincide with the end of the line. There are numerous syntactic parallelisms (e.g., "kość rozkrusza, mózg zaciska" and a pronounced anaphora "ona . . . ona . . . ona" in lines 6, 7, and 9). The boundaries
of the words tend to coincide with those of the feet ("ona wlewa w żyły ołów," for
example), a tendency that reaches a climax at the end. All these devices are
supported by a highly organized sound pattern, based on the repetition of *w, l, ł,*
and *ż,* as well as of stressed *o.* The sound play has obvious semantic import: thus,
ołów (lead, line 6) and *słowa* (words, line 12), related as cause (suffering) and
effect (poetry), are also linked phonetically. They also mark the beginning and
the end of the second half of the poem.

    This emphasis on boundaries and enclosing patterns is in accord with the
central image of the poem. The entire text has an iconic quality, becoming, as it
were, a figure for the mythical shirt of Nessos, confining and imprisoning the
narrator as well as the narration.

    Wat employed for his poem the story of the death of Hercules, known
primarily from Sophocles' *Trachiniae.* The centaur Nessos (Nessus) attempts to
abduct and violate Deianeira, wife of Hercules, but is killed by Hercules. Before
dying, Nessos offers Deianeira his blood and advises her to anoint her husband's
shirt with it secretly. He says that it will serve as a love-charm and so protect her
from Hercules' unfaithfulness. In this way, Nessos enacts a terrible revenge: his
blood, tainted by the hydra's poison of Hercules' arrow, is deadly. When Deianeira gives the shirt to Hercules, the poison causes him unbearable pain. But he
cannot rip off the shirt without tearing away his flesh as well, laying his bones
bare. Unable to bear his suffering, he immolates himself on a pyre, while the
repentant Deianeira hangs herself.

    The shirt of Nessos signifies the narrator's torment, brought about not
only by his illness but also by remorse over the blunders of his life (and consequently similar to both Hercules' and Deianeira's agonies). His bones and brain
are affected equally; somatic and spiritual suffering grow together indissolubly,
just like the shirt and the flesh.

    The poem opens with a series of negations whereby the validity of the myth
is denied: the ancient story does *not* correspond to the experience of contemporary human beings. Nothing remains of it except the shirt—that is, the pain
itself, which assumes the status of an everlasting human condition. In a demythologized universe, the only remaining metaphysical reality is that of suffering
and death. Wat places the key word *nigdy* (never) at the end of a line, in the same
position as the mythical names, as well as in the center of the poem.[68]

    Characteristically, Wat employs metonymy rather than metaphor. The
shirt, by contiguity, becomes a figure for skin, whose symbolic role in Wat's

poetry has been noted by several critics.[69] Skin plays a profoundly ambiguous role in Wat's poetic psyche. In one of his last poems, "Ode III," a poem in prose, he writes:

> With my skin I experienced a Creation full of gifts, of friendly surfaces, of light's smiles, of smells and sounds, all that was pleasing to the senses. With my skin I experienced Creation from the first morning till late evening, till the nightfall, while it was bringing testimony to itself: "It is good" . . .
>
> With my skin I was your constant companion in the stench of prisons and hospitals, my skin responding, vibrating, echoing to the sufferings of your skins. . . .
>
> Therefore I bequeath to you, my brethren, my skin, naked skin, for what else do I have? with a humble prayer, to tan it for the binding of this collection of stanzas.[70]

A window on the universe of purity and corruption, skin is simultaneously a narrow confine, a prison wall.[71] It is thus a metonymic image for both soul and body: considered opposites in everyday language, they merge in Wat's poetic language and in his metaphysics. The final proposal heightens the ambiguity to the extreme: an ultimate sacralization of the skin (what purpose could be nobler than enclosing the Book—that is, the essence of the poet's life?); but also an ultimate blasphemy, a chilling reference to the activities of Nazi war criminals.

Whereas the skin separates the Self from the non-Self, the tormenting shirt belongs to both the alien universe and the personal world: it is both Self *and* non-Self, the locus of their interpenetration, the surface through which the evil of being invades the inner life. The shirt becomes an active force, virtually a living creature endowed with demonic powers that pierce ever deeper layers of the body, reaching to the core of the psyche. It evokes a response that is both somatic and spiritual: a bloody sweat and a poem, the latter a sort of bodily excretion. Thereby, the opposition of outer versus inner and body versus soul is fully transcended. This synthesis is the high point of Wat's somatic mysticism.

The final line, "słowa słowa słowa," is, of course, a quote from Hamlet's dialogue with Polonius: "What do you read, my lord?—Words, words, words." A reader who knows *Hamlet* well, as Wat did, cannot fail to remember that the answer of the Prince of Denmark is given in the rich context of a scene that deals with aging, approaching death, madness, and imprisonment.

The ending, however bitter, strikes a characteristic note. Pain, for Wat, is the essence of the universe, and imprisonment constitutes the context of life. Nevertheless, the shirt of Nessos can be destroyed by *words,* even if only for a moment. The tight symmetry of the poem is violated by the atypical—and alien—last line. Cut off abruptly, and consisting of absurd repetition, it opens the perspective of annihilation—and, simultaneously, the space of speech.

Another shorthand for suffering is presented in the more extensive, complicated poem "Być myszą" (To Be a Mouse),[72] which proposes a myth of escape:

Być myszą. Najlepiej polną. Albo
    ogrodową—
nie domową:
człowiek ekshaluje woń abominalną!
Znamy ją wszyscy—ptaki, kraby,
    szczury.
Budzi wstręt i strach.
    Drżenie.

Żywić się kwiatem glicynii, korą
    drzew palmowych,
rozgrzebywać korzonki w chłodnej
    wilgotnej ziemi
i tańczyć po świeżej nocy. Patrzeć na
    księżyc w pełni,
odbijać w oczach obłe światło
    księżycowej
      agonii.

Zaszyć się w mysią dziurkę na czas,
    kiedy zły Boreasz
szukać mnie będzie zimnymi palcami
    kościstymi,
by gnieść moje małe serce pod
    blaszką swego szponu—
tchórzliwe serce mysie—
    kryształ palpitujący.

To be a mouse. Preferably a field
    mouse. Or a garden mouse—
but not the kind that live in houses.
Man exudes an abominable smell!
We all know it—birds, crabs, rats.
He provokes disgust and fear.
    Trembling.   5

To feed on wisteria blossoms, on the
    bark of palm trees,
to dig up roots in cold, humid soil
and to dance after a brisk night. To
    look at the full moon,
to reflect in one's eyes the sleek light
    of lunar   10
      agony.

To borrow in a mouse hole against
    the time when wicked Boreas
will search for me with his cold, bony
    fingers
so he can squeeze my little heart
    under the blade of his claw—
a cowardly mouse heart—   15
    a palpitating crystal.[73]

The poem obviously refers to Wat's experience of 1939 in the Soviet-occupied Lwów region. In his memoirs, he described the most advisable course of action under the circumstances in the words: "I would have to hide somewhere, in a mouse hole."[74] He did not succeed, because he was searching for his lost wife and son.[75] The result was the disgrace of the Lwów episode.

"Hiding in a mouse hole" is an idiom that has lost its figurative meaning—a worn-out metaphor, as a formalist would say. Wat restores its power by developing it into a sort of plot referring to the classical topos of metamorphosis.[76] Usually metamorphosis signals regression: a human being turns into an animal, a plant, or some other natural entity such as a river, a spring, or a stone.[77] The concept was widely used by modernist writers, who, as a rule, loaded it with grim, horrifying overtones.[78]

A close parallel to Wat's poem is "Lamarck" by Osip Mandelstam, written at the outset of the wave of Stalinist terror that soon counted the author among its victims.[79] Its narrator undergoes the reverse of the Darwinian process, de-

scending the evolutionary ladder and joining the world of lower beings. He
gradually loses his sight, his hearing, his warm blood and opts for "the spider's
deafness" and the "corneous mantle" of primordial sea creatures. The poem has
provoked controversy among Mandelstam scholars: whereas many read it as a
premonition of the coming totalitarian night, others have interpreted it as a
transformation of the Romantic myth of the protean poet who returns to the
source and merges harmoniously with nature.[80] Either way, the historio-political
subtext of "Lamarck" is obvious, whether one reads it as a praise of spontaneity
and chaos—that is, rebellion against the dogma of determinism and progressive
evolution in nature and in society—or as a terrifying prophecy of dehumanization about to happen.

"To Be a Mouse" is marked by the same ambiguity as Mandelstam's poem.
The hero's metamorphosis into a mouse may be interpreted as his dissolution
into nature, his opting for a lost paradise in preference to the vile world of
society, or as his ultimate humiliation and disintegration.[81]

The poem consists of three stanzas of approximately equal length, and the
rhythmical design may be described as "organized *vers libre.*" The long lines
resemble regular Polish syllabic verse with their caesuras and feminine endings.
But this pattern is broken by the short final lines of each stanza, each of which,
with growing strength, invokes the motifs of tremor and agony. The rhythmic
uniformity of the stanzas is juxtaposed with a syntactic diversity, the tempo of
speech increasing continuously.

There are virtually no tropes in the first half of the poem, but the unusual
form of the opening sentence is striking. Impersonal, consisting of an infinitive
and a noun in the instrumental case ("być myszą"), it conveys a sense of agitated,
broken speech and the immediacy of a magic incantation, both portraying and
summoning forth the desired metamorphosis.

The rest of the stanza, however scientific in tonality, follows the singular
logic of myth. The rejection of the human universe and alliance with the realm of
nature is expressed in spatial terms: *house* is opposed to *garden* and *field,* and the
middle world of men to the marginal world of animals, be it celestial (birds) or
chthonic (crabs and rats). Then, the sensory code is introduced.[82] If the inhabitants of the marginal world frequently offend the human sense of smell, the
converse must also be true. Here, Wat employs a device that is lost in translation.
The words *ekshaluje* and *abominalną* in the third line are far from standard
Polish.[83] The line strikes the reader—and outraged some of the critics—on
account of its bizarre quality. What kind of language is this: the grossly exaggerated language of a scholarly treatise or the macaronic speech typical of Polish
baroque poetry and prose, in which more than half the words were often in
Latin? Be that as it may, the line introduces an element of grotesque pathos
which dislocates the mood of the poem: Wat parries the temptation to self-pity
with his usual weapon of self-mockery.

The second half of the poem, much more lyrical and figurative than the first,[84] also employs the language of myth, albeit on the level of classical allegory. The touching, if funny, utopia of the mice is subject to annihilation. "The full moon," attribute to a chthonic deity, brings with it the theme of impending death; eyes that reflect "the sleek light of lunar agony" bring to mind the eyes of a dead animal. Destruction seemingly gains the upper hand. "Wicked Boreas" plays a similar role to the shirt of Nessos in the previous poem. The demonic incursion takes place. One is reminded here of the Gnostic imagery of *Pug Iron Stove*—the "hirsute paw of the Demiurge" and the "boreal moon."[85]

The metamorphosis is finally complete: the heart of the poet has turned into a "cowardly mouse heart," which becomes at the end of the poem "a palpitating crystal."[86] The last line may be read in two different ways. On the one hand, it signifies the last step on the ladder of regression, the transformation of a heart into a stone. On the other hand, "crystal" connotes fragility as well as firmness,[87] thereby signaling that the core of the self remains resistant and alive, if "palpitating." As so often in Wat's poetry, we are dealing here with *discordia concors*, the simultaneous development of two opposed themes, which collide at the end of the piece. The collision opens the way to the resolution of the conflict and to catharsis, which gains in power by dint of the residual ambiguity. "To Be a Mouse" is a remarkable example of this technique, considered to be the definitive trait of baroque poetry (and, perhaps, the mark of any true lyric).

In fact, the very image of a mouse was pivotal to Wat's creative imagination. In *Diary without Vowels*, he confessed: "I have always identified myself with a worm, a mouse, since such is my fate and its harmony with my inner personality."[88] In this one sees just one more instance of *le moi haïssable*. Still, the mouse is more than that, and its connotations affect the meaning of the poem.[89] On a mythological level, it is connected with poetry, there being a semantic and etymological link between *mouse* and *Musa*,[90] with a round dance of mice (see line 9) paralleling the round dance of the Muses. The "palpitating crystal" of the mouse's heart may be identified with the poem as a whole, the rhythmic and stanzaic pattern of which is reminiscent of a hard, albeit uneven, heartbeat.

The poem "Przed weimarskim autoportretem Dürera" (Before a Weimar Portrait of Dürer)[91] consists of two dissimilar parts (reflected in its subtitle "In two versions"):

I

Twoje ciało zielenieje z przerażenia
gdy budzisz się w nocy. By grozie stawić czoło
godnie,
nagi stajesz przed lustrem ze świecą w ręku.
5   Każde włókno ciała
z grozy omdlewa
ze strachu truchleje.
Jak strasznie jest spotkać w nocy własny obraz,
gdy to budzi cię w nocy: "Przyjdź" wola "Przyjdź, kotku".

10   A potem bez ceregieli: "Wróć!"
          Jak kapral do rekruta, co łudził się zejść z pola walki.
                         Daremnie.
                Piece już rozpalone. Dymy idą ku niebu.
                         "Wróć"
15   rozkazuje kapral. A ty wiesz, że donikąd.
                         Do nicości.
              Która jest skłębieniem przerażeń
          podnoszącym włosy na głowie praarchaiznej Meduzie.

                            II
     "Skąd?"—"Od śmierci."—"Dokąd?"—"Do śmierci."
20   "A ty?"—"Z życia. Do życia."
     "Kto ty jesteś?"—"Ja jestem Ty.
     Jak w lustrze:
     ty jesteś moim odbiciem.
     Albo odwrotnie."
25   —"Jak ustalić, kto czyim jest odbiciem?"
     —"Nie ustalisz. Lustra nie ma."

     Lustra nie ma. A przecież widzę swoje ciało przerażone
     oblewane wolno spływającymi dreszczami lęku
     w liturgicznej zieleni świecy.
30   Lustra nie ma. Jest tylko oczarowanie.
     Jest tylko echo, które nie wie, czyim jest echem?
     Czy czyimś jest echem?
     Zawsze słyszało tylko głos swój własny,
     zawsze z siebie się tylko odradza, Feniks przedziwny,
35   wieczna zjawisk partenogeneza.
     Dokąd? Do śmierci. Dokąd? Do życia.
     Jest tylko ja, lecz i ono nie wie, czyim jest ja?
     Czy czyimś jest ja?
     A nadzieja? Ona, owszem, odzywa się jak ptaszę w nocy,
40   gdy wszystkie głosy zmilkły, gdy wszystko śpi,
     gdy wszystko umarło i wszystkie nadzieje wygasły.

                            I
     Terror turns your flesh green
     when you wake up at night. In order to meet fear proudly
     you stand naked before the mirror, a candle in your hand,
     every fiber of your body freezes with fear.

     How awful it is to meet your own image at night,
     when it wakes you at night: "Here," it calls, "here, kitty."
     And then with brutal abruptness: "Back!"

Like a sergeant to a new recruit who hoped to escape the battlefield. In
   vain.
Furnaces are already lit, smoke ascends to heaven. "Back,"
the sergeant orders. And you know he calls you nowhere, to nothingness.
Which is a tangle of horrors
lifting the hair on the head of a pre-archaic Medusa.

II

"From where?'—"From death."—"Where to?"—"To death."
"And you?"—"From life. To life."
"Who are you?"—"I am You.
As in a mirror:
you are my reflection.
Or the other way round."
—"How to determine who is a reflection of whom?"
—"You won't tell that. There is no mirror."
There is no mirror. And yet I see my body, terrified,
bathed in slowly steaming tremors of fear,
lit by the liturgical green of a candle.
There is no mirror. There is only this spell.
There is only an echo which does not know whose echo it is,
whether it is even an echo of somebody at all?
It has always heard only its own voice,
it is always reborn out of itself, a wondrous Phoenix,
eternal parthenogenesis of phenomena.
Where to? To death. Where to? To life.
There is only I, but life does not know whose it is either.
Whether of somebody?
And hope? Oh yes, it makes itself heard, like a bird at night,
when all voices are silent, when everything sleeps,
when everything has died and all hopes are extinguished.[92]

The portrait in question is a pen-and-brush drawing in the castle of
Weimar, which Wat probably saw in 1949.[93] One of Dürer's lesser known works,
it is considered to be the self-portrait most true to reality.[94] The portrait would
be striking in any era: the artist is represented in the nude against a dark
background, with his genitalia depicted in detail. Dürer probably used a small
mirror to reflect his body down to the knee: the dimensions of the mirror would
also explain his somewhat forward-leaning posture. His face is wrinkled, drawn
in quick strokes, his eyes wide open, his gaze intense; the folds of his skin, his
pubic hair, his hanging penis and scrotum are depicted with the extreme care
characteristic of Dürer's drawings. The artist was probably in his late thirties at
the time, but his taut face, flabby skin, and the shape of his penis have led some to
suggest that the portrait represents a man of fifty-odd years—by some accounts,
stricken with syphilis.

It was easy for Wat, an ill man engaged in a painful quest for self-cognition, to identify himself with the figure portrayed by Dürer. Two months before writing the poem, he described his condition in a letter to a friend: "I left a movie house with Ola, and suddenly I faced (in a big mirror, although I did not make that out straight away) an old man pulled out from a coffin, with features so tragically smashed, crushed, that they had even become undecipherable, etc., etc. That was I, the true one."[95]

The mirror is the pivotal motif of the poem, as well as its main constructive principle. Wat sees in Dürer (who draws himself using a mirror) a mirror image of himself. It is impossible to say who exactly the speaker and the addressee of the first part of the poem are or who the participants in the dialogue of its second part. Is it Dürer speaking to himself, either in a mirror or in the portrait? Or is it Wat speaking to himself, as reflected either in a movie-house mirror or in Dürer's self-portrait? Or is Wat addressing the long-deceased German artist? Or is it Dürer who is addressing the Polish poet by means of his drawing, across the abyss of four hundred and fifty years? "You won't tell that. There is no mirror." There is only the endless play of reciprocal signification.

The concept of the mirror is embodied even in the design of the poem. The two parts, or "versions," face each other like an image and its reverse, presenting similar content in opposite forms. The first part uses the device known as *carmen figuratum*, a device employed by a number of Renaissance and Baroque poets and one that Wat utilized more than once. It consists in arranging the lines of a poem in such a way that they take the form of the subject being discussed in the text, in this case, the human body with its mirror symmetry (an aspect lost in the English translation). As in Dürer's drawing, the body ends with its knees set wide apart.[96] In the second "version," the image of the body disappears, but there is a series of repetitions that could easily be called "mirror reflections." Repetitions of words in a slightly transformed or inverted shape[97] are juxtaposed with exact reiterations, thereby creating the effect of proliferating images in facing mirrors or of an unending echo. The reflections cancel each other out, resulting in a void filled only with words. This interplay of presence and absence is brought to a climax in the final self-contradictory sentence, in the hope that makes itself heard when all hopes are extinguished.

Wat's imagery, in particular the image of the echo, takes us to the myth of Narcissus and Echo as told in Ovid's *Metamorphoses*. There, Narcissus falls in love with his own reflection in a pool and dies exhausted while observing it, whereas the nymph, Echo, whose desire Narcissus did not respond to, pines away for love until she becomes only a voice. Both stories deal with the same theme of mirror reflection through the use of two different codes, visual and aural. The end is the same: annihilation of everything but a sign (the voice of Echo, the narcissus flower that represents the dead boy). This defines the structure and message of the poem.

The mirror connotes the solipsistic self-contemplating ego, the multiplicity of the soul, as well as the soul transcending itself and passing "to the other side." Hence, the fear of reflection common to many cultures (and obvious in the poem), as too the motifs of the double and the apparition, closely connected with the mirror. The mirror may also symbolize the power of the unconscious to give an individual an unexpected view of his or her self.[98] It is the most obvious image of the paradox of signification (identity versus nonidentity), illusion, and metaphysical emptiness. Finally, it is an image of *art,* the sign phenomenon par excellence.[99]

The lack of poetic figures in the poem corresponds to its meaning, as well as to the deliberate spareness of Dürer's self-portrait. The man faces himself—his suffering and nonbeing—completely alone, with neither mask nor clothes. There is no God to help; he must rely solely on his own power and dignity. The only color in the poem is the "liturgical green" of the candle by whose light the dying body is seen. The only figure is metonymy: fibers of the body stand for the entire person, and hair tangled by horror becomes "a tangle of horrors."

The key image in the first part is that of Medusa, the mythic woman who had serpents for hair and such a terrifying face that those who gazed at it were turned to stone. She was eventually killed by Perseus, who did not look at her directly, but used her reflection in his shield to guide him (once again, the theme of the mirror image). "Pre-archaic Medusa" may refer to the famous metope of Selinunte, in which Perseus decapitates a bizarre monster depicted in a static preclassical style. The more likely reference, however, is to the painting by Caravaggio that Wat may have seen in the Uffizi in the fall of 1949. The circularity of the picture imitates Perseus's shield with Medusa reflected in it. Medusa's tormented face with wide open mouth emitting a cry is painted in typical *chiaroscuro* manner, its intensity heightened by a dark background consisting, in part, of a furious tangle of black serpents. Wat renews the archetype by juxtaposing it with a scene that is striking in its contemporaneity: "Furnaces are already lit, smoke ascends to heaven." The furnaces are perhaps those of Buchenwald, near Weimar. The sergeant (in the original, he is a corporal) who sends the victim to the furnace—or to the battlefield?—is lance-corporal Hitler.[100]

The "I" disintegrates, lost in the abyss of mirrors and in the vicious circle of a dialogue in which the difference between the self and its reflection is annihilated. Yet, the Kierkegaardian leap of faith that restores the "I" is never denied to the human being. Art, from this perspective, is self-contradictory. An endless interplay of signs, it becomes something more than that: in reflecting the anxiety of time, it opens the way to transcendence. "There is no mirror. There is only this spell." Or, perhaps, there is the *ultimate* mirror of the white surface on which Dürer draws his self-portrait, the white page on which Wat writes his poem. Nothingness that turns a person into stone is petrified by its own reflec-

tion; and, as the myth has it, Pegasus, symbol of artistic inspiration, is born from
Medusa's decapitated body.

The long poem "Poranek nad wodą" (A Morning over the Water), singled
out by several critics as one of the most important in Wat's book of 1957, takes
the form of a surrealist vision:[101]

Tu plaża jest urągliwa. A z wody bestie wychodzą.
Tak było już we śnie Daniela. Ciemno. Czarno było. Nieprzenikliwie.
Tylko że z dawień już dawna stała umowa że
widzialność jest tutaj dobra.
Nikt przeto nie ma prawa powiedzieć: 5
ja tu nic nie widziałem . . .

Pierwsza bestia był koń. Ci-devant perszeron. Teraz całkiem skapcaniał.
Przykucnął, przednie skrżyzował kończyny, wyciągnął z pyska protezy,
wypiął język, który był długi i wąski, bardzo długi i cienki.
Ten koń sapał. Przyjaciele, jak ten koń sapał! . . .   10

Drugą bestią był pasikonik. Owszem, wyolbrzymiony, ale pasikonik,
sprawiał wrażenie więc czegoś zwinnego i bardzo małego mimo niezwykłych
    rozmiarów.
Siadł u nóg konia, przeciągnął się, ziewnął—a tak boleśnie,
ze zachodziła obawa, iż szczęki już mu się już mu się już się mu nigdy nie
    zewrą . . .
Znudził mnie temat pasikonika: o nim dość, dosyć! . . .   15

Trzecią bestią, która z wody wyszła, był ptak—ptaszysko z pogruchotanym
    skrzydłem.
Kuśtykał i biegał po plaży tam i nazad,
"Zabijaj, kradnij, cudzołóż" syczał "kradnij, cudzołóż, zabijaj."
Ale nie jest, nie było i nie będzie nigdy wiadomo, czy adresował to do nas—
biednej garstki ludzi, którzy ukryci w szuwarach   20
obserwowali—nic więcej, obserwowali—i tylko, niestety tylko, i nic i nigdy
    już więcej!
(wolno nas zatem uważać li tylko za obserwatorów).

Na koniec gdy ptak zmęczony zasnął na jednym szponie,
wyszła bestia piąta—larwa: cień człowieka,
co umarł lat temu dosyć.   25
Znałem go—nie cień oczywiście, człowieka:
dziewczyna o skośnych oczach, piersi wysokiej, z czołem ładnie sklepionym,
miała braciszka, na imię mu bylo Pietrek, strzelał z procy, lubił irysy,
puszczał latawce, motylom obrywał skrzydła, jego masturbowała, gdy księżyc
    zachodził w pełnię.

Mówiono o niej we wsi: panienka zadaje się oho-ho-ho-ho-ho z kozłami,   30
wiosną o zaranku spotykano ją ponoć jak wracała z hali
kulejącą, posiniaczoną, w zaszarganej koszuli.
Pachniała terpentyną. Plastrem miodu nakrywała nagą chleba pajdę,
częstowała parobków. Żaden nie brał. Z wyjątkiem jednego.
Nazajutrz poszedł na wojnę. Nie wrócił z wojny ten Jasio.   35

Potem spoza wody wysunął się księżyc równie zielony i duży
i wszystko: plaża i koń, pasikonik i ptak, i larwa dziewczyny
pogrążyło się w jego świetle jak w czerni poczekalni Sądu Ostatecznego. Jak
    kamień w wodzie.
W istocie wszystko wróciło do wody! Wróćmyż i my
do wody, przyjaciele, do wody, do wody. Z niej bowiem wszystko wyszło.   40
Wianek na niej odpływa. Czas go unosi. Czas go uniesie. Czas unosi
    wszystkie wianki ofelii.
I każdą chmurę z nieba. I wszystkie uśmiechy z ust. I wszystkie łzy poezji.
Pani poezji, matki naszej, która płacze syna swego umęczonego
na początku i teraz i zawsze i na wieki wieków amen.

Czas unosi wszystko,   45
jedynie dreszczyk nieśmiały marszczy powierzchnię przestrzeni,
dreszczyk—zwiastun poranka, zwykłego poranka nad wodą.

Here the beach is outrageous. And the beasts come up from the water.
Thus it was already in Daniel's dream. It was dark. It was black. Non-
    transparent.
Still, ages ago it was agreed that
visibility here was perfect.
Therefore, nobody has the right to say:
I saw nothing here . . .

The first beast was a horse. One-time percheron. Now, it had no kick left in
    it.
It squatted, crossed the forelegs, pulled its dentures out of its mouth,
stuck out its tongue, which was long and narrow, very long and thin.
The horse wheezed. My friends, how that horse wheezed! . . .

The second beast was a grasshopper. Well, monstrously overgrown, but still
    a grasshopper,
it looked therefore like something agile and very small notwithstanding its
    uncommon size.
It sat at the horse's feet, stretched itself, yawned—so morbidly
that one feared its jaws would never more would never more would never
    more clench. . .
I am bored by the topic of the grasshopper: enough of it, enough! . . .

The third beast that came up from the water was a bird—a large bird with
  a broken wing.
It hobbled and ran about on the beach, here and there,
"Thou shalt kill, thou shalt steal, thou shalt commit adultery," it hissed,
  "thou shalt steal, thou shalt commit adultery, thou shalt kill."
Still, it was not, it is not and it will be never known, whether it addressed
  us—
a poor handful of people, who hid in the rushes
and observed it—observed, nothing else—that's it, alas, that's it, and
  nothing else, and never more!
(therefore, one might consider us simply observers).

At last, when the tired bird fell asleep on one claw,
there came up the fifth beast—a ghost: a shadow of a person
who died quite a few years ago.
I knew her—not the shadow, of course, but the person:
a girl with squinted eyes, high breasts and beautifully vaulted forehead,
she had a little brother, his name was Peter, he hurled stones from a
  slingshot, liked toffees,
flew kites, tore off butterflies' wings, she would masturbate him during the
  full moon.
The villagers gossiped about her: the lady mingles, oh-oh-oh-oh-oh, with
  the goats,
in the springtime at dawn they supposedly met her returning from the
  alpine meadow,
limping, bruised, in a tarnished petticoat.
She reeked of turpentine. She used to put a honeycomb on a bare chunk of
  bread
and treat farmhands to it. Nobody took it. Except one boy.
Next day, he went off to war. Johnny never came back from the war.

Then the moon, also green and large, came up from behind the water,
and everything: the beach and the horse, the grasshopper and the bird, and
  the ghost of the girl
sank into its light, as into the blackness of the waiting room of the Last
  Judgment. Like a stone into water.
Actually, everything returned into water! Let us return as well
into water, friends, into water, into water. Since everything came up
  from it.
A wreath floats away on it. Time carries it away. Time will carry it away.
  Time carries away all the ophelias' wreaths.
And every cloud in the sky. And every smile on all lips. And all the tears of
  poetry.
Of Lady Poetry, our mother, who weeps over her tortured son
in the beginning, and now, and always, and for the ages of ages, amen.

Time carries everything away.
Only a timid quiver wrinkles the surface of the space,
a quiver—herald of the morning, the usual morning over the water.

As the second line indicates, the poem is a semi-parodic rendering of the vision of Daniel. In the Book of Daniel, four beasts appear: the first is "like a lion," the second "like to a bear," the third "like a leopard." The fourth beast considerably exceeds the previous three in size and significance: "After this I saw in the night visions, and behold a fourth beast, dreadful and terrible, and strong exceedingly; and it had great iron teeth: it devoured and brake in pieces, and stamped the residue with the feet of it: and it was diverse from all the beasts that were before it; and it had ten horns" (Dan. 7:7). According to tradition, the beasts symbolize the four kingdoms that in turn enslaved Israel. The beast that St. John saw (Rev. 13:1–10) seems to be a composite of the four.[102] The beasts come out of the sea. John's vision opens with the words "And I stood upon the sand of the sea," which corresponds to the "beach" and "water" of the poem.

It would be an exercise in futility to search for such an allegorical interpretation of Wat's beasts. What counts here is the *degeneration* of myth and symbol.[103] As is often the case in twentieth-century literature, entropy replaces eschatology.[104] The monsters in "A Morning over Water" are deprived of all dignity and grandeur. Rather than look for their correspondences in history, one should see them as ironic symbols of the self.[105] The tired, toothless horse may stand for the body, commonly compared to a beast of burden in the Christian tradition. The grasshopper, agile but overgrown, with wide open, omnivorous jaws, yet overpowered by ennui, may symbolize the mind. But this interpretation should not be taken too literally. Insects in mythology and human imagination are often connected with demonic forces.[106] Wat's monstrous grasshopper is one of a kind with the chthonic creatures of Hieronymus Bosch, the spiders of Dostoevsky, the transformed Gregor Samsa of Kafka's *Metamorphosis*, and, last but not least, the terrifying grasshoppers in the paintings of Max Ernst and Salvador Dali.[107]

The lame bird is no less demonic: its frenzied sermon is the sermon of the Antichrist. In it can be discerned a symbol of the guilt of a self that has succumbed to the totalitarian temptation. This theme, which was of immense personal significance for Wat, is developed throughout the first half of the poem. Everyone has participated in the crime, if only by observing it.[108]

Perhaps the most remarkable aspect of the poem is the absence of a fourth beast. After the horse, the grasshopper, and the bird, the "fifth beast" appears, but this obviously belongs to a different order. It is improbable that Wat would have overlooked such a glaring omission in the course of diligent editing. Most likely this absence is charged with semantic value.[109] The beast omitted by Wat may be something (or, rather, no-thing) that inspires the deepest horror: the finiteness of the self, the source of Kierkegaardian despair. The rupture in the development of the theme would then reflect the metaphysical rupture, thereby pointing to a threat that is beyond our means of signification while simultaneously evoking a creative response.[110]

This response may be incarnated in the ghost of the peasant girl. An odd vision, which does not correspond to anything in the Book of Daniel, it is profoundly disquieting. What we have here is a folkloric archetype traditional in Polish poetry, that of the witch, the attractive, tempting, but malevolent fairy. The girl mediates between the human world and the world of animals and demons, representing both the power of sex and the allure of sexual transgression. The moon image links her with Astarte or Hecate; she is also related to the lower goddesses of the Slavic pantheon, *vilas* and *rusalkas*. She might be called Wat's muse. Like him, she is the perennial outsider, a nonparticipant in the stable world. Vulgar yet noble, vital yet deadly, she connotes, perhaps, poetry itself.

All the visions eventually disappear into the water, the significance of which in Wat's imagination has been discussed by more than one critic.[111] This is the water of Thales (the single underlying substance of the universe) and of Heraclitus (symbol of the change that in turn is the basic principle of reality). In this poem, water signifies, first and foremost, the flow of time. Nevertheless, poetry is beyond time. Associated first with a dubious witch figure, Lady Poetry becomes the Immaculate Virgin who eternally mourns her crucified poet-son. Thus, the Book of Daniel opens up to the Gospel.[112]

Technically, the poem is at the opposite extreme to such minimalist works as "A Bit of Mythology." A long, proliferating, narrative text, it is written in semi-prosaic paragraphs that bear a faint resemblance to biblical verse. Freely mixing humor and parody with magic imagery, it is not unlike Wat's early texts. Wat plays incessantly with his addressee, employing such devices as a dialogue with an imaginary audience and comic, "iconic" repetitions that stretch the patience of the reader to the limit. This contributes to the overall artistic effect of the poem, created by the interplay of tonalities surrounding the central break. Each element is countered by its opposite, each tension by an opposite tension: the horse is opposed to the grasshopper, the beasts to the girl, and poetry as witchcraft to poetry as Calvary.

Another dream poem, "Podróż" (A Journey), shorter and less intricate, is based on Wat's Soviet experience.[113] In the posthumous *Lumen Obscurum*, it was provided with the subtitle "A prisoner's dream" and an authorial commentary: "A journey through Kiev, in the late fall of 1940, in a tin enclosure of a Black Maria (I could see Kiev through a crack), from prison to prison, until the sixth one agreed to take me."[114]

Zamknięty głucho, zaszpuntowany w ogromnej pustej beczce
staczam się w dół ulicami wąskimi
prowincjonalnej dziury N***
Wszystkie są strome. I ani żywego ducha.
Są tam co prawda muchy. Aż czarno od much w powietrzu.   5
I to nazywają tam nocą! To śmią nazywać nocą!
Skoro noc została skasowana administracyjnym zarządzeniem raz na zawsze.
Nie będzie zatem nocy w N***!
I nigdy już nikt nie zaśpiewa: "Jak cicha jest noc w N***"
Domy w tym mieście ledwie mrugają kagankami przez wąskie szczeliny   10
    strzelnicze:
bo czujność tam obowiązuje, w tym podłych mieście N***!
A w takim razie gdzie, na Boga żywego, straż nocna?!
Straży nie widać w tym martwych mieście!
Zresztą, skądby straż nocna, skoro już nie ma nocy?
Także chodników nie ma. Jezdnią kocie łby.   15
Łatwoż więc sobie wystawić, z jakim hurgotem
dudnieniem
rumorem
beczka to w dół się toczy, to się gramoli pod górę.
Pod górę—jużci!—pod górę!   20
Owo "pod górę" zmysłów jest tylko złudzeniem
: w istocie ulice w N*** zawsze spadają w dół.
Wciąż tylko w dół. W dół i basta!
A temu w dół końca końca końca końca nie widać.

Biją dzwony najpierw klasztorne. Na jutrznię. Potem zegarne—godziny.   25
Noc się skończyla, noc—ci-devant, oczywiście.

A oto i czarny kruk mój stanął u bramy więziennej.

Tightly locked, bunged in a tremendous empty barrel,
I tumble along the narrow streets
of the provincial hole N***.
All of them are steep. And not a living soul.
True, there are flies. The air just black with flies.
And here, they call it night! They dare to call it night!
You see, the night is cancelled once and for all by administrative decree.
Thus, there will be no night in N***!
And nobody will ever sing: "How quiet is the night in N***."
The houses in this city faintly twinkle with oil lamps through the narrow
    loopholes:
since vigilance is mandatory there, in this city of the mean, N***!
But in such a case, where is, by Jove, the night watch?!

One sees no watch in this city of the dead!
By the way, whence the night watch, since there is already no night?
There are also no sidewalks. A cobblestoned pavement.
Therefore, it is easy to imagine, with what din
rumble
racket
the barrel rolls downward here, climbs upward there.
Upward—sure thing!—upward!
This "upward" is just a delusion of the senses
: actually, the streets of N*** always go downward.
Invariable, downward. Downward, that's it!
And one sees no end no end no end no end of that downward.

First, the bells of the convents ring. For matins. Then the bells of the
    clocks strike the time.
The night is over—the one-time night, of course.

And here my Black Maria pulled up at a prison gate.

The most obvious source text here is the *Divine Comedy*. The city of Kiev becomes the "city of the mean" and "city of the dead," a Dantesque *città dolente*.

The bulk of the poem consists of the questions and exclamations of a bewildered man as he observes his grotesque environment. It is not easy to distinguish reality from hallucination. This is highlighted by the punctuation: a colon shifts from its rightful place at the end of the line 21 to the beginning of line 22, both lines, significantly, dealing with the "delusion of the senses".

The city is evidently medieval, an impression created by the narrow cobblestoned streets and fortress-like houses lit by oil lamps and further reinforced by "the bells of the convents"—a sound scarcely possible in Soviet Kiev, the result, perhaps, of an auditory illusion. At the same time, it is a twentieth-century city with the code name N***, as in modern military dispatches, thus bringing to mind the anonymous cities of Giorgio de Chirico and Kafka. A Kafkaesque touch is furnished by the statement that the night here is "cancelled once and for all by administrative decree." Wat alludes to the Soviet cliché concerning "the night of capitalism," supposedly abolished forever by the victorious proletariat. On the other hand, the bureaucracy appears to wield absolute power in the city—so absolute that it is able to tamper with time itself.[115] Or maybe this is just a case of linguistic manipulation: night still exists but has been renamed—an act given an ironic tinge by using the nonnative (French) expression *ci-devant* in line 26.[116]

All this is in full accord with the image of the città dolente. Hell, in Dante's poem, was more often than not Florentine; by the same token, Kafka's Hell was, first and foremost, the Hell of a totalitarian bureaucracy. There are further indications of the city's infernal character. Flies in mythology are commonly related to the chthonic and diabolical world.[117] The words "ani żywego ducha" (not a living soul, line 4), echoed by another idiomatic expression, "na Boga żywego" (by Jove—literally, "by the name of the living God," line 12), intensify the ominous tonality: this is the city of dead souls and a dead God, of the damned and the Devil. But the most distinctive feature of the city is its distortion of space and time. Time loses direction and turns into a frozen eternity of repetitions, whereas space becomes unidirectional: in Wat's inferno, one can move only *downwards*, a reference to Dante's moral topography,[118] which presents hell as a crater where the worst offenders occupy the lowest positions. The faded metaphor of "the provincial hole" assumes a specific connotation, relating to the Dantean image of the crater in general, as well as to the *Malebolge* (the evil holes) of Canto XVIII. The tumbling of the narrator repeats and parodies the descent of Dante and Virgil toward the icy depths where Lucifer dwells. Moreover, the space is closed. The narrator finds himself in a barrel, which suggests both the isolation of a prison cell and a medieval—and hellish—mode of punishment.

All this is, perhaps, only a dream, as suggested by the poem's subtitle. The dislocations of the world found here may be the result of dream logic. Things merge and exchange traits; the police car turns into a barrel then a raven (the Russian slang term for "Black Maria" is "black raven"—an image that appears in the last line and may be read metaphorically as well as literally). The narrator is observed closely, yet there is nobody around; the night is present, yet absent; time is stagnant, yet flows; logical trains of thought lead to preposterous conclusions.

In oneiric literary texts, ringing bells traditionally mark awakening. In the *Divine Comedy*, the lowest point of the Inferno marks an exit from the crater, by which Virgil and Dante leave the subterranean world to see the stars. All the signs suggest that the hellish journey described in the poem may be the dream of a *former* prisoner, who wakes up in his own bed. In the last line, Wat rejects the cliché: the narrator merely exchanges one place of imprisonment for another. To quote another poem of 1956, "Z perskich przypowieści" (From Persian Parables):

> Nothing is ever over
> —the helmsman's voice was hollow—
> and there is no bottom to evil.[119]

There is nothing but dreams within dreams—that is, a succession of prisons, each worse than the previous one.

The short poem "Wielkanoc" (Easter),[120] one of most powerful in the book, deals with the Holocaust:

W dwukonnej karecie	In a two-horse carriage
starozakonny staruszek	an Old Testament little old man
w cylindrze na głowie	with a top hat on his head
jedzie z synagogi	rides from a synagogue

kiwa się, mówi do siebie: rocks and says to himself: 5
królem jestem, królem jestem, jestem   I'm the king, I'm the king, the king
   królem.   am I.

Mężczyzni stoją szpalerem   Men stand lined up
Kobiety wyglądają z okien   Women look from the windows
Dzieci wieszają girlandy   Children hang garlands
Żandarmi klękają na bruku.   Gendarmes kneel on the pavement.   10

Wtem Jahwe wyciągnął rękę   Then Yahweh extended His hand
zdarł jemu z głowy cylinder   tore the top hat of his head
nasadził ciernistą koronę.   put a crown of thorns on it.
Zaczem karetą dwukonną   Then in the two-horse carriage
staruszek starozakonny   the Old Testament little old man   15
wjechał prosto do nieba.   rode straight to heaven.

Dymy stoją nad miastem   Smoke rises over the city
Dzieci wieszanych girlandy   Garlands of hanged children
Kobiety leżą na bruku   Women lie on the pavement
Żandarmi stoją szpalerem.   Gendarmes stand lined up.   20

"Easter" consists of short, simple lines of free verse which form syntactic and semantic units like traditional stanzas. In this, it is a throwback to medieval Polish presyllabic versification.[121] Yet the verse is highly organized. The line boundaries always coincide with the syntactical and intonational boundaries, a precept that such postwar Polish poets as Herbert and Tadeusz Różewicz frequently violated. Most of the lines consist of eight syllables and many are rhythmically identical.[122]

The story has the structure of a Hasidic parable: it is simple yet bewildering, narrated in the straightforward manner of a *shtetl* simpleton yet striking in its intensity and depth. It also has personal overtones. The short monologue of the little old man repeats the words spoken in "Loth's Flight" by Commercial Councillor Samuel Loth as he prepares for his imminent death. For Wat, the image of a king was related to his father. Both Samuel Loth and the hero of "Easter" are incarnations of the pious Kabbalist Mendel Michał Chwat and, by extension, a significant aspect of Wat's psyche. The wordplay in line 2 should also be noted. *Starozakonny*, translated "an Old Testament man," is, in Polish tradition, a polite term for Jew. Highlighted by the repetition of the root (*star*-ozakonny *star*uszek) and by an inner rhyme (*dwukonnej—starozakonny*), it gains in weight. The old man stands for the entire Jewish people—and also for God.

The poem consists of two equal, symmetrical parts. The first is not lacking in humorous and grotesque overtones. It depicts, in sprightly verse, a congenial semi-Victorian scene—the apotheosis of a little old man. His proud statement of kingship evokes, in his somnolent imagination, the worship of all the inhabitants

of the town; characteristically, the gendarmes, representing an alien, not necessarily friendly power, indulge in the most conspicuous obeisance. The scene has
the quality of a Bakhtinian "mock apotheosis."[123]

The second part transforms the mock crowning of the first part into a
veritable crowning on Golgotha. All the signs change valence. This negative
symmetry works on all levels of the text: the present tense changes to the past,
the word order is inverted, and so on. The true king, Yahweh, appears in place of
the mock king, who is nevertheless transformed by this event.

The fourth stanza is a complete reversal of the second. The syntactic
structure is, on the whole, preserved, and many of the same words are used; but
the meanings have all changed emphatically. The old man's fantasy is replaced
by the reality of the Holocaust. The shuffling of sentences and words creates the
effect of an absurd kaleidoscope, culminating in the unspeakable image of
hanged children.

The treatment of God in this poem has commonalities with the Kazakhstan
poem "For So Long I Protected Myself from Thee."[124] Yahweh appears as an
executioner who condemns the little old man—and many, many others—to
death. At the same time, the old man is identified with Elijah, who entered
heaven in a fiery chariot (2 Kings 2:1–12), and Jesus, whom Wat considered to be
an archetypal symbol of Jewish fate. The message of the poem is thus a tragic
paradox that transcends human understanding. God's ways are inscrutable, and
the only possible response to the apparent absurdity of the universe lies in our
memory and words, however imperfect they may be. The lapidary lines of
"Easter," so different from the colloquial profuseness of Wat's longer poems,
have the quality of an inscription on a monument: they give a formula for an
experience beyond articulation.

11

Emigration, 1957–1967

The two years, from July 1957 to July 1959, that the Wat family spent in their old apartment on Niemcewicz Street were but a break between two sojourns in the West. Their second long journey to Italy and France, which began in 1959, developed into permanent exile. Wat's transition to the status of political émigré was thus a gradual one. For all practical purposes, the period immediately preceding Wat's departure should be considered part of his émigré years, although at the time he was an "internal émigré," a condition characteristic mainly, if not exclusively, of Communist countries.

After 1956, the political situation in Poland deteriorated steadily, with the reformists losing ground every month. Whereas the change in public spirit that had taken place proved to be permanent, the cultural atmosphere became stifling once again. For more than one writer, going west seemed the only option. The first writer to rebel openly against the new cultural reality was Marek Hłasko, one of the leaders of *Point-Blank* and an idol of youth similar in his views and comportment to the American "beat generation." In 1958, he published two of his highly critical stories in the West and, as a consequence, had to stay abroad, joining for a time the circle of *Culture* in Paris.

Although Wat was still engaged in literary projects in his native country, he was now forced to contemplate permanent emigration more seriously than at any time before. This option was still difficult for him. "Contrary to all appearances, it turns out that I am not a cosmopolitan," Wat confessed to Iwaszkiewicz.[1] Moreover, there were financial problems and the problem of securing an exit visa for Andrzej. Only in 1959 did these appear to be solved. By then, Wat was receiving an adequate income from Polish and Western sources, and Andrzej was able to leave for Brussels and Paris.

Wat's return to literature was consolidated by a new, albeit truncated edition of *Lucifer Unemployed*, published in 1960.[2] He also had several more ambitious projects in mind. In 1958–59, Wat proposed to "The Reader" no less than four books: "Kartki z notatnika" (Leaves from a Diary), "Pieśni" (Songs), "Król

Lear z Defy" (King Lear of the Security Service), and "W poranek warszawski" (On a Warsaw Morning). The contracts were duly signed,[3] but Wat came through on these projects only in part. "Leaves from a Diary" developed into *Scraps of Paper in the Wind*. "Songs" turned into *Wiersze śródziemnomorskie* (Mediterranean Poems), the last book that Wat published in Poland before breaking with the regime. "On a Warsaw Morning" seems never to have proceeded beyond the stage of vague intention. The fourth, "King Lear of the Security Service," was to be a collection of short stories, according to a note dated 26 May 1959: "Time, place, subjects; quite variegated (the interwar period, the war, XVIII century, ancient times; Warsaw, Zamość, Jurata, Paris, Weimar, Rome, the environs of Naples, Syracuse; the literary milieu, physicians, the papacy, prisons, hospitals, a Warsaw courtyard, Goethe's house, the Hitlerites, their victims, the ghetto, an episode of the Peloponnesian war; several stories from the collapse of the unfinished novel *Loth's Flight* and from the play *The Women of Monte Olivetto*)."[4]

The project went beyond the merely preliminary stage. In the Wat archive (file 19) is a notebook that gives the titles of thirty-seven stories. The last section of the book was to consist of a single text entitled "Po śmierci" (After Death), described by Wat as "an unfinished long short story which cannot be finished." In the notebook mentioned above and in another one are either partial or complete drafts of many stories, the four most polished and legible of which were published by Krzysztof Rutkowski in 1988. The most interesting story, "After Death," remains in manuscript form, however.

All the stories appear to have been drafted in 1953–54, in the wake of Wat's first bout of illness. They are the same kind of intellectual fiction as most of Wat's early prose works and hark back to Voltaire, Jonathan Swift, and Anatole France. Parables devoid of psychological analysis, they mostly explore the paradoxical consequences of a given situation or set of ideas, reveling in irony and malicious dialectic. A story with the title "Ulysses of the Whorehouses" would seem to belong in *Lucifer Unemployed*. But there is a difference: in general, the new stories are more concise then the prewar ones, approaching fables or poems in prose in their texture.

The story "A Sultan's Doubts," a one-page Oriental tale, is based on a logical paradox. Sultan Saladin declares that he will convert to the faith of any man who will accept martyrdom as a condition of the Sultan's conversion. A monk succeeds in winning him over to Catholicism. When the monk, who had counted on Saladin's clemency, becomes aware of his miscalculation, he attempts to make the Sultan change his mind, but he is executed nonetheless as a crook. His death convinces the doubting ruler of the truth of Christianity— since, in Saladin's words, a God who punishes unworthy servants must be great indeed. An even shorter story, "Something on the Power of Poetry," is about a Jewish prisoner who manages to survive by reciting Goethe's "Erlkönig" to a

Nazi overseer; the latter is ashamed of his lack of education and esteems people who know Goethe by heart. Unfortunately, he is replaced by a new overseer who has a doctorate in classical philology; since he cannot be intimidated in this way, the prisoner is sent to the gas chamber. The semi-autobiographical "Death in a Hospital" is based on a motif reminiscent of that developed by Jorge Luis Borges in his story "El milagro segreto" (1943). A dying poet, who has not practiced his craft for many years, creates a work of genius in his agony but is unable to write it down—or perhaps the brilliance of the work is just an illusion.

All these plots are manifestly Borgesian. Employing unusual twists and turns of action in order to reach an ambiguous and disturbing resolution, the stories address Wat's principal concerns—religion, totalitarianism, poetry, and death—with a nihilistic mockery worthy of *Lucifer Unemployed* and *Pug Iron Stove*. Yet, they bring to a logical end Wat's striving for brevity and compression (which he also shares with Borges). At about this time Wat wrote: "Perhaps in our Western prose the same process of condensation will begin its work such as occurred in Chinese poetry a thousand years ago. A combination of a couple or several words will become the symbolic equivalent of many combined situations in multistage and multilayered systems of meaning, of allusions, insinuations, suggestions."[5]

Such compactness is absent only in "After Death." This story belongs to a genre that was popular in antiquity (with Lucian and others) and was later developed by writers such as Rabelais and Mark Twain: namely, a satirical description of the otherworld. The hero, Aleksander, dies in a hospital and finds himself in a pleasant park reminiscent of a sanatorium. He is overjoyed, since death has saved him from unbearable pain. But gradually certain disquieting aspects of his new environment become apparent. In a small pavilion, Aleksander is questioned by an officer, who orders him to fill out several forms and explains that the surrounding country is inhabited by the people who died between 1873 and 1953. After eighty years in limbo, the deceased disappear; in all probability, they are transferred to the next level of the otherworld, although nobody knows for certain what happens to them. Bodily functions, such as eating and sleeping, are redundant in the otherworld and therefore cease. Aleksander, an old philanderer, inquires anxiously about the possibility of female company but soon notices that libido is irrelevant after death. Moreover, after the interview with the officer, Aleksander becomes invisible (as do all dwellers in limbo). He can communicate vocally with his companions in distress but all their voices are changed, so that the deceased will not be able recognize their acquaintances, friends, and relatives. For this reason, mention of one's name or the circumstances of one's earthly life is formally banned.

Wat's concept of the otherworld has traits in common with ancient mythology, which, starting with Homer, presented Hades as a region of tedium in which shadows wander aimlessly, pining for full-blooded existence, and with

twentieth-century dystopias, which depict a universe ruled by an ominous bureaucracy, more often than not of quasi-scientific bent. Still, Wat's version
alludes not so much to literary precedents as to his own misfortunes in the
USSR and in postwar Poland. It is precisely the interplay of traditional imagery,
modernist subtexts, and personal experience that makes "After Death" artistically unique.

Only gradually does Aleksander become aware that he is in Hell. The
process of discovery is punctuated by ironic details: for instance, the only game
played by the deceased is "diabolo," a seemingly innocent pastime that consists
in spinning an hourglass-shaped top on a string between two sticks. He finds the
environment to be unbearably monotonous:

> All the avenues, all the streets, all the pavilions, all the trees here are as similar
> as twins, if not identical (perhaps not, since one knows that there are no two
> identical objects), they have no names or numbers . . . therefore nobody here
> can gain an understanding of space, moreover, it is impossible to know the
> particulars of time, since . . . there is no sun, no moon, no time of day, no
> seasons. . . . When Aleksander asked . . . how one could measure the time
> spent in the city, a passerby answered, that the numbers and terms were
> broadcast by special loudspeakers, albeit irregularly and unpredictably. . . .
> Some, added the passerby disdainfully, claim that they have an intuition of the
> passage of time, thanks to the function of their kidneys, yet *primo*, kidneys here
> do not function at all, since there is no need, *secundo*, this is simply boasting.[6]

The emptiness of such an existence frequently drives the inhabitants of
Hell to suicide—which is pointless, because they are already dead. The invisible
dead hang themselves on numerous trees and are periodically removed by a
machine, to which they give cordial thanks.

This bizarre time-space continuum inevitably brings to mind the well-
ordered, albeit impenetrable, maze of Lubyanka's cells and corridors, where
psychological coercion was aggravated by a loss of any sense of time and a
complete lack of knowledge as to one's future. Yet, simultaneously, it represents
a Communist utopia, which, according to Wat, is identical to an ideal prison: a
world of absolute equality and stasis, where the atomization of society has been
brought to perfection. The relationship of that system to all preceding social
systems is expressed in the laconic image of "mud huts and the Tower of Baal,"[7]
in which Babel, symbol of confusion, is replaced by Baal, the false god.

Wat develops his metaphor of the totalitarian universe in great detail.
Religion in Hell is, predictably, banned. At the same time the otherworld imitates and parodies various precepts of the Gospel: "There is neither Greek nor
Jew, neither priests nor pastors, neither rabbis nor lamas—all of us are equal
here, in the face of the Universal Computer."[8] There is also no police. "What do
we need police for? We represent perhaps the highest stage of societal development. The society which is no longer a society but a set of individuals devoid of

any common links, since they are devoid of any needs."[9] This is a virtual embodiment—and ironic inversion—of Stalinist formulas describing the radiant future when the state would wither away and everybody would be satisfied "according to his needs." Wat's God substitutes—the "Universal Computer" and the "Great Card Index"—bring his fantasy close to contemporary science fiction such as Aldous Huxley's *Brave New World*—or the Polish novels of Stanisław Lem, written later than "After Death," however. At the same time, the ominous universe depicted in the story remains metaphysically perplexing, as Wat's Kabbalistic and Gnostic interests once again come to the fore: "You see, transcendental Being is founded on the principle that there is no final 'there,' and after each 'there' follows a higher 'there,' which in turn determines our fate. How may one think about anything else, especially since nobody knows for sure what is considered by a certain 'there' to be virtue and what guilt. . . . It is quite possible that one transcendental instance evaluates something as merit, while the next one, a higher one, counts it as a crime—who knows?"?[10]

The philosophical parable nevertheless yields to satire. The otherworldly courts that evaluate one and the same deed in opposite ways may easily be interpreted as a parody of Stalinist justice, with its grotesquely unpredictable oscillations according to the vagaries of the political winds.

Not only is the story unfinished: as already mentioned, Wat described it as a text "which cannot be finished." At its close is a summary of events to follow—including Aleksander's stint in a punishment cell, where his nose is gnawed off, supposedly by rats[11]—and various passages to be inserted earlier in the text. In one of the latter, Aleksander meets a professor, who engages in dialogue with him:

> —Can't you understand that the Great Card Index, which is never examined by anybody and will never be used by anybody, as well as everything else here is just a perfected and ideal method of exerting power over the people? That it is an ideal structure resulting from the maximal and ideal development of the concept of power over the people?
> —But what for? Who needs that power?
> —That I don't know,—answered the Hegelian professor (as he had introduced himself) and said nothing more. Still, he did not disappear, since he sniffed from time to time.[12]

The words of the Hegelian echo the divagations of O'Brien, the agent provocateur turned investigator in Orwell's *Nineteen Eighty-Four*, whose cynical lecture about the party exercising power for power's sake culminated in the dictum: "If you want a picture of the future, imagine a boot stamping on a human face—forever."[13]

Whereas "After Death" may be defined as Wat's first attempt to come to grips with Stalinism, his play "The Women of Monte Olivetto," mentioned in the summary of "King Lear of the Security Service," represents a temporary surrender to Stalinist literary dogma. The typescript of the play survives in the Wat archive. On its title page are the words: "Written in a moment of fatigue after hospital, of capitulation—a lie, yet luckily never brought into being."[14] He did not discuss "The Women of Monte Olivetto" in his memoirs and apparently wished to consign it to oblivion. The play is nevertheless not devoid of interest, if only as a testimony to the climate of the era.

While writing "After Death," a merciless satire of Stalinism that most likely could not be published in newly post-Stalin Poland, Wat apparently toyed with the idea of emerging from "internal emigration" with an ideologically acceptable work. But in contrast to more than one writer, he resisted the temptation, aided perhaps by the obvious artistic weakness of "The Women of Monte Olivetto."

The action of this full-length play takes place in an imaginary Italian township close to Naples in the fall of 1949 (the time of Wat's first visit to the Neapolitan coast) and spring of 1950. The name of the town alludes to the Mount of Olives, and the pattern of the biblical myth is discernible in the play, though hardly manifest. "The Women of Monte Olivetto" follows the precepts of bourgeois melodrama, albeit with a socialist realist tinge.

The heroine, Rachele Damia, is a self-made businesswoman. Having lost her husband and children in the war, she founds the League of Lonely Women for those who share the same fate and employs them in a sweatshop. Her enterprise thrives, due to scanty wages and a rigid discipline. Posing as benevolent matriarch, she sets her sights on transforming the League into a global organization. Arguably the most interesting character in the play, Rachele seems to be patterned on Gorky's heroines—for example, the strong-willed shipowner Vassa Zheleznova. (Wat and Ola published their translation of Gorky's drama of that title in 1951.)

The play opens with the arrival of Vittorio Bardini, a returning emigrant from the United States, who reveals his identity as Rachele's only living son. Vittorio's tangled fate has transformed him into an antiwar activist and a Communist sympathizer. The happy reunion of Rachele and Vittorio predictably turns sour. Formerly docile, Rachele's employees begin to stir, incited by Vittorio, who, on top of everything, enters into a liaison with one of them, a Polish girl called Wanda. After a heated argument, Rachele turns Vittorio out of the house. In the third act, which takes place seven months later, Vittorio organizes a protest of dockers against a shipment of American arms, and the women of Monte Olivetto actively support him. Although Vittorio lands in prison, his cause triumphs: thus, the Christian archetype is repeated, albeit in specifically socialist realist form. Rachele, who has become a staunch supporter of American imperialism, is devastated by these events and is finally struck by paralysis. Her life is summarized in a melodramatic monologue by her secretary Paola:

—You wanted to be the heroine of a tragedy. To place your destiny above all other destinies. And Fate played a cruel game with you. . . . At first, it elevated you beyond measure. And gave you back your son, whom you considered to be dead. This was the first warning! . . . Fate warned you, yet you were blind. You rejected your son, you violated the laws of maternity. And then fate suddenly turned against you and delivered you a mortal blow by the hand of that son. . . . Fate cast him against you just when you were about to achieve your greatest moment, your glory. . . . And who are you now? Helpless, with a dead tongue, dead limbs. Only your eyes and ears are alive in order to see and hear your defeat, your tragic and trivial epilogue.[15]

A second archetype comes into play here: the myth of Oedipus, albeit in inverted form, since the mother is substituted for the father and the parent's guilt for the son's guilt. Accordingly, punishment by self-blinding is replaced by a paralysis that leaves the eyes open. But Wat's masterful manipulation of mythical themes does not save the play: the epilogue is more trivial than tragic.[16]

The play has many supporting characters, the most fascinating of whom is a degraded man of letters, Dr. Adolf Schweigedoch, a Jew who lost his wife and son at Auschwitz. Schweigedoch furnishes an ironical commentary on the events of the plot, never sparing Vittorio and his Communist ideology. Clearly an autobiographical character, he shares Wat's most private experiences and thoughts. Wat provides him with a caricature last name meaning "shut up,"[17] as if he were addressing his own iconoclastic self. Still "Mr. Shut Up" remains the only attractive figure in the play, as is often the case with similar characters in Gorky's works.

The play's manifest deterioration toward the end is striking. Whereas the first act is a passable dramatic opening (sprinkled with Schweigedoch's parables) and the second includes a convincing clash of characters, the third seems offhand and full of sloganeering. At the beginning, Wat appears to have taken "The Women of Monte Olivetto" seriously, using it to vent some of his genuine concerns. Then, after realizing that such a play had no chance of being accepted, he rounded it off in the hated socialist realist manner—and subsequently repudiated it altogether.

On 28 April 1959, Wat received an invitation to go to France, aided by the Ford Foundation.[18] Since Andrzej was already in the West, Aleksander and Ola could at long last leave for Paris. They settled in Maisons-Laffitte, the Paris suburb where *Culture* had its headquarters. There, they were assigned a three-room apartment with kitchen and bath. For a time, they shared the apartment with the filmmaker Roman Polanski, a semi-émigré who was soon to become famous and who needed his room only at night.[19]

The family postponed applying for refugee status, since an abrupt break with the regime in Poland might have harmed Ola's relatives and Broniszówna. This, in turn, impeded Aleksander's work and reduced his chances of making a living. A considerable portion of the émigré community treated the Wats with suspicion. Nor did close ties with *Culture* go unnoticed by the Polish authorities, who nevertheless continued to play a cat-and-mouse game with Wat and, for a time, avoided turning him into a nonperson, as they had done Miłosz, Hłasko, and others.

There were also some successes. Less than two months after his arrival in Paris, Wat went to the Fourth International Biennale of Poetry at the Belgian seaside resort of Knokke-le-Zoute, 3–7 September 1959. Here, he made a speech that had an unmistakable, if moderate, anti-totalitarian ring. Several of his poems were translated into French and appeared in the prestigious Belgian periodical *Le Journal de poètes* with an introduction by Jeleński.[20] A lively interest in Polish poetry, generated by the events of 1956 and the following years, worked to Wat's advantage, and he gradually gained recognition, especially in the narrow but influential circle of Western writers and intellectuals concerned with East European affairs. He also had a group of close Polish friends, all of them associated with *Culture*. Closest among them was perhaps Zygmunt Hertz, a kind, witty man who provided the Wat family with much help.[21]

At the end of 1959, the Genoese industrialist Umberto Silva started a publishing house with the express goal of presenting East European authors to an Italian audience. Józef Zaremba, the Polish cultural attaché in Rome, knew Silva well and recommended Wat for the position of editor.[22] With his many years working for Gebethner and Wolff, as well as in the publishing industry of postwar Poland, Wat was well qualified for the job. Silva invited him to Genoa, where he and Ola arrived on 22 January 1960.[23] They stayed in a hotel in Nervi. The environment reminded them of Menton-Garavan and Vence, where Wat had worked so successfully three and a half years before: "the beauty of Italian sea, of its colors, mimosa, palms, small harbors with brightly colored boats. The air was soft and fragrant, and at night in the bushes the fireflies shone."[24]

Unfortunately, the relationship with Silva soon began to sour. For a time Silva was fascinated with Wat's idea of publishing sumptuous multivolume editions of Mickiewicz, Krasiński, and Norwid—"not as precursors but as modern writers, preying upon modern problems—authors who are accessible and even revealing for a sophisticated Western intellectual of our time."[25] But after two months, it became clear that it would not be possible to find enough translators for such an enterprise.[26] In addition, Wat and Silva rubbed each other the wrong way. Moreover, Wat's erudition and enthusiasm now came up against the limitations imposed by illness.

In September 1961 Wat was appointed literary representative of Silva Editore in France, responsible for Russian and Polish collections and a consultant on French, English, and German publications. For this, he was paid the meager salary of 600 francs a month.[27] Before long, the family left Italy and joined Andrzej, who was now married and living with his wife in Paris.

Thereafter, Wat received a temporary reprieve, thanks to the efforts of Hertz and Miłosz. In 1960, Miłosz had left France for the United States. The following year, he received a grant from the New-Land Foundation. Since he was already established as a tenured professor of Slavic literatures at the University of California at Berkeley, he requested that the grant be transferred to Wat. The foundation complied.[28] In July of the following year, Wat asked for the grant to be extended, informing the foundation that he was writing three books: one dealing with Stalinism in literature, another with the prospective title "The Fang and the Key," and the third, a book of memoirs entitled "The Hostage on the River Ili."[29] An extension of one year was granted,[30] which allowed Wat to terminate his unsatisfactory employment at Silva Editore.

"Old Wat started to write and has fallen into a trance. Ola says that she has not seen Aleksander in such good shape for many, many years," Hertz wrote to Miłosz on 25 August 1961.[31] On 19 October of the same year, he continued: "You just don't imagine how great your services to God and mankind are. I mean the case of Wat. As a writer, the guy was dead as a nail: the volcano's inactivity was caused by a feeling of censorship, a muffling of the voice, and justified by his disease. . . . Suffice it to say: it turned out that Aleksander after many years of fasting has got a taste for writerly life. . . . I observe his swelling belly like an old midwife, though do not see the baby's kicks as of yet."[32]

During 1961–63, the Wat family lived mainly in Paris, though their stays there alternated with long winter sojourns in the south, at La Messuguière, a holiday resort for intellectuals, of which Ola wrote: "The exceptional beauty of the landscape, the town of Cabris close by, on a hill, a nice road under a high ridge. Clearings with big rocks, some of them of a tremendous size, as if arranged into heathen cult patterns by human hand. . . . Greenness, old twisted olive trees, old ruined sheepfolds of grey stone; one could still see traces of bonfires. On clear mornings, the coast of Corsica was visible. . . . Such an unusual, powerful and pure palette of colors. Aleksander's favorite place."[33]

Aleksander and Ola stayed at La Messuguière from December 1961 to early April 1962 and again from January to April 1963. Immediately upon his first arrival at Cabris, Wat wrote to Józef and Maria Czapski: "One could not dream of anything better. An immeasurable silence, one does not even hear the birds."[34] Conditions were ideal for work, and there was also a good library.[35]

During Wat's first sojourn in Cabris, he wrote two long poems—or rather, lyrical cycles—which must count among his best work: *Pieśni wędrowca* (Songs of a Wanderer) and *Sny sponad Morza Śródziemnego* (Dreams from the Shore of the Mediterranean). These were complemented by the short lyrical text "Poezja" (Poetry), dedicated to Gordon Craig on his ninetieth birthday.[36] At the end of the year, Wat's second book of poetry, *Mediterranean Poems*, was published, comprising all three texts.

The book generated as much interest among readers as had his *Poems* of 1957. "2,000 copies of my really difficult, enigmatic (for others, and on a deeper level even for myself) *Mediterranean Poems* were sold," Wat noted, not without surprise, in *Scraps of Paper in the Wind*.[37]

Wat's presence in Polish literary life was nevertheless nearing an end. He was determined to pursue his main goal of trying to understand and interpret Stalinism. No censorship, external or internal, must be allowed to interfere with the execution of this task, which entailed becoming a nonperson in his native land. Not without reason, Wat considered himself a unique witness, whose testimony might prove to be particularly valuable. Not least, he was a survivor. Almost all those who had undergone experiences similar to his had either perished in the purges, as did Jasieński and Steklov, committed suicide, like Mayakovsky and Borowski, or simply died. In the early 1960s Wat lost the last two of his friends who had succumbed to the Communist temptation: Stawar died in Paris on 5 August 1961, and Broniewski in Warsaw on 10 February 1962.

Wat worked intensively, filling hundreds of pages with his almost illegible handwriting. He used every inch of space, including the margins and covers of his exercise books: this was due partly to haste and fits of pain, partly to the lingering habits of a prisoner, who expected searches and was always short of writing materials.[38] A book with the tentative title "Kilka rysów do przyszłego portretu Stalina" (Some Strokes for a Future Portrait of Stalin) lacked only the three final chapters when Wat—because of a deep aversion to his topic, he said—was forced to discontinue the work due to persistent eczema.[39] A hint of this has been preserved in his *Songs of the Wanderer:*

> I prattle. Grow muddy with drinks. Covered
> with sweat, yes, sweat, eczema, mycosis.
> My clothes are filthy. No fragrant oils
> from Grasse will help; not all the perfumes of Arabia can clean them. Nor
> will the breath of my little sister mimosa under the window
> undo anything.[40]

In 1961, Wat made his first significant contribution to uncensored Polish literature. The occasion was the appearance of several stories and an essay signed by Abram Terts (the name of the hero of a famous thieves' song), which began to leak across the Soviet border in 1959 and were translated into major Western languages almost immediately. A stinging critic of Stalinism and socialist realism, Abram Terts continued the grotesque, phantasmagoric tradition of Russian modernist fiction. Wat contributed to the translation of Terts into Polish. In 1961, a Polish version of Terts's *Fantastic Stories* appeared in Paris, together with a comprehensive introduction entitled "Czytając Terca" (Reading Terts) by

Wat. Still reluctant to break his links with Poland, Wat followed the author he was discussing by concealing his identity under a pen name, Stefan Bergholz. He was less than enthusiastic about the Russian's writing (even if it had points in common with his own early fiction). Not without grounds, he considered Terts a product of a Communist education and susceptible to the mental deformations and illusions engendered by the Soviet system. Nevertheless, the introduction furnished an opportunity to expound, for the first time, his long-incubated thoughts on the singular qualities of Stalinist doctrine and the character of Soviet art.[41]

"Reading Terts" was followed by a paper presented at an Oxford conference on Soviet literature, convened under the auspices of St. Antony's College and the periodical *Survey* on 1–8 July 1962. The title of Wat's paper was "Quelques aperçus sur les rapports entre la littérature et la réalité soviétique" (Some Notes on the Relations between Literature and Soviet Reality). Its main points were summarized in *Dialogue*, a quarterly bulletin published by the Congress for Cultural Freedom in Paris, in fall 1962. Contributing to this strictly anti-Communist venture was virtually synonymous with breaking with the regime.[42]

In Oxford, Wat met several leading scholars of Russian and Soviet literature, including Sir Isaiah Berlin and Gleb Struve. The meeting with Struve proved especially fruitful: Struve was greatly impressed by Wat's paper and arranged for him an invitation to the University of California at Berkeley, where he himself taught.[43]

In April 1963, on his return to Paris from his second sojourn at La Messuguière, Wat found himself legally in limbo. At the end of the preceding year, he had applied for an extension of his Polish passport.[44] But the Polish consulate in Paris issued him instead a new document, which entitled him to stay in France but simultaneously deprived him of his rights to his Warsaw apartment. The Communist government of Poland thereby gave the Wats a clear signal that they were to consider themselves *de facto* émigrés. Extension of the document to allow him to travel to the United States was refused. Nevertheless, even though a person *non grata*, his *Mediterranean Poems* scored a critical success in Poland. Several reviews appeared in early 1963, most of them enthusiastic.[45]

The Wat family finally became fed up with this cat-and-mouse game. Ola approached the Polish consul and stated their position in no uncertain terms: both were intending to apply for refugee status. The consul asked her to postpone the decision until 10 A.M. the next day, when the answer from Warsaw was expected. It never came. Then, she wrote, "without hesitation, we initiated the procedure for obtaining the *Certificat de refugié* and *titre de voyage*. We were free. The world stood open before us, we could go to Berkeley. One of my sisters, who then worked at the State Publishing Institute, lost her job soon after our break with Poland. Even Broniszówna for some time did not play as often as before, and not the same roles. . . . This 'cutting of the umbilical cord,' as Aleksander would say, was in any case tragic. He took it to heart very much."[46]

Wat registered in Paris as a stateless person on 28 May 1963.[47] Two days before, he had become a grandfather, when a son, François, was born to Andrzej and his wife.

The trip to the United States did not materialize until December because of further bureaucratic hassles. The Wats remained in their apartment in Paris, enjoying their new-found freedom and entertaining various friends. Among them was Miłosz, now established in Berkeley but in France frequently on visits; he was to become the first and most important critic of Wat's new poetry.[48] Someone else who was close to Wat at this time was Jan Lebenstein, a Polish artist whose paintings and drawings, which made ample use of somatic grotesquerie and diabolic imagery, were similar in tonality to Wat's works.[49]

In November, Słonimski came to Paris. "It was a tremendous joy for us— he is the only person from the prewar milieu to whom I feel attached,"[50] Wat noted in *Diary without Vowels*. "Witty, charming, delicate," Słonimski brought the news that most Polish intellectuals understood and respected Wat's decision to become a political émigré.[51] This was a source of relief, since Wat had been profoundly hurt by the gross, if predictable, slanders of virtually the entire Polish press, to which some estimable cultural figures had contributed.

There was also at least one representative of the youngest generation of Polish letters: the critic Wojciech Karpiński, who came to Paris for the first time, became enamored of Wat's works published in *Culture,* and asked Hertz to introduce him to the author—a wish Hertz fulfilled.[52] Talks with Karpiński could not but confirm the words of the old Skamandrite.

People in Poland were, then and later, the audience that Wat most desired: "I'll never find a common language with the émigrés, I'll always remain alien, a problematic Pole for them. I have left the only Poles who understood me in the old country. We were brought together by a common experience, even at the times when they were high on the top and I was in the pits, and I'll sooner come to an agreement with an ex-Stalinist who oppressed me than with the émigrés, whose beliefs I shared so ardently. For what are beliefs, when the same words express diametrically opposite experiences?"[53]

The group of those who understood each other immediately included visitors from other Eastern European countries. In 1963, Wat met his old acquaintance from Alma-Ata, Konstantin Paustovsky, who had come to Paris on a tourist visa with his stepdaughter, Galya Arbuzova, and another Russian writer, Viktor Nekrasov. Both Paustovsky and Nekrasov belonged to the liberal elite of the Soviet Union. Galya was representative of the younger Russian generation, well educated, open-minded, and strongly critical of the regime. Traces of discussions with these visitors, who brought to Paris a sense of the changing spiritual climate in the USSR, are scattered throughout Wat's writings.[54]

After obtaining a French permit of residence for three years, on 23 November 1963,[55] Wat was free to visit Berkeley. At the same time, he learned about the assassination of John F. Kennedy. Shocked enough to compare Kennedy's death to the assassination of Julius Caesar and even to the Crucifixion, Wat considered writing a novel about Lee Harvey Oswald, patterned on Dostoevsky's *Notes from the Underground, The Adolescent,* and *The Possessed*—one of the many projects never brought to fruition.

Finally, in the middle of December, the Wats left for Berkeley, where they were greeted by Gregory Grossman, chairman of the Center for Slavic and East European Studies. The first days in California were happy. Wat was intrigued by San Francisco, a city he had longed to see in his youth and had celebrated in *Pug Iron Stove:* "Waves with foam like loose flowing white hair, and distance— something that I need for living and understanding myself, almost a snail in the immense world."[56]

Wat's physical suffering diminished in Berkeley for the first time in eleven years. This alleviation of pain proved to be temporary, but during his first winter in California he was quite euphoric. He gave talks on the Berkeley campus and continued work on his major projects concerning Stalinism and Soviet literature. There were also new poems—and the best pages of *Diary without Vowels,* the book Wat began in Paris, probably after his defection, were written in Berkeley.

The euphoria was nevertheless punctuated by bouts of acute depression. Notes from even the earliest months in Berkeley are frequently marked by feelings of failure and of the absurdity of life. Wat's first poem in the United States, "Z kosza" (From a Basket), was about old men in a hospice in San Francisco, with whom he clearly identified.

> A huge basket of abundance, our beautiful city of Saint Francis.
> Something smells bad here. Like a grass snake which I once kept
> imprisoned in a jar. . . .
>
> I will humbly knock at the hospice on Mission Street:
> beyond the pane in the lobby old men sit, a senate of near poverty,
> they keep silent, look at the wall. Now newspapers on sticks hanging from
>   their hands
> like flags lowered in mourning. Like a turned-down flame of Eros.
> They are burned out, as the saying goes. . . .
>
> I, too, don't want to write the way I do. Would like it to be perfect,
> clear, sacral, as in Bach. And out of grief that I cannot,

I am jotting down this poem as a grass snake imprisoned in a jar would
  write.
Or, another time: as a crab would write,
the one pulled out of the basket by a gray-haired black woman's old hand.
That's just the way it happened to me.[57]

In spring 1964, the pain returned, worse than before, leaving him "without
a trace of any desire except that of eternal nonexistence, without a shadow of any
sensibility except the desperate anxiety concerning the fate of Ola and Andrzej."[58] Wat's predicament was aggravated by a sharp sense of moral bank-
ruptcy. He had not come through on his commitment to the New-Land Foundation, and now he was unable to carry out his duties at Berkeley. Several new
literary plans, including "Stalin's Diaries," a "project for a best-seller,"[59]
amounted to no more than wishful thinking. He filled hundreds of pages with his
scrawl, the most legible part of which consisted of sorrowful confessions and
severe self-criticism:

> Despair, senile twaddle; all that seemed to me muscular, verbally and
> mentally energetic, is nothing more than rambling, sticky logorrhea.[60]

> I grew old many years ago, yet only here, in America, after short weeks of a
> second youth, did I become an old man—here, on this American soil. And I'm
> mortally tired every evening—this fatigue never abates, and yet it is only in the
> evening, around eight o'clock, that I pray stubbornly and fervently not to wake
> up in the morning.[61]

Aleksander and Ola jointly considered suicide.[62] Gregory Grossman in
vain attempted to convince Wat that his self-reproaches were overstated. He
managed to extend Wat's stay in Berkeley for another half-year. Finally, realizing
that Wat was on the verge of a breakdown, he proposed a singular remedy. If Wat
was stricken by writer's block but still capable of lively conversation, which in
fact temporarily alleviated his pain, why not record on tape his reminiscences?
This might be a valuable form of therapy and restore in Wat a sense of purpose
and self-esteem, and at the same time it would give rise to a completed book,
which otherwise seemed an unattainable, Kafkaesque goal. Miłosz agreed to take
on the duties of interviewer and interpreter.[63]

In the early months of 1965, Wat and Miłosz undertook a series of taping
sessions, each of which lasted an hour and a half. Ola was usually present too and
sometimes added comments. By the beginning of summer, a substantial number
of recordings had been made; but "Wat considered this no more than half or even
a quarter of what he wanted to say,"[64] according to Miłosz. Grossman and others
tried to persuade Wat to stay on in California until the end of the year, but Wat
rejected this offer of an extension: his savings would suffice for several years of
moderate living in France, and he wanted to avoid what seemed to him contin-

ued trespassing on the university's hospitality.[65] After a department party with farewell speeches, the Wats left for Paris, on 2 July 1965.[66] Miłosz went too, in order to make further recordings. Altogether, thirty-nine sessions were taped. These converted into almost two thousands pages of typescript and covered Wat's life from his futurist years to early 1943.

Wat's friendship with Miłosz had its ups and downs, but their collaboration proved to be exceptionally fruitful. "It is hard to find a more considerate, more intelligent and stimulating listener than Miłosz,"[67] Wat wrote. "Our philosophies are contrary, but does that do any harm? So much the better."[68] Miłosz, in turn, was an appreciative audience. As he himself wrote: "Something remarkable occurred, even during the initial sessions: I listened as if enchanted, and the greater the attention Wat saw in my eyes, the higher he would soar. . . . I quickly realized that something unique was transpiring between us. There was not a single other person on the face of the earth who had experienced this century as Wat had and who had the same sense of it as he. . . . No one in his generation, I thought, was leaving historians a gift of this sort, in this field."[69] The different world views, characters, and generational experiences of Miłosz and Wat only served to spark their fascinating exchange. Deliberately relegating himself to the background, Miłosz was nevertheless very much present in the book, even in its blanks and silences.

Ola was the third person responsible for the final shape of *My Century*. It was she who transcribed the tapes. Of this endeavor, she wrote: "I will always remember his first reaction, when he heard his own voice, entered the room where I worked, and having listened to some small fragment went out fast, closing his ears and saying: 'But it's awful, awful.' Later, he never wanted to be present during my typing, he would not listen to his own utterances. . . . He knew that the tremendous amount of work and time necessary for bringing the recordings to a state at least minimally corresponding to his intents and ambitions was beyond his abilities."[70]

On their return to Paris, Aleksander and Ola rented an apartment in the suburb of Antony.[72] This was to be Wat's last home. It was a comfortable place, with a large balcony and a garden. But Wat's health was deteriorating rapidly. Still, he continued to write. *Scraps of Paper in the Wind* was produced in the years 1966–67: a valuable complement to *My Century*, it contained many pages of Wat's best prose. He also created poems, though he was increasingly unable to write them down. Ola notes: "In a cage, our small bird Maciuś chirped incessantly, and one always hears his twitter in the background of the poems recorded by Aleksander. . . . Waking up in the night because of pain, he often switched on the tape-recorder and softly read the poems aloud—the 'tape-recorded whispers' which I discovered only after his death."[72]

Death hung over him as a never-ceasing presence, however. Describing his frame of mind in these last years, he wrote:

> When death is in me, more and more evident and materialized, when it grows inside me, and I can already touch it with my fingers, which resist the gesture, when it brings me closer to the threshold with every day, with every passing moment, the fear approaches as well. Fear of fears, that fear which is *the* fear in all other fears.[73]

> I must endure that death in the same way as I have endured the hardest trials of my life: all my life's value depends on it. . . . I must die facing death, my adversary or my brother, up to the last hour: but I must stand on my feet, up to the very last moment. It will be a great injury for me, a great irremediable injury, if I die in torpor, passively, helplessly sliding down.[74]

> My last battlefield: poems against physical suffering. Or: intelligence against suffering? *Kto kogo?*[75]

For some time, Wat considered returning to Poland, if only to die on native soil. In his correspondence with Broniszówna, he cautiously hinted at such a possibility. The topic was so sensitive that Wat wrote about it in secret (if transparent) code in Russian.[76] But he hardly meant it seriously: the situation in the Communist world was far from conducive. He was again grossly attacked in the Polish press, on the occasion of a French anthology of Polish poetry edited by Jeleński and published in 1965. Wat, who helped Jeleński in preparing and editing the book, was represented by eight poems, a fact that gave rise to fits of anger on the part of Przyboś and the semi-official critic Artur Sandauer. Przyboś said: "How diluted is the book by the empty talk of that malingerer! (He feigned sickness so as to make the naive People's Poland pay for his and his wife's long stays abroad, and finally 'chose freedom') . . . It is a most obvious propagandistic and political bias. A prize for non-poetic services."[77]

But there were some brighter moments too. As before, Wat spent winters in the south: in 1966 and 1967 he stayed in Palma de Mallorca, together with his brother, Moryc, and niece Roma Herscovici, who, between them, paid for the hotel.[78] There, Wat felt slightly better and was able to work more intensively. In Palma, he edited his definitive volume of poetry, *Lumen Obscurum*, which included early futurist verses, fragments of *Pug Iron Stove*, both postwar collections and new poems written in 1963–67. He did not live to see the book come out, however, in 1968.

While in Palma de Mallorca in early 1967, Wat wrote his last piece on literary theory, "O przetłumaczalności utworów poetyckich" (On the Translatability of Poetic Works). The occasion was the simultaneous publication of three anthologies of Polish poetry in three different languages.[79] Wat's article may be classified as a mini-treatise. It consists of sixty-eight numbered paragraphs arranged in strict logical order, in the manner of Ludwig Wittgenstein's *Tractatus Logico-philosophicus.* Brief and condensed, they present a coherent theory of the translation of poetry and summarize in passing Wat's views on metrics, rhyme, verse phonetics, semantics, intertextuality, poetic conventions and their automatization, the attitude of the poet to the native tradition, the relation between poetry and prose, and so forth.[80] Among the particularly original features of the article is Wat's suggestion that anthologies be arranged in reverse chronological order:

> Supposed advantages: an explorer who goes from the delta of the river's mouth to the sources would discover more easily, and in a quite specific way, what is permanent and what is ephemeral in a given national poetry: he would more exactly retrace the design of the branches, the mouths of the alien tributaries. The panoramic landscape would present itself to him in a new and more interesting form.
>
> More important: when a good reader starts perusing the anthology with good contemporary poets (who, in my opinion, are intimately closer to a *good* contemporary reader), he finds which qualities of the old poets were of essential, real and permanent value, beyond the textbook evaluations and interpretations.[81]

On 10 April 1967 Wat wrote a letter to the PEN Club concerning the role of exiled writers in the new situation of dialogue with the East, a dialogue that was to develop across borders and independently of political systems.[82] Hopes for such a development were soon undermined by a new political crisis: the Six-Day War between Arab countries and Israel in June 1967. The defeat and humiliation of the Arabs stirred strong feelings in the Communist camp. These were complemented by the anti-Semitism endemic to many East European countries. Then, as in 1953, anti-Semitism broke out—unashamedly—and this time it was the Polish government that took the lead.

The new post-Holocaust wave of anti-Semitism in Poland was, for Wat, the ultimate disgrace. By upsetting the balance between Jewishness and Polishness that he had struggled to establish from his earliest years, it undermined the very roots of his existence. Polish émigré writers published a statement concerning the Arab-Israeli war, which Wat signed. On 30 May 1967, he wrote an individual statement as well, under the heading "O solidarność z Izraelem" (On Solidarity with Israel), which was published in the *News* on 2 July. It was Wat's last contribution to the press, a fitting one for someone who, in his own words, always felt himself "a Jew-Jew and a Pole-Pole."

Of this period, Ola wrote: "From a balcony sheltered by a red awning Aleksander saw lawns, colorful beds of flowers and high poplars. The flat was nice and comfortable. Yet he did not want to go out when I urged him, he said that even I was unaware of his state. . . . He spent much time in an armchair, looking somewhere, silent, absent. Often, he entreated me to ask him no questions, wrote on the card 'I cannot converse,' let his eyes rove after my bustle, took his meals mechanically."[83] Her diary of 1967 consists mainly of short entries:

I. 3. A terrible day, a terrible evening. Suffering.
I. 5. Listening to Bach. . . . Relief.
II. 4. Good walk. He feels well.
III. 21. A great suffering. . . . Grief. Hopelessness. And the spring in its very bloom![84]

Secretly, Wat made arrangements concerning his only property—his books and the tapes of *My Century*. He considered most of his work trash that might, at best, be of use to Ola should she decide to write an autobiography. In July 1967, he wrote his last poem, which was found later among his papers:

I clad myself in the armor of silence:
all the words are already taken away except for one.

Perhaps they were only on loan?

Perhaps they were only displayed
to tempt the eyes of a passerby?
and now is night, the dead of night?

That word, the last remaining one,
I am not allowed to pronounce it:
birds in the air would fall!
and thunder from the clouds
would strike the heart of my friend!
yet she is to visit my grave
so that both of us could find consolation
in silence
without words.[85]

On the evening of 29 July 1967, Wat said good night to Ola as usual. After she left to go to her room, he put his last notebook on his bed and took forty sleeping pills. Before switching off the light, he wrote: "For God's sake. Do not save my life by any means. I should have already done what I now do."

His funeral was attended by a group of friends. Zygmunt Hertz described it in a letter to Miłosz as follows: "A short passage to the cemetery—bald and empty, without trees, bushes, vegetation, a sort of transit camp in a desert on the way to heaven, hell or purgatory."[86]

12

A Critique of Stalinist Reason

The prose works that Wat write during the last fifteen years of his life can be divided into three groups. First, there is *Moralia*, a kind of notebook or literary diary, which probably dates from the mid-1950s, after Wat's first bout of illness. Secondly, there are numerous essays about Stalinism and its historico-cultural context. Third, there is his main book of memoirs, *My Century*, complemented by *Scraps of Paper in the Wind* and *Diary without Vowels*, which concentrate, respectively, upon Wat's childhood and last years, periods that are largely disregarded in *My Century*.

The boundaries between the three groups, as between individual works within each group, are fluid. The entire corpus of Wat's late prose may be described as one long monologue revolving around the magistral themes of totalitarianism, suffering, conscience, and death. Each topic accumulates related texts and connotations, expanding into infinity yet entering into relation with one or all of his principal concerns.

Stylistically, Wat's late prose works seem disorderly. This is partly due to the circumstances of their composition. Most of them are either rough drafts arranged in a provisional order by publishers or "thinking aloud" transcribed from tapes. Yet, Wat actively cultivated a philosophy of fragmentariness. If a synthesis were attainable at all, it could be revealed only in moments of blinding insight. In this, the Gnostic element in Wat's personality and Weltanschauung once again came to the fore. A contemporary critic has stated: "Wat was one of those people who desire to enclose all truth in one concept and all language in one word. That is, he was one of the 'illuminati,' to whom the great unity revealed itself through the individual impulse of a thought, image or verbal figure. He was endowed by a *naturaliter* mystical consciousness, of which, as one may suspect, he was never completely aware."[1]

Thus, Wat's striving for ultimate certitude led him in two directions simultaneously: first, to endless variations on a given theme, parerga, and paralipomena; second, towards the aphorism, the short, clear formula, the all-embracing, though unattainable, Word. Both strategies were aimed at defeating the Interferer; yet both were self-defeating. Wat's desire for synthesis could never be satisfied: the world of the pleroma was forever broken into slivers and splinters, and the Interferer was only a personalized metaphor for this irredeemable break.

Moralia belongs to an ancient literary genre practiced by Pascal, La Rochefoucauld, Schopenhauer, and Nietzsche, among others. It consists mainly, though not exclusively, of thoughts jotted down in a careless manner and oscillates between unprepossessing table talk and profound generalizations on the human condition and human behavior. It also includes numerous anecdotes and witticisms of the Stalinist era.

A close parallel to Wat's *Moralia* is found in the writings of Vasily Rozanov, a Russian philosopher and journalist who made his name primarily through two idiosyncratic books of disjointed aphorisms and short essays, *Solitaria* (1912) and *Fallen Leaves* (1913–15).[2] Rozanov, a fiercely independent thinker, was preoccupied, first and foremost, with religion, gender, and sexuality, all of which he discussed in an uninhibited way. Wat was aware of Rozanov's work from at least the 1920s, but it was only after writing *Moralia*, already an émigré, that he became seriously interested in it. At that stage, he wrote: "If only I had known Rozanov in time, in my younger years! I knew him, yet I never really contemplated the topic: Rozanov and myself. Only Józio's preface[3] directed me to that. Naturally, I find no similarity between us, I detest him, though in a quite different way than I detest myself, his thoughts are alien and somewhat disgusting to me. But his difficult fate? but sharp, twisting meanders of his public life, but its unhappy end? And the presence of his wife at his side—her wisdom, purity, strength."[4]

The form of a notebook, which characterizes not only *Moralia* but also most of his other essays, proved to be a most appropriate vehicle for Wat's thought.[5] At once intimate and anecdotal, provocative and terse, *Moralia* touches on much the same range of subjects as *Fallen Leaves* and *Solitaria*, even if problems of gender, which were of primary importance to Rozanov, are largely replaced in Wat's work by those of imprisonment and illness. Like Rozanov, Wat always begins in medias res, and his monologue, like Rozanov's, is of a profoundly dialogic nature: "I think, therefore I maintain a dialogue with myself. That is, any thinking presupposes the splitting of 'I' into 'I' of a different order and 'non-I.' Inner and pronounced monologues are only a certain rhetorical form of dialogue: I convince someone, I oppose someone, I subordinate myself to someone, I negotiate with someone—such is thinking, in its archaic and magical forms as well as at its Socratic heights."[6]

This emphasis on an other as a requirement for consciousness and meaning conforms to modern insights concerning the nature of language and thought. In Polish letters, a counterpart to Wat's stance is provided by Gombrowicz, who devoted his entire life and work to a scathing analysis of the relationship between "I" and the "other." Nevertheless, Wat's and Gombrowicz's approaches differ considerably. Whereas Gombrowicz concentrated on unmasking inauthenticity (yet considered authenticity unattainable and empty) and on ridiculing a consciousness inhibited by social conventions, Wat—not unlike Rozanov— attempted to look beyond inauthenticity, toward true selfhood. He was not so much interested in undermining the traditional concept of personality as in searching for its transcendental roots. The moral dimension of his inner dialogue gave it a quality of religious meditation. Wat's aphoristic prose, not unlike his poetry, often became confession and prayer, in which the "someone" with whom he argued and to whom he subordinated himself was God.

Rozanov's last book, *The Apocalypse of Our Times* (1917–18), included a vision of impending disaster but did not examine it in detail. The author of *Moralia* could be described as a post-apocalyptic Rozanov—Rozanov after the totalitarian experience.

Wat's notes vary greatly in length. Some of them take up only one or two lines, whereas some spread over several pages. They include bitter aphorisms— "Thou shalt love thy neighbor as thyself? Can one love oneself? Does one actually love oneself? Try to love thy neighbor as intensely as thou hate thyself"[7]—and brief, pessimistic fables—"On a highway, a road-roller moves. A ladybird puts its forelegs on the roller and says: 'Wait a minute, let's discuss. . . .' For God's sake, who is there to hold discussions? The road-roller with the ladybird? And about what?"[8] Many of them are based on patterns elaborated by Wat's predecessors in the art of paradox, such as Oscar Wilde—"And here is the peculiarity of our century: Caliban, having seen his face in a mirror, fell in love with himself."[9] There are also dialogues and narratives, psychological novellas, metaphysical and aesthetic divagations, personal portraits, descriptions of dreams, and, finally, drafts of poems and complete poems.

One of the most interesting sections of *Moralia* consists of stories belonging to Wat's favorite genre of "novel-notes,"[10] which develop a paradoxical conceit in a limited space, dispensing with descriptions and dialogues and including only what is absolutely necessary. Like many other stories by Wat, they resemble Borges's synopses of longer works that were never written. Some were obviously intended for inclusion in the collection "King Lear of the Security Service," which Wat proposed to "The Reader" in 1959.[11] On the other hand, *Moralia* includes the outline of an entire novel, the action of which was to take place in the ancient Egypt of Akhenaten and Tutankhamen. Resembling *Joseph and His Brothers* by Thomas Mann and alluding to the earlier, classic Polish novel *Pharaoh* (1896) by Bolesław Prus, it was to be a transparent allegory of Stalinism and its gradual breakdown. Arguably, the best of the stories is the one that tells of a German philosopher who, because of his professional activities, is

subjected to an unusual punishment: he must live in a luxurious hotel surrounded by a death camp and constantly observe exhausted and tortured prisoners who, however, cannot see him.

Another layer of *Moralia* consists of personal reminiscences and meditations, many of which concern Wat's physical suffering. There are also prison
reminiscences, camouflaged as stories told by someone else.[12] More than one
note concerns the narrator's tortured memory of his evil deeds, which may seem
insignificant yet reveal his less acceptable human qualities, such as indifference,
disloyalty, and a striving for petty advantage at the expense of others. A similar
poignancy permeates shrewd but less than flattering portraits of fellow writers,
including Witkacy, Tuwim, and Broniewski. The tenor of Wat's reflections on
his life and times is summed up in the keen maxim: "Essentially, I practice usury:
I collect my sweet interest, bitterness, from everything."[13]

Only rarely, and hence all the more impressively, does different tonality
gain the upper hand. Such are the almost Proustian epiphanies of prewar Warsaw, Italy, or a fleeting moment in the Polish countryside—an escape from
history, suffering, and death into the paradisiacal world of pure sensual perception:

> Looking from the balcony over the beach, X . . . thought: I shall not forget
> four overturned kayaks on the shore, the red color of their bottoms, the tall girl
> in the white bathing suit, the wizard with a bunch of gray hair on a hollow
> chest, I shall not forget any of these wicker baskets, this small green flag, the red
> buoy on greenish grey waves, the blue booth, the olive-colored tufts of grass, all
> the patches: red and blue, and yellow, and orange, and green, and white, and
> indigo—I shall not forget anything ever—for that approaching time, when I
> will dwell for the ages of ages in nothingness, reliving my memories![14]

Moralia, together with the story "After Death," represents Wat's earliest
approach to the phenomenon of Stalinism, which casts its shadow on every other
topic he treats. It is this that ensures *Moralia*'s intrinsic unity, even more than its
overall pessimistic mood.

Wat attacks Stalinist reality from various standpoints and by various means.
He becomes, as it were, an ethnographer and anthropologist of communism,
describing everyday patterns of life and behavior in East European countries and
revealing their profoundly distorted character. He perforates, deflates, and dis-
credits Stalinist ideological doctrines and clichés. He condenses the essence of
totalitarianism into polished maxims and at the same time immerses himself in
elaborate philosophical and sociological discussions of its development and
structure. Wat is as perspicacious and pessimistic an observer of human foibles
as was La Rochefoucald; but whereas the seventeenth-century moralist considered selfishness to be the primary motivation for all human behavior, Wat notes
other motives as well, including an innate, all-pervading striving toward uniformity and simplification.[15]

In *Moralia*, the main focus of Wat's attack on Communist dogma is its narrowly rationalist character:

> Nothing disproves subjective idealism and nothing proves the objective existence of the world better than the bankruptcy of macrosocialism. Since it is an attempt to deduce the world from a couple of arbitrarily accepted and developed premises. An attempt, carried out with such an inordinate cost in power, means, human lives and violence, that it would be sufficient for the realization of the most farfetched idea. Therefore the way in which rationalism and logic turn into their "dialectic" opposite expressly shows that there is a certain objective reality, which does not allow one to impose "ideas" on it and lives by its own rules, never coinciding with the structure of mechanical (deductive-rationalist) logic.[16]

Here, Wat remains within the bounds of the Marxist philosophical paradigm and its terminology, taking aim at the totalitarian project, as it were, "from inside" (a technique that he also used in "Anti-Zoilus," written several years before *Moralia*). Any orthodox student of Marx and Lenin would readily accept Wat's conclusion that "being—from whatever level one looks at it—is full of contradictions, moves, lives, exists, develops in contradictions. *Polemos pater panton* (contradiction begets everything), said Heraclitus."[17] In Wat's view, communism is an attempt to cancel the interplay of contradictions and subordinate everything to a uniform set of principles; hence it is doomed to failure.

Stalinism imposed a common denominator on sets of ideas, values, and customs that were incomparable and incommensurable.[18] Its main and fatal weakness consisted in the merging of "humanist, socialist or universal ideals— these are three different names for virtually one ideal—with tribal laws."[19] (According to Wat, this was the point at which communism parted with Nazism, which openly proclaimed the omnipotence of tribal law.) The unnatural amalgam of two opposing slogans, one announcing happiness for everyone, the other demanding death for the enemies, constituted an incurable split between Communist theory and practice, which, ultimately, led to the system's self-destruction:

> The sign of equality was written down instead of the sign of contradiction. Hence the seemingly exaggerated, irrational significance which Stalin assigned to artisans of the word. This unity could exist only on a purely verbal level: the word is, in any case, obedient, flexible, polysemantic for the so-called engineers of human souls who can denote black as white and vice versa. Hence the paradox, that in the land of the dictatorship of the proletariat a man of letters was paid incomparably better than a worker—he was at the top of the *happy few*, yet woe to him if he did not fulfill his duty.[20]

Here, Wat approached the original line of reasoning that was to become his trademark in subsequent essays. Throughout the last years of his life, he practiced a critique of communism that might best be termed *linguistic* and *semiotic*.

Wat considered publishing *Moralia*, if not in its entirety, then in parts. But in fact it was published—even then in slightly abridged form—only post-humously, in 1986. He took up many of its threads again in the essays on Stalinist ideology and civilization that he wrote during the 1960s. However much Wat may have insisted on the dividing line between "poetry-poetry" and "prose-prose," his essays are clearly the work of a poet, saturated with metonymies, hyperboles and witticisms, symbols and quotations. Usually employing long, meandering sentences with endless digressions, Wat at the same time practices the art of ellipsis and suggestion. He freely juxtaposes the languages of theology, philosophy, history, science, and belles lettres. In short, the essays are no less baroque than is Wat's mature poetry.[21]

The Stalinist mystery related to the metaphysical problem that had always fascinated Wat: that of the source and nature of evil. Perhaps they could be revealed fully only in symbolic, abstract visions in the spirit of Kafka and Camus—not without reason, these two writers more than any others interested Soviet intellectuals engaged in trying to interpret their country's fate.[22] Still, Wat opted for an analytical procedure. However elliptical and disorganized his essays were, they followed the rules of logic and strove to demythologize the Communist phenomenon in a scientific way.

The first avenue of research might be described as genetic. More than one thinker had looked for the roots of Stalinism in Russia's past—in particular, in Russian intellectual history, and Wat accepted some of the previous findings. The specific, highly idiosyncratic development of a great Eurasian country could not but leave abiding traces in the nation's present. Thus, the simplistic pseudo-scientific Weltanschauung typical of Russian nihilists of the nineteenth century was embraced by most Russian revolutionaries. Another factor that merged with naive scientism, thereby giving birth to some of the worst Stalinist excesses, was Russian *"pensée sauvage,"*[23] a semi-mythological folk world view fraught with memories of age-old oppression as well as es-chatological hopes.

But Wat did not subscribe to the popular view that Stalinism was a direct continuation of Russia's past—or of any other country's past, for that matter.[24] Such a reading would, in his opinion, underestimate its power and potential. Stalinism was to be studied structurally, not genetically, on its own terms, not on the terms of preceding systems.

Wat summarizes his argument in two short paragraphs:

> *Stalinism consists of the semantic instrumentalization of everything.* Of the world of people, and of the world of things. Of all economic, social and spiritual human activity. Of human being as such. Of his consciousness, thought and word. And, finally, even of this very doctrine.
>
> Instrumentalization and not instrumentalism, since we are speaking about a process and not about a philosophical trend. A process, the end of which, its only and final end, consists in the process itself.[25]

The instrumentalization of society was achieved by the instrumentalization of the human being, who, according to Soviet precepts, was to become a cog in society's machine. This, in turn, was accomplished by transforming human consciousness (which is founded on language and inseparable from it). This means that "language—language in its entirety, as language-speech and language-writing—must first of all yield to instrumentalization,"[26] Wat noted in his essay "Some Notes on the Relation between Literature and Soviet Reality."

Any civilization, including that of pre-revolutionary Russia, assumes a degree of mutual interdependence between the universe of words and the universe of things, so guaranteeing a modicum of objectivity of meaning. Hence, semantic arbitrariness is unacceptable. In the paradoxical world of Stalinism, however the opposite obtained. Here, semantic values were elastic, changeable, and amenable to control, in accordance "with the will of the Lord—*Logos Spermatikos*, to use the Gnostic term."[27]

The new totalitarian language, unlike the specialized language of a science, diplomatic jargon, or thieves' slang, could not be reduced to a limited repertory of conventions or codes relating to a particular part of the universe. It was a *global* phenomenon that affected the fundamental relationship between word and thing, *signifiant* and *signifié*, as well as between truth and falsehood.[28] It involved the abuse and corruption of language at its core.

One cannot but recall here, as Wat did, modernist experimentation with language aimed at undermining its ability to convey any sense at all. Wat's *Pug Iron Stove*, one of the most radical avant-garde texts of its era, was an attempt at global desemanticization in its subversion of linguistic habits and expectations, its generation of purely verbal objects, and, in general, its repudiation of mimesis in favor of semiosis. Now, his playful experiment revealed its perilous side: there was something in common between the avant-garde artist and the totalitarian dictator, both of whom assumed the mantle of the dark Gnostic demiurge, generating and destroying meaning at will. However approximate an analogy, it was far from fantastical. Even the well-documented animosity of totalitarian leaders to "degenerate art" might be explained, up to a point, by their intolerance of any competition.

Wat's poetic experience allowed him to examine the phenomenon of totalitarianism from a particular angle. At the same time, it could not but deepen his predicament. Stalin, the forbidding father figure, the very thought of whom filled Wat with an abhorrence that resulted in bouts of illness, assumed the features of Wat's mirror image. This was the most perverse trick of the Interferer and the one that drove Wat to despair more than any other. "My clothes are filthy: no fragrant oils / from Grasse will help; not all the perfumes of Arabia can clean them."[29]

The transformation of language began with its impoverishment. But although Wat paid attention to this most obvious trait of Stalinist discourse,[30] he insisted that there was more to the transformation than a narrowed vocabulary, simplified grammar, and predictable style. Specific techniques that deformed the entire logical and semantic framework of language were also operative. First, Stalinism misinterpreted and perverted "a certain set of general names, abstract works, recurring expressions—such as Man, People, Freedom, Humankind, Happiness, Socialism, Peace, Justice, etc., etc. (and also their opposites), separating them, with intentional brutality, from their usual meanings, which had been previously verified within the limits of evolutionary oscillation by the old tradition of *common sense.*"[31] This semantic purification, so-called, overturned meanings, identifying peace with the desired military superiority of the Soviets, the common weal with a lack of goods, and so on. More specific words, such as "bread" and "father," were then subordinated to the perverted universals, becoming matter for compulsory metaphors.

Second, a series of paralogistic operations were employed, starting with operations habitual for "savage"—and, incidentally, poetic—thought. For instance, a favorite Stalinist device was a variant of metonymy: namely, synecdoche, a figure of speech commonly defined as *pars pro toto.* The part of humankind, that supposedly expressed its common will to achieve the final eschatological goal—that is, the proletariat—was substituted for humankind in its entirety. Then the proletariat was replaced by its own vanguard, which in turn was replaced by the Communist party. The party was then identified with its leadership, and the leadership with the leader. Thus, the dictator came to be endowed with the magical qualities of a mythical king, in whom the entire power of humankind was concentrated and on whom its good totally depended.[32] What counted was the general law: all such operations "lost their *paralogical character, as they established their 'place' and rank within the specific logic of global Communist thought.*"[33]

An important aspect of the Stalinist semantic universe was its striving for absolute dichotomy. Totalitarian language explicitly divided the world into white and black: "either comrade or enemy, either *in-group* or *out-group*, either struggle for or struggle against, either adoration or hatred, either obedience or obliteration, etc."[34] This led to the characteristic practice of a double standard: "their" nuclear bomb was genocidal, while "ours" was beneficial; "their" prisons were inhuman, while "ours" were liberating. The mind trained in Stalinist semantics could not see the fallacy here. Wat knew this well, since he had yielded to this same double standard in 1931 in his argument with Słonimski concerning Polish and Soviet prisons.[35]

According to Wat, there were two stages in the development of Stalinist language politics and its implicit theory. For a time, it was furnished with a basis by Nikolai Marr, a linguist who asserted that transitions between social formations were marked by the complete overturning of semantic values. But in 1950, Stalin found that Marr's theory limited his options, since it posited a correspondence between the structure of society and that of language, thus placing restrictions on semantic arbitrariness. This, in Wat's option, was the reason for Stalin's famous attack on Marr in his pamphlet "Marxism and Problems of Linguistics."

An innovation that, according to Wat, proved Stalin's genius, was *"the transference of human language beyond truth and falsehood, beyond good faith and lying* (and, therefore, the breaking of the dialectical relationship between good faith and lying)."[36] The leader's words became a meta-reality, an object of belief that could not be questioned (just as the metaphysical concepts of transubstantiation and bodily resurrection cannot be questioned by the Catholic faithful). This secured the final ambition of the system: the complete replacement of transcendental authority by the earthly authority of the dark Demiurge.

One of the earliest of Wat's essays on Stalinism, "The Key and the Hook," reflects in its title the dichotomy between goal and means: "the key is the doctrine or, to be precise, its aspirations for power over the words, the hook is the terror employed as a tool of social pedagogy."[37] There is feedback between the two: the doctrine clears the way for terror, while terror secures the doctrine's impact. Wat gives several vivid examples of Stalinist education. When in Poland in the 1950s, due to a sudden, harsh money reform, people lost their entire savings in a single day, the papers came out with the headline "Workers and peasants express their satisfaction." This exercise in semantic inversion was justified by a private remark of someone in charge of the media: "It must be done this way, so that they'll get used to it as soon as possible." Another example given by Wat is even more eloquent. A Soviet prisoner—probably Wat himself—appeals to the freedoms proclaimed in Stalin's constitution, whereupon the man interrogating him displays a big stick, adding calmly: "Here is Stalin's constitution for you." The restructuring of consciousness in the two cases depends on the same process. A person is suddenly faced with a shattering truth, whereupon all signs lose their usual meaning and value and are now defined according to the will of the authorities.

This quasi-Zen revelation was imprinted on minds by repetition under duress. Here, the second member of Wat's dyad, "the hook," had its day. A person undergoing reeducation could in fact be spared the actual experience of terror: "The *real* confrontation with the investigator is not necessary. . . . It is sufficient for him to be omnipresent *in effect*. It is sufficient if the man in the street notices gaps in his environment that appeared during the night."[38] Prison camps indeed served as educational institutions; but rather than educating the inmates (who had already been written off), they shaped the thought and language patterns of the millions living *outside* them.

The next step was the reduction of signs to signals: that is, the lowering of their semiotic rank. Symbols were no longer to function as symbols but as stimuli conditioning behavior.[39] Praise of the dictator was to call forth immediate applause; standard formulas of denunciation were to provoke an explosion of hatred. Both reactions would be sincere since individuals, as well as collectives, needed violent emotions, as well as a sense of participation in order to avoid total psychological collapse in a hallucinatory universe.[40] In fact, the categories of sincerity and insincerity lost their applicability here, and the world of empty signs obtained sacral dimensions. The leader's pronouncements were interiorized at the level of the latter-day superego. The outcome was thus a profound semiotic psychosis.

Since an authentic work of art cannot be created employing a depraved, degraded language, socialist realist art, in Wat's view, was a contradiction in terms. (This pertained to all art—to literature, visual art, music, and the rest—since all sign systems were perverted by totalitarianism, if in varying ways.) The function of socialist realism was purely instrumental. Writers and artists were to combat the entropy caused by semantic arbitrariness by creating a quasi-reality and *"restoring to words . . . their old natural emotional auras."*[41] In this way, a semantic Frankenstein was born: empty signs were furnished with a pseudo-content that, in extreme cases, could inspire heroism and sacrifice.

Yet art was, at the same time, the only thing that could initiate a semantic revolution and so promote healing of the psychosis. In Wat's words, the reinterpretation of language was the most compelling task of literature in Communist countries. He had in mind not formal innovations—at least, not only such. His goal was more challenging if, in a sense, simpler: to promote a return to former, nonperverted language and its natural semantics.

Wat saw the way back as starting with what he called "winking words," a phenomenon characteristic of all Communist countries but perhaps most pronounced in Poland. These were expressions and statements that outwardly followed the rules of the mandatory ideological discourse but were used for smuggling politically dubious messages. Wat had practiced the art of double entendre in his review of Kruczkowski's *The Germans* and in "Anti-Zoilus." Externally like Stalinist exercises in the reversal of meaning, it was actually their opposite. It was free of the former's schizoid qualities, comprising instead a refined play on differences between direct and figurative senses—a game that sharpened writer's and reader's minds, making both less susceptible to Stalinist reeducation. In this, the Great Deceiver was himself deceived.

True, the game sometimes became dubious, a first step to capitulation. But as a rule, it aimed—and succeeded—at reinstating common sense and natural meanings under the guise of the Stalinist perversion of meaning, not vice versa. It was practiced originally by former anti-Fascists of the 1930s who joined the postwar mainstream in the hope of humanizing the regime. (Many people connected with the *Forge* belonged to this category.) Later, writers of the younger generation such as Sławomir Mrożek transformed the game of "winking words" into a full-fledged Aesopian language, with profoundly liberating effect.

In Russia, where Stalinism had more time to take root and was imposed more forcefully, Aesopian language did not develop to such a significant degree.[42] Nevertheless, it was Russian literature, in the persons of Pasternak and Solzhenitsyn, that completed the task, overturning the Stalinist semantic revolution and restoring natural meanings in full. Both Pasternak and Solzhenitsyn directly continued the literary tradition of the nineteenth century. In Wat's view, one might have expected a resurrection of the baroque in Russia, given that it had flourished there in the seventeenth century and had influenced writers of the 1920s such as Pilnyak. But, in contrast to Poland, where the baroque was amply echoed in the literature of the thaw, it did not thrive in Russia,[43] its place being taken by "immediate, cathartic Realism."[44]

Wat's discussion of Stalinist language was far from scholarly, being neither precise nor exhaustive, and its weak points stand out. Wat was not very attentive to the links (and differences) between Stalinist discourse and other kinds of Marxist discourse, often treating the former as something that had appeared in full armor directly from Stalin's brain, as Athena from Zeus's head. His juxtaposition of Stalinist language with totalitarian languages of non-Marxist provenance leaves much to be desired. It could also be argued that Wat's reduction of Stalinism to the language that embodied it was a poetic overstatement; for there is little doubt that numerous extra-linguistic factors contributed to the development of the Communist way of life. Finally, Wat, like many Sovietologists before and after him, ascribed virtual omnipotence to "the key and the hook," thereby exaggerating the staying power of Stalinism. His own resistance to its doctrine and terror was one of many proofs that the Stalinist phenomenon would not necessarily be long-lived.

Be that as it may, Wat carved out a particular niche of speculation in his essays—a niche hardly occupied, at the time, by any existing discipline. Located at the intersection of linguistics and philosophy, as well as several other branches of learning, including theology, his discussion was an early attempt to develop a new approach to the unique social phenomena of the twentieth century. Wat's approach could be termed proto-semiotic. Before Wat, there had been only a few attempts to analyze totalitarian society from the perspective of language: among them, Victor Klemperer's notes on Nazi language entitled "Lingua Tertiae Imperiae,"[45] the famous essay on "newspeak" appended to *Nineteen Eighty-Four* by George Orwell, and some chapters in *The Captive Mind* by Czesław Miłosz. With the possible exception of Klemperer's essay, they were as devoid of scientific rigor as Wat's work. It should also be noted that Wat predated, if only by a few years, the birth of the modern theory of sign systems, which approached the same problems in a more methodical way. There are numerous resemblances between his insights and the arguments of semioticians such as Umberto Eco and Roland Barthes, who studied contemporary techniques of persuasion and rhetorical manipulation, the clichés and mythologies of everyday life, and, in general, the tyranny of (not necessarily totalitarian) discourse. Wat can easily be placed within the framework of deconstructionist trends, which attempt to demystify language as a strategy of power—though his critique of totalitarianism also points to the excesses of deconstruction, with its reversals and undercutting of meanings.[46]

As for concepts and ideas that parallel Wat's thought, the Russian semiotic school should once again be mentioned; its representatives shared with Wat the experience of life within a totalitarian universe (Western scholars' obvious good fortune in escaping such an experience may also be construed as their limitation).[47] Thus, the concept of a secondary semiotic system, developed by Lotman and his colleagues,[48] can help to elucidate Wat's analysis of Stalinist language. In totalitarian states, the secondary system of ideology, founded on the primary system of natural language, tends to replace it and, at the same time, to eliminate other semiotic systems. This secondary language is closed and exempt from all criticism: there can be no appeal to a metalanguage or another language outside "our" own. All such "foreign" languages are proclaimed incorrect and, moreover, fraught with magical, dangerous power: they are repressed by strict censorship and, theoretically, must cease to exist. To use Lotman's terms, linguistic pluralism (a necessary condition for a living, developing culture) is replaced by monolingualism; or, in the terms of Bakhtin, dialogue yields to the monologue of the triumphant power. All speakers are confined by a single sign system with claims on universality. Its isolation from rival sign systems facilitates the overturning of values, which parodies the liberating practice of Bakhtinian carnival.[49]

Wat's praise of art as the main, if not the only, way to return to natural meanings and values may sound exaggerated, but it contains a measure of truth. It should also be pointed out that Wat's own art became a means of escape from the deadly grip of Stalinism. His constant argument with himself, his setting the same ideas in different contexts, thereby changing their hue and impact—in short, the multi-voiced quality of his writing—was the very opposite of the monolingualism enforced by the leader.[50]

The essay "Nine Notes Concerning a Portrait of Joseph Stalin," written in Berkeley, stands by itself. It is unfinished: of the nine chapters planned, Wat completed only five, dealing mainly with Stalin's literary style and social policy. Yet it may be considered the best among Wat's essays.[51] An unusual interpretation of the dictator as artist, it is one of the most convincing studies of Stalin ever written. As already noted, Wat's approach to Stalin testifies to an at least partial, if unconscious, identification: the poet, master of signs and meanings, confronts his opposite and twin, the Great Perverter and Depraver of signs.

"Nine Notes" abounds in unique and fascinating observations concerning

Stalin's style, cultural background, and literary antecedents. Wat traces his links with folklore, in particular Russian folk epic, which paradoxically draws Stalin the writer close to Mayakovsky (whom he hardly understood). The formal, scriptural framework perceptible in most of Stalin's works makes him a counterpart to another all-powerful Russian ruler who indulged in writing, Ivan the Terrible—a better stylist, one must concede. There was also the strong influence of pre-revolutionary Russian bureaucratic discourse, as well as Russian nineteenth-century literature, which Stalin knew very well. Wat goes so far as to hint that Stalin may have shaped the Soviet totalitarian system, perversely, following the precepts elaborated by the negative characters of Dostoevsky and Saltykov-Shchedrin.[52]

Wat also dwelt at length on Stalin's humor, which, for all its trivality, masterfully utilized the semantic ambivalences and inversions presupposed by totalitarian discourse. Mainly for this reason, Stalin's language, mechanically transformed into dead clichés by his myriad followers, never lost its energy when employed by Stalin himself.

Through skillful manipulation of semantics and exploitation of all kinds of corrupted meanings, paralogistic arguments, and empty signs, Stalin was able to enforce an unprecedented social system in which he mediated all communication. One of the most interesting aspects of Wat's analysis pertains precisely to Stalin's role as intermediary, perversely reintegrating atomized society. By contrast with Milovan Djilas, Wat denied the existence of a "new class" of bureaucrats in the USSR before Stalin's death. In his view, Stalinism aimed at the destruction of *any* collective bodies, whether existing or only coming into being. The unifying impulse was furnished by the dictator, and only by him. "The first principle: where two are gathered together, there am I in the midst of them. . . . Brother becomes brother, husband becomes husband, neighbor becomes neighbor, colleague becomes colleague, son becomes his father's son not directly, immediately, yet through the Party, that is, through the incarnation of Stalin. This system of the 'third present' found its symbol in the person of Pavlik Morozov, who denounced his parents, caused their execution and, after being himself killed by his grandfather, reigns in all Soviet pedagogy."[53]

Wat's approach to Stalinism as a communicative phenomenon again and again reveals the totalitarian leader as an artful parody of God. The very striving of Stalin for impersonality and anonymity, which manifests itself in his famed "modesty," marks him out as an embodiment of nothingness.[54] As befits the Devil, Stalin acts freely; but this freedom is a cruel parody of divine (and human) freedom: "It is the highest degree of liberty on the antipodes of anarchy: his, Stalin's liberty is measured by the sum of the liberties he took away from others. From all of us."[55]

The same critique of totalitarian reason can be discerned in *My Century*, the book that did most to bring Wat posthumous recognition. Wat's memoirs give the reader much more than his essays, however. They set his critique of Stalinism in a profoundly personal perspective; like most memoirs, they refract their philosophical message through the lens of psychological crisis. In the words of Jean Starobinski:

> . . . one would hardly have sufficient motive to write an autobiography had not some radical change occurred in his life—conversion, entry into a new life, the operation of Grace. If such a change had not affected the life of the narrator, he could merely depict himself once and for all, and new developments would be treated as external (historical) events. . . . It is the internal transformation of the individual—and the exemplary character of this transformation—that furnishes a subject for a narrative discourse in which "I" is both subject and object. . . . The narrator describes not only what happened to him at a different time in his life but above all how he became—out of what he was—what he presently is.[56]

My Century—together with *Diary without Vowels* and *Scraps of Paper in the Wind,* which should be considered its indispensable appendices—concentrates on just such a radical change in Wat's life, on his internal transformation against the background of history and against history. Like *Pug Iron Stove,* it is the story of a self. But unlike *Pug Ivon Stove,* it does not make use of confused surrealist imagery or openly violate the rules of narrative: quite the opposite, it proceeds in a realist manner, ostensibly aiming at historical truth. Nevertheless, a similar metaphysical framework may be discerned in the poem written by the young Warsaw futurist and the book dictated by the ailing émigré on the verge of suicide. *Pug Iron Stove* documents the hazardous adventures of a self in the face of nonbeing on a quest for salvation that is eternally denied, whereas Wat's memoirs present the history of a self tempted by totalitarian nothingness and almost reduced to anonymity, yet finally regaining identity—which does not necessarily equal salvation—by sheer force of conscience and reason.[57]

At the same time, external events that affected the narrator's life are pictured amply in *My Century.* Wat's struggle with history takes place in concrete circumstances described with verve and perspicacity. He dwells on three unusual loci of life: first, the colorful artistic, literary, and political milieu of prewar Poland; second, the rapidly disintegrating society of Lwów under Soviet occupation; third, the "counter-world" of numerous prisons where the narrator undergoes his rite de passage. In Proustian terms, the first two belong to the realm of *le temps perdu,* the third to the sphere of *le temps retrouvé.* Having lost himself in a universe of false values, the narrator restores his personal wholeness in an antiuniverse that imposes ultimate isolation yet calls for the establishment of authentic contacts between human beings.

Wat's memoirs are a veritable mine of information for both Polonists and Sovietologists, and it is no wonder that they generated quite a stir in the literary and academic world when they first appeared. Like all memoirs, *My Century* is not devoid of bias and factual errors, many of which were immediately noted either by critics or by Wat's fellow survivors; moreover, certain facts—and indeed entire periods—seem to have been erased from Wat's memory, no doubt for psychological reasons. Still, the information given in *My Century* is largely in agreement with our knowledge of the era. Wat's book abounds in vignettes and anecdotes which convey a sense of one of the most unusual historical dramas that humankind has played out. It also provides countless intellectual and moral portraits of the *dramatis personae,* from Soviet dignitaries to common criminals, from writers to members of the secret police, from aristocrats to beggars—not to mention numerous instances of these classes overlapping. In addition to its main topic of Stalinism, it touches upon religion, ethnic relations, literature, music, friendship, and many other subjects. Thus, it is a polythematic and polyphonic work, "all about everything," to quote Jeleński.[58] Last but not least, it is one of the most important works on the phenomenology and sociology of prison life ever written, an outstanding link in a line extending from Silvio Pellico through Dostoevsky to Solzhenitsyn.

Like any autobiography, *My Century* is problematic generically. It is situated on the border between literature and nonliterature. In the first place, there are visible traces of its oral provenance. Miłosz and subsequent editors did not erase all the lexical idiosyncrasies, anacolutha, rough syntactical structures, improvisational patterns, and repetitions in Wat's text; nor did they wish to do so. The narrator follows the chronology of his story only in the most general sense: there are endless flashbacks, digressions, and interruptions of the narrative.

In the words of Georges Gusdorf, an "autobiography cannot be a pure and simple record of existence. . . . A record of this kind, no matter how minutely exact, would be no more than a caricature of real life."[59] Autobiography involves conscious choices on the part of the writer, "who remembers and wants to gain acceptance for this or that revised and corrected version of his past, his private reality."[60] Hence it includes numerous rationalizations. Finally, autobiography becomes coherent by dint of a dense network of cross-references and allusions to linguistic, literary, and cultural memory.

While sharing these traits with all or most autobiographies, *My Century* is nevertheless distinguished by the fact that it is a work born in the process of direct communication. It is, most emphatically, part of the linguistic practice that envelops and transcends it, a segment of living speech that neither begins nor ends at the boundaries of the book. Wat addresses an other (Miłosz), who takes an active part in the creation of *My Century* as in the ancient art of maieutics—helping the narrator become aware of his latent memories, form his concepts, and articulate his thoughts. This ongoing contact with a living person who directly reacts to the narrator's confession is perceived by Wat as a safeguard against untruth. He professes a particular aesthetics (and ethics) of voice, as opposed to an aesthetics of sight: "Many of our intellectual civilization's problems, our intellectual problems, arise because people do not read aloud. An enormous percentage of literature would simply vanish if the authors had to read their works aloud, only aloud. They would be ashamed; the falsehood would be obvious."[61]

Although it is due to extra-literary reasons that Wat's memoirs are unfinished, open-endedness is in fact one of their inherent qualities. *Diary without Vowels* and *Scraps of Paper in the Wind* are also open in this way, requiring the direct collaboration of the reader, who is invited to fill in the gaps and take up the lines of narration and thought, even though this is a task fraught with the prospect of failure.

In recent criticism, there has been a tendency to dismiss the factual content of autobiographies and to treat them as virtually fictional exercises in self-creation or as strictly intertexual games, in which established conventions of self-depiction are applied, played with, and subverted.[62] Such a view may be an exaggeration, but one cannot disregard the tension between the historical and the mythical in Wat's book, between the professed aim of presenting objective testimony of the author's era and life and the fact that Wat, like anyone else, must make his text conform to certain conventions. Wat was aware of the difficulties of the genre he had chosen. *My Century* includes self-reflective and self-critical passages that might be called meta-literary:

> WAT: Today we ask ourselves if the novel is possible, but we'd be much more justified in asking ourselves the general question whether autobiography is possible, as pure autobiography, memoirs, or confessions. By analogy with what is happening in physics, just as the atom has ceased to be the simplest unit, subject to no further reduction, so has the event, the fact, become incredibly complex. . . . And what's more in things that touch on the human condition, the individual, humanity in some way, opinions about facts are completely and intrinsically enmeshed in value judgments, attitudes, stances. And so an autobiography, which is supposed to present the history of a soul or the fate of a person, encounters at every step (of course, blessed are those who are not aware of this) the multidimensionality of facts that contain their own contradiction. . . .
>
> MIŁOSZ: In the past, biography held to certain conventions. And authors did not attempt to tell absolutely everything; they simply accepted the conventions and they made a selection. They knew that selection was inevitable and did not reflect badly on us. Today there is a desire to tell absolutely everything.
>
> WAT: There's simply no faith in any definite principle of selection.[63]

> WAT: The sin, the error of historiography today (I mean the best historiography, the one produced by writers) is that it confuses those two basic styles of speaking about one's times. It mixes St. Augustine with Livy. If we take Machiavelli, for example, his meditations on Livy provide tremendous

intellectual pleasure. Their line of reasoning and thought is exceptionally pure—not the least like St. Augustine's. But from Rousseau on we again see history confused with autobiography. And isn't that one of the signs of our illness? The muddying of history with biography. Isn't that a sin?[64]

Wat here touches on several sensitive issues. The facts recounted by the narrator of an autobiography are intrinsically tainted by evaluation and myth-ologization: "the illusion begins from the moment that the narrative *confers a meaning* on the event which, when it actually occurred, no doubt had several meanings or perhaps none."[65] The conventions of autobiography that, prior to the twentieth century, enabled the narrator to keep his narrative under control have now loosened; consequently, mythologization is no more confined within limits prescribed by the genre. Autobiography is an attempt to structure one's being in time, but the lack of strict principles of selection leads to arbitrariness and chaos. The delimitation of biography and history, at least in modern writing, is all but impossible. Contemporary theory of autobiography has expounded this dilemma in philosophical terms: "If autobiography is in one sense history, then one can turn that around and say that history is also autobiography, and in a double sense: the makers of history, or those through whom history is made, could find in their autobiographies the destiny of their time achieved in action and speech; and the writers of history organize the events of which they write according to, and out of, their own private necessities and the state of their own selves."[66]

Wat deals with the predicament of the autobiographer in a specific way. Rejecting most of the age-old conventions of the memoir genre, he nevertheless consciously and emphatically applies certain principles of selection. One of the most noteworthy features of *My Century* is its discretion in private matters: "It's not an autobiography because, to take one example, I'm not dealing with the erotic, the sexual, things that are so important in my life and most people's lives. And besides, I don't think anyone has ever succeeded in speaking of that. Being candid about it leads to a certain degradation of the author himself."[67] The book may be read as a touching story of family love victorious over incredible ordeals, but this is decidedly not its formative quality (by contrast with Ola's memoirs). Wat focuses on the public realm, if not as one of "the makers of history," then at least as a participant, one of "those through whom history is made" and who pay for its forward advance with their mutilated lives.

Further, Wat employs in *My Century* certain conventions of the novel and drama. However freely and spontaneously the book was generated, an overall artistic pattern may be discerned in it, which influences the hierarchy of nar-rated events and, to a degree, weighs on their veracity.[68] This makes the question of the genre of Wat's memoirs even more problematic but at the same time helps the narrator to resolve the aforementioned tensions.

As we have seen already, Wat emphasizes the crisis situations of his life. One such crisis takes place in the early 1920s, when his disgust with his social and cultural environment provokes in him an iconoclastic revolt that proves to be spiritually unbearable. The next obvious crisis occurs in Lwów, where Wat opts for sheer survival and, consequently, a conformist stance. He is now a being fully determined by social forces, motivated solely by fear and the dictates of anonymous state power. He is saved from this indignity only by his arrest, which amounts to a coup de grace. His main spiritual crisis takes place in Saratov prison, where, exhausted almost to the point of death, Wat faces evil personified:

> One night, I couldn't sleep because of the light bulb. I heard laughter, a flourish of laughter that kept approaching and receding. A vulgar laugh, actually. . . . It was then that I had a vision of the devil. I won't even try to reconstruct that night because I wouldn't succeed. But it was then that the breakthrough occurred. . . . Well, I saw a devil with hooves, the devil from the opera. I really did see him—it must have been a hallucination from hunger, but not only did I see him, but I could almost smell the brimstone. My mind was working at terribly high revolutions. It was the devil in history.
>
> And I felt something else, that the majesty of God was spread over history, over all this, a God distant but real. . . .
>
> A strange night, very strange. I didn't sleep the entire night. And what was the laughter? It was a patrol boat. I suspected right away that there was a patrol boat out on the Volga that night that kept approaching and receding, and the laughter was its anti-aircraft alarm.[69]

Was it a "real" vision or a hallucination? Did it occur at all, or was it only imagined later? Such questions are beside the point: what counts is that it assumes a pivotal position in the artistic economy of Wat's memoirs, allowing him to structure his life. An image of the operatic Devil, chilling by virtue of its very triviality, refers, as Wat admits, to Gounod's Mephisto. Simultaneously, it attains the texture and immediacy of the visions experienced by Dostoevsky's characters: the shabbily dressed Russian gentleman in his fifties who confronts Ivan Karamazov, the small red spider that Stavrogin sees while awaiting the self-inflicted death of the girl he has seduced.

My Century is patterned on certain texts of world literature dealing with the motifs of crime and punishment, temptation and repentance, and the disintegration and renewal of the individual. In this context, Proust has already been mentioned. The narrator may also be linked with those among Dostoevsky's heroes who err and are subsequently resurrected to a new life—Raskolnikov would be the first choice here, because of his iconoclastic predisposition and the fact that his redemption takes place in prison, in the depths of Russia, and on the bank of a wide, wild river. The corresponding Polish text, as Jacek Trznadel has noted,[70] is Mickiewicz's *Forefathers' Eve*, whose protagonist, Konrad, consumed with humanist and revolutionary fervor, confronts the Devil in a prison cell, falls into his trap, and is then exiled to Russia and eventually redeemed by the suffering he shares with the people.[71]

The motif of spiritual crisis and redemption was to be given a final touch in

the never-written chapter on the narrator's revolt in Kazakhstan. But even
without this chapter, *My Century* has a clear structure founded on two opposed
movements: the loss of self and the arduous process of piecing the self back
together. The process is never finished, because the self as such is continuous
becoming; or, to put it another way, the final product is a book that embodies this
self in the process of becoming.

The contradictions that afflict the autobiographer are resolved through the
medium of metaphor. The requisite metaphor, as James Olney puts it, may be
described as the "order-produced and order-producing, emotion-satisfying"[72]
theory or myth that lends unity to the autobiography, merging personal life and
history, self and world, into a whole. Using this line of reasoning, it could be said
that Wat's memoirs revolve around two master metaphors. The first, a great
theological and eschatological metaphor, subsumes the narrator's experience
and the experience of entire peoples and countries under the concept of the
"Devil in history." The second controlling metaphor, which also has theological
connotations, is that of imprisonment.

Wat is primarily concerned with the phenomenology of the totalitarian
prison. He describes the rules and practices of the Gulag system in its several
variants with a near-scholarly precision that rivals that of Solzhenitsyn's depictions. But in Wat's writing imprisonment may also be interpreted more generally
and figuratively, as it is by Auden in his famous epitaph for Yeats. A human being
is confined by his or her condition: the social environment, the finitude of being,
time and space, disease and death. One of most obvious facts of that captivity is
the "prison house of language," which, paradoxically, may be destroyed by
language itself.

It is worth examining in some detail the literal imprisonment depicted by
Wat (and also by many other critics of Soviet "Gulag civilization").[73] A distinctive characteristic of the totalitarian prison, which makes it different from
prisons in nontotalitarian conditions, is the absence of well-defined boundaries
between prison and the outside world. No longer a microcosm governed by its
own laws, the prison becomes a center toward which the macrocosm gravitates. It
is within the prison that the laws of the macrocosm are expressed with greatest
clarity.

To begin with, Wat is inclined to see his misfortune in terms of the Romantic notion of imprisonment.[74] "All previously read descriptions of prisons come
to my mind: Silvio Pellico, the leaden dungeons of Venice, Chillon, Con-
ciergerie, princess Tarakanova,[75] Schlüsselburg."[76] But this way of looking at
things works only in rare circumstances, such as the solitary cell in Lubyanka
where Wat was held for a short time, where the perfect isolation and silence
predisposed him to meditation. More often, the opposition between "outside"
and "inside" dissolves to some extent. The totalitarian prison, although closed
and well guarded, then merges with the "big zone," which encompasses the

entire country, closed and guarded. When Wat is driven through Kiev in a Black Maria, he perceives the city as consisting almost exclusively of prisons, so much so that he loses count of them: the fifth (or maybe the sixth), which agrees to take him in, mirrors the city itself: "We drove into something almost like a town, quite extensive. The buildings were solid, heavy, well proportioned, decently kept up."[77]

The boundary between "outside" and "inside" is blurred not only in space, but also in time. One finds oneself in prison without fully understanding one's condition; the transition is gradual and diffuse. The story of Wat's bizarre arrest is a good example. Later, in Saratov, Wat marches in a column that is herded through empty streets and does not know the precise moment at which he entered the prison courtyard. His subsequent release is likewise incomprehensible; nor does it improve his situation very much.

Thus, the prison archipelago is not separate from the rest of the country. There is hardly more coercion (and perhaps less fear) in Zamarstynów than in the "free" space of Lwów where Wat is forced to contribute mendacious articles to the *Red Banner* and practice so-called self-criticism. Totalitarian confinement is brought to crystalline perfection; prison and country reflect each other infinitely. The reader observes a series of prisons, almost identical yet inserted inside one another.

But the totalitarian universe has another striking trait: although boundaries between its compartments are diffuse and the compartments themselves mirror each other, there is no communication between them. A person can cross the border, usually in only one direction; a message cannot. Conditions of life in other "Dantean circles" belong to the domain of folklore—until one enters them (and this takes place unexpectedly, for no obvious reason). In Lwów, a Georgian who had experienced Soviet prisons fifteen years before tells Wat: "They'll send you to Moscow for sure. If you are lucky, you'll end up at Lubyanka. Lefortovo is the worst. And Sukhanovka is even worse. It's in the forest. No one comes out of there."[78] More frightening information follows, leading Wat to expect that he will be tortured in Moscow. But this does not happen. Nevertheless, the world of torture is close by: passing an office door, Wat hears a woman scream, "a beautiful contralto voice."[79] The scream is the only signal that penetrates the boundary between two levels of prison experience; yet what if it was stage-managed for the sole purpose of subduing other inmates? One is not supposed to know. The all-embracing prison obtains phantasmagoric and metaphysical dimensions. Communication—the vocation of the writer—proves fatal.

The main effect of imprisonment on a human being is "mental restructuring."[80] Prison routine, depicted by Wat in precise, naturalistic detail—*My Century* includes "a rather extensive treatise on the psychology of bedbugs"[81]—

leads to a profound psychological shift. The nature of that shift, as described by Wat, is ambiguous. The communicative blockage established by the authorities is designed to crush personality. The microcosm of the prison, which is but a concentrate of the totalitarian macrocosm, applies increasing pressure to its inmates, "in order to drive the prisoner, through mental devastation and moral degradation, into a universe which is not imaginary, as people often assume, but which is fundamentally different."[82] The prisoner must become acclimatized to the distortion and twisting of meanings and the overturning of values—in short, to arbitrary Stalinist semantics. This can result in moral insanity, but also in clinical insanity, as in the case of Wat's cellmate Dunayevsky. On the other hand, sensory deprivation, the status of a prisoner as "living dead," and the very time-space continuum of the prison, reminiscent of the sacred time-space of the otherworld, may lead to an enhancement of perception and a deeper under-standing of the world and oneself. The outcome depends on the strength of the individual. Ultimately, it is determined by a metaphysical choice, similar if not identical to that posited by Kierkegaard.

My Century, like most previous books on prison experience, emphasizes the motif of prison time and its paradoxes. Wat's divagations on this topic are as fascinating as they are numerous:

> A . . . thing that is particularly hard to bear and that is experienced to perfection in Lubyanka in cells that are absolutely walled off from the world are those paradoxes of time when the present becomes incredibly distended, ex-panded like an accordion, while the time behind you, the past, contracts. It seems that the days you have behind you, the past, are only a single day, that time contracts, has little content, whereas the time ahead of you is a wasteland, totally terrifying.[83]

> The pendulum of prison time swings between agony and nothingness.[84]

This agony of time, its distension and contraction, the "pure present" of imprisonment, is accompanied by an intensified perception of harshly restricted space. Subversion of time-space configurations was, in Wat's view, an essential aspect of the Stalinist realm. In Lubyanka, this subversion reached its limits. Here, time and change were canceled. Thus, prison parodically embodied the coming state of eschatological harmony, devoid of thesis and antithesis. "Dos-toevsky has Svidrigailov imagine eternity as a room with a spider web in one corner, but in Lubyanka our room was clean and swept. But one room. Abso-lutely hygienic. No trace of any spider web."[85]

One of the main goals of Stalinist jailers was to induce in their victims what might be called a time psychosis, parallel to the semantic psychosis. Still, the ambivalence remains: "You had to be vigilant in defending your inner life in that place where everything was tidy, discreet, quiet. But was I up to the task?"[86] For those who were, imprisonment did not empty the mind but filled it with mean-ing. The limited space and the nonlinearity of time brought into play the faculty of memory and the gift of moral judgment: "And you don't know whether you are doing the judging or if it's that *judex ergo cum sedebit* in you that's speaking. . . . The highest judge, the omnipresent."[87] In prison, the narrator experiences numinous moments of spiritual growth, the widening of his psychic capabilities, communion with his personal past and the past of his entire people, be they Polish or Jewish, and, finally, restitution of his self after confrontation with the Devil in history:

> Everything was one that night. The main thing was the feeling of the oneness of the experience and my oneness with it. Before then I had felt mostly discord within myself, but that night I had such a feeling of monolithic unity, of a sort I was never to experience again in my life. As if I only became myself at that moment. That night, I truly was one, one and indivisible. It was a very long night. That night certainly transformed me and also the way I acted in prison. I have the impression that it was only after that night that I became human and was able to live in society with people.[88]

The metamorphosis is far from final, since new challenges lie ahead. (Wat's illness will constitute the next imprisonment, just as his yielding to communism in the early 1930s constituted the previous one.) But this experience leads him out of Svidrigailov's "room with a spider web" into the space of communion with the other. Here, another trait of the prison chronotope comes to the fore: the paradox of communication.

In Romantic literature, prison is tantamount to solitude, which allows the prisoner to plunge into the depths of his own soul; in Gulag literature, by contrast, the prisoner finds himself permanently immersed in alien voices. Wat depicts two kinds of prison. In the Polish, pre-totalitarian kind, the narrator is by no means cut off from the world: he communicates with his wife in sign language, receives her letters in herrings' heads, gets messages of sympathy (and gourmet food) from people outside, and so on. Nevertheless, this kind of prison is closer to the Romantic type: not without reason, Wat likens it to solitary "monks' cells,"[89] one of which is assigned to him (although he can meet his fellow inmates during an hour's walk). In a totalitarian prison, communication with the outside world is all but absent, yet solitude is likewise virtually nonexistent. "A tin can of sardines: the prisoners sit for months or years in one cell, always the same people. They know nothing about their near ones. And there is nothing except interrogation, and the prisoner faces the alternative: either the investigator or he himself has gone crazy."[90]

This "tin can" metaphor applies equally to Zamarstynów, where Wat shared 38 square feet with twenty-eight others; to the discreet otherworld of Lubyanka, where there are just three other inmates in his cell; and to Saratov, where "numerous clubs" formed in a cell containing at least a hundred prisoners.[91] Prison entails incessant presence of the other. As Jean-Paul Sartre stated in his play *Huis Clos*, this, perhaps, is the definition of Hell. But, strangely enough, Hell does not fully materialize, if only because the groups of prisoners are in continuous flux. The narrator faces "large collectives," as the narrator of Dostoevsky's *Notes from the House of the Dead* did before him;[92] he enters into social intercourse with them and adds his voice to theirs.

The all-embracing prison of Stalinist society, however, is the prison of language. Only one language is permitted, and this language is completely closed. Apt here is the famous maxim in force during prisoners' marches: a step to the side is considered an attempt to escape. In *My Century* Wat repeats most of what he says about Stalinist language in his essays, albeit with an emphasis on its numbing effect. Just as a human being is reduced to a mechanical component, so signs are reduced to stimuli with a view to annihilating human speech altogether. The Devil whom the narrator sees in Saratov, does not say a word: he simply laughs.

In the totalitarian universe, inhuman language imprisons; and, conversely, human languages are imprisoned. Stalinism consists in a monologue; the language of those silenced equals "a host of dialogues, an entire network of dialogues intersecting in an incredible tangle."[93] Most if not all of the prisoners are there because they deviated from the official discourse, and their universe remains a realm of heteroglossia. Here, the narrator meets people who become his mentors and help him to shape his thought in a continuous dialogical exchange.[94] Last, but not least, the ethnic backgrounds of the prisoners are as diverse as everything else. Ethnic languages and social jargons cross and recode each other, and unusual hybrids arise in the process.[95]

Like many texts about Gulag life, *My Century* thematizes language. Not only are the peculiarities of the prisoners' speech diligently recorded, a practice habitual to Wat even in the prewar years;[96] linguistic discussions form a considerable part of the book. Dunayevsky's amateurish exercises in etymologizing, which eventually become a symptom of his madness, have "an enormous indirect effect"[97] on Wat, inducing him to rethink his attitude to semantic nihilism. Several fascinating pages touch upon the linguistic phenomenon of graffiti and in so doing allude to the Romantic topos of the inscription on a prison wall:

> I was most impressed by philosophical maxims, which I was also to find later on in every provincial prison.

> Bud' proklyat kto vydumal nazvanie
> Ispravitel'no-trudovye lagerya.

> A curse on whoever invented the name
> Corrective Labor Camps. . . .

"A curse on whoever invented the name. . ."—anger about a name, the meaning of words, semantics. The loss of freedom, tyranny, abuse, hunger would all have been easier to bear if not for the compulsion to call them freedom, justice, the good of the people.[98]

In a vacuum of dehumanization, the lowest point is the point at which a nonarbitrary meaning is once again attached to a sign and silence overcomes itself.

In her rush "forward through space, backward in time,"[99] Stalinist Russia destroyed its nineteenth-century-style penitentiaries (which, according to Michel Foucault, were the most representative symptom of a shift in the direction of modern culture[100]) and brought back the old-style *katorga*, characterized less by loneliness and surveillance than by crowding and chaos. One may speak here of a partial restoration of the "carnival subculture" typical of the traditional, unreformed prison.[101] Thus, the Bakhtinian theme of carnivalistic renewal appears once more, even if prison is an extremely gloomy carnival indeed. At the very bottom, in the universe of the living dead, fear disappears. As in Roman Saturnalia, the system turns free men into slaves—who, paradoxically, become free. Hell becomes Purgatory, and the Babel of imprisoned languages is transformed into Pentecost.

Wat shares this mythology of prison with Solzhenitsyn and many other authors who have described the Gulag experience. Up to a point, it is precisely that: a mythology that enables them to come to terms with an absurd, hopeless situation. Yet, there is also a certain truth in the perception of prison as a sanctuary of human authenticity and dignity in a topsy-turvy world—one of those "islands, and not only islands, rocks against which all that reforging of souls was smashed to pieces."[102] Prison, in Wat's book, reveals the social and personal dimensions of a human being as they really are. Often the prisoners, like Wat's Ukrainian cellmates in Zamarstynów, share a feeling of almost mystical brotherhood: "A beautiful human solidarity reigned among them, sudden and beautiful banishment of all egotisms and egoisms. And they had absolutely nothing of the barracks spirit."[103] This atmosphere, which reminds one of the early Christians in the catacombs, is a significant factor in the narrator's overcoming of his inner crisis.

In the carnival chorus of the prison universe, one can discern the voices of ever-doubting reason, wise buffoonery, folk proverb, and also art. The passages of *My Century* devoted to Wat's reading in prison and to his listening to Bach's *St. Matthew Passion*, the sounds of which, however incredible it might seem, reached him on the roof of Lubyanka during a twenty-minute walk, are among the best in the book. Art is, for Wat, the most concentrated form of human solidarity, transcending the boundaries of space and time. Art is also definitive proof of the system's failure: "if this exists, then how ephemeral, what a nonentity, all the might of the empire must be, that might that a beautiful Polish carol says 'quakes in fear.'"[104] Finally, art is a communicative phenomenon, a manifestation of language at the peak of its intensity. And this is the domain of the narrator's freedom: in prison, he composes poems in his mind. If the Devil is devoid of language and reduced to laughter, the narrator is not.

13

Endgame: The Poetry of Exile

"Let the critics discourse on the structure of poetry, linguistic entropy, metonymy—poetry fulfills itself when it is an act of heroism. That lesson on the ontological meaning of poetry was not lost on me," Wat said in his memoirs.[1] First and foremost, he was thinking of the poems he composed and committed to memory in Zamarstynów prison. Through his ordeal, the unique nature of poetry became palpable to him: "I could detect its presence with my fingertips, even though poetry's spiritual content is perhaps even purer than that of religious experience since the latter contains psychological elements. . . . Poetry, however, can feed on those elements too, but it can also do without them. Perhaps poetry can do without everything and is a state of nirvana, not meaning nothingness, but, on the contrary, the highest fullness."[2]

These words pertain equally to the poems that Wat wrote in his last years. In his slow descent towards death, he was deprived of his natural environment, the context of his native language, and hope: the result was poetry hovering on the verge of silence, purified of everything but its self.

The alienation of exile is a paradigmatic motif in Polish letters. In the nineteenth century, four of the most outstanding Polish Romantic poets—Mickiewicz, Słowacki, Krasiński, and Norwid—chose the fate of an émigré. In the twentieth century, the experience of emigration was repeated by major literary figures such as Miłosz and Gombrowicz, as well as by lesser figures such as Lechoń and many others, including, for a time, Tuwim and Słonimski. In the modern period a similar fate befell the literary people of almost all Eastern European countries, as well as Germany and Spain. What makes the Polish case unique, however, is the continuity between the nineteenth and twentieth centuries. In Poland, the very concept of the poet became almost conterminous with the concept of the "exiled one" in the mind of the reader.

Needless to say, the reality of emigration never entirely conformed to the elevated exilic myths. In the following excerpt from a letter of 1 March 1964 to another Polish émigré, Józef Wittlin, Wat is only repeating Mickiewicz's complaints of a century earlier: "[My decision was] not easy, but necessary. I was in constant agony there, I could no longer exist under communism, even if it were mollified and human with respect to me. Yet here bitterness is never lacking, and while I observe, for example, Russian émigrés, I am becoming convinced that this is a Polish quality. . . . To impede life for each other, to make it more repugnant and flavor it with bitter condiment. Yet, while there is perhaps no ethnic group less fit for emigration than Poles, malicious fate forces them to emigrate in the greatest numbers."[3]

There was another problem that disturbed Wat far more than the proverbial émigré squabbles: namely, the rupture of ties with his readers in Poland, whom he valued all the more in that he had found them so late in his life. As a result, Wat's poetry became mainly, if not exclusively, a dialogue with himself. Yet the lack of an immediate audience did not deprive him of the "providential reader," to use Mandelstam's phrase.[4] Moreover, it contributed to Wat's originality. He was as far as anybody from the traditional image of a Polish émigré poet as a prophet and leader of his people promoting a feeling of identity and granting a Messianic hope. Nor was he inclined towards the kind of nostalgic, emotional poetry that one finds in Mickiewicz's *Pan Tadeusz* and, to some extent, in Czesław Miłosz. Wat's last poems developed the metaphysical tradition present in his entire postwar poetic work; they were primarily analytical, examining the phenomenon of exile in philosophical and moral terms.[5]

Wat was always an alien in one way or another—a Jew among Christians, a Christian among Jews; a man imprisoned in prewar Warsaw for his Communist views and in wartime Alma-Ata for challenging the Soviet authorities; an iconoclastic futurist in a traditional cultural setting and an avowed enemy of socialist realism in the literary milieu that had disgracefully yielded to Zhdanovist precepts. A relentlessly eccentric soul, forever marginalized and excommunicated by society, his experience of exile began while he was still on his native soil; and he remained an outsider in both France and the United States.

Wat's anomalous situation in the Polish exile community deserves to be discussed in some detail. Politically, as well as aesthetically, Wat was attracted most by the circle of *Culture*, which itself consisted of outsiders.[6] However, even Wat's relations with *Culture* and its editor Jerzy Giedroyc were ambiguous and marked by bitterness on both sides.[7] To make matters worse, Wat found himself in a chronological "no man's land."

The *terminus a quo* of Wat's emigration cannot be established with certainty. His first long stay in the West already had the flavor of exile. Typically exilic moods and motifs are found in many of the poems included in his book of 1957, especially those relaying his impressions of Italy and France. Wat's transition to the status of exiled poet remained reversible for a long time. Such a situation was not uncommon in the nineteenth century, but was less usual—and, in the view of many émigrés, improper—in the twentieth. But, it is relatively unimportant where one locates the start of Wat's exile, whether in 1955, 1963, or some year in between, since leaving Poland for the West was a rare occurrence during this entire period and contributed to Wat's social and psychological isolation.

The first wave of Polish postwar émigrés consisted mostly of people who had fought the Nazis in Western Europe and refused to return to their native land after the Communist takeover. The second wave followed only in 1968, as a result of an anti-Semitic campaign conducted by the Polish authorities; while the third wave consisted primarily of activists in the Solidarity movement, who were cut off from their country by martial law in December 1981. Each of these groups had its own distinctive physiognomy. Wat did not belong to any of them, a fate he shared with Miłosz. But, by contrast with Miłosz, he did not live to see the second wave, which included many of his former acquaintances, or the third, which included many of his readers and admirers. Because of this, as well as because of his nonconformism, Wat, who had been an internal émigré in Poland, retained that bizarre status in emigration: "an exile among exiles," comparable to Tsvetaeva or Brodsky.[8]

Even in the strictest sense, there were two exiles in Wat's life: one in the East, the other in the West. Instead of contrasting his uprooted condition to a golden age spent in his motherland, as émigré poets usually do (and as he himself did in "Willows in Alma-Ata"), Wat in his later poems juxtaposed two layers of exilic experience. Images of Kazakhstan, appearing through images of the Mediterranean or the Pacific, impart a palimpsestic quality to many of these works. There was no exit from the layrinth. In the last analysis, exile became identified with the human condition. Far from being merely the personal misfortune of Aleksander Wat, exile and uprooting were perceived as the fate of all mankind in this totalitarian century and, moreover, as the metaphysical state of a universe that has lost contact with God. Of course, in this, Wat follows a long biblical and Gnostic tradition. But he takes the ancient paradigm and implants it into both his experience and his poetics, thereby making it his own.

A strong foretaste of exile was present already in the long narrative poem "Evening—Night—Morning" included in the book of 1957 as the coda to its fourth cycle, *Alien Places, Alien Faces*. Written in Taormina, it was about the Sicilian landscape, its people, and its mythic past, all apprehended as the epitome of foreignness. Sicily evoked an ambiguous feeling in Wat: "better just to dream about it, it's a depressing, although fantastically beautiful country," he wrote to Wittlin from Rome on 12 June 1957.[9] Like most of Wat's Italian poems, "Evening—Night—Morning" refers back to the genre of "meditation on the ruins" particularly popular in Renaissance and Baroque poetry. It was brilliantly represented in Polish letters by Mikołaj Sęp Szarzyński, whose "Epitaphium Rzymowi" (Epitaph to Rome) followed in the footsteps of an Italian humanist poet born in Sicily, Ianus Vitalis:

Look at the rings of walls, the theaters, the churches,
Turned into rubble and broken columns:
They are Rome. . . .
Look, what tricks Fortune plays. What was immobile,
Is in decay, what was in movement endures.[10]

Wat's poem elaborates essentially the same motif. The poet enters an alien
world that is holy yet decayed. This is the realm of death, where only the
impervious universal rhythm persists:

Zdejm sandały. Te kamienie	Take off your sandals. These stones
święte są. Martwa jaszczurka	Are sacred. A dead lizard
legła jak klejnot z nieba rzucony.	lies as a jewel thrown from the sky.
Tymi schodami uciekał Orestes.	By these steps Orestes fled.
W łodzi z rudymi żaglami	In a boat with brown sails,
Erynie ścigają go. . . .	the Erinyes pursue him. . . .
Królestwo nocy! Nim księżyc	The realm of night! Until the moon
wzejdzie—	rises—
Królestwo nocy! Wszechświat się	The realm of night! The universe
kurczy	contracts
ale królestwo nocy się rozkurcza.	yet the realm of night dilates.
Skurczu-rozkurczu rytm wiekuisty.	The eternal rhythm of contraction
I tak pulsuje co jest i co nie jest	and dilation.
w Zgodzie.	And thus throbs what is and what is
Poza tym jest Niezgoda.	not
	in Concord.
	The rest is Discord.

The poem is supplemented by an extensive commentary in prose, in the
manner of T. S. Eliot. The matricidal exile Orestes is dismissed in the commentary with a disregarding gesture (which in fact emphasizes his pivotal role in the
poem): "The story of Orestes is still remembered, so there is no need to summarize it. As far as is known, Orestes never visited Sicily." Concord and Discord are
defined as "the basic concepts of the philosophy of Empedocles." Concord, or
Love, is the force of union, whereas Discord, or Hatred, the force of division,
breaks the unity established by Concord until everything becomes individual.
The substratum of Concord is water, whereas the substratum of Discord is fire.
The two serve as a counterbalance to each other, alternating in an endless
cycle.[11] It should be noted that Wat inverts the Empedoclean conceptual framework, bringing it into line with the Gnostic motifs of the pleroma and its loss,
unity, and individualization. Concord in the system of Empedocles provides the
impetus for combination and is conducive to the development of all higher
forms; Discord breaks the resulting complex structures, so giving rise to an

amorphous state.[12] In Wat's commentary (and in the poem itself) the opposite takes place. Moreover, there is a certain ambiguity with regard to Discord. On the one hand, it is one of the two forces that maintain the "eternal rhythm of contraction and dilation," life and death; on the other, it is situated beyond the universal rhythm of nature. By dint of some paradoxical logic, both "what is and what is not in Concord" participates in the balance of the universe, whereas Discord does not.

The title of the poem connotes a passage through darkness to a joyous return of light, that is, life. Yet, Wat's poetic meditation retains its somber tonality to the very end. The wanderer belongs to the realm of Discord and gives it a voice. He is unable to escape his past: his encounter with history, *sacrum*, and myth only intensifies his predicament.[13]

It is worth looking at the poem (only two stanzas of which have been given above) more closely. Written in free verse, it oscillates between the oneiric and the ironic mood. Visionary images of the Sicilian landscape alternate and merge with scenes of daily life in contemporary Taormina. Lexical rarities coexist with a conversational tone, mystical symbols and allegories with reportage; the artificiality of poesis docta competes with the straightforward idiom of modern poetry. The internal rhythm of the poem is created by a repetition of motifs and passages that are transformed in accordance with the movement of time: the snows of Etna becoming red and then gray at sunset, a deer and a wolf running out from the ruins of the Greek theater and wandering through the town, fishermen leaving for the night's catch and returning, a naked baby lying in the shrubs "as in a wicker basket." Most such passages are fraught with mythic allusions, even if they are only vague and sometimes contradictory. Eras overlap, as Greek imagery mingles with Judeo-Christian and the temple of Apollo, to which Orestes comes, is transformed into the San Pancrazio church that is built over its foundation. In a line that is repeated four times in varying forms throughout the poem, the lamps of Taormina are transformed into ampules of blood, and vice versa. This line is striking by dint of its multilayered symbolism; it refers at once to the blood spilt by Orestes; the melted rock of Etna, where Empedocles perished; the blood of St. Januarius, which is preserved in an ampula in Naples; and the trivial artifact of modern civilization. The Erinyes become "wild Buicks with headlights turned on," and black-clad Demeter, looking for her daughter, is transformed into a black beauty from an Oklahoma music hall—the only fictional person in the poem, Wat states emphatically. It is hard to tell what is going on here: whether we are dealing with an ironic subversion of myth or an oneiric ennobling of everyday existence such that archetypes shine through.

Two main narrative lines are closely interwoven, one of which concerns the fishermen on their night trip (Luigi is going to sea for the last time). The nightly experience reflects the universal rhythm of Empedocles. The monotonous eleven-syllable lines, striking sound organization, and abundance of repetitions should be noted.

Płomyczki w ogrom wkroplone ciemności na morzu drgają maleńkie czółenka. . . .	Small flames sprinkled into the enormity of darkness little boats tremble on the sea. . . .
Królestwo nocy żyje z naszych śmierci każda śmierć nasza jej obszar poszerza. Ogrom królestwa rybaków przeraża. . . . Każda śmierć nasza jej obszar poszerza, nawet śmierć w ratach, z której się budzimy do świata złudzeń, pod słońce pozoru, w ciągłej pulsacji nocy i dnia.	The realm of night lives by our deaths our every death widens its area. The realm's vastness scares the fishermen. . . . Our every death widens its area, even the pro-rated death from which we wake up for the world of illusions, under the sun of irreality, in the permanent throbbing of night and day.

The force of union is symbolized by the expanse of the nightly sea (note the onomatopoeic sequence *poszerza—przeraża—poszerza,* in which the ends of the lines, saturated with sibilants, iconically represent the foaming crests of the waves); the force of division, the substratum of which is fire, by the "small flames" of the boats, which find an echo in the electric light bulbs of the city. "And thus throbs what is and what is not in Concord."

"The rest is Discord." The second narrative line concerns Orestes, the "blood-stained man" of the *Eumenides.* Throughout the evening, night, and morning, he strives in vain for the purification that would allow him to reunite with his people. His mad flight infringes upon the universal harmony. The rhythm of the passages about Orestes presents a contrast to the rhythm of the seascape:

Gdy matkobójca wbiegł do miasteczka, Erynie długą zmęczone podróżą padły na skałki. . . .	When the matricide ran into the town, the Erinyes exhausted by a long journey fell on the rocks. . . .

The variable length of the lines and flexible metrical pattern, which appear whenever the narrator is telling of Orestes, clearly allude to Greek tragedy[14]— and indeed, the ruins of the Greek theater in Taormina play a conspicuous role in the poem. The tragic Greek chorus becomes in Wat's hands a boisterous chorus of poor women from a contemporary Sicilian city:

Szwaczka Giovanna śmieje się, śmieje się matka jej wdowa, śmiech kobiet pluszcze jak fala jonijska.	Giovanna the seamstress laughs, her widowed mother laughs, the laughter of women splashes like an Ionian wave.

The story of Orestes gives narrative form to all the issues of guilt, alienation, and uprooting that are crucial for Wat's exilic poetry. In the tragedy of Aeschylus, Orestes, who killed his mother, Clytaemnestra, in revenge for his father's murder, wanders over land and sea pursued by a troop of the Erinyes. Tormented by the deeds of his past, Wat easily identified with Orestes. Like him, Wat fled from city to city and faced the prospect of never returning home. Sicily, a profoundly alien land saturated with mythic resonances, could not but be conducive to this identification.[15] Moreover, in psychoanalytical terms, Orestes the matricide symbolizes the émigré anguished by the rejection of his motherland and the danger of losing his *Muttersprache*.[16]

The contrapuntal development of the two themes in "Evening—Night—Morning" does not lead to any clear resolution. The fishermen participate in the ongoing movement of nature, the supposed death of Luigi being no more than an element in the circular pattern of annihilation and renewal. But for Orestes, there is no renewal, nor even death. He roams the streets of the town, while the Erinyes take a short rest on the rocks where they have spread out the blood-stained cloth, as part of their gradual transformation into the laughing women presided over by "Giovanna the seamstress." During the night, Orestes commits a new crime: he sleeps with a black beauty, then strangles her, since "throats had always fascinated him." When, in the silver and gold of the morning, a blind hunter with a bow and a lyre—perhaps Apollo Archagetas, patron of the earliest Greek colonists in Sicily—appears, it is "too late for purification":

W czarne płótna obleczone odpływają Erynie. Orestes z nimi. Żegnaj Orestesie. Boże uwolnij od grozy istnienia.	Clothed in black linen, the Erinyes sail off. And Orestes with them. Farewell, Orestes. O Lord, liberate us from the horror of existence.[17]

The narrator's statement, "The path between sin and repentance is obstructed by a cliff similar to that of Tarpeia," is supplemented by a poignant ironic comment: "Everybody knows this by experience." The experience, of course, is Wat's. The modern age disproves both Empedocles and Aeschylus: the Erinyes cannot be laid to rest, Concord and Discord cannot be reconciled and integrated in a universal scheme of being—except, perhaps, by creating a poem in which they have their preordained place.

The oneiric and metaphysical patterns of "Evening—Night—Morning" are further developed in *Mediterranean Poems*. This book was produced in record time: Wat wrote the texts in Cabris and Vence between January and April 1962; they were given to the printer that August and reached readers in November.[18] The edition numbered 2,250 copies, which, for a book of poetry in Poland, was unusually high. This may have been because the authorities, aware of Wat's intent to become a political émigré, wanted to prevent the looming scandal by persuading him to remain loyal. However that may be, Wat reckoned with the prospect of his *Mediterranean Poems* being confiscated and planned a new edition of the book abroad, under the auspices of *Culture*. But there was no need to implement that plan, and Wat's draft of a preface to that unrealized edition, written on 27 January 1963, remains in his archive. It is of considerable interest, however, since it explains the circumstances under which the poems were created, as well as much of their imagery:

> I spent the winter of 1962–63 in a locality, the description of which the reader will find in the poem [*Songs of a Wanderer*] and its commentary. Before my eyes spread a panorama as extensive as it was violent: the distant expanse of the sea, chains of bare mountains, as well as forested hills and ravines, the abodes of rocks and people, and all this in a poignant tonality of ceaseless erosion, of living and inanimate matter growing old, of a descent towards decay, degradation, death—and I was particularly sensitive to this tone and mood because of the verdict of my years and erratic fate. Elsewhere, degradation and old age appear before us in a foul shape, on muddy roads. Here, however, they were fully present in beauty, a poignant beauty, in splendor and attraction, in the sadness and haughty glory of sublimity.[19]

A dissonance once again intruded on that harmonious if contradictory universe. Wat was in the midst of writing his book on Stalinism, which brought him back from space to time, from the metaphysics of nature to the agony of history:

> Anyhow, I undertook that difficult, penitentiary work (and I'm still far from its conclusion), and just when the poem already germinated in me as a yet vague mixture of meanings, impulses and language, I received from Paris the bulky volume of the French report from the XXII Congress of the [Soviet] Communist party.[20] . . . I would not advise anyone to take it into their hands. A couple of months later I got the Polish variant: expurgated of the most ignominious, juicy words, it does honor to Polish Communists and their feeling of elementary decency. The French edition . . . gives a measure of the impudence and baseness of those responsible for it: leaders, editors, translators, indeed, of proofreaders.[21]

Thus, *Songs of a Wanderer* developed as a meditation on ontology and history.[22] The Demiurge of the visible world merged with the Soviet totalitarian dictator, a metaphorical amalgam characteristic of Wat's mature imagination.[23]

Like many late texts by Wat, the poem is heterogeneous in the extreme. It is but one half of a diptych, whose second part, *Dreams from the Shore of the Mediterranean*, is even more obscure. I do not intend to analyze it in detail: suffice it to say, there are numerous similarities and resonances between the two poems, which may be understood as variations on a single topic, if distant ones. Yet the highly complicated structure of *Songs of a Wanderer* is obvious enough, even without taking into account its concave-convex mirror image, *Dreams from the Shore of the Mediterranean*. Wat bridges the gap between abstraction and concreteness with admirable ease: in this, he is comparable only to Eliot, who was undoubtedly his model and whose level of artistry he rivaled, albeit in a different language.

Songs of a Wanderer consists of eleven items of varying length and structure. The first song, which is echoed by the tenth, is a concise apostrophe to Wat's wife and son, written in trochaic trimeter and replete with the rhetorical questions and parallelisms typical of Polish folklore:

Komu gaj sądzony?	For whom is the garden fated?
Komu w gaju miło?	Who is happy there?
W czyich oczach tonąć?	Whose eyes will be my haven?
Kto się do mnie skrada?	Someone steals towards me.
Co zapada w otchłań?	What falls in the abyss?
Skąd się krzyk rozniesie?	A scream resounds.
Ręka czyja pnie się?	A hand gropes upward.
Podaj rękę, synu	Give me your hand, my son.
Żono, patrz mi w oczy.	Wife, look into my eyes.[24]

The garden is the traditional *locus amoenus* of ancient and Renaissance poetry, as well as of folksong. Nevertheless, from the very beginning it is placed under a question mark and undermined by abyss imagery.[25] It is the Garden of Eden, with its inescapable sequence of innocence, temptation, and fall—the latter translated into strictly physical terms: a body descending, a resounding scream, a hand groping for something to hold onto. The song becomes a stylized magical incantation. The penultimate tenth song repeats it, albeit with slight variations and in a minor key. The final lines are rearranged, hope being replaced by acquiescence:

Nie patrz w oczy, żono	Don't look at me, my wife.
Synu, opuść ręce.	Son, let my hand go.

Between, Wat depicts, on a large scale, the world immersed in evil, organic as well as historical.

The second song is the longest. It forms a strong counterpoint to the opening apostrophe by its narrative swing, disquisitional tone, and heavy, slow-moving, semi-prosaic lines. The poet, facing the prospect of annihilation, looks for a metaphysical center where God and self coincide and all change ceases. He appears to find it in the stone of the surrounding mountains and ravines.

Zbrzydzony wszystkim co żywe oddaliłem się w świat kamienny: tutaj
myślałem, wyzwolon, z góry a bez pychy będę oglądał tamtych rzeczy
zwichrzenie. . . .
Po prostu: serce kamienia. Po prostu:
sny kamienia. Być w sercu kamienia—jak ja tego pragnąłem!
W sercu kamienia, bez skażenia, które przez nasze skażone żyły
wchlapuje się w głąb naszych serc i wrasta, czyniąc je materią wskroś gnilną,
poddaną wszelkim rozkładom.
                    Sny kamienia! jak ja pragnąłem widzieć sny
kamienia, jego kamiennym wzrokiem! . . .
Co kamieniowi po bogactwie? Zapewne, w bogactwach prześcignieliśmy
kamienie, przez miliony lat naszego bytowania na ziemi. Ale im—co
    bogactwa?
W ich świecie wewnętrznym ubogo, jak to ubogo nazwiemy wyklutymi
    oczami
naszej mowy. Ale wszystko tam znaczące i czyste, wszystko tam wszystkim.
Tylko tam. Jeśli jest Bóg, tam jest. W sercu kamieni. Także—w ich
    snach. . . .
Aetas serenitatis. Zatem zbrzydziwszy
sobie świat żywych, jego urodę zwróconą do śmierci, psowaną, z martwych
wstającą w robactwo, w szczaw, w mierzwę dla chłopskich rąk, zatem
uciekłem w świat kamienny.

Disgusted by everything alive I withdrew into the stone world: here
I thought, liberated, I would observe from above, but without pride, those
    things
tangled in chaos. . . .
Simply: the heart of a stone. Simply:
the dreams of a stone. To be in the heart of a stone—how much I desired
    this!
In the heart of a stone, without the flaw which through our tainted veins
slushes deep into our hearts and grows, making them totally putrid matter,
subjected to all decay.
                    The dreams of a stone! how I wanted to see the dreams
of a stone, through its own stony eyes! . . .
What are riches to the stone? Yes, in riches we surpassed
stones during our million years' existence on earth. But what are riches to
    them?
In their inner world nothing but poverty—as we call it, using the gouged-
    out eyes
of our poor speech. But everything there is meaningful and pure,
    everything there is everything.

Only there. If God exists, he is there. At the heart of stones. Also—in their
   dreams. . . .
Aetas serenitatis. Thus, disgusted
with the world of the living, its beauty turned toward death, decaying, rising
from the dead as vermin, as acrid weeds, as manure for peasant hands, thus
I fled into the stone world.

The verse is free, with lines reminiscent of Homeric hexameter lines,
though usually surpassing them in length. Words fill the page to capacity, as if to
create an icon of an extensive, immovable, opaque substance. The next level is
created by parallelisms and repetitions, which divide the song into large compositional units, three of which relate to "the heart of a stone," "the dreams of a
stone" and "the thought of a stone," thereby revealing consecutive layers of a
stone's interior universe. The vocabulary is in part philosophical, in part naturalistic, with a perceptible tinge of Old Polish.

Stone has always symbolized cohesion, unity, strength, and harmonious
reconciliation with self.[26] It also represents the divine essence—such are the
precious stones frequently enumerated in the Bible. The symbolism of stone,
although shorn of the biblical diversity of colors, forms, and textures, is of
primary importance to Wat. For him, stone is Absolute, "a sovereign monad"
untainted by disintegration, sin, and guilt—indeed, outside all intentionality.[27]

                       Erozja? myślałem, co ona
kamieniowi? Co niszczenie jego wewnętrznych struktur? Serce kamienia
nie w strukturach i nie w stosunkach czaso-przestrzeni, ono, szczodre,
odbudowuje struktury, gdy czas, bezsilny, je niszczy. Serce kamienia
nie podległe zniszczeniu, śmierci wszystkiego, co się staje.

                    What's erosion, I thought,
to a stone? What's the crumbling of its inner structures? The heart of a
   stone
is not in structures, in space-time relations, it is generous,
rebuilding structures, while time, impotent, disintegrates them. The heart
   of a stone
does not submit to annihilation, to the death of everything which becomes.

Withdrawal into the world of stone means both liberation from deception
and unity with the metaphysical realm. Stone knows nothing of the wrenching
agony of existence and therefore provides a counterweight to the narrator's
ontological and historical exile.[28]

In Wat's poetic universe, stone is opposed, first and foremost, to skin, as the
realm of essence to the realm of becoming, of change, suffering, and decay. The
other symbolic opposition manifested in *Songs of a Wanderer,* is stone versus tree.

        Nawet drzewo, twór najdoskonalszy demiurga,
gdy jeszcze nie zasnął . . .
nawet ono, gdy—osiłek, drąży, rozsadza kamień dzikim, obrosłym
nieczystościami i robactwem korzeniem; kiedy wyciąga z ziemi matki
i bez wstydu wynosi na światło jej sny uroczne: listowie, ptactwo, ziarno,
zawsze gotowe ku odlotom, ku wirowaniu, ku frenezji!—nawet drzewo,
powtarzam, najpiękniejszy z pomysłów demiurga na krawędzi zaśnięcia—
nawet ono, cóż ono może kamieniowi?

        Even the tree, the most perfect creation of the demiurge
just before he fell asleep . . .
when, like a strong man, it wedges into the stone and splits it apart
with its savage, dirt-covered, worm-covered root; when it pulls out of
    Mother Earth
and shamelessly brings to light her magic dreams: leaves, birds, seeds,
even the tree, always prepared for flights, vibration, frenzy—even the
    tree—
I say again, the most beautiful creation of the demiurge while on the edge
    of sleep—
what can it do to the stone?

The tree, often identified with the poet, in general in Wat's poetry, signifies creativity and freedom and mediates between the earthly world and the heavenly world. Here it acquires new qualities: filth, aggressiveness, fierceness, as well as a magical beauty that is, nonetheless, "shameless" and suspect. Incarnation of the Dionysian principle, it belongs to the temporal realm created by the Demiurge, not to the atemporal sphere of the pleroma.[29] Thus, it participates in the universal rhythm of contraction and dilation from which stone is supposedly exempt.

But is it? The next two songs undermine the concept of stone as pure Absolute, gradually placing even stone under the dominion of the evil Demiurge. The symbolic structure is transformed. The poet slowly falls asleep with a stone under his head[30] and becomes "a stone among stones."[31] Then comes a moment of enlightenment:

                    . . . zbudził mnie zgiełk tych,
        których przeżyłem.
                    Pamiętaj! Pamiętaj!
        Nie szpalerem obstawili mnie; nie w karocy
mam minąć ich tego, co przeżył: nie suknie włożyli świąteczne
i nie wianki na ich głowach. . . .
Pamiętaj! Pamiętaj!—krzyczą: a chcą być zapomnieni.
Pamiętaj! krzyczą: a chcą wiecznej niepamięci.

                    . . . I was awakened by the din of those
        whom I survived.

Remember! Remember!
Not in a double row did they surround me: not in the carriage
of a survivor must I pass them: no holiday dresses do they wear:
no wreaths on their heads. . . .
Remember! Remember!—They shout: and they want to be forgotten.
Remember!—They shout: and they want eternal oblivion.

This is a transformation of the motif of Jacob's ladder and the converse of
the Buddhist awakening into nirvana. The self-contradictory voices of those
who perished remind the poet of his responsibility. A survivor, he must not
forget the millions of victims. "Naked, though tightly swathed in the lava /
of clay," they come from the ovens of Auschwitz, as well as from the permafrost of
the Gulag. Their voice is the voice of Discord, from which there is no escape,
into either the beauty of a tree or the purity of a stone.[32] Paradoxically, it is only
at the moment when the poet takes upon himself the guilt of the survivor that he
becomes consubstantial with the (suffering) God:

I pogubiwszy
w trudnym z gór zejściu wszystko, com wiedział, znów jestem tym,
którym jestem.

And having lost
everything I knew in that difficult descent, I am again what
I had been.[33]

Whereas the narrator loses his knowledge, stone loses its quality of eternal
stasis. It is no longer the "petrified music of creation"[34] but reveals instead its
link with infirmity and death. A disquisition on stone in the fourth song concentrates on "inanimate matter growing old," "ceaseless erosion," and "the monotonous agony of space," motifs emphasized by Wat in his preface and commentary.[35] Stone now merges with repulsive human flesh.

Nie erozja. Nie osiedla, przysiółki, dukty, drogi w przeplotach. Ale
egzema. Ale egzema ziemi, grzybica ziemi. Starzenie się ziemi. Rozpadowe
   procesy
ziemi. Śniedź na ścierwie kamiennym. Złuszczenie, parszywienie
   skrofulicznego
jej dziecięcia.

Not erosion. Not hamlets, farms, fire trails, interlacing roads. But—
eczema. But—eczema of the earth, mycosis of the earth. Decrepitude of
   the earth. Processes of the earth's
disintegration. Black blight on a stone carcass. The scaling and psoriasis of
   her scrofulous
child.[36]

The shift that takes place in the semantic structure of *Songs of a Wanderer* may be described as a passing from Parmenides to Heraclitus, from the universe of *hen ta panta* (all things are one) to the universe of *panta rhei* (all things flow). The rocks and mountains of Provence are now perceived as just one more transitory creation of the Demiurge, who assumes the mask of cruel Yahweh, appearing in the poem under the name Vengeful Hand—"A not sufficiently exact translation of '*Beyod hazoko,*' containing the idea of might and violence, but certainly of vengeance as well," Wat notes in his commentary.[37] The self-contained interior of stone is no longer contrasted to the borderline of skin: both stone and skin are afflicted by the same disease, the innumerable names of which—eczema, mycosis, black blight, psoriasis, scrofula—are but ritual euphemisms (metonymies) for leprosy, the "uncleanliness" of the Book of Leviticus. The axis of the poem's symbolic system now changes: the metaphysical opposition between the absolute and the transitory is replaced by an existential opposition between the absurd and ineradicable human dissent.

The fourth, fifth, and sixth songs deal with various facets of the world of history—or rather, with history in varying degrees of proximity, here in panoramic outline, there in close-up. The fourth song introduces a human element, a blind old woman waiting for her son to return from work. Described in detail and located in time and space (her son "has a job in Grasse, / at Grasset's perfume factory"), she is evidently a symbolic figure, though her role remains vague. She may in fact be one of the Parcae, an incarnation of destructive time and the absurdity of history. On the other hand, she is "Mat' Syra Ziemla" (Cold Mother Ziemla), an image of earth taken from Russian folklore, which Wat learned well in Soviet prisons. As such, she connotes both death and Our Lady. Her song ("And I bore you, son, for eternal dying / And I raised you, son, for painful rest"), stylized as a Slavic prayer or charm and incongruous on the lips of a Frenchwoman, brings these connotations to the fore.

The next song presents an instant photograph, as it were, a minute segment of historical time—a "pedantically realistic"[38] street scene in Cabris in February 1962. Wat marks the moment precisely (it is early February, the feast of the Epiphany having taken place less than a month before) and fills the text with numbers and names: "a fountain circa 1900," "600 km., 20 kg. load," "38 C.," Mr. Fevrard "in a smooth Aronde," a laborer "in a red Peugeot," "Monsieur Maxime." The dramatis personae include an innkeeper, some soldiers, a hunter who lost his leg in the war, and the owner of a gift shop, each absorbed in his or her daily routine. The song is patterned, to some extent, on the final section of Eliot's *A Game of Chess*, which takes place in the trivial environment of an inn, and is as multilayered as Eliot's piece. At the beginning, the embroidered skullcap of Monsieur Maxime, a local drunkard, reminds the narrator of his earlier exile in Central Asia. Images of "violet-colored mountains" and "a rider-philosopher, / a knight in tatters, girt with the scarlet / of Kashmir" overlap with imagery of Provence, as in a doubly exposed snapshot, telescoping past and present and furnishing the two-dimensional scene with historical depth. The soldiers who march in single file, releasing gas and roaring vulgarly, evoke the memory of war and the premonition of future disasters. The next layer is that of mythology. A hunter symbolizes death—a meaning made obvious in the sixth song:

Zielony myśliwy	The green hunter
z czujną lufą,	with a vigilant barrel
z psem niemową	with a deaf-mute dog
na stanowisku.	at his post.
Nie pytaj kto, wiem	Don't ask who. I've known
od dawna.	for a long time.[39]

If the "deaf-mute dog" of the hunter is a close relative of Cerberus, the demon of the pit, the innkeeper's dog, Diane, merges with her owner in the mythic image of Queen Diana Hecate Luna, goddess of sorcery and witchcraft. Hecate, in turn, overlaps with the Queen in *Alice's Adventures in Wonderland*, who whimsically demands that her subjects be beheaded.

Here, a new stratum of meaning is introduced. Imagery of exile, agony, and execution points to the totalitarian experience. The sixth song transfers the reader from an inn to a similarly trivial environment in which the banality of evil continues its play. "Three good buddies, around a samovar with vodka and cucumbers," who drink, belch, and scribble notes on pieces of paper, do not differ in any essential way from the people in the Cabris scene. But here we are dealing with history, as "machine of hell" and "masterpiece of Satan." The drinkers are Stalin, Molotov, and Kaganovich, who look through the dossiers of their victims and sentence them to capital punishment with a scorn and thoughtlessness that rival those of Lewis Carroll's Queen (her words "Off with his head" are once again echoed here). Wat quotes almost verbatim the speech of Aleksandr Shelepin, the KGB chief under Khrushchev, delivered at the Twentieth Congress of the CPSU, in which he exposed the unsavory details of Stalinist justice. The case is that of Army Commander Yona Yakir, who, following arrest in May 1937, sent a letter to Stalin from his cell, asserting that he was innocent and would die with words of love for the great leader, the party, and the country on his lips. "Stalin wrote on this letter: 'Scoundrel and prostitute.' Voroshilov added: 'A perfectly accurate description.' Molotov put his name to this and Kaganovich appended: 'For the traitor, scum and [next comes a scurrilous, obscene word] one punishment—the death sentence."[40]

The entire scene echoes the call "Remember" of the third song, albeit in a darker mode.

Toward the end, *Songs of a Wanderer* strives for resolution of its oppositions. The seventh song is a bitter yet humorous debate on the theological question *unde malum* (whence evil)—the question Wat had discussed in Lubyanka with his companion in distress Mikhail Taitz.[41] In commemoration of these semi-Augustinian disputes, it is presented as a casual conversation between the inmates of a prison cell. The narrator's attempt to distinguish Satan, who rebelled "out of concern for man," from the Devil, who "runs errands for God"—and the absolute evil of Stalin's rule from the relative evil of Khrushchev's thaw—parodies Marxist formulas and ends in tragicomic failure:

> Złe jest poznanym Dobrem. Może
> odwrotnie. Tak czy owak, Złe to Dobre na niższym że tak rzeknę
> etapie POSTĘPU. Czemu utożsamia się Szatana z diablem?—
> abo ja wiem. Zagadka, na naszym przynajmniej etapie, ludzi
> z loszków. Dlatego siedzimy. Nasz to pech. Spytaj zresztą
> Schaffa.

> Evil is apprehended Good. Perhaps
> the reverse. Anyhow, a Good at a lower, so to speak,
> stage of *Development*. Why is Satan identified with the devil?—
> How should I know? A riddle, at least, at our stage, of people in the clink.
>   That's
> why we are locked up. Our tough luck. Besides, ask Schaff.[42]

The eighth song has the same tinge of self-irony. Its message is unambiguous: either willingly or unwillingly, the narrator participates in the trivality of evil. A victim, he also identifies himself with his tormentors: he swears obscenely, grows "muddy with drinks," plays with his cronies; his skin, afflicted with eczema, becomes like Stalin's pockmarked skin.[43] The ritual of purification, patterned after the Roman *februatio* (the action, let us remember, takes place in February, the month of the festival of expiation in ancient Rome), is unsuccessful:

> Okadź się siarką, wełną, ogniem,
> gałęzią jodłową, w jedwabiach sakralnych
> zasiądź przy lichtarzu z Seneką . . . Aetas
> serenitatis; za starości przełęczą
> pogoda. Słowa, słowa. Seneka już dawno wypadł ci z ręki.
> Marzysz, stary grzybie, marzykujesz, marzykulujesz.

> Purify yourself with censers of sulphur, wool, fire,
> fir twigs, in sacral silks
> meditate by a candle, with Seneca. *Aetas
> serenitatis;* beyond the pass of old age
> there is peace. Words, words. Seneca fell from your hand long ago.
> You dream, old fogy, you daydream, daydrumdream.

"Words, words" is a reference both to *Hamlet* and to Wat's poem "A Bit of Mythology," where it is employed in connection with the motif of disease (and burning skin).[44]

Sudden shifts of mood in this song are followed by an even more unexpected shift after its closure. The ninth song, which takes for its motto Andrew Lang's words, "It is the nature of the highest objective art to be clean. The Muses are maidens," is a virtual paean to purity and youth. Motifs of inner peace, serenity, and reconciliation with the self appear once again, now related not to the world of the stone, but to the sky, air, and trees.

This latest reversal of the poem's symbolic structure finds expression in two metonyms. In the eighth song the narrator turns, by dint of contiguity, into a "stone which does not fall,"[45] while in the ninth he becomes, synecdochically, a hand that remembers that it was once a wing. In both cases, he is suspended between heaven and earth; but whereas the stone gravitates downward, the wing connotes upward movement. In this can be discerned the archetypal symbolism of the duality of human nature.

Now the meaning of the preceding songs (from the third on) becomes clearer. The faculty of memory, which superimposes one era on another, enables the poet to create a universe in which nothing is transient. In this universe, human suffering, though unredeemed, is never senseless; the power of conscience, while revealing the guilt of the self, at the same time enables the self to ascend to a level above absurdity. Acceptance of memory, together with compassion and responsibility, also entails acceptance of anguish and a sense of one's finitude, which is indispensable for liberation. This is, in a general sense, a religious—and, in particular, a Christian—world outlook, one that has found its most powerful literary advocate in Dostoevsky; yet it is not incompatible with atheist thought, as Camus demonstrated. Wat oscillated between Camus and Dostoevsky to the very end. It might be said that for him it was art, not religion or philosophy, that mattered in the final analysis.

The ninth song ends with an oxymoronic formula that subsumes the experience of exile: "It's bitter to die on foreign soil. / It's sweet to live in France." The poem has come full circle, and the tenth song, as we know, repeats the first, introducing a note of acceptance of death. Still, the frame is violated: a last, eleventh song breaks out, resolving the unstable equilibrium of the poem in a short hymn of love.[46] It answers the unarticulated yet crucial question *unde bonum* (whence the good), thereby furnishing a necessary conclusion. It glorifies family, "the golden division of the species," the embodiment of renewal, and ends in the tonality of prayer:

Górski potoku	O, mountain stream
I dna bazalcie	Basalt beneath
Wzlotu opoko	Bedrock of flight

Domu wahadło	Pendulum-home
Serca imadło	Vise of the heart
Konwalio duszy	Lily of the soul
Ciszy kontralto	Contralto of quiet
I wierny całun	And faithful shroud.
Smutku fiolecie,	Violet—sorrow,
Gdy zima prószy.	In winter flakes,
O, ciepła ziemio	O, you warm earth
Szczytów i dolin!	Of peaks and valleys!
W doli-niedoli	In sickness and in health
Siostro moja syjamska	Siamese sister
Oblubienico.	My Bride.

This mystical outpouring is perfectly baroque; partly rhymed, full of contradictory and idiosyncratic images, it employs motifs culled from the Psalms and the Song of Songs.[47] Now, the motif of the Virgin bringing the hope of salvation is fully developed. She is mother and wife simultaneously, but also "Siamese sister"—that is, part and symbol of the androgynous self as it appears in Gnostic doctrine. She points to a coniunctio oppositorum that is beyond all names; she is also the motherland and the native tongue, both of which welcome the prodigal, exiled son.

The posthumous collection of Wat's poems that was published in Paris in 1968, the year after his death, encompassed almost his entire poetic opus, and was arranged, albeit with exceptions, in chronologically reverse order, but framed by poems from his final exile. The person responsible for its final shape was Ola, assisted by Miłosz, Jeleński, Pierre Emmanuel, and others. It was a structure that corresponded to Wat's will, and all the changes in the published texts of the poems were changes that he himself had made. Some fifty other poems written during the period 1963–67 were omitted and found their way into print only much later, mainly in *Zeszyty Literackie* (Literary Notebooks), the principal periodical of the third wave of Polish emigration of the 1980s,—for whom Wat was a veritable cult figure, and some only in the definitive collection of Wat's poetry edited by Anna Micińska and Jan Zieliński that was published in Kraków in 1992. During his last exile, Wat wrote more than a hundred poetical texts, some quite extensive. The creative upsurge that began in 1956 continued unabated to the very end, even gaining strength in the years immediately preceding his death.

The title of Wat's posthumous collection, *Ciemne świecidło,* merits discussion. It has usually been translated into English as *Dark Trinket,* but this literal rendering does not convey Wat's full meaning. *Ciemne* is indeed "dark," and *świecidło* denotes a "spangle, tinsel, trinket," which gives the title a poignant sense of "empty show." Yet this is only part of the semantic game. In interpreting the import of these two words, their appearance in at least two poems in the book should be taken into account. The first poem, with the same title as the collection, was written on 6 November 1963, on the eve of the anniversary of the October Revolution:

Platon kazał nas wyświecić
z Miasta, w którym Mądrość rządzi.
W nowej Wieży z Kości (ludzkich)
dziś Astrolog trutynuje
gwiazd koniunkcję z Marsem, oraz
z Oekonomią bied i brzydot.
Mrok zapada i Minerwa
śle swe sowy do Wyroczni.
Platon kazał mnie wyświecić
w noc bez Światłych Filozofów.
Kwiaty szczęściem oddychają,
chmura ciepło deszczem pachnie,
w ciszy słyszę swoje kroki,
idę a i nie wiem dokąd?
Platon kazał mnie wyświecić
z Miasta, w którym rządzi Zmora.

Plato decreed to throw us out
of the City in which Wisdom rules.
In a new Tower of (human) Bones
an Astrologer now considers
the conjunction of stars with Mars,
and
with the Oeconomy of misery and
shabbiness.
The darkness grows, and Minerva
sends her owls to the Oracle.
Plato decreed to throw me out
into the night without Enlightened
Philosophers.
Flowers breathe happiness,
a cloud smells warmly of rain,
in the silence, I hear my own
footsteps,
I go, and do not know whither.
Plato decreed to throw me out
from the city in which Nightmare
rules.

A joyful celebration of exile, the poem has for its immediate source text the well-known passage from Plato's *Republic*, which Wat quotes in abridged form by way of commentary. The utopia of Plato, harbinger of all proto-Communist and Communist utopias, entails a system requiring total obedience that hardly yields to either Orwell's fantasies or Shigalyov's project in its mix of perverse equality, militarism, and mental manipulation. Moreover, art is certainly not compatible with it. This passage from the *Republic* (III. 398A–B) is an unrivaled picture of institutional hypocrisy and callousness.

Then what if someone should arrive in our city who is clever enough to play all sorts of roles and to imitate anything? If he proposes to put on a performance and recite the poetry he has brought with him, we shall certainly bow to him and pay him homage, calling him sweet, blessed, and wonderful, and say that there is none like him in the city. But we shall also say that the law forbids his kind to remain in the city. Then we shall anoint him with myrrh, garland his head with wool, and send him away to some other place. For our part, and for the good health of our souls, we shall continue to employ poets and storytellers who are less amusing and more austere. They will speak in the style of the good man and will tell their stories in accordance with the rules we laid down at the beginning when we first began to describe the education of our soldiers.[48]

A human being—other than a very peculiar kind of philosopher, perhaps—would scarcely be capable of living in such a system. Banishment from Plato's city is a fortunate circumstance indeed: not without reason does Wat rhapsodize it in a dancelike trochaic tetrameter. The humorous (if ambivalent) mood is achieved, among other means, through idiosyncratic archaisms, such as *trutynuje* (considers), and outdated spelling, such as *Oekonomia*. The Old Polish word *wyświecić* means "to throw out, to send into exile." Its Slavic root, *svĭt-* relates it to the concept of light; thus, primarily, it means "to expel ignominiously by candlelight." The narrator is excommunicated from the world of enlightenment and dubious wisdom and thrown into the world of outer darkness, a world of blossom and life-giving rain. He treads diffidently, but he is happy and not alone; moreover, the owl of Minerva, the true wisdom, hovers over his head.

Thus, darkness and light exchange attributes. The Apollonian state reveals itself as a horrifying wasteland, in which the proverbial ivory tower (in Polish, "wieża z kości słoniowej") is replaced by a tower of human bones ("wieża z kości ludzkich"); and the Dionysian night becomes a source of renewal. Here, the secondary connotations of the word *wyświecić* come into play, for it may also mean "to lead out from the dark," "to enlighten, to educate."[49]

In this context, the words *ciemne świecidło* acquire several contradictory meanings. On the one hand, they could refer to the empty pretensions of the utopian state; on the other, to the narrator, the poet thrown into the night of exile, whose art, however dark, gives off light for both himself and others. This second meaning is the one corroborated by the second poem, which is addressed to noted critic and journalist Leopold Łabędź, who admired Wat's poetry while considering his essays overly metaphoric and vague.[50]

> What can I do if for you I am
> *lumen obscurum?* Believe me, in myself
> I contain my whole self as a bright point.
> Even transparent. But
>   a misunderstanding,
> semantic, today reigns over all and sundry.
>
> Yet I do not forget, my Hippolyte:
> we are both well-behaved boys
> in straw hats and white middy blouses
> with navy-blue trim, who early in the morning
> went chasing butterflies. But who, at nightfall,
> run after zigzags of lightning,
> painting, exhausted. In vain . . .

                              For not even those zigzags
will tear through Chaos! Nothing will tear Chaos
apart. It tears itself apart. Eating into
itself, piece after piece, insatiable.
            And there's nothing I can do about it,
dear friend.[51]

The poem is furnished with a motto from Hegel: "frisst der Grimm seine
Gestaltungen in sich hinein" (fury itself devours its own forms). Addressing
several of Wat's favorite themes—the perverted semantics of modern times, the
destructive passion of cognition and repentance—it defines the poet and poetry
as *lumen obscurum,* "dark light." This light, for Wat, is inextricably bound to the
chaos of the unconscious, the self-devouring fury of which is represented in the
poem iconically: the word "insatiable" breaks in the middle, is torn asunder, as it
were.

"Dark light" may be related to the Gnostic concept of primeval light
imprisoned in the material world, as well as to the archetypal symbol of the black
sun manifested in Gerard de Nerval's "El desdichado," several of Mandelstam's
poems, and in dozens of other texts, including the Upanishads, the Old Testament, the Talmud, and some medieval Christian and alchemical literature.[52] In a
particularly meaningful way, it appears in the story of Calvary, which formed the
pivot of Wat's mature poetry. The black—that is, eclipsed—sun signifies the
Crucifixion. Thus, the title of Wat's last book is a reference to his preoccupation
with suffering, sacrifice, and art and might best be rendered *Black Sun* or, more
cautiously, *Lumen Obscurum*—the Latin expression that Wat himself employed.[53]

Lumen Obscurum, as well as other late poems that were not included
therein, develops the poetics manifested in Wat's book of 1957. The metaphysical and baroque qualities here become, if anything, even more pronounced, as
does the grotesque and absurd streak of surrealist provenance.[54] The dominant
trait is one of open-endedness: thus, the border between rough draft and finished poem is not always clearly established. The unifying element is furnished
primarily by the sense of the author: employing various masks and producing
incongruous collages of alien texts, Wat is nevertheless present to the reader as
an easily recognizable "I," rooted in concrete historical and biographical circumstances. Technically, free verse is the order of the day. Only eight poems follow
classical patterns, but among them are poems that are significant: for example,
"Ewokacja" (Evocation), which treats Wat's prison experience more frankly than
ever before, and particularly "Hölderlin," a magnificent monologue by the
insane German poet, who clearly merges with Wat's own persona:

    I lifted the black lid of the harpsichord
    And tore off the strings. Until just two remain.

I will perform my farewell concert on them,
playing YES on the first, and on the second—NO.

YES—I sing enraptured for Her, the Unchangeable One,
and for you always: Nein, Altesse. . . .

One is struck by the density of allusions at the beginning of the poem. First, there are references to Hölderlin's life. As Wat notes in one of his essays, Hölderlin, in a fit of insanity, once tore half the strings out of the piano presented to him by Prince von Homburg and improvised on the remaining ones, "very similar in this way to socialist realist writers." He answered "no" to all questions, invariably adding "Sir" or "Altesse Royale," thereby mixing negation with homage.[55] The "farewell concert" most likely points to Mayakovsky, the epitome of a socialist realist writer, who developed this very motif in his pre-revolutionary poem "The Backbone Flute." In Wat's verse, however, Hölderlin plays on only *two* strings, on which he distinguishes between negation and affirmation with utmost clarity. His emphatic YES and NO clearly allude to the biblical text "But let your communication be, Yea, yea; Nay, nay: for whatsoever is more than these cometh of evil" (Matt. 5:37). This is a self-representation of the mature Wat, who makes straightforward distinctions, rejecting semantic confusion and conformism. Like a tuning fork, "Hölderlin" establishes the pitch for Wat's "farewell concert." The entire book oscillates between praise and satire, between enraptured homage to the ideal mother and bride of *Songs of a Wanderer* and an abrupt *non serviam* to the powers of evil.[56]

A significant motif of *Lumen Obscurum* is a trimming down to the essentials: black and white, plus and minus, yes and no. This may take the form of uncovering and baring. Such is the poem "Śród nocy o tej samej wciąż godzinie" (In the Middle of the Night, Always at the Same Hour), where Wat speaks of his last day, which will undress him, "taking off the rags." A more sophisticated development of this theme occurs in the poem "Skóra i śmierć" (Skin and Death), dedicated to Jan Lebenstein. "Skin and Death" starts with the words "A self-respecting skeleton never shows up stark naked" and goes on to describe a skeleton in such a way that the design of the words on the page represents this very subject from the front, an arrangement reminiscent of Lebenstein's paintings, in which bizarre, sinister semi-human figures are also usually presented in full front view.[57] Deprived of skin and muscles, the skeleton signifies a truth that leaves no room for self-deception: Wat refers here to the old topos of the Dance of Death.

Several poems in the book focus on the positive pole, the pure "yes" of being. They are usually short, like "Żmije i ważki w dobrej zgodzie" (Snakes and Dragonflies in Good Concord), which is about reconciliation with death and in which the weeping of a widow becomes a lullaby for her departed husband. A similar poem has all the conciseness of a Japanese tanka and, at the same time, of a Christian prayer:

> The super earthly beauty of things
> When the last glance falls on them: a silver
> plate on a mahogany table,
> a pink shred of clouds and sky, a twitter
> of our small bird Maciuś
> and my wife's face. Her eyes
> for the ages and ages amen.

For the most part, however, uncovering essentials means becoming aware of suffering and evil in the world. The powerful poem "Inwokacja" (Invocation) becomes a baroque dialogue between Wat and his weak, rotting, cruel body, ending on a virtually blasphemous note:

> Dano ci nadzieję zmartwychstania
> > błogosławione ludzkie ciało,
> w radość wiekuistą,
> > ciesz się ciało
> bólu. Wiekuistego.

> Thou wast given the hope of resurrection
> > blessed human body
> into the eternal glory
> > exult body
> of pain. Eternal.

The irregular syntax of these lines creates an ambiguity: the last word, *Wiekuistego* (Eternal), may relate either to resurrection and new life, in which case, *ciało bólu* would mean "body of pain," "suffering body," or to pain, in which case, "body" in the penultimate line would remain without a modifier.

Trimming the pattern of existence to its essence results in a juxtaposition of giving and taking. This is the topic of the opening poem, "Buchalteria" (Book-keeping). Life's beauty and exultation must be paid for in accordance with rules that transcend reason:

> I paid. For everything. With my body and my soul.
> For the sky, for the wind, for the stanza, for the girls' smile, even for those
> > two
> cruel hands which do not allow me to drown. True,
> the usurer's interest has accrued so much, that I'll pay not earlier
> than at the Last Judgment.

The same juxtaposition of essentials, of being and nonbeing, marks the odes, long poems in a biblical style of verse that almost obliterates the difference between poetry and prose. We have already looked at Ode III, an ambiguous paean to human skin.[58] Ode I takes for its subject Shakespeare's Prospero, who has lost both Miranda and Ariel and remains alone on his island (which Wat places in the vicinity of Sicily). Ode II, dedicated, like "Skin and Death," to Jan Lebenstein, is one more "meditation on the ruins," a typical exilic poem employing imagery from the prophetic books of the Old Testament.

> Where will I find signs of our tribal encampments,
> where do we have our wells, our roads and crossroads,
> our gates and cities, our oracles, pillories?
>
> What remained of Ur, Babylon, Nineveh?
>
> Sands have buried their wild splendor, gods
> have decomposed in mortuaries of museums,
> and their inhabitants, long ago turned to dust,
> vibrate in the sand, forever.
>
> Only the embittered longing of my heart remains . . .

The passage of time bares the skeletons of cities, just as it bares the human skeleton, stripping it of flesh and skin. History is reduced to the implacable rhythm of decay, and all that remains is alienation. This age-old motif exerts a powerful hold on Wat, merging into one his three self-images: of a Jew sharing the fate of his scattered people, of a Pole ejected from his country, and of a repentant iconoclast who longs for the unity with the universe and himself that he lost through his demonic rebellion.

Ode II belongs to a sizable group of Wat's late poems that refer directly to the Bible. As in Wat's earlier poetry, Old Testament topics are interwoven with motifs from Greek and Roman myths; but the latter now take a distant second place as Wat, in his last years, became more aware than ever of his links with Judaism.[59]

Much of Wat's imagery related to Jewish topoi is vague, sometimes traceable to Haggadic and Kabbalistic sources, sometimes rooted solely in his personal mythology. He creates quasi-biblical characters, such as a princess of Israel who looks into a golden mirror reflecting her coffin and a "shepherd from the Negev desert" who betrays his sheep and goes to the city to meditate on his death. With regard to the last, the time is far from clear: the style and mood recall the Old Testament, yet a kibbutz is mentioned, suggesting that the action may be set in modern Israel. In the poem "Na spacerze" (Taking a Walk) two women appear at "the edge of Eden, this side of the barbed-wire wall." They are "Temeh, Cain's wife, and Tirzah, Abel's widow,"[60] who discuss endlessly their husbands' row. The barbed-wire wall and the toil of Cain's sons, who, under surveillance by guards, extract gold from the biblical river Pison (Wat inserts the reference "Genesis 2:11" in the middle of the line), obviously point to modern times.

As frequently in Wat's poetry, myth turns into reality, and reality into myth. In the process, myths are, ironically, often travestied and distorted. Different eras overlap and transpire through one another. A poem on John F. Kennedy's assassination, written on 22 November 1963, starts out with two lines from Isaiah:

> Take a harp, go about the city,
> thou harlot that has been forgotten.
> When they murder the King, the infamy falls
> upon all. And the stains multiply
>   on our roofs.
>
> Thou harlot that has been forgotten,
> History of passing instants. A black sail
> arrives from overseas. The herald
> arrives in a hurry. And the signs multiply,
>   written in blood. . . .

Prophetic and apocalyptic images blend, characteristically, with Greek ones. The black sail, signifying disastrous news from overseas, comes from the story of Theseus (who, returning victoriously from Crete, forgot his promise to hoist white sails instead of black ones, thereby inadvertently causing his father's suicide); and the herald who comes running belongs to the world of Greek tragedy.

The "harlot that has been forgotten" (Isa. 23:16) is a symbol used by Wat on a number of occasions. Here it relates to time; in Ode II, it appears in the spatial context of the "world of galuth." The Hebrew word that signifies the condition of the Jewish people in the diaspora becomes, for Wat, synonymous with any experience of exile and, first and foremost, with the visible world, rooted in the Fall, which is what separated it from the pleroma. The "desert of galuth" of Ode II is localized in the alleyways and cul-de-sacs of Paris, which stink of humiliation and abuse.

> . . . in the ill-smelling alleys
> of your rues de Beausire flocks of harlots
> reproduce in every generation, they alone—O shame!—
> old civilizations;
> only here the unaging face of the Babylonian whore,
> gestures of priestesses of the Lady of Biblos,
> at the street corners a biblical prostitute—and, had
> a Median warrior hot from battle with his quiver
> and arrows stood before her, she would have led him

to a hotel as she does a neighboring shopkeeper.

So on that desert of galuth where I languish away,
day after day, I am stuck
—O shame!—
in a stinking joint, among pimps and sluts,
and in their loathsome company
I visualize myself in my city, Nineveh,
at the time of my prophet,
Jonah.[61]

Ode II is in fact an excerpt from *Small Delilah,* a narrative poem that describes sympathetically a prostitute from Lebanon eking out a living in Paris. It may be noted that Wat returns here to the imagery of his early futurist works. Rue de Beausire is a variant of Krzywe Koło (Crooked Circle) in *Pug Iron Stove,* and the prostitute herself, although depicted in a realist vein, recalls the corrupted Beatrices who people Wat's surrealist poem. She may be interpreted as yet another incarnation of Sophia, Divine Wisdom, suffering under the guise of a whore of the lowest rank.[62] Similarly, Wat's identification with the prophet Jonah is not without precedent in his early verse (where sea monsters are mentioned more than once).

Wat continues here a tradition well rooted in medieval, baroque, and modernist texts. But his mix of Old Testament imagery with twentieth-century trivia is truly unique. A good example is the poem entitled "Hymn" (Paean). It is about Berenice, queen of Palestine and amour of the Roman emperor Titus, who was at the latter's side during the siege of Jerusalem and witnessed the destruction of the city. Yet Berenice is combined with another Berenice, wife of Ptolemy III Euergetos, after whom the constellation Coma Berenices (Berenice's Hair) is named. Moreover, she becomes a relative of the young Wat, his aunt's daughter, although he becomes aware of her fate only when he reads Racine's tragedy, in August 1914, listening to the rattle of peasants' carts on a Warsaw street.

As Miłosz has noted, Wat's mature poems always start with a "real place and real event, transmuted, elevated, frequently nobilitated by humor."[63] Their texture is extremely dense. The oscillation between straightforward and ironically distanced narratives, the overlapping of spatiotemporal layers, and their erudite allusions frequently renders them unintelligible without an autobiographical key, sometimes provided by Wat himself, either next to a poem or concealed in his memoirs or essays, and sometimes lost.

The motif of the Passion now assumes a particularly prominent place. Christ becomes not simply one among many mythical and historical masks employed by the poet, like Orestes and Jonah, but the very pivot of his meditations. Wat's treatment of the Gospels remains unorthodox, often as not border-

ing on heresy and blasphemy.[64] Whereas for a metaphysical poet, the Crucifixion is the paradigm of freely accepted sacrifice and obedience unto death,
crowned by resurrection, for Wat, it primarily symbolizes senseless and never-
ending suffering. Passion scenes merge with other depictions of God inflicting
absurd pain. In a poem "Tej znów nocy . . ." (This Night Again . . .) God,
whose taboo name is signified by only two letters, P.B., comes in the Kafkaesque
form of an immense earthworm and strangles the narrator, whose final statement
"You know: whatever He does, He does out of love for me" has a preposterous ring.

As we saw earlier, the crucified Christ was, for Wat, a symbol of the Jewish
fate. Christ's kenosis, his self-abasement in becoming man, furnished a figure for
both metaphysical and historical exile. Finally, the Crucifixion expressed and
signified in its very shape the extreme tension between the opposite poles of
death and life, immanence and transcendence, human transgression and divine
grace. It possessed the ultimate ambivalence sought by Wat.

References to the Passion theme in *Lumen Obscurum* and other late poems
of Wat are variegated and related to different experiences. "Pejzażyk 1939" (A
Miniature Landscape, 1939) takes up a traumatic memory: the narrator mockingly crucifies himself on a pine tree and later considers the gesture to be the
cause of his misfortune. A short rhymed piece entitled "Skoro wiesz. . ." (Since
You Know . . .) speaks of three crowns that the poet must accept: an iron crown
signifying pain, a leaden one signifying remorse, and finally, like Christ, a crown
of thorns. The poem "Gdy drżał w śmiertelnych potach . . ." (While He Trem-
bled Agonizing in Sweat . . .) blends Christ's experience with the experience of
the apostles, among whom Wat sees himself, whose dream is abruptly transformed into a premonition of death. In the poem "Druhowie jedli . . ." (The
Companions Ate . . .) the Gospel story is similarly complemented by an unexpected addition: Jesus, carrying his cross, recites the Kaddish (Jewish prayer for
the deceased) for his father, Joseph the carpenter, "since it happened exactly on
Pesach." Moreover, the symbolism of the Passion is here filtered through the
reality of the Holocaust: the "companions," indifferent to Christ's suffering, eat
and drink with Roman centurions from vessels that once belonged to murdered Jews.
At the end of the poem, Wat superimposes the skull emblem ("death's head") of the
SS on the traditional imagery of Golgotha, "place of a skull" in Hebrew:

> It was fair and idyllic around the hills,
> called the upland of Death's Heads. Until
> the darkness came, suddenly. Golden goblets,
> silver plates fell from the table.
> They did not break, naturally.
> It would be a pity to lose so many valuable utensils.

The most impressive treatment of the Crucifixion in Wat's poetry was
never included in *Lumen Obscurum:* it is the poem "W Wielki Piątek . . ." (On

Good Friday), written on 8 June 1967, a month and a half before Wat's death. It subsumes the main motifs of Wat's religious thought: an idiosyncratic amalgam of Judaism and Christianity coupled with an obvious failure to reconcile the two faiths, an identification with doubting Thomas, and, finally, an awareness of absurd suffering that nevertheless opens the way to a spiritual vision symbolized by Christ's wounds:

> On Good Friday, when the bells are already ringing midnight,
> I withdraw from the altar. I leave the community of the faithful,
>   their sweet converse with the saints is not for me.
>   They'll start to seek me
> already on Holy Saturday and Happy Easter, and then
>   on the Last Thursday of the Carnival
> —with knives—among these, whom the nice old lady
> (she who added brushwood to the pyre of Hus)
> saw pricking the Holy Host.
> I would like to return barefoot, on the sharp rocks, to the Wailing Wall.
> My place is there. I shall not withdraw from it.
> Perhaps I would just run off to the road to Emmaus.
>   If I only could put my numb fingers
> into the wounds of Man. These truly do not heal. Ever.
> The rest is silence.

Lumen Obscurum includes a short untitled farewell poem, which forms a counterpart to "On Good Friday." The Crucifixion is here replaced by the archetypal motif of *pyrosium* and *cataclysmum*, which predates both Jewish and Christian symbols. The poem has a motto from Lucan (*Pharsalia*, VII: 814–15): "Communis mundo superest rogus ossibus astra mixturus" (there remains a conflagration which will destroy all the world and bring the stars and dead men's bones together).[65] Lucan is referring to the universal conflagration predicted by Zeno of Citium: according to Zeno's doctrine, this will reabsorb souls into God, the infinite ocean of energy, one more name for the Gnostic pleroma. Wat speaks about this same final cataclysm, though for him it merges with the great conflagration of his own century, which he had first predicted in his futurist poems and had then had to live through:

> Fire of stars and fire of our
> bones: the common fire.
> Smoke rises high.
> A seagull flew by.
> Farewell, wife.
> Farewell, bird.
> Farewell, cloud.

The nouns once again juxtapose oppositions: heaven and earth, fire and water, life and death. Is fate accepted in the final consummation? Are the contradictions of being resolved? Or is the poem just an outcry of hopelessness? However that may be, exile ends: everything is dissipated in a cloud of smoke, and then the cloud itself vanishes—into silent letters, into empty space on a page.

In his memoirs, Wat returned to the bizarre experience of his youth that he had earlier transferred to Gabriel Moor, hero of his story "Seller of Dreams." If *I* return to it now, it is because it is the most succinct statement that Wat ever made about what it meant to him to be a poet.

> In the night, I had a dream: somebody very slowly, with perfect diction recited to me a poem—the arch-poem, that only poem, the creation of which is the highest achievement and happiness. I understood that and in rapture, dazzled by its beauty, told myself that I must impress every word of it upon my memory. Immediately after the last word I woke up, actually by effort of will. . . . Groping, I found pencil and paper—I already remembered, alas, only dispersed sentences and words, yet these I started to write down feverishly, in letters as big as possible and with big intervals. Then, happy, I fell asleep once again. In the mourning I found a chaos of deformed signs on paper, I managed to decipher only a couple of words. . . . I cite this event as a weak and clumsy analogy for the existence of a poet: it is an unceasing search for the forgotten, immense arch-dream, which fills up our universe.[66]

Notes

Preface

1. See Włodzimierz Bolecki, "Pisarze niedocenieni—pisarze przecenieni," 175.

Chapter 1: Prehistory, 1900–1918

1. "I was a stubborn opponent of Piłsudski's politics, but I also felt the unusual, unique in modern times personal appeal of that dictator. (That is, I have never met him personally, I have seen him just once, from afar, in Aleje Ujazdowskie.)" Wat, *Moralia*, in *Pisma wybrane* (1986), 2:30.

2. Wat, "Początek autobiografii" (Beginning of an Autobiography), Wat archive, file 46.

3. Ibid.

4. Wat, *Dziennik bez samogłosek*, in *Pisma wybrane*, 2:94. See also Jan Zieliński, "Spowiedź syna królewskiego," in Wat, *Wiersze wybrane* (1987), 6.

5. "Zeszyt łososiowy z teczki IV (1)," Wat archive, file 46.

6. Wat, *Kartki na wietrze*, in *Pisma wybrane*, 2:211.

7. On him, see Gershom Scholem, *Major Trends in Jewish Mysticism* (New York: Schocken Books, 1978), 244–86, 407–15.

8. On him, see, e.g., Martin Buber, *Hasidism* (New York: Philosophical Library, 1948).

9. Wat, *My Century* (1990), 116.

10. Many years later, on 28 November 1963 in Paris, Wat recorded in his diary a Kierkegaard-style dream about an imagined sin of his father. See Wat, *Dziennik bez samogłosek*, 83–84.

11. Wat, *Kartki na wietrze*, 195.

12. Ibid.

13. Wat, *Dziennik bez samogłosek*, 91.

14. Watowa, *Wszystko co najważniejsze* (1990), 12.

15. Wat, *Kartki na wietrze*, 194.

16. Ibid., 193.

17. Ibid., 184–85.

18. Wat, *My Century*, 94–95.

19. The Social Democratic Party of the Polish Kingdom and Lithuania (SDKPil), founded in 1900, differed from the Polish Socialist Party (PPS) in its internationalist stance and professed indifference to the cause of Polish national independence (Feliks Dzierżyński was one of its leaders). Still, friendly contacts between members of these competing groups were far from uncommon at that time.

20. Wat, *Kartki na wietrze*, 185.

21. Watowa, *Wszystko co najważniejsze*, 133.

22. Ibid., 133–34.

23. See Wat, *Ciemne świecidło* (1968), 194.

24. Wat, *Mój wiek* (1981), 2:334.

25. See chap. 7.

26. Watowa, *Wszystko co najważniejsze,* 19.

27. Wat, *My Century,* 95.

28. Ibid., 290.

29. Wat, *Kartki na wietrze,* 195–96.

30. Wat, "Początek autobiografii," n.p.

31. Wat, *Dziennik bez samogłosek,* 143.

32. Ibid., 146.

33. Ibid., 147.

34. Wat, *My Century,* 71. See also id., *Kartki na wietrze,* 184.

35. See Wat, *Mój wiek,* 2:51; id., *Kartki na wietrze,* 184.

36. Wat, *Mój wiek,* 1:55.

37. Wat, *Kartki na wietrze,* 189. Wat speaks here about the 300th (not 250th) anniversary of the Romanov dynasty, in 1913, four years before the Revolution.

38. Osip Mandel'shtam, *Shum vremeni* (*The Noise of Time*), in his *Sobranie sochinenii,* 2d ed. (New York: Inter-Language Literary Associates, 1971), 2:99.

39. It is interesting that Wat's younger contemporaries and friends, the well-known poets Adam Ważyk and Czesław Miłosz, mention the same books among their earliest literary impressions. In fact, Miłosz wrote a collection of poems under the title *Bobo's Metamorphosis.*

40. Wat, *Kartki na wietrze,* 185.

41. Ibid., 193.

42. Ibid., 185.

43. Watowa, *Wszystko co najważniejsze,* 132.

44. See Wat, *Mój wiek,* 2:47–49; id., *Kartki na wietrze,* 185–86.

45. Wat, *Kartki na wietrze,* 215.

46. Ibid., 194, 215.

47. Przybyszewski's impact on Wat's early writings seems obvious enough, even if his overstrained style and hysterical characters were for Wat no less an object of parody than *Forefather' Eve.*

48. Wat, *Kartki na wietrze,* 184.

49. Ibid., 189.

50. See Wat, *Mój wiek,* 1:360–61, and id., *My Century,* 154.

51. Wat, *Mój wiek,* 2:335; id., *Kartki na wietrze,* 188.

52. Menahem Mendel Beilis, a Jew from Kiev, fell victim to a blood-libel charge; he was acquitted by a jury of Russian peasants, but the court proceedings provided a great opportunity for anti-Semites to vent their feelings publicly.

53. Wat, *Moralia,* 7.

54. Wat, *Kartki na wietrze,* 197.

55. Ibid., 170.

56. Ibid., 190.

57. Wat, *Moralia,* 41.

58. Wat, *Mój wiek,* 2:328.

59. Watowa, *Wszystko co najważniejsze,* 132.

60. *Kartki na wietrze,* 190. "Le moi haïssable" (the odious I) is a concept taken from Pascal.

61. Ibid., 192.

62. Wat, *My Century,* 238. Origen was an early Christian writer who castrated himself.

63. Wat, *Mój wiek,* 1:55.

64. Ibid.

65. Wat, *Kartki na wietrze*, 185.

Chapter 2: Futurism, 1919–1924

1. Wat, "Wspomnienia o futuryzmie" (1930), 68.

2. In his mature years, Wat maintained that his early work was closer to dadaism than to futurism.

3. Ważyk, *Dziwna historia awangardy*, 52.

4. Wat, *Dziennik bez samogłosek*, in *Pisma wybrane*, 2:84. This fantastic idea—a Jewish youth becoming bishop of Rome—several years later because the plot for one of Wat's short stories in the famed *Bezrobotny Lucyfer* (Lucifer Unemployed).

5. Wat, *Moralia*, in *Pisma wybrane*, 2:35–36.

6. See Wat, *My Century*, 3.

7. Wat, *Kartki na wietrze*, in *Pisma wybrane*, 2:180.

8. Tuwim appreciated Wat's futuristic attitude to language. He even imitated—with characteristic caution—his younger colleague's neologisms and linguistic games. The strategy proved successful in his cycle of poems under the virtually untranslatable title *Słopiewnie*, which is made from two Polish roots, *word* and *song*.

9. Wat, "Tuwim," Wat archive, file 32, 1.

10. See Daniel Gerould, *Witkacy: Stanisław Ignacy Witkiewicz as an Imaginative Writer* (Seattle: University of Washington Press, 1981); Anna Micińska, *Witkacy: Stanisław Ignacy Witkiewicz, Life and Work*, translated by Bogna Piotrowska (Warsaw: Interpress Publishers, 1990).

11. Wat, "Stanisław Ignacy Witkiewicz, pogromca tradycyjnego teatru" (1926), 11.

12. Ibid.

13. Wat, *Mój wiek*, 2:77.

14. Ibid., 1:213.

15. Portraits of Ola and Aleksander, painted by Witkacy in his idiosyncratic manner, occupied a place of honor in Wat's Warsaw apartment, but were lost in the first days of World War II. See Wat archive, file 67.

16. Wat, *Mój wiek*, 1:155.

17. Ibid., 128.

18. See ibid., 40 n., and Wat, "Wspomnienia o futuryzmie," 76.

19. For a partly analogical development in the history of Russian literature, compare David M. Bethea, *Khodasevich* (Princeton, N.J.: Princeton University Press, 1983), 28ff. Wat's notion of a kinship between decadence and totalitarianism is amply demonstrated in his memoirs and essays.

20. Wat, "Wspomnienia o futuryzmie," 71.

21. The spelling of the Polish words *wieczór* (evening) and *urządzony* (organized) was "phonetical" (deliberately distorted), and the word *Murzynów* (Negroes) had a small letter instead of the required capital. Orthography of this kind became a hallmark of many Polish futurist texts. I refrain from trying to imitate it in my English translations, however.

22. Wat, "Wspomnienia o futuryzmie," 71. Jarosław Iwaszkiewicz, who was present at the reading, claimed that the not-too-courageous man in the nude was Stern himself. See his *Książka moich wspomnień*, 217.

23. Watowa, *Wszystko co najważniejsze*, 132.

24. Wat, "Wspomnienia o futuryzmie," 74.

25. See Jarosiński, "Wstęp," xxxvii–xxxviii.

26. Iwaszkiewicz, *Książka moich wspomnień*, 217.

27. Wat, "Wspomnienia o futuryzmie," 72.

28. On him, see Nina Kolesnikoff, *Bruno Jasieński: His Evolution from Futurism to Socialist Realism* (Waterloo, Ont.: Wilfred Laurier University Press, 1982), and Edward Balcerzan, *Styl i poetyka twórczosci dwujęzycznej Brunona Jasieńskiego* (Wrocław: Zakład Narodowy im. Ossolińskich, 1968).

29. Wat, *Mój wiek*, 1:48.

30. Ibid.

31. Wat, "Wspomnienia o futuryzmie," 72.

32. See, among others, Bereś, "Futurystyczna baśń o cywilizacji," 40–46.

33. Wat, *My Century*, 5.

34. Mandelstam's formula (pertaining to Acmeism) was recorded by Anna Akhmatova. See "Mandel'shtam" in her *Sochineniia*, vol. 2 (New York: Inter-Language Literary Associates, 1968), 185.

35. Wat, *Mój wiek*, 1:56.

36. Wat, "Wspomnienia o futuryzmie," 70–71.

37. Ibid., 75. It has to be admitted that Polish futurists displayed much naïveté in their attempts to catch up with "modernity." Their none-too-sophisticated experiments were mocked and parodied by many critics, including Witkacy. The celebrated poem "Moskwa" (Moscow), by Stanisław Młodożeniec, consisted essentially of two words: *tum* (I'm here) and *tam* (there), repeated throughout the text in slightly varying forms. They were to suggest the peal of Moscow bells or, perhaps, the radio call sign. The outcome of the experiment was nothing more than a primitive onomatopoeia, slightly amusing at best. See Janusz Sławiński, "Poezje Młodożeńca," *Twórczość* 5 (1959), 124, and Carpenter, *Poetic Avant-garde in Poland*, 50–51.

38. Wat, "Wspomnienia o futuryzmie," 71.

39. See chap. 3.

40. The word *gga* was virtually unpronounceable as well as untranslatable. From the text of of the manifesto one could infer that it was a bizarre onomatopoetic permutation of the noun *gęganie* (cackle).

41. I use the translation by Richard Lourie (*My Century* [1990], 10–11), albeit introducing some corrections and additions and attempting to preserve strictly all the peculiarities of spelling and punctuation of the original.

42. One of the figures rejected is Nietzsche, who was considered a paragon of antitraditionalism by almost all cultural figures of the era. "The great iridescent monkey known as dionysus" refers to his famous opposition of the Dionysian and Apollonian elements of the creative process; Dionysianism was celebrated, among others, by Young Poland writers and Skamandrites.

43. See their manifesto, reprinted by Vladimir Markov in *Manifesty i programmy russkikh futuristov* (Munich: Wilhelm Fink Verlag, 1967), 53–58.

44. The manifesto resembles the dadaist manifesto published by Louis Aragon in *Littérature* in the same year, 1920. See also Zaworska, "Futurystyczne koncepcje sztuki dla mas," 81–82.

45. In 1964, Stern qualified this quasi-ecological statement as completely fortuitous, as stemming either from his interest in the races or from a happy trip with a girl in a horse-drawn carriage. See Anatol Stern, *Poezja zbuntowana*, 2d ed. (Warsaw: Państwowy Instytut Wydawniczy, 1970), 52.

46. Viacheslav Ivanovich Ivanov and Mikhail Osipovich Gershenzon, "A Corner-to-Corner Correspondence," in *Russian Intellectual History: An Anthology*, edited by Marc Raeff (New York: Harcourt, Brace & World, 1966), 374–75.

47. This prefigures the concepts of Witold Gombrowicz, who was influenced by the futurists. See Wat, "Coś niecoś o Piecyku," in *Ciemne świecidło*, 231.

48. Wat noted that the anticivilizational ardor of the futurists was reiterated, to a degree, in Polish poetry after World War II (Tadeusz Różewicz, Miron Białoszewski). See *Mój wiek*, 1:41–42.

49. Ibid., 23.

50. Ibid.
51. Wat, "Wspomnienia o futuryzmie," 76.
52. Wat, *Mój wiek*, 1:39.
53. For an extensive analysis of Kraków Vanguard theory and poetic practice, see Carpenter, *Poetic Avant-garde in Poland*, 79–165.
54. See Wat, "Metamorfozy futuryzmu" (1930), 121, 125.
55. Kwiatkowski, *Literatura Dwudziestolecia*, 25.
56. Wat, *Dziennik bez samogłosek*, 108.
57. Wat, "Nad koleżką profesora Heisenberga—rozmyślanie" (1958).
58. Wat, *Mój wiek*, 1:294; 2:179–80; id., *My Century*, 276.
59. See Wat, *Mój wiek*, 2:180.
60. Bruno Jasieński, "Exposé do Nog Izoldy Morgan," in id., *Utwory poetyckie, manifesty, szkice,* compiled by E. Balcerzan (Wrocław: Ossolineum, 1972), 219.
61. Jan Żyżnowski, "Futuryzacje," *Rzeczpospolita* 60 (1921), quoted in Bereś, "Wokół futurystycznego zmierzchu," 48.
62. M. Wierzbiński, "Głupota czy zbrodnia," *Rzeczpospolita* 341 (1921).
63. *Kurier Polski* 205 (1922); *Skamander*, 22–24 (1922), 458; see also Jarosiński, "Wstęp," lxxv.
64. Wat, "Metamorfozy futuryzmu," 126.
65. Ibid:, 125–26.
66. See text in Jasieński, *Utwory poetyckie*, 93–97.
67. Wat, *My Century*, 7.
68. Ważyk, *Dziwna historia awangardy*, 69.
69. Wat, "Metamorfozy futuryzmu," 128.
70. Wat archive, file 65.
71. In the words of a Polish scholar, the manifesto proved to be the main achievement of the agency. See Jarosiński, *Literatura i nowe społeczeństwo*, 29.
72. See Jarosiński, "Wstęp," xxxiii.
73. Wat archive, file 7.
74. Wat, *Kartki na wietrze*, 210.
75. See Wat, *Ciemne świecidło*, 209–18.
76. Ważyk, *Kwestia gustu*, 65.
77. I reproduce here the original text; the text printed in *Ciemne świecidło*, 211, differs slightly, since Wat re-created it from memory.
78. There may also be an indirect reference here to *The Blue Bird* (1909), a symbolist fantasy by Maurice Maeterlinck that was immensely popular before World War I, especially in Russia, where it was successfully staged by Konstantin Stanislavsky. A Polish translation by Jan Kasprowicz (*Błękitny ptak*) appeared in 1913. *The Blue Bird* represented everything in art that was odious to a futurist.
79. Because *on* in Polish means both "I" and "it," the subject of the second line could also be *krok* (stride). At first glance, this would overstrain even futurist poetics; nevertheless, the possibility of an alternative reading cannot be excluded. *Krok* is commonly used as a metonymy for *krocze* (crotch). Hence, one can read the second line as "I have blue crotch"—although in standard Polish one would say "Ja mam niebiesko w kroku" rather than "Ja mam niebieski krok." Because "crotch," in turn, is a metonymy for "penis," and "bird" is a metaphor for the same organ, the entire poem may contain an obscene meaning as a description of masturbation, after which the "blue bird" loses its vigor. Such a reading would fit nicely with the aforementioned poem by Stern, as well as with the general proclivity of Polish futurists for scenes of self-abuse. Nor is it incompatible with the first reading, so taking the mockery of passéism to the extreme.
80. I reproduce only part of the poem, as printed in *Ciemne świecidło*, 210. My analysis makes use of that final version.

81. It should be noted that this attitude is more symbolist than futurist in the strict sense.

82. Krystyna Pomorska, *Russian Formalist Theory and Its Poetic Ambiance* (The Hague! Mouton, 1968), 96–97.

83. See Ważyk, *Dziwna historia awangardy*, 52.

84. See the extensive analysis of this motif in V. V. Ivanov and V. N. Toporov, *Issledovanija v oblasti slavjanskix drevnostej* (Moscow: Nauka, 1974), 86–125.

85. In addition to these mythological source texts, one suspects literary ones: viz., the second part of *Forefathers' Eve,* where an evil landlord is pecked by birds, and a popular story by Żeromski entitled "Rozdziobią nas kruki, wrony" (We will be pecked to pieces by ravens and crows).

86. At this point, the symbolism of fish reveals its manifold nature, a fish in early Christian iconography connoting Jesus.

87. The last image in the poem corresponds to the topos of world fire employed by many twentieth-century Russian poets, including Blok (The Twelve") and Mandelstam ("A Poem about an Unknown Soldier").

Chapter 3: *Pug Iron Stove*

1. Wat archive, file 7.

2. See Wat, "Coś niecoś o Piecyku," in *Ciemme świecidło,* 230.

3. Wat, *Mój wiek,* 2:181.

4. See, e.g., Wat, *My Century,* 98.

5. Wat, *Mój wiek,* 2:337.

6. Wat asserted that he knew at the time, four people who liked the work. But it provoked serious interest among young poets (including Miron Białoszewski, who allegedly copied it by hand) only after World War II. See Wat, *Kartki na wietrze,* in *Pisma wybrane,* 2:174, 178.

7. See ibid., 179–80.

8. Witkiewicz, "Aleksander Wat."

9. Hereafter, it is the text reprinted in H. Zaworska, *Antologia polskiego futuryzmu i Nowej Sztuki* (Wrocław: Zakład Narodowy im. Ossolińskich, 1978), 225–71, to which I refer; the numbers in parentheses indicate pages.

10. Wat, *Dziennik bez samogłosek,* in *Pisma wybrane,* 2:111.

11. Mayakovsky's favorite (and celebrated) garment during his futurist years. See also n. 61.

12. Wat, *Dziennik bez samogłosek,* 113; id., *Kartki na wietrze,* 183.

13. For more on this, see the end of this chapter.

14. *Les Chants de Maldoror* by Lautréamont is another literary work that comes to mind in this context.

15. Arthur Rimbaud, *Complete Works, Selected Letters,* translated, with an introduction and notes, by Wallace Fowlie (Chicago: University of Chicago Press, 1966), 307.

16. See Wat, *Dziennik bez samogłosek,* 113.

17. The rather uncommon slang phrase *szwendać się* (loiter) appears in the poem three more times: in the passage on Africa quoted, in the opening line ("Happiness loiters behind us joyless essential indispensable and golden," 225), and in the section title "A corpse loitering around midday." It is tempting to read all three as alluding to Rimbaud.

18. Africa, the paradigmatic locus of singular events and exotic passions, plays a particularly prominent role in Wat's poem (253, 261, 262). The influence of Nikolai Gumilyov, Russian poet and traveler well known to Polish futurists, may also be suspected here.

19. Quasi-quotation is a typical device in *Pug Iron Stove* (e.g., 249, 250).

20. On this topic, see, e.g., Robert Greer Cohn, *The Poetry of Rimbaud* (Princeton, N.J.: Princeton University Press, 1973), 9–10.

21. Wallace Fowlie, *Rimbaud's Illuminations: A Study in Angelism* (London: Harvill Press,

1953), 26. See also Jean-Louis Baudry, "Le Texte de Rimbaud," *Tel Quel* 35 (1968), 46–63, and 36 (1969), 33–53.

22. See C. A. Hackett, *Rimbaud: A Critical Introduction* (Cambridge: Cambridge University Press, 1981), 82.

23. See Hugo Friedrich, *Die Struktur der modernen Lyrik: Von Baudelaire bis zur Gegenwart* (Hamburg: Rowohlt, 1956), 23–24.

24. Among Polish precursors of Wat, critics mention such Young Poland writers as Jan Lemański and Roman Jaworski, both rather modest practitioners of the genre of grotesque. See Bolecki, "Od potworów do znaków pustych." Antecedents can be found in world literature—e.g., in German romanticism—and echoes of this kind of writing crop up in futurist and subsequent works (including those of Witkacy and Witold Gombrowicz). Still, the combination of ingredients concocted by Wat remains unique.

25. See the classic study M. Bakhtin, *Tvorchestvo Fransua Rable i narodnaia kul'tura srednevekov'ia i Renessansa* (Moscow: Khudozestvennaja literatura, 1965). An ample literature develops and qualifies Bakhtin's ideas on carnival and the overturning of values: see, e.g., Umberto Eco, V. V. Ivanov, and Monica Rector in *Carnival!* edited by Thomas A. Sebeok (Amsterdam: Mouton, 1984); Richard M. Berrong, *Rabelais and Bakhtin: Popular Culture in Gargantua and Pantagruel* (Lincoln: University of Nebraska Press, 1986); Gary Saul Morson and Caryl Emerson, eds., *Rethinking Bakhtin: Extensions and Challenges* (Evanston, Ill.: Northwestern University Press, 1989); Michael Holquist, *Dialogism: Bakhtin and His World* (London: Routledge, 1990); and Michael Gardiner, *The Dialogics of Critique: M. M. Bakhtin and the Theory of Ideology* (London: Routledge, 1992).

26. However contrived this unseemly episode may appear, it is in fact taken from Cellini's memoirs, as Małgorzata Baranowska proved in "Trans czytającego młodzieńca wieku (Wat)," 228–30.

27. Wat may be targeting the mannerist, pretentious novel *Faunessy* (Faunesses), by Maria Jehanne Wielopolska (1884–1940), published in 1913. See Baranowska, "Transfiguracje przestrzeni w twórczości Aleksandra Wata," 288–89.

28. This love-hate attitude to Young Poland has its perfect counterpart in the ambivalent attitude toward symbolism characteristic of Russian futurists. See Krystyna Pomorska, *Russian Formalist Theory and Its Poetic Ambiance* (The Hague: Mouton, 1968), 53.

29. See Wat, *Kartki na wietrze*, 174–75, 209.

30. Wat, "Coś niecoś o Piecyku," 234.

31. See Roland Barthes, *Sade, Fourier, Loyola*, translated by Richard Miller (New York: Hill and Wang, 1976), 36–37.

32. Carpenter, *Poetic Avant-Garde in Poland*, 71.

33. See ibid., 72.

34. See Pomorska, *Russian Formalist Theory*, 94ff.

35. Wat, "Coś niecoś o Piecyku," 230–31. It might also be noted that *ponuro* and *konuru* form a rhyming pair in the famous poem "A Cloud in Pants" (1915) by Mayakovsky, undoubtedly known to Wat at the time.

36. Wat, *Kartki na wietrze*, 209.

37. Wat, "Tuwim," 15.

38. The literature on Gnosticism is enormous. For the following analysis, see esp. Wilhelm Bousset, *Hauptprobleme der Gnosis* (Göttingen: Vandenhoeck und Ruprecht, 1907); Hans Jonas, *Gnosis und spätantiker Geist*, 2 vols. (Göttingen: Vandenhoeck und Ruprecht, 1934–54); Kurt Rudolph, *Gnosis: The Nature and History of Gnosticism*, translated by Robert McLachlan Wilson (San Francisco: Harper & Row, 1987); and Giovanni Filoramo, *A History of Gnosticism*, translated by Antony Alcock (Oxford: Basil Blackwell, 1990).

39. See Filoramo, *a History of Gnosticism*, xvi–xviii; also Harold Bloom, *Poetry and Repression: Revisionism from Blake to Stevens* (New Haven and London: Yale University Press, 1976); and

Paul A. Cantor, *Creature and Creator: Myth-Making and English Romanticism* (Cambridge: Cambridge University Press, 1984).

40. On Towiański, see H. Desmettre, *Towiański et le messianism polonais* (Lille, 1947); Wiktor Weintraub, *Literature as Prophecy: Scholarship and Martinist Poetics in Mickiewicz's Parisian Lectures* (The Hague: Mouton, 1959); Adam Sikora, *Towiański i rozterki romantyzmu* (Warsaw: Wiedza Powszechna, 1969).

41. On the relationship between sacredness and sacrilege, see Laura Makarius, *Le Sacré et la violation des interdits* (Paris, 1974).

42. Wat, *Kartki na wietrze*, 190–92.

43. Ibid., 191.

44. A reference to *The Golden Legend*, by Jacobus de Voragine.

45. The role of the number 3 in Dante's poem is well known. The number 13 (with its ominous connotations) serves as both counterweight and parody of 3 in Wat's text.

46. Iseult la Blanche Mains is presented by Wat, characteristically, as "Iseult of the White House."

47. See Gershom Scholem, *Origins of the Kabbalah* (Princeton, N.J.: Princeton University Press, 1987), 235, 295–96, and his *On the Kabbalah and Its Symbolism* (New York: Schocken Books, 1965), 163, 182.

48. See Rudolph, *Gnosis*, 76–83; Filoramo, *History of Gnosticism*, 147–52, etc. Cf. a Nag Hammadi document: "I am the honoured and the despised. I am the prostitute and the respectable woman. I am the wife and the virgin" (quoted in Rudolph, *Gnosis*, 81).

49. See the well-known analyses by Roland Barthes (in particular, his *Sade, Fourier, Loyola*).

50. See Barthes, *Sade, Fourier, Loyola*, 182.

51. See Pomorska, *Russian Formalist Theory*, 113.

52. See Barthes, *Sade, Fourier, Loyola*, 137–38.

53. See Wat, *My Century*, 178. Licentiousness, transgression, and crime as means of purification and cognition of divinity are aspects of an age-old notion, spread, among others, by some offshoots of Gnosticism. See, e.g., Rudolph, *Gnosis*, 247–50 (on the sperm cult and the consumption of the embryo, 253–57); Filoramo, *History of Gnosticism*, 185–89. It is tempting to relate this attitude also to the teachings of Jacob Frank, a Jewish sectarian who praised sin as a means of overcoming sin. The Frankists (who later renounced the most offensive part of their founder's dogma) remained active in Polish society until the uprisings of 1831 and 1863. Adam Mickiewicz probably had some Frankist connections.

54. It should be remembered that Wat cited illness as a constitutive factor in his work on *Pug Iron Stove*. On the general economy of disease in art, see Susan Sontag, *Illness as Metaphor* (New York: Farrar, Straus and Giroux, 1978).

55. On fascination with abnormality and disease in modern poetry, see Friedrich, *Die Struktur die modernen Lyrik*, 28, 58–60, etc.

56. See also "Braciszek słońca uśmiecha się jak idiota" (Little brother of the sun smiles like an idiot, 258).

57. On violence in ritual and art see, e.g., René Girard, *La Violence et le sacré* (Paris: Bernard Grasset, 1972). On violence in futurism, see Erich Fromm, *The Anatomy of Human Destructiveness* (New York: Holt, Rinehart and Winston, 1973); John J. White, *Literary Futurism: Aspects of the First Avant-Garde* (Oxford: Clarendon Press, 1990).

58. See, e.g., Rudolph, *Gnosis*, 121.

59. Wat, "Coś niecoś o Piecyku," 233.

60. In this passage may be found, besides an obvious reference to Ibsen's *Peer Gynt*, several allusions to Shakespeare, whose name is ingeniously hidden in the text by being translated into Polish.

61. The garment in question is Mayakovsky's famous "yellow jacket." Yellow is the dominant

color in *Pug Iron Stove* (e.g., 229, 231, 244, 245, 247, 250, 265) and usually has ominous connotations. See Baranowska, "Transfiguracje przestrzeni," 292–93, and her "Trans czytajacego-młodzieńca," 207. Compare the similar role of yellow in works by Gogol and Andrei Belyi: see Andrei Belyi, *Masterstvo Gogolia* (Moscow and Leningrad: Gosudarstvennoe izdatel'stvo khudozestvennoj literatury, 1934), 307–9.

62. Compare Khlebnikov's self-appointed title "The President of the Globe."

63. An obvious reference to Nietzsche, *Die fröhliche Wissenschaft*. Originally, "the joyous science" (*Gai saber*) referred to a mystical trend in Provençal literature of the late Middle Ages.

64. The Polish verb *uprzestrzenić się* is a neologism.

65. See nn. 11 and 61.

66. See Rudolph, *Gnosis*, 109 (the world as prison), 119–21 (the state of the subject as sleep or drunkenness).

67. Ibid., 118–19, 177–79; Filoramo, *History of Gnosticism*, 40.

68. Filoramo, *History of Gnosticism*, 39. See also Rudolph, *Gnosis*, 95: "Redemption consists in the awakening of Adam to the knowledge of his true origin and of the worthlessness of the Demiurge."

69. See P. Heller, *Dialectics and Nihilism* (Amherst, Mass.: University of Massachusetts Press, 1966), 289; quoted in Filoramo, *History of Gnosticism*, xvii.

70. Filoramo, *History of Gnosticism*, 135.

71. It also features in Wat's short poem "Płodzeńe" (Breeding) (1921) and forms the semantic axis of his story "Hermafrodyta" (The Hermaphrodite), included in *Lucifer Unemployed*.

72. On the serpent in Gnosticism, see Rudolph, *Gnosis*, 247.

73. Filoramo, *History of Gnosticism*, 61.

74. Ibid.

75. Ibid., 90–92.

76. There is an ample literature on anagrams: see, e.g., Jean Starobinski, "Les Anagrammes de Ferdinand de Saussure," *Le Mercure de France*, February 1964, 243–62.

77. Filoramo, *History of Gnosticism*, 41. For a Christian, the divine messenger is naturally identified with Jesus. Cf. Rudolph, *Gnosis*, 148–50.

78. Filoramo, *History of Gnosticism*, 41.

79. Ibid., 141.

80. See George Poulet, *Exploding Poetry: Baudelaire / Rimbaud*, translated with an introduction by Françoise Meltzer (Chicago: University of Chicago Press, 1984), 94–95.

81. A similar cluster of motifs may be found in many poetic texts, from T. S. Eliot's *The Waste Land* (end of part 3) to Russian symbolist poetry (e.g., D. Segal, "Poeziia Mikhaila Lozinskogo: simvolizm i akmeizm," *Russian Literature* 13, no. 4 (1983), 333–414).

82. Compare Rudolph, *Gnosis*, 151 (separation of Jesus and Christ), 169–71 (Christ as onlooker at the crucifixion of Jesus).

83. The idiosyncratic adjective *mopsożelazny* (pug iron) looks like one more dadaist grimace. Nevertheless, it is prepared by several appearances of *mops* (pug) in the text of the poem (240, 252). It may be noted that Mayakovsky uses *mops* in "A Cloud in Pants" (the hero of the poem, in a fit of *mania grandiosa*, promises to take a walk with Napoleon on a chain, like a pug). A wise Professor Mopsus figures among the characters of the grotesque and parodic work *Tańce śmierci* (Dances of Death), written at the end of the nineteenth century by Felicjan Faleński (see Bolecki, "Od potworów," 95–97) and perhaps known to Wat. It is also possible that Wat is employing here an "interlinguistic" pun (pig iron—pug iron), intelligible only to English readers.

84. See Poulet, *Exploding Poetry*, 101–04.

85. See Friedrich, *Die Struktur die modernen Lyrik*, 52–53.

86. Cohn, *Poetry of Rimbaud*, 9.

87. Ibid.

Chapter 4: Radical Left, 1924–1928

1. First published in French translation, edited by Boris Souvarine, in *Le Contrat social* 6 (1963), 322–30; then in the Polish original in *Kultura* 1 / 2 (1964).

2. Fyodor Dostoevsky, *The Devils*, translated by David Magarshack (Harmondsworth: Penguin, 1985), 404.

3. Ibid.

4. M. K. Dziewanowski, *Poland in the Twentieth Century* (New York: Columbia University Press, 1977), 93–94.

5. See the interesting discussion with a writer of Jewish origin, Julian Stryjkowski, in Jacek Trznadel, *Hańba domowa: Rozmowy z pisarzami* (Lublin: Test, 1990), 151–52.

6. See Simoncini, "Ethnic and Social Diversity in the Membership of the Communist Party of Poland: 1918–1938," 65–66, 90.

7. Ibid., 59.

8. See Roman Loth, "'Kultura Robotnicza'—'Nowa Kultura' 1922–1924. Szkic z dziejów prasy kulturalno-oświatowej KPRP," *Przeglad Humanistyczny* 1 (1965); Jarosiński, *Literatura i nowe społeczeństwo,* 107ff.

9. On him, see Wanda Papiewska, *Jan Hempel: Wspomnienia siostry* (Warsaw: Książka i Wiedza, 1958); Jan Szmyd, *Jan Hempel: Idee i wartości* (Warsaw: Książka i Wiedza, 1975).

10. Wat tells an instructive story about his discussion, *ca.* 1922, with Tadeusz Kotarbiński, a leftist professor of philosophy: "I remember how I, still a student, asked Kotarbiński once . . . : 'what do you think, Professor, about Lenin's Empirio-Criticism?' Kotarbiński answered with a smile: 'I do not think anything at all, that is a book written by an amateur.' Then both of us burst out laughing" (*Mój wiek*, 1:79). The book in question is Lenin's *Materialism and Empirio-Criticism* (1911), a work of some philosophical ambition devoted to polemic with Ernst Mach and his Russian followers.

11. See, e.g., Jarosiński, *Literatura i nowe społeczeństwo,* 148–54.

12. Wat, *Mój wiek*, 1:21–22. Maria Konopnicka was a populist, rather sentimental poet.

13. Wat included the text in *Ciemne świecidło*, thereby acknowledging that it had been important for his inner development.

14. Wat, *My Century*, 6.

15. Jan [J. Hempel], "Kultura Robotnicza," *Kultura Robotnicza* 1 (1922); quoted in Jarosiński, *Literatura i nowe społeczeństwo,* 130.

16. It should nevertheless be noted that leading leftist writers valued Wat's contributions to *New Culture* highly. See *Od bliskich i dalekich: Korespondencja do Władysława Broniewskiego*, vol. 1, edited by Feliksa Lichodziejewska (Warsaw: Państwowy Instytut Wydawniczy, 1981), 103, 108.

17. B. K. [J. Hempel], "Nieporozumienia literackie."

18. Wat and Broniewski became acquainted at the end of 1921: see Broniewski, *Pamiętnik 1918–1922,* 278–79, 289.

19. Wat, *Mój wiek*, 1:28.

20. See ibid., 155, 172, 174.

21. See Wat, *Moralia*, in *Pisma wybrane*, 2:12.

22. Kwiatkowski, *Literatura Dwudziestolecia*, 399.

23. Wat was financial manager of the periodical. See Stawar's letter to Broniewski of 15 August 1927, in *Od bliskich i dalekich*, 1:361.

24. Watowa, *Wszystko co najważniejsze*, 140.

25. Ibid., 9.

26. See chap. 7.

27. Wat, *My Century*, 30, 33.

28. Wat, *Mój wiek*, 1:101.

29. Ibid., 2:32.

30. Watowa, *Wszystko co najważniejsze*, 10.

31. Wat, *Kartki na wietrze*, in *Pisma wybrane*, 2:206–8.

32. Anonymous review in *Droga* 11 (1928), 1094.

33. Wat, "Nim ją reskrypt do życia powoła" (1927).

34. Wat, *Mój wiek*, 1:282.

35. Ibid.

36. Wat, "Teatr w dzisiejszej Rosji Sowieckiej" (1926).

37. Wat, "Nieporozumienia krytyki literackiej" (1928).

38. Wat, *Mój wiek*, 2:262.

39. Ibid. Only much later was Kafka introduced to a Polish readership by the great modernist author Bruno Schulz.

40. Witold Wandurski, "Majakowski i polscy poeci," in *Włodzimierz Majakowski*, edited with an introduction by Florian Nieuważny (Warsaw: Państwowe Zakłady Wydawnictw Szkolnych, 1965), 282. The text first appeared in Ukrainian in *Żyttia i revolucja* 7 (1931), 75–86.

41. Wiktor Woroszylski, *Życie Majakowskiego* (Warsaw: Państwowy Instytut Wydawniczy, 1965), 619. This was, of course, a futurist commonplace. See, e.g., Vladimir Markov, *Russian Futurism: A History* (Berkeley: University of California Press, 1968), 185, 335.

42. Woroszylski, *Życie Majakowskiego*, 613.

43. Vladimir Maiakovskii, *Polnoe sobranie sochinenii*, vol. 8 (Moscow: Gosudarstvennoe izdatel'stvo khudozhestvennoi literatury, 1958), 331.

44. Arutcheva, "Zapisnye knizhki Maiakovskogo," 384.

45. Wat, *Kartki na wietrze*, 217.

46. Wat, *My Century*, 24.

47. Watowa, *Wszystko co najważniejsze*, 15.

48. Ibid., 17.

49. Wat, *My Century*, 44.

50. Wandurski, as quoted in Woroszylski, *Życie Majakowskiego*, 612. Andrzej Pronaszko was a painter active in Polish theater. What is being referred to here is "the miracle on the Vistula" whereby the Polish army defeated the Bolshevik troops.

51. There is a considerable literature dealing with Mayakovsky's psychological and political predicament, most of which owes much to the classic study by Roman Jakobson, "O pokolenii, rastrativshem svoikh poetov," first published in *Smert' Vladimira Maiakovskogo* (Berlin, 1930). See the English translation by Roman Jakobson, "On a Generation that Squandered Its Poets," in *Major Soviet Writers: Essays in Criticism*, edited by Edward J. Brown (Oxford: Clarendon Press, 1973), 7–32.

52. Wat, *My Century*, 44. See also Watowa, *Wszystko co najważniejsze*, 16–17.

53. Wat to Wiktor Woroszylski, 1 March 1963; archive of Alina Kowalczykowa.

54. Wat, *My Century*, 45.

55. Watowa, *Wszystko co najważniejsze*, 16. See also Wat, *Mój wiek*, 1:141.

56. [Bengt Jangfeldt], "Vvedenie," in *V. V. Maiakovskii i L. Iu. Brik: Perepiska, 1915–1930*, compiled and edited with introduction and commentary by Bengt Jangfeldt (Stockholm: Almquist & Wiksell International, 1982), 36–37.

57. See his telegram of that date to Lili Brik, in *V. V. Maiakovdskii i L. Iu. Brik*, 183.

58. V. Katanian, *Maiakovskii: Khronika zhizni i deiatel'nosti*, augmented 5th ed. (Moscow: Sovetskii pisatel', 1985), 459.

59. Wat, *My Century*, 44; Watowa, *Wszystko co najważniejsze*, 15–16.

60. See chap. 7.

Chapter 5: The Early Fiction

1. A king of that name ruled Spain from 1886 and was deposed in 1931, nine years after the publication of Wat's work. In 1921 or 1922, Wat signed one of his letters ("virtually a crazy story") to Izabela Hertzowa "King Alfonso XIII." See *Od bliskich i dalekich*, 1:67. One suspects here a reference to Gogol: the titular hero of "Diary of a Madman" considers himself to be the Spanish king Ferdinand VIII and signs himself accordingly. Use of this name may also be a mocking gesture towards Peiper, known for his Spanish sympathies.

2. The drama "R.U.R." by Karel Čapek, which introduced the concept of the robot, was published at almost the same time as Wat's story, in 1921.

3. See Wat, *My Century*, 92.

4. Ibid., 148.

5. Ważyk, *Dziwna historia awangardy*, 52.

6. See Kwiatkowski, *Literatura Dwudziestolecia*, 214–16.

7. In a sense, "Seller of Dreams" is a philosophical counterpart to "A Story." If the former deals with exteriorization (and communicates its inherent perils), the latter investigates "the treachery and the danger of interiorization," as Wat put it in *My Century*, 92. Moreover, both texts might be called Gothic tales—the first thoroughly modernized, the other retaining a Romantic coloring.

8. Note his "fantastically large" hat and beard, typical attributes of Peiper mentioned in *Mój wiek*, 1:39.

9. In its structure and message, "Seller of Dreams" anticipates some well-known stories by Jorge Luis Borges: "Tlön, Uqbar, Orbis Tertius" (about two juxtaposed realities and their menacing interaction), "Las ruinas circulares" (about the universe as a dream), and "El milagro segreto" (about the search for an ideal text).

10. Wat, *Mój wiek*, 1:78.

11. Wat, "Od autora," in id., *Bezrobotny Lucyfer* (1960), 8.

12. "Przedmowa do drugiego wydania," Wat archive, file 35.

13. Leon Pomirowski, "Bezrobotny Lucyfer," *Wiadomości Literackie* 10 (1927).

14. Wat, *My Century*, 81; id., *Mój wiek*, 1:213.

15. Wat, *Mój wiek*, 1:82.

16. See also the discussion on pp. 99–100.

17. Chesterton visited Poland in 1927.

18. Ważyk, *Dziwna historia awangardy*, 69–70.

19. Wat, "Co zawdzięczają pisarze polscy literaturom obcym?" (1927).

20. John Coates, *Chesterton and the Edwardian Cultural Crisis* (Hull: Hull University Press, 1984), 1.

21. It is possible that the title of Wat's book contains an allusion to Chesterton's novel *The Ball and the Cross*, in which a Professor Lucifer plays a significant role.

22. They appeared in *Wiadomości Literackie*, respectively nos. 18 and 25 in 1927 and no. 42 in 1928.

23. Wat, "Uwagi o Chestertonie" (1927).

24. A reference to Mickiewicz's early ballad "The Romantic," considered a manifesto of Polish Romanticism: "Faith and love are more discerning / Than lenses of learning."

25. Wat, "Czego broni Chesterton" (1927).

26. Ibid.

27. Wat, "Chestertonica" (1928).

28. All quotations from the stories in *Bezrobotny Lucyfer* are taken from Lillian Vallee's translation (1990).

29. One cannot fail to note here a satirical reference to Feliks Dzierżyński, known for his unflinching cruelty as well as for his sentimentality.

30. Wat was particularly interested in Krasiński's philosophy of history during 1937–38 (see *Mój wiek*, 2:85). Later, in the 1960s, he produced around 150 typewritten pages dealing with various aspects of Krasiński's writing. Parts of that unedited manuscript were published under the title *Szkice o Krasińskim (Essays on Krasiński)* in 1988. See Wat, *Pisma wybrane*, 3:188–221.

31. Wat, *Moralia*, 5.

32. Ibid., 4.

33. In 1927, Wat's idea did not look particularly outlandish. For many years, the fate of the czar and his family, shot in Ekaterinburg in July 1918, gave rise to wild speculations. In 1920, an unknown young woman attempted suicide in Berlin; she was hospitalized and later recognized by some as the czar's daughter Anastasia, who had, it seems, survived the ordeal of Bolshevik execution. The story of "Anastasia"—who in fact died in 1984—made headlines in European newspapers, including Polish ones, at the time.

34. See his novel *Penguin Island*, a satrical allegory of French history.

35. The first edition of *Petersburg* appeared in 1916; Wat probably knew it in the second, more concise edition of 1922.

36. Leftist writers sometimes transformed the myth of the "yellow peril," giving it positive connotations: e.g., the hero of Jasieński's *I Burn Paris*, a Chinese revolutionary named P'an Tsiang Kuei, appears as the proletarian savior of the city.

37. Jusuf (or Yusuf) ben Mchim was a real-life person, an African friend of the Polish futurists who took part in their grotesque poetry reading on 8 February 1919. The name Chang Wu Pei is a conflation of the names of two Chinese warlords, Chang Tso-lin and Wu P'ei-fu, whose activities were making headlines during the 1920s.

38. One cannot but be amazed at the uncanny accuracy of Wat's prediction: during World War II, he was to scratch out a meagre living as a deportee teacher in a workers' settlement in Kazakhstan, close to the border of China.

39. This passage resembles the famous "courtyard scene" in the final volume of Proust's *Remembrance of Things Past* (which in fact, could not have been known to Wat at the time, since it appeared in the original only in 1927).

40. Czesław Miłosz, Foreword to Wat, *Lucifer Unemployed*, xii.

41. Mikhail Bulgakov should also be mentioned in this connection. His masterpiece, *The Master and Margarita*, written during the 1930s but not published until 1967, makes use of the same device and testifies to a somewhat similar attitude to (Soviet) culture.

42. Wat, *Mój wiek*, 1:59.

43. Ważyk, *Dziwna historia awangardy*, 41.

44. Ważyk, *Kwestia gustu*, 96.

45. Wat, *Mój wiek*, 2:251.

46. See chap. 10.

47. Kwiatkowski, *Literatura Dwudziestoleucia*, 207–8.

Chapter 6: Communism, 1928–1939

1. Wat was impressed by *A Start in Life*, a typical socialist realist film about the reeducation of juvenile criminals (made in 1931). By a twist of fate, the film glorified (in a rather adroit manner) the Soviet prison camp system that Wat was later to experience firsthand. See *Mój wiek*, 1:135–36.

2. Ibid., 136.

3. Ibid., 137–38.

4. Ibid., 86.

5. Wat, *My Century*, 20.

6. Wat, *Mój wiek*, 2:330–31.

7. Ibid., 1:81.

8. See Czesław Miłosz, *The Captive Mind*, translated by Jane Zielonko (New York: Alfred A. Knopf, 1953), 9 ff.

9. Wat, *Mój wiek*, 1:64.

10. Ibid. 1:76, 159–60; id., *My Century*, 52.

11. Wat, *My Century*, 18.

12. Wat, *Mój wiek*, 1:73, 76.

13. Ibid., 76.

14. See *Leon Schiller: W stulecie urodzin, 1887–1987*, edited by Lidia Kuchtówna and Barbara Lasocka (Warsaw: Państwowe Wydawnictwo Naukowe, 1990), 159–60. Wat mentions Daszewski as scene-painter for the show, although that is not corroborated by the only surviving playbill.

15. Leon Schiller, "Upadek teatru burżuazyjnego," in his *Teatr Ogromny*, edited with an introduction by Zbigniew Raszewski (Warsaw: Czytelnik, 1961), 65–66; quoted in Schiller, *W stulecie urodzin*, 159. On "facto-montage," see also Edward Csató, *Leon Schiller* (Warsaw: Państwowy Instytut Wydawniczy, 1968), 392–96.

16. Wat, *My Century*, 28.

17. Wat to Irena Schiller, 14 October 1956, quoted in her "W związku z artykulem Leona Schillera" (1959), 20.

18. Wat, "Dola robotnicza" (1929), 7.

19. The story of the play and its closing are reported in "Echa Wystawy Krajowej," "Sztuka prześwietla politykę społeczną," "P. Prystor w roli cenzora."

20. Wat, *My Century*, 29. See also id., *Mój wiek*, 1:99–100.

21. Wat, *Mój wiek*, 1:108, 111.

22. *Mój wiek*, 2:211, 351. The later date is corroborated by Daszewski's letter to Broniewski, 19 July 1929 (*Od bliskich i dalekich*, 1:488). Also, *Social Policy of R. P.* was staged in 1929, and Wat could not have received his royalties earlier. He mentions two visits he made in Berlin: to the office of *Die Linkskurve* (a periodical that started in 1929) and to a movie house showing *Sunny Boy* (a picture released that same year). Further, in 1928, Besedovsky was still trusted by the Soviet authorities.

23. Wat, *Mój wiek*, 1:103.

24. Ibid., 1:104; 2:351.

25. Csató, *Leon Schiller*, 359–62.

26. Wat, *My Century*, 30.

27. Ibid.; Wat, *Mój wiek*, 1:100–102; 2:351.

28. See Wat, *Mój wiek*, 1:107.

29. Ibid., 2:351.

30. Ibid., 1:111–12.

31. Ibid., 1:108, 111. See Grigory Besedovsky, *Revelations of a Soviet Diplomat*, translated by Mathew Norgate (London: Williams & Norgate Ltd., 1931); Gordon Brooke-Shepherd, *The Storm Petrels: The first Soviet Defectors 1928–1938* (London: Collins, 1977), 85–106.

32. Wat, *Mój wiek*, 1:21.

33. Wat, *My Century*, 15–16; id., *Mój wiek*, 1:68.

34. Wat, "'Zazdrość' Olieszy" (1929).

35. Wat, "Literatura faktu" (1929).

36. Wat, *Mój wiek*, 1:158.

37. The set of *The Literary Monthly* with the inscriptions has been preserved in the Wat archive. Quoted in Watowa, *Wszystko co najważniejsze*, 147; Wat, *My Century*, 13.

38. See Wat, *Mój wiek*, 1:76–77, 121; id., *My Century*, 19.

39. Watowa, *Wszystko co najważniejsze*, 12.

40. Wat, *Mój wiek*, 1:88.

41. Ibid., 1:64, 88, 180; Wat, *My Century*, 58.

42. Wat, *My Century*, 13.

43. Jerzy Putrament, *Pół wieku: Młodość* (Warsaw: Czytelnik, 1969), 201.

44. The text of the poem has never been found, though Putrament claimed that it had been published. See Jan Zieliński, "Wiersze dla Wata," in *Pamięć głosów: O twórczości Aleksandra Wata*, 137. See also Wat, *My Century*, 59.

45. Roman Werfel, interview, in Teresa Torańska, *Oni* (London: Aneks, 1985), 83.

46. See Sander L. Gilman, *Jewish Self-Hatred: Anti-Semitism and the Hidden Language of the Jews* (Baltimore: Johns Hopkins University Press, 1986).

47. Wat, *My Century*, 54–55.

48. Wat, *Mój wiek*, 1:155.

49. Ibid.

50. Słonimski, "Kronika tygodniowa."

51. "Metody przedrzeźniania się p. Słonimskiego," *Miesięcznik Literacki* 2 (1930), 117. An answer written and signed by Wat, "Klusownictwo frazesów," was considerably milder.

52. See Wat, *My Century*, 52.

53. Wat, "Poeta rewolucji Majakowski" (1930).

54. Ibid., 287–88.

55. Wat, *Mój wiek*, 1:90.

56. Wat, "W pracowniach stylu" (1931).

57. Ibid., 779.

58. Ibid., 773.

59. Wat, *My Century*, 58.

60. The ritual repetition of Stalin's name was not yet considered a proof of loyalty, as in the late 1930s and 1940s (and excessive repetition would have drawn the attention of the Polish censors). Therefore, the *Literary Monthly* avoided the name (a fact perceived by Wat in his later years as having, for him, a certain personal significance) but hardly the spirit. See *My Century*, 48.

61. Wat, "Reportaż jako rodzaj literacki" (1930).

62. Wat, "Jeszcze o reportażu" (1930).

63. This mixture of judicious sociological and literary analysis with sectarian excess is reminiscent of Georg Lukács (whose views on fiction, and on the novel in particular, were for the most part consonant with Wat's).

64. See Jarosiński, *Literatura i nowe społeczeństwo*, 209.

65. Wat, "Reportaż jako rodzaj literacki," 330 n.

66. Wat, "Literatura faktu" (1929).

67. *Belomorsko-Baltiiskii kanal imeni Stalina: Istoriia stroitel'stva*, edited by M. Gorky, L. Averbakh and S. Firin (Moscow: Gosudarstvennoe izdatel'stvo "Istoriia fabrik i zavodov," 1934). The book has become a rarity. An English translation by H. Smith and R. Haas (under the title *Belomor: An Account of the Construction of the New Canal between the White Sea and the Baltic Sea*) was published in 1935. For a discussion of the book, see Aleksandr I. Solzhenitsyn, *The Gulag Archipelago, 1918–1956: An Experiment in Literary Investigation*, III–IV, translated by Thomas P. Whitney (New York: Harper & Row, 1975), 80–100.

68. Wat, *Mój wiek*, 1:156.

69. Wat, *My Century*, 56.

70. Wat, *Mój wiek*, 1:157.

71. Ibid., 167.

72. Wat, *My Century*, 19, 57.

73. See Wygodzki, "Spotkanie z 'Miesięcznikiem Literackim'"; also Wat, *My Century*, 19.

74. Poles at that time were mostly ignorant of Ukrainian literature, translations being almost nonexistent.

75. Wygodzki, "Spotkanie," 409.

76. Ibid., 406.

77. Ibid., 408.

78. On "Tom," see Krystyna Dolidowska, *"Książka" i "Tom": Z dziejów legalnych wydawnictw KPP, 1918–1937* (Warsaw: Centralne Archiwum KC PZPR, 1977); Henryk Cimek and Lucjan Kieszczyński, *Komunistyczna Partia Polski, 1918–1938* (Warsaw: Książka i Wiedza, 1984), 431–32.

79. Wat, *Mój wiek,* 1:216–17.

80. The titular "King Staś" was Stanisław Poniatowski, the last king of Poland, who reigned in the eighteenth century and was invoked in the appeal of the Polish PEN Club as benefactor of the arts and spiritual patron of the gathering.

81. See Wandurski to Jasieński, 11 November 1930 in Lewin, "Polonica w dziale rękopisów Instytutu Literatury Światowej im. Gorkiego w Moskwie."

82. A Ukrainian writer and stage director of Communist persuasion.

83. Wat, *Mój wiek,* 1:177.

84. See *Miesięcznik Literacki* 15 (1931), 703.

85. Wat, *My Century,* 62.

86. Ibid., 23.

87. The number was mentioned in Wat's poem "Przed Breughelem starszym" (Before Breughel the Elder) in 1956. See chap. 8. For different numbers, see Wat, *Dziennik bez samogłosek,* in *Pisma wybrane,* 2:75.

88. See *Kurier Warszawski,* 12 September 1931; *Gazeta Warszawska,* 12 September 1931; and other Polish newspapers of that date. See also Wat, *My Century,* 62–65; Watowa, *Wszystko co najważniejsze,* 18.

89. Wat, *My Century,* 63–64.

90. Słonimski, "Kronika tygodniowa."

91. Boy-Żeleński, "Nekrolog sądów przysięgłych."

92. Wat, *My Century,* 67.

93. Ibid., 66.

94. Watowa, *Wszystko co najważniejsze,* 18–19.

95. Wat, *My Century,* 76; see also *Od bliskich i dalekich,* 2:42–43.

96. Wat, *My Century,* 79.

97. Ibid., 79–80.

98. See his obituary by Mieczysław Fuksiewicz in *Księgarz* 4 (1981), 38–41.

99. Cf. ibid.; see also Wat, *Mój wiek,* 1:247.

100. Wat, *Mój wiek,* 1:245. See also id., *Kartki na wietrze,* in *Pisma wybrane,* 2:185.

101. Watowa, *Wszystko co najważniejsze,* 13–14.

102. Ibid., 144. After World War II, Kruczkowski, a novelist and playwright of some talent, became an influential figure in Polish political and cultural life. He showed his gratitude to Wat by helping him through his postwar misfortunes, albeit with caution. See Wat, *Mój wiek,* 1:251, 2:118.

103. Wat, *Mój wiek,* 1:250–51; id., *Kartki na wietrze,* 185.

104. Wat, *Mój wiek,* 1:215.

105. Ibid., 1:221, 251.

106. Ibid., 1:239.

107. Watowa, *Wszystko co najważniejsze,* 14–15.

108. Wat, *Mój wiek,* 1:249–50.

109. Watowa, *Wszystko co najważniejsze,* 19.

110. Wat, "Za porozumieniem" (1935).

111. Wat, *Mój wiek*, 1:229.
112. On the Congress and its background, see among others, Lazar Fleishman, *Boris Pasternak v tridtsatye gody* (Jerusalem: Magnes Press–Hebrew University, 1984), 236–66; Ewa Bérard, *La Vie tumultueuse d'Ilya Ehrenbourg* (Paris: Ramsay, 1991), 179–86.
113. Wat, *Mój wiek*, 1:229.
114. See Szczygielski, "Internowanie 'S'."
115. Wat, *My Century*, 226.
116. Wat, *Mój wiek*, 1:220–21, 240.
117. Ibid., 1:221.
118. Ibid.; also Wat, *My Century*, 247.
119. The sheer number outweighed any comparison. The authorities in interwar Poland had destroyed the lives of less than a hundred Communists; the Nazis were responsible for the deaths of several hundred. See Norman Davies, *God's Playground: A History of Poland* (Oxford: Clarendon Press, 1981), 2:545.
120. Wat, *My Century*, 90.
121. Watowa, *Wszystko co najważniejsze*, 20–21.
122. Wat, *Mój wiek*, 1:238.
123. Wat, *My Century*, 97.

Chapter 7: Prison and Kazakhstan, 1939–1946

1. See Watowa, *Wszystko co najważniejsze*, 23–24, 131; Wat, *My Century*, 98.
2. As did many of Witkacy's friends, Wat became aware of his fate only after the war.
3. Wat, *Mój wiek*, 1:258.
4. See Jan Gross, *Revolution from Abroad: The Soviet Conquest of Poland's Western Ukraine and Western Belorussia* (Princeton: Princeton University Press, 1988), 3–70.
5. See ibid., 145–46.
6. *Documents on German Foreign Policy*, vol. 8, edited by R. J. Sontag (Washington, D.C.: U.S. Government Printing Office, 1954), 166.
7. Adolf Rudnicki, *Żywe i martwe morze*, 3d ed. (Warsaw: Czytelnik, 1956), 58–59.
8. See Winklowa, *Boy we Lwowie 1939–1941*, 229; also Wat, *Mój wiek*, 1:277.
9. Winklowa, *Boy we Lwowie*, 229.
10. F. Istner, "Kronika," *Czerwony Sztandar* 20 (1939); quoted in Gross, *Revolution from Abroad*, 85, and Winklowa, *Boy we Lwowie*, 13.
11. Wat, *My Century*, 326–27; also id., *Mój wiek*, 1:277. See also Nadezhda Mandel'shtam, *Vospominaniia* (Paris: YMCA Press, 1970), 89–90.
12. See Wat, *Mój wiek*, 1:86, 289; id., *My Century*, 106.
13. Borwicz, "'Inżynierowie dusz'," 160.
14. See *Czerwony Sztandar* 25 (1939).
15. Winklowa, *Boy we Lwowie*, 16–17, 230; Rudnicki, *Żywe i martwe morze*, 61; Wat, *My Century*, 100–101, 124.
16. After the war, a Polish newspaper of the same kind (with the same name) appeared in Vilnius (Wilno), capital of Soviet-occupied Lithuania.
17. "Przyłączenie do Związku Radzieckiego oto wola narodów Zachodniej Ukrainy," *Czerwony Sztandar* 24 (1939); quoted in Winklowa, *Boy we Lwowie*, 9.
18. "Pisarze polscy witają zjednoczenie Ukrainy," signed by Wat, *Czerwony Sztandar* 48 (1939).
19. A strictly pro-Soviet account of the Lwów experience (abounding in telling details) may be found in Jerzy Putrament, *Pół wieku: Wojna* (Warsaw: Czytelnik, 1969), 15 ff.
20. Stryjkowski, *Wielki strach*, 64.

21. See interview with Stryjkowski in Trznadel, *Hańba domowa*, 152.
22. Stryjkowski, *Wielki strach*, 84.
23. Wat, *My Century*, 101.
24. On him, see Borwicz, "'Inżynierowie dusz'," 132–34.
25. See Winklowa, *Boy we Lwowie*, 19–21; Borwicz, "'Inżynierowie dusz'," 152–53.
26. See Gross, *Revolution from Abroad*, 147, 288 n. 12; Winklowa, *Boy we Lwowie*, 22–23.
27. Wat, *Mój wiek*, 1:314.
28. See, e.g., Borwicz, "'Inżynierowie dusz'," 148–49, and id., "List do Redakcji 'Zeszytów Historycznych'," *Zeszyty Historyczne* (Paris: Instytut Literacki, 1964), 5:249–50. Cf. Wat, *Mój wiek*, 1:268.
29. Wat, *My Century*, 105–6; id., *Kartki na wietrze*, in *Pisma wybrane*, 2:219.
30. Borwicz, "'Inżynierowie dusz'," 127.
31. Wat, *Mój wiek*, 1:277.
32. "W pracowniach pisarzy."
33. Wat, "Kobieta radziecka" (1939).
34. Wat, "Pomost do literatury radzieckiej" (1939).
35. Wat, "Delegatka ze Lwowa" (1939).
36. Wat, "Przemysł materiałów budowlanych" (1940).
37. Wat, "Pol'skie i sovetskie pisateli" (1939).
38. Wat, *My Century*, 112.
39. See Trznadel, *Hańba domowa*, 153.
40. Wat, *Mój wiek*, 1:274.
41. See Stryjkowski, *Wielki strach*, 66–69.
42. Wat, *My Century*, 103.
43. See the brilliant analysis of the phenomenon in Gross, *Revolution from Abroad*, 117–22.
44. Stanisław Vincenz, *Dialogi z Sowietami* (London: Polska Fundacja Kulturalna, 1966), 125; quoted in Gross, *Revolution from Abroad*, 144.
45. See Gross, *Revolution from Abroad*, 194.
46. Wat, *My Century*, 236.
47. For an alternative account, see Ważyk, "Przeczytałem *Mój wiek*," 48–50.
48. Janusz Kowalewski, quoted in Winklowa, *Boy we Lwowie*, 37.
49. Wat, *My Century*, 118–22; Watowa, *Wszystko co najważniejsze*, 31–35; Borwicz, "'Inżynierowie dusz'," 134.
50. Winklowa, *Boy we Lwowie*, 233.
51. See *Czerwony Sztandar* 104 (1940). Kolski, who perished during the war, appears to have been an admirer of Wat and Broniewski (Borwicz, "'Inżynierowie dusz'," 139).
52. Gross, *Revolution from Abroad*, 155.
53. Wat, *My Century*, 126.
54. Ibid., 133.
55. Borwicz, "'Inżynierowie dusz'," 136.
56. See Ważyk, "Przeczytałem *Mój wiek*," 51.
57. Watowa, *Wszystko co najważniejsze*, 39.
58. Ibid., 29.
59. Wat, *My Century*, 109; id., *Mój wiek*, 1:214; Watowa, *Wszystko co najważniejsze*, 35.
60. Watowa, *Wszystko co najważniejsze*, 39–44.
61. Gross, *Revolution from Abroad*, 155.
62. Davies, *God's Playground*, 2:567.
63. Watowa, *Wszystko co najważniejsze*, 54.
64. Ibid., 66.
65. Wat, *Mój wiek*, 2:39.

66. Ibid., 5; Wat, *My Century*, 113, 148.

67. Wat, *My Century*, 63, 196; see also Watowa, *Wszystko co najważniejsze*, 135.

68. Wat, *My Century*, 144; id., *Mój wiek*, 2:91.

69. Wat, *My Century*, 144.

70. This poem was never included in editions of Broniewski's collected works printed in Communist Poland. This English translation is by Burns Singer and is taken from Jerzy Peterkiewicz and Burns Singer, *Five Centuries of Polish Poetry, 1450–1970*, 2d ed. (London: Oxford University Press, 1970), 106; quoted in an adapted version in Davies, *God's Playground*, 2:546.

71. Wat, *Mój wiek*, 1:297.

72. Ibid., 2:19.

73. See Gross, *Revolution from Abroad*, 179–81.

74. Wat, *My Century*, 188.

75. Ibid., 213–14. See also N. Mandel'shtam, *Vospominaniia*, 82–83. See also chap. 12.

76. Wat, *Mój wiek*, 2:38–39.

77. Wat, *My Century*, 246–49; see also id., *Mój wiek*, 2:132–38.

78. For more on Wat's "meeting with the devil," see chap. 12.

79. A. Krakowski to Ola Watowa, quoted in Watowa, *Wszystko co najważniejsze*, 71.

80. On the delegation and its work, see Więcek, "Po lekturze *Mojego wieku*," 61–62.

81. Wat, *My Century*, 316.

82. See Wat to Ola, 19 January 1942, in Watowa, *Wszystko co najważniejsze*, 74.

83. Wat, *Dziennik bez samogłosek,* in *Pisma wybrane*, 2:144.

84. Watowa, *Wszystko co najważniejsze*, 83.

85. Wat, *My Century*, 329.

86. Watowa, *Wszystko co najważniejsze*, 85–86.

87. Wat, *Dziennik bez samogłosek*, 144.

88. Wat's testimony regarding this view of Soviet intellectuals is corroborated by many memoirists, including Ehrenburg.

89. Watowa, *Wszystko co najważniejsze*, 86.

90. Wat archive, file 44.

91. Wat, *Mój wiek*, 2:251. See also chap. 5.

92. Wat, *My Century*, 328. A manuscript on Mayakovsky, in Russian, survives in the Wat archive, file 11.

93. "Projekt w sprawie zbierania poloników w ZSRR," Wat archive, file 17.

94. See Wat, *Kartki na wietrze*, 172.

95. Ibid., 171.

96. "Irys, dziennik literaturze i historji poświęcony" Wat archive, file 3. The proposal was advanced in April 1945.

97. Wat, "Śp. Stanisław Rogoż" (1942).

98. Ibid.; see also Wat, *My Century*, 354.

99. Wat, *Mój wiek*, 1:303.

100. Watowa, *Wszystko co najważniejsze*, 74.

101. Wat, *Mój wiek*, 2:241.

102. Ibid., 2:268.

103. It appeared in a periodical printed in Warsaw by the Polish resistance movement, *Nurt* (The Stream) 4 (1943).

104. Watowa, *Wszystko co najważniejsze*, 88–89.

105. L. Trotskii, *Moia zhizn': Opyt avtobiografii* (Moscow: Kniga, 1990), 2:300.

106. Wat, *Kartki na wietrze*, 205.

107. Wat, *Mój wiek*, 1:147–48.

108. "Epilogue: A selection from the memoirs of Paulina Wat," in Wat, *My Century*, 362.

109. Ibid., 365.

110. "Omarchadżew," in *Pisma wybrane*, 3:141.

111. Wat, *My Century*, 356. See also id., *Dziennik bez samogłosek,* 141.

112. See "Epilogue," 375 ff.

113. Wat attempted to write such a novella at the end of his life but left it unfinished (see the quotation from it given in the text). See his *Pisma wybrane*, 3:141–45.

114. Wat, *Mój wiek*, 2:221; see also id., *My Century*, 300.

115. In a strange telling coincidence, Wat's revolt took place at the same time as the uprising in the Warsaw ghetto (April–May 1943), of which he was, of course, unaware.

116. "Epilogue," 374.

117. Wat, *Kartki na wietrze*, 197.

118. Wat, *Dziennik bez samogłosek*, 143; id., *Kartki na wietrze*, 207.

119. Watowa, *Wszystko co najważniejsze*, 35–36.

120. Wat archive, file 12.

121. English translation taken from *With the Skin* (1989), 87.

122. Compare Wat, *Dziennik bez samogłosek*, 116.

123. Wat, *Moralia*, in *Pisma wybrane*, 2:26.

124. Ibid., 30.

125. See *Na melodie hebrajskie*, 2 (*Hebrew Melodies*, 2), a poem of 1956 that might be considered both counterpart and comment on "Willows in Alma-Ata."

126. Compare the similarly non-standard *obezliścił* ([he] stripped [me] of leaves) in the poem "Like a rotten tree," in the context *z żony obezliścił* (that is, the leaves are identified with the persona's wife).

127. See Wat, *Kartki na wietrze*, 186.

128. It should also be noted that *żegnani* is highlighted by a persistent sound interplay with *żegluje* ([it] sails) and *żeglugi* (sailings). The pattern of repetition and alliteration in the poem is exceptionally rich: compare, among others, *wierzby–wszędzie–wierzbami–wierzbo–wierzbo–warszawska–wierzba–walcząca Warszawo–Warszawo; tatrzański–tianszański*.

129. The dreamlike tonality is reinforced by the polysemic verb *roiłem*. *Roić* can mean "to daydream, to imagine things" and "to swarm, to teem," especially in the reflexive form *roić się*. The two meanings merge in Wat's usage, which is slightly ungrammatical.

130. Wat, *Kartki na wietrze*, 186.

131. See Łukaszuk, *. . . i w kołysankę*, 21–22.

132. This archetypal theme was amply represented in *Pug Iron Stove*.

133. See Łukaszuk, *. . . i w kołysankę*, 22.

134. One might even interpret the God of the poem as a totalitarian dictator (or a totalitarian doctrine personified). The fate of the revolutionary crushed by—and submitting to—the Stalinist dictatorship was a popular topic of the period, and, like many writers of the twentieth century, Wat was deeply preoccupied with it, both consciously and unconsciously.

135. Wormwood here constitutes a semantic rhyme with absinthe (line 5), a liqueur made with wormwood oil.

136. Wat, *Dziennik bez samogłosek*, 137.

137. Wat, *Kartki na wietrze*, 198.

138. Thomas à Kempis, *The Imitation of Christ*, edited with an introduction by Edward J. Klein (New York: Harper & Brothers, 1941), 85.

Chapter 8: In Postwar Poland, 1946–1957

1. Wat, *Dziennik bez samogłosek*, in *Pisma wybrane*, 2:65.

2. See, among others, Gömöri, *Polish and Hungarian Poetry, 1945 to 1956*, 31–63.

3. The article, by Leon Gomolicki, entitled "Andrzej Żdanow—teoretyk realizmu soc-jalistycznego," appeared in *Kuźnica* on 19 September 1948; quoted in Fik, *Kultura polska po Jalcie,* 104.

4. See chap. 7.

5. Ważyk, "Troska o człowieka."

6. Wat archive, file 69.

7. Wat archive, file 12.

8. Watowa, *Wszystko co najważniejsze,* 125.

9. Ibid.

10. See Wat to Władysław Kowalski, 13 June 1945, and Ważyk and Bronislaw Szoł to Wat, 1 August 1945: Wat archive, file 12.

11. See also Watowa, *Wszystko co najważniejsze,* 26.

12. Ibid., 127.

13. Wat archive, file 69.

14. Watowa, *Wszystko co najważniejsze,* 131–32.

15. Wat, *Mój wiek,* 1:60; see also id., *My Century,* 114.

16. Wat, *Dziennik bez samogłosek,* 162–63.

17. Watowa, *Wszystko co najważniejsze,* 134.

18. Ibid., 135.

19. Wat, *My Century,* 27; Watowa, *Wszystko co najważniejsze,* 136.

20. See his autobiography, 7 January 1955, Wat archive, file 69.

21. See Wat, *My Century,* 59.

22. Wat, *Kartki na wietrze,* in *Pisma wybrane,* 2:200.

23. Wat, *Mój wiek,* 1:56. In 1950, *Rebirth* and the *Forge,* which had distinct, partly opposed programs, were merged into the faceless *Nowa Kultura* (*New Culture*), the title of which mimicked that of the old Communist weekly from which Wat was expelled in the 1920s.

24. Wat, " 'Klub Krzywego Koła' " (1963). "Marranos" were Spanish Jews forced to accept Christianity formally, who nevertheless continued privately to observe the Jewish law. Wat applied this medieval term to people of liberal persuasion who only formally subscribed to the party line. See also *Moralia,* in *Pisma wybrane,* 2:6.

25. See Wat to Ola, 31 May 1947, archive of Alina Kowalczykowa.

26. The speech, which could not be delivered in Zurich for technical reasons, was finally made at a press conference in Bern and was widely referred to in the Swiss press. See Wat, "Nil nisi veritas" (1947).

27. Wat, "Przemówienie Aleksandra Wata na zjeździe PEN Clubów" (1947).

28. Wat, "Bitwa pod Zurychem" (1947).

29. Letter to Ola, 29 May 1948, archive of Alina Kowalczykowa.

30. Wat, "Od Zurychu po Kopenhagę" (1948).

31. Ibid.

32. See Wat to Ola from Brussels, [summer 1948], archive of Alina Kowalczykowa.

33. Wat, *My Century,* 241–42.

34. See chap. 9.

35. Postcard to Ola, 9 September 1949, archive of Alina Kowalczykowa.

36. Wat to Ola, 18 September 1949, same archive.

37. Wat considered the Congress "somewhat hollow, meaningless." See Wat to Andrzej, 7 September 1949, same archive.

38. Wat to Ola and Andrzej, 3 October 1949, same archive.

39. Same archive.

40. Wat, *Moralia,* 29.

41. Wat, "Kronika, ale nie-dobrowolska" (1948).

42. See Fik, *Kultura polska po Jalcie,* 109.

43. Wat, *Dziennik bez samogłosek*, 162.

44. *Nowiny Literackie*, 2 (1948).

45. *Kuźnica* 8 (1948).

46. See chap. 10.

47. Wat, "Oto jest miasto śpiewne" (1949).

48. Wat, "Druga zbrodnia Salome" (1948), 8–10.

49. See below on Wat's "Anti-Zoilus."

50. *Po prostu* 1 (1947); quoted in Fik, *Kultura polska po Jałcie*, 83.

51. See, among others, Alicja Lisiecka, *Pokolenie 'pryszczatych'* (Warsaw: Państwowy Instytut Wydawniczy, 1964).

52. *Kuźnica* 6, 7 (1948). Quotations are taken from the text reprinted in *Pisma wybrane* 3:149–77.

53. Wat, "Antyzoil albo rekolekcje," 151.

54. On socialist realism, in its mode of "literature of the fact," see also chap. 6.

55. Wat, "Antyzoil albo rekolekcje," 167.

56. Ibid., 166.

57. Ibid., 167.

58. Ibid.

59. Ibid., 167–68, 176.

60. Ibid., 176.

61. *Po prostu* 2 (1948); quoted in Fik, *Kultura polska po Jałcie*, 93.

62. Żółkiewski, "Spór po rekolekcjach."

63. Wat, "Sprostowanie Aleksandra Wata" (1948).

64. Wat, *Mój wiek*, 1:62.

65. Wat, *Kartki na wietrze*, 176.

66. Wat, *Dziennik bez samogłosek*, 71.

67. Information furnished by Alina Kowalczykowa.

68. Trznadel, *Hańba domowa*, 92.

69. Wat, *Mój wiek*, 2:186.

70. Ibid., 2:187.

71. Mieczysław Jastrun. See Wat, *Moralia*, 47.

72. Wat, *Kartki na wietrze*, 203.

73. Wat, *Mój wiek*, 1:250.

74. The Nineteenth Congress of the Communist Party of the Soviet Union (CPSU) took place in October 1952, immediately preceding Stalin's death.

75. Wat, *Moralia*, 48.

76. Watowa, *Wszystko co najważniejsze*, 138.

77. Wat, *Moralia*, 47.

78. Ibid., 18.

79. Ibid., 19.

80. Watowa, *Wszystko co najważniejsze*, 145–65; Wat, *Moralia*, 16.

81. Watowa, *Wszystko co najważniejsze*, 146.

82. See Wat, *Dziennik bez samogłosek*, 154.

83. Wat, *Moralia*, 24.

84. See ibid., 23; Wat, *Dziennik bez samogłosek*, 65, 71, 143, 156; id., *Kartki na wietrze*, 205.

85. Wat, *Dziennik bez samogłosek*, 117–18.

86. Ibid., 89.

87. See ibid., 160; Wat, *Mój wiek*, 2:336–38; Watowa, *Wszystko co najważniejsze*, 159–62.

88. Wat, *Kartki na wietrze*, 205.

89. See chap. 5.

90. Wat, *Dziennik bez samogłosek*, 113.

91. Ibid., 62.

92. See Alina Kochańczyk's extensive analysis of *Diary without Vowels:* "'Dziennik bez samogłosek'—Aleksandra Wata studium do autoportretu," in *Pamięć głosów*, 85–101.

93. In Polish letters, this view was most memorably expressed by Krasiński; in European letters of the twentieth century, its main proponent was Thomas Mann (who drew on Nietzsche). See Victor Erlich, *The Double Image: Concepts of the Poet in Slavic Literatures* (Baltimore: Johns Hopkins University Press, 1964), 38–67.

94. Kochańczyk, "'Dziennik bez samogłosek'," 90.

95. Wat, *Moralia*, 22.

96. Wat, *With the Skin*, 27.

97. Wat, *Dziennik bez samogłosek*, 156.

98. Quoted in Jan Strękowski, "Umarł jak każdy z nas," *Tygodnik Solidarność*, 5 March 1993.

99. Later, the *Universal Weekly* was arbitrarily turned over to "loyal Catholics" who changed its tenor, though that proved to be only temporary.

100. Wat, *Kartki na wietrze*, 203–4.

101. Ibid., 159.

102. Oral information provided by Andrzej Wat.

103. Wat, *Mój wiek*, 2:335.

104. Ibid., 2:334.

105. See Ibid., 2:329.

106. Ibid., 2:335.

107. Wat, *Dziennik bez samogłosek*, 159–60.

108. See Micińska, "Aleksander Wat—elementy do portretu," 80.

109. See Wat to Broniszówna of that date, archive of Alina Kowalczykowa.

110. See Wat to Andrzej, 17 June 1957, same archive.

111. Watowa, *Wszystko co najważniejsze*, 154. The daughter of Wat's brother Moryc, Roma Herscovici, took on some financial responsibility for Aleksander's and Ola's well-being. (Wat had no qualms about being supported by the Polish government—which, in his opinion, was simply paying him a small part of its debt for years of harassment—but the official support was meagre.)

112. Letter of 9 September 1956, archive of Alina Kowalczykowa.

113. Watowa, *Wszystko co najważniejsze*, 163. A letter from Craig and a book with a dedication to Wat have been preserved in the Wat archive, file 73.

114. See Wat to Broniszówna, 9 May 1957, archive of Alina Kowalczykowa.

115. See Wat to Andrzej, 6 February 1957, same archive.

116. See Wat to Broniszówna, 13 November 1956, and Ola to Broniszówna, 3 April 1957, same archive.

117. See Ola to Broniszówna, 16 December 1956, same archive.

118. The words of Przyboś, Słonimski, and Witaszewski are quoted from Fik, *Kultura polska po Jalcie*, 232–33.

119. Gömöri, *Polish and Hungarian Poetry*, 222–23.

120. Arnold Szyfman, a theater director.

121. Watowa, *Wszystko co najważniejsze*, 27–28. See also Wat, *Kartki na wietrze*, 181.

122. See *Poznański Czerwiec 1956*, edited by Jarosław Maciejewski i Zofia Trojanowiczowa, 2d ed. corrected and enlarged (Poznań: Wydawnictwo Poznańskie, 1990).

Chapter 9: "Loth's Flight"

1. Work on the novel began in October 1948. See Wat to Ola, 5 February 1949, archive of Alina Kowalczykowa.

2. Wat, "Dosyć dyskusji! Realizm trzeba realizować" (1949).

3. Ibid.

4. Wat, *Kartki na wietrze*, in *Pisma wybrane*, 2:198.

5. Wat, "Bitwa pod Zurychem" (1947).

6. Kazimierz Wyka emphasized the similarities between "Loth's Flight" and Mann's fiction in an enthusiastic letter to Wat of 21 July 1949, Wat archive, file 49.

7. Wat, *Moralia*, in *Pisma wybrane*, 2:15.

8. Ibid., 10.

9. Wat, *My Century*, 241–42.

10. Gerald Fleming, "Engineers of Death," *New York Times*, 18 July 1993, E19.

11. Interestingly, a senior engineer named Willibald Prüfer figures in Wat's notes to the novel, where there is also mention of his "sudden death."

12. Wat, *Kartki na wietrze*, 198–99. See the above mentioned letter to Ola of 5 February 1949: "Now, I have begun to strongly dislike much of what I have written."

13. "Ucieczka Lotha: Powieść historyczna z niedawnej przeszłości," Wat archive, file 72.

14. The reconstruction would be more accurate if Wat's notebooks were deciphered in their entirety or, at least, in large part (a task that seems next to hopeless because of his illegible handwriting). However, the overall design of "Loth's Flight" underwent change in the course of Wat's work, which complicates matters enormously.

15. "Ucieczka Lotha," in *Pisma wybrane*, 3:119.

16. "Ucieczka Lotha," typescript, 115.

17. There is a striking parallel between Erika Pokorny and Nietzsche's sister, Elisabeth Förster-Nietzsche, who adulterated her brother's works with anti-Semitic passages: an uncanny coincidence, since Förster-Nietzsche's forgeries were exposed only in 1958.

18. "Ucieczka Lotha," in *Pisma wybrane*, 3:105.

19. Ibid., 3:128.

20. See chap. 12.

21. "Ucieczka Lotha," in *Pisma wybrane*, 3:109.

22. "Ucieczka Lotha," typescript, 75.

23. Another text that may be being alluded to here is Kafka's short story "A Hunger Artist."

24. Theoretically, Loth could "escape" also by suicide, but this possibility is never mentioned by Wat: on the contrary, he said in the *Evening Express* that Loth was to be "miraculously saved."

25. See M. M. Bakhtin's analysis in the best-known book on the topic: *Problemy poetiki Dostoevskogo*, 4th ed. (Moscow: Sovetskaia Rossiia, 1979). For a contemporary evaluation and development of Bakhtin's concepts, see chap. 3, n. 25.

26. "Ucieczka Lotha," typescript, 3.

27. Yashar Toledot, 51b–52a.

28. "Ucieczka Lotha," typescript, 8.

29. See, e.g., Donald Ward, *The Divine Twins: An Indo-European Myth in Germanic Tradition* (Berkeley: University of California Press, 1968); Victor Witter Turner, *The Ritual Process: Structure and Anti-Structure* (Chicago: Aldine, 1969). It should also be noted that Loth's daughters are twins.

30. There is a large and continuously growing body of studies on this topic: e.g., Karl Miller, *Doubles: Studies in Literary History* (New York: Oxford University Press, 1985); Paul Coates, *The Double and the Other: Identity as Ideology in Post-Romantic Fiction* (New York: St. Martin's Press, 1988); Susan Gillman, *Dark Twins: Imposture and Identity in Mark Twain's America* (Chicago: University of Chicago Press, 1989). See also the instructive remarks on the double and mirror image in Iu. M. Lotman, *Kul'tura i vzryv* (Moscow: Gnozis, 1992), 112–26.

31. "Ucieczka Lotha," typescript, 8–9.

32. Ibid., 1.

33. Ibid.

34. Ibid., 120.

35. Ibid., 73–74.

36. Among the many hidden references to Ivan Karamazov in "Loth's Flight," the persistent motif of "sticky leaves," object of Ivan's adoration, should be mentioned.

37. Traces of a Gnostic theme may be detected in a long passage in which Glücks, after the death of his baby daughter, feeds flies and ants to a cistern full of amphibians, which disgust and fascinate him simultaneously. In a contemporary remnant of Gnosticism, Mandean mythology, primordial "black stinking water" from which "arose and appeared evil things" is a central cosmogonic image: see E. S. Drower, *The Mandeans of Iraq and Iran* (Oxford: Clarendon Press, 1937), 254–55. Glücks here seems to represent the superior Deity, repelled by the world but awaiting its return to the pleroma.

38. Wat had had the unenviable opportunity to observe such atomization in Lwów: see chap. 7.

39. Aleksander Wat, " 'Niemcy'—Leona Kruczkowskiego" (1949). The quotation from Hölderlin is taken from the English translation by Willard R. Trask, adapted by David Schwarz, in Friedrich Hölderlin, *"Hyperion" and Selected Poems* (New York: Continuum, 1990), 128.

40. Wat, " 'Niemcy'—Leona Kruczkowskiego."

41. "The wild forest," a quotation from the opening of Dante's *Divine Comedy*.

42. "Ucieczka Lotha," typescript, 103–4.

43. "Ucieczka Lotha," in *Pisma wybrane*, 3:115.

44. In 1949, Wat took pains to visit the Am Kerker Hall in Erfurt where the exchange between the poet and the emperor had taken place. See Wat, *Moralia*, 15.

45. "Ucieczka Lotha," in *Pisma wybrane*, 3:113–15.

46. Ibid., 3:118.

47. Ibid., 3:116–18.

48. See n. 25.

49. Wat, *Kartki na wietrze*, 199.

50. "Ucieczka Lotha," typescript, 134–35. Voigt cherishes the naive hope of "civilizing" the Nazi regime, a motif reminiscent of the illusions of Żółkiewski and his circle (see chap. 8).

51. Wat archive, file 18.

52. Wat, *Kartki na wietrze*, 173.

53. Ibid., 199–200. Cf. the parallels and mutual influences of avant-garde art and totalitarianism posited by some historians of culture. See esp. Boris Groys, *The Total Art of Stalinism: Avantgarde, Aesthetic Dictatorship, and Beyond,* translated by Charles Rougle (Princeton, N.J.: Princeton University Press, 1992). See also chap. 12.

54. "Ucieczka Lotha," typescript, 91–93.

55. See chap. 1.

56. "Ucieczka Lotha," typescript, 113.

57. Ibid., 101–3.

58. Ibid., 71.

59. See the brilliant analysis of the interplay of points of view in several classical novels by B. A. Uspenskii, *Poetika kompozitsii* (Moscow: Iskusstvo, 1970), esp. 135–58.

60. Wat's interest in psychoanalysis, marked by a certain distrust and irony, found expression not only in the character of Langleben but also in several descriptions of Loth's dreams, which present much material of interest to a Freudian. Incidentally, Langleben figures in "Loth's Flight" either as Kurt or as Adolf; this is almost the only case of authorial oversight in the entire novel, something a Freudian would consider significant.

61. Johannes Thyl was to write a short about the papacy, which brings to mind Ivan Karamazov's tale of the Grand Inquisitor, as well as Wat's *The Eternally Wandering Jew.*

62. "Ucieczka Lotha," typescript, 72.

334 NOTES TO PAGES 198-206

63. It is interesting to note that Loth and Glücks are both about the age that Wat was during his Calvary in Ili and Alma-Ata: Loth is forty-four, Glücks in his forties.

64. One suspects that the name of the presumed narrator, Johann Sebastian, is an allusion to Bach.

Chapter 10: The New Poetics

1. The period of the so-called thaw resulted in a significant upsurge in the publication of poetry in Poland. During 1957, around 80 new collections of poems appeared, 30 by first-time authors (in the preceding year, the respective numbers were 60 and 14). The average size of the editions was, 1,000 copies. See Matuszewski, "Liryka. Poemat," 20.

2. Wat, *Kartki na wietrze*, in *Pisma wybrane*, 2:180.

3. Wat to Józef Czapski, 22 March 1963, archive of Alina Kowalczykowa.

4. For the first time since the war, the books of some—though by no means all—émigrés were considered for the prize as well—e.g., the first volume of Gombrowicz's *Diary*—although Miłosz's *The Poetic Treatise*, a no less important achievement, was passed over in silence.

5. Wat, *Mój wiek*, 2:213. See also Watowa, *Wszystko co najważniejsze*, 155.

6. Wyka, "Super flumina Babylonis," 98.

7. Drawicz, "Przerwane milczenie."

8. The term "Turpists" was invented by Przyboś for polemical purposes: those to whom it was applied, though visible enough, never existed as a formal group.

9. Grochowiak, "Pokusy cnotliwe. A. Wat."

10. Maciąg, "Poezja rozstrojonego instrumentu," 3.

11. Contemporaries maintained that Maciąg's review was actually written by Przyboś. See Jastrun, "Dzienniki," 46.

12. Wirpsza, "Wiersze Aleksandra Wata."

13. Ibid.

14. Czesław Miłosz, *The History of Polish Literature*, 2d ed. (Berkeley: University of California Press, 1983), 412.

15. Two highly talented young poets who perished in the Warsaw Uprising should also be mentioned here: Krzysztof Kamil Baczyński and Tadeusz Gajcy.

16. Wyka, "Super flumina Babylonis," 99.

17. Ibid., 100.

18. Ibid., 106.

19. Kamieńska, "Poezja tragizmu i mądrości," 3; Kłak, "Wat z tej i z tamtej strony," 2–4.

20. Jeleński, "The Dilemma of the Polish Intellectuals," 257.

21. Jeleński, introduction to "Voici Aleksander Wat," 3.

22. Herling-Grudziński, "Czysta czerń."

23. Wat, *Kartki na wietrze*, 183.

24. Ibid.

25. Wat, *My Century*, 284.

26. Wat to Andrzej, 1 November 1956, archive of Alina Kowalczykowa.

27. See esp. C. G. Jung, *Aion: Researches into the Phenomenology of the Self*, translated by R. F. C. Hull (*The Collected Works of C. G. Jung*, vol. 9, part II [Princeton: Princeton University Press, 1968]; *Psychology and Alchemy*, translated by R. F. C. Hull (*Collected Works*, vol. 12 [Princeton: Princeton University Press, 1968]); Carl G. Jung, M.-L. von Franz, Joseph L. Henderson, Jolande Jacobi, and Aniela Jaffé, *Man and His Symbols* (New York: Doubleday, 1976). Cf. Dieter Wyss, *Depth Psychology: A Critical History: Developments, Problems, Crises* (New York: Norton, 1966).

28. We have already noted Wat's kinship with such poetry of meditation and repentance in the course of analyzing his poem "For so long I protected myself from Thee." See chap. 7.

29. Wat, *Dziennik bez samogłosek*, in *Pisma wybrane*, 2:73.

30. Wat to Józef and Maria Czapski, 12 February 1963, archive of Alina Kowalczykowa.

31. Wat, *Dziennik bez samogłosek*, 109.

32. Wat, *Kartki na wietrze*, 177.

33. Ibid., 210.

34. Ibid., 215.

35. Ibid., 175.

36. Wat, *Dziennik bez samogłosek*, 106.

37. See Wat, *Moralia*, in *Pisma wybrane*, 2:9–10.

38. Wat, *Dziennik bez samogłosek*, 92. This statement of 1963 was echoed by Miłosz in one of his best-known poems, "Ars poetica?" (1968).

39. See chap. 1.

40. Wat, *Dziennik bez samogłosek*, 88.

41. Wat, *Moralia*, 25.

42. Ibid.

43. W[at], "Posłowie od autora" (1967).

44. Ibid.

45. See Wat, *Kartki na wietrze*, 220.

46. See ibid., 215.

47. See W[at], "Posłowie od autora."

48. Wat, *Moralia*, 32.

49. Wat, *Dziennik bez samogłosek*, 109.

50. See Iu. M. Lotman, *Lektsii po struktural'noi poetike* (*Uchenye zapiski Tartuskogo gos-udarstvennogo universiteta*, vol. 160 [1964]); *Struktura khudozhestvennogo teksta* (Moscow: Iskus-stvo, 1970); *Analiz poeticheskogo teksta: Struktura stikha* (Leningrad: Prosveschchenie, 1972).

51. Wat, *Dziennik bez samogłosek*, 107.

52. Ibid., 108. See also chap. 2.

53. See Roman Jakobson, "Randbemerkungen zum Proza des Dichters Pasternak," in *Selected Writings*, vol. 5 (The Hague: Mouton, 1979), 416–32.

54. Wat, *Dziennik bez samogłosek*, 111.

55. Wat, *Kartki na wietrze*, 173.

56. This approach is quite similar to Jakobson's: see esp. his "Randbemerkungen" and "O pokolenii, rastrativshem svoikh poetov" (cited in chap. 4, n. 51).

57. The circumstances of his imprisonment are never made explicit, though they were known to many contemporary readers. This omission turns into ellipsis, a deliberate device that gives to Wat's images an air of Kafkaesque universality.

58. A reference to *The Star of Satan* (*Sous le soleil de Satan*), a novel by Bernanos that Wat had translated in 1928.

59. See Miłosz, "O wierszach Aleksandra Wata," in *Prywatne obowiązki*, 68.

60. Wat, *With the Skin*, 19.

61. See 1 Kings 9:28, 10:11; 2 Chron. 8:18.

62. See Watowa, *Wszystko co najważniejsze*, 30–1.

63. See chap. 13 for a fuller discussion.

64. Written in Menton in February 1956, it was first published in *Twórczość* 11 (1956).

65. Translation by Stanisław Barańczak.

66. See Barańczak, "Four Walls of Pain," 176: "Most of his critics have noticed that from the stylistic viewpoint poems from his later phase represent, as it were, two different models of writing—so different that one could suspect these poems of having been written by two different authors."

67. See Edward Stankiewicz, "Centripetal and Centrifugal Structures in Poetry," *Semiotica* 3/4 (1982), 217–42. See also Barańczak, "Four Walls of Pain," 177.

68. This word order, which emphasizes the eternal character of suffering, appears only in the second version of the poem; in the first, line 5 reads: "już się nigdy nie pozbędę."

69. Zieliński, "Spowiedź syna królewskiego," in *Wiersze wybrane,* 18–19; Karpiński, "Aleksander Wat—krajobrazy poezji," *Zeszyty Literackie* 18 (1987), 66–67; see also the analysis in Barańczak, "Four Walls of Pain," 178–81.

70. Wat, *With the Skin,* 81–83.

71. See Barańczak, "Four Walls of Pain," 179.

72. Written in Menton-Garavan in April 1956 and printed in *Twórczość* 11 (1956) together with the previous poem.

73. Wat, *With the Skin,* 15.

74. Wat, *Mój wiek,* 1:258.

75. See chap. 7.

76. Compare totem and animal disguise in primitive societies.

77. See Łukaszuk, . . . *i w kołysankę,* 135.

78. The best-known example is *The Metamorphosis* by Kafka, where the alienation of the hero, Gregor Samsa, is symbolized by his unexpected transformation into a gigantic insect. Bruno Schulz, a friend of Wat's who was influenced by Kafka, used the plot in one of his stories, in an inverted form: there it is the father who turns into a cockroach, whereas in Kafka's book it is the hero who assumes an entomological form and is, not necessarily willingly, killed by his father.

79. Wat might have known "Lamarck," which was published in 1932 in the popular Soviet periodical *Novyi Mir.*

80. See Osip Mandel'shtam, *Sobranie sochinenii,* 2d ed. (Washington, D.C.: Inter-Language Literary Associates, 1967), 1:499–501; Jennifer Baines, *Mandelstam: The Later Poetry* (Cambridge: Cambridge University Press, 1976), 51–55; Boris Gasparov, "Tridtsatye gody—zheleznyi vek (k analizu motivov stoletnego vozvrashcheniia u Mandel'shtama)," in *Cultural Mythologies of Russian Modernism: From the Golden Age to the Silver Age,* edited by Boris Gasparov, Robert P. Hughes, and Irina Paperno (Berkeley: University of California Press, 1992), 167–71.

81. One cannot help but be reminded here of Wat's escape into illness.

82. Like Mandelstam, Wat emphasizes the "lower" senses (smell, taste, and touch) as characteristic of the nonhuman universe, in which hearing and vision are present only obliquely.

83. The usual words would be *wydziela* and *odpychającą.*

84. Its particularly tight sound organization (*oczach obłe* . . . *księżycowej agonii; zaszyć się* . . . *zły* . . . *zimnymi,* etc.) should be noted.

85. See chap. 3.

86. The appearance of the pronoun *moje* (my) in line 14, signifying the identification of the narrator with the mouse, should be noted.

87. "In many dreams the nuclear center, the Self . . . appears as a crystal. The mathematically precise arrangement of a crystal evokes in us the intuitive feeling that even in so-called 'dead' matter, there is a spiritual ordering principle at work" (Jung et al., *Man and His Symbols,* 209).

88. Wat, *Dziennik bez samogłosek,* 72.

89. There is, e.g., a tradition that brings together the themes of the mouse and the Jew. This became a veritable obsession with Tuwim and was recently employed by Art Spiegelman.

90. See V. N. Toporov, "Mousai 'Muzy': soobrazheniia ob imeni i predystorii obraza (k otsenke frakiiskogo nachala)," in *Slavianskoe i balkanskoe iazykoznanie: Antichnaia balkanistika i sravnitel'naia grammatika* (Moscow: Nauka, 1977), 28–86.

91. Written in Paris in July 1956 and also printed in *Twórczość* 11 (1956).

92. Wat, *With the Skin,* 17–18.

93. See chap. 8.

94. See Franz Winzinger, *Albrecht Dürer in Selbstzeugnissen und Bilddokumenten* (Reinbek bei Hamburg: Rowohlt, 1971), 141, 147.

95. Wat to Pawel Hertz, 16 May 1956, archive of Alina Kowalczykowa. See also Wat, *Moralia*, 10. This meeting with himself had in fact been foretold in *Pug Iron Stove* as early as 1919: "*Behind a counter, you will see your own pale image. How terrible it is to meet one's own pale image at midnight. What?*"

96. Interestingly, hair, represented by the first line, is mentioned in the last line of this first part (line 18), once again, a mirror symmetry.

97. The inversion may be either semantic (*skąd–dokąd*) or semantic and graphic simultaneously (*od–do*).

98. Jung et al., *Man and His Symbols*, 205.

99. On symbolism of the mirror see: J[uan] E[duardo] Cirlot, *A Dictionary of Symbols*, 2d ed., edited and translated by Jack Sage (London: Routledge and Kegan Paul, 1962), 211–12; Ad de Vries, *Dictionary of Symbols and Imagery* (Amsterdam and London: North-Holland Publishing Company, 1974), 323; Umberto Eco, "Mirrors," in *Iconicity: Essays on the Nature of Culture: Festschrift for Thomas A. Sebeok on his 65th Birthday*, edited by Paul Bouissac, Michael Hertzfeld, and Roland Posner (Tübingen: Stauffenburg Verlag, 1986), 215–37; Iu. I. Levin, "Zerkalo kak potentsial'nyi semioticheskii ob'ekt," in *Trudy po znakovym sistemam*, vol. 22 (*Uchenye zapiski Tartuskogo gosudarstvennogo universiteta*, vol. 831 [Tartu, 1988]), 6–24.

100. He could also be the "little corporal" Napoleon, or Stalin, or death itself.

101. First printed in *Nowa Kultura* 48 (1957), date and place of composition unknown.

102. See Jay Braverman, *Jerome's Commentary on Daniel: A Study of Comparative Jewish and Christian Interpretations of the Hebrew Bible* (Washington, D.C.: Catholic Biblical Association of America, 1978), 84–94; Eric William Heaton, *The Book of Daniel: Introduction and Commentary* (London: SCM Press, 1956); Harold Henry Rowles, *Darius the Mede and the Four World Empires in the Book of Daniel: A Historical Study of Contemporary Theories* (Cardiff: University of Wales Press Board, 1959); see also Uriah Smith, *The Prophesies of Daniel and the Revelation* (Nashville, Tenn.: Southern Publishing Association, 1946).

103. See Łukaszuk, . . . *i w kołysankę*, 93–94.

104. See, e.g., Zbigniew Lewicki, *The Bang and the Whimper: Apocalypse and Entropy in American Literature* (Westport, Conn.: Greenwood Press, 1984).

105. Compare Jung et al., *Man and His Symbols*, 207: "The Self is often symbolized as an animal, representing our instinctive nature and its connectedness with one's surroundings."

106. Interestingly, there is a mythological relation between insect and incest, insects in myths sometimes being born of an incestuous relationship; cf. lines 28–29.

107. See Erwin Schimitschek, *Insekten in der Bildenden Kunst im Wandel der Zeiten in psychogenetischer Sicht* (Vienna: Naturhistorisches Museum, 1977).

108. Another text may be being alluded to here is Dante's *Divine Comedy*. "Midway in the journey of life," at the beginning of the poem, Dante faces three beasts: a leopard, a lion, and a she-wolf, which represent three sins, variously interpreted as luxury, pride, and avarice or fraud, violence, and incontinence.

109. Compare the notions of Derrida on the dialectic of presence / absence and these of Iser on the blank as the essential agency in evoking a reader's response. See Jacques Derrida, *Of Grammatology*, translated by Gayatri Chakravorty Spivak (Baltimore: Johns Hopkins University Press, 1976); Wolfgang Iser, *The Act of Reading* (Baltimore: Johns Hopkins University Press, 1978).

110. On hiatus as a constructive principle in the practice of modern Russian poets, see R. D. Timenchik, "Zametki ob akmeizme II," *Russian Literature* 3 (1977), 281–300.

111. Kryszak, "Ból mój, mój demon," 136; Łukasiewicz, "W dwudziestoleciu (O poezji Aleksandra Wata)," 16–19; Barańczak, "Four Walls of Pain," 181–83.

112. Significantly, Christian commentators, from Jerome to John Donne, considered Daniel the preeminent prophet of Christ's coming.

113. First published in *Przegląd Kulturalny* 50 (1956), date and place of composition unknown.

114. See Wat, *My Century*, 165–67.

115. Compare Solzhenitsyn: "Mean to say that the sun up in the sky must bow down to decrees, too?" (*One Day in the Life of Ivan Denisovich*, translated by Ralph Parker [New York: E. P. Dutton, 1963], 69).

116. It was also used in "A Morning over the Water," in the description of the horse (line 7).

117. The biblical name of Satan, Beelzebub, means "Lord of the Flies."

118. See esp. the insightful analysis of Iu. M. Lotman, "Zametki o khudozhestvennom prostranstve. 1. Puteshestvie Ulissa v 'Bozhestvennoi komedii' Dante," in his *Izbrannye stat'i v trekh tomakh*, vol. 1: *Stat'i po semiotike i tipologii kul'tury* (Tallinn: Aleksandra, 1992), 448–57.

119. Wat, *With the Skin*, 25. Wat's words might also be translated "Nothing is ultimate [. . .] / and there's no bottom to the worse."

120. Written in Menton in April 1956 and first printed in *Twórczość* 11 (1956).

121. On this type of verse, see Zbigniew Siatkowski, "Wersyfikacja Tadeusza Różewicza wśród współczesnych metod kształtowania wiersza," *Pamiętnik Literacki* 3 (1958), 119–50.

122. Especially noteworthy are the rhythmic patterns of line 12, which describes the violent movement of Yahweh's hand, and lines 16–17, which mark the moment of the old man's fiery apothesosis.

123. See chap. 3.

124. See chap. 7.

Chapter 11: Emigration, 1957–1967

1. Wat to Iwaszkiewicz, 24 August 1956, Wat archive, file 55.

2. As in his avant-garde years, Wat distinguished himself at this time as a translator of controversial modern literature. He became the first Polish promoter of Jean Genet. Wat's translation of "The Maids" appeared, in 1959, in the liberal periodical *Dialog* (*Dialogue*).

3. Wat archive, file 44.

4. Wat archive, file 19. Zamość is a town in eastern Poland, Jurata a Polish spa on the Baltic Sea.

5. Wat, *Moralia*, in *Pisma wybrane*, 2:5.

6. "Po śmierci," typescript, Wat archive, file 41, 10.

7. Ibid., 3.

8. Ibid., 17.

9. Ibid., 18–19.

10. Ibid., 15.

11. Compare the famous torture scene in Orwell's *Nineteen Eighty-Four*.

12. "Po śmierci," 21–22.

13. It is not known whether Wat was familiar with Orwell's novel (first published in 1949) at the time of writing "After Death," in 1953–54. This may be a case of literary convergence.

14. "Kobiety z Monte Olivetto," typescript, Wat archive, file 14.

15. Ibid., 88–89.

16. On mythical patterns in socialist realism, see Katerina Clark, *The Soviet Novel: History as Ritual* (Chicago: University of Chicago Press, 1981).

17. Like Schweigestill in *Doctor Faustus*.

18. Wat archive, file 49. See also Watowa, *Wszystko co najważniejsze*, 155.

19. Watowa, *Wszystko co najważniejsze*, 155–56.

20. At approximately the same time, some of Wat's poetry was translated into German by Karl Dedecius and into Italian by Teresa Jeleńska and Cesare Vivaldi.

21. See Watowa, *Wszystko co najważniejsze*, 155, 167.

22. See ibid., 156; Hertz, *Listy do Czesława Miłosza, 1952–1979*, 80.

23. Wat archive, file 67.

24. Watowa, *Wszystko co najważniejsze*, 156–57.

25. Wat to Pawel Hertz, 9 April 1960, archive of Alina Kowalczykowa.

26. Wat to Pawel Hertz, 3 June 1960, same archive.

27. Wat archive, file 58. Wat's relationship with Silva Editore is amply documented in file 51 and elsewhere.

28. See Hertz, *Listy do Czesława Miłosza*, 100–102.

29. See Wat to Robert Wolf, 11 July 1962, Wat archive, file 56.

30. Wat archive, file 56.

31. Hertz, *Listy do Czesława Miłosza*, 92.

32. Ibid., 100–101.

33. Watowa, *Wszystko co najważniejsze*, 163–64.

34. Wat to J. and M. Czapski, 5 December 1961, archive of Alina Kowalczykowa.

35. Ola to Broniszówna, 10 January 1962, same archive.

36. *Songs of a Wanderer* appeared in *Twórczość* 7 (1962), albeit in abridged form: the censors cut the sixth song, which referred directly to Stalinist crimes.

37. Wat, *Kartki na wietrze*, in *Pisma wybrane*, 2:180.

38. See Rutkowski, "Nota redakcyjna," in *Pisma wybrane* 1:9.

39. Wat, "'. . . jak upiór staję między wami i pytam o źródło złego'" (1966). See also Wat, *Mój wiek*, 2:202.

40. Wat, *With the Skin*, 58.

41. Abram Terts was actually Andrei Sinyavsky, a Moscow critic and literary scholar born in 1925, who had made his name through a study of Pasternak's poetry. Together with a friend, Yuly Daniel (who wrote under the pseudonym Nikolai Arzhak), Sinyavsky conducted his private war with the Communist regime for several more years. The identities of Terts and Arzhak, known to very few, and certainly not to Wat, were finally uncovered by the Soviet authorities in 1965. Their trial in 1966 became a turning point in the history of the Russian dissident movement, since they both refused to retract, and their imprisonment stirred strong public protests not only in the West but also inside the country. Wat, by then an émigré, took part in the campaign for their release, which became one of his last public actions.

42. A complete Polish translation of the paper appeared only in 1985, in London, in *Pisma wybrane*, 1; but part of it was published in the émigré periodical *Aneks* 21 (1979), 56–70.

43. Watowa, *Wszystko co najważniejsze*, 168.

44. Wat archive, file 65.

45. J. J. Lipski, "Noc ciemna," *Twórczość* 4 (1963), 58–60; Łapiński, "Sny nasze powszednie;" Międzyrzecki, "Poeta nowy." There was only one lukewarm review: Wilkón, "Wata pieśni rozlewne."

46. Watowa, *Wszystko co najważniejsze*, 169.

47. Wat archive, file 44.

48. See Wat, *Dziennik bez samogłosek*, in *Pisma wybrane*, 2:71–74.

49. Lebenstein subsequently designed the cover for Wat's posthumous book of poetry, *Lumen Obscurum*. On the book's title, see chap. 13.

50. Wat, *Dziennik bez samogłosek*, 79.

51. See ibid., 84.

52. See Karpiński, "Aleksander Wat—krajobrazy poezji," 56; also Karpiński to Wat, 7 October 1965, Wat archive, file 50.

53. Wat, *Dziennik bez samogłosek*, 69–70.

54. See, e.g., *Kartki na wietrze*, 216–17. See also the unpublished part of "Dziennik bez samogłosek," Wat archive, file 30.

55. Wat, *Dziennik bez samogłosek*, 76.

56. Ibid., 93.

57. Wat, *With the Skin*, 94.

58. Wat, *Dziennik bez samogłosek*, 111.

59. Ibid., 140.

60. Ibid., 121.

61. Ibid., 124.

62. Ibid., 102, 105.

63. See *Kartki na wietrze*, 205; Miłosz, Foreword to Wat, *My Century*, xxi–xxii.

64. Miłosz, Foreword to *My Century*, xxii.

65. See Wat, *Kartki na wietrze*, 205–6.

66. Wat archive, file 67.

67. Wat, *Kartki na wietrze*, 206.

68. Wat, *Dziennik bez samogłosek*, 79.

69. Miłosz, Foreword to *My Century*, xxii–xxiii.

70. Watowa, *Wszystko co najważniejsze*, 170.

71. Their address was at first given as Parc de Sceaux (Antony and Parc de Sceaux are contiguous suburbs).

72. Watowa, *Wszystko co najważniejsze*, 173.

73. Wat, *Dziennik bez samogłosek*, 149.

74. Ibid., 152.

75. Wat, *Kartki na wietrze*, 220. "*Kto kogo*" (Who—whom): a quotation from Lenin.

76. See Wat to Broniszówna, 30 November 1965, archive of Alina Kowalczykowa.

77. "O 'Antologii poezji polskiej' mówią: Julian Przyboś, Artur Sandauer, Maciej Żurowski i Janusz Wilhelmi," *Kultura* [Warsaw] 3 (1966).

78. Oral communication of Andrzej Wat. See also Wat to Broniszówna, 8 December 1966, Wat archive, file 7.

79. One was the aforementioned French anthology edited by Jeleński; Miłosz published the one in English, Karl Dedecius that in German.

80. See chap. 10.

81. Wat, "O przetłumaczalności utworów poetyckich," in *Pisma wybrane*, 3:186. The idea came to Wat in Zamarstynów prison: see *My Century*, 141.

82. Wat archive, file 8.

83. Watowa, *Wszystko co najważniejsze*, 174.

84. Wat archive, file 67.

85. Aleksander Wat, *Poezje zebrane*, compiled by Anna Micińska and Jan Zieliński (Kraków: Znak, 1992), 436.

86. Hertz, *Listy do Czesława Miłosza*, 245.

Chapter 12: A Critique of Stalinist Reason

1. Nowicki, "Aleksandra Wata porządek myślenia," 117.

2. On Rozanov, see Anna Lisa Crone, *Rozanov and the End of Literature: Polyphony and the Dissolution of Genre in "Solitaria" and "Fallen Leaves"* (Würzburg: Jal-Verlag, 1978); A. Siniavskii, "*Opavshie List'ia*" *V. V. Rozanova* (Paris: Syntaxis, 1982).

3. Wat has in mind here Józef Czapski's preface to the French translation of Rozanov's book *La Face sombre du Christ* (Paris: Gallimard, 1964).

4. Wat, *Dziennik bez samogłosek*, in *Pisma wybrane*, 2:123.

5. The title *Scraps of Paper in the Wind* refers directly to Rozanov's *Fallen Leaves*.

6. Wat, *Moralia*, in *Pisma wybrane*, 2:35.

7. Ibid., 54.

8. Ibid., 5.

9. Ibid., 13. See also chap. 2.

10. See chap. 5.

11. See chap. 11.

12. See Wat, *Moralia*, 25.

13. Ibid., 6.

14. Ibid., 24.

15. See chap. 6.

16. Wat, *Moralia*, 37.

17. Ibid., 26.

18. See ibid., 30.

19. Ibid., 45.

20. Ibid.

21. "Mad Baroque, uncontrollable *art nouveau* as a tool of cognition" is their main distinguishing feature, in the words of Karpiński ("Aleksander Wat—klucz i hak," *Zeszyty Literackie* 19 [1987], 64).

22. See Wat, "Klucz i hak," in *Pisma wybrane*, 1:3.

23. Wat here refers to *The Savage Mind*, the influential book on the thought and mythology of primitive peoples by Claude Lévi-Strauss.

24. See chap. 9.

25. Wat, "Kilka uwag o związkach między literaturą i rzeczywistością sowiecką," in *Pisma wybrane*, 1:114.

26. Ibid., 116.

27. Ibid.

28. See Wat, "Klucz i hak," 11.

29. See chap. 11.

30. See esp. Wat, "Dziewięć uwag do portretu Józefa Stalina," in *Pisma wybrane*, 1:139–42, 148.

31. Wat, "Klucz i hak," 12.

32. See ibid., 13; also Wat, "Kilka uwag," 117.

33. Wat, "Klucz i hak," 13.

34. Wat, "Kilka uwag," 113.

35. See chap. 6.

36. Wat, "Kilka uwag," 115.

37. Karpiński, "Aleksander Wat—klucz i hak," 64. Wat took the dichotomy of "the key" and "the hook" from Pascal but transformed both concepts significantly.

38. Wat, "Kilka uwag," 119.

39. See Umberto Eco, *La struttura assente* (Milan: Bompiani, 1968), 90.

40. See Wat, "Kilka uwag," 120.

41. Wat, "Klucz i hak," 13.

42. Abram Terts could perhaps be considered one of its representatives, although Wat had many reservations about his writing.

43. This observation was in general true in 1963, when Wat made it; but baroque trends subsequently became apparent in new Russian writing, especially in the poetry of Joseph Brodsky, which paralleled, to a degree, Wat's poetry and may have been influenced by it. (Brodsky had translated Wat into Russian.)

44. Wat, "Klucz i hak," 33.

45. Victor Klemperer, *LTI: Notizbuch eines Philologen* (Berlin: Aufbau-Verlag, 1947).

46. See Jonathan Culler, *On Deconstruction: Theory and Criticism after Structuralism* (Ithaca, N.Y.: Cornell University Press, 1982); Christopher Norris, *Deconstruction: Theory and Practice* (London: Methuen, 1982); G. Douglas Atkins, *Reading Deconstruction, Deconstructive Reading* (Lexington: University Press of Kentucky, 1983); John M. Ellis, *Against Deconstruction* (Princeton, N.J.: Princeton University Press, 1989).

47. See chap. 10.

48. The concept was introduced in the ground-breaking article by A. A. Zalizniak, V. V. Ivanov, and V. N. Toporov, "O vozmozhnosti strukturno-tipologicheskogo izucheniia nekotorykh modeliruiushchikh semioticheskikh sistem," in *Strukturno-tipologicheskie issledovaniia: Sbornik statei* (Moscow: Izdatel'stvo Akademii Nauk SSSR, 1962), 134–43.

49. See chap. 3. This is particularly striking since Wat had almost certainly never read the Russian thinker, whose principal work, *Problems of Dostoevsky's Poetics*, became available to the general public only in 1963 (its first edition of 1929 went unnoticed outside Russia and was soon suppressed). By that time, Wat's essays on Stalinist language had already been written. Wat, as far as I know, never mentioned Bakhtin in his works.

50. See Dorota Mazurek, "Metafora 'klucza i haka' w eseistyce Wata," in *Pamięć głosów*, 103–4.

51. See e.g., its evaluation in Gorczyńska, "Komunizm oczami poety," 142.

52. Wat, "Dziewięć uwag," 153–55; id., "Dostojewski i Stalin," in *Pisma wybrane*, 1:188.

53. Wat, "Dziewieć uwag," 170. Cf. id., *My Century*, 145–46.

54. See Wat, "Dziewięć uwag," 161.

55. Ibid., 157.

56. Jean Starobinski, "The Style of Autobiography," translated by Seymour Chatman, in *Autobiography: Essays Theoretical and Critical*, edited by James Olney (Princeton, N.J.: Princeton University Press, 1980), 78–79.

57. To quote a contemporary analysis of Christian autobiographies: "the encyclopedic mirror reflects what leads the individual to model himself on Christ; and what draws him away from his model when he, a sinner, allows himself to be inveigled into imitating the Devil. The medieval mirror encodes an ambivalence, and the need for choice—it evokes the risk inherent in every human destiny oriented towards salvation" (Michel Beaujour, *Poetics of the Literary Self-Portrait*, translated by Yara Milos [New York: New York University Press, 1991], 30).

58. Jeleński, "Lumen obscurum: O poezji Aleksandra Wata," quoted incorrectly in Miłosz, Foreword to *My Century*, xx.

59. Georges Gusdorf, "Conditions and Limits of Autobiography," translated by James Olney in *Autobiography*, 42.

60. Ibid.

61. Wat, *My Century*, 73–74.

62. See Jerome Hamilton Buckley, *The Turning Key: Autobiography and the Subjective Impulse since 1800* (Cambridge, Mass.: Harvard University Press, 1984), vii.

63. Wat, *My Century*, 9.

64. Ibid., 13.

65. Gusdorf, "Conditions and Limits," 42.

66. James Olney, *Metaphors of Self: The Meaning of Autobiography* (Princeton, N.J.: Princeton University Press, 1972), 36.

67. Wat, *My Century*, 287. In fact, Wat becomes much more frank about his erotic life in *Scraps of Paper in the Wind* when he recounts his early sexual experiences, and *Diary without Vowels* presents as much material for a psychoanalyst as any modern autobiography.

68. See Zieliński, "Powrót do rzeczy," 11.

69. Wat, *My Century*, 291.

70. See chap. 1.

71. In a broader perspective, these patterns may be traced to ancient allegorical narratives describing a spiritual quest punctuated by meaningful encounters (e.g., *Perceval, Divine Comedy*, and *Pilgrim's Progress*). See Angus Fletcher, *Allegory: The Theory of a Symbolic Mode* (Ithaca, N.Y. Cornell University Press, 1964).

72. Olney, *Metaphors of Self*, 30.

73. The following discussion draws on certain concepts first formulated in Tomas Venclova, "Prison as Communicative Phenomenon: The Literature of Gulag," *Comparative Civilizations Review* 2 (1979), 65–73. It also owes much to the unpublished dissertation by Elizabeth Anne Cole, "Towards a Poetics of Russian Prison Literature : Writings on Prison by Dostoevsky, Chekhov, and Solzhenitsyn" (Yale University, 1991).

74. See Victor Brombert, *La Prison romantique: essai sur l'imaginaire* (Paris: J. Corti, 1975).

75. A pretender to the Russian throne imprisoned by Catherine the Great. According to legend, she perished during a flood that inundated her cell.

76. Wat, *Mój wiek*, 2:32.

77. Wat, *My Century*, 167.

78. Ibid., 185.

79. Ibid., 213. See also chap. 7.

80. Ibid., 218.

81. See Wat, *Mój wiek*, 2:181.

82. Ibid., 2:38–39. Cf. chap. 7.

83. Wat, *My Century*, 66.

84. Ibid., 206.

85. Ibid., 264.

86. Ibid., 187.

87. Ibid., 152.

88. Ibid., 292.

89. Ibid., 79.

90. Wat, *Mój wiek*, 2:39. See chap. 7.

91. Wat, *My Century*, 277.

92. See Viktor Shklovskii, *Za i protiv: Zametki o Dostoevskom* (Moscow: Sovetskii pisatel', 1957), 107.

93. Wat, *My Century*, 266.

94. This exchange continues in the closed world of the Alma-Ata hotel, which recalls a prison, if a relatively luxurious one, in more than one respect.

95. See, e.g., the almost "transrational language" of Kim, the Korean whom Wat meets in Lubyanka.

96. See Wat, *Mój wiek*, 1:198.

97. Wat, *My Century*, 219.

98. Ibid., 173.

99. Ibid., 178.

100. See his *Surveiller et punir* (Paris: Gallimard, 1975).

101. For more on this, see John Bender, *Imagining the Penitentiary: Fiction and the Architecture of Mind in the Eighteenth Century* (Chicago: University of Chicago Press, 1965).

102. Wat, *My Century*, 230.

103. Wat, *Mój wiek*, 1:336.

104. Wat, *My Century*, 241.

Chapter 13: Endgame

1. Wat, *My Century*, 210.

2. Ibid., 209.

3. "'Twarzą zwrócony do śmierci'," 12–13.

4. See Mandelstam's essay "O sobesednike" (On the Addressee, 1913) in his *Sobranie sochinenii*, vol. 2 (New York: Inter-Language Literary Associates, 1971), 233–240.

5. On this, see Wojciech Ligęza, "Wat—poeta emigracyjny," in *Pamięć głosów*, 50.

6. It gradually became a pivotal feature of the Polish émigré community, but this process reached fruition only after Wat's death.

7. See "'Twarzą zwrócony,'" 10–12.

8. See David M. Bethea, *Joseph Brodsky and the Creation of Exile* (Princeton, N.J.: Princeton University Press, 1994), 46.

9. "'Twarzą zwrócony,'" 4.

10. Translation by Miłosz.

11. In *Moralia*, Wat confesses that he introduced the motif of Concord and Discord into the poem spontaneously, without any prior thought of Empedocles and his system. See *Moralia*, in *Pisma wybrane*, 2:9–10.

12. See, e.g., Helle Lambridis, *Empedocles: A Philosophical Investigation* (University: University of Alabama Press, 1976), 48–52.

13. On the failure of Wat's attempts to escape his past, see Julian Kornhauser, "Jak czytano 'Wiersze śródziemnomorskie' Aleksandra Wata," in *Pamięć głosów*, 126–27.

14. Wat employs here the traditional Polish rendering of the meters of Greek tragic choruses. It may be noted, for example, that the first ten-syllable dactylotrochaic line of the passage quoted coincides rhythmically with the famous opening lines of the apostrophe to the boat sung by the chorus of Trojan maidens in Jan Kochanowski's tragedy *Odprawa posłów greckich* (The Dismissal of the Grecian Envoys), published as early as 1578: O białoskrzydła morska pławaczko, / Wychowanico Idy wysokiej . . . / (O white-winged sea-swimmer, / Brought up by the lofty Mount Ida).

15. In both the poem and its commentary, Wat mentions nightmares haunting tourists in Taormina in conjunction with Jung's claim that immigrants in the United States frequently saw in their dreams symbols of pre-Columbian mythology.

16. See Julia Kristeva, *Étrangers à nous-mêmes* (Paris: Fayard, 1989), 13–14; Bethea, *Joseph Brodsky*, 41–42.

17. The last line, as Wat notes in the commentary, refers to *Oresteia*.

18. Kornhauser, "Jak czytano," 117.

19. "Na wypadek konfiskaty 'Wierszy śródziemnomorskich.' Przedmowa," Wat archive, file 13, 1.

20. The Twenty-Second Congress of the CPSU, which took place in 1961, gave rise to a denunciation of Stalin and his henchmen, limited but more extensive than that of 1956.

21. Wat, "Na wypadek," 2.

22. See Pietrych, "Obraz natury w 'Pieśniach wędrowca' Aleksandra Wata," 74.

23. See Wat, "Na wypadek," 3: "Without demonizing, I saw Stalin in the colossal perspective of the menacing demiurge of the universe."

24. All the translated fragments of *Songs of a Wanderer* are taken from Wat, *With the Skin*, 47–61.

25. The point of departure for the poem was the fine garden at La Messuguière, which Wat elsewhere described as marked by "an immeasurable silence" (see chap. 11), and which looked out at the panorama of the Provence mountains.

26. See Cirlot, *Dictionary of Symbols*, 314; de Vries, *Dictionary of Symbols and Imagery*, 443.

27. It is tempting to interpret the symbol of stone as also connoting the Catholic Church, built on the rock of St. Peter: see the New Testament pun on his name in Matt. 16:18.

28. Wat's paean to stone has many analogies in twentieth-century poetry, including that of Poland. The first and, in many respects, most important collection of Mandelstam's poems bears the title *Stone*, referring to both the immutable Logos of ancient philosophy and the firmness and durability of medieval architecture. One possible influence on Wat's description of stone could be the lyrical studies of everyday objects (including a pebble) by Francis Ponge. Simultaneously with *Songs of a Wanderer*, the poem "Rozmowa z kamieniem" (A Talk with a Stone) was published by Wisława Szymborska, one of the most significant Polish poets of the younger generation. Szymborska's poem focuses on a stone's imperviousness and isolation from the human universe. Among more distant analogies might be noted the work of visual artists who took a particular interest in matter, its substances and textures, such as Jean Fautrier, Antonio Tapiés, and Alberto Burri, who rose to prominence in the 1950s and 1960s.

29. See Pietrych, "Obraz natury," 78-79.

30. An obvious reference to Jacob's pillow: Gen. 28:11.

31. Significantly, the words *na krawędzi zaśnięcia* (on the edge of sleep) are introduced into the scene, echoing the preceding mention of the demiurge, creator of the transitory world of beauty, birth, and decay.

32. See also Wat's memoirs: "My road to Damascus was impeded by an obstacle, certainly not the only, but an imperative one: the voice of my father, *remember, remember*" (*Mój wiek*, 2:334). See chap. 8.

33. In the English translation, the biblical allusion is less than obvious. Polish "jestem tym, którym jestem" refers to God's words to Moses, *'ehyeh-'asher-'ehyeh*, "I am that I am" (Exod. 3:14). See Łukasiewicz, "W dwudziestoleciu," 15; Pietrych, "Obraz natury," 81. It should be noted, however, that the biblical formula appeared only in the final version of the poem that was included in *Ciemne świecidło;* in the edition of 1962, the line read: "jestem tym, którym byłem" (I am what I had been).

34. Cirlot, *Dictionary of Symbols*, 314.

35. See above and Wat, *With the Skin*, 73. The same motifs are amply represented in *Dreams from the Shore of the Mediterranean* and in other poems by Wat, starting with his "Fragment" of 1946, which describes the Uchkurgan valley in Soviet Central Asia.

36. The motif of eczema is, as mentioned in chap. 11, strictly autobiographical.

37. Wat, *With the Skin*, 73.

38. Ibid., 74.

39. The hunter also plays a crucial role in *Dreams from the Shore of the Mediterranean*.

40. A. N. Shelepin, speech to the Twenty-second Congress of the CPSU, quoted in Robert Conquest, *The Great Terror: Stalin's Purge of the Thirties* (Harmondsworth: Penguin, 1971), 305.

41. Wat, *Mój wiek*, 2:339.

42. Adam Schaff, a Polish Marxist philosopher.

43. In his commentary, Wat cites here a letter by Niccolò Machiavelli, alluding to the popular definition of Stalinism as latter day Machiavellism.

44. See chap. 10. Interestingly, the eighth song also quotes *Pug Iron Stove*.

45. Compare the motif of falling in the first and tenth songs.

46. It is virtually a separate piece, dedicated to Ola on their thirty-fifth wedding anniversary, and therefore presumably written on or before 24 January 1962, earlier than the bulk of *Songs of a Wanderer*.

47. Technically, it is patterned after the Catholic litany to the Virgin Mary (the so-called Lorettan litany, officially approved in 1601), which consists of a long series of invocations; it is also reminiscent of the "song of the bones" (which in turn is modelled on the Lorettan litany) in the second part of Eliot's *Ash Wednesday*.

344 NOTES TO PAGES 298-307

48. Plato, *The Republic*, newly translated by Richard W. Sterling and William C. Scott (New York: W. W. Norton, 1985), 95.

49. The most specific meaning of *wyświecić,* "to emit in the shape of light," is attested by Mickiewicz's *The Great Improvisation,* in which Konrad states that his will, emitted in a mighty burst, would light up a hundred stars.

50. See Jeleński, "Lumen obscurum."

51. Wat, *With the Skin,* 98. In the published English translation, one sentence of the original is omitted. The end of the first part of the poem should read: "Even transparent. On the streak of Chaos, / which is, of course, dark. But / a misunderstanding, / semantic, today reigns over all and sundry."

52. See Iurii Ivask, "Ditia Evropy," in Osip Mandel'shtam, *Sobranie sochinenii* (New York: Inter-Language Literary Associates, 1969), 3:x–xi; "Chernoe solnce," ibid., 404–11; A. Ia. Syrkin, *Nekotorye voprosy izucheniia upanishad* (Moscow: Nauka, 1971), 81–85; Gregory Freidin, *A Coat of Many Colors: Osip Mandelstam and his Mythologies of Self-Presentation* (Berkeley: University of California Press, 1987), 311–12; see also V. B. Mikushevich, "Opyt lichnogo bessmertiia v poezii Osipa Mandel'shtama," in *Slovo i sud'ba: Osip Mandel'shtam, Issledovaniia i materialy* (Moscow: Nauka, 1991), 307–11.

53. See Stala, "Od czarnego słońca do ciemnego świecidła;" Wojdyło, "Malarstwo i kolor w poezji Aleksandra Wata," 115–16.

54. A good example of a surrealist poem with a strong satirical tinge is "Elementy do portretu" (Elements for a Portrait), perhaps related to the essay with a similar title, "Some Strokes for a Future Portrait of Stalin." In it, a veritable "metonymic madness" reigns, and disjointed parts of the body frolic in a Daliesque landscape, dreaming in vain about consolidation into a painting in formal Soviet style. Another instance is "Król i sny królewskie" (A King and His Dreams), an occasional, purely nonsensical poem that makes fun of Jerzy Giedroyc and the staff of *Culture,* the title of which is anagrammatized in the text (see Zieliński, "Spowiedź syna królewskiego," 8).

55. Wat, "Prawdziwy początek Iwana Denisowicza," in *Pisma wybrane,* 1:231.

56. Compare *Moralia,* 33: "And, besides, 'to serve.' Personally, I don't like it, even in a figurative sense. *Non serviam.*"

57. Interestingly, this same device was employed in a parody of Wat's poetry written by Józef Mondschein and published as early as 1921. See Zieliński, "Wiersze dla Wata," 134–6. Cf. chap. 10 on the Dürer poem.

58. See chap. 10.

59. Thus, the poem "Z Hezjoda" (From Hesiod) imitates closely Hesiod's rendering of the myth concerning the four ages and four races of men (golden, silver, bronze, and iron) yet is replete with references to Genesis and the prophets.

60. These names were probably invented by Wat (Tirzah was a daughter of Zelophehad: Num. 26:33, 27:1). The Jewish tradition does not assign names to Cain's and Abel's wives, but, according to Muslim tradition, they were Kelimia and Lubda.

61. Wat, *With the Skin,* 79–80.

62. See chap. 3.

63. Miłosz, "O wierszach Aleksandra Wata," 72.

64. See Aleksander Fiut, "'Uwierzytelnić swą nieprzynależność," in *Pamięć głosów,* 19–20.

65. Lucan, *The Civil War (Pharsalia),* with an English translation by J. D. Duff (Cambridge, Mass.: Harvard University Press, 1977), 429.

66. Wat, *Mój wiek,* 2:80.

Select Bibliography

Works by Wat are listed in chronological order, works about Wat in alphabetical order.

Works by Wat

BOOKS (in Polish and in English)

JA z jednej strony i JA z drugiej strony mego mopsożelaznego piecyka. Warsaw: Nakladem B. Skra-Kamińskiej, 1920.

Bezrobotny Lucyfer. Opowieści. Warsaw: F. Hoesick, 1927.

———. Warsaw: Czytelnik, 1960.

Wiersze. Kraków: Wydawnictwo Literackie, 1957.

Wiersze śródziemnomorskie. Warsaw: Państwowy Instytut Wydawniczy, 1962.

Ciemne świecidło. Paris: Libella, 1968.

Mój wiek: Pamiętnik mówiony. Foreward by Czesław Miłosz. Prepared for publication by Lidia Ciolkoszowa. 2 vols. London: Polonia, 1977.

———. 2d rev. ed. London: Polonia, 1981.

———. Warsaw: Niezależna Oficyna. Wydawnicza, 1980 [1983]. [Underground rpt. of 1977 edition.]

———. Warsaw: Wydawnictwo Krąg, 1983. [Underground rpt. of 1981 edition.]

———. Warsaw: Czytelnik, 1990.

Ewokacja. Kraków: Wydawnictwo KOS, 1981. [Underground edition.]

Świat na haku i pod kluczem: Eseje. Vol. 1 of *Pisma wybrane.* Compiled by Krzysztof Rutkowski. London: Polonia, 1985.

———. Kraków: Wydawnictwo -x-, 1988. [Underground reprint.]

Dziennik bez samogłosek. Vol. 2 of *Pisma wybrane.* Compiled by Krzysztof Rutkowski. London: Polonia, 1986.

———. [Kraków]: Oficyna Literacka, 1987. [Underground reprint.]

———. Warsaw: Czytelnik, 1990.

Pisma wybrane. Compiled by K. Rutkowski. Warsaw: OW Reduta, 1986. [Underground edition.]

Rapsodie polityczne: Eseje. Wrocław and Warsaw: Wers, 1987. [Underground edition.]

Ucieczka Lotha: Proza. Vol. 3 of *Pisma wybrane.* Compiled by Krzysztof Rutkowski. London: Polonia, 1988.

———. Oficyna Wydawnicza Margines [Oficyna Literacka], 1989. [Underground reprint.]

Wiersze wybrane. Selected and compiled by A. Micińska and J. Zieliński. Warsaw: Państwowy Instytut Wydawniczy, 1987.

Poezje zebrane. Compiled by Anna Micińska and Jan Zieliński. Kraków: Znak, 1992.

Bezrobotny Lucyfer i inne opowieści. Selected and compiled by Włodzimierz Bolecki and Jan Zieliński. Preface by Włodzimierz Bolecki. Warsaw: Czytelnik, 1993.

Mediterranean Poems. Edited and translated by Czesław Miłosz. Ann Arbor, Mich.: Ardis, 1977.

My Century: The Odyssey of a Polish Intellectual. Edited and translated by Richard Lourie, with a foreword by Czesław Miłosz. Berkeley: University of California Press, 1988.

———. New York: W. W. Norton, 1990.

With the Skin: Poems of Aleksander Wat. Translated and edited by Czesław Miłosz and Leonard Nathan. New York: Ecco Press, 1989.

Lucifer Unemployed. Translated by Lillian Vallee, with a foreword by Czesław Miłosz. Evanston, Ill.: Northwestern University Press, 1990.

UNCOLLECTED ARTICLES AND OTHER MATERIALS

"Prymitywiści do narodów świata i do polski." manifesto, written with Anatol Stern. *gga. pierwszy polski almanach poezji futurystycznej. dwumiesięcznik prymitywistów.* Warsaw: Futur Polski, 1920; rpt. in A. Lam, *Polska awangarda poetycka. Programy lat 1917–1923,* vol. 2: *Manifesty i protesty. Antologia,* Kraków: Wydawnictwo Literackie, 1969, 170–72; H. Zaworska, *Antologia polskiego futuryzmu i Nowej Sztuki,* Wrocław: Zakład Narodowy im. Ossolińskich, 1978, 3–6.

"Plastyka." *Nowa Sztuka* 2 (1922), 28.

"St. I. Witkiewicz: *Szkice estetyczne.*" Review. *Nowa Sztuka* 2 (1922), 29–30.

"Bosel, Chaplin, Dempsey, Edison i M-elle Mimi." *Almanach Nowej Sztuki* 1 (1924), 19.

"Stanisław Ignacy Witkiewicz, pogromca tradycyjnego teatru." *Ekran i Scena* 11 (1926).

"Teatr w dzisiejszej Rosji Sowieckiej." *Ekran i Scena* 14 (1926).

"Uwagi o Chestertonie." *Wiadomości Literackie* 18 (1927).

"Czego broni Chesterton." Review. *Wiadomości Literackie* 25 (1927).

"Nim ją reskrypt do życia powoła." *Wiadomości Literackie* 43 (1927).

"Co zawdzięczają pisarze polscy literaturom obcym?" Answer to a questionnaire. *Wiadomości Literackie* 47 (1927).

"Poezje Czyżewskiego." Review. *Wiadomości Literackie* 16 (1928).

"Ce que les écrivains polonais doivent aux littératures étrangères: Enquête de la 'Pologne Littéraire.'" Answer to a questionnaire. *Pologne Littéraire* 23/24 (1928).

"Chestertonica." Review. *Wiadomości Literackie* 42 (1928).

"Nieporozumienia krytyki literackiej." *Wiek XX* 1 (1928).

"Dola robotnicza: Scena z faktomontażu teatralnego pt. *Polityka Społeczna.*" Fragment of a play. *Pobudka* 53 (1929).

"'Zazdrość' Olieszy." Review. *Wiadomości Literackie* 31 (1929).

"'Literatura faktu.'" Review. *Wiadomości Literackie* 35 (1929).

"Pacyfistyczna literatura w Niemczech." *Miesięcznik Literacki* 1 (1929), 21–32.

"Klusownictwo frazesów." Polemics with A. Słonimski. *Miesięcznik Literacki* 2 (1930), 117–19.

"Wspomnienia o futuryzmie." *Miesięcznik Literacki* 2 (1930), 68–77.

"Metamorfozy futuryzmu" *Miesięcznik Literacki* 3 (1930), 121–28.

"E. Glaeser: *Rocznik 1902.*" Review. *Miesięcznik Literacki* 3 (1930), 159–60.

"Z. Nałkowska: *Dom kobiet.*" Review. *Miesięcznik Literacki* 5 (1930), 272–73.

"Odpowiedź Redakcji." Polemics with T. Peiper. *Miesięcznik Literacki* 5 (1930), 280.

"Poeta rewolucji Majakowski." *Miesięcznik Literacki* 6 (1930), 281–88.
"Reportaż jako rodzaj literacki." *Miesięcznik Literacki* 7 (1930), 330–34.
"Łosoś w majonezie, Liga Narodów i radosny cień króla Stasia." *Miesięcznik Literacki* 9 (1930), 410–12.
"Jeszcze o reportażu." *Miesięcznik Literacki* 10 (1930), 425–26.
"W pracowniach stylu." *Miesięcznik Literacki* 17 (1931), 773–80.
"Za porozumieniem." Signed with other authors. *Lewar* 11 (1935), 2.
"Pisarze polscy witają zjednoczenie Ukrainy." Signed with other authors. *Czerwony Sztandar* 48 (1939).
"Kobieta radziecka." *Czerwony Sztandar* 61 (1939).
"Pomost do literatury radzieckiej." *Czerwony Sztandar* 65 (1939).
"Pol'skie i sovetskie pisateli." *Literaturnaia gazeta* 66 (1939).
"Delegatka ze Lwowa." *Czerwony Sztandar* 81 (1939).
"Przemysł materiałów budowlanych." *Czerwony Sztandar* 90 (1940).
"Śp. Stanisław Rogoż." Obituary. *Polska* 12/13 (1942).
"Przemówienie Aleksandra Wata na zjeździe PEN Clubów." Speech. *Odrodzenie* 23 (1947).
"Bitwa pod Zurychem." *Odrodzenie* 27 (1947).
"Łzy i słuszna miara." *Przekrój* 118 (1947).
"Nil nisi veritas." Polemics with S. Kisielewski. *Tygodnik Powszechny* 122 (1947).
"Sprostowanie Aleksandra Wata." Polemics with A. Włodek. *Dziennik Literacki* 8 (1948).
"Błahy komentarz do rzeczy wielkich." *Odrodzenie* 13/14 (1948).
"Od Zurychu po Kopenhagę." *Nowiny Literackie* 31 (1948).
"Quelques vues sur la littérature polonaise d'aujourd'hui." *Kuźnica* 34/35 (1948).
"Druga zbrodnia Salome: Szkic scenariusza do filmu w technikolorze." Script. *Przekrój* 181 (1948), 8–10.
"O Lucjanie Rudnickim." *Odrodzenie* 50 (1948).
"Kronika, ale nie-dobrowolska." *Nowiny Literackie* 33 (1948).
"Dosyć dyskusji! Realizm trzeba realizować. . . ." Interview. *Express Wieczorny* 22 (1949).
"'Oto jest miasto śpiewne.'" *Odrodzenie* 34 (1949).
"'Niemcy'—Leona Kruczkowskiego." Review. *Odrodzenie* 44 (1949).
"Nad koleżką profesora Heisenberga—rozmyślanie." Polemics with J. Przyboś. *Nowa Kultura* 16 (1958).
"Dwa głosy poetów." Statement. *Wiadomości* 42 (1959).
"'Klub Krzywego Koła.' O książce Witolda Jedlickiego." Review. *Na Antenie* 9 (1963).
"Le 'réalisme socialiste.'" *Le Contrat Social* 7 (September–October 1963), 271–73.
"La mort d'un vieux bolchévik: Souvenirs sur Stieklov." *Le Contrat Social* 7 (November–December 1963), 322–30.
"Oświadczenie." Statement. *Kultura* 11 (1963), 106–7.
"O wolności." *Kultura* 11 (1963), 46–48.
"'. . . jak upiór staję między wami i pytam o źródło złego' . . . Głos Aleksandra Wata." *Na Antenie* 43 (1966).
"Posłowie od autora." Author's afterword. *Oficyna Poetów* 2 (1967), 16.
"O solidarność z Izraelem." Statement. *Wiadomości* 27 (1967).

TRANSLATIONS

J. Cocteau. "Sekrety zawodowe (Wybór fragmentow)." *Almanach Nowej Sztuki* 2 (1925), 67–69.
L. Bruun. *Białe noce (Primabalerina Jego Cesarskiej Mości)*. Novel. Warsaw: Rój, 1927; several reprintings.

M. H. Dupuy Mazuel, *Gracz w szachy*, 2 vols. Warsaw: Rój, 1927.

I. Erenburg [Ehrenburg]. *Trzynaście fajek*. Stories. Warsaw: Rój, 1927.

O. Henry. *Bluff*. Stories. Warsaw: J. Mortkowicz, 1927.

―――. *Opowieści*. Stories. Warsaw: Rój, 1927.

―――. *Romans na promie*. Stories. Warsaw: Rój, 1927.

―――. *Szlachetny farmazon*. Stories. Warsaw: Rój, 1928.

G. Bernanos. *Pod słońcem szatana*. Novel. Warsaw: Rój, 1928; rpt. Warsaw: Pax, 1949.

F. Dostojewski [Dostoevsky]. *Bracia Karamazow*. vols. 1-4. Novel. Warsaw: Rój, 1928; several reprintings.

O. Henry. *Kryjówka Czarnego Billa*. Stories. Warsaw: Rój, 1928.

F. Dostojewski [Dostoevsky]. *Zimowe notatki o wrażeniach z lata*. Essays. Warsaw: Rój, 1929.

―――. *830 dolarów*. Stories. Warsaw: Rój, 1929.

P. Benoit. *Aksela*. Novel. Warsaw: Rój, 1930; rpt. Warsaw: Rój, 1936.

E. Glaeser. *Rocznik 1902*. Novel. Warsaw: Rój, 1930.

P. Istrati. *Rzeź na pustyni*. Novel. Warsaw: Biblion, 1930.

J. Wassermann. *Krzysztof Kolumb: Don Kichot Oceanu*. Novel. Warsaw: J. Mortkowicz, 1931; rpt. Poznań: Wielkopolska Ksiggarnia Wydawnicza, 1949.

P. Omm. *Podziemna dyktatura: Wojna alkoholowa w Stanach Zjednoczonych*. Essay. Warsaw: Gebethner i Wolff, 1932.

I. Erenburg [Ehrenburg]. *Fabryka snów*. Essay. Warsaw: Rój, 1933.

―――. *Dzień wtóry*. Novel. Warsaw: Rój, 1935; rpt. Warsaw: Iskry, 1954, 1956.

H. Mann. *Młodość króla Henryka Czwartego*. Novel. Warsaw: Rój, 1936; several reprintings [vol. 1 in Wat's translation].

J. Roth. *Falszywa waga*. Novel. Warsaw: Rój, 1939; rpt. Warsaw: Państwowy Instytut Wydawniczy, 1961.

A. Gajdar [Gaidar]. *Czuk i Hek*. Children's story. Warsaw: Nasza Księgarnia, 1949; several reprintings.

O. Henry. *Ostatni liść*. Stories. Warsaw: Książka i Wiedza, 1950.

M. Gorki [Gorky]. *Wassa Żeleznowa*. Play [with O. Wat]. Warsaw: Państwowy Instytut Wydawniczy, 1951; rpt. in M. Gorki, *Pisma*, vol. 10, Warsaw: Państwowy Instytut Wydawniczy, 1956.

A. Gajdar [Gaidar]. *Timur i jego drużyna*. Children's story. Warsaw: Nasza Księgarnia, 1952; several reprintings.

―――. *Dalekie kraje: Tajemnica wojskowa*. Children's stories. Warsaw: Nasza Księgarnia, 1954.

―――. *Los dobosza*. Children's story. Warsaw: Nasza Księgarnia, 1954; rpt. Warsaw: Nasza Księgarnia, 1957.

A. Ostrowski [Ostrovsky]. *Panna bez posagu*. Play. Warsaw: Państwowy Instytut Wydawniczy, 1954.

I. Turgieniew [Turgenev]. *Nowizna*. Novel. Warsaw: Państwowy Instytut Wydawniczy, 1954.

A. Gajdar [Gaidar]. *Błękitna filiżanka i inne opowiadania*. Children's stories. Warsaw: Nasza Księgarnia, 1955.

―――. *Niech świeci*. Children's story. Warsaw: Nasza Księgarnia, 1955.

P. Tursun. *Nauczyciel*. Novel. Warsaw: Nasza Księgarnia, 1955.

A Czechow [Chekhov]. *Opowiadania*, vol. 2. Stories. [The story *Chameleon* translated by J. Wyszomirski]. Warsaw: Czytełnik, 1956.

R. Leonhard. *Śmierć Donkiszota*. Stories. Warsaw: Wydawnictwo Min. Obrony Narodowej, 1956.

W. Rozow. *Stronica życia*. Play. Warsaw: Czytelnik, 1956.

A. Gajdar [Gaidar]. *Trzy opowiadania*. Children's stories [with M. Górska]. Warsaw: Nasza Księgarnia, 1959.
J. Genet. *Pokojówki*. Play. *Dialog* 6 (1959), 56–75.
A. Terc [Tertz; A. Sinyavsky]. *Opowieści fantastyczne*. Stories [translated by J. Łobodowski and S. Bergholz (A. Wat)]. Paris: Instytut Literacki, 1961.

PUBLISHED CORRESPONDENCE

Letter to the International Conference of Revolutionary Writers in Kharkov, 21 October 1930. In P. Lewin, "Polonica w dziale rękopisów Instytutu Literatury Światowej im. Gorkiego w Moskwie," *Przegląd Humanistyczny* 4 (1962), 167.
"'Twarzą zwrócony do śmierci . . .' Listy Aleksandra Wata do Józefa Wittlina." *Znak* 2 (1991), 3–16.

Works about Wat

BOOKS

Łukaszuk, M. . . . *i w kołysankę już przemieniony płacz. Obiit . . . Natus est w poezji Aleksandra Wata*. London: Kontra, 1989.
Pamięć głosów: O twórczości Aleksandra Wata. Studies edited by Wojciech Ligęza. Kraków: Universitas, 1992.
Watowa, O. *Paszportyzacja*. Gdańsk: Wydawnictwo Inicjatywa Podziemia, 1983. [Underground edition.]
———. Warsaw: Wydawnictwo Międzyzakładowej Struktury "Solidarności," 1984. [Underground edition.]
———. [Wrocław]: Agencja Informacyjna "Solidarności Walczącej," [1984]. [Underground edition.]
———. *Wszystko co najważniejsze . . . Rozmowy z Jackiem Trznadlem*. London: Puls, 1984.
———. [Warsaw, 1985]. [Underground rpt.]
———. [Warsaw]: Międzyzakładowa Struktura "Solidarności" V, 1985. [Underground rpt.]
———. [Warsaw]: Zona [1985]. [Underground rpt.]
Watowa, Ola. *Wszystko co najważniejsze.* . . . Warsaw: Czytelnik, 1990.

ARTICLES

Aaron, Jonathan. "Without Boundaries." *Parnassus: Poetry in Review* (Spring/Summer 1981), 110–28. Review of *Mediterranean Poems*, 115–19.
a.k.w. "'Niech żyje Europa!'" *Comoedia* 9 (1926).
"Aleksander Wat et l'avant-garde poètique polonaise." Obituary. *Le Monde*, 23 August 1967.
"Aleksander Wat laureatem nagrody 'Nowej Kultury' za rok 1957." *Nowa Kultura* 1 (1958).
Ambroszko, J. "'Mój wiek' Aleksandra Wata: Dzieje duchowe autora i rozrachunek z komunizmem." *Warsztaty Polonistyczne* 3 (1992), 6–14.
Arutcheva, V. A. "Zapisnye knizhki Maiakovskogo." In *Literaturnoe nasledstvo*, vol. 65: *Novoe o Maiakovskom*, Moscow: Izdatel'stvo AN SSSR, 1958, 325–96. [On Wat, 384.]
Baliński, St. "Śmierć poety." Obituary. *Dziennik Polski i Dziennik Żołmierza*, 9 August 1967.
Baranowska, M. "Poeta mimo woli." Review of *Ciemne świecidło. Teksty Drugie* 1–2 (1991), 185–90.
———. "Trans czytającego młodzieńca wieku (Wat)." In id., *Surrealna wyobraźnia i poezja*, Warsaw: Czytelnik, 1984, 187–230.

———. "Transfiguracje przestrzeni w twórczości Aleksandra Wata." In *Przestrzeń i literatura: Studia*, edited by M. Głowiński and A. Okopień-Sławińska, Wrocław: Zakład Narodowy im. Ossolińskich, 1978, 281–96.

Barańczak, St. "Four Walls of Pain: The Late Poetry of Aleksander Wat." *Slavic and East European Journal* 33 (Summer 1989), 173–89.

———. "A Masterpiece of Memory." Review of *My Century. New Republic*, 5 September 1988, 34–35.

——— [B. Stawiczak]. "Trzy złudzenia i trzy rozczarowania polskiego futuryzmu." *Znak* 304 (1979), 995–1006. Rpt. in his *Etyka i poetyka*, Paris: Instytut Literacki, 1979, 71–82.

Bayley, J. "In God's Playground." *New York Review of Books*, 19 July 1990, 23–24.

Bereś, St. "Futurystyczna baśń o cywilizacji." *Miesięcznik Literacki* 12 (1979), 35–51.

———. "Wokół futurystycznego zmierzchu." *Miesięcznik Literacki* 12 (1980), 45–62.

Bieńkowski, Z. "Motyka i słońce." Review of *Dziennik be samogłosek. Wokanda* 5 (1991), 12.

Bolecki, W. "Od potworów do znaków pustych: Z dziejów groteski: Młoda Polska i dwudziestolecie międzywojenne." *Pamiętnik Literacki* 80 (1989), 73–121. Rpt. in his *Preteksty i teksty: Z zagadnień związków międzytekstowych w literaturze polskiej XX wieku*, Warsaw: Państwowe Wydawnictwo Naukowe, 1991, 102–58.

———. "Pisarze niedocenieni—pisarze przecenieni: Ankieta Kultury." *Kultura* 7/8 (1992), 153–85. [On Wat, 174–75, 180.]

———. "Regresywny futurysta." In Aleksander Wat, *Bezrobotny Lucyfer i inne opowieści* (1993), 5–18.

Borejsza, J. "Kawiarniani klasycy." *Odrodzenie* 9 (1948).

Borwicz, M. "'Inżynierowie dusz.'" *Zeszyty Historyczne*, vol. 3. Paris: Instytut Literacki, 1963, 121–63.

———. "'Mój wiek' Aleksandra Wata." *Zeszyty Historyczne*, vol. 43. Paris: Instytut Literacki, 1978, 225–28.

Boy-Żeleński, T. "Nekrolog sądów przysięgłych." *Wiadomości Literackie* 42 (1931).

Brakoniecki, K. "Światłość w ciemności: O wierszach Aleksandra Wata." Review of *Ciemne świecidło. Poezja*, 10 (1982), 6–22.

Breiter, E. "Bezrobotny Lucyfer." Review. *Robotnik* 68 (1927).

Breza, T. "Jak tu uciec od polityki? Kongres w Kopenhadze." *Odrodzenie* 27 (1948).

Brodzki, J. "Łakomstwo wyobraźni." Review of *Bezrobotny Lucyfer. Głos Prawdy* 50 (1927).

Bujnicki, T., and M. Stępień. "Krytyka poetycka w czasopismach: 'Kultura Robotnicza,' 'Nowa Kultura,' 'Dźwignia,' 'Miesięcznik Literacki.'" *Ruch Literacki* 2 (1961), 76–87; 3 (1961), 135–48.

Burek, T., Żytkowicz, H. "Aleksander Wat." In *Literatura polska w okresie międzywojennym*, vol. 3, Kraków: Wydawnictwo Literackie, 1993, 71–98.

Cameron, J. M. "Prophet of Lubyanka." Review of *My Century. New York Review of Books*, 8 December 1988, 26–28.

Carpenter, B. Review of *Lucifer Unemployed. World Literature Today*, 65 (Spring 1991), 328–29.

———. Review of *Mój wiek. World Literature Today* 53 (Winter 1979), 145–46.

Cieński, A. "'Esencje jego czarne. . . .'" Review of *Wiersze. Odra* 4 (1958).

Czapski, J. "Nad grobem poety." Funeral speech. *Wiadomości* 36 (1967).

Czaykowski, B. "From Rhythm and Metaphysics to Intonation, Experience and Gnosis: The Poetry of Boleslaw Leśmian, Aleksander Wat and Czesław Miłosz." In A. Czerniawski, ed., *The Mature Laurel: Essays on Modern Polish Poetry*, Bridgend, Glamorgan: Seren Books, Chester Springs, Pa.: Dufour Editions, 1991, 36–87.

Davis, B. Review of *Lucifer Unemployed. Wilson Library Bulletin* 65, no. 2 (1990), 120–21.

Drawicz, A. "Przerwane milczenie." *Księgarz* 10 (1958), 234–35.

Duszka, W. "Bruliony Aleksandra Wata." Review of *Pisma wybrane*. *Tygodnik Powszechny* 9 (1988).

"Echa Wystawy Krajowej." *Pobudka* 40 (1929), 8–9.

Feuerman, E. J. "Uwagi na marginesie książki Aleksandra Wata pt. 'Mój wiek.'" Letter to the editor. *Zeszyty Historyczne* 45 (1978), 234–36.

Gelbard, P. S. "Lucifer Unemployed." *New York Times Book Review*, 25 March 1990.

Gömöri, G. Review of *Ciemne świecidło*. *Books Abroad* 44 (Spring 1970), 325–26.

[Gorbanevskaia, N.] Review of *Mój wiek*. *Kontinent* 15 (1978), 387–88.

Gorczyńska, R. "Komunizm oczami poety." *Kultura* 4 (1986), 141–44.

Górecki, M. "W zgiełku dręczonych wyrazów." *Wezwanie* 4 (1983) 29–36.

Greń, Z. "Nowości z dwudziestolecia: 'Bezrobotny Lucyfer' Wata." Review. *Życie Literackie* 33 (1956), 5.

Grochowiak, St. "Pokusy cnotliwe: A. Wat." Review of *Wiersze*. *Żołnierz Polski* 1 (1958).

Gross, J. T. "Nasz wiek." Review of *Mój wiek*. *Wiadomości* 27 (1978).

———. "Poland: How It Was." Review of *My Century*. *New York Times Book Review*, 13 November 1988, 30.

Gryczanka, M. "Do krytyka, p. Włodzimierza Maciąga." On *Wiersze*. *Życie Literackie* 11 (1958).

[Grydzewski, M.]. "Lumen obscurum K. A. Jeleńskiego." On *Ciemne świecidło*. *Wiadomości* 49 (1968).

Grzybowska, K. "Przeciwko przepisom." On *Wiersze*. *Życie Literackie* 11 (1958).

[Hempel, J.] B. K. "Nieporozumienia literackie." *Nowa Kultura* 11 (1924).

Herling-Grudziński, G. "Czysta czerń." Review of *Wiersze*. *Wiadomości* 11 (1958).

Hirsch, E. "Songs of a Wanderer." Review of *With the Skin*. *New Yorker*, 16 July 1990, 79–85.

Horzyca, W. "W kraju idej." Review of *Bezrobotny Lucyfer*. *Epoka* 15 (1927).

[Hulka-Laskowski, P.] "Livres nouveaux." Review of *Bezrobotny Lucyfer*. *Pologne Littéraire* 15 (1927).

Hyde, G. "Poetry in a Stony Place." Review of *My Century* and *With the Skin*. *Times Literary Supplement*, 20 September 1991.

———. "Settling Down to Stasis." Review of *Lucifer Unemployment*. *Times Literary Supplement*, 23 November 1990.

Irzykowski, K. "Uwagi: Trzy sprostowania." *Europa* 6 (1930), 188–89.

Iwaszkiewicz, J. "O nagrodach literackich." *Twórczość* 2 (1958), 172–73.

Jarosiński, Z. "Wstęp." In H. Zaworska, ed., *Antologia polskiego futuryzmu i Nowej Sztuki*, Wrocław: Zakład Narodowy im. Ossolińskich, 1978.

Jastrun, M. "Dzienniki." *Res Publica* 1 (1987) 44–61. [On Wat, 46.]

Jeleński, K. A. "Aleksander Wat." Polemics with A. Pospieszalski. *Wiadomości* 3 (1978).

———. "The Dilemma of the Polish Intellectuals." *Partisan Review* 24 (1957), 247–60. [On Wat, 257.]

———. Introduction to "Voici Aleksander Wat." *Le Journal des poètes* 7 (1959), 3.

———. "Lumen obscurum: O poezji Aleksandra Wata." Review of *Ciemne świecidło*. *Wiadomości* 45 (1968); rpt. in his *Zbiegi okoliczności*, Paris: Instytut Literacki, 1982, 250–61.

———. "Odpowiedź na partyzantkę krytyków." Polemics. *Kontynenty* 88 (1966), 4–10. [On Wat, 4–6.]

"Jerzy Bernanos: 'Pod słońcem szatana.'" Review. *Droga* 11 (1928), 1093–94.

J. H. F. "Pamiętnik mówiony Aleksandra Wata." Review of *Mój wiek*. *Jedność* 12 (1977).

Kaliszewski, W. "Dzieło nienapisane." Review of *Pisma wybrane*. *Więź* 5 (1988), 112–16.

———. "O dzienniku, diable i Aleksandrze Wacie." *Twórczość* 11 (1988), 119–22.

———. "Wyjść poza ciemność, o Aleksandrze Wacie." Review of *Ciemne świecidło*. *Powściągliwość i Praca* 7–9 (1988), 12–13.

Kamienska, A. "Poezja tragizmu i mądrości (O wierszach Aleksandra Wata)." Review of *Wiersze. Spojrzenia* [supplement to *Gazeta Pomorska*] 33 (1958).

Karpiński, W. "Aleksander Wat—klucz i hak." *Zeszyty Literackie* 19 (1987), 60–68; rpt. in his *Książki zbójeckie*, London: Polonia, 1988, 70–77.

———. "Aleksander Wat—krajobrazy poezji." *Zeszyty Literackie* 18 (1987), 56–69; rpt in his *Książki zbójeckie*, London: Polonia, 1988, 57–69.

Kijkowska, Z., "Do Redakcji 'Kuźnicy.'" *Kuźnica* 8 (1946).

Kijowska, M. "Das mopseiserne Öfchen oder Wer war Wat?" *Süddeutsche Zeitung*, 17 April 1991.

[Kisielewski, St.] Kis. "Wata i lipa." *Tygodnik Powszechny* 26 (1947).

———. "Moja trzecia siła." *Tygodnik Powszechny* 153 (1948).

Kłak, T. "Wat z tej i z tamtej strony." Review of *Wiersze. Kamena* 6 (1958), 2–4.

Kochańczyk, A. "Poeta w piekle XX wieku." *Akcent* 4 (1989), 16–22.

Kołakowski, L. "Pamięć i myśl." Review of *Mój wiek. Kultura* 11 (1977), 115–18.

Koryl, J. "Emigracyjny obrazoburca?" Review of *Wiersze wybrane. Polonistyka* 9 (1989), 628–30.

Kowalczyk, A. S. "Staliniada Aleksandra Wata." Review of *Świat na haku i pod kluczem. Znak* 1 (1989), 91–94.

Kozielski, M. "Czerń, śmierć i ciemność: Fragment książki 'Obroty utożsamień Aleksandra Wata.'" *NaGłos* 5 (1991), 27–46.

[Kozikowski, E.] E. K. "Bezrobotny Lucyfer." Review. *Czartak* (1928), 197.

Krasuski, K. "Twórczość Aleksandra Wata." *Ruch Literacki* 3 (1991), 278–81.

Kryszak, J. "'Ból mój, mój demon.'" Review of *Wiersze. Poezja* 7/8 (1974), 135–38.

Lasota, G. "Wat, Jasieński i inni." *Polityka* 40 (1987).

Lichniak, Z. "Podejrzliwość nieunikniona." Review of *Wiersze. Kierunki* 39 (1958); rpt. in his *Monologi kibica literackiego*. Warsaw: Pax, 1959, 73–74.

Ligęza, W. "'Homo patiens' Aleksandra Wata." *Znak* 2 (1991), 17–24.

Lipski, J. J. "Noc ciemna." Review of *Wiersze śródziemnomorskie. Twórczość* 4 (1963), 58–60; rpt in his *Szkice o poezji*, Paris: Instytut Literacki, 1987, 27–31.

Litwinowicz, A. "'Mój wiek' Aleksandra Wata." Review. *Tydzień Polski* [appendix to *Dziennik Polski*], 11 (1978).

Lourie, R. "Introduction" to *My Century: The Odyssey of a Polish Intellectual*. Foreword by Czesław Miłosz. Berkeley: University of California Press, 1988, xxvii–xxx.

"Lucifer sans travail." Review of *Bezrobotny Lucyfer. Pologne Littéraire*, 15 (1927).

Łapiński, Z. "Powrót do liryki." Review of *Wiersze. Tygodnik Powszechny* 15 (1958).

———. "Sny nasze powszednie." Review of *Wiersze śródziemnomorskie. Tygodnik Powszechny* 11 (1963).

Łobodowski, J. "Dzieje tragicznego poety." Review of *Mój wiek. Tydzień Polski* [appendix to *Dziennik Polski*], 32–34 (1977).

Łukasiewicz, J. "W dwudziestoleciu (O poezji Aleksandra Wata)." *Pismo* 5/6 (1981), 9–24.

———. "Wizje, obrzędy i skazy." *Tygodnik Powszechny* 26 (1992).

Maciąg, W. "Poezja rozstrojonego instrumentu." Review of *Wiersze. Życie Literackie* 5 (1958).

———. "Szanowna Pani Marto. . . ." On *Wiersze. Życie Literackie* 11 (1958).

Maciejewski, J. "Katastrofizm na wesoło." Review of *Bezrobotny Lucyfer. Twórczość* 9 (1961), 122–25.

Maciejko, P. "Aleksander Wat: narodziny Fausta." *Ogród* 2 (1992), 265–78.

Mackiewicz, A. "Poezja Aleksandra Wata." *Warsztaty Polonistyczne* 3 (1992), 6–18.

Martin, T. Review of *My Century. Antioch Review* 47 (1989), 245–46.

Matuszewski, R. "Gałąź późno rozkwitła." Review of *Wiersze. Nowa Kultura* 17 (1957).

———. "Liryka: Poemat." *Rocznik Literacki*, 1957, esp. 25–27.

Mazurek, D. "Aleksandra Wata poezja doświadczenia i doświadczania." *Akcent* 4 (1989), 120–29.

Micińska, A. "Aleksander Wat—elementy do portretu." In Aleksander Wat, *Poezje zebrane*, Kraków: Znak, 1992, 5–109.

———. "Wszystko co najważniejsze." *Tygodnik Powszechny* 13 (1991).

Międzyrzecki, A. "Poeta nowy." Review of *Wiersze śródziemnomorskie*. *Przegląd Kulturalny* 18 (1963).

———. "Skala widzenia." Review of *Wiersze*. *Nowe Książki* 4 (1958), 193–96.

Miłosz, C. Foreword to Aleksander Wat, *Mediterranean Poems*, 1977, vii–x.

———. Foreword to Aleksander Wat, *Lucifer Unemployed*, 1990, ix–xii.

———. "Introduction à la poésie d'Aleksander Wat." *Preuves* 201 (1967), 24–29.

———. "On Aleksander Wat." *Antaeus* 60 (Spring 1988), 41–45; rpt. as Introduction to *With the Skin*, 1989, 7–12.

———. "O wierszach Aleksandra Wata." *Kultura* 9 (1967), 3–14; rpt. in his *Prywatne obowiązki*, Paris: Instytut Literacki, 1972, 62–73.

———. "Poeta Aleksander Wat." *Tygodnik Powszechny* 34 (1992).

———. "Przedmowa." In Aleksander Wat, *Mój wiek: Pamiętnik mówiony*, 1977, 5–18; rpt. in subsequent editions, with English translation in English editions.

"Nad książką." Review of *Bezrobotny Lucyfer*. *Głos Prawdy*, 22 (1927).

"Na marginesie książki Aleksandra Wata." Review of *Bezrobotny Lucyfer*. *Nasz Przegląd*, 6 February 1927.

Napierski, S. "O rewolucji w poezji." *Wiadomości Literackie* 11 (1924).

Nastulanka, K. "'Bezrobotny Lucyfer' czyli przygoda intelektualna lat dwudziestych." Review. *Nowe Książki* 21 (1960), 1302–3.

"Nieprzyzwoity wybryk." *Życie Warszawy*, 2 March 1948.

Nowicki, Sz. "Aleksandra Wata porządek myślenia." *Kontakt* 1 (1987), 116–26.

Nyczek, T. "Bach na dachu Łubianki." In his *Emigranci*, London: Aneks, 1988, 11–31.

"O 'Antologii poezji polskiej' mówią Julian Przyboś, Artur Sandauer, Maciej Żurowski i Janusz Wilhelmi." *Kultura* (Warsaw) 3 (1966).

Ołbromski, M. "Czarodziejska kula: Inspiracje antyczne w powojennej liryce Alesandra Wata." *Zeszyty Naukowe KUL* 3–4 (1986), 45–66.

"Oświadczenie i odpowiedź." *Życie Warszawy*, 16 March 1948.

Peiper, T. "Listy do redakcji." *Miesięcznik Literacki* 5 (1930), 278–80.

Pevear, R. "Poetry Chronicle." *Hudson Review* 30 (1977), 457–66. [On *Mediterranean Poems*, 464–66.]

Pietrych, K. "Obraz natury w 'Pieśniach wędrowca' Aleksandra Wata." *Prace Polonistyczne*, ser. 46 (1990), 73–87.

———. "Wyznanie dziwiącego się poetry." Review of *Dziennik bez samogłosek. Powściągliwość i Praca* 9 (1989), 6.

PMK. "Aleksandra Wata ABC komunizmu." Review of *Mój wiek*. *Res Publica* 1 (1979), 87–90.

Podgórecki, A. "Moralne bezhołowie." *Oficyna Poetów* 56 (1980), 25–27.

Polsakiewicz, Z. "Druga młodość poety." Review of *Wiersze*. *Gazeta Pomorska*, 16 February 1958.

Pomirowski, L. "'Bezrobotny Lucyfer' Wata." Review. *Wiadomości Literackie* 10 (1927).

Pospieszalski, A. "Kim był Aleksander Wat?" Review of *Mój wiek*. *Wiadomości* 49 (1977).

"P. Prystor w roli cenzora." *Pobudka* 44 (1929), 4.

Prokop-Janiec, E. "'Żyd Wieczny Tułacz': dialektyka, publicystyka, katastrofa." *Teksty Drugie* 5 (1992), 79–84.

Przyboś, J. "W sprawie artykułu A. Wata." *Kuźnica* 10 (1948).

Pytasz, M. "Wat jakiego nie znamy." *Literatura na Świecie* 7 (1983), 337–39.

Radzilowski, T. "Oral History and Biography: *My Century.*" *Oral History Review* 18 (1990), 106–9.

[Redakcja] RDC. "'Słowo' i 'rzecz' czyli casus Aleksandra Wata." *Kultura* (Warsaw) 15 (1963).

Reszczyńska-Stypińska, M. "Na marginesie poezji Aleksandra Wata." *Tydzień Polski* [appendix to *Dziennik Polski*], 46 (1968).

Rettinger, M. "Bezrobotny Lucyfer." Review. *Przegląd Współczesny* 21, no. 60 (1927), 154–546.

rk. "Rekolekcje antyzoila." *Nowiny Literackie* 11 (1948).

Rutkowski, K. "Słowo o Wacie." *Twórczość* (1991), 82–88.

Rymkiewicz. A. "Dobra sztuka zawsze ma ojczyznę." *Kierunki* 14/15 (1958).

[Sadkowski, W.] sad. "Wiersze Wata." Review of *Wiersze*. *Trybuna Ludu* 79 (1958).

Sanford, G. Review of *My Century*. *Political Studies* 40 (1992), 179–80.

Schiller, I. "W związku z artykulem Leona Schillera." *Teatr* 8 (1959).

Semil, E. "Bezrobotny Lucyfer XX wieku." Review. *Polityka* 47 (1960).

Shenfel'd, I. "Aleksandr Vat o sovetskix pisateliax." *Novoe Russkoe Slovo,* 31 December 1978.

Simoncini, G. "Ethnic and Social Diversity in the Membership of the Communist Party of Poland, 1918–1938." *Nationalities Papers* 22, suppl. 1, 55–91. [On Wat, 65–66, 90.]

S. K. "Z ostatnich nowości wydawniczych." Review of *Bezrobotny Lucyfer. Kuryer Literacko-Naukowy* 11 (1927).

Skubalanka, T. "Polska poezja futurystyczna w oczach językoznawcy: Przyczynek do przemian poezji współczesnej." *Przegląd Humanistyczny* 5 (1979), 1–17.

Słonimski, A. "Kronika tygodniowa." *Wiadomości Literackie* 49 (1929).

———. "Kronika tygodniowa." *Wiadomości Literackie* 38 (1931).

Spectator. "Świat koncentracyjny." *Wiadomości* 7/8 (1978).

Stala, M. "Buchalteria." *NaGłos* 5 (1991), 76–82.

———. "Od czarnego słońca do ciemnego świecidła." *Teksty* 6 (1980), 105–21. [On Wat, 118–21.]

Stasiński, P. "Wat—opis walki." Review of *Pisma wybrane. Res Publica* 5 (1987), 107–14.

Stern, A. "Futuryści polscy i inni." In id., *Poezja zbuntowana,* 2d ed., Warsaw: Państwowy Instytut Wydawniczy, 1970, 5–97.

———. "O poetach Nowej Sztuki. List do redaktora 'Almanachu.'" *Almanach Nowej Sztuki* 2 (1924), 45–6.

———. "Start." *Wiedza i Życie* 2 (1958), 113–16.

Sterna-Wachowiak, S. "Gnothi seauton: Pamięci Aleksandra Wata." *Przegląd Powszechny* 12 (1988), 385–97.

Stryjkowski, J. "Olbrzymia czarna przestrzeń." In J. Trznadel, *Hańba domowa.* Lubin: Test, 1990, 148–61. [On Wat, 152–53.]

Sulikowski, A. "Poszukiwania metafizyczne Aleksandra Wata." *Odra* 9 (1992), 44–50.

Szaniawski, K. "Metafizyka zniewolenia—świadectwo Aleksandra Wata." In *Literatura źle obecna (Rekonesans),* London, Polonia, 1984, 67–77.

Szczygielski, Z. "Internowanie 'S.'" *Polityka* 33 (1962), 11.

Szpakowska, M. Review of *Mój wiek. Twórczość* 4 (1991), 97–105.

"Sztuka prześwsietla politykę społeczną." *Pobudka* 41 (1929), 5.

Tishmaneanu, V. Review of *My Century*. *Orbis* 33 (1989), 299.

Tomaszewski, M. "Pisarz i kat." Review of *Świat na haku i pod kluczem. Zeszyty Literackie* 15 (1986), 142–48.

Trznadel, J. "Glosy do wspomnień Aleksandra Wata." *Puls* 33 (1987), 70–76.

———. "Krótka pamięć." *Tygodnik Solidarność* 32 (1993).

———. "O Aleksandrze Wacie." *Zeszyty Literackie* 4 (1983), 19–23.

———. "Złe z dobrem w przeplocie (o poezji Aleksandra Wata, ciąg dalszy)." *Kultura Niezależna* 33 (1987), 24–30.

Tyczyński, T. "Wat—ciemne świadectwo." *Społeczeństwo Otwarte* 6 (1993), 33–35.

Venclova, T. "Aleksander Wat: Three Futurist Poems." In *Literary Tradition and Practice in Russian Culture*, edited by Valentina Polukhina, Joe Andrew, and Robert Reid, Amsterdam: Rodopi, 1993, 246–61.

———. "Gnostyczny 'Piecyk' Aleksandra Wata." Translated by Joanna Zach-Błońska. *Teksty Drugie* 2 (1994), 54–75.

———. "Was Mayakovsky in Warsaw Once or Twice? Futurist Friends Vladimir Mayakovsky and Aleksander Wat." In *The Mayakovsky Centennial: 1893–1993: A Commemoration of the Life, Work and Times of Vladimir Mayakovsky*, edited by Anne D. Perryman and Patricia J. Thompson, New York: Lehman College, 1993, 19–27.

Wat, A. [Andrzej]. "Jeszcze jedno oszczerstwo Sandauera." Polemics. *Kultura* 5 (1984), 150–51.

"Wat Aleksander." *Oficyna Poetów* 2 (1967), 2.

"Wat Aleksander." In *Słownik współczesnych pisarzy polskich*, compiled and edited by Ewa Korzeniewska et al., vol. 3. Warsaw: Państwowe Wydawnictwo Naukowe, 1964, 443–46.

Watowa, O. "Wielki los, który przychodzi." Interview with B. Sulek. *Tygodnik Solidarność* 44 (1992).

Ważyk, A. "Przeczytalem *Mój wiek.*" *Puls* 34 (1987), 48–55.

———. "Troska o człowieka." *Kuźnica* 3 (1946).

Weinzicher, M. "Na marginesie książki Aleksandra Wata." Review of *Bezrobotny Lucyfer*. *Nasz Przegląd* 37 (1927).

Werfel, R. Interview. In T. Torańska, *Oni*, London: Aneks, 1985, 72–104. [On Wat, 83.]

Wielopolska, M. J. "Do Aleksandra Wata." *Wiadomości Literackie* 44 (1927).

———. "Dopuszczalne metody na niedopuszczalne metody p. p. Millera i Wata." *Głos Prawdy* 15 (1928).

Więcek, K. "Po lekturze *Mojego wieku.*" *Puls* 33 (1987), 58–67.

———. "Wszystko, co mogę powiedzieć zgodnie z prawdą." *Kultura Niezależna* 29 (1987), 78–92.

Wilkoń, A. "Wata pieśni rozlewne." Reviw of *Wiersze śródziemnomorskie*. *Życie Literackie* 18 (1963).

Wirpsza, W. "Wiersze Aleksandra Wata." Review of *Wiersze*. *Nowa Kultura* 49 (1957).

Witkiewicz, S. I. "Aleksander Wat." In id., *Teatr. Wstęp do teorii czystej formy w. teatrze. O twórczości reżysera i aktorów. Dokumenty do historii walki o czystą formę w teatrze. Dodatek: O naszym futuryzmie*, Warsaw, F. Hoesick, 1923, 240–48; rpt. in id., *Pisma filozoficzne i estetyczne*, vol. 1: *Nowe formy w malarstwie. Szkice estetyczne. Teatr*, compiled and edited by J. Leszczyński, Warsaw: Państwowe Wydawnictwo Naukowe, 1974, 404–9.

Włodek, A. "Jeszcze o Nieborowie." *Dziennik Literacki* 9 (1948).

———. "To więcej niż obiady czwartkowe." *Dziennik Literacki* (1948).

Wojdyło, M. "Malarstwo i kolor w poezji Aleksandra Wata." *Ruch Literacki* 2 (1985), 109–25.

Woroszylski, W. "Myśmy żyli w literaturze." In J. Trznadel, *Hańba domowa*, Lublin: Test, 1990, 86–105. [On Wat, 92–93.]

"W pracowniach pisarzy." *Czerwony Sztandar* 54 (1939).

Wróblewska, T. "Przypominamy dwudziestolecie." Review of *Bezrobotny Lucyfer*. *Orka* 16 (1961).

"W sprawie poziomu polemik." *Życie Warszawy*, 3 April 1948.

Wygodzki, St. " 'Mój wiek' Aleksandra Wata." Review. *Nowiny-Kurjer*, 17 March 1978.

————. "Spotkanie z 'Miesięcznikiem Literackim.'" *Polityka* 38 (1958); rpt. in *Księga wspomnień, 1919–1939*, Warsaw: Czytelnik, 1960, 402–11.

[Wyka, K.] "List Kazimierza Wyki." *Nowa Kultura* 1 (1958).

————. "Super flumina Babylonis." Review of *Wiersze. Twórczość* 3 (1958), 98–113; rpt. in his *Rzecz wyobraźni*, Warsaw: Państwowy Instytut Wydawniczy, 1959, 413–40; 2d ed., enlarged, 1977, 341–60.

Zaleski, M. "Aleksander Wat i zło." *Zeszyty Literackie* 18 (1987), 70–79.

Zawada, A. "Udręczone wiersze Wata." Review of *Wiersze wybrane. Twórczość* 4 (1989), 88–96.

Zawodziński, K.W. "Spory teoretyczno-literackie." *Dziś i Jutro* 12 (1948).

Zaworska, H. "Futurystyczne koncepcje sztuki dla mas." *Pamiętnik Literacki* 58, no. 3 (1967), 79–107.

————. "Lucyfer bezrobotny i rozczarowany." Review. *Nowa Kultura* 7 (1961).

Zdanys, J. "Voices from the Other Europe." *Yale Review* 79, no. 3 (1990), 467–82. [On Wat, 478–80.]

Zieliński, J. "Leopold Łabędź o Aleksandrze Wacie." *Puls* 26 (1985), 100–7.

————. "A Polish Intellectual." Review of *My Century* and *With the Skin. Partisan Review* 58 (1991), 733–36.

————. "Powrót do rzeczy." Review of *Mój wiek. Oficyna Poetów*, 4 (1979), 11–15.

————. "Spowiedź syna królewskiego." *Twórczość* (1984), 77–87; rpt. in A. Wat, *Wiersze wybrane*, Warsaw, 1987, 5–27.

Zieniewicz, A. "Kalejdoskop Aleksandra Wata: Style rzeczywistości w quasi-pamiętniku." *Państwo i Kultura Polityczna* 6 (1989), 7–50.

Zychowicz, J. "Medytacje o świecie bez wzoru: O figurach poezji Aleksandra Wata." *Poezja* 4–6 (1990), 73–82.

Żółkiewski, S. "Spór po rekolekcjach." *Kuźnica* 8 (1948).

Books That Mention Wat

Broniewski, W. *Pamiętnik, 1918–1922*. Compiled from the manuscript with an introduction and commentary by Feliksa Lichodziejewska. Warsaw: Państwowy Instytut Wydawniczy, 1984.

Carpenter, B. *The Poetic Avant-garde in Poland, 1918–1939*. Seattle: University of Washington Press, 1983, esp. 64–77.

Czachowski, K. *Obraz współczesnej literatury polskiej, 1884–1934*, vol. 3: *Ekspresjonizm i neorealizm*. Warsaw and Lwów: Nakładem Państwowego wydawnictwa książek szkolnych, 1935, 548–50.

Fik, M. *Kultura polska po Jalcie: Kronika lat 1944–1981*. London: Polonia, 1989.

Gömöri, G. *Polish and Hungarian Poetry, 1945 to 1956*. Oxford: Clarendon Press, 1966, 254–58.

Hertz, Z. *Listy do Czesława Miłosza, 1952–1979*. Paris: Instytut Literacki, 1992.

Iwaszkiewicz, J. *Książka moich wspomnień*. Kraków and Wroclaw: Wydawnictwo Literackie, 1983.

Jarosiński, Z. *Literatura i nowe społeczeństwo: Idee lewicy literackiej dwudziestolecia międzywojennego*. Warsaw: Cytelnik, 1983.

Kwiatkowski, J. *Literatura Dwudziestolecia*. Warsaw: Państwowe Wydawnictwo Naukowe, 1990.

Lam, A. *Polska awangarda poetycka: Programy lat 1917–1923*, vol. 1: *Instynkt i ład*. Kraków: Wydawnictwo Literackie, 1969.

Leon Schiller: W stulecie urodzin, 1887–1987. Edited by Lidia Kuchtówna and Barbara Łasocka. Warsaw: Państwowe Wydawnictwo Naukowe, 1990, 159–60.

Miłosz, C. *Rok myśliwego*. Paris: Instytut Literacki, 1990, 201–2.
Od bliskich i dalekich: Korespondencja do Władysława Broniewskiego, vols. 1–2. Compiled by
  Feliksa Lichodziejewska. Warsaw: Państwowy Instytut Wydawniczy, 1981.
Pomirowski, L. *Doktryna a twórczość: Rzecz o współczesnej krytyce, najnowszej prozie polskiej i
  dramacie*. Warsaw: J. Mortkowicz, 1928, 142–44.
Stępień, M. *Ze stanowiska lewicy: Studium jednego z nurtów polskiej krytyki literackiej lat
  1919–1939*. Kraków, 1974.
Stryjkowski, J. *Wielkistrach*. Zapis 14 (1980), 64, 84, 94.
Ważyk,A. *Dziwna historia awangardy*. Warsaw: Czytelnik, 1976.
———. *Kwestia gustu*. Warsaw: Państwowy Instytut Wydawniczy, 1966.
Winklowa, B. *Boy we Lwowie, 1939–1941*. Warsaw: Pokolenie-Rytm, 1992.

Index